THIRTEEN
SENSES

THIRTEEN

SENSES

A Memoir

Victor Villaseñor

rayo

An Imprint of HarperCollins*Publishers*

HarperCollins books may be purchased
for educational, business, or sales promotional use. For information, please write:
Special Markets Department, HarperCollins Publishers Inc.,
10 East 53rd Street, New York, NY 10022.

Printed on acid-free paper

FIRST EDITION
Designed by Fritz Metsch

Library of Congress Cataloging-in-Publication Data is available upon request.

ISBN 0-06-621077-1

01 02 03 04 05 RRD 10 9 8 7 6 5 4 3 2 1

To Women of Substance this book is dedicated, to women who've put their hands on their hips like my mother and my grandmothers and taken up ground, saying this is my Sacred Piece of Mother Earth and from Here I will not be moved! From *mi familia* to your family, *gracias,* embrace the Stars!

Contents

Part Six
HEAVENTALKING

Part Seven
EARTHTALKING

Part Eight

ILLUMINATION

Part Nine

REBIRTHING

Preface

THROUGHOUT THE AGES, tales have been passed down within families, keeping intact oral histories that weld one generation to the next. This is my family's tale of love, adversity, magic, and wonderment.

Growing up, I was told by my father time and again that a good story could save our life. Then he'd explain to me how he and his sisters had been dying of thirst and hunger as they made their way north from Mexico to the United States during the Mexican Revolution of 1910. "We were ready to lay down and die," my father told me. "Cannons were blasting all around us. People were screaming and dying. The creeks ran red with blood, but then when the sun went down, your grandmother would brush the snakes and scorpions out of the way with some brush and fix a place for us to sleep for the night. She'd give us a smooth little rock to suck on if we had nothing to eat, and she'd tell us stories about the stars, the moon, the she-fox, and soon we'd forget our hunger and we'd be traveling with her words through a world of wonder.

"God was with us. He was our best friend and He was smiling to us with the stars and the moon, and little by little all our troubles of the day would disappear."

My father, a big strong man from *los Altos de Jalisco,* would cry and cry and tell me that his mother, a little old bag of Indian bones, knew a life that few people knew—a life so full of the Holy Breath of the Almighty that no one could ever lose hope. My father told me that they'd go to sleep there in the rocks and dirt, feeling full of hope and love and the complete understanding that tomorrow would be another gift straight from God, and so all would then be possible no matter how harsh their day had been—for life was a dream to live, not a reality to fear.

This, then, is a history of a people—a tribal heritage, if you will—of my Indian-European ancestors as handed down to me by my father and mother, my aunts and uncles, my cousins and family friends.

Back at one time, we were all Indigenous People, and the time has come to circle back to when the Mother Earth was young, the Heavens spoke, and people listened.

Like my grandmother used to say, there are no strangers, once we get to know each other's story. Enjoy. *Gracias*. Thank you.

Victor E. Villaseñor
Rancho Villaseñor
Oceanside, California
Spring 2001

Part One

WEDDING

VOWS

August 18, 1979

Oceanside, California

I

---

*Such a man and woman aren't measured from their heads to
their feet, but from their heads to the sky, for these people are
giants — who know the Thirteen Senses of Creation!*

WAS IT LOVE?
Had it ever really been love?

For fifty years they'd been husband and wife. For fifty years the Father
Sun had come and gone. For fifty years the Mother Moon had risen and
disappeared. For fifty years they'd loved, fought, and lived together, and
now, here they were standing before the priest once again, ready to renew
their wedding vows.

Juan Salvador Villaseñor, the nineteenth child of his family, was
seventy-five years old. Maria Guadalupe Gomez, the eighth child of her
family, was sixty-eight years old. Salvador now turned and took the hand
of the woman standing beside him. Lupe turned and looked into Salvador's eyes.

The priest began his words, and Salvador and Lupe's children and
grandchildren and great-grandchildren looked on with love, respect, and
gusto. It was a small wedding this time with just family and a few friends,
being done in the living room of the great house that Salvador and Lupe
had designed and built nearly thirty-five years before.

Sunlight streamed in through the large windows behind Salvador and
Lupe as the priest continued his words. People's eyes filled with tears.
This was a magic moment, where everyone in the room just knew that
God's blessing was with them.

The groom was dressed in his favorite dark maroon suit with a striped
tie of silver and gold. The bride was wearing a beautiful three-quarter-
length white dress with intricate lace and interwoven ribbon of yellow

gold. Salvador's hair was white and full and still curly. Lupe's hair was mostly gray, too, yet sprinkled with beautiful long strands of black.

The priest continued, and the small gathering of family and friends listened to every word. This time, different from last time, the priest was much younger than the couple getting married. "Juan Salvador Villaseñor," the young priest was now saying, "do you take Maria Guadalupe Gomez to be your wife? Do you promise to be true to her in good times and in bad, in sickness and in health, to love and honor all the days of your life?"

Lupe turned and stared at Salvador's lion mane of hair and the huge, long, white moustache on his upper lip. It moved like a fat worm as he spoke. "Yes, I do," he said.

Hearing this, she realized how different these words now felt compared to last time. When she'd heard these words fifty years before, she'd been so young and naïve that she'd taken his "Yes, I do" to mean so much more than she did this time. Last time, she'd thought these words meant that she would have someone with her through good times, bad times, sickness, health, and there would always be love and honor. What a fool she'd been! If the truth were known, sometimes she would've been better off without him.

Then, she realized that the young priest was speaking to her. "And you, Maria Guadalupe Gomez," said the young man of God, "do you take Juan Salvador Villaseñor to be your husband? Do you promise to be true to him in good times and in bad, in sickness and in health, to love him and honor him all the days of your life?"

At first Lupe didn't answer. My God, this was exactly what she'd done for all these years. But had he? Had Salvador been true to her and honored her? Or, had he ever really even loved her?

Then she suddenly remembered how these words "in bad times" had almost stopped her last time. Even back then, when she'd been eighteen years old, she'd wondered if it was wise for any woman to agree to this statement.

"Say, 'yes, I do,' " said the young priest, leaning in close to Lupe.

Lupe almost laughed. This was exactly what the priest had done last time. Only then the priest had been old, and he'd looked so full of authority that she'd been intimidated. But she wasn't intimidated in the least this time, and so she just looked at this young priest and smiled.

Juan Salvador saw her smile, that little smile of hers that was so full of mischief. He grinned, squeezing her hand.

Feeling her hand being squeezed, Lupe turned and looked at this gray-haired, old man standing beside her, and she saw his grin. She grinned, too.

"Okay," she said, squeezing his hand in return. "Yes, I do."

Everyone in the room looked greatly relieved, except Salvador. He'd never had any doubt.

Then it was Lupe's turn to repeat the words of holy acceptance, but when she came to the passage, "To have and to hold from this day forward, for better, for worse, for richer, for poorer, in sickness and in health, until death do us part," tears came to her eyes. After fifty years of marriage, she could now see that these were the very words that had given her the power to endure all the hardships of the years.

Why, these words "until death do us part" were the very foundation of every marriage. And she could also see that yes, even back then, fifty years ago, she'd had the wisdom to see that these were the words that had given her beloved mother, Doña Guadalupe, the strength to rise up like a mighty star and bring her *familia* back from the dead, time and again during that awful Mexican Revolution!

She could now see so clearly that these words "until death do us part" were the words that gave each and every woman the power, the vision to accept the Grace of God and gain the absolute conviction of mind that she and her family would survive—no matter what—just as her beloved mother-in-law, Doña Margarita, had so well explained to her only days before their first wedding back in 1929.

Lupe now understood very clearly that these words were the secret with which every ordinary woman became extraordinary, giving her the wisdom and confidence within herself to rise up like a mighty eagle and see her family through their darkest of hours of life, *la vida*.

Tears streamed down Lupe's face just as they'd streamed down her face fifty years ago at their first wedding, which had taken place up the coast in Santa Ana, California, at the Holy Catholic Church of *Nuestra Señora de Guadalupe* on Third Street and Grand. The whole *barrios* of Corona and Santa Ana had attended that wedding. Archie Freeman had barbecued a whole steer. Fifty chickens had been cooked in *salsa de mole* by Lupe's *familia*. Salvador had paid for Lupe's wedding dress, her sister Carlota's maid of honor dress, and the yards and yards of material for other maids' of honor dresses, too. It had been a celebration that had lasted for three days. People had come from Mexico and all over the Southland.

Lupe couldn't stop crying. She and this gray-haired old man standing beside her had seen so much life together, so much suffering and turmoil, and, also, so much joy and wild adventure.

A big part of her now loved Salvador more than ever before, because she'd been with him for more years than she'd been with anyone. Why, she'd only been with her own parents the first eighteen years of her life.

And yet, even though this was true, there was still another part of her that despised him. He'd broken her heart time and again. It was sometimes hard for her to even just look at him, if she let her mind go racing off into all the terrible situations that he'd put her through.

Then it was time for them to exchange rings, but this time they were only adding a simple gold band to their original wedding rings.

And once more—she couldn't believe it—the priest had Salvador say "to love and cherish for the rest of their lives," but then, when he turned to her, he said for her to say "to love, cherish, and obey."

Lupe's heart stopped. "Oh, no," said Lupe, startling the young priest. "I will not say obey! How dare you!"

"But you must, if you want to—"

"I must," she said. "I must! And he doesn't have to! Oh, no, you don't! You don't talk to me like this after fifty years of marriage, and I now knowing what I know!"

"Good for you, Lupe!" said Carlota, Lupe's older sister, who was sitting with Lupe's children and grandchildren. "He was no good when you married him the first time, and he's still no good today!"

"Keep quiet, Carlota!" said Lupe, turning on her sister, who was wearing a black lace dress and a large blond wig and white powder on her dark, wide Indian face. "This is my wedding, not yours, and I will speak for myself."

"I was only trying to help," said Carlota, who had been married to Archie Freeman, but they'd never had any kids, and so she considered Lupe's children like her own.

Lupe turned back to her husband. Smiling, she soothed Salvador's hand, reassuring him that everything was all right. Then she turned to the priest and said, "Father, I will not say 'obey' and not have him say 'obey,' too." She spoke calmly. "What do you think marriage is, a beautiful little ceremony and then everything is wonderful thereafter? Marriage is—"

"Hell!" shouted Carlota, cutting in once again.

"Carrrrr-lota!" said Lupe, rolling the "r" of her sister's name with its full Spanish sounding power. "You will leave the room if you can't keep still."

Carlota began to cry. "Oh, I'm sorry, Lupe," she said. "It's just that all his life, Salvador has been a no-good, lying—"

"Carlota, 'quiet,' means 'quiet!' " snapped Lupe. "In the name of God please keep quiet! And you," she said, now turning back to the priest once again, "as I said, I will not say 'obey,' and you will not tell me what I must or mustn't do, do you hear me?"

The young priest didn't know what to do.

"I will say 'love and cherish,' just like my husband said," continued Lupe, "but I will not say another word."

"Well, yes," said the priest, trying to accommodate, "but I don't know if this is acceptable, unless Salvador is in agreement to this."

"Oh," said Lupe, "then you are telling me that I need a man's approval for what I can say or not say!"

She was really angry now. Everyone in the room could see it.

"No," said the priest, "I didn't mean that." He was beginning to sweat. Never had he had a simple marriage ceremony turn into a situation like this. And these two people had looked so old and nice and decent before they'd started the ceremony. "Look, what I'm trying to say," he now said, pulling at his collar, coughing, and clearing his throat, "is that, well, in any agreement between two people—men or women—they both need to be in agreement if a change in normal procedure is going to be made."

"Oh," said Lupe, calming right down, "this I can understand." She turned to Salvador. "Okay," she said, "so do you agree with me, Salvador, that I don't have to say 'obey' if you didn't have to say it?"

All this time, Salvador had only been grinning, but now he laughed. "Look," he said, turning to the priest, "I know you've never been married, Father, so you don't really understand what's going on. But believe me, to tell any woman, who's alive and breathing, that she must obey is so ridiculous that only men who've never married in one hundred generations would have ever come up with such an ignorant idea! Of course, she doesn't have to obey me! She never has in fifty years, so why in the hell would I be stupid enough to think that it was going to be any different now?"

"All right," said the priest, taking out a white handkerchief to wipe his forehead. "Then Maria Guadalupe, will you love and cherish for the rest of your lives?"

"Why, sure," she said, "of course." And her eyes danced with merriment. Oh, she'd truly come a long ways in the last fifty years.

"Say, 'I do,' " whispered the priest, but very cautiously this time.

"I do," said Lupe.

Salvador now slipped the wedding band on Lupe's finger, and then licking his lips, he suddenly grabbed his bride and gave her a big, wet kiss. At first Lupe resisted, trying to push him away, but when he wouldn't be pushed away, she began kissing him, too.

Cameras flashed, and everyone applauded! Champagne bottles exploded open, and people were laughing and yelling.

THE FATHER SUN, the blanket of the poor, was going down. The whole tribe of the Villaseñors went outside to have their picture taken.

Carlota, *"Tia Tota,"* as all the children called her, moved quickly with her cane in hand and took the main chair in the middle of the picture, sitting to Salvador's right and forcing her sister Lupe to sit on Salvador's left. And so this was how Salvador and Lupe's golden anniversary picture was taken, with *Tia Tota* sitting proudly in the center with her five-foot-two frame looking so large and tall and imposing as she faced straight into the camera.

Tia Tota really thought that she was the queen of the whole show, with her large, blond wig, white-powdered face, and a huge white flower pinned above her heart area, wanting so desperately to hide her dark Indian blood and look All-American White.

Salvador was looking off into the distance toward his right, holding his black, thick-rim glasses on his lap with both of his hands. Lupe had one grandchild and one great-grandchild on her lap. She was completely oblivious to their picture being taken—she was so happy playing with these newest additions of *la familia.*

And standing behind Salvador and Lupe were their four children, Tencha, Victor, Linda, and Teresita, and their families.

It was a telling picture.

THE FATHER SUN WAS NOW GONE, and the Mother Moon was coming up, and the Child Earth was cooling. Everyone was done eating, and they were now talking and drinking and visiting.

The women were gathered in the living room next to the grand piano. The men were in the long formal dining room, right off the living room where Salvador was in the process of lighting up a big, fat cigar, a ritual that he did very slowly with long, wooden matches.

Gorjenna, Salvador and Lupe's second oldest granddaughter, was loud and tipsy. Ever since she was a child, Gorjenna had loved horses and riding. She'd never gone in for dresses and stuffed dolls like her sister RoseAna, who was two years older than she.

"Oh, *grandmama*," Gorjenna was now saying, with her big blue eyes so excited that they just looked like they were going to pop off her lovely, smooth-skin face, "I was so scared that you weren't going to say 'I do' that I almost wet my pants. I mean, my dress," she added, laughing, realizing that today she wasn't wearing her Levi's.

"Me, too!" said RoseAna, laughing equally nervously.

Both of these young women, Gorjenna and RoseAna—Tencha's children—looked totally All-American, without a bit of Mexican Indian blood in them, but, also, they'd been taken down to Guadalajara, Mexico, and *los Altos de Jalisco* enough times as youngsters by their grandparents, so that they were both proud of their Mexican ancestry.

"Tell us, *grandmama*," continued Gorjenna, "if you had it all over to do, would you still marry *grandpapa?*"

Hearing this, Linda, Salvador and Lupe's second daughter, almost spilled her champagne.

And Lupe, feeling wonderful with all the Mumm's champagne she'd drunk, looked at Gorjenna and all these young women standing before her. "Yes, of course, *mi hijitas*," she said.

"But *grandmama*," said RoseAna, "you have to admit that there was a moment when it looked like you weren't going to say your vows."

"Yeah," said Gorjenna, smiling happily, "my sis is right. You weren't going to say 'obey,' *grandmama!*"

"And she didn't," said Teresita, Salvador and Lupe's third daughter, "so let bygones be bygones."

"Of course, I didn't," said Lupe, "I'm not a child."

"Then *grandmama*," Gorjenna said, "you don't think that wives should obey their husbands?"

"Of course not, *mi hijita*," said Lupe. "How did you ever get that in your head?"

"Well, because, men—I mean, we, women, are taught, *grandmama*, that men are—"

"Are what?" said Lupe, cutting off her granddaughter, "weaker than we women when life really gets tough? Oh, I've told all of you girls since you were babies," continued Lupe, "that I saw my mother in the middle of the Revolution keep our family alive and together with her power! Not my father. No, he ran away. Then I saw my sisters do the same thing. It was never the men, *mi hijita,* who kept our families together. God as my witness, men fall apart when children are crying with hunger. Ask your *grandpapa,* Salvador; he will tell you the very same thing. It was his mother who got them through the Revolution, not his father. Please, do not ever believe all these lying, romantic movies of the men being so big and strong and the women being weak and scared and not knowing what to do.

"Do you think for one minute that Salvador and I would have ever gotten this far and built this fine home here if I'd left things up to him? Why, it's taken me these fifty years to civilize him, I tell you, and make him into the man he thinks he is today—a fine, great man with his airs of fine cigars and all his show-off ways."

"You tell them, Lupe, you tell them!" shouted Carlota. "These girls need to know! All men are cowards and liars and no good! But what can we women do? A dog can't give us what we want, so we're stuck needing to do what we can with men!"

The screeching that now erupted from the young women in the living room was so loud, it even startled the men in the next room.

"Carlota!" said Lupe. "That kind of talk helps no one! What these girls need to know is that life was never meant to be easy, and especially not easy for us women, ever since God chose for us to be the carriers of life here inside of our bodies, and not the men. Oh, no man knows the joys of pregnancy or the pains of birthing," added Lupe, "and so they can't possibly have the respect and understanding of life that women have!"

"Exactly," said Carlota. "This is why I chose to never have children, and I don't care what any priest tells me—because priests are men, too, and they don't know—I wasn't going through all that suffering that I saw my mother and sisters go through just because they had a few moments of pleasure with a man, but the man—the no-good—can just run off abandoning what he created, and continue his own pleasure!"

"On this, I entirely disagree with my sister Carlota," said Lupe. "But, I will say that I wish I could've spoken up fifty years ago as I spoke up to this priest today. Because life will continue to be—not just difficult for us women—but completely unfair if we allow people like this young priest to get away with getting us to use words like 'obey' and not the men!"

"Tell them, Lupe, tell them!" shouted Carlota, waving her cane in the air. "This is good! Really good! Now you're talking! And girls, any time your husband says to you, 'Oh, no, honey, you just don't understand, because you're a woman,' the truth is that he is hiding something and trying to make a fool of you! Mark my words, I know. I had to steal money from Archie, just so I wouldn't always be penniless, and I swear that I worked at our businesses as many hours as he did, or more!"

"I'm sorry to say," said Lupe sadly, "Carlota is right. But I never needed to steal from Salvador, because in our marriage, I handled all the banking and bookkeeping, but—oh, was I in for questioning when any monies were missing! Then, so help me God, every time it turned out that Salvador, himself, had spent that money, but it never stopped him from trying to blame me the next time.

"I swear," said Lupe, "I now realize that every marriage is like returning to the Garden of Eden, and there is Adam again, trying to blame Eve for his own shortcomings. So what you girls need to know is that it is absolutely not for any wife to obey her husband, and it has never been! It is for a wife to understand that above all else, she is a mother, and as a mother, ours is to attend to the survival of our children and of the home. And a home, *mi hijitas,* is not a fine house with great walls and roof, but a piece of the Mother Earth where a woman has squatted down to give birth, and in doing this sacred act, she makes that piece of Earth Holy before God," added Lupe with power.

"Lupe is right," said Carlota, tears coming to her eyes, "we had nothing but sticks with mud for walls for our home in Mexico, and our floor was dirt that we swept and watered down every morning and afternoon and polished smooth with the sweat and oil of our bare feet. But oh, what a home we had. The finest home in all the world, because our mother—God bless her soul—showed us love and the way to God every day! And our laughter, and our fights; oh, we were poor, but so happy with our love of *la familia!*"

Carlota couldn't go on—she was crying so much. There was not one dry eye among all the women in the room.

IN THE NEXT ROOM Salvador was leisurely smoking his long, fat cigar. The husbands of Linda, Gorjenna, and RoseAna were also smoking cigars. But they were puffing on their cigars like a person does with a cigarette, causing their fine cigars to burn too hot and fast. The whole room was filling up with smoke. Victor, Salvador and Lupe's only son, got up to open the side door. Victor hardly ever smoked, and the smoke was bothering him. Glancing into the next room, he saw that their Aunt Carlota's face was full of mischief as she talked to the younger women.

"I'm not joking," she was saying. "We women have to know how to get our way with men or we don't got a chance. Everything is organized to their side. Not ours. So the best way for us to get our way is by rolling our eyes and hips like this and pretending to be obedient, but we are not! No, we're thinking and planning all the time. It's hell, I tell you, living with men!"

And as she said this, Carlota rolled her big, painted-up eyes to the heavens and gave such a smile with her powdered-white face as she moved her hips suggestively that the young women were all busting with laughter.

"*Tia Tota!*" screeched Gorjenna, blushing. "I didn't know you could still move like that!"

"You're just terrible!" said RoseAna, wiping her eyes—she was laughing so hard.

"Oh, no, she's not terrible! She's good!" yelped Teresita, shuffling her feet and doing a little dance. "And roll those hips again, *Tia Tota*! Roll 'em and roll 'em! And keep those joints loose and young!"

Carlota did as her niece Teresita said, holding on to her cane with her right hand and raising her left hand to dance and roll her hips, like a real ballroom sex machine.

"Well," said Lupe, "I was always very different from my sister Carlota, as all you girls know, so I never rolled my eyes and did those other things to get my way in my marriage. What I did was speak up very frankly, saying what I was thinking, as I'd seen our mother do with our father. But I'll tell you, it wasn't always easy, especially when we first got married and I was so young and I knew nothing. And Salvador, like a typical man, just thought that he knew everything.

"And why do men think this, God only knows," continued Lupe. "When it's so obvious, as my mother-in-law, Doña Margarita, explained to me, that it was us, the women, that God entrusted with the carrying of life here in our womb, so He obviously thought a great deal of us.

"I loved that old woman so much," added Lupe. "I tell you, a mother-in-law can be a great asset to a young wife, if the wife is wise and open-minded, and that mother-in-law knows how to give advice from a distance."

"But Lupe," said Carlota, smiling, "you have to admit that this is the very reason God gave men such big heads, the truth is that the poor fools are really good for nothing. You kept this family together, not Salvador!"

"Well, then, *grandmama*," said Gorjenna, sipping her champagne, "are you saying that maybe you wouldn't have even married *grandpapa*, if you had it all over to do today?"

RoseAna slugged Gorjenna on the shoulder so hard that she almost knocked her younger, smaller sister off her feet.

"Gorjenna," said Linda, hitting her niece on her other shoulder, equally hard. "When are you going to learn to watch your mouth!"

"Stop hitting me, you two!" yelled Gorjenna back at them. "Or I'm not joking, I'll hit back and hard, too! Who are you guys kidding? This is what we all really want to know!"

"She's right," said Teresita, making a face at her sister Linda, "so you two guys stop hitting her, or I'll join Gorjenna and we'll knock you old fogies for a loop! She is only asking the juicy question that we all really want to know, but don't have the guts to ask. So come on, *mama*, tell us," added Teresita, turning to her mother, "if you had it all over to do, would you marry *papa*?"

The room went silent and Linda's eyes filled with tears, but she never made a sound.

"You want to know the truth?" said Lupe, taking a big sip of her champagne. Her eyes suddenly lighting up with *gusto*. "Eh, you girls really want to know?"

"Yes!" said Teresita, Gorjenna, and RoseAna excitedly.

Tencha and Barbara—Victor's wife—only nodded, saying nothing.

Linda shook her head, saying, "No, please, dear God, no," but she said it all so softly that no one heard.

And across the room Victor, who'd been smiling, quit smiling and took a big breath.

"No, of course not," said Lupe to her daughters and granddaughters. "If I'd known Salvador back then, like I know him now—I would never have married him. He lied to me! He tricked me!"

"And I warned you!" shouted Carlota, shaking her cane up at the ceiling. "I told you that he was a liar and a bootlegger before you married him! But no, you wouldn't listen to me! You believed him instead!"

Linda had to grip the piano to steady herself. She was getting physically ill.

"Quiet, Carlota!" said Lupe. "This is for me to say! Not you!" Lupe was high on champagne and she wasn't going to be stopped. "Salvador swore to me days before our wedding," she continued, "that he was an honest, hardworking fertilizer mover, and that he didn't drink or gamble. And Carlota is right, I did believe him, and we got married. Then it wasn't until after I was pregnant that he had the guts to tell me the truth that he was a bootlegger, a gambler, and he drank and carried a gun! Everything that we were brought up to detest in our home!"

Linda now quit holding on to the piano for support, stood up straight, and screamed: "Lies! Nothing but lies! Oh, I detest how you two are going on with this one-sided complaining about *papa*, without owning up to your own damn responsibilities!

"Papa loves you, *mama*! He has always loved you! If my husband ever showed me half the love *papa* always shows you, *mama*, I'd drag my ass across burning fire just to be with him! And yes, we all know that *papa* isn't perfect, but damn it—oh, you should be ashamed, both of you!"

And saying this, Linda threw her champagne glass across the room, shattering it against the fireplace; then she turned and walked out the front door, slamming it so hard that the whole house shook.

In the playroom, the kids had stopped watching TV, and they came racing through the house to see what was going on.

In the living room, Teresita was howling with laughter, and then she, too, threw her crystal glass of champagne across the room against the fireplace.

"Welcome to our *familia*," said Teresita, laughing *con carcajadas*. "Welcome to our crazy-*loca familia*!"

Gorjenna was the next one to drink off her champagne and throw her glass with a scream. Then everyone got into the act, even Carlota.

In the next room, Salvador calmly continued smoking his big, fat cigar, burning red-hot like a hardwood log that took a long time to turn into ashes.

But not all the men felt as comfortable as Salvador with this crazy behavior of the women. Some of the young men were getting very anxious—especially Linda's husband, Roger. He was squirming. He just couldn't find any reason for women to behave so wildly.

But Salvador, the lead bull, was through with trying to educate sons-in-law, so he just kept smoking, not saying one word as the younger men continued squirming and smoking their cigars too fast.

Outside, Linda looked up at the stars. It was a beautiful night. Then catching her breath, she came back into the house, slamming the front door again. She walked into the living room, right up to the women.

"Okay," she said, "let's settle this thing once and for all! Come on, let's not be chickens! Let's go into the other room and ask *papa*!"

"Ask him what?" said Gorjenna, looking startled.

"Gorjenna!" screamed Linda. "Don't act innocent! Come on, you started this whole damn thing!"

"You mean, that you now want me to go ask *grandpapa*, if he had it all over to do, would he marry *grandmama*?"

Linda nodded, wiping the tears from her eyes. "Exactly," she said.

"Oh, no," said Gorjenna. "I've screwed up enough for one day. I'm now gonna keep my mouth shut, just like *Tia Tota* here. Eh, *Tota*, you and me, we don't talk no more, no matter what we're thinking."

"Yes, I think you're right," said Carlota. "Because no matter what I say, even if it's the truth, everybody just—"

"*Tota!*" snapped Teresita. "You heard *mama*. Quiet! Not one more single word! Lips closed, like this, only opening them to drink champagne!" she added, laughing. "Come on, what the hell; Linda is right. Let's not be chickens and do things halfway! Let's use all the crystal, get refills, then go and ask *papa*, too!"

"But he'll only lie," said Carlota, "you know that. Lupe was so beautiful that she could have had her pick of anyone, even that *gringo* Mark, who was educated and his parents were wealthy, but what did she do, she—"

Lupe saw it first.

Lupe was the first one to see that Linda, with tears streaming down her face, now stepped forward to slap her aunt across the face. And Linda was strong, so this slap would be no little ladylike slap.

But Lupe was able to step in front of her daughter before this great tragedy could occur. She grabbed her daughter Linda's hand, stopping her in midswing. Then Lupe whirled on her sister. "CARLOTA!" yelled Lupe. "I forbid you to say one more bad thing about my husband while you are under his roof!"

"But—"

"No buts!" screamed Lupe into her sister's face. "Don't you see how your words offend his children? Are you so blind in your hate that you can't see what you've been doing all these years! Why, you've insulted their very blood!"

"But, Lupe, they also came from you," said Carlota, still not able to let go. "That's why they're good."

"It's okay, *mama*," said Linda, drying her eyes and gripping her forehead with the hand with which she'd been prepared to slap her aunt. "Let her go on talking. I'm leaving, and I'm never setting foot in this house again as long as I live!"

And saying this, Linda quickly turned to leave once again, hurrying across the large, spacious living room toward the front door, but Gorjenna and Teresita caught her.

"Come on, Linda," said Gorjenna, blocking the front door with her body, "I'll ask *papa*. I'll do it! But damnit, I just never meant all this to happen."

"Linda," said Teresita, taking her sister in her arms, "I love you. We all love you. Remember, no matter what, we're *familia*, and we will always be *familia*! Hell, don't you remember, *papa* always said that half the time his mother would say that it was better to have pigs than relatives, because at least you could kill the pigs and eat them, but what could you do with relatives when things got wild?"

"*Papa's* mother didn't say that," said Linda, wiping her eyes. "It was *mama's papa* who always said that, and he said it about kids; not relatives."

"Well, whatever," said Teresita. "Now, come on back, and we'll ask *papa*. But first, more champagne!"

"Oh, Lupe, God forgive me!" Carlota was saying at the other end of the room. "I never meant to offend your children, it's just that Salvador has always been a liar and a no—"

"Can't you keep quiet, Carlota?" yelled Lupe. "You see how you offend, and yet you just keep talking! He wasn't your husband, Carlota, he was mine, and still is, have respect!"

Opening up another couple of bottles of Mumm's champagne, Tencha and Barbara filled everyone's new crystal glasses, and then they all started across the living room to the dining room, where the men were sitting around the long dining table, smoking cigars.

This time Carlota didn't try to take the lead as she'd done when they'd gone outside to do the family portrait. She stayed behind, along with Lupe.

At the far side of the long, narrow dining room sat Salvador in his large, burgundy, all-leather office chair that he'd purchased especially to use in the dining room. He just loved to lean back between bites and leisurely chew his food like a bull chewing his cud in a peaceful, green meadow.

He was now leaning back in the tall-back chair, smoking his long, fat cigar, truly enjoying to look at the gray-white smoke rising from the burning end of his fine Mexican cigar made in the state of Veracruz.

"*Papa,*" said Teresita, who even as a child had always had a very quiet, strong way about her, "we've come to ask you something very important."

"What might that be?" said Salvador, looking up from his cigar at this youngest daughter of his. He could see that they all looked nervous; all these young women who stood here before him, ranging in age from their early twenties to late forties. He saw their anxiousness, their excited faces, and yes, their apprehension, too. He breathed, taking a deep breath. He could see that Lupe and Carlota had stayed behind in the other room.

"So ask," he added.

"Papa," said Teresita, "we want to know that if you had it all over to do, would you still marry *mama*, knowing her like you know her now?"

"Of course," he said, "absolutely!"

"But *papa*," continued Teresita, "would you still lie to *mama* if you had it all over to do?"

"Lie?" said Salvador, now glancing around at all the young men, who were anxiously listening, too.

"Yes, about your bootlegging and gambling," said Teresita.

"Oh, that! Of course," he said, laughing with *gusto*. "How else can a man catch an angel?" He looked at Lupe in the next room. "Just look at your mother. She was so young and innocent when we got married."

Everyone turned and looked across the dining room to the living room, where Lupe had remained to play with her grandchildren and great-grandchildren. And there she was, old and gray, but still looking like an angel as she sat telling a story to the children.

"I was an outlaw!" shouted Salvador with power. "A bootlegger! Everything that Lupe had been raised to hate, but once she saw that we were married and going to have a baby, I saw this young angel of mine rise up with the power of a shooting star to protect her nest!

"This is a woman to live for with all your heart! How do you think men have been getting good women to marry them since the beginning of time. All men lie, *mi hijita*."

"See!" shouted Carlota from the other room. "I told you so! He even admits it! He lied! He's a liar! And he's no good!"

"Oh, shut your damn stupid mouth!" bellowed Salvador, leaping out of his grand chair and the cords of his old, wrinkled-up neck coming up like ropes. "At least I'm honest about my lies! But you, you lie to yourself so much that you couldn't see the truth if it hit you! Admit it, you've always been jealous of your sister since the day she was born, and still are!

"It takes guts for any woman to marry, have children, and make a home! You're nothing but a loudmouth, coward *pendeja!* Men are good! Nothing wrong with a real *macho a lo cabrón!* Let's not play the constipated fool! You show me a man, Carlota, who's all nice and wonderful like you women pretend that you want 'em, and I'll show you a man who you women don't wet your pants for when he touches you!"

"Salvador!" said Lupe, having come rushing into the room behind her sister once she'd heard Carlota's voice, yelling at Salvador. "Have respect! These are your daughters and granddaughters who are listening to you! Isn't it enough that you ruined my life?"

"RUINED YOUR LIFE, HELL!" bellowed Salvador. "Admit it, Lupe, you've loved your life with me, and still do! It's just all this *caca de toro* that's put into women's heads by stupid, romantic books and movies that has ruined everything!" And saying this, he smashed his cigar into his ash-tray and came across the room. Everyone moved aside. "Lupe," he said, "come, let's make the kiss!"

"No, you're drunk! And you stink of cigar!" she added.

"So, what's new?" he said. "Men drink and smell like goats; this is the real perfume of life, those juices BETWEEN OUR LEGS!"

And he reached out for her . . . softly, gently, tenderly, gazing into her eyes the whole time. And she didn't move away. No, she held still as a hummingbird, fluttering in midair. He touched her cheek with his finger-tips, ever so gently, but didn't move in any closer. You could hear a pin drop, the whole room had become so quiet.

"Lupe," he said, gliding his fingers across her cheek and neck, "come, let's make that kiss, *mi amor*."

"No, Salvador!" she snapped.

"Lupe, Lupe," he said softly, never taking his eyes off her eyes as he continued to stroke her oh, so gently, "come on, just one little kiss."

She shook her head, then moved her weight from one foot to the other, but still she didn't move away. No, she held close to him, behaving just like a mare in heat by shifting her weight, and keeping in close.

And Gorjenna, having bred many mares, caught it first, then so did Linda and Victor. This was so basic, so natural, if people just knew anything about their animal husbandry.

"Come on, Lupe," Salvador now said, "let's see that little smile of yours, that little, cute, twisted smile." He grinned.

"No," she snapped, being annoyed and stomping her foot, "I will not smile! I am not your toy!"

Gorjenna had to cover her mouth to not shriek. This stomping of the foot was right on schedule in the mating game between a stud and a mare. She glanced at Linda and Victor—who were also into horses—and she saw that they had seen it, too.

"Not even one little, tiny smile?" continued Salvador.

"No!" snapped Lupe again, moving the whole of her hips.

"Oh, yes, here, here it's coming, Lupe. It's coming, that little smile," he said, showing his teeth with a big grin, just as a stud would now do.

"Oh, Salvador!" said Lupe, not being able to stand it anymore. And she now suddenly smiled, showing her own teeth, and she stuck her tongue out at him. "I don't want to smile! Because, well, it's all still true," she said, hitting him, "if I'd known you then, as I know you now, I never, never would've married you, and that's the truth, and you know it! Those first few years of our marriage were awful!"

"Yes, of course they were," he said, calmly. "I agree completely; those first two or three years were awful, and yes, you never would've married me, and I knew that, and so that's why I lied. Oh, *querida mia*, you are still my angel! Just look at you, your eyes, your lips, your little smile—even when you don't want to smile—and your hands.

"I was watching your hands, *querida,* when you were in the other room playing with our grandchildren as you told them a story, and the way your hands moved, flying like birds as you spoke to them—oh, Lupe, you still fill my heart with as much love today as you did the first day I saw you! *Ah, te amo con todo mi corazón!*" he shouted with *gusto*.

There wasn't a dry eye in the whole room. Even the guys were choking.

"But Salvador, you were MONSTROUS! I can't forgive you for some of the things you did! The distillery blowing up in Tustin, and the police sirens were coming, and I thought you were dead, and Tencha here, still breast-feeding, and oh, it was awful!"

"DON'T FORGIVE HIM!" yelled Carlota from across the room. "You should've married Mark, Lupe! He was good! He was decent! He didn't eat like a pig! He had table manners!"

Salvador exploded! "My God, I'm going to kill this woman yet! Not one moment of peace have we had with her around! And where she gets this mouth of hers, I don't know. Your mother, Lupe, she treated me with respect and intelligence!"

Saying this, Salvador let go of Lupe and started across the room to grab Carlota by the throat and choke her to death. But Carlota was fast, and she quickly shuffled out of the room with her cane in her hand, scurrying across the living room and down the long hallway.

And she was so fast, so quick with her bad hip and all, that everyone started laughing, even Linda. Life, *la vida,* was so full of turns and twists! And there went *Tía Tota*, running with that old cane of hers, and Salvador after her.

"Why did you marry a man like Archie," he was yelling, "if you hate men so much! He was a bull! Then in Oceanside down by the pier, you were always flirting with all those young men who came into that bar, leaning up over the pool table to fix the balls for them with your short skirt so high that they could see up your underwear! You were *el escándalo del barrio!* A hypocrite, and a liar!"

"Salvador!" Lupe was shouting. "Stop it! Please, stop it! One of you has to have the intelligence to keep respect!"

Everyone was laughing now. The whole thing was hilarious.

"RESPECT, HELL!" Salvador shouted. "Yes, I agree with you, Lupe, the first few years of our marriage were AWFUL, like they are for most married people when they finally really start getting to know each other after all that bullshit goodie-goodie shit of courtship! But," Salvador added with power, "it wouldn't have been so awful if this damn sister of yours hadn't been there at every turn putting in her two cents!

"Admit it, Lupe, if she hadn't been there with us, we could have planted our Holy Seeds of marriage in the first three years of *nuestro matrimonio*, as my mother told us that every young couple must plant, instead of always having to listen to this little barking-bitch-voice of your crazy-*loca* jealous sister!"

"Lupe, don't listen to him!" yelled Carlota from down the hallway, waving her cane as she spoke. "He's lying! You two wouldn't be here today with all your wonderful children if it wasn't for me! Who forced Archie to wire you money when the distillery blew up and you two were running from the law! Who loaned you the money when you wanted to buy this ranch that we're standing on right this very minute? It was me, me, me, Salvador! And you know it!"

"No, I don't know it!" Salvador yelled back at Carlota. "All I know is you got a tongue so big and fat and twisted that even the words that come out of your mouth don't know their own origin!"

"*ABORTO del DIABLO!*" screamed Carlota. "That's what you are! An abortion of the Devil!"

Lupe had tears running down her face, she was so upset. Salvador came back across the room and took her in his arms.

"Lupe," said Salvador, "Lupe. Lupe. Lupe. It's okay," he added, stroking her gently. "It's all right. God's just having a little fun with us like He always does, that's all. Kiss me. Come on, let's make the kiss."

She nodded, and they were kissing softly, gently, and fully.

Linda had tears running down her face.

Teresita, Gorjenna, RoseAna, they were all crying, too.

This was love!

This was the key of living between a man and a woman . . . after fifty years of marriage to kiss and kiss again with an open heart and soul!

Part Two

HONEYMOON

August 18, 1929

Santa Ana, California

2

And so he, the nineteenth child, having come to his mother
at fifty years of age, now found his second truelove, and . . .
they married.

C OMING OUT of the Holy Catholic Church of *Nuestra Señora de Guadalupe* on Third Street and Grand in Santa Ana, California, Salvador and Lupe were met by a crowd of well-wishers who showered them with rice and flowers.

Cameras flashed!

People shouted with *gusto!*

Lupe and Salvador lowered their heads, hurrying down the steps of the church, and quickly got into their beautiful ivory-white 1926 Moon automobile and drove to their reception across town.

And it was a huge, glorious reception with an abundance of food, announcing to all the people of the *barrio* that the terrible days of the Mexican Revolution were over, and it was now time for all of them to start a new life in this fine country of the United States!

Deputy Sheriff Archie Freeman, who was dating Carlota, had barbecued a whole beef *à la* Archie Freeman. And Doña Guadalupe, Lupe's mother, had cooked fifty chickens in *mole*, her specialty. There were barrels of rice and beans and chopped-up *salsa*. And next door, hidden from the nondrinkers—particularly Lupe's family, who were totally against drinking—was a ten-gallon barrel of Salvador's finest bootleg whiskey.

People had come in from all over the Southland and Mexico. Manuelita's family—Lupe's closest female friend since childhood—had come in from Arizona, too.

For months Salvador and Lupe had planned this event, wanting to see their two families finally intermingling, and especially their two great, old mothers, Doña Margarita and Doña Guadalupe. Salvador and Lupe were each the baby of their *familia*, and so this celebration—after so much hardship—was now the crowning event of their two mothers' lives, a pure blessing straight from God!

The Father Sun was going down when Lupe and Salvador were finally able to steal away from the wedding crowd. They went behind Lupe's parents' home into the walnut orchard to be alone. Here in the privacy of the walnut trees, they finally began to really kiss after months of courtship and preparation for their great wedding.

The light of the world was going, and the magic of the night was coming, and they were finally alone, married—having taken their wedding vows before God and all the world—and they were now putting a fire of passion to their very center.

Salvador gripped Lupe close, smelling deeply of her long, dark, beautiful hair, but then—just as they were both beginning to tremble with desire—Lupe turned away.

"Look," said Lupe, pointing Indian-style with puckered lips for Salvador to turn.

He did so, and there walking together were their two grand, old mothers, looking so beautiful, each carrying a cup in her hand as they made their way away from the lights of the party. Their old mothers were laughing with such *gusto*.

Salvador's whole chest swelled up with pride. Only twelve years before, he and his mother and sister, Luisa, had been at the Texas border, caught in a sandstorm, choking to death, but his short, dark, little Indian mother had never given up. No, she'd taken him in hand—when he'd been ready to roll over and die—and she'd sworn to him before the Almighty, that they would live and she'd see him grow and marry and . . . she had.

Tears came to Salvador's eyes, and he turned Lupe, placing her in front of himself so they could both keep watch over their mothers, then he pressed Lupe up against himself, and lowered his head, smelling her naked neck.

Lupe shivered, feeling his hot breath on her neck, and she rolled her head back, wanting to get more of his hot, good breathing on herself. After all, they were married now and so whatever they did together was sacred— her sisters had explained this to her.

Salvador started kissing her ear, using his tongue ever so lightly. Quickly, she turned her head around to face him, and they began kissing once again, as his hands moved smoothly over the small of her waist, stroking her full *Latina* hips.

Now she could feel the fire of Salvador's loins getting hard as molten lava as he pushed up against her backside. Oh, she was on fire, too!

But then suddenly, Lupe broke from her truelove's arms, just like that, without any explanation, and rushed out of the orchard, going past the party, and into her home.

Salvador was left standing in the walnut orchard feeling like a fool. People were glancing at him, wondering what had happened.

Doña Guadalupe, seeing her daughter Lupe rush into their house, quickly followed her.

Salvador went over to his own mother, shrugged his shoulders, and then together they walked next door to where the whiskey was hidden to have a couple of good shots.

"What happened?" asked his mother, Doña Margarita.

"I don't know," said Salvador.

"Don't worry," she said, stroking her son's arm. "Just look around. God is with us. It has been another wonderful day in paradise here on Mother Earth."

But everything didn't feel that wonderful for Salvador or Lupe right now.

When Salvador had rubbed his molten hardness up against her *nalguitas* and he'd begun touching the inner part of her ear with his tongue— quick little hot-flashes had gone shooting all through her body. Suddenly, Lupe had trouble catching her breath, and she'd felt something break inside of her. She'd jerked her ear away from Salvador, tore loose from his arms, and ran with terror as fast as she could for the back door of her parents' home.

Bursting in through the back door of her parents' home, Lupe immediately rushed to the bathroom, which, thank God, was empty, and she'd no more than pulled up the yards and yards of her wedding dress, jerking them to the side and sat down on the toilet, than all these molten-hot juices had come pouring out of her, hitting the toilet bowl with a mighty bang!

Lupe didn't know if she was pissing, or having her period, or if she'd just—God forbid—had her first sexual experience that she'd heard her sisters and girlfriends talking so much about in the last few weeks.

All she knew was that if she'd stayed in Salvador's arms for one more second, she would've never had the presence of mind to leave his embrace. When he'd put the tip of his thick tongue into her ear, that had been—oh, she'd felt all these little quick wonderful hot-flashes go shooting through her!

"*Mi hijita,*" Lupe heard her mother calling her through the door, "are you all right?"

"I don't know, *mama,*" said Lupe. "I think I am."

"Can I come in?"

"No, please," said Lupe, flushing the toilet and trying to get to her feet. But she felt so lightheaded that she immediately had to sit back down on the toilet.

"I'm coming in," said Doña Guadalupe.

"Oh, *mama,* I don't know what happened," said Lupe, taking her mother's hand. "We were so happy, then I suddenly felt something break and had to rush to the bathroom."

"Don't worry, *mi hijita,* a woman's body can have many complications. This is nothing new," her mother told her. "In fact, this often happens with a young woman when she is a virgin. After all these years of yearning, her female body just bursts open," she added, laughing. "Why, one of your very own sisters—but which one I will not say—had so much going on before her wedding night, that she burst like a ripe watermelon, not really knowing if she'd peed, or had a sexual outburst. After all, our female openings are all pretty close together, whether goats, pigs, cows, or us women. So *calmate, mi hijita,* for you are not the first or the last to be a little overwhelmed with your body's reactions on your wedding day."

"But, *mama,* what should I do? I'm afraid of going to bed on those fine sheets that my *nina* Sophia hand-embroidered with pink flowers and little, tiny green leaves and vines, and soil them."

The older woman burst out laughing. "Spoken just like a real woman! Of your husband, you are not even thinking, but of those pretty sheets that make up your nest—you are thinking completely!"

Lupe's eyes filled with tears. Being with her mother felt so safe.

"Look, *mi hijita,*" said her mother, "you don't have to go on your honeymoon if you don't want to, *querida.* The truth is that half the women I know would have been better off, if they'd met their husbands a week later. With the preparation of a wedding, and the men all drinking, it's a wonder any marriage ever gets off on the right foot. Rape is more often what happens on a girl's first night, if the truth be known."

"But *mama,* Salvador has worked so hard to prepare our house in Carlsbad."

"So?" said the tough, old, warrior-woman, refusing to be moved. "Then all the more reason for you to go when you are ready and he's not crazy from all these activities!"

"But what will I tell him?" Lupe asked.

"I'll tell him for you," said her mother. "Don't you worry about that. You'll have plenty of opportunity over the course of your marriage to have to speak up for yourself, but . . . that doesn't have to start today. Now, tell me, *mi hijita,*" she added in a gentler tone of voice, "what was it that you flushed; blood, pee, or *el caldo de miel?*"

Oh, Lupe would've died if her mother had spoken to her like this just a week ago. For *"el caldo de miel"* meant "the soup of honey," as the sexual juices were referred to in Mexico. But something had happened to Lupe with the preparations for the wedding, and so she wasn't embarrassed at all. It was as if, well, in some way she and her mother had become more like friends over the last few weeks, than mother and daughter.

"I think maybe all three, *mama,*" said Lupe, blushing all red, then laughing. "But I don't know. It almost felt like all my female parts just burst open! And I didn't really want to take a good look at it before I flushed."

"Did it feel good, or did it burn when it burst?" asked her mother.

Lupe blushed. "A little of both, *mama,*" she said, recalling how it had felt so wonderful when Salvador had pressed his body up against her backside and put his tongue in her ear. Oh, she'd almost died!

"Then I don't think we have anything to worry about; you're okay."

Lupe then went to her mother's arms, hugging her and feeling so good to have such a wonderful, wise woman as her mother.

GOING BACK OUTSIDE, Doña Guadalupe approached Salvador and his mother, explaining to both of them that everything was fine, but that Lupe wouldn't be able to go on her honeymoon.

"She's going to have to stay home for a few days," she added, glancing at Salvador's mother, Doña Margarita.

"It is as it is," said Doña Margarita, raising up her cup of whiskey. "I might have had a better marriage too if my own mother had kept me home for a few days after our wedding. He was drinking. We were dancing. Even the livestock got wild our celebration was so noisy.

"*Mi hijito*," added the short old Indian woman, turning to her son, "you have a fine, smart, wise mother-in-law, *gracias a Dios!*"

"Thank you, señora," said Salvador to Lupe's mother, and he tried to smile and see how all this was for the best, but he was too upset. My God, he'd been looking forward to their wedding night for months. This, he'd thought, was to be the highlight of their lives.

Salvador decided to get stinking drunk, and so he did and everything was going well, until a few of his male friends started to tease him. Salvador viciously knocked one down and silenced the rest by telling them that in the mountainous area of Mexico where he was from, it wasn't uncommon for an inexperienced bride to stay home for instructions before joining her husband.

The teasing stopped.

After all, among *los Mejicanos* the purity of an inexperienced virgin was the highest honor that any man could ever hope to bring to his bridal bed.

Also, if anyone had continued to tease Salvador, there would have been guns drawn.

NOW, IT WAS the following morning and Salvador was waking up in Corona—some sixty miles east of their wedding in Santa Ana, California. His mouth tasted awful. He had a terrible hangover, and he just couldn't wake up.

He could feel someone kissing him and tickling his ear, ever so softly. At first, he thought it was Lupe, his truelove, kissing him in their little cottage in Carlsbad—along the coast south of Santa Ana. But, then, he remembered that she hadn't come on their honeymoon. He opened his eyes and here was his old mother before him, tickling him in the face with a long rooster's tailfeather. And to his shock, it wasn't his truelove in bed with him. No, it was his sister Luisa's mangy old dog who was with him, licking his neck and ears.

Salvador leaped out of bed! The dog smelled foul! "*Mama*, stop it!" he yelled. "Oh, my God! My head hurts!" he added, almost losing his balance and falling.

"Good, you deserve it," she said, laughing *con carcajadas*. "It's way past noon! You've been kissing that dirty dog all morning."

Hearing this, Salvador rushed out of the little shack, spitting in pure revulsion. Outside, he massaged his forehead as he leaned against the avocado tree by his mother's outhouse and started peeing. The pain in his head would not subside.

After relieving himself, Salvador went back inside his old mother's shack. He was still shaking. His mother had a cup of coffee ready for him.

"I put some hair of dog in your coffee for you," she said, handing him a steaming mug.

He made a face. "Hair of Luisa's dog, *mama*?"

The old woman laughed. "No, not Luisa's dog. This is what our priest, Father Ryan, says in English, 'hair of the dog,' when he puts a little whiskey in his coffee to help him get over his hangover. English, I swear, the more I learn, the more I have to laugh. Did you know that in English they call liquor, 'spirits'? I love it! Anyway," she added, "how are you feeling, *mi hijito?* Pretty bad, eh?"

"Yes, *mama*," he said, "awful! I'd like to loan my head to my worst enemy!"

"Well, all right," she said, "sit down and sip your coffee and feel awful if you want for an hour or two, but then no more, because I've figured out that this is the perfect opportunity—when everyone thinks you're on your honeymoon—for you to do some very interesting work. Remember, there is no bad from which good doesn't come in life, if we just open our eyes and see past our limited vision. Who knows, maybe this situation has actually saved your marriage in the long run, eh?"

"Oh, please, *mama*, I don't want to hear any of your old wisdom kind of stuff! Besides, I've heard all you have to say a thousand times!"

"Oh, only a thousand," she said, refusing to be intimidated, "then I guess I need to tell you a few more times. The two greatest sayings of our whole entire Mexican culture are *con el favor de Dios*, with the favor of God, and *no hay mal que por bien no viene*, there is no bad from which—"

"All right, all right, I heard you, *mama*! But please, no more! I'm in pain!"

"Okay, then not another word. But I want you to know that I'm only giving you another couple of hours to feel bad, then that's it. No more. You get out and start scratching the dirt, looking for seed like any other hungry, healthy chicken.

"Remember, one hour a day of feeling bad or sorry for yourself is good and healthy. Two hours is okay, but three fists of Sun and you need your food and water taken away, so thirst and hunger can then become your teachers. Life was never meant to be easy here on earth, but a lesson learned either by love or *chingasos!*" she added, laughing *con carcajadas!*

"*Mama;* please, no more!" said Salvador, going back outside. His head was pulsating with pain. He didn't want to hear any more of his mother's old stuff. My God, sometimes he just wished that she'd shut the hell up!

Going back outside, Salvador sat down on an old orange crate under the huge avocado tree between his mother's shack and his sister Luisa's house. The Sun was high overhead, and sipping his coffee with the whiskey and plenty of sugar, little by little, he began to feel better.

"Hair of the dog," he said quietly to himself. He'd never heard this American expression before. "Hair of a dirty, mangy dog," he now said, remembering how he'd awoken with Luisa's dog in his bed, kissing him.

Finishing his coffee, Salvador began to see that maybe his crazy old mother was, indeed, correct. There really were no accidents in life, *la vida*, so maybe this was, in fact, the perfect opportunity . . . for him to take care of some very important unfinished business before he began his life as a married man. After all, none of his bootlegging competitors would ever expect a lightning-fast attack from a man on his honeymoon.

FOR SEVERAL MONTHS NOW, two guys had been coming down from Los Angeles to Carlsbad, trying to cut into Salvador's bootlegging territory. Everyone knew that Salvador's territory included all of North County San Diego, then the areas of Lake Elsinore and Temecula. The areas of Riverside and San Bernardino he shared with two other medium-size bootleggers, and San Clemente, San Juan Capistrano, Tustin, and Orange he also shared. In Los Angeles, Salvador was completely out of the picture. That huge area of the City of the Angels, with its thick density of population, was an area strictly taken care of by the big boys, the Italians, who were out of Fresno. They were in a whole other league than Salvador.

This big organization from Fresno—in the San Joaquin Valley in central California—had connections from the East Coast, and the power to bring in the finest liquor makers from Italy. They had the exclusive rights to all of Los Angeles, San Francisco, and Sacramento.

With these big boys, Salvador wanted no *problemas*. In fact, he was in their debt, because, after all, it had been one of their finest liquor makers from the old country, Al Cappola, who'd originally taught Salvador how to make "bootleg" liquor when they'd been spending time together in jail in Tulare, just outside of Fresno.

There in the jail of Tulare, everyone had been fighting each other like cats and dogs, when Salvador had been put into the tank. In no uncertain terms, with a lightning-fast attack, Salvador had demolished the biggest troublemaker, a big bully redneck farmboy, and then he'd had an election taken among all the prisoners, including the Chinaman, electing a judge and three enforcers, and all the bullying and sexual abuses had instantly been brought to a stop.

That was when the dignified, old Italian had seen Salvador's worth and so he'd immediately befriended him. And when Salvador learned what it was that the old man did for his livelihood, Salvador had offered to pay him a few dollars per day—a huge sum—if this great magician from Italy would teach him the art of making fine liquor.

At first old man Al Cappola had stared at Salvador with his huge, lioned face, saying absolutely *nada, nada,* nothing. But then he'd finally spoken. "If any other man would ask me this, I'd spit in his face, but . . . seeing how you are a man of high intelligence, who immediately brought peace and respect to this tank of fools, then I say, yes, I will teach you," the old man had added with a power. "But with the understanding that you will never do any business in a territory that belongs to our organization of the *amigos Italianos!*"

Salvador had agreed and after that, he and Al Cappola had become very good friends, *paisanos* as they say, and so the big organization out of Fresno respected Salvador and he respected them. This was why he, Salvador, couldn't figure out who were these two guys who were coming down from Los Angeles and trying to move into his territory.

But who knew? Management changed hands in every organization, and a bootlegger's territories were as vital to a bootlegger's survival as hunting territories were to a tribe of hunter-gatherers.

Sipping his second cup of coffee, a large part of Salvador just felt like hunting down these two guys, killing them both, and that would be that, bringing an end to the whole thing. What really made him mad was that these sneaky bastards had only started moving into his territory once he'd started making plans for his wedding.

The world of men truly didn't respect a man in love.

To marry, that was okay, but to really fall in love with the woman you planned to marry, this was a sure sign—among men—that you'd lost your marbles and joined the world of women and children.

And then began the jokes, "Hey, *mano,* has she put the ring in your nose, yet? Who wears the pants, eh? Have you been told to squat when you pee so you don't mess the hole of the outhouse?"

The list of these remarks was endless, and none of them were innocent, his mother had explained to him. These remarks were well-thought and were all aimed at you, a newlywed, to make you feel stupid and weak because you were in love.

"And so, *mi hijito*, above all else," his mother had told him, "this is why each new married couple must be very careful of their friends who are single or embittered in their own marriage. These vultures will try to drag you down into their own world of discontent, because—to see you happy—threatens their entire world!"

Breathing deeply, Salvador glanced up at his old mother who'd come outside to water her plants. Oh, how he loved this old bag of Indian bones. He smiled. Sunlight was coming down all about her as she went from plant to plant, humming and giving love to each.

Watching his mother, it truly angered Salvador how these two snakes from Los Angeles had no respect for love or family, and they'd come in, trying to take away his livelihood once they'd seen that he was getting married.

But, still, if he killed them both, then it turned out that they were, indeed, part of that big outfit out of Fresno, he'd be in big trouble. His heart began pounding. He'd have to be very careful.

After all, he was now really a married man, and so he couldn't just take the chances that he'd taken as a single man.

He breathed. Either way, his mother was right, this was the perfect opportunity to catch those two guys by surprise, because nobody but nobody figured that a man on his honeymoon would have murder in his heart.

STRETCHING, waking up the day after her wedding in her parents' house in Santa Ana, California, Lupe realized that she felt a lot better than she'd felt the night before when she'd run away from Salvador. But she now wondered if she'd really done the right thing to let her mother talk her out of going on her honeymoon.

Because, yesterday when he'd been holding her in his arms—it had felt like heaven with all those little hot-flashes shooting through her body. Lupe continued stretching as she awoke. Oh, she'd slept so well. All night long she'd dreamed of holding Salvador in her arms, hugging him and kissing him and smelling of him so warm and close.

She wondered how Salvador had spent his night. Had he also dreamed of making love to her all night long? She hoped so. And she wondered if her truelove was right now, at this very moment, thinking of her, too.

AND, INDEED, at that very instant, Salvador was thinking of Lupe, too. He was thinking of how he'd awoken in bed this morning with a mangy old dog instead of his bride. But he now put all his thoughts of Lupe and the dog out of his mind and he started to figure a plan of how to get these two guys from the City of the Angels who thought that he'd become easy pickings because he'd gotten married.

Salvador finished off his third cup of coffee with some hair of the dog, had a little breakfast, then he quickly got dressed in his old, worn-out work clothes and was out the door. He was ready.

It was late afternoon. Somehow, the day had just slipped away. The Father Sun, the blanket of the poor, was now only five fists off the distant horizon in the west, and so he had to move quickly.

"And where are you going in such a big hurry?" asked his old mother, Doña Margarita, who was coming in after having run Luisa's chickens out of her garden. "Eh? Tell me. I want to know."

"Look, I'm busy, *mama,*" said Juan Salvador. Hell, he'd already visited with his old mother nearly half a day, then they'd had breakfast with his sister Luisa and her two sons Jose and Pedro in the front house. He was in a big hurry. "I got to go. I'll explain things to you when I get back tonight."

He had his jacket and his snubnose .38 Special Smith and Wesson in hand and headed for his truck. He wouldn't be taking his Moon automobile for this job.

"I'm going with you," said the old woman, seeing his jacket and gun.

"*Mama,* damnit, I'm twenty-five years old and a married man, surely I can go out on my own for the afternoon," he said. "I'm sorry to talk to you in this way, but I'm in a hurry, and I don't have time to have you tagging along with me today! Maybe tomorrow you can come with me, okay, *mama?*"

"No, it's not okay!" shouted the old, toothless woman. "I'm getting my shawl and rosary and I'm going with you right now, and that's that!"

She set her hoe by the front door and hurried inside her tiny one-room shack, got her shawl and rosary and was out the door. Salvador rolled his eyes to the heavens. But there was just no arguing with this stubborn, old Indian woman when she got like this.

Luisa's two older boys Jose and Pedro were in a rocky field beyond their two houses, playing baseball with the other neighborhood kids. At thirteen years old Jose Leon—who'd been named after Luisa's first husband Jose-Luis—was a big, strong kid who was already taller than Salvador. But Pedro, on the other hand, at eleven years old was small and cute like Luisa's second husband Epitacio, whom Luisa now lived with in the run-down, four-room house in front.

Epitacio worked part-time for Salvador.

Salvador had trained Epitacio Leon in the art of making liquor, but Epitacio had nothing to do with the selling of the whiskey. Epitacio, Salvador had found out to his surprise, was a good, solid, hardworking man who didn't complain about the long hours of the distillery process, which often had to go around the clock for seventy-two hours at a time. But for the sales of the bootleg whiskey, Epitacio didn't want anything to do with it. He hated guns and violence and also Luisa didn't want him to have anything to do with it.

Luisa had already lost her first husband to violence, and so she didn't want to lose her second. Plus, Epitacio Leon also just wasn't that brave when it came to weapons and strong-arm competitors—even though his last name was lion.

Juan Salvador now waved to Luisa and Epitacio, who were out in the back working on their chicken coop, because—not only were their chickens getting into Doña Margarita's garden—but lately the *coyotes* were also killing their chickens. Salvador helped his old mother get in his Model T truck and they were off.

When Salvador made deliveries, he never used his beautiful, ivory-white Moon automobile or his fancy suits. No, that kind of showy stuff was only for the movies as far as he was concerned. For deliveries, Salvador liked to look like what he was, a worker, a deliveryman, and so he dressed in his oldest, dirtiest clothes and covered his barrels of whiskey with horse manure so no one would ever suspect what it was that he really did.

Cowshit, he'd found out the hard way, was too wet and didn't wash off the barrels very well. Chickenshit smelled too strong. And why chickenshit was so strong was because birds—chickens, hawks, turkeys, all birds—didn't pee separately, so when they crapped they were also peeing at the same time, making it a very strong manure.

Horseshit was best, Salvador had found out, and not just for hauling whiskey, but for his mother's plants, too. It was a weaker shit. Horses didn't have two stomachs and rechew their food like cows or goats—all split-hoof animals, except the pig family—and they, also, pissed separately. Knowing your shit could really help a man or woman in more ways than one, Salvador's mother had told him all of his life, and he could see that she was absolutely right. A person's shit told you not just what that person was eating, but if they were relaxed and taking the time to chew their food. Farts, *pedos,* these were also a very telling story.

Getting on the highway, Salvador headed southeast into the hill country between Corona and Lake Elsinore. There he turned off the road into some oak trees, got out, walked around, made sure they weren't being followed, then he took some brush and brushed out the tracks of his Model T truck and headed downstream, driving alongside the dry riverbed.

Parking in some thick brush, his mother got out and stretched her legs and Salvador went down into the dry riverbed with a shovel and dug up a stash of six ten-gallon barrels of whiskey.

Salvador had been running-in-panic for the last six weeks. His ex-partner Julio, a good man, had gotten himself killed, along with his crazy, arrogant, foul-mouth wife, then Salvador's older brother, Domingo, had gone to prison just days before the wedding.

La bootlegada was no joke. Bootlegging was a dangerous business. Salvador had had to lie to Lupe a few days before they'd married about all his businesses. Lupe and her family really had no idea what it was that he did for a living. They all thought that he was an honest manure hauler, who worked moving fertilizer for the different ranches in the area.

In fact, just before their wedding, Lupe had finally straight-out asked Salvador if the rumors were true that he was a bootlegger, and he'd looked at her right in her face and said no.

Having loaded the six barrels, Salvador was unable to turn the Model T around in the loose, sandy soil. He let a little air out of the rear tires, then getting better traction, he was now able to turn the truck around and get back on the two-lane dirt highway.

Just this side of Riverside, Salvador pulled off the two-lane highway into a horse ranch where he knew the Mexican ranch-hands very well. But coming up to the barn, he saw that there was a group of young Anglo cowboys moving cattle into the corrals where he normally stopped to get his load of horse manure to cover his whiskey barrels.

"Damnit!" said Salvador, hitting the steering wheel.

"What is it?" asked his old mother.

"Well, usually there's no one around this time of the day, so I was figuring I could just pull in and get the horse manure I needed to cover my barrels. But now, I see that I don't know all these cowboys, except for that one Moreno brother, so I can't have all these *gringos* see my barrels in the truck, and—oh, if only I would've gotten the manure first like I usually do, but I was in a hurry so I thought that I'd save time by getting the barrels first, then this way I would've had to unload the manure, load the barrels, then put the manure back on the barrels."

Doña Margarita laughed. "What have I told you a thousand times, *mi hijito?* There are no 'ifs' in life. For if my aunt had balls, she'd be my uncle! And laziness, remember, is always the first step to letting the Devil near."

"No more, *mama,* please," said Salvador, gripping his forehead. "Not now." He quickly put the truck in reverse and got back on the highway. "Also, I didn't know how many barrels I'd find in that riverbed. That damn Julio and his stupid, greedy wife stole so many barrels from me, that I really don't know what I have or don't have."

"May God bless their souls," added his mother, making the sign of the cross over herself, "and forgive you for speaking of the dead without any compassion. Lack of compassion, this is the next step after laziness to letting the Devil near."

Salvador just shook his head, truly wishing that his mother hadn't come along. This was all she ever talked about, the Devil this and the Devil that, and God this and God that, and all these lessons that we mortals had to learn from life or we'd get the shit kicked out of us.

Then, they were just coming into downtown Riverside, when a police car suddenly came up behind them, signaling for Salvador to pull over.

Salvador's whole heart leaped into his mouth!

He thought of going for his gun and shooting the cop. But no, absolutely no! There was other traffic on the highway, and he had no fight with the cops. He was a businessman, after all, performing the service of selling quality merchandise to people who were adults and wanted his whiskey of their own freewill!

And that's when he saw it.

That was when he saw that his old mother had her rosary in hand and she was in a trance praying.

"He will not see the barrels," she was saying. "Do You hear me, God? He will not see the barrels! My son just got married and he's starting a new life so he needs Your help right now! Not tomorrow, not next week, but right now, and so You will help him now, God, and that's that! He will not see the barrels!"

Salvador pulled the truck to a stop off the side of the road by a huge old tree.

"Do You hear me, God?" continued Doña Margarita with her eyes closed in concentration. "You owe me one, God, and so You will help us now, or I swear You will have me to answer to when I get to Heaven, and we both know that *Maria* is on my side, and so You better pay close attention to me right now! He will not see the barrels! He will not see the barrels! Do You understand, *Papito Dios*? You owe me one, and so he will not see the barrels!

"You just stay calm," she said, opening her eyes and turning to Salvador. "You stay calm and everything is fine and he will not see the barrels, *con el favor de Dios!*" she added, kissing the crucifix of her rosary. "Do you understand me, *mi hijito*, God owes me one, and so you just stay calm and everything will be as it is already; perfect!"

"Yes, *mama,*" said Salvador, taking a deep breath. But oh, his heart was going a million miles an hour! In his rearview mirror, he now saw the huge cop climb out of his car, adjust his gun belt, and walk toward them with a slow, easy gait.

Salvador thought of his .38 snubnose again.

"No!" she said. "You will not have any such thoughts! Do you understand? You will just keep calm like I said. God and I are handling this one for you, but from now on, as a married man, you will need to start making your own daily miracles!"

Salvador nodded and was saying, "Yes, *mama,*" when the cop came up to their truck, and he glanced into the bed.

"Well," said the cop, looking puzzled, "I pulled you over because your rear tires look pretty low, so I figured you had quite a load, but I can see that you're not hauling anything, so I guess you just need to put some air in your tires." And, saying this, he tipped his hat. "Drive carefully, and get some air in those tires at the next station."

Salvador couldn't speak. All he could do was nod, and so he nodded again and again, then finally blared out, "Thank you, officer!"

"You're welcome," said the cop, and he looked into the truck bed once more, then returned to his vehicle.

Salvador said nothing, thought nothing, until the policemen had driven off. Then he got out of the truck, looked in the bed of the Model T, saw the six barrels sitting there in plain sight, and he rubbed his forehead, and paced back and forth by the side of the vehicle.

"*Mama,*" he said, finally stopping and staring at her, "how do you do this? My God, in the Revolution, bullets were flying all about us, splattering in the rock and dirt, and I was sure we were going to die, but then you'd have us kneel on the ground and pray to God and—poof, those bullets wouldn't hit us and we'd be safe."

She nodded. "Exactly, *mi hijito*, you quiet the heart here inside of yourself with prayer, this is the first step in all miracle making."

"And you say that now that I'm a married man, I'm going to have to learn how to make my own daily miracles?"

"Exactly," she said. "To enter into the World of Creation is exactly what every married man and woman must know how to do.

"Why do you think the institution of marriage was created in the first place? It was created, *mi hijito,*" she said, closing her eyes in concentration, "to give each man and woman the foundation for the understanding of the powers of God here on earth. A man alone can never realize the full power of the Almighty any more than a woman alone. You just watch, *mi hijito,* in the next three years you and Lupe are going to travel to places that you two never dreamed of before. I know, believe me, your father and his high-feeling, arrogant, European ways forced me into a world of forgiveness and compassion that I never dreamed of traveling." She smiled, making the sign of the cross over herself. "You're on your way now, *mi hijito,* this is the last miracle that God and I are doing for you. It's all up to you and Lupe now, *con el favor de Dios,*" she added.

"Oh, *mama,*" said Salvador, starting to pace once again. "Oh, *mama, mama!* All of my life you've been our everything for us children. I don't know anything about making my own miracles! That cop, I swear, I was so scared and confused that if you hadn't been with me, I might have shot him."

"No, you would not have shot him."

"How do you know?"

"Because," she said, closing her eyes in concentration once more, "I raised you to have love, here in your center, and it takes the power of love to have the guts to not go around shooting people to settle matters."

"But I thought of doing it, *mama.*"

"Of course, you're a man, *mi hijito.* But to think is not to do. To think is small potatoes compared to doing. And here inside of you, you are strong in knowing this difference. No, you would not have killed in cold blood," she added.

He nodded. "And you knew that a cop was going to pull me over, and that's why you insisted to come with me?" asked Salvador.

"Oh, no, I'm not God," she said, laughing. "I didn't know what was going to happen to you in complete detail, but as a mother, as a woman of substance, I did have the feeling here in my heart," she said, breathing deeply, "that you were going to need my help, and so that's why I insisted on coming with you."

"Oh, *mama,* you are such a mystery to me," he said, pacing back and forth under the huge, old tree by the side of the road. "I'll never forget as long as I live, we were crossing the desert on our way north to the Texas border, and it was getting dark when we finally got to the water hole. But the hole was completely dry, and we were all dying of thirst. And yet you and all these old women didn't panic. No, you all just got together and had us children kneel down and begin to pray as the last sunlight disappeared. And miracle of miracles, fresh water began seeping out of the ground that night, filling the hole with water by daybreak. How do you do it, eh? I was so scared when the cop came up and yet you were so calm and my God, he really didn't see those barrels!"

"Easy," said Doña Margarita, "when I pray, I just give myself over to God, completely, and He then gives of Himself to me. And God can do anything, so then can I."

Standing under the great old tree, Salvador nodded. "I see, simple as that, eh?"

"Yes, simple as that," she said, nodding to the tree. "Once we give up the ghost."

"Ghost?"

"Yes, *la ilusión* that we really have any separation whatsoever between us and Holy Creation," she said, kissing the crucifix of her rosary.

"*Mama,*" he said, "my God, who are you to know so much?"

"Who am I? Well, *mi hijito,* since you always seem to keep forgetting, then I'll tell you again," she said. "I am your mother. I am the woman who brought you forth with life from here between my legs, and so you will never get rid of me when I decide to be with you!

"Because, as I've told you time and again, even after I'm dead and gone and the worms have eaten my earth-body and you're so old and deaf that you can't hear your own farts, I'll still be here inside your heart and soul like *una GARRRRRAPATA,* a tick up a dog's ass, scratching at you, clawing at you, giving you great discomfort, every time I see you or one of your offspring get lazy and allow the Devil to come near! Do you understand now? This is who I am, your ancestral TICK UP YOUR SPIRITUAL ASSHOLE FOR ALL ETERNITY! So you don't get lazy on me again," she added. "GET YOUR SHIT FIRST!"

Salvador burst out laughing. What else could he do?

THE NEXT DAY, Salvador was down in Carlsbad, delivering whiskey, when his good friend Jerry Bill told him who the guy was who'd brought the two men down from Los Angeles to try to take over his territory. Why, it was Tomas, a good friend of Salvador's, a man who'd sat across the table from Salvador in many a poker game and then had had breakfast with him in the early hours of the morning.

And the two men that Tomas had invited down were no other than . . . the *Filipino* and the *Italiano,* the two guys who'd cut Salvador's throat a few years back in Corona, leaving him for dead, and then they'd also been the sons-of-a-bitches who'd gotten Salvador arrested in Hanford, for gambling. That's how he'd ended up spending time in the Tulare jail.

These two stool pigeon bastard-*cabrones,* Salvador was going to kill immediately, and he didn't give a good damn if they were *amigos* of the big boys out of Fresno, or not!

But then, that night as Salvador slept alone in Carlsbad in the little white house that he'd especially prepared for his honeymoon with Lupe, his mother, Doña Margarita, appeared to him in his dreams. *"Mi hijito,"* said the old Indian woman, "I didn't raise you up all these years for you to now just go out and do your revenge like a stupid, typical man!

"You must think deeper, *mi hijito,* much deeper than the wolf or the *coyote,* and come up with a plan as cunning as the little She-Fox herself, the Female Force who helps God reign the Heavens."

And saying this, his old mother then turned into a little She-Fox in Salvador's dream, and whispered to him so quietly that his sleeping male-brain now thought that these were his very own thoughts.

"Sleep, my child-darling, sleep," whispered the little She-Fox, "and let all the wisdom of the ages come to you. Remember the story of how the little She-Fox fooled the big strong *coyote* when he was going to eat her babies. She took the big, hungry *coyote* down to the lagoon and convinced him that the reflection of the full Moon in the water was the biggest, most delicious cheese in all the world. Greed did all the rest, *mi hijito.* The coyote drank the water, wanting to empty the lagoon so he could get to the cheese, and he choked to death. Remember, greed can be a person's best friend when the other has it and you don't."

"Yes, *mama,"* said Salvador to the She-Fox in his dream, "I remember that story well, but I'm a man, *mama,* so I don't know what to do, except kill these two *cabrón*-bastards!"

"Then sleep some more, *mi hijito,"* said his old Indian mother to him in his dream, "and believe me, you'll soon come up with a plan so fantastic that it will give you a greater reputation than just the killing of two mere mortals. And also remember the formidable powers of the mother pig, the only farm animal capable of returning to the wild and surviving, because she never lost her wild instincts. And it is within our wild instincts that lies the key to our soul.

"Dream, *mi hijito*, dream, and know that our soul is our doorway to God. *Coo-coo rrroo-coo coooooo, dijo la Paloma!*" his mother continued singing.

And Salvador continued dreaming as he slept, and all these Ancient Powers came to him in the Great Open River of *Papito Dios*.

In the morning, just as the dawn of the new day was coming forth, Salvador awoke with such strength and clarity of mind that he leaped out of bed, bursting with energy!

He was ready!

He was full to the brim!

It was already done, finished, and completed here inside of his being!

The Heartbeat of his Ancestry was beat, beat, beating, pounding inside of him. He was now in that Holy State of Being *Aprevenido!*

Salvador washed, dressed, and drove whistling up to Tustin to see Archie Freeman, who was a deputy sheriff in both Orange and San Diego Counties.

Immediately, Salvador told the huge lawman that he'd give him a free barrel of whiskey, if he'd just come down to Carlsbad this afternoon and say hi to him.

"And I'll be waiting for you east of town," said Salvador, "you know, over in that old barn by the Kelly Ranch."

"Just come and say hi?" said Archie, grinning. "Hell, just what kind of a fool do you figure me for, Salvador?"

"A smart one," said Salvador, not flinching.

He and Archie had done a lot of business together over the last few years. And lately, Archie had been getting sweet on Lupe's sister Carlota, so—who knew?—they might end up being brothers-in-law yet.

"Look, Archie," continued Salvador, "you're the law, so truthfully, it's best that I don't tell you what I'm doing. You just come by and say 'hi, how's everything going,' and then leave immediately, and I'll handle everything, and this way you're not involved in any way."

Archie reached up to his long, dark, California Indian face with his huge, thick right hand and scratched himself, then began pulling at his right ear, the chewing-over-information ear, then he scratched the left side of his face. "Just come by and say, 'hi, how's everything going,' and leave immediately, eh?"

"That's right," said Salvador. "But you got to tell no one that you've even seen me, because I'm still on my honeymoon, okay? And you do this, and I'll deliver you a free, ten-gallon barrel tomorrow."

"Of real whiskey?"

"Of my best!"

"You mean, that 12-year-old stuff?"

"You got it!"

"Okay," said Archie, licking his chops, "you've got yourself a deal, but I'll tell you, I smell a mighty big rat here somewhere."

"From me? Oh, no, Archie, I'm a married man now."

On this one, Archie burst out laughing. "Married, my ass! You still look like the same son-of-a-bitch *cabrón* I met the first day I saw you! So tell me," added Archie, "all business aside, why aren't you on, well, your honeymoon?"

If anybody else had asked, Salvador would've gone into a rage, because he wasn't going to allow any pair of hanging balls to tease him about his love for Lupe. But Archie was almost like family; or maybe even better than *familia*.

"Archie," Salvador now said, "Lupe's mother came out and told me after the wedding that Lupe wasn't feeling well, so could I please wait for a few days before she joined me for our honeymoon. But like I told you, no one must know, not one person, okay?"

"You got it," said Archie.

"Then we got a deal?" asked Salvador, wanting to make sure, because the law was a very big part of his plan—for this whole thing to work. "I'll see you late this afternoon, just before sunset in that shack by those horse corrals just this side of the Kelly Ranch on the old El Camino?"

Archie nodded, and they shook hands. And now that Salvador had accomplished this deal with Archie, he quickly drove over to Corona, bought himself a couple of young, male pigs, and hired two of the Moreno boys to help him—at such a price that they couldn't refuse.

Then he quickly went to his mother's place, got Luisa's two older boys to wash his Moon automobile for him as he bathed, shaved, and got all dressed up. The boys did a wonderful job. Jose, his nephew, was turning into a very responsible young man. Salvador then offered to pay the two boys. Pedro immediately accepted the money, but Jose didn't.

"Uncle," said Jose, "you do so much for us all the time, that it's a pleasure to just be able to do something for you. We don't want your money. Do we, Pedro," he said, turning to his younger, smaller brother.

Pedro really didn't want to, but he returned the money. "Jose is right," he said. "We don't want your money! Ah, shit!"

Salvador laughed, then looked at his nephew Jose in the eyes. Blood was really blood. This boy had never even met his great big father—who'd been killed back in Mexico by two stupid, little, scared soldiers at the dinner table as they ate—but he had his father's size and looks and sense of justice, balance, and the larger, fuller picture of life.

Salvador hugged both boys in a big *abrazo,* kissing them, then he got in his fine, newly-washed Moon automobile and took off for Carlsbad with the Morenos following behind him in his truck with the two pigs.

He was wearing a gorgeous suit and great tie. Salvador knew that he had to look the part for what he was now going to do. It was no accident that a good lawyer spent as much time and thought on his dress as a good prostitute. Clothes, about fine clothes, Salvador had also learned in Montana when he'd been hiding from the law and Lady Katherine, the English madam of the finest whorehouse in the whole Northwest, had taken him under her wing.

In the *barrio* of Carlsbad, Salvador immediately found Tomas Varga, who'd brought in those two guys from Los Angeles.

"*Cómo estas*, Tomas," said Salvador, stepping down out of his grand car and smiling to this man that was well known all through the *barrio* as a small-time, two-bit gambler. "I need to have a little talk with you. I got a little business deal for you, so you can make a few extra dollars."

"Oh, no, I'm too busy, Salvador," said Tomas, already looking nervous. "I can't go with you right now."

Just then, the two Moreno boys were at Tomas's side, and Salvador drew close and put his .38 snubnose into Tomas's gut. "We insist," said Salvador quietly. "Just keep still, and nothing is going to happen to you, *te juro.* I promise, we just need to talk a little bit."

Getting Tomas in the front passenger's seat alongside Salvador, the two Moreno brothers got in the truck. Salvador drove slowly out of the *barrio de Carlos Malo*—as Carlsbad was referred to by the Mexican people, meaning the neighborhood of Bad Charles—and east up the hill, by the Carlsbad forest and over to El Camino, the old, abandoned dirt road that the *padres* had used when they'd first come into California over two hundred years ago.

Salvador headed south, and he could see that Tomas was getting more and more frightened as they went. Salvador loved it. His mother was right, why be a huge, powerful wolf or *coyote* when you could be a quick, agile, little, cunning She-Fox, and allow the frightened man's imagination to do it all for you.

"But where are we going, Salvador?" Tomas was saying. "I'm just a gambler, you know that, Salvador. I never had anything to do with—" He stopped his words.

"You never had anything to do with what?" asked Salvador, acting innocent and turning the knife in a little deeper. Imagination could do so much more than the wildest reality. His mother always said that a frightened person's mind was the Devil's finest playground.

"Relax," said Salvador, "just relax, *amigo,*" he added, reaching out and stroking Tomas's leg like you'd do for a woman. This he'd seen done in prison. This small, innocent-looking act caused a frightened man's balls to draw completely up into his body, leaving him as available as any female who'd lost all self-respect.

"It's all right, *amigo mio,*" continued Salvador, talking softly, gently, "I know that you didn't intentionally mean any harm. But, well, you know how it is, a man's livelihood is a man's livelihood, and just because—" Salvador now had to swallow hard to keep himself calm, "—I got married doesn't mean that I still can't take care of business."

Salvador wanted to scream, to turn into a jaguar and rip this man's throat out with his teeth, but he didn't. He calmed down, breathing easy like a reptile in the hot midday desert.

Up ahead, in the canyon, Salvador pulled off the dirt road of El Camino and took a trail across a meadow toward some abandoned horse corrals.

Inside the barn were the two little pigs, which Salvador and the Morenos had brought by earlier when they'd checked things out. And now, in no time at all, the Moreno boys had a good little fire going.

By now Tomas was so confused, not knowing what was going on, that he just couldn't shut up. Salvador just loved how the unknown rattled people, particularly those who weren't at home with themselves. The changing forces of living life, *la vida,* could kill a man who didn't have his feet well planted into the Mother Earth.

"But Salvador, I never brought them down here!" Tomas was now saying. "You need to believe me! I swear it on my mother's grave! I respect a man's territory!"

Salvador almost laughed on this one. Years ago he'd learned, that anytime a man swore to something, especially over his mother's grave, this meant that then this was exactly what this man was lying about. Lies were such good company to fear.

"Yes, you respect a man's territory," said Salvador. "But do you respect a man's marriage?"

"But what are you talking about?" yelled Tomas, eyes jumping.

"Marriage," said Salvador, "do you respect a man who's gotten married? Or do you—like so many little two-bit pimps who handle women with a slap in the face—think a man's gone weak in the head when he's in love and he marries?"

"Salvador, I swear, I don't know what you're talking about! I have never even spoken to this girl you married. I—I—oh, God, I think there's been a misunderstanding here! I deal in cards and, you know, prostitutes; not in decent women, Salvador!"

Salvador only smiled. "Exactly. I know. I know," he said as he continued to sharpen his knife, realizing that yes, indeed, he'd struck pure gold here inside this man's private hell.

Why, it was this little two-bit Tomas who'd told the *Filipino* and the *Italiano* that the North County San Diego was for the taking because Salvador was getting married and couldn't control his area anymore. Why, this little son-of-a-bitch had probably even told 'em, "Come on, hurry, before someone else moves in! For we all know that a man who marries has lost his nerve!"

Salvador turned and looked at Tomas, and yes, Tomas was tall, well-built, and very handsome with a rugged appearance to him. But looking at his eyes, especially into his left eye, the female eye, it was easy to see just how very little Tomas really was.

Why, Tomas was nothing but a rabbit, a cottontail, facing his worst nightmare, the She-Fox, herself!

Salvador now rolled up the left sleeve of his own shirt, and licked the hairiest part of his forearm, then he put the blade of the knife that he'd just sharpened to this licked part of his forearm to test the sharpness of the blade. The knife shaved a little, two-finger-wide portion of his forearm as clean and smooth as a baby's ass.

"Pretty good, eh?" said Salvador, seeing how Tomas had watched the whole procedure very carefully. "But I think I should still strap it first."

"But what are we going to do?" asked Tomas, having finally got caught up in the details of what was going on about him.

Salvador loved details; they were the lifeblood of any well-laid plan.

"Well, of course, I'm going to castrate these two little pigs," said Salvador.

Tomas glanced at the two little pigs, who were rooting happily in a corner of the barn, digging at the earth with their noses. They looked so cute and happy and peaceful.

"Poor little things," said Tomas, suddenly looking greatly relieved. "But then why did you bring me along? I don't understand."

Just then, Archie's big Hudson car came roaring up outside, right on schedule.

"Who's that?" asked Tomas.

"Archie," said Salvador, "but don't worry. I'll tell him that everything is okay."

The barn door burst open and in stepped Archie, filling the entire doorway like a big studhorse. "Just stopped by," he said, full of power, "to say hi and see if everything is okay."

"Everything is fine," said Salvador, calmly.

"Oh, yes, everything is fine," said Tomas, looking even more relieved to see the law.

"Good, then I'll be seeing you," said Archie, and he turned and left as quickly as he'd come, and they could all hear his big Hudson changing gears as it went roaring back up on El Camino and headed north back to town.

"But I don't get it," said Tomas, feeling very confident now. "If you're just going to castrate some pigs, then why did you bother to bring me all the way out here?"

"Because," said Salvador, suddenly stepping in close, as the two Moreno boys—who were some of the greatest horsemen in all the Southland—now roped Tomas with the *riatas* that they'd been playing around with, before he ever knew what was happening, "I'm going to cook up those pigs' balls and feed them to you, before we castrate you and feed your own *tanates* to you, too!"

All the blood left Tomas's face.

"No man," continued Salvador, "should have to eat his own balls before knowing if he likes balls cooked with *salsa verde* or *salsa colorada!*"

Tomas screamed to the heavens, startling the two little pigs, as the Moreno boys tied him in a chair and then tied the chair to one of the horse stalls and jerked down his pants.

Then when the first little pig was caught and his legs were held wide apart for his cutting, you couldn't distinguish the screams of Tomas from the little pig's SCREECHES!

The first pair of balls were tossed in the frying pan of the little fire with *salsa verde*, because no matter how much Salvador kept asking Tomas which *salsa* he preferred to start with first, he couldn't speak, he was screaming so much as Salvador shoved the first burning-hot pig's ball down his throat, almost choking him to death!

By the time Salvador and the two Moreno boys dropped Tomas back off in the *barrio de Carlos Malo,* he was no longer ever going to be a Doubting Thomas again for as long as he lived! He was a true believer now, for he'd seen *el Diablo* as sure as he breathed.

Half crazy-*loco* out of his mind, that very night Tomas drove up to the City of the Angels, and with a gagging, burned mouth and throat, he told his two partners to never venture to the North County San Diego again, for the Devil lived!

And the Devil's name was Juan Salvador Villaseñor, and Archie, the law, was in full partnership with *el Diablo,* and my God, he prayed for the day that he'd be forgiven for ever having dreamed of interfering in another man's territory!

By the end of that week, after taking care of . . . well, a little more unfinished business, Salvador's reputation grew in such leaps and bounds that people now said that his blood ran backward from his heart and his earth-body cast no more shadow in the full Moon, for his soul was now at one with the Devil, himself!

3

And so she, the child who'd been conceived on the night that
a meteorite struck the Earth, was now a married woman and
she was in love!

FOR THREE MORNINGS Lupe slept in late, while the rest of her family got up before sunrise so they could go to work in the fields. And each morning Lupe would get herself a cup of coffee and go out on the front porch to watch the light of the new day.

Lupe had never done this before in all her life. She and her family had always been at work in the fields before the first light of the day. But now, being a newly married woman—who was getting herself healthy and ready for her husband to come and get her on Friday so they could go on their honeymoon—she had leisure time for the very first time in her life.

Several people came by that week to visit with Lupe, wanting to tell her of the rumors that were spreading like wildfire about Salvador having castrated a man and tortured another one to death, but Lupe always cut them short, saying, "No, not one word!" For her mother had taught her that a smart woman never listened to gossip, and she wasn't going to start now.

After all, she and Salvador had taken their wedding vows before God, and he was now her husband and she loved him with all her heart and soul, and so she wasn't going to allow even one ill word spoken about him in her presence.

Sitting on her parents' porch with a cup of coffee with plenty of sugar and milk, Lupe watched the coming of the new day. Oh, this was such a luxury! Lupe had never known that sleeping in late and getting up slowly felt so good! Lupe now sat here on her parents' porch steps, all cuddled together in her nightgown and robe, warming her hands with her cup of coffee and watching the morning sunlight come in through the tree branches and dance on her mother's flowers, herb garden, and beautifully scented plants.

For as long as she could remember, her mother had explained to Lupe and her sisters that a woman had to talk to her plants and trees and flowers on a daily basis in order to feel complete. For *Papito Dios* had made woman from the plant-world, just as He had made man from the mineral-world.

Lupe could now see so clearly that her mother had, indeed, been correct. It was a miracle how each tree branch, each flower, each plant took on the life of the coming of the Sun. Why, the plants were beginning to smile, to sing, to whisper good tidings to Lupe as she sat sipping her coffee, mesmerized by the coming of a whole new day.

"Hello," said Lupe to the plants all around. "Good morning. I hope you all slept well."

The plants purred and Lupe knew they'd had a wonderful night. Lupe continued to sip her coffee. *Papito Dios* had truly been very wise when He'd taken the strength from the tree, the beauty from the flower, and the healing powers from the herbs to make woman strong, beautiful, and a healing force. *Papito Dios* had also truly been very wise when He'd taken wind, rock and the molten fire to make man. That was why men liked to be on the move like wind and go to rock caves to find peace. Where women, on the other hand, went to their garden of *maize, frijoles,* and *yerbas buenas* to reconnect themselves with these quiet, invisible, holy mysteries of life, *la vida.*

"Always remember that men are mineral," her mother had told Lupe and all her sisters ever since Lupe could remember, "and women are vegetation. That's why the two will always have difficulties. Men were formed from the clay along the river's edge. Women were formed from the roots of the great tree that grows on the river's edge. It's a miracle that they ever come together at all."

Having heard this story all of her life, Lupe now felt so happy that her mother had had the wisdom to not let her go on her honeymoon when she'd been passing blood and not feeling well—for now, on Friday, when Salvador came to get her, she'd be feeling well and clean and ready.

She could hardly wait!

She was, after all, now a married woman!

Her heartbeat quickened with just the thought of the delicious kisses that they'd had in the walnut orchard behind her parents' house. Then, when Salvador turned her about, so that the backside of her body came up against the full length of his—she'd truly understood for the first time in all her life why men came from rock and molten hot fire!

She shivered, sipping her coffee, and remembered Salvador's kisses and the feel of his body up against her buns as she now watched the early-morning light giving color and life to her mother's garden.

IT WAS FRIDAY, and Salvador was washing up and changing his clothes so he could go and pick up his bride over the coastal hills from Corona to Santa Ana. He was at Luisa's. There was no running water in his mother's little shack in back, so Salvador was bathing and getting dressed in his sister's house in the front.

"Salvador," Luisa was now saying as she watched Salvador prepare to shave his face in front of the old, broken mirror, "forget Lupe! Don't go get her! Admit that you were a fool to have ever married that girl! You spent a fortune on that fool girl. Nobody ever bought me a diamond ring!" shouted Luisa. "Nobody ever got me furniture and set up a house for me. Then her mother came out to tell you that Lupe wasn't ready to go on her honeymoon, this is an outrage! She didn't have the guts or decency to come out and tell you herself!"

"Calm down, Luisa," said Salvador, strapping his straight razor so he could start shaving. His face was lathered with soap and soft-feeling from having taken a hot bath. This would be a very good, close shave, so when he and Lupe kissed again, they could also rub cheek to cheek without his beard scratching her. "You're talking crazy, Luisa. I'm already married, and everything is going to be wonderful!"

"Oh, no!" she continued shouting. "I know what I'm talking about! This is the future being put in your face, and you know it, Salvador!" Luisa was eight years older than Salvador, and she was really upset. "I tell you, you should have married a real woman like the ones I've introduced you to! But no, not you, you got blinded by a pretty virginal girl, thinking it's so beautiful to train *una inocente* to your own ways," she added sarcastically, "instead of getting a real woman who already knows the ways of the world, and would appreciate you for the real man you are!

"You fool, Salvador!" she said. "Don't go get her, I tell you! Listen to me, Lupe is only going to make you miserable for the rest of your life! And you'll never be appreciated for the man you really are! Mark my words, I'm a woman, and I know what I'm talking about!" she added, shouting with power. "Lupe isn't for you!"

regretted my life with your father, Don Juan, even amid all the great pain and great suffering that came between us, for just look at you children who came from our union!"

"But, *mama*," said Luisa, "you don't understand! There are a dozen wonderful women who'd marry Salvador in a second with all their heart and soul! The whole trouble with Salvador, *mama*, is that he picked a woman with his head, wanting to train her, instead of choosing her with what is between his legs!" she added in frustration.

"That's enough, Luisa!" said their mother. "You got the mouth of a witch!"

Still refusing to be stopped, Luisa burst out laughing. "I, the mouth of a witch!" she said. "Why, *mama*, all our life it's been you who has told us that this is exactly what men say of any woman that they can't handle—that she's a witch!" And she continued laughing and laughing, truly loving it. Then she wiped her eyes and said, "Oh, Salvador, *mama* is right, I love you so much, and I know you got big balls, so I'm just afraid this *inocente* is never going to be able to give you what you really need. What do you think keeps a marriage alive, eh? Why do you think Epitacio returned to me after being lost for all those years? It's all here in the center of a woman," she said, gesturing vulgarly between her legs, "where life itself begins, that a man's *tanates* finally find refuge, inside a woman's warm juicy nest of honey!"

"*Ayyyiii!*" said their mother, laughing, too. "I think you've been around me too long! But your sister is right, Salvador, love comes and goes, but what keeps a marriage alive and well over the years is respect of the bed, which takes the sting out of our everyday disappointments."

"Okay," said Salvador, "out, out, out! Both of you! It's a miracle that I haven't cut my throat with all the talk that's going on."

Putting his mother and sister out of the bathroom, Salvador quickly dressed and was out the door. He was feeling ten feet tall! He had won his territories back in a lightning-quick attack, and now he was on his way to pick up his bride, the love of his life!

SALVADOR WAS DRIVING down the tree-lined street of Lupe's house in Santa Ana when he saw Archie's big Hudson parked in front. Immediately, Salvador smelled trouble, and his heart took flight, pounding inside his chest like a great drum.

He took a few deep breaths, calming himself down. He parked his

Salvador said nothing. What could he say? He began to shave with long, upward strokes at the neck, and small, downward strokes at the cheek. The truth was that Luisa had never liked Lupe from the start, as Carlota had never liked him from the start, either. And besides, if he wasn't careful, he could cut his throat with his straight razor.

Just then, their mother, Doña Margarita, came in the back door. "What is all this shouting about?" asked the old lady. "I could hear you all the way to my own house, Luisa!"

"Oh, *mama!*" yelled Luisa. "I'm telling Salvador that he shouldn't go to pick up Lupe! That she's only going to make him miserable all his life! Look, what she already did—she didn't even go on her own honeymoon!"

"Luisa, Luisa," said their mother, closing her eyes in concentration, "do you not see what is really happening? Are you so blind with your jealousy that you can't see what you are really saying?"

"But I'm not jealous!" shouted Luisa louder than ever. Salvador almost cut himself. "I love Salvador! We've been through hell together, but we always supported one another! We never hid behind our mother's skirt, and didn't face reality!"

"*Mi hijita,*" said the skinny, old woman, "and what is jealousy if not the other side of love, eh? Of course, you love your brother very much and want the best for him, but—and this is a very big 'but'—love without reins is a love without brakes. And love without brakes is a love without trust, and a love without trust will consume any person's mind. Why do you think that even the Devil, himself, fears to travel the voyage of love, because he well knows that if he ever lets himself rise up in love, he'll then never have the brakes to stop until he has rejoined God!

"So put the reins of faith and trust in God, on this love that you have for your brother, or *mi hijita*, you will only end up getting near the Devil and speaking like a jealous, frightened sister, undermining your brother's home, instead of being the strong, good-hearted sister that I know you are.

"Now, no more! For remember, my own father, the great Don Pio, was also against my marriage to your father. And your grandfather warned me that if I married this red-headed man of pure Spanish blood, that my life with him would be pure misery, because every time he'd anger, he'd throw it up in my face that I was nothing but a lowlife, ignorant, backward Indian savage—and your grandfather was, indeed, correct," added the old woman with her eyes suddenly filling with tears, "for such became the case.

"But still, *mi hijita*, I want you to know that there was never a day that I

Moon automobile behind Archie's big, black car and went up the steps to Lupe's parents' home. He was good now, he was good, but also he was unarmed. He breathed, keeping himself alert and ready, come what may.

Carlota answered the door. She was all smiles and big happy eyes. Now, Salvador just knew for sure that he was in for some big *problemas.*

"Hello, Sal," said Archie, sitting in the front room sipping tea from a little white cup with Lupe, Carlota, and their father and mother. "I thought you'd be coming along just about now, so I came by to invite you two newlyweds to go out to dinner with me and Carlota to that new amusement park over in Long Beach."

Salvador glanced at Lupe. My God, she was beautiful! And he saw that she had her bags packed and was ready for them to go on their honeymoon. "Well, I don't know," said Salvador. "You see, I'd like to drive Lupe down to Carlsbad before dark to our new house, so, well, she can see the flowers that I planted in the front yard and the—"

"You got your whole lives to do that," said Archie, cutting Salvador off, as he got to his feet. It was always very impressive when Archie stood up. He wasn't really a giant, but the way he took up ground when he stood up and the size of his huge California Indian face, well, he just dwarfed men who were six-feet tall. "So," he was saying, "why don't you just come along with Carlota and me for dinner. I think it's important, Salvador," he added with that special grin of his.

Having added the word "important," Archie now knew that he'd made his point, for Salvador's whole face shifted.

Archie laughed and laughed, finishing off his tea. The tiny teacup looked so ridiculous in his huge, thick-fingered hand. Archie sucked down the last of his tea with a big, long, air-sucking sound.

Salvador breathed, realizing that he'd been had. "All right, Archie," he said, "if it's all right with Lupe, then, well, we'll be happy to join you and Carlota."

Just then, as Salvador turned to his bride, Lupe made a little face that would endear her to his heart for years to come. For she made this cute, little face, puckering her lips together like she was really disappointed, but then she smiled this grand smile like a gracious lady, and said, "Yes, of course, Salvador, for we really do have the rest of our lives together, *querido.*"

The word *"querido,"* meaning "sweetheart," sent Salvador shooting through the Heavens! And that little, quick face of puckered-up lips told Salvador that, yes, indeed, she truly did want to be with him, and not go out with these people for dinner. But that she'd do it anyway, for he was her *querido,* her sweet love.

It became a whole experience for the four of them to say good-bye to Lupe's two old parents, Don Victor and Doña Guadalupe, and go out the door. Because now that his bride was ready to go off with him alone, her every look, her every touch, or just the brush of her hand sent him flying!

ARCHIE AND CARLOTA got in the front of Archie's big, black Hudson and Lupe and Salvador climbed in the back. A new amusement park had opened up out in Long Beach, and this was where Archie was taking them.

Salvador and Lupe held hands and didn't talk much the whole way out. They were both too nervous. But Archie and Carlota, on the other hand, weren't nervous at all, and they talked the whole way, telling jokes and laughing happily.

Long Beach was warm and beautiful. Catalina Island looked to be just a couple of miles out to sea. They walked along the boardwalk and looked out at the sea, four well-dressed young people.

Then Archie and Carlota went on the roller coaster. Salvador and Lupe laughed with *gusto* every time they caught sight of their terrified faces. Once, laughing so hard, Lupe lost her balance and started to fall, but Salvador caught her in his arms. Their eyes met. They held, not moving, just holding there looking at each other, and then Salvador drew Lupe close, kissing her ever so lightly. To his surprise, Lupe now grabbed him, kissing him in return with such open, wild passion that he jerked back—eyes wide-open!

She saw his startled look and laughed. "We are married, you know," she said, eyes full of mischief.

"Well, yes, but I thought that you were—"

"What? Afraid?" she said, laughing all the more.

"But the whole drive out you hardly came near me," he said.

"Well, you acted like you were mad at me," she said.

He grinned. "Me mad at you, oh, no!" he said.

"Well, then, let's kiss some more," she said. "That was delicious!"

He licked his lips, glancing around. He'd never expected this. But Lupe, she never once took her eyes off of him, as they now drew close together once more, kissing again and again, then again! They were both beginning to tremble and feel very light-headed, when Carlota and Archie came walking up.

"Didn't I tell you," said Archie, slipping his arm around Carlota, "leave them alone a minute and they'll be at it like real lovebirds, eh? Come on," he added, "let's all go throw some baseballs at those clowns, then eat. I'm starved! You know, I could've made it to the Yankees if they'd allowed half-breeds to play."

They all threw some baseballs at the clowns. Salvador and Lupe couldn't stop glancing at each other. Archie was really good and he won a big stuffed bear. Then they went down the boardwalk to find a place to eat. They came to a Chinese restaurant with a big red dragon painted at the entrance. Carlota and Lupe had never been to a Chinese restaurant before. Archie immediately decided that they'd all eat Chinese.

"But I don't talk Chinese, except sew-sew cho-cho, which means 'where's your hot sister?' " laughed Archie, towering above everyone as they went inside. "So how are we going to order?"

"I talk a little Chinese," said Salvador.

"You do?" said Lupe.

"Sure," said Salvador.

Sitting down Salvador asked to speak to the owner and when the owner came, he spoke to him in Chinese, ordering things that weren't on the menu. Lupe and Carlota weren't the only ones who were impressed.

"Where in the hell did you learn Chinese?" asked Archie.

"In *Mexicali*," said Salvador.

"Then," said Archie, "you must be that son-of-a-bitch that no one's been able to catch who's been smuggling in all those slant-eyed bastards!" And saying this, Archie started laughing, then grinning ear to ear.

But Salvador gave Archie nothing. "I don't know what you're talking about," said Salvador. "I just have a few good friends over in *Mexicali*, that's all."

"What do you do, smuggle 'em from *Mexicali* over to Chinatown in Hanford in the central valley of Fresno, or all the way to San Francisco?" said Archie. "A bunch of hot, slanted-eyed girls, eh?" And he would have continued talking and laughing if he hadn't seen the sudden look of death that flashed across Lupe's face. "Hey, man, I'm only kidding, Lupe," he added quickly. "No harm meant. Shit, man, Salvador's probably a virgin as far as I'm concerned!"

Saying this, Archie started laughing again. He just couldn't help himself because—in his estimation—he'd just found out how Salvador got all his money. The son-of-a-bitch was a Chinaman importer! A much bigger crime than bootlegging!

Salvador still said nothing. He now knew why Archie would always be a deputy, and never the sheriff himself. He was a stupid big-mouth. He and Carlota truly deserved each other. Neither one of them knew when to keep their mouths shut. Hell, if Archie had been smart, he should never have tipped his hand and just let him, Salvador, keep on talking like a fool, and he could've then maybe found out how truly big this whole Chinese smuggling business really was. And it was huge!

Yes, Salvador knew how to speak a little Chinese, and he also knew how to speak a lot of Greek. This country was made up of people from all over the world. Spanish and English weren't enough to help a man get into people's hearts in this fast-growing nation.

Salvador also spoke a little Yaqui and a little of the native tongue of his mother's people from their village in Oaxaca, Mexico. He never could have gotten his smuggling jobs in *Mexicali* if he hadn't spoken several languages. It was a very poor man, indeed, who couldn't at least pronounce another's name in his own native tongue.

When the food arrived, it was a banquet. There was a whole duck roasted to a beautiful golden color, a platter of rice covered with beautiful vegetables and big succulent shrimp, and another platter of gravy and chicken and nuts. And then, the most special of all, here came the owner himself, carrying the biggest platter with an entire fish baked in a golden-orange sauce and decorated with greens and fruit.

"Oh, beautiful!" said Salvador, smiling proudly at the owner. "It's even more than I expected!"

"Good!" said the owner, full of pride and elegance.

"A fish?" said Carlota, making a face of pure disgust as the owner set the elegant platter down in the middle of the table. "That's disgusting!"

Lupe kicked her sister under the table. But Carlota wasn't to be silenced.

"Don't kick me!" she yelled. "Its eyes are open and it's staring at me!"

Archie let out a howl of laughter that could be heard across the entire restaurant. "Great!" he said, winking at the ashen-faced owner, "that just leaves more for me to enjoy!"

Saying this, the huge lawman dug into the big fish. Salvador was glad that Archie had come along. Oh, he'd felt ready to flatten Carlota across the face! Why, she was the most stupid, self-centered human being he'd ever met!

Lupe took Salvador's hand underneath the table, petting him gently. He turned and looked at her and she looked so kind and gentle and understanding that all his anger disappeared. He just couldn't believe that Lupe and Carlota were really sisters—they were so different.

Going home that night, Lupe and Salvador rode in the back of the big Hudson and they held each other close and watched the Mother Moon follow them home, slipping between the clouds.

GETTING OUT OF THE BIG HUDSON, Lupe went inside with her sister to get her things so she and Salvador could now drive down to Carlsbad to start their honeymoon. Archie and Salvador stayed outside. Archie suggested that he and Salvador take a little walk down the street and stretch their legs.

"All right, you son-of-a-bitch!" said Archie, letting Salvador have it once they were out of earshot from Lupe's house. "You used me, you bastard! Now the word is out all over the Southland that I'm in cahoots with you—and my God, you really were gonna castrate that sorry son-of-a-bitch, weren't you? He still can hardly talk—his throat's all burned—and he's still terror-stricken!"

But then, before Salvador could say anything, Archie, who'd been raging-angry—just a second ago—was now happy and laughing to beat hell. "You're a genius, Salvador!" he said. "Even I never thought of using baby pigs to work a man's mind! Good God, can those little pigs scream! You're lucky he didn't die on you from a heart attack or choke to death with those hot burning balls you shoved down his throat! It's gonna cost you two more barrels, Sal!"

Salvador breathed deeply. Why, this wild Indian, deputy son-of-a-bitch was never going to fail to amaze him. He wasn't angry with what he'd done to Tomas; oh, no, he was jealous!

"All right," said Salvador, now laughing, too, "two more barrels it is, but I can't give 'em to you for a few weeks, Archie, 'cause I'm short right now, and, well, we still got to go on our honeymoon."

"All right," said Archie, calming down, "I'll buy that, but also, I want you to know that your little war ain't over yet. Those two guys, the *Filipino* and *Italiano,* they're still fishing. I just don't know what it is between you guys. But don't worry; I didn't leave you out to dry. People really think I'm backing you, you son-of-a-bitch, *cabrón* genius!"

"Thanks," said Salvador, smiling. "It really did go pretty smooth."

"But next time, you let me in on what you're doing—you crazy Indian son-of-a-bitch! Little pigs, my God!"

Just then Lupe's brother Victoriano came walking up, saying that their mother needed to speak to him, Salvador.

Archie started laughing, saying under his breath to Salvador as they all headed back up the street to Lupe's house, "That's why I'd never marry a virgin," he said. "Hell, I don't want a woman running in terror when I drop my pants, showing my studhorse!"

It took all of Salvador's power to not whirl about and slug the huge law-man in the face. My God, what was wrong with everyone? Didn't anyone have respect for the Holy Sacrament of Matrimony anymore?

AND SO IT CAME TO PASS one more time Salvador was told that Lupe wasn't feeling very well again, and she wanted to stay home for another night, so could he please come by and pick her up in the morning.

"Also," said Lupe's mother Doña Guadalupe, "I think she wants to arrive at your little house in the daylight, so she can see the flowers that you told her you planted for her." The old Yaqui Indian woman then took Salvador's hand. "Please be patient, Salvador," she'd added. "Lupe is a fine young woman, and strong, too, you'll see, when the difficult times of life come, she will not fail you."

Salvador breathed deeply, looking at Lupe's mother's dark, wide-set eyes. He well knew that this old Indian woman, who was sitting before him, came from the Yaquis of Northern Sonora, and that many of them had relocated across the border to Tucson, Arizona, after the terrible Yaqui-Mexican War of the eighteen hundreds. Salvador knew, that when this old lady said that her daughter Lupe was strong and that she wouldn't fail him when the hard times of life hit them, she really knew what she was talking about. The Yaquis had endured the same terrible kind of fate that his own mother's people had endured down in the lower boot of Mexico.

"All right," said Salvador to Doña Guadalupe, "then tomorrow it is, so tell Lupe that I'll be by for her about midmorning, and to please be ready."

"I'll tell her, and you won't regret this, Salvador," she said. "Believe me, many a marriage has been ruined at the start because of the man's impa-tience."

Saying this, she took a deep breath, and Salvador well knew that she was trying to tell him volumes of information, and no doubt that this was the catastrophe that had happened to her in her own marriage.

But, also, Salvador figured that this was only half the story, because his own mother had always told him that it took two people to make or ruin a home, and that as many marriages were ruined by a woman's indecision as by a man's aggression.

He said nothing of this. He got in his Moon automobile and drove off, feeling pretty damn disappointed once again. He headed east out of Santa Ana over toward Corona to spend another night with his mother and his sister Luisa. But then, on the way there, he decided that he really didn't want to have to face his sister's words again of how he'd married the wrong woman.

He turned south, headed for Carlsbad. He'd spend another night of their honeymoon alone in the house that he'd fixed up for Lupe and himself.

Getting past San Juan Capistrano and coming out along the sea just north of San Clemente, Salvador saw the Mother Moon dancing on the flat, rippling water, and a surge of frustration ripped into his body.

Salvador almost turned around, to go to that famous whorehouse in Pasadena so he could get himself to calm down!

He didn't want to wake up with aching balls again!

Maybe his sister Luisa was right. He'd made a terrible mistake in marrying Lupe. He should have married a woman of experience who wouldn't be playing these damn stupid little games with him! Because, if the truth be known, he was going crazy-*loco* with wanting Lupe so much that—oh, my God, he was hurting between his legs.

Just south of San Clemente, Salvador pulled over to relieve himself. Standing there, he saw the moonlight dancing on the sea, then he spotted a dozen well-fed horses below the bluff on the shoreline.

It looked like a mare was in heat, and two studs were fighting to see who would get to her. One stud looked dark and lean and compact. The other looked speckled-white and fuller and larger. The two male animals looked truly magnificent rearing up on their hind legs as they pawed at each other with the bright moonlight dancing on the rippling sea behind them.

It was a magic moment of pure beauty with the Mother Moon giving a silvery glow to the horses and glistening sea. And the stars, oh, they were out by the millions dancing on the water, too!

Southern California was still, for the most part, an uninhabitable land of *ranchos* and open space. There weren't any city lights to dilute the bright vastness of the Heavens.

Salvador finished relieving himself.

Oh, God, how he yearned for Lupe. All his life, his old mother had put him to sleep, telling him that it was written in stars how one day each of us would find our truelove and marry.

"But how will I know her?" he'd asked his mother.

"Her hands will fly like birds when she talks, her eyes will dance like leaves in the breeze when she looks at you. She will be the most beautiful woman in all the world to your eyes! And her voice will soothe the worries of the day from your mind."

Tears now came to Salvador's eyes. For it had all come true. Lupe's hands did fly like birds when she spoke and her eyes did dance like leaves in the breeze when she looked at him. And yes, indeed, she was the most beautiful woman in all the world and when he closed his eyes and listened closely her voice soothed his very soul.

Below, one of the studs had won and he was now sniffing underneath the mare's tail. With a screeching scream, he mounted her—and oh, my God, it made Salvador dizzy just to watch!

GETTING INTO THE OCEANSIDE-CARLSBAD AREA, Salvador couldn't bring himself to go to their honeymoon cottage alone again. He decided to stop by and see old man Kenny White at his garage and give him some of the money he owed him. Salvador wouldn't have had the money for his wedding, if it hadn't been for that old *gringo*.

Salvador could now see that his mother was right, there was no bad from which good didn't come if a person just kept going and didn't get bitter. Hell, if it hadn't been for his brother Domingo's stupid behavior—which almost got them both put in jail—then he, Salvador, would have never discovered who were his real friends when all the chips were down.

And it wasn't his own people, *los Mejicanos*, who'd come through for him; oh, no, it had been an Anglo, a Jew, and the German couple Hans and Helen who'd come through for him.

Not Archie, not his Mexican friends whom he'd helped so many times over the years. No, it had been Kenny, an Anglo, who'd loaned him the money, and Harry, a Jew, who'd helped Salvador get Lupe's diamond wedding ring and then had given Salvador credit for all of the wedding clothes, and then it had been the German couple Hans and Helen who'd given him six months' free rent and helped fix up the little white house for Lupe and him.

It shocked him.

It truly amazed him. It was as if his own people really didn't have much faith in their own *gente*.

It was well after midnight when Salvador pulled up in front of Kenny's garage. He was now glad that he hadn't gone all the way up to that famous whorehouse in Pasadena where they had those beautiful, young women who looked and dressed like the movie stars of the day.

He needed time to himself. Oh, tonight when he'd held Lupe in his arms there in the backseat of Archie's big Hudson, it was crazy, but he'd felt more wonderful than when he'd had sex with any woman!

IT WAS ALMOST DAYBREAK when Kenny White came out of his garage and found Salvador asleep. "Up and at 'em!" yelled Kenny, pounding on Salvador's window. "Jerry Bill came by yesterday, and wants to know if you're still in business?!?"

"Jerry?" said Salvador, sitting up and rubbing his eyes. He felt terrible. There was a Mexican *serape* over his body.

"I put that Mexican blanket over you last night after you came in," said Kenny. "You were tossing and turning, so I figured you was just cold. What happened to your honeymoon, anyway? The woman ain't supposed to throw you out 'til you've been married at least a couple of weeks."

"She didn't throw me out," said Salvador, yawning. "I haven't even brought Lupe home yet."

"I'll be," said Kenny, his eyes suddenly full of mischief. "But now tell me, were you really gonna cut that guy? Pigs, I'll be damned! When I told old Archie, he got jealous that he hadn't thought of that trick himself. So I guess they'll now be keeping some pigs down at the jail in Oceanside when they wanna get a prisoner to talk.

"Come on in," added Kenny, "I got the coffee brewing. Man, I feel good! Hell, if I felt any better, I'd get my ass arrested! The world just can't stand to see a man too happy! You look terrible, Sal!"

Salvador nodded and got out of the Moon and walked around to the back of the garage to take a leak, before going inside. Kenny's garage was just east of the railroad tracks, down the street from the Twin Inns Hotel.

"Jerry Bill said that he'd probably be up today to see you," added Kenny.

Jerry Bill was a good friend of Salvador's. Jerry Bill and Fred Noon, Salvador's big-time lawyer from San Diego, were both good, solid, straightforward, hard-drinking men. It was strange, but ever since Salvador had learned the art of liquor making, he was hiding from the law, on the one hand, but he was also in close with more good, solid, leading citizens than he could've ever met with any legitimate job.

This was a fine country for an outlaw, as long as you had a good mechanic to keep your car and truck ready to go, and a big-time lawyer to cover your ass if your car or truck wasn't fast enough.

Inside, Salvador had a cup of coffee with Kenny, and he handed the old man fifty dollars. "Here's a little more of the money I owe you," said Salvador.

"Hell, no," said Kenny, sipping his steaming hot coffee. "You keep that money 'til your marriage is on its feet! You're a real man, Sal. And your word is good enough for me."

"Kenny, you're the best," said Salvador. "The absolute best!"

"All right, I'll accept that," said Kenny, putting his coffee down, "but now don't start any of your damn hugging *abrazos,* Sal." Kenny put both of his hands out in front of himself, so Salvador wouldn't try to hug him. "I wasn't raised up with all these compliments and hugs—make a man nervous is what they do!"

But Salvador was an experienced horseman, so he shifted his eyes to look over Kenny's right shoulder, and said, "Who's that?" in a sudden tone of voice. When Kenny turned to look, Salvador grabbed him in a big *abrazo,* hugging him close. Kenny fought it, but only for a split-second, then he was hugging Salvador in return with such power that Salvador had to hold strong to not have his ribs broken.

Over the years, Salvador had found this to be true with so many *gringo* men, they just didn't like to be touched or hugged. It seemed to threaten their manhood. But then once they got hugging, then my God, it was like they were so hungry for male contact, that they'd hug back in desperation.

It was eight o'clock by the time Salvador started up the coast to pick up Lupe. He'd stopped by their little honeymoon house in the orchard—four blocks north of the *barrio,* where someday the new Carlsbad post office would be built—and he'd shaved, showered, and changed clothes.

He just didn't know what had gotten into him last night. But he'd felt lost and lonely inside. He'd actually begun to resent Lupe.

It was good that it was daytime now, because the things of the night just didn't seem to sit well with a man when he was in love.

Salvador was just north of Oceanside when he remembered the two stallions of the night before. He had to pull at his crotch. What a beautiful sight that had been!

———

WHEN SALVADOR PULLED UP to Lupe's home in Santa Ana in his Moon automobile, both of her parents were playing cards on the front porch. Doña Guadalupe and Don Victor each had a pile of pinto beans in front of them and they both looked very intent on the game.

"Quick, come here," said Don Victor, when he saw Salvador come up the stairs. "Look at the predicament that this old woman has got me into! I got good cards, take a look, but she's beat me so many times in the last few days that I'm even afraid of betting on these!"

Salvador nodded hello to Doña Guadalupe, tipping his small-brim Stetson, then he took a look at Don Victor's cards. The white-haired old man held two kings and two tens. They were good cards. But still, Salvador would've thrown them away without a moment's hesitation if he'd been having bad luck.

"Remember the saying," said Salvador to the balding old man, "the worst curse of the gambler is having the second best hand."

"Yes, of course, we all know that," snapped Don Victor. "The best thing is to have the best or the worst, so then you won't be tempted to bet, if you don't have the winning hand.

"But you tell me, Salvador," he said, looking at his son-in-law in the eyes, "how can a man know that his hand is second best unless he bets?"

Salvador's whole heart came up into his mouth. Oh, these words, these thoughts, they were what haunted every loser every day of his life. Lady Luck, after all, was a very dangerous woman if a man didn't know how to court her shapely, beautiful curves.

"Myself, that's why I don't gamble," said Salvador. "I put my money only on a sure thing."

And here, Salvador, who was in actuality a professional gambler, had said it all, telling the old man the real secret about gambling. But still, even as he, Salvador, told this secret to Lupe's father, he well knew that this old man would only laugh, and never take this advice to heart. For you could see it in his eyes, especially his right eye, the male side; he loved the feel of risking! This was what got him flying. Not the winning, not the figuring and planning, but simply the risking it all to the wild winds of life, with no plan or scheme for the odds of survival, whatsoever.

But, on the other hand, Salvador could well see that his wife, Doña Guadalupe, did understand. You could see it in her left eye, and so this was why she was the real breadwinner of their family. She, the woman, with the power of the mother pig, had the absolute focus of mind to know when not to buck the odds and, and yet, she also knew when to risk every-thing, even her own life for the survival of *la familia*!

"Ha!" continued Lupe's father, laughing happily. "I'm not going to chicken-out now! I'm a man, and so I'm betting!"

With a gleam in his old eyes, he turned around facing his wife and pushed in his whole pile of beans, betting everything he had. Salvador could see his own father doing this type of *macho* bravery, and it was so stupid, and completely unnecessary!

Reluctantly, Doña Guadalupe saw his bet, pushing in an equal amount of beans. "Three queens," she said.

"Three queens!" yelled the old man, throwing down his cards in dis-gust. "Damnit! I lost again!"

Don Victor got to his feet, pulling his pants up angrily . . . just as Lupe came out the door, suitcase in hand, wearing her royal blue dress and full-length coat with the fur collar that Salvador had bought for her. And she looked so beautiful, so breath-taking elegant. There was no movie star who even came close to Lupe's natural beauty.

"Oh, how I just hope I get rich once before I die, so I can choke this old woman to death with money!" continued Lupe's father, half-angry, but still laughing at the same time. "So she'll realize once and for all, just what kind of man I am!"

"But I know what a good man you are already," said Lupe's mother Doña Guadalupe, smiling as she drew in all her winnings.

"Look at her," snapped the old man. "She has the mouth to say that even as she takes all of my *frijoles!*"

The roar of *carcajadas* that came from Lupe's old mother as her father mentioned his beans, was so loud, so contagious, that Lupe and Salvador started laughing, too, and then Don Victor was laughing, also.

The two old people laughed until they had tears in their eyes, and their stomachs ached. And then Doña Guadalupe and Don Victor looked at their daughter—standing here before them with her suitcase beside her—and they suddenly realized what the moment was really all about.

They weren't laughing because of their *frijoles*; oh, no, they were laugh-ing these painful *carcajadas* because they were losing the baby of the fam-ily, and soon they'd also lose Carlota and Victoriano, and then they'd be all alone.

The two old people dried their eyes and took each other's hand as they stood looking at Lupe and Salvador—two old people who were still at odds with each other, two old people who saw love in this young couple's eyes, and it caused them to remember that love in themselves.

"Well, well," said Don Victor, drying his eyes with the back of his hand and reaching for his daughter, "I guess this is it." And he took Lupe into his old, thin arms, giving her *un abrazo.* "And only yesterday you were chasing after your deer up and down the hillsides in *la Lluvia de Oro* as agile as a Tarahumara Indian—oh, my God, how the years have flown by!"

He was crying and crying and hugging his daughter, and then Doña Guadalupe joined them and she was crying, too.

Salvador watched these two old parents hugging their daughter, and he now once more knew, down deep inside of himself, why he'd chosen Lupe above all other women to be his wife; not only was she beautiful, but she knew love deep in her center.

"Please," said Lupe, kissing her mother and father, "tell my *nina* Sophia that I'm sorry I didn't get to see her, but we'll be back soon, and Salvador and I will spend time with her then."

Salvador had no idea what Lupe was talking about. But Lupe was very upset. Sophia was Lupe's oldest sister and she was also Lupe's *nina*, meaning her godmother, and so Sophia and Lupe were very close, but still Sophia and her husband, Julian, hadn't come to Lupe's wedding. Sophia had sent their older children to Salvador and Lupe's wedding, but she and Julian hadn't come, because these were hard times and they hadn't thought that they had the proper clothes.

It had bothered Lupe tremendously, but she also hadn't dared to ask Salvador to buy them clothes—fully realizing that he'd already spent a fortune as it was. And besides, her sister Sophia was as stubborn as she was tiny and cute, and once she'd made up her mind, that they needed special clothes to come to Lupe's wedding, she just wouldn't change her mind.

"Of course, *mi hijita,*" Doña Guadalupe now said to her daughter, "please don't worry about your sister Sophia anymore. As soon as Victoriano gets another truck, things will be better for all of us again."

"Excuse me," said Don Victor to Salvador, "but while these women talk, I'd like to see you alone, Salvador."

"But they need to be going," said Doña Guadalupe anxiously. "You can talk to him some other time."

"Look at her," snapped Don Victor. "During your courtship, she'd steal you for three hours at a time—ruining your ears! But now I only wish to speak to you for a moment and she says no! Women, I swear, they're impossible! But what can we do? Pigs are only good for eating!"

Saying this, the old man put his long, thin arm about Salvador's thick, heavy shoulders and walked away with him. "Tell me," he said, taking a little stone out of his pocket and rubbing it with his thumb and index finger, "do you remember me telling you about all the gold that's still left in the canyon where we came from in Mexico?"

"Yes," said Salvador. "I remember well."

"Well, see this little stone," said the balding old man, "I picked it up on the trail when we were walking out of the canyon. Look, it's got color, and if you look close, you can see little spiderwebs of interlaced gold. In any other place, this stone would have been considered wonderful ore, but in our canyon, we had such a wealth of pure gold nuggets, that stones like this we just threw away."

He laughed. "Look at it, look at it real closely. I'll tell you, all these years this little stone is what has given me the heart to go on." He breathed. "My wife, she brought her wild lilies, but I, I brought this little stone, and whenever times get too hard for me to handle, I just take this little stone out of my pocket, and rub it between my thumb and fingers. I feel good when I rub this little stone!" He breathed again. "Salvador, it has always been my dream that before I die, I return to Mexico, and dig for gold again! And not for a rich Mexican or for an American company like last time, but for myself, this time! With my own two hands and arms! And I want you, Salvador, to come with me so we can dig deep into the Mother Earth and get rich together!"

"Sounds good to me," said Salvador, seeing the old man's eyes aglow with fire.

"Really?" said the old man, surprised by his son-in-law's quick response. "You'll then go with me!?!"

"Sure, why not? Then we'll all be rich!" added Salvador, giving the old man exactly what it was that he wanted, fully realizing that the old man was really all talk, all bluff, just like he was in cards. But what the hell? We all had our dreams, and dreams were such an inexpensive gift to give, his mother always told him. And then, also, who knew? Miracles did happen. And dreams were to miracles like manure was to a plant, giving them each the power with which to grow.

Well, the joy, the *gusto* that now came into the old man's eyes, lit up his whole face. "Then it's settled!" he said with a sudden rush of newfound vitality. "And we'll take Victoriano, too, and then we'll all come back like kings! And I'll buy *frijoles* by the truckload, so this damn old lady won't be able to win them all from me even in a million years!"

Lupe's old father now laughed with *carcajadas*, pumping Salvador's hand up and down on the deal, and—in this moment of supreme joy and feeling of abundance—he handed Salvador the little stone that he'd held so dear for all these years!

"For you!" he said with tears coming to his old, wrinkled-up eyes. "That you will be a better man with my daughter than I was with my wife. For the truth is, Salvador, that I've never been *un hombre* much good at cards, or gambling, or even at life, itself. But you, oh, you are different than me, I can see it in your eyes, your clothes, your confidence. You are a man among men, a real *macho!*"

And saying this, the tall, thin, old man hugged Salvador close, kissing him on his right cheek, then on his left. Salvador's eyes filled with tears, too, holding the little stone in his right hand. His own father—a powerful giant—had never shown him such love and honor! But still, taking this old man's little stone made Salvador feel a little bit uncomfortable.

"No," said Salvador, "you keep the stone. It is yours, Don Victor."

"Mine?" asked the old man. "You take our heart, the soul of our family, with the taking of our baby daughter, but now you don't accept this stone? Here, take it, Salvador, and rub it like this between your thumb and fingers when life gets tough. Please, I've been where you are going, and we men need our little stone, or else we never stop playing with our *tanates,*" he added, laughing.

Salvador breathed. "Well, then, I accept," he said.

"Good," said Don Victor, smiling grandly.

All this time Lupe and her mother had been watching, and they didn't really know what the two men were talking about, but it made them feel very good to see such joy and warmth between them.

It had been a long time since Don Victor had shown any spark of his old self.

Salvador picked up Lupe's two bags and carried them down the steps to the Moon. Putting the suitcases in the back, Salvador then opened the car door for Lupe and got her inside. Then he waved his good-byes to his in-laws, and walked around, jumped in the Moon, started the motor, and they were off.

He took Lupe's hand as they sped away. And just the touch of her sent him flying!

Part Three

MOONTALKING

End of August 1929

Carlsbad, California

4

*And so they'd now entered into the Garden of Eden, God's
first couple — a man and a woman who of their own freewill
chose the way of the Almighty!*

WITH HER OPEN HAND, Lupe played with the passing breeze
outside her window as they drove down the coast from Santa Ana
to Carlsbad. The breeze had never felt so delicious on her naked skin. She
just couldn't get over it; she was now a married woman going off on her
honeymoon. And here was her husband, *su esposo,* sitting beside her,
looking so handsome at the wheel of their grand automobile. Lupe
purred.

But then, just south of San Clemente, as they came into the great Santa
Margarita *Rancho*—which would one day be the Marine Corps Base of
Camp Pendleton—Lupe had a problem. She needed to pee, but there was
no gas station or any other facilities. And of course, all of her life she'd
relieved herself behind bushes and trees when she and her family had followed the crops, but this was different. She was all alone with this man, a
stranger, and her mother and sisters weren't here to help give her privacy
with a blanket.

But then she once more remembered that Salvador wasn't a stranger.
He was her husband. Her *esposo!* She started laughing.

"What is it?" asked Salvador.

"Oh, nothing," she said. "Just please pull over. Quick."

Salvador pulled over to the side of the road. Lupe got out and went
behind the Moon automobile to relieve herself, but then she realized that
she could be seen by oncoming traffic. She quickly walked across a little
slope toward the sea. Here, she found a tree and some tall brush.

Finding a small clearing near the end of the slope, Lupe decided that this was a good place. She turned and saw that Salvador was watching her. She waved for him to please turn around. He did so, and when she squatted down to relieve herself, she'd never heard herself pee so loudly. My God, she sounded like a waterfall.

Finishing, she realized she had no paper, so she didn't know what to use to dry herself. Standing up, there was a little white butterfly flying about her. She laughed. Then glancing around, she saw that a whole swarm of these butterflies were coming toward her.

Her face lit up with joy, remembering the tens of thousands of great big orange butterflies that had come into her family's canyon every year back in Mexico.

A hawk now flew over Lupe's head, giving a great cry. It was a Redtail Hawk, which was known to many Native People of the Southwest as the Red Eagle—a human's guide.

Breathing in of the butterflies, Lupe suddenly felt so blessed as she now looked out across the gray-green-brown landscape all about her and to the glistening, dancing, vast blue sea. The Redtail called to her again, telling her that she was surrounded by the Almighty Creator's Beauty!

Laughing, Lupe raised up her arms and the white butterflies danced all about her like Angels. She laughed all the more and the butterflies came in so close that some began to land on the naked skin of her arms. Why, she could hear these butterflies speaking to her, singing to her, whispering good tiding to her just as her mother's plants had whispered to her when she'd drank her coffee on her parents' porch, watching the break of the new day.

Then miracle of miracles, up came a mother deer and her two little yearlings, standing at the edge of this swarm of white butterflies.

Lupe couldn't stop smiling—she was so happy!

The Red Eagle screeched again and again and Lupe felt like she'd been magically transported back in time to her childhood when the whole world had been full of magic and wonder! A time when she and her girlfriends had lived in the Daily Miracle of all plants breathing in and out of the Holy Creator and all animal life was glowing with the Union of Creation.

A time when she and Manuelita, Uva, and Cuca—her best friends growing up—and her sister Carlota had raced up and down the *barrancas* of their box canyon, when the soldiers of the Revolution weren't trying to catch them and rape them.

Lupe now felt so blessed—she COULD BURST! She waved for Salvador to come across the slope and join her.

Love was in every breath she took!

Love was in every sight she saw: the trees, the brush, the sea, the breeze, the butterflies, the deer, and of course, the calling Red Eagle.

Taking her husband's hand, Lupe stepped with Salvador over the dark wet-spot where she'd peed and they walked down to the seashore. The butterflies followed them like they were Angels sent by God.

Suddenly, a covey of quail exploded in a quick-burst, flying from a big bush down by the sand. Lupe and Salvador took off their shoes and walked along the shore. Every step they now took, they walked in God's Beauty. They'd entered Heaven on Earth.

The Father Sun was going down by the time they got back to their car and drove into Oceanside. They stopped on the bluff above the Ocean-side pier and got out of their Moon. There were a few silky-thin clouds out over the sea where the Father Sun, the Right Eye of the Almighty, was set-ting.

The closer and closer the Father Sun drew to the sea, the whole west-ern sky lit up in colors of pink and gold, red and orange, and the clouds took on beautiful colors of silky-silver.

People gathered on the bluff and watched the miracle of light giving clo-sure to another magnificent day, truly a Gift from the Almighty.

Salvador held Lupe in his arms up against his body as they both watched the Sun now touching the sea and begin to go slipping, sliding into the great Pacific. He could feel the warmth of Lupe's firm, well-rounded *nalguitas* up against him. It was delicious!

Then boom, the Right Eye of God was going, going, gone, and here held a little pyramid-like flash of greenish-blue light for a split-second!

Suddenly, it was much cooler.

Quickly, Salvador and Lupe got back in their car.

By the time they got to Carlsbad—only three miles south of the pier—Lupe was going crazy with hunger! It had taken them nearly six hours just to drive down from Santa Ana, and usually this drive only took about an hour. And her sister Maria had warned Lupe of this timeless time and hunger of love.

In fact, both of Lupe's older married sisters, Maria and her *nina* Sophia, had explained to her of this woman's hunger, of this woman's timeless sense of time that took place when a man and woman united in the full commitment of Holy Matrimony.

Time stood still and all living life burst forth in abundance! And a woman became so hungry that she had to be very careful, for if she opened up, really opened up to her full powers of love too quickly, on her wedding night, why, she could devour the man—skin and bones and all—taking him into her body again and again, until there'd be *nada, nada*, nothing left of the man for even the buzzards.

And it was true, for everything that Lupe now saw, she just wanted to take it and put it in her mouth, chew it up, and pull it down deep into her starving, aching body!

Holding Salvador's hand as they drove—she was tempted to bite the fingers off his hand, one by one, sucking them first, then chewing them, devouring them as she took them deep inside of herself!

By the time they pulled off the road into the tiny town of Carlsbad, Lupe was so hungry, that she knew she was dangerous!

"Tell me," she said, trying to keep calm, "do we have anything at home so I can fix something for us to eat?"

"No, I don't think so," said Salvador. "But we can go out to eat later."

"Later? Oh, no!" she said. "I'd like to stop and buy groceries, so I can fix our first meal for us in our new home."

That was the other thing that Lupe's two older married sisters, Maria and Sophia, had told her to do: stock the house with plenty of food before they went to bed. "Or else," Maria had told her, "newlyweds have been known to devour each other, only to be found dead and stinking up the house weeks later!"

"Oh, all right," said Salvador, turning onto the main street of Carlsbad. "There's a new market just down the street from our house. My friend Kenny—you know, you met him at the wedding—loaned Eisner the money to get his little store started."

"Didn't Kenny loan you money, too?" asked Lupe.

"Yes, that's right," said Salvador. "Kenny's a good man."

A few weeks ago, Salvador had begun telling Lupe about his fertilizer business. After all, he wanted to start building a little trust between them before he stopped all of his lying.

My God, Lupe really had no idea that he was a gambling man, a bootlegger, drank alcohol and carried a gun. She had married him, really thinking that he just moved fertilizer for a living.

The truth was going to shock her. Lies just weren't good traveling companions with love for very long.

Buying two whole bags of groceries—which came to thirty-five cents—they drove back down the main street of town, turned left, went east one block, then they turned left again up a dirt road, and right into an orchard where their little house was located. Salvador had rented the house from his good friends Hans and Helen Huelster, the German couple who owned the Montana Café. Hans and Helen had met Lupe at their wedding. Helen thought Lupe was the most naturally beautiful woman she'd ever seen.

It was a good-size, two-bedroom house with indoor plumbing that Salvador had picked up for fifteen dollars a month—a fortune! A dog and two cats had come with the house and a little vegetable garden in back and an enclosed, white picket fence surrounded the whole place. There were roses in the front yard, plus all the fresh flowers Salvador had planted. Their closest neighbors were two blocks away.

Getting out of the car, Salvador didn't know if he should carry in his bride first, or the two bags of groceries that Lupe just kept clutching to her breasts as if she was afraid of losing them.

"Lupe," he finally said, laughing. "I don't think I can carry you over the threshold, if you don't let go of those groceries."

Blushing, Lupe put the two bags down and Salvador picked her up in his arms. Looking into each other's eyes, they now drew close, and oh, just the touch of their lips sent them flying!

Quickly, Salvador opened the little, white gate with one hand, then holding the gate open with one foot, he took his young bride through the fence and toward the house. But then, out of nowhere, here came the little dog that belonged to the house and he didn't recognize Salvador and Lupe, and he began growling and snapping.

Salvador yelled at the dog, then made the terrible mistake of trying to kick him away.

The tough, little dog now leaped at him, grabbing Salvador by his pant leg, and he and Lupe both fell to the ground. Salvador was mad as hell, but Lupe couldn't stop laughing. The little, brown dog was now looking so proud of himself that he was actually smiling, and saying, "Look, I may be small, but I'm a real tough little dog, so you two will never have to worry, 'cause I can keep guard with no *problema!*"

Still feeling pissed off at getting his pant leg ripped, Salvador now made the mistake of taking yet another kick at the dog. Instantly, the little beast quit smiling and attacked Salvador again, biting him. Salvador yelped out in pain. And he was such a tiny dog, hardly any larger than the two cats that now came up to be loved, rubbing up against Salvador and Lupe as they lay there on the ground.

Salvador quit kicking the dog and started laughing, too. Instantly, the dog was smiling once again.

"Just look at that little *cabrón* bastard!" said Salvador, laughing. "He's actually proud as hell that he knocked us down!"

"Yes, he is," said Lupe, "and the way he bit you when you tried to kick him, he looks like a real little—" she stopped her words.

"Go on, what were you gonna say?" said Salvador.

"Oh, nothing," said Lupe, blushing as she lay there on the ground next to Salvador, petting the two cats and the dog.

One cat was a mousy-brown color, and the other had three different colors, and so, of course, this last one had to be a female cat. For a male cat to have three colors was as rare as a four-leaf clover.

"Come on," said Salvador, "what were you going to say?"

Lupe blushed all red again. "I was going to say—" But she couldn't say the word, for she'd never used any swear words in her life.

"Come on, Lupe," said Salvador, taking her chin in his hand and gently raising up her face so they could see each other eye-to-eye, "what were you gonna say? Remember, you're a married woman now, you can say and do whatever you want."

"I can?"

"Sure, you are an adult now, a responsible person, ready to start your own home. So tell me, what were you going to say?"

"*Chingon*!" she said quickly, never having said this word before. "I was going to say that the little dog looks like a real *chingon*!"

The laughter, the *carcajadas* that erupted from Salvador's body was so huge, that it startled the two cats and dog—who'd obviously all been raised together the way they treated each other so well—and Lupe hit Salvador in the stomach to stop him from laughing at her, but then she was laughing, too. Oh, it had felt so good to say that forbidden word.

"So that's what we'll call him from now on," said Salvador, "*el Chingon, our great protector!*"

Salvador and Lupe couldn't stop laughing. Then they drew close, held, looking at each other with so much feeling, and began kissing and kissing, here on the ground outside of their honeymoon cottage. Lupe didn't mean to—but oh, my God, she bit Salvador on the neck so hard that he screamed out in pain!

"You bit me!" he yelped. "First the damn dog, and now you!"

"Oh," she said, "I'm sorry! I don't know what got into me, but, well, I think you better feed me, Salvador . . . real quick!"

Seeing her eyes, he didn't laugh. Oh, there was a look of hunger in

Lupe's eyes that would've terrified most men. Salvador rubbed the place where she had bit him, then got to his feet and went to get the groceries.

Petting the two cats and the little dog, Lupe then got to her feet, too. She hated to admit it, but a large part of her had really liked biting Salvador. It had made her feel like, well, a really *chingona*!

She winked at the little dog, and he smiled at Lupe, then Lupe followed Salvador inside.

The house was all dark. Salvador lit a match, searching for the light switch, but couldn't find it. The house was quiet and spooky-feeling, especially every time they moved and the floor screeched. Lupe's whole mood quickly changed. They could each hear the other's breathing. Finally, Salvador found the light switch and turned on the lights.

Lupe glanced around and the first thing that came to her mind was how truly large the rooms were. She'd never been in such a large, spacious home. It made her parents' house look like a little shack, and her sister Sophia's house look like nothing but a migrant tent.

"Well, how do you like it?" asked Salvador, proudly.

"It's really big," she said.

"Yes, I thought you'd like it," he said, "and it has indoor plumbing, too, not just electricity. Come, let me show you the bathroom and the kitchen."

Lupe followed Salvador. The other light switches weren't as difficult to find.

"Like you said, Lupe," Salvador continued speaking as they went into the kitchen, then the bathroom, "a place away from both our families, so we can get to know each other without interference."

He loved taking Lupe from room to room. Most of the furniture that they'd picked out together had already arrived and she was in awe as she saw the different rooms with all their furnishings.

"You know," said Salvador, "my mother was very impressed when I told her that one of your first requests was that we live alone, without either one of our families close by for the first year. She told me, that for you being so close to your family, and yet to have the wisdom to want us to be alone is remarkable—but what are you doing?" he asked, interrupting himself. "Does the house smell bad or something?"

"No, not really," said Lupe. She was sniffing at the room. They were now in the little bathroom. "It's just, well, strong," she said, lying, because the truth was that the whole house smelled awful.

"The owners, Hans and Helen, you know, they're German," said Salvador. "And they were cleaning."

"Well, it's spotless," she said, "I'll say that for them. But it smells so strong of soap that—could we open the windows while I start dinner? Tomorrow, I'll bring in some flowers from the garden to give fragrance to the house."

"Yeah, sure," said Salvador, shoving the bottom half of the two windows upward. "But couldn't we eat afterward?"

"After what?" said Lupe, slipping off her coat as they went back into the kitchen. But, then, she turned and saw Salvador's face and she realized what he meant. "Oh, that," she said, turning a dozen different shades of red as she put her coat over the back of one of the kitchen chairs. "No," she said very strongly, "I have to feed you first."

"You have to feed me first," he repeated. "What am I, a horse?"

"Well, no, of course not," she said. "But you see, my sister Maria, well, she explained to me that—" Lupe stopped her words, turning an even deeper shade of red. She couldn't tell him what her sister had explained to her. She glanced down at the polished hardwood floor, avoiding her husband's eyes.

Once more, Salvador became very intrigued. "Just what exactly is it that Maria told you?" he asked, coming closer to her with a twinkle in his eyes.

"No," said Lupe, pursing her lips together and keeping her head down. "I can't tell you."

"But why not?" he asked, truly enjoying her predicament.

"Because," she said, glancing up, ready to tell him the truth. But then she saw that his eyes were dancing. He was making fun of her. "No!" she now said angrily. "I won't tell you now! You get out of my way, while I start cooking, and that's that!"

He heard her tone of voice, saw her stance, and he could still feel where she'd bit him, so he backed off. His bride could be a tiger. He started laughing.

"Don't you dare laugh at me!" she snapped. "I might not know much about marriage yet, but I've seen what happens to male pigs during the mating season!"

The howl, the scream of laughter that came ripping out of Salvador's body was so great, that even the dog, *Chingon,* outside began to bark once more.

"Oh, oh, oh, oh!" screamed Salvador. "So that's why we had to get groceries, so you could feed me first! So I don't waste away to skin and bones like a male pig in rut!"

Lupe's cheeks now flushed so red that her face burned of fire. "Well, it's true," she said. "Even Sophia told me the same thing; not just Maria! 'Women have to be careful to not wear out their husbands on their honeymoons, or they get so weak that they can't go to work!' "

Hearing this one, Salvador fell down on the floor, laughing, kicking, and banging his fists—howling! Outside *Chingon* ran around the house, barking wildly and then the other dogs of the neighborhood began barking, too. Finally Lupe couldn't help it, and she lost her anger and was laughing, too.

Sobering up, Salvador lay there on the floor looking at Lupe's long, strong, well-shaped legs as she stood here leaning back against the stove, wiping the tears from her eyes from laughing so hard.

Lupe looked at Salvador's eyes. She saw how his eyes were devouring her, eating her up leg by leg, thigh by thigh, breast by breast; oh, my God, Almighty, why, he was as hungry for her as she was for him!

It was really frightening, because if his hunger was anything like the hunger that she, herself, was feeling when she looked at him—then, oh, my God, her sister Maria's stories were absolutely true . . . and newlyweds had, indeed, been found dead, because they'd consumed each other to death!

He, Salvador, was now slowly getting to his feet, saying, "Lupe," as he now came closer to her, "I'm strong, *querida*. Believe me, you don't have to worry about me dying for at least—" he grinned, "—three days."

Saying this, he came to her, pressing his body against her body as she'd leaned back on the stove, and his open mouth was on her mouth, and they were kissing, mouthing! And she could feel his rock-hard, molten-fire growing and growing, pressing up against her, getting huge! Then he was picking her up in his powerful arms, and they hurried down the hallway, where he kicked open their bedroom door with a bang!

And on the sheets, that Lupe's sister Sophia had embroidered for her with pink roses and green leaves and vines, Salvador lay her down across the length of the wide bed. His breathing changed, becoming long, and hot, and very heavy.

Lupe could now truly understand that the Almighty had, indeed, made men of rock and molten fire, for Salvador was just burning on top of her, kneeling over her body. His eyes alone were burning hot coals; a fire just wanting to consume her!

Then he was kissing her softly, gently, slowly, on the mouth, the cheeks, the neck, and she now also knew why God had made woman from the flower and the tree. For she could feel her whole body now opening up to Salvador *como una flor a la lumbre del Sol,* like a flower to his fire of the Sun, as she arched her back to him, wanting him all deep inside of her as quickly as she could!

He was her Sun!

She was his Moon!

He was her Day!

She was his Night!

And the Almighty Holy Creator was now here with them both, equally, guiding them, helping them, into a Creation of their very own *Paraiso!*

Time disappeared. And this Miracle of the Union between a Man and a Woman began.

Yes, something had, indeed, happened since they'd left Santa Ana.

All their Senses had begun changing, changing, growing, expanding from the moment that Salvador and Lupe had decided to get married and to leave their parents' homes; two people, two hearts, two souls, preparing to enter into their own Kingdom *con Papito!*

Adam and Eve all over again!

Lupe now felt the roughness of his shaved face as she pulled Salvador down to herself, smelling him as she put her arms about his neck, feeling his wide, thick body pushing down on her.

Lupe thought of taking off her royal blue dress before it got wrinkled, but decided against it and she listened to the dogs barking outside—much like the dogs that had always barked outside their lean-to back home in *la Lluvia de Oro* in Mexico. She now ran her fingers through Salvador's thick mane of curly-black hair as she arched her back up to him, and he . . . and he continued kissing her in quick, little nibble-like kisses.

Her skin was beginning to glow, to sweat, as he continued kissing, nibbling, whispering tender words of endearment.

Then suddenly her skin was alive and beginning to sing! To tingle in hot, little-quick-rushes all over her face and neck and shoulders, then travel down, down between her shoulder blades, the length of her whole body!

No one had ever told her about this!

Oh, this was wondrous!

She began to open her mouth wide just to breathe, and pull his face down to hers so she could mouth him, bite him, eat him all up! Miracle of miracles, the rushes continued, and Lupe got so hot that she had to push him away so she could breathe.

"Are you okay?" he asked.

"Yes," she said between gasps for air. "I'm all right. I'm just, well, hot."

And she was, indeed, so hot that she now had to pull back her long, dark hair before she could continue kissing again.

"Okay," she said, having caught her breath and reaching out for him again. And here they were again, kissing and mouthing and breathing together, and it was like their two separate bodies were now becoming one.

As if they were now becoming one huge mass of feeling, one huge body of wonderment, of delicious, marvelous . . . oh, oh, oh, and these strange feelings were building, building up inside her, feelings she'd never known before in all her years of yearning, dreaming, and wanting!

Then, suddenly, she was on FIRE!

AFLAME!

She could feel his hard stone of molten lava pulsating up against her through her dress, and she felt a sudden, hot—hurting sensation begin at the base of her skull, slowly at first. Very slowly. Then faster and faster . . . as it all came shooting down her spinal column . . . in a volcano of explod- ing fire!

She heard a SCREAM!

From whom this scream had come, she had no idea, 'til she realized that she was the one who was gasping to catch her breath. She screamed again!

She could now feel her body BURSTING OPEN, and she was now all wet at the center of her being!

She began to go wild with fear, thinking that she was going to get sick again and have to rush to the bathroom. But she didn't. No, she could feel that this time, different than last time, she'd actually become more alive than she'd ever been before in all of her life!

She'd burst through into a whole new world of feeling!

Now she was ready to the root of her being to burst open and take this man deep inside of her, to levels of feelings she'd never felt before!

Then she heard a series of low, growling cries, and at first she thought that these cries came from the dogs outside. But then, as they grew louder, closer, and more numerous, she suddenly realized these were also coming up from deep inside her . . . as she now grabbed at Salvador with such terrible power that she thought she'd crushed him.

Lupe could hear herself SCREAMING so loud, then giving tight cries as she'd never heard herself give before!

Her whole body was breaking, EXPLODING, ERUPTING in WILD SPASMS with each SCREAMING CRY!

Then, suddenly, she couldn't stand it anymore and she just flung Salvador away from herself across the bed and to the floor, so she could catch her breath again!

"I'm sorry!" she yelled, desperately trying to catch her breath. "I hope I didn't hurt you again."

This time, she hadn't just pushed Salvador away. Oh, no, this time she'd flung him clear across the entire length of the bed to the floor, where he now lay staring at her in disbelief. He was shocked. He outweighed her by a good fifty pounds, and yet she'd tossed him away like a toy.

He shook his head, grinning. "No, you haven't hurt me yet," he said, smiling. "I think I'm still okay."

"Good," she said, taking one more big breath, trying to calm her pounding heart. "Then come back on the bed," she said, reaching out to bring him close again. Oh, she was so hungry! She truly had to be careful. She was starving!

He took her outstretched hand. He was now very glad that they'd had over a week to cool off after their wedding. Two people truly could kill each other on their wedding night.

Moonlight was coming in their bedroom window, moontalking to them through the white lace curtains. The Mother Moon was truly every young lover's best friend, helping them, guiding them in this miraculous moment of power and youth.

"I don't want to hurt you," said Lupe, as she helped him back in bed. "But I really thought I was going to die, so I had to push you away."

He nodded. "You don't have to explain," he said. "I'm okay."

"Really?" she said.

"Yes, really," he said, smiling. "Like I said, don't worry, I can take this for two or three days. You don't frighten me. But I'll tell you, I've never been tossed across a bed like a little toy doll before."

"Well, maybe I don't frighten you," she said, smiling, "but I'm kind of frightening myself," she added, truly enjoying the thought of her own power.

She now took hold of him again, pulling him across the wide bed to herself, licking her lips. She was feeling real *chingona*. And, oh, just the touch of him, sent her skin itching, singing, glowing, burning hot all over again!

Suddenly, Lupe forced herself to stop. "Wait. Please, stop. I want to undress now," she said, not wanting to ruin her dress any more. And saying this, Lupe got up and went into the privacy of the bathroom, while he began to strip so he could get under the covers.

In the bathroom, Lupe undressed, folded her clothes, and slipped the beautiful beige-white gown over her naked body that Harry's wife, Bernice—the Jewish couple that Salvador had introduced her to—had given her as a wedding gift.

"This gown, you change into on the first night of your honeymoon in the privacy of the bathroom after you've made him hot with kisses," had said Bernice, a woman who kept herself so shapely and well that she looked twenty years younger than her age. "Then you turn off the light, my dear, as soon as you come back into the bedroom, because this quick little sight of you in this gown, your husband will treasure with excitement even after fifty years of marriage!

"For a honeymoon, after all, is for the building of memories that help keep us married people together in the years to come. And if he says to turn the lights back on so he can see you, you say no! And say it with conviction! But then add very suggestively, 'Later, honey, please, when I'm less shy.' But you are not shy, my dear," had explained Bernice. "Oh, no, you know what you are doing. You are building the foundation of the fantasies that every successful marriage is based upon!"

Lupe sat down on the toilet, listening to her waterfall-like pouring, then she wiped herself, flushed, washed her hands, fixed her hair, drank some water from the sink with her cupped hand—when she could find no glass—then she breathed, looking at herself in the mirror, and by God, it truly surprised Lupe to see how truly beautiful she was every time she looked in the mirror.

After all, she'd never been one to spend much time before mirrors. Why, she, Lupe Gomez—no, Lupe Villaseñor—was a breathtaking beauty . . . and she was a married woman!

She laughed, she smiled, she giggled, and she thanked God, made the sign of the cross over herself, and came out of the bathroom, let Salvador feast his eyes on her for only a split second, then she turned, turning off the light of the bedroom.

"But, Lupe," said Salvador, "don't turn off the lights! I want to see you; you look so beautiful!"

"No!" she snapped. "I will not turn them on! Please, Salvador, later, maybe, when I'm, well, you know, not so shy," she added, softly.

"Oh," he said, truly loving the sweet, innocent tone of her voice.

She, Lupe, now slipped under the covers with Salvador, her truelove, and they drew their two bodies close together on the cool, smooth sheets, then began to kiss and smell each other. He was naked, and she'd never smelled a naked man before.

She giggled, liking it!

And so He, the Day ended and She, the Night began, as the Mother Moon spoke to them, Moontalking.

5

The Devil saw their happiness, their joy of being in Holy
Union with the Almighty, and so he smiled, creeping down
from the Tree of Knowledge to intercept them.

FOR THREE DAYS AND NIGHTS, Salvador and Lupe were together in their little honeymoon cottage, moontalking to the stars and getting to know each other as they'd never known anyone else ever before.

Lupe told Salvador stories of her childhood, of what it had been like to grow up in a gold mining town in Mexico . . . high in the mountains of *la Barranca del Cobre,* which was owned by a big American company. She told him of her pet deer, of running up and down the steep hillsides with her deer, like a wild Indian.

Salvador told Lupe stories of growing up in *los Altos de Jalisco,* where the Earth was red and all men carried a gun, and of his pet bull, Chivo, the greatest fighting bull in all the region, and how life had been a happy, wild adventure 'til the Revolution of 1910 had come exploding into their mountainous area when he'd been nine years old.

They talked and made love and talked some more, little by little coming to feel so close together that it almost felt to them as if they'd known each other forever.

Two hearts becoming one.

Two minds becoming one.

And soon their stories intermingled in each other's dreams, and their bodies began taking on each other's smells.

Smells and dreams uniting them into a feeling of oneness that they'd never known before.

Dreams and smells, two very powerful means of communication, and here, at this crossroads of smells and dreams, the whole world disappeared, and they were now all-new and so happy, so very happy giving love and more love to each other again and again!

They slept when they were tired and they talked when they awoke, and little by little, this stranger that they'd married became each other's best friend.

Lupe now felt safe enough to ask Salvador questions about sex and men and life that she'd always been too embarrassed to ask her mother or sisters. And he, too, little by little, told her things about his life that he'd never told anyone before.

But it wasn't until the third night, when they'd worn themselves to exhaustion, that they finally shed their outer skins like snakes in the springtime, and they forgot all their past lives, and now nothing else existed, but this new, brave world that they'd created between themselves in lovemaking.

And the smell of their bodies, and the smell of their wet-scented bed, became a Universe for them to explore as they came to know each little curve, each secret little crevice of their two bodies.

They continued to make love again and again.

Slowly, gently, Lupe came to know for the first time in her young life, why the Sun was always referred to as a male member when he came rising up with his hot-burning power each morning, just before he burst forth, shooting sunlight to all the Female Earth!

Love! Love! *Amor* was the mating of Heaven and Earth!

Lupe now took Salvador deep inside of herself again and again, finally beginning to satisfy that growling hunger that she'd been feeling ever since they'd left her parents' home.

Now, here they finally were, a man and woman of One Soul: the First House of every Home.

The First House of the Three Sacred Worlds of Creation, the place where *Papito Dios* resided with each New Couple, breathing in and . . . breathing out.

The drums were beating!

The Drums were beat, Beat, BEATING!

They, Lupe and Salvador, had re-united with the Heartbeat of the Universe; One Song, One Verse, the SYMPHONY of CREATION!

THEN, THERE CAME A KNOCKING on their front door.

It was midmorning, and Kenny White had come to tell Salvador that

Fred Noon was in town and that he needed to see him, something about his brother, Domingo, in prison.

"All right," said Salvador, glancing behind himself, wanting to make sure that Lupe hadn't overheard. "I'll be over at your place in an hour."

"An hour, eh?" said Kenny, grinning. "Hell, I remember the days when you'd be ready in two minutes! Just joking," added Kenny. "We all know you're on your honeymoon. Don't worry. I'll go have breakfast with Fred over at the Montana Café. We'll meet you there. Also, I think it's about time I took your car in for service."

"Thank you, Kenny," said Salvador, rubbing his face and trying to get the sleep out of his eyes, "you're a good *amigo.*"

"Hell, you keep me in the best liquor since I last tasted Canadian Whiskey," whispered Kenny with a big, shit-eating grin. "See you, Sal! Man, if I felt any better, I'd get arrested!"

"Who was that?" asked Lupe, when Salvador came back into the bed-room.

"Kenny," said Salvador, rubbing his eyes and still trying to wake up. My God, he almost hadn't recognized Kenny when he'd first opened the door. It was like he and Lupe were so far away . . . in another world! "He came to tell me that, well, my attorney, Fred Noon, from San Diego is up here to see me."

"You have an attorney?" asked Lupe. "But why would you need one for moving fertilizer?"

Salvador took a deep breath. Lupe was really quick. She was no dummy. She'd put two and two together real fast. He'd have to be very careful around her while he was hiding all these lies from her. Lies and love didn't mix very well. Love just opened you up too much.

"When I get back, we'll talk," he said. "There are, well, quite a few things that I need to explain to you."

"Like what?"

"Not now," he said. Damnit, she was fast! "I have to meet Fred and Kenny in an hour."

"In an hour," she said, snaking her left leg out from under the warm covers and hooking him gently between his legs with her foot, "then we still have a little time, don't we?"

"Lupe," he said, feeling excited and yet pushed, "I need to clear my head and think. My God, I almost didn't recognize Kenny when I saw him at the door. It feels like, well, we've been drugged, or, well, at least lost for years or something."

She pursed her lips together, not liking it, looking a little hurt, but still she didn't release him with her foot. She wiggled her toes. It felt so delicious being *chingona*. It felt so all daring, and new to her.

Feeling her toes playing with his private hanging parts, Salvador grinned. "Okay," he said. "But only a quickie. I got to bathe and dress. Man, I bet we smell worse than two deer in rut."

She nodded, remembering when her pet deer had come in rut and how he'd become so wild and unmanageable and yes, smelly. Wiggling her toes, she now drew him close to herself, then with a smile, she reached out with her hand, grabbing hold of him. And Salvador loved it.

In the last three days and nights, Salvador had truly come to learn why it was that all through the ages men had put such a high value on a virgin wife. Lupe had blossomed before his very eyes, becoming almost a slave to her own sexuality.

She was like a beautiful, young filly coming into her own, a flower, *una flor,* opening petal by petal, a fruit tree sprouting forth with its new leaves and blossoms—just bursting with vitality!

Just the look of her eyes sent his heart dancing!

SALVADOR WAS DRESSED and ready to go out the door.

"But how long will you be gone?" asked Lupe. "I want to cook for you."

"I won't be gone long," he said to her, trying to get out the door. "I'll be right back."

"Promise?" she said.

"Absolutely," he said, "it should only take me an hour or two at the most to see Fred Noon, then pick up a little money that's owed to me."

"Well, all right," she said, drawing close to him and giving him another long kiss. "But don't stay any longer. I'm fixing you a special supper."

"I promise," he said, "not a minute longer."

And she started to hug him again, but he managed to slip under her grasp and get to the door.

She laughed good-naturedly. Oh, she was purring! Why, her whole body hadn't stopped singing ever since their lovemaking had begun.

Lupe followed Salvador out the door to his car. He started the motor. "Hurry back!" she yelled. "I'll be waiting!"

He turned their Moon automobile around and started down the driveway. She waved good-bye to him. She felt so happy to be married and waving good-bye to her husband as he went off into the world that tears came to her eyes.

The little dog, *Chingon,* came up to her. Lupe squatted down, petting him as she wiped her eyes and watched Salvador, her truelove, drive down the long driveway between the avocado trees, then turn left toward town.

All her life Lupe had been told that love was the most wondrous thing in a person's life, and that the act of lovemaking itself was what kept a woman young and healthy. But she'd never understood until now—that she'd been with Salvador again and again for days on end—that lovemaking not only released all of a woman's vital juices, but awoke a woman's skin, like from a long sleep, becaming so soft and smooth as it sang and tingled with life.

She could still feel Salvador here, all over her skin.

TURNING LEFT toward downtown Carlsbad, Salvador reached under his seat and checked his .38 Special. He had absolutely no idea what this was all about, but it sure as Hell couldn't be any good, he figured.

Walking into the Montana Café, Salvador immediately spotted Helen serving coffee. Seeing him, the German woman let out a shout. "Look, Hans," she yelled to her husband who was behind the counter in the kitchen, "Salvador has risen from the dead!"

"Good!" yelled Hans, who was dressed all in white and cooking. "Feed him our special, so he don't die!"

"Hi, Helen," said Salvador. "Hi, Hans!" he shouted to the kitchen.

Hans and Helen had become two of Salvador's best friends. Then Salvador saw that Fred Noon and Kenny were waiting for him over at a corner table. Archie was with them, too. It looked like they had just finished eating and were now drinking their coffee.

Salvador took a deep breath. My God, it truly seemed like two or three years had passed since he'd last seen any of these people. He still had the full smell of Lupe here in his nostrils and the feel of her body all over his body. A man in love was truly a lost creature. His balls, his *tanates,* they were still hanging loose and tingly, feeling so good with each step he took. He smiled.

"Well, now there's a man who's done nothing but enjoy himself for days," said Archie in a loud, happy voice. "Just look at him! Hell, he looks younger and better than I've ever seen him!"

"He's just sober for a change," said Kenny White. "That's what he is, sober, because Lupe don't allow drinking! Why, the crazy son-of-a-bitch stared at me when he came to the door, like he couldn't remember who the Hell I was!" added Kenny, laughing.

"Don't let their teasing get to you, Sal," said big, tall, rawboned Fred Noon. "We're all proud of you! Sit down! Join us! Hell, it's not often a man manages to pull his life together, especially after what you've been through in the last few months, and marry the woman of his dreams.

"So how is Lupe?" added Fred Noon respectfully. Noon was dressed, like always, in a very fine-looking suit and tie. Success, wealth, they just seemed to radiate from the man.

Taking a deep breath, Salvador looked at Fred Noon in the eyes, and nodded. All three men burst out laughing.

"That good, eh?" said Archie. "Well, I'll be damn! I guess I was all wrong! Them virgins are good stuff, after all!"

Saying this, Archie was laughing and laughing and slapping his leg. And normally, Salvador would've taken offense at what Archie had just said, and he would've told the big lawman off for being so disrespectful, but now, for some reason, he wasn't offended by Archie's remark at all. No, he could see that Archie was just Archie, and he hadn't really meant anything. Hell, he was in admiration of what he, Salvador, had done. He'd pulled together—against great odds—a life of hope and love.

Just then, Helen came to the table with a huge plate of eggs, pork chops, and potatoes. "Here," she said, "on the house! Hans says we got to keep your strength up, Sal." She laughed. "Hans always likes to brag how I almost killed him on our honeymoon. I didn't know anything. I met Hans when I was thirteen, and we married when I was sixteen, so I had no idea a woman can kill a man!"

The four men laughed. Hans and Helen were different from any couple that Salvador had ever met. They just weren't married; no, they worked together, too. And he was the boss, there was no doubt about that, but also she was free to voice her opinions about anything. Theirs was the first marriage that Salvador had ever seen where they actually called each other "partners," as if they were in business together. And Helen was dark. This always puzzled Salvador, because he'd come to assume that all Germans were blond with light skin, like Hans. And Hans, oh, he was a bull! Why, Salvador had once seen Hans come from behind the counter with his huge butcher knife and discipline these big *gringo* boys who hadn't finished their food and were being too noisy.

Seeing the three eggs, the two thick, juicy, pork chops, and the big mountains of sliced potatoes, Salvador was suddenly so hungry that his mouth began to salivate. He glanced at Hans behind the counter, waved to him, thanked Helen, then he attacked the food with *gusto,* as if he hadn't eaten in years!

Kenny and Archie burst out laughing.

"My God, Sal," said Kenny, "don't she feed you?"

"Feed you, my eye," said Archie. "She never lets him get out of bed!"

Fred Noon joined them, laughing, too.

All three of these men were in their early forties, and they had only the highest regard for Juan Salvador Villaseñor, who, at twenty-five years of age, had managed to carve out a life for himself in a very treacherous, rough-and-tumble world. And they all knew that he'd done it with honor, meaning that he was a man of his word, *un hombre de su palabra!* A man of respect. And respect had no patience for people who weren't on their toes. Money didn't accompany fools for long.

GOING BACK INSIDE their little white cottage, Lupe put on some water to make herself a cup of coffee, and she decided to bathe and wash her hair. It was a warm, sunny day, one of the last days of August, and she could smell the sea coming in with the breeze through their open windows. She could hardly get over the fact that this was really her home, *su casa*; not her parents' home, not her sister's home, but hers, Lupe's, a married woman's.

She began to whistle as she went from the kitchen to the bathroom. She felt so happy and safe and all warm and good, deep inside of herself. She could smell the roses from the garden in front. She could hear *Chingon* chasing one of the cats. These smells, these sounds, they were now the smells and sounds of her home, *su casa.*

Lupe turned on the water to the tub, testing it with her fingers until it was just right, then she tied up her hair and stripped. She would soak in the tub with her cup of coffee, relaxing for a while before she washed her hair. She could really do anything she wanted. After all, she was now an adult, a responsible person, as Salvador had said. She smiled, feeling so good.

The dog barked.

But no, Lupe didn't panic. She just simply held still and listened, quickly realizing that it was a happy, playful bark, and decided everything was okay. She wrapped a towel about herself and went into the kitchen to get her cup of coffee so she could start bathing.

Looking out the kitchen window, she saw that *Chingon* was playing in the front yard with one of the cats like they were best friends. She felt proud of herself that she hadn't panicked with the dog's barking. It had been years since all those terrible abuses of war and destruction, but still she was always very alert and ready.

Getting her coffee, she was going back down the hallway to the bathroom when she decided to go back and lock the front door. Yes, she was an adult, a married woman, but also she was . . . a child of war.

AFTER SALVADOR FINISHED his breakfast, they all went outside, and Fred Noon excused himself from Kenny and Archie, saying that he needed to speak to his client Salvador privately.

Kenny nodded and said that he'd see them all back at his garage. Archie said that he'd mosey his way through town, take care of a few things here and there, and maybe catch them later.

"Sal," said Fred Noon as they walked alone over to his Buick, which was parked across the street in front of the Twin Inns Hotel, "I just don't have the connections up in L.A. like I have down here in San Diego, so these racist sons-of-a-bitches are going to stick your brother with all they can! I'm sorry," he added, "but I really thought I was going to be able to break their asses, but I wasn't."

Salvador nodded. They were standing alongside the statues of the great big white chickens at the entrance to the famous Carlsbad hotel. The truth was that Salvador had half expected this, because the whole deck was stacked against *los Mejicanos* in this country from the word go.

Ever since he and his family had crossed the border at El Paso, Texas, it had been nothing but war. Not an open war of cannons and guns like it had been in Mexico during the Revolution, but a hidden war of laws and companies twisting everything in favor of the *gringo* and totally against the Mexicans. But, also, he was finding out that not all *gringos* were in cahoots with these laws and companies; no, some Anglos were pretty good, fair-minded people.

Salvador now looked up into Fred Noon's face and said, "Don't worry, Fred. You're a good man. You don't bullshit me or hide, so I'm sure that you did everything you could. I respect you, and so does my family. We will get through this one way or another, don't you worry."

"Damnit," said Fred, "if this don't beat all! I bring you bad news, and you turn it around, trying to give me comfort. I really love doing work for your people, Sal. I bring news like this to an Anglo client, and he's all over the place in panic and ends up trying to blame me. You people got guts," added Fred Noon, "I'll say that for you!"

Salvador laughed. "Well, what else can we have, Fred, when we've been knocked down for so long, that it all looks up to us."

Fred Noon laughed, his bright blue eyes losing their fierce-looking, hawk-like fire. "I guess you're right, and maybe this is the real strength of this country, its immigrants, who've had it so bad elsewhere that everything here looks good."

"That, I don't know about," said Salvador. "All I know is that nothing is free in this land of the free, especially for us *Mejicanos*. So, well, we got to take our chances, and sometimes it works and sometimes it don't."

Fred moistened his lips, looking at Salvador in the eyes. "I'll keep you posted, *amigo*," he said in Spanish. Fred spoke perfect Spanish. He liked going fishing down to Baja California a lot. "And if I see any break, I'll call you. Give my best to your bride," he added, "and say hello to your mother. You got two fine women with you, Salvador, two fine women."

"I know," said Salvador. "That was always the plan, ever since *mi mama* started telling me how to pick a wife, and I was only about four years old. Do you need a couple of bottles, Fred?"

"Sure, I could always use some, Sal. Best damn whiskey in the whole area! And those bastards up in L.A., they had their feet up on their desks, drinking your whiskey, and laughing how they'd done in some *chile*-belly greasers! Oh, I wanted to get 'em! But Los Angeles is a whole other ball-park from San Diego, especially when the Feds get involved."

"So what do I tell my mother about Domingo?" asked Salvador. "Two years?"

"No," said Fred, licking his lips. "I'm sorry, but you better tell her three, four, maybe even five."

"I see," said Salvador. This was a tough sentence. Domingo had only been caught with liquor. "Then that son-of-a-bitch from Washington, he's going to get away with having used barbwire on my brother's face?" asked Salvador, suddenly getting angry as he remembered how Domingo had been worked over in such a vicious, cowardly way! Salvador would've loved to get that FBI guy alone for just five minutes and teach him what was what.

Fred Noon nodded. "Yeah, Sal, and I almost had the racist bastard, if I could've just convinced the judge that we were talking about a White man, because your brother has blue eyes and red hair."

"So then if you could've convinced the judge that my brother was a White man, it would've been against the law for that FBI guy to beat him with the barbwire?" asked Salvador.

"Yeah, that's right," said Noon.

"So then to beat White men with barbwire is against the law, but to beat Mexicans like dogs with barbwire while they're handcuffed and can't fight back is okay?"

Fred Noon nodded.

"And the darker the Mexican, the more it's okay?"

Fred Noon shrugged, but then thought a second, licked his lips which had gone very dry, and he nodded again.

Salvador took a deep breath, and then another. He was raging. He didn't need to hear anymore. He was boiling! White people, oh, they were really protected in this country in or out of jail. But Mexicans, Indians, Blacks, and especially the Chinese, they didn't count for shit!

"Okay, Fred," said Salvador, now licking his own lips, too. Rage quickly dried out a body. "So how much do I owe you?"

"Not a damn thing!" said Fred. "Consider it a wedding present from me to you and Lupe. I swear, Sal, I do believe that Lupe must be the most elegant, beautiful young lady I've ever laid eyes on, and these two old eyes of mine have taken in a lot of beautiful women!"

Salvador nodded. "Yeah, I think you're right. But she's not just beautiful, Fred, she's quick and smart, too."

"Does she know about your business?"

"No, not yet."

"Oh," said the tall, well-known attorney, arching up his right eyebrow, "this might prove very interesting. Be careful, Sal, that agent Wessely son-of-a-bitch is still in the area."

"Thank you," said Salvador, remembering how Fred Noon had found out that this Wessely guy had been a Texas Ranger before joining the FBI. And he'd been taken in and raised by a Mexican family, after his parents had died, then he'd raped their thirteen-year-old daughter. This was when he'd started hating Mexicans. He had snake-eyes, like so many *hombres* who'd sold their eyes to the Devil, so they wouldn't have to see who they were or what it was that they'd done.

SALVADOR AND HIS ATTORNEY, Fred Noon, drove their cars down to Kenny's garage, just down the street on the other side of the railroad tracks. Archie was gone. Salvador went to the back of the garage, where old man Kenny White kept a couple of cases of whiskey hidden for him. He gave Fred Noon six bottles of his finest 12-year-old whiskey.

"Oh, your 12-year-old!" said Noon, grinning ear to ear.

"The best!" said Salvador.

Immediately, Fred Noon opened a bottle and took a swig. "Ah, that's good!" he said. "Hey, you wouldn't mind telling me just how much longer it takes you to make this 12-year-old, would you?"

"No way," said Salvador, "good whiskey is like a good woman, and if you don't keep the mystery, then the magic is gone."

"Okay, I'll buy that," said Fred. He capped the bottle, put the box with the six bottles of whiskey in his trunk, then he gave Salvador a big *abrazo* and took off.

Old man Kenny White and Salvador stood there and watched him drive off. Fred Noon was a real man's man, who lived with honor and eyes open, hiding from no one, especially not from himself. Fred Noon wasn't one of these educated men who hid behind their professional title, refusing to dirty their hands in the aches and pains of the world.

"So tell me, Sal," said Kenny as they went back into the garage, "how much longer does it take? And I know it ain't no twelve years! Shit, you didn't have any 12-year-old a couple of weeks back, and now you got five cases."

Salvador only smiled. "See you, Kenny," he said, changing the subject. "I got to go see a man about a little money."

"Be careful, Sal!" said the gray-haired old man, laughing. "And don't forget, it's about time for me to service that car."

Al Cappola, the great magician from Italy, had told Salvador very carefully to never let the customers know the secret to fine liquor making. Hell, with a good professional needle, a man could age a barrel of new whiskey into 12-year-old in less than half a day. All you did was put the whiskey in a charcoal-burned oak barrel, insert your long heating needle, and keep the whiskey at a steady temperature just a few degrees below boiling, so it could take on the flavor of the barrel. Then you added a little coloring and brown sugar, but just a pinch, and let the barrel settle for twenty-four more hours, and you then had whiskey as smooth and well-aged as any 12-year-old from Europe.

If the truth be known, this was the way it was done all over the world, Al Cappola had explained to Salvador. And it didn't matter if it was cognac from France, whiskey from Ireland, scotch from Scotland, or *tequila* from Mexico, liquor was liquor. No magic. No big secret. And yet it was very important to keep it all a secret, or the magic of the aging process was, indeed, lost. Why, even old Archie, who knew a little about bootlegging himself, was in awe when it came to Salvador's fine 12-year-old whiskey.

"Look," Al Cappola told Salvador, "the priest has his tricks for keeping the truth of God all full of mystery, women have their tricks for keeping a man excited for more years than it's worth, but the greatest magician of all is the fine liquor-maker!"

And it was true. For this big organization outside of Fresno, which controlled most of the West Coast, had brought in Al Cappola from Italy and treated him and his family like he was a king!

Knowledge was power!

IT WAS EARLY YET. Lupe wasn't expecting him home for about an hour, and so Salvador decided to drive up to San Clemente and collect the money that Carlitos Chico owed him. Carlitos was behind three payments, so no doubt, he, too, like Tomas, figured that Salvador was out of the picture now that he had gotten married. But was Carlitos Chico in for a surprise.

Salvador lit up a cigar, truly enjoying his drive up the coast. Then arriving at Carlitos Chico's place, a little ranch house just this side of San Clemente—in the big, fertile valley where a lot of farming was done for the Santa Margarita *Rancho*—Salvador got the idea that he'd just put a scare into this little bastard Carlitos, like he'd done with Tomas. So that once and for all, everyone would stop counting him out just because he was in love and married!

Parking down the hill from Carlitos's house, Salvador got out of his car, .38 in hand, and came walking up quietly, then suddenly kicked open the front door, yelling, "I've come for my money, you son-of-a-bitch!"

And there was Carlitos Chico, meaning "Little Tiny Charles," or "Chuck" as you'd say in English, naked and down on one knee, making a fire in his little wood-burning stove with a naked woman lying on his bed.

Seeing Salvador come crashing into his home with pistol in hand, Carlitos leaped to his feet like a tiger, yelling, "*Mira! Mira! Cabrón*! You found me hot and hungry!"

Salvador's eyes shot huge, staring down at the largest human organ that he'd ever seen hanging on a male human. Some thousand pound horses didn't have a cock on them like this!

The damn fool little *Indio cabrón* from Guanajuato now came rushing forward, attacking Salvador with a piece of firewood in hand, and his huge, thick organ swinging from side to side like a third leg between his skinny thighs.

"But I'm armed, you fool!" yelled Salvador. "Don't you see?"

"I see your gun," yelled back the naked man, "and I'm going to take it away from you and shove it up your ass! I, too, know how to castrate pigs!"

Well, Salvador was now the one who was in shock and he backed up toward the door as he fired two times into the floor to stop the crazy little Indian—not wanting to kill him, because Carlitos, was, in fact, a good man. A foreman on the Santa Margarita *Rancho*. A man of respect! But the two bullets didn't slow the little crazy-*loco* Indian down and he took a swing at Salvador's head with the piece of firewood.

Salvador was experienced, so he ducked, taking the blow with his left shoulder as he stepped in, hitting Carlitos Chico across the side of his skull with the .38 Smith and Wesson.

The man went down hard, and at first Salvador thought that maybe he'd killed him, but he checked his breathing and found that he was all right. What a fool he, Salvador, had been! What had ever possessed him to come charging into a man's house. Carlitos, damnit, had done the right thing in defending his home.

Then Salvador remembered the naked woman, and he glanced over and realized that she hadn't made a sound. No, she'd just covered herself with the blankets and now lay there quietly.

He nodded to the woman, put his gun away, finished making the fire, and put on the coffee. Then he hunched down Indian-style, warming his hands to the fire. He waited until Carlitos came around.

"How's your head?" asked Salvador.

"How do you expect, you son-of-a-bitch!"

The woman came over with a blanket wrapped around herself, and she took Carlitos in her arms, covering his nakedness with her blanket, too.

"You had no right breaking in like that, Salvador! I owe you money, but this isn't right!"

Salvador nodded. "You're right. I was wrong. I'm sorry."

"I'm no two-bit pimp like Tomas," continued Carlitos. "I'm a foreman! A worker! A man of respect! You come in like that on me, then you got to be prepared to kill me!"

Salvador nodded again, fully realizing that Carlitos was absolutely right, but also, Salvador realized that if they'd been alone, Carlitos would have already accepted his apology. With this woman present, Carlitos had to put on a big show. And he was right to put on this show. After all, no woman wanted a man who wasn't *un hombre de estaca*!

"You're right again," said Salvador, "you are a man of respect, and I did wrong. But that damn Tomas, he told me that you decided not to pay me, and well—"

"But you're no fool," said Carlitos Chico, cutting Salvador off, "so how could you take that pimp's word without coming to see for yourself? I got your money ready for you. I'm a man, damnit, *un macho*!"

"You are," said Salvador, glancing at the woman. And he suddenly thought that he'd seen this woman before, but he couldn't place her. She was in her late twenties, probably just a few years older than Carlitos, and she had a hard look to her like she'd been around, but you could also see that she had a lot of respect for her man. She was tough. The whole incident had not unnerved her.

Salvador felt like such a fool. What if someone had burst in on him and Lupe? It was true, they would have had to kill him.

"Look, Carlitos, I agree with you, I did wrong; I'm sorry, and I tell you what I'll do. How much do you make per day working as a foreman at the Santa Margarita *Rancho* right now?"

"Well, I don't get paid by the day anymore, Salvador," he said, proudly. "I get paid by the month."

"Okay, well how much a month?"

"It's a lot, Salvador."

"How much?"

"Thirty dollars, month in and month out," said Carlitos, proudly. "Rain or shine, it don't matter."

"Oh, that is a lot," said Salvador. "But what the Hell! I made a big mistake and so I'll pay for it. You pay me the money you owe me, and we'll deduct one month's wages that you don't pay me."

"All right!" said Carlitos, "now you're talking! But you remember who I am next time, Salvador! I'm not some little run-away pimp who abuses women and who's afraid of work or guns or castration!"

Carlitos then paid Salvador the money that he owed him, deducting the thirty dollars, and said that he needed another barrel. They parted *como hombres de estaca*. But, also, Salvador fully realized that when this story got out, it was going to hurt his reputation, opening up the door for a lot of fools to think that they, too, could challenge him.

But what could he have done? Kill Carlitos when it had been he, Salvador, who had been entirely in the wrong? The ins and outs of power had to be reevaluated on a daily basis, or reality, she did it for you in a very forceful, unceremonious way. Long ago, he'd learned that Lady Luck was not a woman who accepted the courtship of fools for long.

The Sun, *la cobija de los pobres*, was slipping, sliding into the sea by the time Salvador started back down the coast. He'd been a fool! A stupid fool! Tomas was one thing, but this Carlitos Chico was a whole other animal! And this animal, my God, had the biggest human cock probably in the whole world, and guts, too! Why, Salvador had never seen anything like that on any human being!

Suddenly, Salvador remembered where he'd seen that woman before. She was the wife of the owner of the big, famous Mexican restaurant up in San Juan Capistrano. She wasn't in her late twenties. Hell, no! That woman was probably closer to forty years old, but my God, after being with Carlitos, he'd ironed out all of her wrinkles from inside out, making her look twenty years younger.

Salvador now felt very happy. Carlitos wasn't going to tell anyone about their little incident. And she wasn't either. Because her husband was a big shot—not just among *los Latinos,* but *los gringos,* too—and so there was no way that Carlitos or that woman wanted anyone to know about their wild excursions.

Just north of Oceanside, Salvador pulled over to take a leak. The stars were out by the millions. Life was truly full of twists and turns. Never would he have guessed what Carlitos was really famous for—he was such a small-bone, wiry, little Indian.

Salvador got a pint bottle out of his trunk, and took a few good swigs, then capping the pint bottle, he breathed deeply. Hell, Carlitos was a regular walking, talking fountain of youth for a woman whose husband called himself Spanish, when he was really a Mexican from Zacatecas and was well known for chasing after every new, young waitress he hired.

It was dark by the time Salvador came into downtown Carlsbad, and he realized that he was late, but so much had happened. He hoped Lupe wouldn't be too mad at him. But, well, what could he have done? After he'd pistol-whipped the man, he'd had to stick around and work things out.

Then he remembered his .38 and he slipped it out of his pants and put it under his seat as he turned right into the orchard where their little cottage was located.

He could see that the lights were on inside of their *casita* at the end of the driveway. His heart-*corazón* leaped with anticipation!

FOR HOURS LUPE HAD BEEN WAITING for Salvador. She'd taken her bath and fixed up the house, then she'd gotten so hungry that she wanted to eat, but no, she had a special meal in mind for him, and so she hadn't wanted to spoil her appetite.

Finally she hadn't been able to wait any longer, so she'd made herself a couple of quick, little *quesadillas* to hold her over. But eating her second *tortilla* with the melted cheese and homemade salsa, she'd looked out the kitchen window for the hundredth time and she'd suddenly seen all the orange trees, lemon trees, and avocado trees—as if for the first time—and so she'd rushed outside to pick herself a bunch of avocados.

She made two more *quesadillas* and added avocado this time, and they'd tasted so good! But still she'd been starving, so she'd heated up three more *tortillas de maiz*! After eating these, she'd decided to go outside and pick some flowers and try to calm down. She'd put a few flowers in the bedroom and some others in the kitchen, then she'd gone back outside again—so she wouldn't be tempted to make more *quesadillas*—and she'd sat down on the front steps with their little dog *Chingon* and the two cats.

By now the Father Sun was going down behind the orchard in the west. Suddenly, she didn't know why, but she could feel, here, inside, that something was happening to Salvador right at this very moment.

She gripped her stomach, closing her eyes, and she could see that he was in danger. She could really see-feel it here, inside of her mind's eye. She opened her eyes and picked up the calico cat, holding her to her breasts. Salvador, her truelove, was in trouble, and she just knew it. Tears came to Lupe's eyes and she quickly made the sign of the cross over herself and sent God's love to him, so that he'd have the power to get himself out of whatever trouble he was facing.

After all, her mother had explained to her time and again, that love wasn't just love for a woman. No, for a woman when she was in love, she then became an instrument of feelings, of intuitions, of a Sacred Knowingness that came straight from the Almighty.

For a woman to be in love meant that her whole *corazón* was open, and an openhearted woman had the Holy Eyes of Creation!

Lupe now continued hugging the cat to her breasts as she sent all of her love to Salvador who was in trouble. Oh, she could feel it, she could see it, she could see-feel it here with her heart-eye inside of her self that her true-love was in danger.

Then suddenly it was gone—just like that!

Salvador was no longer in danger. He was safe now. She just knew it here, in her *corazón*. She'd helped him. She'd helped him as surely as her mother had helped them all to survive those terrible days of the Revolution.

She smiled, feeling good that she'd been able to help her husband out of his danger, but also, there was a part of her that just hated him for not being home on time and putting her through all this pain.

Lupe dried her eyes and put the cat down and went inside. It was beginning to get cold. She began to whistle. She just knew that everything was better now, and Salvador, her husband, her *esposo*, would soon be home and he was okay. She decided to start dinner.

It was dark when she looked out the kitchen window and saw her love's headlights turn in their driveway. She felt like going out the front door screaming and scratching his eyes out for making her worry so much! But no, she didn't. Instead, she simply smoothed out her apron as she'd seen her mother do a thousand times, and she began to hum to herself as she went to the stove, turned on the gas, and began to fix their special dinner for them.

She was not going to be one of these emotional, always-yelling wives. No, she was going to keep calm and have dignity, then after they'd eaten, that's when she was going to let him have it with this hot frying pan between the eyes!

Lupe laughed. Just the thought of hitting him with the hot pan that she now had in her hands made her feel much better.

She was humming, singing when *Chingon* started barking at the oncoming car. Then the headlights went out, the motor of the Moon stopped, and she heard the door of their automobile open and shut. *Chingon*'s barking changed to sounds of welcoming.

She dried her eyes again. She'd been so frightened for Salvador, but no, absolutely no, he would not see her tears. And he wouldn't see her anger, either. She was going to be a good wife. After all, it wasn't just the dog who'd bit him. She'd bit Salvador, too, and so she could do it again if she so chose.

She laughed, feeling much better.

She'd truly enjoyed how he'd screamed out in pain when she'd put her teeth to him like a real *chingona*!

WALKING IN THE FRONT DOOR, Salvador was smiling and feeling no pain. Hell, he'd drunk most of the pint bottle of whiskey driving down the coast, fully realizing that once he got back inside his home there'd be no more drinking. But he really didn't mind that; after all, he was in love.

But then, coming in the front door, he wondered about his breath. She was in the kitchen, and it smelled good, but he didn't know what to do about his breath.

"You're just in time!" she said, so full of *gusto*. "I've started supper!"

He went into the kitchen. What else could he do? And there she was, his love, and she had a flower in her hair and she came across the room, away from the stove, with open arms to kiss him. He quickly turned his face away so she wouldn't smell his breath.

"Let me wash up first," he said. "I'm all dirty."

"Oh, all right," she said, feeling a little disappointed.

He looked over her shoulder and saw that she'd also set the table for them in the front room with flowers and white linen. It was beautiful. Their home, their *casa*, their nest. Never in his life had he known such pleasure. Why, all the sex that he'd had with other women didn't even compare a little bit to what he was now feeling with this young bride of his who was here standing before him, looking at him with such love!

He rolled his tongue around inside his mouth. From now on, he'd have to keep some candy or something in the car, so he could get the taste of the liquor out of his mouth before he came inside their *casita*.

He took Lupe in his arms, wanting to kiss her, to taste of her, but not until he'd washed his mouth.

"Oh, I missed you so much," he said.

"I've missed you, too," she said. "I feel like you were gone for years, Salvador! I was getting worried!"

"I'm sorry," he said, "but you see, well, I . . . ah, had a little trouble collecting the money this guy owed me."

"Oh, Salvador," she said, suddenly feeling her heart beginning to pound again, "you have to be careful of people who don't want to pay what they owe! My *nino*, my sister Sophia's first husband, whom I was very close to, his father was killed by a man who owed him money. It was awful, this man shot my *nino's* father, right there in front of my *nino's* eyes who was only ten years old, just because he didn't want to pay the money he owed.

"You need to be very careful, Salvador," said Lupe, tears coming to her eyes. "Money can do wild things to people's minds. I just knew you were in trouble! I could feel this pain here in my stomach! I don't want you getting killed, you hear me, Salvador, and especially not for money!"

He smiled. Her eyes were full of passion. "It's okay," he said. "Believe me, *querida,* you don't have to worry. I'm not going to get killed."

"You better not, Salvador, because, well, I . . . I . . . we're married," she said, "and we have a home to build and a future and . . . and people are depending on us."

"And you, you love me, right?" he said, smiling, guessing that this was what she'd really started to say at first, for he was beginning to see that she often had trouble saying these words.

"Yes, that, too," she said, and she kissed him fully on the lips, then turned, going to the stove. "Now, you get out of here! I don't want you seeing what I'm cooking 'til I'm ready."

"Why not?" he asked, taking off his coat.

"Because, well, I've just discovered that maybe I don't know how to cook as well as I thought," she said.

"You mean you don't know how to cook?" he said, suddenly realizing that the pint bottle of whiskey was in his jacket.

"No, I didn't say that," she said. "I said maybe. But just the same, don't you come into the kitchen 'til I call you."

"All right," he said, glancing around the room, trying to decide where to hide the bottle but still have it handy. He looked at the big stuffed chair in the front room and decided that would be a good place, under the pillows.

"I'm going to go wash up," he said.

"Okay, but don't be too long," she said. "This is really special."

"Great," he said, going out of the room, then—when he saw that Lupe wasn't looking—he slipped the pint bottle under the two pillows that Hans and Helen had made especially for them with their names, Sal and Lupe, embroidered on them.

He was in the bathroom washing, whistling happily, when he suddenly heard a terrible scream, and he saw his eyes go wide with terror in the mirror.

Instantly, he turned, rushing down the hallway, wishing that he'd brought his .38 inside instead of that stupid pint bottle. He continued racing into the kitchen, not knowing what to expect. Smoke was everywhere. He couldn't see what was going on!

"What is it?" he yelled.

"Nothing!" she shouted. "I'm just cooking."

"Cooking!" he said, opening the back door and waving the smoke out of the room with a dishrag.

"Yes, everything is fine," she said. "Just fine! It's just that, well, the cheese slipped a little bit out of the *chile* is all."

"The *chile*?"

"Yes, I'm making your favorite, *chiles rellenos*. Don't you remember? You once told my mother that *chiles rellenos* are your favorite, so I—"

And there it was again.

Lupe dipped the next *chile* stuffed with cheese into the batter, put it in the sizzling hot pan, and the whole thing exploded! The *chile* went flying one way, the cheese another, and the pan caught on fire with batter!

Salvador burst out laughing. This had to be the funniest thing, he'd ever seen!

And there was Lupe stomping her foot, jumping up and down, yelling at the *chile* to stop it.

"Stop it, *chile*!" she shouted. "What's wrong with you? Don't you know you're supposed to stay in the pan so the cheese can melt!"

Salvador fell back against the wall, howling with laughter!

Then she was crying. "Oh, Salvador, I so much looked forward to cooking this special meal for you all day, but then I got so hungry that I ate, I think, a dozen *quesadillas* with avocado, and—oh, stop laughing! I swear, or I'll hit you with this frying pan!

"You were late, Salvador!" she added. "You were late! And I got so worried for you that my stomach hurt!"

"I'm sorry," he said, trying to stop his laughter. "I'm really sorry, but I was all the way up in San Clemente, and—you ate a dozen *quesadillas*," he said, in astonishment. "Well, maybe, that's why your stomach hurt."

She heard his words and her eyes narrowed and suddenly she was so mad because, well, what he said made sense, but she'd been so sure that her stomach had hurt because she'd been worried for him.

"Oh, you don't love me," she said. "Or you wouldn't say such an awful thing! My stomach hurt because you were in trouble, Salvador, and I could feel it here in my heart! Not because of those *quesadillas*!"

He didn't know what to say or do.

"Didn't you feel a sudden calmness come to you," she continued, "when you were in danger collecting your money?"

"Yeah, sure, after I knocked him down," he said.

"You knocked him down?" she said.

"Well, yes," said Salvador, realizing that he was digging himself in as he spoke. But what could he do? "He came at me with a piece of firewood and I didn't want to kill him, so I hit him to the side of the head with my gun."

"You had a gun?" said Lupe, staring at Salvador full in the face. Oh, her heart was beginning to pound once again.

He took a big breath. He'd really dug himself in deep. Love and lies just didn't mix. "Look, Lupe," he said, "we'll talk later, okay?"

"And when is later?" she asked.

He looked at her. He swallowed and looked at her. Why, my God, this young, innocent-looking wife of his could be a tiger. "Well, later is when—let's eat, then we'll talk. I have a lot to tell you. You see, I was raised in *los Altos de Jalisco,* and up there all men carry guns. And remember, you, yourself, just said that your *nino's* father was killed when he went to get money that was owed to him, and I'm sure he was without a gun. Guns aren't bad, *querida,* they're just another tool like, well, a saw or knife or—"

"No, Salvador," said Lupe, smoothing out the apron on herself, "guns were made just for killing, nothing more." She wiped the tears from her eyes. "I saw what guns did to our village every time soldiers came," she added. "Now, sit down while I make you the *chiles rellenos,*" she continued, "and we'll talk later, like you said. Oh, I was so sure that I knew how to cook these darn *chiles* after eating my mother's all of my life."

And saying this, Lupe pursed her lips together and gave that special, little look of hers, looking so cute, and yet, determined.

Salvador took a deep breath, loving her calm, respectful style. He took her in his arms and kissed her, and oh, just the taste of her was Heaven! She began to kiss him back, too. Then suddenly they were both so hungry for each other that they were BURNING once again.

THAT NIGHT, they went to the Montana Café to eat dinner. Kenny White—who'd been eating by himself—came over to their table to say hello. With a grand feeling of abundance, Salvador asked him to join them. Little by little, Lupe got to know the white-haired, old man and appreciate his humor. Then, when they'd finished eating, Helen brought them a freshly baked apple pie that she'd just taken out of the oven.

"This pie you take home with you," she said. "It's your honeymoon present from Hans and me." And saying this, the big German woman then drew in close to Lupe, kissing her on the cheek. "I'd thought you were so beautiful at your wedding, Lupe, like all brides are, but oh, I never expected to see an angel when you're in just your regular street clothes. You were blessed by God, my dear!"

Lupe blushed. All her life she'd heard words like this and she'd never known what to say, because as far as she was concerned, every person was equally blessed by God and so her good looks had never really meant much to her. "Thank you," she simply said.

"And you make sure that he takes good care of you," added Helen. "You two have a good, happy life together. Hans and me, that's what we always make sure we do for ourselves, no matter how hard we work, we also make sure to have a good life together." Then smiling, she turned and patted Salvador's hand. "And, Sal, no bill tonight. Hans, he told me, so no argument, because he's the boss!" she added with pride.

Salvador waved to Hans behind the counter and Hans waved back with a big, grand smile. Hans was also a drinking man. In fact, he and Helen drank together on their day off. Salvador would stop by later, in a couple of days, and give Hans and Helen a bottle of his 12-year-old.

Going home that night to their *casita* in the orchard, Lupe kept going over Helen's words inside of her head. "Have a good, happy life together," she'd said. "That's what Hans and I always make sure we do for ourselves, no matter how hard we work."

Lupe had never heard of such a thing in all her life.

No, all her life she'd only heard about needing to work, needing to be strong, needing to be careful, needing to have faith in God, but she'd never heard anyone ever say anything about having a good, happy life.

And not just a little happiness here and there, where chance might happen to give it to you; no, this German woman had actually said that she and her husband made sure to have a good life together, no matter how hard they worked.

Well, then, what did this mean, that happiness could actually be planned for ahead of time like one planned for work? And a celebration didn't just happen because there was a death in the family or it was some religious holiday.

Lupe's whole head was spinning as she held the warm apple pie on her lap and they drove home to their *casita*. Also, Helen had said "we make sure to have a good life together," as if implying that a man and a woman could be together in having a good time, and not the man just going off with the men and the woman with the women.

A whole new world was opening up for Lupe, and she was now feeling more at home here in Carlsbad than she'd ever felt in any community in all the years that she and her family had been living in the United States.

Why, tonight she'd felt welcomed and at home with Kenny and Hans and Helen, people who had roots in their community, people who weren't just passing migrants searching for work.

For the first time in all of her life, Lupe had a sense, a feeling that maybe this country of the United States could really be her homeland, after all.

THAT NIGHT, after eating a slice of warm apple pie in the kitchen of their little *casita,* Salvador pulled out the roll of money that Carlitos Chico had paid him.

"What's that?" asked Lupe, never having seen such a large roll of money in all her life.

"The money the man owed me," he said. "Would you count it for me? I know you're good at numbers."

"Well, yes, of course," said Lupe, licking her lips with a sudden nervousness. And she didn't know why, but she actually felt like she was seeing a rattlesnake lying alongside the uneaten portion of apple pie as she now looked at this roll of money on their kitchen table.

Salvador saw her look. "*Querida,* it won't hurt you," he said.

"I know that," said Lupe. "But it's so much. I mean, I've never seen that much money in all my life. How could this be? Did he owe you for a whole year or something?"

"No, not exactly," said Salvador. "You see, I do favors for people now and then, too."

"What kind of favors?" she asked.

He took a deep breath. Once again he'd put his foot in his mouth. If he wasn't careful, he was going to lose her. "Why don't you just count the money first," he said, "so we can put it safely away, then we can talk, okay?"

"Well, all right, but my God, Salvador, my family is working all the time, and they never bring home money like this."

He nodded. "Yes, I know. My family, too. Just count it, Lupe, so you can put it away in a safe place for us."

"Me?" she said. "Me, put it away?"

"Yes," he said. "You."

She swallowed. She'd never been given such responsibility. Why, in most Mexican homes, the woman wasn't even allowed to touch the money. In fact, this was one of the points that her mother and father had constantly argued about in their home, until their father had finally left.

"All right," said Lupe, reaching across the table and taking hold of the big roll of money.

She unrolled it, smoothed out the pile of green bills, and began to count, putting the ones in one pile, the fives in another pile, and the tens in a third pile. Twenties, they were unheard of back in these days. And a fifty or a hundred-dollar bill, these were only tales that the working people heard of that maybe existed among the rich.

It scared Lupe to handle all this money, but, also, in a strange way, it felt exciting.

Salvador never once took his eyes off of her, watching her every move. His young bride didn't know it, but she'd been completely right, when she'd said that money did crazy things to people's minds.

He continued watching her. He well knew that he was being the lead horse in their marriage right now, guiding them through a needle's eye where there would be no return.

The die was cast.

The Devil had, indeed, been welcomed into their Garden, but Salvador had no fear. After all, it was he who'd opened their door wide for *el Diablo*.

The monies Lupe counted that night came to $137, including the money Salvador had had in his pocket before he'd collected his money from Carlitos. Salvador thanked Lupe for counting it, then he told her to give him twenty for himself, take what she needed for groceries and housekeeping, then to put the rest away for safekeeping.

At first Lupe didn't know what to do. Never in her life had she ever heard of a husband asking his wife to do this.

"Go on, Lupe," said Salvador, "give me the twenty I need and take what you need."

"But I don't know how much I need," she said.

"What did our groceries cost the other day? Almost a dollar, right?" he said.

She nodded in agreement.

"Well, then, Lupe, take ten dollars," he said, "and keep it in your purse."

"Ten dollars!" she said. "Salvador, that's what my parents pay for a whole month's rent!"

"It's okay, Lupe," said Salvador calmly. "Money doesn't spoil like tomatoes or get smelly like meat going bad. Money is paper, just paper, so it keeps very well. Take ten," he repeated, giving her a little wink of the eye for reassurance.

She saw his wink and breathed. "Okay," she said, taking five ones, then a five dollar bill. She put them in her purse. "But now what will we do with the rest?" she asked.

"You figure it out, *querida,*" he said, giving her lots of free rein so she could find her head. After all, a good lead horse didn't want the horses that followed him to have no mind of their own, especially if the terrain was as rocky and broken as the ground Lupe and he were traveling. "Remember, this is your *casa,*" he added.

Hearing this, Lupe's whole chest swelled up with pride. "*Casa,*" the word had never sounded so good to her! Why, she could now see that a woman's home was so much more than she'd ever dreamed. It wasn't just a private place for a young couple to make love, it was also a place that took thinking and planning, a place in which their dreams could take root and grow to . . . the Heavens!

Lupe got up, glanced around, then went over to the cupboards below the kitchen sink to search for a place to put away their money.

Salvador watched, never taking his eyes off of her. His mother had well explained to him—time and again—that on a honeymoon, it wasn't just a time for a man and woman to make love, but to give each other wings!

Finding an empty can under the sink, Lupe washed the can, dried it, then put the money in the can and covered the can with a dry dishrag.

Salvador smiled. Yes, Lupe was innocent, but she was also very, very brave. Everything was going to work out, if he just kept calm and let his good friend, the Devil, do his work.

After all, fear of the unknown was always very scary . . . at first.

Part Four

SUNTALKING

September 1929

6

*And so their mothers had, indeed, taught them both about
Love and God, but it was now Life, la Vida, that was to
teach them the lessons of el Diablo!*

THE WHEELS WERE TURNING.
The huge iron wheels of the train were turning slower and slower, and Juan Salvador was staring at the huge iron wheels and trying to figure out what to do.

He was in Mexicali, Mexico, just across the border from Calexico, California, and it was early morning, still dark, but already it was hot and muggy—completely different from the cool, ocean air of Carlsbad, over the mountains to the west, where he'd left Lupe the day before.

Yesterday, Salvador had driven up to Lake Elsinore for just a few hours to check on his distillery . . . which his brother-in-law Epitacio was attending to while he, Salvador, was on his honeymoon. When he got there, Epitacio had told him that his mother, Doña Margarita, needed to see him immediately, that it was urgent!

Driving up to Corona, Salvador's old mother had told him that she'd had a terrible dream of Domingo in prison, and then sure enough, here had come this Chinese man from Hanford, California, needing to see Salvador right now, *pronto*; something about if Salvador could help them, then they, in turn, would help him with his brother, Domingo, in prison.

Hearing this, Salvador had immediately driven over to San Bernardino, just a few miles east of Corona, to see the Chinese man from Hanford, California.

This Chinese man and Salvador had spent time in jail together and knew each other very well. The man had quickly explained to Salvador that some problems were cooking up in San Quentin, but for him not to worry, for they handled the laundry in the prison like they did in most prisons in all of California, so they could help him with these upcoming *problemas* if he, Salvador, brought this Chinese doctor for them across the border from Mexicali.

"You deliver this doctor for us to Hanford right now, tomorrow, for this emergency we got," said the Chinese restaurant owner, "and we'll pay you five hundred dollars in cash when you deliver him alive and well."

Salvador's whole heart leaped into his mouth. My God, five hundred dollars was a fortune! And this restaurant owner's word was as good as gold. When they'd done their time together in the Tulare jail, it had been this Chinaman who managed to get the supplies into the jail, so Al Cappola could give Salvador his final lesson on how to make fine liquor. Why, the guards themselves had gotten drunk with them. Every business dealing that Salvador had ever done with the Chinese people had been nothing but straight-up dependable and honest.

"What emergency is this?" asked Salvador.

"My people are dying in Chinatown," said the restaurant owner.

"I see," said Salvador, remembering how the influenza had hit the people in the *barrios* of Arizona, Texas, and California a few years back and the American doctors wouldn't come to see them. It had been his own mother, Doña Margarita, who'd thrown open the windows, gotten the people out of their blankets, and had them drink the special herbs that she'd picked in the fields of God's Garden. "And you'll be able to help me with my brother?"

The man nodded. "No problem. But we need this doctor quick. My own daughter, she's sick," said the man, his face suddenly twisting with fear. "And my wife, she already died."

Hearing this, Salvador nodded. "I'll do it, what the hell!"

So throwing caution to the wind, ignoring everything that Archie and his attorney, Fred Noon, had told him about needing to be careful and lay low because this FBI agent Wessely was still in the area and gunning for him, Salvador said yes, that he'd do it. But what really bothered him wasn't the law or the dangers of the job; no, what really hurt him here in his heart-*corazón* was that he wouldn't be able to go home to Carlsbad and tell Lupe, his truelove, that he'd be gone for a couple of days and nights.

And poor Lupe, why, he'd simply told her—when he'd left home yesterday morning—that he'd only be gone a few hours.

Salvador now quit watching the huge, iron wheels of the different boxcars going slower and slower as they came in to be loaded with fresh produce. He got back in his Moon automobile. He and the big doctor looked very out of place at the railroad yard in their fine suits and grand car, but Salvador didn't care. He was in a hurry to get this Chinese doctor across the border so he could collect his money and get home to Lupe, but also . . . he had to be very careful, or he could end up going to prison again.

"Okay," he said to the big, tall Chinese doctor, whom he'd picked up in Mexicali's Chinatown the night before, "we'll go back to the border stop and take one more look around, but if it still doesn't look good, then we're coming back to this train yard and figure things out one way or another, *a lo chingon!*"

"Okay, *a lo chignon*, however you speak," said the big doctor.

This was the first Chinaman who spoke any English that Salvador had ever smuggled into the United States. He was also the biggest, tallest, strongest-looking Chinaman that Salvador had ever seen.

Starting the motor of his Moon automobile, Salvador turned on his headlights and gave it the gas. Ever since Salvador had first started buying cars, he'd always made sure to get vehicles that had plenty of horsepower, so that they could really move in case he ran into any *problemas.*

Approaching the little border stop in Mexicali, Salvador could see that there were still several American guards at the crossing station. Driving by, he headed west, staying on the Mexican side of the border, thinking that maybe he'd just drive out across the desert and circle the whole town.

But then, getting to the first little group of hills west of town—there was some color in the Father Sky of the approaching day—and Salvador could just begin to make out the towering black mountains in the distance, the mountains that separated the California deserts from the coast.

He lit up a cigar, smoking leisurely, and ahead he could also begin to see the huge, flat, dried-up salton sea just this side of the black, towering mountains. Salvador turned to the right, and in much closer to himself, maybe only a half a mile away, he saw the dark outline of a car parked on top of a little hill. A man was standing tall alongside the vehicle, silhouetted against the night sky.

"Damnit!" said Salvador, tossing his cigar out his window. "The Border Patrol! I guess we're going to have to do this *a lo chingon!*"

"*A lo chingon!*" repeated the big, tall, dignified-looking man, once again repeating Salvador's words with such a terrible mispronunciation that this time Salvador burst out laughing.

Salvador turned the Moon around, driving into a little *arroyo*, and here, in the wash, he cut his headlights. Now, they were completely out of sight, and the first light of day was just starting to break in the east, but already it was so damn hot that Salvador was pouring with sweat. He'd hoped to get this job done last night, but all night the border had been swarming with officers, as if they were expecting something special.

"All right," he said to the big Chinese doctor, getting out of the Moon. "Get out quick! Quick! I need to put you in the trunk of the car!"

The big doctor got out and came around the back and looked at the little trunk of the Moon. He shook his head. "Oh, no, I don't think I like this *a lo chingon*," he said, mispronouncing the words again. "I'm too long, too big for the back of this car."

"Look," said Salvador, taking off his suit jacket and throwing it inside the Moon, "just get your damn feet in there, and I'll cram you down with the lid."

"Oh, no!" said the doctor. "It too hot and I can't breathe in here!"

"Damnit," said Salvador, pulling out his .45 automatic, which he always carried for big jobs, "we don't have much time! Just get your ass in there, now!" And he jumped up with the .45, hitting the doctor on the head as hard as he could, wanting to knock him out, but the man was so strong that he didn't go down.

"No!" protested the doctor, rubbing his head as if he'd just been bit by a *mosquito*. "They don't pay you to hit me on head! I'm going to be indebted for twenty years!" He began to cry. "I die, if I get in here. And I have wife and kids, and little, little baby boy," he added, crying all the more.

"Aaaaah, shit!" said Salvador. "I got family, too! I just got married, in fact, and I was only trying to knock you out so you wouldn't suffer in there, but, man, you're one big, strong son-of-a-bitch!"

"Here, you want to breathe?" said Salvador, raising up the .45 again, "I'll fix it for you to breathe!" He shot two quick bullet holes through the open trunk lid of his beautiful new car, while the doctor stared at him as if he'd just gone completely crazy-*loco*.

"There," yelled Salvador, "now you got air holes, so get your ass in there, you big *cabrón*, before I shoot you, too! I could get ten years for smuggling your Chinese ass across!"

He raised his .45 to hit the doctor again, but this time the big, tall man just jumped into the trunk by himself, squeezing down as best he could. Salvador slammed down the lid, banging the doctor two or three times on the head before he could get it completely closed.

He was really a big man, and all the time, he kept yelling, "I don't think I like *a lo chingon!* I don't think I like *a lo chingon!*"

Salvador was laughing. This big doctor was a good man. In fact, all the Chinese people that he'd smuggled in over the last few years were good, honest, hardworking people. Salvador just couldn't figure out why the United States government was so dead set against the Chinese.

Putting his .45 away, Salvador wiped the sweat from his face and let a little air out of each back tire so he could go across the sandy soil without getting stuck. Then he got back in his Moon and drove out of the *arroyo* with his headlights off. Quickly, he glanced around, didn't see the car up on the little hill anymore, and so he gave the Moon the gas, going north out across the flat, sandy desert.

"Okay, here I go, running across the border *a lo Gregorio Cortez!*" said Salvador, feeling the excitement of the chase coming into his heart as he referred to the popular ballad of the day about a Mexican cowboy who'd outrun all the Texas Rangers a few years back over in Texas.

So, there was Salvador, really moving across the sandy, hot land, when suddenly, out of nowhere, right in front of him, was that damn car he'd seen up on the hilltop.

And one of the officers had his gun drawn, as the Moon came leaping out of the little dry riverbed, and the other officer then jumped out of their vehicle, pointing his weapon at Salvador, too.

But Juan Salvador had been dodging bullets all his life, and so he now just gave his fine automobile the gas and went flying straight at the two officers, turning away only at the very last moment, just as the first gunman leaped out of the way, firing wildly.

Salvador was grinning, feeling full of the Devil, having one hell of a wild, good time as the two officers now opened fire on him as he sped away.

Then he remembered the doctor in his trunk and he hoped to God that a stray bullet hadn't killed him. He turned left and started northwest out across the sandy, flat desert.

"Are you all right?" he yelled at the doctor, but the man didn't answer him as they went bouncing, leaping out across the broken desert.

Then, out of nowhere, there were two more dark cars with glaring headlights, right up ahead of him next to some tall cactus.

Salvador glanced back around and saw that the other car was headed his way, too. He braked, slowing down. He didn't know what to do. All around him was sand and brush and treacherous, little *arroyos*.

Then in the early morning light, he saw those famous, orange and white sand hills at the base of the huge, towering, black mountains, and in closer, toward him, he then saw that long, white salt flat of a forgotten sea.

Salvador turned, heading for the flat, dry sea and the little orange and white hills. He hoped to God that the doctor hadn't been shot. He now gave his Moon all the gas, wanting to make it to that flat, dry sea before the officers caught him.

But as soon as the officers saw him turn toward the sea, all three lawmen gave their vehicles the gas, too, hoping to cut him off.

Seeing this, Salvador quit smiling. "Oh, please, dear God, help my car fly away like an eagle from these no-good Texas Ranger sons-of-a-bitch. Give me the wings of an eagle, *Papito Dios*!"

Just then Juan Salvador heard the screech of a great Golden Eagle, "EEEIII-EEEEEE!" as he went leaping, bouncing across the beautiful, open desert toward the salt flat. But the two cars in front of him had a shorter distance to go, and they were closing in on him fast, jumping, bouncing, lifting clouds of dust.

"Oh, *mama, mama*, help me! You, too, Lupe, help me with our love!" yelled Salvador, feeling a rush of wild excitement.

The Golden Eagle screeched again and Salvador now knew that his old *mama* had come to help him in the form of an eagle because she, too, really didn't want him to be caught.

After all, he was a married man now, and his *mama* wanted him to live and have a life with Lupe, and not be doing any more of these crazy, wild things that he'd been doing for survival ever since they'd had to leave their mountainous area of *Jalisco*.

But, also, he had to start making his own miracles. And all miracle making, his *mama* had told him, started by bringing peace to your heart.

He breathed, trying to calm down, but then he couldn't believe it. From the car that was closing in on him, on the right, an officer was now hanging out of his window, trying to shoot him.

For the life of him, Salvador couldn't figure out what was going on in this crazy man's head. Hell, he hadn't robbed a bank. He hadn't hurt anyone. All he, Salvador, was doing was trying to get a doctor across the border so he could help his people.

The officer was so close now that Salvador could see his young, sunburned, face. His blue eyes were full of wild excitement as he took careful aim at Salvador, firing once, twice, just barely missing him.

Quickly, Salvador began to pray, remembering how his dear old mother had taught them to kneel down and pray when the bullets of the Revolution had showered like rain all about them.

Immediately, Salvador's heart calmed and the whole world slowed down, giving him time to think. Instantly, he knew what to do. He slammed on his brakes, cutting viciously to the right, directly toward the two oncoming officers.

The Moon behaved beautifully, and the driver of the vehicle was taken by such surprise—seeing the Moon coming straight at him—that he braked hard and cut away and his red-faced partner with the gun flew out the window of their car, face-first into some cactus!

Seeing the shocked man's face as he went flying out the window into the cactus, Salvador laughed with *carcajadas*, feeling wonderful, as he now turned around and headed back toward Mexico.

The officers had won!

They'd stopped him from getting across the border, but also, Salvador felt good about getting the gun-happy, young officer full of cactus thorns.

Hitting the smooth, dry salt flat, Salvador was gone.

The two remaining cars were just no match for his grand automobile. Salvador now left the six officers behind in the distance as he sped away back into Mexico, across the smooth, white, forgotten sea.

The Sun, *la cobija de los pobres*, the blanket of the poor, was just coming up in the east and shooting rays of golden light across the land. It was a magnificent sight with the light dancing all around Salvador's automobile with a wonderful display of silvery brightness.

Approaching the end of the lagoon, Salvador glanced up at the sky to the west, and to his complete surprise, he saw the Mother Moon. And she was huge and full, holding there in the pale blue sky of the coming day.

Juan Salvador was filled with such a feeling of wonderment, that he hit the brakes!

The Sun was rising and the Moon was setting, and he could see them both at the same time!

The Right and Left Eyes of the Holy Creator!

Salvador opened the door of his car and got out in the middle of the dry sea and he suddenly just knew . . . here inside of his soul that yes, indeed, Lupe, his new truelove, had been praying for him when he'd been in trouble. Yes, she, too, had been sending him her *amor* just as his mother had come to help him in the form of an eagle.

Realizing this, Salvador heard the Golden Eagle screech again and he glanced up and here she was, just barely above him, looking huge. Why, he could actually see her dark, magnificent eyes, she was so close.

Tears of joy came to Salvador's eyes as he looked at Mother Moon, holding here in the pale blue sky of the coming new day. He could now see so clearly that all the world was alive and singing to him. The Moon was moontalking to him, telling him deep inside of himself that Lupe was still praying for him at this very moment, just as his sacred mother had prayed for him all these years.

His eyes filled with tears and he stood here rooted to this white, flat, forgotten-sea with the Father Sun coming up on his left and the Mother Moon going down on his right, and he just knew to the very depths of his soul that we, human beings, were instruments of God's love when we prayed.

Smiling, Salvador felt a gentle breeze caress him. He now sent his love to Lupe, too, telling her that he was fine, that he was out of danger.

Instantly, he realized that Lupe had, indeed, gotten his message.

His mother had always told him, that the conversations of the heart knew no distance for they traveled through the Almighty!

Then Salvador heard a knocking, a banging. He glanced about himself, and saw that the banging sound was coming from the trunk of his car. He suddenly remembered the doctor and opened up the trunk and let the doctor out. The man was pissed! And he was pouring with sweat and blood. He wanted nothing more to do with Salvador.

"I almost got killed and cooked to death!" yelled the doctor. "Bang, bang, up and down! Bang! BANG! BANG! Up and down! Look at my head, it's all bloody and cut and—oooooo, it hurts!"

And why, Salvador didn't know, but he started laughing.

"NOT FUNNY!" screamed the big doctor. "*A lo chingon*, not funny! NOT FUNNY, *A LO CHINGON!*"

"Look," said Salvador, still not able to stop laughing, "just thank God, you weren't shot. So we're doing fine. And now, guess what I've decided to do," said Salvador, grinning, "I'm going to buy a whole railroad car of lettuce just for you, so you can hide in that lettuce, and I can then ship you in luxury all the way to Los Angeles, California. No more *problemas* from now on," he added with a smile, wondering where this whole idea of lettuce had come from. Hell, he'd never thought of buying a railroad car of lettuce. "You just sleep and rest on a nice, cool bed of lettuce, and I'll get you across in no time!" added this voice within him, talking as if it had a life all of its own.

"Oh, no!" yelled the big doctor. "I want our money back! You're a bad man! Very bad, bad, bad *a lo chingon*—you!"

"Bad, me?" said Salvador. "Hell, I'll show you bad!" And he drew his .45 again, firing by the man's feet. "Get the hell back in that trunk, you chickenshit bigmouth!" he yelled. "Hell, I've taken Chinese women across the border with more guts than you! Old women!"

"You mean you bring old Chinese women across the border?" asked the doctor, looking suddenly very interested.

"Absolutely! And these old women had a lot more guts than you," added Salvador.

"Okay, I'll go then," said the big doctor. "But oh, I don't like any more of this *a lo chingon*," said the tall, dignified man. "I ride with you up front. And I'm hungry! I no eat!"

Salvador laughed, closing the trunk lid. They were on the Mexican side of the border, so it would be okay for the doctor to ride up front with him, but there was no way that he was going to take the doctor back into China-town in Mexicali to eat, and maybe run the risk of him running out on him.

Driving off across the dry, white, flat sea with the doctor at his side, Salvador just knew that something quite extraordinary had happened to him.

He'd been shot at, he'd barely escaped with his life intact, and yet he felt so calm, so relaxed. He suddenly knew that he'd finally come to this Blessed Place between the Sun and Moon where his mother Lived and Miracles were Created.

There were no accidents.

He was on his way, learning how to be a married man of Daily Miracles.

All those truckloads of lettuce that they'd been loading on those rail-road cars this morning before dawn came flashing to his mind. He really would buy a railroad car full of lettuce, hide the doctor in the sea of pro-duce, and ship him across the border to wherever the train was going. Oh, life was so easy, so effortless once you "saw" with the clarity of God.

Salvador made the sign of the cross over himself, saying, "Thank You, *Papito*. Thank You, God, *gracias*."

BUYING THE BOXCAR of lettuce cost Salvador all the cash he had, so there'd be no going back now.

He then drove down to the river, way south of town, so they could cool off, and the doctor wouldn't get the idea of running out on him. And together they washed in a stream and then covered the whole car with mud, hiding the two bullet holes that Salvador had shot through the trunk lid. Miraculously, yes, miraculously, not even one bullet from the officers' guns had hit the vehicle.

They rested on the river's bank and a couple of times the big doctor asked Salvador if those old Chinese women that he'd taken across the border had really been tougher than him.

Salvador laughed, seeing the big man's concern, then assured him that yes, they had been a whole lot tougher than him. The doctor was much quieter after that. Then it was dark and they headed back to town.

Getting to the railroad yards, they looked around, making sure that no one was watching. Then Salvador checked his receipt to be sure he had the right boxcar, and he had the big man climb into the railroad car and, in the light of the full Moon, dig his way down into the lettuce.

"And keep still like a brave, old woman," said Salvador to him. "Understand, no move 'til I come and call you, eh?"

Salvador then drove to the border stop in town and saw that there was only one guard on duty. The man checked Salvador's papers, searched his car, and passed him on through.

It was after midnight when Salvador watched the long train come across the border, heading north. He drove along the highway, catching glimpses of the train now and then as it sped across the desert. The Mother Moon hung low in the night sky, talking gently to Salvador as she played in and out among the clouds. Salvador thanked Lupe again and again. He could just feel the steady flow of Lupe's love coming to him as she prayed. Love truly didn't know any distance when it was sent through God.

Just before daybreak, the train stopped at a place at the foot of the towering, dark mountains to refuel. Here, Salvador had them unhitch his boxcar of produce, telling them that he had his own personal trucks coming for his lettuce. As soon as the train started up the grade, Salvador climbed up on the boxcar and started looking for the doctor, but he couldn't find him.

"The son-of-a-bitch ran out on me!" yelled Salvador. "You no-good, crazy-*loco cabrón*! You crazy-*loco* fool didn't have the guts to stay put *a lo chingon* like a good woman!"

"*A lo chingon* like a good woman I do, too!" Salvador heard a weak little echo come up to him from out of the lettuce.

"*A lo chingon!*" repeated Salvador.

"*A lo chingon!*" came the echo again. "I tough like good woman!"

"Oh, you crazy-*loco* son-of-a-bitch!" said Salvador joyfully. "So you did stay put like a good woman!"

"Yes, you crazy son-of-a-bitch," said the echo as the lettuce started moving under Salvador's feet. "I stay put *a lo chingon* like a good woman!"

Salvador started laughing, and when he saw the doctor's big face suddenly erupt out of the lettuce, he took the doctor's face in his two hands and kissed him on the lips. "You're absolutely beautiful!" he said.

"Beautiful, oh, no, *a lo chingon!*" said the doctor, smiling ear-to-ear. "I no good woman that way, you crazy-*loco* son-of-a-bitch!"

And they started laughing and laughing. They'd done it! They'd really done it! They'd gotten across the border!

IT WAS DARK when Salvador and the big doctor pulled into Chinatown in Hanford, California—fifteen hours to the north. And all the way, the big doctor and Salvador drank *tequila* and talked.

Salvador came to learn a lot about China and Chinese medicine and herbs and these things called pressure points. Salvador told the doctor that his own mother was *una curandera*, meaning that she was a healer who healed people with local weeds and the massaging of the bottoms of the people's feet, which mirrored the soul, his mother always said.

"You see," said Salvador, "my mother is old and walks barefoot a lot. She says that for good health, people need to get rooted to the dirt, *la tierra*, every day with their bare feet, so that the love of the Mother Earth can keep them strong with power inside!"

"Your mother is yes, right," said the doctor. "The bottoms of the people's feet work all the pressure points of the whole body. This is why they brought me from China. The American doctors are good for bones broken, but don't understand our Chinese medicine, which brings good healing to the mind and soul, not just the body."

Then he showed Salvador a little box in which he kept pieces of bark and dirt and tree leaves.

"Yes," said Salvador very excitedly, "just like *mi mama!* Then you people also know that men are rock and mineral, and women are tree and bark and leaves!"

"Yes," said the doctor, "ying and yang!"

"You mean, men and women?"

"Yes, ying and yang, men and women, the same!"

"Ooooooooh," said Salvador. "I see! I see! You know, I'll bring my mother to meet you. She, not the American doctors, saved the lives of hundreds of people in Arizona when the influenza hit the *barrio*," continued Salvador. "The American doctors didn't know what to do, but my mother did. She cooked up all these tomatoes with different *yerbas* and then wrapped the people's feet and chest, opening up all the windows so they could breathe in fresh air. And the American doctors got so mad at my mother, saying that they'd told everyone to close their windows, and she was going against their orders."

"Yes, and American doctors are mad at me, too," said the big Chinese doctor, drinking down another shot of *tequila*. "That's why I couldn't get legally into country. I want to meet your mother," he added. "Maybe we can teach each other."

"Sure," said Salvador. "My mother loves talking *yerbitas*. You know, she ended up saving the lives of hundreds of Americans, too. Oh, were the American doctors mad!"

By the time they pulled up in front of the restaurant in Chinatown in Hanford, California, Salvador and the big doctor were best friends, and they were singing Mexican songs together. Salvador went inside to get the owner. The man was thrilled to see Salvador and came racing outside with three other people to see the doctor.

Seeing the big, tall man, the restaurant owner got so excited that he began shouting at the doctor. The other people explained to Salvador that this man was a famous doctor in China, and that they were so proud that he'd finally agreed to come to be with them here in the United States.

And now, of course, they were also eternally grateful to Salvador, for once more he'd been able to miraculously get someone across that treacherous border for them.

The owner of the restaurant had a big feast prepared in honor of Salvador and the doctor.

"One thing," the doctor said to Salvador, "we want no lettuce, please!"

Salvador laughed *con carcajadas*. "Yes, driving up here," he said to the restaurant owner, "we ate lettuce until it was coming out of our ears!"

For dessert, the owners paid Salvador the remainder of the five hundred dollars that they'd agreed upon, then presented him with this little, hand-carved wooden box.

Inside was something Salvador had never seen before. It was a huge mother-of-pearl, but so shiny, so polished that it looked almost translucent. Salvador thanked the man over and over again. Why, the stone was almost hypnotic if you looked at it too long.

Leaving Hanford that night, Salvador felt so happy that he continued singing. After so many years of bloodshed and suffering, it truly seemed like the Heavens had finally opened up for him.

Why, he had money in his pocket, and he was on his way to see his *esposa*, his wife, his truelove, the most beautiful woman in all the world; the woman who had moontalked to him in his hour of need.

And here was the Mother Moon, *la Luna Madre*, lighting his way once again as he sped homeward in his grand automobile.

RIGHT AFTER SALVADOR HAD LEFT, Lupe found the pint bottle of whiskey under the pillows that Hans and Helen had given them when she'd started straightening up the house.

She looked at the bottle hidden underneath the pillow for several moments before picking it up. What did this mean, a bottle of whiskey here and a gun that he'd hit a man across the head with? Lupe suddenly remembered the man that she'd seen in Corona at Salvador's sister Luisa's house, before she'd met Salvador, and how this young man had stood there so calmly with his back to her and he'd had a gun handle sticking out of the back pocket of his pants.

The thought now sent chills up and down Lupe's spine—that young man had reeked of violence!

"Oh, my God," she said aloud, "could it be that I, I, I have married that man, and I don't know it?"

Terror gripped Lupe's heart with such power, that she suddenly felt ill!

Quickly, she picked up the bottle with her fingertips and took it outside and threw it in the trash. But, then, she suddenly remembered that roll of money, too, and how she'd felt like she'd seen a rattlesnake when she'd first seen that money lying there on their kitchen table alongside the apple pie.

She ran back inside, got the can with the money from under the sink, and ran back out the front door and threw the money into the trash, too.

And it felt good! She'd cleaned house!

She'd cleaned house, and the Devil be warned, for she was going to protect her nest just as she'd seen her mother do time and again all through the Revolution, and then here in this country, too!

Lupe breathed and glanced around, looking at the trees, the grass, the flowers, the sky. They seemed very different to her now that she'd cleaned her nest!

She decided to take a little walk and visit this property on which they lived, and as she walked, she breathed deeply, beginning to calm.

At the back end of the property, Lupe found an old eucalyptus tree.

The huge trunk of the tree was knotted up with bulging twists of white and brown bark. The bark was coarse and rough with smooth places here and there. This was a tree that had seen a lot of life; many wet and dry seasons. High above the leaves danced in the breeze, each leaf looking like a small angel of light against the sky.

Lupe reached out with her right hand, placing it on one of the smooth places on the trunk of the great tree, and instantly she felt a warmth, a power coming to her from the tree.

Tears came to her eyes and she began to pray as she'd seen her mother do thousands of times back home in their canyon, and little by little, she got to feeling much better. After all, every woman needed her own Crying Tree. This her mother had told her ever since she could remember, that women came from the Tree of Knowledge just as men came from the Rock of Fire.

Trees spoke to women.

Rocks and Fire spoke to men.

Suddenly, Lupe felt very tired. All this worry had really gotten to her. She decided to lie down by the trunk of this huge, old tree. Lying down, Lupe looked up through the branches of the great eucalyptus and she watched the leaves dancing against the background of the sky and clouds.

Lupe must've fallen asleep, for the next thing she knew she was dreaming of being up in Heaven with *Papito Dios* and *Papito* was now talking to her, singing to her, chanting to her with the sound of the leaves making love with the sea breeze.

Time passed.

And more time passed and when Lupe awoke, she now felt a confidence and clarity of mind that she hadn't felt before. Now she could see very clearly what it was that she needed to do.

Simply, she had to bring everything to the Light.

She would now go to the trash and retrieve the money and yes, even the bottle. Then she'd put the bottle under the sink along with his money. They were going to have to talk.

Yes, this was exactly what she'd do. Then when Salvador returned, she was going to talk to him about this bottle, then she'd talk to him about how she felt about the money. After all, they hadn't been able to talk the other night after they'd come back from eating at the Montana Café, but they were certainly going to talk now.

Fear of the darkness wasn't going to rule her life.

She was her mother's daughter, after all, and so she wasn't going to hide money or bottles from her husband. No, she was going to keep everything out in the open, and demand to know what this was all about. This was her home, *su casa,* her piece of Sacred Earth.

She would not be moved!

Feeling so much better, Lupe sat up and she breathed deeply. She could now see that the Tree was smiling to her with a thousand little happy faces hidden here and there all over its coarse, rough bark. The whole Tree was glowing with Love, just as her mother had always said that her own Crying Tree had been glowing with *Amor* for her back in Mexico.

Tears came to Lupe's eyes and she was so happy that she was her mother's daughter, and so she wasn't going to continue in a marriage with a man who'd lied to her about his drinking and that he was—oh, she could hardly say the word—a bootlegger, an outlaw, a man who sold liquor to men who should be using that money for their *familias*!

The tears continued flowing from Lupe's eyes. She knelt up, hugging the Tree in a big *abrazo,* embracing the Tree with both of her hands, giving Love to the Tree with all her Heart.

Her sister Carlota had warned her of all these rumors going around about Salvador, but she'd refused to listen, because she'd believed Salvador with all her heart and soul.

She'd trusted him!

She'd trusted Salvador!

She'd put her faith in a man, *un hombre,* and he'd hid a bottle of whiskey in their home, and liquor was the way of the Devil, their mother had always told them. Liquor and cards ruined more *familias* than even war, leaving children hungry and young mothers desperate!

Lupe continued crying and hugging the great old Tree, feeling its rough, tough bark against the soft, inner side of her arms. She and Salvador had been so happy, so much in love, so how could this awful situation have come to be?

Wasn't *Papito Dios* supposed to be helping people in love?

Wasn't love, itself, supposed to be able to keep the Devil at bay?

Suddenly, Lupe felt like somehow it had been her very own love that had kept her blind and allowed the *Diablo* to enter their home.

Lupe shivered all over, and suddenly she just knew that Salvador was in danger once again, but this time a large part of her just didn't care what happened to him.

But he was really in bad trouble! She could feel it here inside of her stomach! Quickly, she pushed past her resentments and began to pray for her husband with all her God-Gifted Powers once again.

"No!" she yelled at the Devil who'd come near, trying to tempt her mind into that Hell of doubt and confusion. "I will not be tempted! I will not be taken down into that world of hating my husband. Be gone, *Diablo*! I love my husband, and we are with God's Holy Light, and we will talk and work things out when he gets home. Please, dear Lord, help me!"

And Lupe made the sign of the cross over herself, here at the side of her Crying Tree and suddenly, once again, she just knew that she'd helped Salvador through his hour of danger. He was safe now. He was good once again. And he would be coming home. Of this, Lupe was sure down deep in her *alma y corazón!*

IN THE COOL, EARLY HOURS of the night, Salvador pulled into Carlsbad, California. He was dropping, he was so tired. He'd been up for three days and nights and he was ready to die.

But, also, he figured that he couldn't just take his grand automobile home looking like this. No, he had to stop by to see old man White, so Kenny could clean up the car, fix the bullet holes, and check over the entire vehicle before taking it home.

Pulling in to Kenny's garage, Salvador couldn't see straight. His eyes just kept closing up on him. His Chinese connections in Mexicali had given him six little envelopes of ground-up white crystal to help him stay awake, but still he was dead tired.

Back in those days, *coca* and *marijuana* were legal on both sides of the border, but also Salvador knew that once the *coca* substance wore off, he'd be more tired than he'd ever been before, so he'd had to be very careful and not be tempted to use any more of the substance for a few months. The human body could very quickly become enslaved to these little, innocent-looking, white crystals.

Parking in front of the garage, Salvador walked around to the back and was just going to knock on Kenny's door, when the door suddenly flew open. And here stood old man White with his 30/30 Winchester in hand.

"Oh, it's you!" said Kenny, lowering his rifle. "Damn, you look terrible, Salvador."

"And I feel worse," said Salvador. "Sorry to wake you up, Kenny, but I wore that car out, and I need to get home. I told Lupe I'd only be gone a few hours, and it's been, well, three days, I think."

"Three days, Jesus Christ!" said Kenny, grabbing Salvador under his left armpit and helping him inside. "You better come on inside and sit while I check your car, and then I'll drive you home."

"Good," said Salvador, letting Kenny lead him across the room, "and by the way, I've got three hundred of the four hundred dollars you loaned me, Kenny."

"Great," said Kenny, helping Salvador to sit down, then he went to get his pants and shoes. He was only in his nightshirt. "I could use it, that Eisner needs a little more help for his grocery store, but we'll talk about that money in the morning, after you've slept. Hell, you might not be able to pay me that much after you speak with Lupe. Remember, you're a married man now, Salvador, and a married man needs to first check things over with his wife, or all Hell can break loose."

"Bull!" said Salvador. "You loaned me that money before I got married, man-to-man, and so I pay you, man-to-man, what I can, when I say I can, and I say now! Here, take three hundred off my roll. I'll still have over a hundred to take home to Lupe. Always remember, Kenny, lettuce is only lettuce, even by the boxcar, but *amigos* who'll walk on fire with you are worth more than gold!"

Kenny had loaned Salvador that money when everyone else had turned him down.

"Hey, I like that, money is only lettuce, but friends are gold," said Kenny, figuring that this was what Salvador had been trying to say. "Okay, if you're expecting a boxcar of this kind of lettuce, then I'll take my three hundred now," he added.

Kenny counted out three hundred dollars, then gave the roll of money back to Salvador. "You better recount your money and make sure I didn't cheat you, Salvador," said Kenny.

"Hell, no!" said Salvador. "Do I check my car when you say you fixed my brakes? No, I trust you, man-to-man, *a lo macho*. And 'trust,' Kenny, is a big, big word! In fact, it's the big, biggest, most important word, next to 'love'!"

"I'll buy that," said Kenny. "Trust really is a big one, and so is love. And Hell, I've failed miserably at both of those many a'time!"

"Bullshit! A man like you never fails!" said Salvador, trying to get up to embrace Kenny, but he fell back in his chair. "Maybe gets knocked on his ass, but a good man always gets up again. And women, they are even tougher, my mother always told me."

"Is that where you've been? To see your mother?" asked Kenny, having met Salvador's mother several times.

"Yeah," said Salvador, lying.

"Fine woman," said Kenny, as he went across the room to his bed, and got Salvador a blanket to wrap himself. The sea was only a few blocks away, and—different than Mexicali—the weather was cool along the coast.

Going up front, Kenny saw that Salvador's Moon was all covered with mud, and so he figured that something pretty bad must have happened, because Salvador always kept his Moon so nice and clean. The keys were still in it, so Kenny tried the motor and it started right up. He opened up his garage door and put the roadster inside.

Coming back to his place in back, Kenny found Salvador washing his face in the sink. "I need to wake up and get home," said Salvador. "Hell, I told Lupe that I'd only be gone a few hours." He was half out of his mind, he looked so tired and worried.

"All right, come on, you crazy newlywed, I'll drive you home," said Kenny, laughing.

"Good," said Salvador. "You're a real *amigo*, Kenny, the best! Even if you are a damn *gringo!*"

Kenny laughed. "Well, you're pretty good, too, Salvador, even if you are a damn Mexican!"

Kenny and Salvador walked out of his house and got into his Ford truck. Kenny lived behind his garage, and the house that Salvador and Lupe were renting was three blocks away, over on the north side of Elm Street—which years later would be renamed Carlsbad Village Drive.

Salvador was sound asleep before Kenny had driven a block.

AS SOON AS LUPE HEARD a vehicle coming down their long driveway, echoing between the trees, she jumped out of bed and ran to the window. Salvador had been gone for three days and nights, and she'd been scared half out of her mind.

And yes, of course, she realized that they didn't have a phone, but still he could have called the Eisner market down the way and had them come and tell her what was going on. She'd been praying day and night, hoping to God that Salvador was all right. They'd been so close, so happy, so why hadn't he come home? Could it be . . . oh, no, not another woman? My God, she hoped not.

But, then, Lupe saw that it wasn't their Moon automobile that was coming down the driveway through the orchard. No, it was a big truck.

"Oh, my God!" said Lupe. "Salvador has been killed, and someone is coming to tell me!"

Quickly, she put on her robe and rushed to the front door. Then she thought that she recognized the truck. It was Kenny White's big truck, and it looked like he was alone.

But then, Kenny parked his truck, and she saw him get out and go around to the passenger side. The blood came back to Lupe's face when she saw that Kenny was helping Salvador out of the truck. Her truelove had come home to her, and he was alive!

"Is he hurt?" she asked Kenny as he brought Salvador inside.

"No, I don't think so. He's just at the end of his rope. He told me he hasn't slept for three days."

"When did he get to your place?" she asked. All her life Lupe had been very shy, but she wasn't shy now.

"Just a little while ago. He had car trouble and dropped the Moon off at my garage."

"I see. Was he in a wreck?"

"No, I don't think so," said Kenny, taking Salvador down the hallway to the bedroom. "Just tired."

Lupe was trying her best to keep calm, but, oh, she'd been sick with worry, and she'd had no one to talk to.

Kenny lay Salvador down on the bed and pulled off his boots.

"Am I home?" asked Salvador, waking up. "I need to get home to Lupe!"

"You're home," said Lupe.

"Lupe! Lupe!" said Salvador, quickly reaching out for her. "I love you so much, and I've been driving and driving and . . . and the Moon followed me, bringing me home. Did you see the Mother Moon tonight? She's beautiful, Lupe, and she spoke to me," he said. "She told me that you were praying for me. And I could feel your love come to me here in my heart, this time," he added, then he was fast asleep again, and snoring quietly.

Kenny laughed. "Well, I guess he had quite a trip, with the Moon and all. I think he was at his mother's place over in Corona."

"I don't know," said Lupe. "Three days ago, he said he was just going out for a few hours on business."

Lupe walked the older man to the front door. She was so upset that she could scream.

"Good night," said Kenny, tipping his hat.

"Good night," said Lupe. "And, well, thank you very much for bringing him home, Kenny."

"You're welcome, Lupe, and, please don't be too hard on him," he began to say, but then he stopped himself. "Sorry, Lupe," he said, "it's none of my business," he added quickly, and left.

Lupe closed the door and took a deep breath. Yes, she knew that Kenny was right and she shouldn't be too hard on Salvador. No, she should be happy and thank God that she'd gotten Salvador back in one piece; but, also, she couldn't just hide the fact that she was angry.

She'd been so worried.

Where had he been, and what had he been doing? Had he really been at his mother's all this time? Then why hadn't either of them thought of calling her?

Once again, Lupe wondered if, well, could it be another woman.

But oh, she really didn't want to have all these kinds of terrible thoughts running around inside of her head. What was wrong with her? It just seemed that ever since she'd found that bottle of whiskey hidden under the two beautiful pillows with their names embroidered on them, her mind was just alive with the Devil's toys of doubt and fear!

She began to cry. She felt overwhelmed.

UP IN CORONA, Doña Margarita was praying with her rosary in hand when she heard her daughter-in-love's crying. Ever since Salvador had come by and she'd given him the message that the Chinese man needed to see him, she'd been praying day and night for God, the Father, to help her son Salvador and his young wife.

A mother's job was never done. A woman of substance wasn't done until her earth-body was returned to the ground from which it had come.

But even then the journey of life, *la vida,* wasn't finished. After human beings finished their work here on Earth, they then returned to the Great Beyond to continue their service in the name of the Holy Creator.

Doña Margarita prayed in her little shack in the predawn of the day using the rosary that had been her father's—the rosary that she'd been carrying from town to town ever since they'd had to leave their beloved *tierra de los Altos de Jalisco.* And in her mind's eye, the old woman suddenly knew that Lupe and Salvador were in danger once again.

Salvador's young wife was crying and the Devil was creeping close, preparing to snatch her love for Salvador away from her the first chance he got.

Quickly, Doña Margarita moved up and down the musical scale of the full Thirteen Senses as she'd done before when she'd turned into an eagle and went to help her son at the border. This time she once more stopped at the Eleventh Sense—called Form-Shifting by many Indigenous People of the Southwest—and she took on the form of an owl this time.

El Diablo was creeping down the branches of the Tree of Knowledge to intercept Lupe's prayers when the old Indian came sweeping down out of the Heavens and took the old Devil by such surprise, grabbing him by his long weasel tail, that he leaped out of the Tree and went screaming up into the Sky, trying to get away. But the She-Owl had a good hold of him, and she rode him through the Heavens until by accident she almost got him through the Gates of Heaven and back with God.

"Get the hell away from me, you smelly old woman!" he screamed.

"Oh, come and give me a quick kiss!" she said. "You know you love me, and to love me is to love God!"

Hearing this, the Devil spat and took off for the depths of Hell!

AND INSIDE of their honeymoon cottage, Lupe suddenly felt this great peace come over her and she felt so happy, so blessed, like all these feelings of doubt and fear had left her soul, and *Papito Dios* was now completely here with her once again.

"Thank You, Lord God, for helping me," she said. "I don't want to keep having all these bad thoughts inside of my head, thinking that my husband's love be false!"

And saying these last words "his love be false," Lupe was suddenly back in her box canyon of *la Lluvia de Oro*. She was seven years old and she and her childhood girlfriends were playing jump rope and singing a song about false love.

> *Naranja dulce, limón partido,*
> *Dame un abrazo, por Dios te pido!*
> *Si fueran falsos tus juramentos,*
> *En algún tiempo se han de acabar.*
> *Toca la marcha, mi pecho llora,*
> *Si tus juramentos serán verdad,*
> *Duran el tiempo que naranjas dulces.*

> Sweet orange, split lemon
> Give me a hug, for the love of God!
> If your promises are false,

Sometime they will end.
The march sounds on, my heart cries out,
If your promises are true,
They'll last as long as oranges are sweet.

The tears streamed down Lupe's eyes, and in Corona some seventy miles away, Doña Margarita smiled, sending love to her daughter-in-love. For the words of "daughter-in-law" had never made much sense to the old Indian woman. It wasn't the "law" that brought new members into one's *familia,* it was the "love." And so tears of joy continued streaming down Lupe's face as her mother-in-love kept praying for her, and Lupe was now sure that everything was going to work out for her and Salvador and their promises were true to each other, so their love would then be sweet as long as oranges were sweet—forever and ever!

Lupe felt better. It was hard to keep full of doubt and fear when you had so many wonderful memories smiling down upon you like kisses from Heaven.

She made the sign of the cross over herself, thanking the Holy Creator.

Then instantly, she remembered the bottle and the can of money she'd thrown in the trash. She'd never gone back to get them! She decided to now go and retrieve them.

She was no longer afraid.

The Devil was gone. She'd brought light into her darkness.

And walking outside, here was the Mother Moon, and she looked so beautiful surrounded by dark sky and bright stars.

"Hello, Mother," Lupe said to *la Luna,* as she'd done every single night back home in their beloved box canyon.

And the Mother Moon smiled back to Lupe, holding in all her glory, the Female Eye *de Papito Dios,* giving Heart-Guidance to women since the dawn of time.

THE NEXT AFTERNOON, Kenny White was washing off Salvador's car so he could start working on it, when he came across the two huge bullet holes in the lid of the trunk. He turned off the hose and opened the trunk very carefully. There were splatters of blood all over the inside of the trunk. Kenny didn't know what to do. Should he go to the law, or should he wait and ask Salvador to explain himself first? He decided to put the car back inside of his garage and have a good-sized drink of whiskey so he could think the whole situation over very carefully.

SALVADOR SLEPT FOR SIXTEEN HOURS STRAIGHT.

Then little by little, as he began waking up, he dreamed that he was being hugged and kissed and it felt so good. Warm, strong, firm legs wrapped all about him and hard, big-nippled breasts pushing against him like a covey of quail running uphill.

He dreamed of gripping his truelove closer and closer, tighter and tighter, feeling her young, hard quail-breasts beating hard against his chest as she jerked him to herself with such hunger and warmth and smooth silkiness.

Then yes, oh, yes, they were gliding, slipping, sliding through that needle's eye of returning toward a memory, a longing of paradise.

All yesterdays disappeared and today stood still . . . not in thoughts, but in feelings of warmth, of juicy wet warmth, and kissing, kissing, holding, and, oh, oh, yes, yes, such soft, tender feelings—truly a Gift from Heaven!

For every little kiss, every little caress of Heart to Heart in the quiet of the Good Night was a journey to the Great Beyond.

In the distance, the ocean waves continued racing up to the seashore like wild stallions. And the Mother Moon rejoiced, giving light and warmth to all young lovers.

And here, in this Blessed Place, the Mother Moon smiled, speaking gently to them, and Salvador and Lupe listened with open hearts, finally letting go, and standing naked before the Universe, having surrendered themselves completely to the journey *de AMOR*!

An owl called outside their window.

In the distance a rooster crowed and flapped his wings.

Another Sacred Night was coming to pass.

THEN IT WAS DAYBREAK and waking up, Salvador remembered that entering Carlsbad, he'd dropped his car off at Kenny's before coming home because he hadn't wanted Lupe to see the car all dirty and . . . with those huge bullet holes in the trunk.

He leaped out of bed! He had to get over to Kenny's garage before the old man found those bullet holes and turned him in to the law! What had he been thinking? Kenny was an Anglo!

"Lupe," said Salvador, "I need to go and see Kenny!"

"But why?" she said, lying naked next to him in bed. "You were gone for three days and nights!"

"Look," he said, looking out their window and seeing the first signs of daylight just coming up over the avocado trees in the east. "I know that last time I said I'd only be gone a few hours and was gone for a couple of days, but, look, it's almost daylight, and this time I'm honestly—"

"You were gone three days and three nights," said Lupe, cutting him off. "And now you've been home two days, but you've been asleep for the whole time."

Salvador stared at her. "What are you saying?" he said, looking completely baffled. "You mean, that I've been sleeping for two days—oh, my God! I've got to get to Kenny's, and fast!"

Salvador leaped up, grabbed his clothes and pulled them on as he went rushing down the hall. "I'll be right back, Lupe!" he yelled. "I'll be right back!"

"Salvador!" screamed Lupe, slipping on her robe. "Don't you dare leave me again! I'd thought that you'd gotten killed! I was going crazy with fear! We need to talk! I found your whiskey bottle!"

"I'll be right back!" he yelled, repeating himself.

"You leave," she screamed, "and this time I won't get your money and whiskey from the trash when I throw them away!"

But he paid her no attention. He was out the door, then glancing around, he saw that he had no vehicle. He suddenly remembered that his truck was being used by Epitacio and his car was at Kenny's place. Quickly, he started down the driveway at a jog, and then he was running, and he was barefoot.

Lupe watched him go. For the life of her, she couldn't figure out what was going on. Why, Salvador was acting crazy. Was she doing something wrong? What could possibly be so urgent about his car's condition? Her brother, Victoriano, had always said that Kenny was a good mechanic, so surely he could figure out what to do with the car without Salvador.

Lupe was so mad that she wanted to scream, and so scream, she did! The rooster next door answered Lupe's screams, and then *Chingon* began barking, too!

AND IN CORONA—some seventy miles to the northeast—Doña Margarita could see with her heart-eye what was going on with her family.

Oh, ever since they'd left their beloved mountains of *Jalisco* the Devil just kept thinking that he could have his way with them but she wasn't about to let the Great Lucifer have his way. She and her people had been fighting with the Forces of Darkness since the dawn of time and so these battles of Creation were nothing new to her.

Sweeping down into Carlsbad in the daylight, Doña Margarita now took on the form of the big red rooster that lived next door to her son's little rented house. She burst out of the chicken coop with a flutter of wings and started through the orchard to get the Devil, who was once more tempting Lupe with his toys of fear and doubt. She wasn't her father's daughter for nothing. Oh, she was ready for battle, as she now came calling and prancing between the trees on her she-rooster legs.

GETTING TO KENNY'S GARAGE, Salvador was out of breath and his feet were hurting. He hadn't run barefoot in years, and the soles of his feet weren't tough anymore.

Immediately, he tried the big garage doors, but they were locked, and Kenny never locked his garage doors. Carlsbad was a little village and everyone knew everyone, and so no one locked their doors. Hell, half of the people in town didn't even take their keys out of their cars, day or night.

Turning around, Salvador suddenly saw that there stood Kenny right behind him with his 30/30 Winchester in hand.

"Good morning, Kenny," said Salvador, feeling his heart up in his throat. The old *gringo* looked mad as hell.

"Good morning, Sal," said Kenny, lowering the rifle.

"I, ah, came over to see you," said Salvador.

"Good, I've been waiting," said Kenny, " 'cause I ain't putting one hand on your car 'til we talk."

"I see," said Salvador. "So you found them?"

Kenny laughed. "Hell, Salvador, them bullet holes are pretty hard to miss. They're as big around as cannon holes, damnit!"

"Yeah, you're right," said Salvador, "they're .45 holes."

"Shit," said Kenny, pulling on his big nose. "What did you do, Sal? Kill someone? There is blood all over the inside of the trunk."

"Damn," said Salvador. "I forgot all about that. But, you see, I was hauling a dead pig for a barbecue and—"

"DAMNIT, SALVADOR!" exploded Kenny. "Don't give me that kind of HORSESHIT! It's been too long a night for me, wondering if I'm abetting a killer, or not!

"Sal," Kenny continued, "you're going to have to be straight with me, if you expect me to be in this thing with you. Hell, I don't know, maybe the son-of-a-bitch needed killing! Maybe he'd been terrorizing your mother and your people . . . I don't know. But damnit, you got me into this thing by bringing your car to me, so now you've got to be straight with me, Sal! And right now, DAMNIT!"

The old man was boiling mad and waving his 30/30 all around. Salvador had never seen him like this before. He breathed and calmly looked at Kenny very carefully for a long, silent moment. "Then you haven't been to the law, eh?" asked Salvador.

"Hell, no!" snapped Kenny. "But I'll tell you, it's crossed my mind more than once."

The skin on the back of Salvador's left hand began to itch. And he could feel the itching start up the whole of his arm and dig into his left armpit. He put his left hand to his teeth, scratching the itch. No, he wasn't going to let fear panic him.

"Okay," said Salvador, "I'll be straight with you, Kenny. In fact, I'll be more straight with you than I've ever been with any man, Mexican or *gringo*." The itching stopped. He felt good now. The Devil hadn't gotten hold of him.

"Good," said Kenny, "I'm ready. Let me have it, Sal. But first, damnit, come on in and let's have a cup of coffee and a shot of whiskey. My mouth has suddenly gone dry. I've been up two nights thinking about this damn situation!"

"But why didn't you just come by and get me?" asked Salvador.

"Because, damnit, Salvador," said Kenny impatiently as they went inside of his place, "you're on your honeymoon, and you're a good man, and so I, just, well—hell, a man only gets one try in a lifetime to make a home, Sal, and so I wasn't going to ruin that for you!

"Besides, you brought me your car in good faith, and that showed a lot of trust in me, man-to-man, and so I wasn't going to sell out that kind of trust to the law. Remember, I was married to a Mexican woman for years. I know how you people get treated. Once the law is brought in, you don't got a fucking chance!"

Going into the kitchen of his little place behind the garage, Kenny immediately reached under the sink and brought out a gallon jug of bootleg whiskey. It was Salvador's product. Sometimes Salvador paid Kenny for his services in bootleg whiskey instead of cash.

"Well," said Salvador, after they'd had a shot and were waiting for the coffee to heat up, "first of all I want to tell you, Kenny, that, well, I really appreciate you not going to the law. You're a good man, Kenny, the best, and—"

"Sal, DON'T BLOW SMOKE UP MY ASS!" barked the old man. "Just tell me what the hell this is all about!"

"Well, okay," said Salvador, "simply, I brought a man across the border and . . . and, well, I shot those holes in the trunk so he could breathe."

With great deliberateness, Kenny now reached for the jug, then slowly, ever so slowly, he served himself another good-size shot. "Shit," he said, "normally I just drink from the jug. So why in the hell am I now serving myself drink by drink?"

He took the shot glass in his huge, thick hand. He was trembling, he was so upset. "Nope," he said to Salvador as he neatly shot the whiskey down his throat, then wiped his mouth with the back of his hand, "sorry, Sal, but that's still a hard one for me to believe. Just too nice a vehicle to be shooting bullet holes through it." He shook his head.

Salvador closed his eyes in concentration. What more could he do? He'd told the truth. And then, suddenly, with his eyes closed in concentration he saw it all so clearly. "Kenny," he simply said, "did you notice that the holes go from the inside out?"

Kenny shook his head. "No, I didn't," he said.

"Well, let's go look," said Salvador. "You see, I had the trunk lid open when I did it, Kenny."

"Yeah, now that you mention it," said Kenny, pulling at his big nose with his huge workman's fist again, "I did notice something odd about those holes. But damnit, Salvador, that story still doesn't hold water. Who the hell could be that valuable, that a man would shoot bullet holes in his own car?"

Salvador took a deep breath. Here, for a change, he was telling the truth, and he was having a hard time getting someone to believe him. It really was like his mother always said, people were more ready to accept a lie with a good story behind it than the truth told to them straight on. Truth really could be a wildcat not easily housebroken.

"He was Chinese," said Salvador.

Hearing this, Kenny burst out laughing. "Now let me get this straight, for a Chinaman you shot your own car? This is what you're telling me?"

"Yeah, Kenny, that's what I'm telling you," said Salvador, and here he held, not saying another word. For what could he say, the Chinese weren't considered to be worth anything in this country.

And also, if Kenny now did believe his story, this was even more dangerous, because the smuggling of Chinese was a much bigger crime than bootlegging. And so if Kenny did believe him, then he'd just given Kenny the rope to hang him with a federal crime if he ever decided to go to the law.

"A Chink?" said Kenny, grinning.

"Yes, a Chinese doctor," said Salvador.

"Well, I'll be," said Kenny, grinning even more. "I never thought I'd be in a position to be helping the Chinks."

"Yeah," said Salvador, "and his people needed him real quick. There's a sickness in Chinatown and they can't tell the authorities. They're afraid that they'll just round 'em up and kill them all, like they did in Los Angeles a few years back, and bury them in that pit out by Pasadena."

Kenny nodded. "I know the story well. Remember, we met working in a rock quarry."

Salvador nodded. "Also, with my brother, Domingo, in prison in San Quentin, they now owe me a favor."

"I'll be damned," said Kenny. "Small world, eh?" He smiled. "Hell, I was about fourteen when I met my first Chink. It was in a mining camp in Colorado. I was just about dead and he fed me and helped me through a bad winter. He had all these great stories of working all over the West. He'd come from China at the age of fourteen—same age as me at that time—but when I met him, he was old and he'd never married or had any friends after he got separated from his people. Shit, these Chinks have had it worse than Negroes. At least the slaves were brought in with their women, too."

Kenny paused for a moment, then added, "But you didn't kill anyone, right?" And he looked Salvador straight in the eyes, but then, before Salvador could answer, Kenny changed his mind and quickly added, "No, don't tell me. Hell, I already know more than I need to know. We never had this conversation, as far as I'm concerned. But I'm sure glad to do my part in helping the Chinks. That old man saved my live."

"You're helping," said Salvador.

"Good," said Kenny, getting to his feet. "So now you want me to just patch up those holes, do you? I really couldn't find anything else wrong with the car, except it needs service and cleaning because of all that cactus and brush you were dragging underneath it. Must've been one hell of a chase." He grinned. "I hope the pay was good, Salvador, 'cause you knocked the shit out of that vehicle!"

"It was, Kenny, like I said, he's an important doctor, and they needed him up in the—"

"Nope, don't tell me. Like I said . . . we never had this conversation," said Kenny. "Come on, the coffee's hot. Let's have a cup." He was much better now.

"All right, but then I need to go home," said Salvador. "Hell, I just ran out of the house barefoot without giving Lupe any explanation."

Kenny burst out laughing. "You sure as hell like living dangerously, is all I can say," said Kenny, serving them each a mug of steaming hot coffee. "My wife almost cut my balls off one night 'cause I'd been gone too long for her taste. These Latin women, man, an *hombre* needs to sleep with one eye open, I swear! Finally, I had to leave her. Almost cut my dick off on another night," he added, laughing.

AT HOME, Lupe was in the kitchen, chopping vegetables with a knife. All her life, as long as she could remember, she'd watched her mother chop vegetables and make *tortillas.*

Finishing with the vegetables, Lupe put them in a bowl in front of her, and she began to hum. She had a dozen rolled-up balls of dough to her left on the counter. Taking the first of these little fist-sized balls, she began rolling the ball of dough out on the cutting board with the dark hardwood rolling pin that her mother had given her when she'd been a little girl. It was the same hardwood rolling pin that Lupe's grandfather, Leonides Camargo, had given to her mother for making *tortillas* when she'd turned nine years old, and then her mother had given to her when she'd turned seven so she, too, could make *tortillas.*

That day, her mother had taken Lupe aside and explained to her that she was no longer a child. She was seven years old now, and so from this day forth she'd have to start working and behaving herself like a young lady, a rosebud on its way to becoming a full rose, or bad things could happen to her.

"*Porque, mi hijita,* there are many dangers for a young girl in this life," her mother had explained to her. "Just as there are many dangers for a deer or a bird in the wild. And so a smart mother doesn't hide these facts from her daughter's eyes, but, instead, opens her daughter's eyes to these dangers so she'll be able to see and be able to take care, just as the deer takes care of itself from the lion and the birds of themselves from the hawk.

"So I'm not saying these things to frighten you or cause you not to enjoy your life, *mi hijita*," her mother had said to her, "but on the contrary, I'm saying these things to you so you can be aware of your surroundings, then you can enjoy life to its fullest!"

Then her mother had reminded her of all the girls from their village who'd been stolen and raped with the awful Revolution, but—thank God—not one of her sisters had come to such a fate.

"And I believe, *mi hijita,* that much of this has to do because I forewarned your sisters of life's twists at a very young age, just as I'm speaking to you now.

"I swear, mothers who are always telling their daughters to be aware of the scorpion or the snake, but don't explain to them that we, women, must be aware of men and their actions—these mothers are fools! For the matters of the heart, *mi hijita,* cannot be entrusted to these ridiculous, silly, modern stories of romance and happiness ever after, but must be understood with open eyes and the knowledge that a woman's heart is her strength! Not her weakness as these stupid songs and books say!

"For no man can ever break a woman's heart, if she has entrusted her heart—not to the man—but to her home! *Su Casa!* Her nest! Using her God-given hands to roll out the *tortillas,* chop the vegetables, keep the fire going under the *comal,* and hum—like this—as she works.

"Work, *mi hijita,* is a woman's power. Her relaxation and sanity. Her way of coming to terms with life's twists and turns, and not lose her way. After all, remember that it is written in the stars that men came from the rock, the wind, and the fire! And we women came from the flower, the tree, the soil, the water, and, hence, any healthy woman can consume a man's fire as easy as water can consume any little flame.

"Why do you think men are so weak and chase the wind, because down deep they know that the time of their molten-hot fire is short-lived. Whereas women are strong, knowing deep inside of themselves that all life comes from them, and they are the eternal soil for planting and the rain that comes from the Heavens and replenishes the rivers and lakes and even the very sea.

"So always know, *mi hijita,* that you are *una lluvia de oro,* a rain of gold, sent by God to do your work for the survival of all humankind. We are the power, we women are *el eje,* the center, the hub *de nuestras familias,* and in this knowledge, then our hearts are INDESTRUCTIBLE!"

Lupe now dried her eyes with the back of her hand, breathing deeply. She would never forget that day that she turned seven years old and her *mama* had told her all these things of being a strong, healthy woman.

Rolling out each ball of dough, Lupe placed the flat, round *tortilla* on the hot *comal* to the right of her, working from left to right as her mother had always done. And she could now see very clearly that her mother had, indeed, been so wise for this was her whole *problema* now. She'd entrusted her whole heart and soul to Salvador, instead of to this home, this *casa,* this nest that they were building together.

And this house that she and Salvador rented from Hans and Helen had a good roof and solid walls and even electricity and yes, indoor plumbing. This was a good *casa,* a fine house, and this little stove, that Lupe was cooking on right now, was the two-burner gas camp stove that Salvador had bought for their wedding, just like the camp stoves that Lupe and her family had always used when they'd followed the crops.

Lupe had so much to be grateful for. She'd never forget the day that she and Salvador had gone shopping for this little stove and their furniture. Why, she'd felt like such a grown-up, holding hands as they'd looked at this and that, buying things for their home with her husband-to-be. They'd also bought a table and four chairs, a sofa, chair, and bed, and then even one set of dresser drawers. Lupe had never had a dresser before in all of her life. At home, they always used crates from the orchards, or open, homemade shelves to put their clothes away.

No, their little rented home hadn't come with a stove, refrigerator, or furniture, but she and Salvador, an engaged couple, had gone out and bought these things and they now had a very nice, little *casita* for themselves.

She heard a rooster call outside her window and she began to sing, to whistle, to feel much better. And the smell of the *tortillas* cooking and the look of the colorful chopped vegetables—they spoke to Lupe, they spoke to her heart as they'd spoken to her mother, and as they'd spoken to her mother's mother, a pure-blooded Yaqui.

The rooster continued serenading their home with sound and Lupe—Maria Guadalupe Gomez; no, Villaseñor—a married woman, now took the next ball of dough and began to roll the ball out with the hardwood rolling pin that had belonged to her mother.

Lupe just knew to the root of her being that women had been doing this for hundreds of thousands of years. Not with flour as she was doing here, but with *maiz,* corn, the staff of all life, *la vida.*

Lupe continued working the dough with her rolling pin with her two hands, then using her right hand to flip over the other tortilla on the *comal* when it was ready. She was feeling better now. It felt to her as if, somehow, a great burden had been uplifted from her shoulders.

Suddenly the rooster, which had been calling outside, screeched a terrible cry, and he came chasing after a weasel-looking animal past Lupe's kitchen window in a fury of fluttering wings!

Lupe laughed; this truly felt like being back home in their village, a rooster screeching and rodents running. She now began to sing as she continued working the balls of dough. Her home was good now. Her nest was safe. The Devil be warned. She had not allowed darkness to take over her heart.

Lupe continued singing and rolling out the *tortillas* with her rolling pin that had been given to her mother by her mother's father—who'd made the rolling pin from the root of a great tree that had been uprooted by lightning. Lupe now dreamed on—not in thoughts—but in feelings of life, *la vida,* that came to her through her hands, her arms, her fingers, as these soft, firm balls of dough in front of her turned into flat, smooth *tortillas*.

Then Lupe heard Kenny's truck coming down the long driveway, echoing between the trees.

Lupe's heart began to pound once again. Oh, if Salvador was seeing another woman, she'd cut his heart out with this knife that she used to chop the vegetables.

Suddenly she was so mad again that it frightened her.

She began to bang at the ball of dough with the rolling pin. Then she began slapping the *tortilla* back and forth between her palms, as she turned over the other tortilla that was cooking on the *comal*.

She breathed and breathed again, trying to calm herself down. No, she would not be one of these always-yelling wives!

She would calm down, greet Salvador, feed him, and then they would talk. And they would talk calmly, reasonably, and get to the bottom of this mess. No, she would not use the big, sharp knife. After all, her mother had never stabbed their father even after he'd lost all their family's money to cards and liquor.

She breathed, calming herself down. She would be a good *esposa*. Yes, she would be a good wife. She was her mother's daughter, after all.

7

*And so shedding their outer skins, they now came to know
each other as only young lovers can who've stepped forward
in the full commitment of matrimony.*

IT WAS DAYBREAK, and Doña Margarita didn't know what to do. Her old friend *el Diablo* was using every trick he knew, trying to get his way with one of her sons. And no one was a more experienced trickster than the old Devil, himself—God's Greatest Angel back at one time.

In the early morning light, Doña Margarita got up and went to relieve herself in the outhouse. It was still too early for her to go over to her daughter Luisa's house and talk with her. But Doña Margarita felt that she needed to talk to someone, because once she'd run the Devil out of Lupe and Salvador's home, then he'd come to her in a terrible dream, showing her how he was going to try to snatch Domingo's soul.

Outside, the Father Sun was just beginning to give glorious colors of rose and yellow and pink to the far horizon. She loved her little old outhouse with the candles and the little altar with a picture of Jesus and the statue of *Maria*. Going inside, she lit a candle, then sat down with her Bible and rosary in hand to do her daily calling and say her rosary. As she prayed she could still feel the Devil trying to get into her mind. He was giving her no rest. He was trying to get her in every way he could. Finally, she'd had it. Enough was enough!

"Aaaah, yes," she said, feeling a long good *caca* coming with a load of *pedos*. "And here comes this big juicy *caca* and bunch of farts especially for you, dear Lucifer."

"Ah, you filthy old lady!" yelled the Devil, leaping out in the open.

"Of shit for you, yes," she said, "but of my soul for God, no!" And she began to laugh with *carcajadas.*

The Devil took off, spitting as he went.

IN CARLSBAD, some seventy miles southwest of Corona, California, Salvador was driving up the long driveway to his home in Kenny White's big truck. His Moon automobile wouldn't be ready for a few days.

Looking out the kitchen window, Lupe saw Salvador come up to their home in Kenny's truck, and, oh, just the sight of him caused a sudden flood of wonderful, deep woman-feelings to pass over her. She just couldn't help it. Salvador was like sunlight to her heart.

She prayed to God that they could talk and work everything out, for she really didn't want to break her wedding vows and leave this man, whom she loved, but, well, she would, if she had to—now, before they had any children. For her mother had well explained to her that once a couple had children, then there was no turning back, especially for the woman.

She greeted Salvador and she served his dinner and they ate, then she put the dishes in the sink, and now she was ready. "Salvador," she said, smoothing out the apron on her lap as she'd seen her mother do all of her life, "we need to talk. You were gone for three days and nights, then you came in and slept like you were dead. What is going on? I need to know. I can't live like this. And also, while I was cleaning house, I found a bottle of whiskey under the pillow that Hans and Helen gave us," she added as calmly as she could.

She stopped. She'd said enough. And also her heart was pounding. But there was no turning back. This was it. All this had needed to be said. And she didn't know if he'd now be angry or what, but she'd said the truth—she couldn't live like this, being worried all the time.

Seeing the look in her eyes, Salvador took a deep breath, trying to gather his thoughts. She'd said a mouthful, and most husbands would now just jump to their feet and yell at their wife, saying that he was the man of the house, that he brought home the money, and so he wasn't to be questioned. But Salvador didn't think this way. After all, he'd been raised by his mother, and so he didn't want to intimidate this young bride of his, and crush her spirit.

That was easy. Any two-bit pimp could intimidate a young woman.

What he now had to do was hold still as a hummingbird in midair, feeling his heart pounding with rage, and yet do *nada, nada,* nothing just like he did in a poker game when he knew the other guy had drawn aces and he only had kings. He had to hold so still, so strong with his two kings, that the man with the aces would figure he had a full house and cave in.

For at this moment, Lupe, his young wife, was, indeed, holding aces and asking nothing short of the impossible of him. Why, she was asking for him, a man, to be straight and truthful with her, a woman, and he wasn't prepared to do this.

Hell, if he was truthful with her, she'd run in panic. For he was a monster. He was everything that she'd been raised to hate. He breathed, and he tried to figure where to begin without losing Lupe. She didn't know anything about his illegal activities. She really thought that he hauled fertilizer for a living.

"Okay, Lupe," said Salvador, licking his lips which had gone dry, "you're absolutely right, you do need to know what's going on."

He took in yet another deep breath, taking in of the Life-Force *de Papito Dios.* In the last few weeks, he and Lupe had become so close. But still, he, Salvador wondered if any man could ever really be completely honest with any woman. And yes, of course, with his mother he was completely honest, and with Lady Katherine, the madam of that house up in Montana, he'd been completely honest, too, but these were women of experience, older than him, and his teachers.

He now looked at this young bride of his and he decided to give it a try. But he'd have to go very, very carefully. And not too fast, or all at one time, either. After all, this was the wisdom of the She-Fox, being careful and going slowly. This was why she was always able to outdo the bigger, stronger *coyote.*

"Look, Lupe, I'm going to talk now, and I'm going to tell you many things, but you are going to have to listen to me patiently. Because you see, I did a favor for some people, but this isn't what will take me away from you now and then for a few days and nights in the future."

Hearing this, it was now Lupe who didn't dare take her eyes off of Salvador. No, she held, watching his eyes and every move.

"And," asked Lupe, refusing to shy away, "who are these people that you did a favor for?"

"Chinese," he said.

"Chinese?!?" she repeated, looking totally surprised. "But how in God's name do you owe these people a favor, Salvador! All my life *mi mama* told us girls to be wary of the Chinese men because they come and trick a family out of their daughters, marry them, then work them to death like slaves!"

Salvador nodded. "And I'm sure that this is true, Lupe, because the Chinese are a hard people, but they've also had it very hard here in this country."

"So have we, but our men don't enslave their wives!" said Lupe. Oh, she was really upset.

"Lupe, Lupe," said Salvador, "please calm down and listen closely; your mother is a fine woman, but she doesn't know the whole story. You see, the Americans here in this country, they brought over the Chinese men by the thousands to build the railroad, but they weren't allowed to bring over any women with them. Then once they were through with these men, they just threw them out like dogs! And they didn't do this to the Greeks and other people. Why, even the Blacks, *los Negros*, were treated better than the Chinese," he added, repeating Kenny's words. "At least they brought them over with their women."

Lupe moistened her lips, never taking her eyes off Salvador. This was so different than she'd been taught to think. And she wanted to ask him so many questions about the rumors that he was a bootlegger, but what popped out of her mouth next, even took her by surprise.

"And . . . and did these Chinese pay you for this favor that you did for them?" asked Lupe.

Hearing this question, Salvador burst out laughing. Never in a million years would he have expected this. "Yes," he said, between *carcajadas* of laughter, "they paid me."

"How much?" she asked.

Well, this next question sent Salvador rolling to the floor with laughter, kicking and yelling and holding his stomach. Oh, Lupe was tough! This young, innocent bride of his really got down to the nitty-gritty no matter how frightened she was. And *pronto*, too!

"Don't you dare laugh at me!" she yelled. "You did it! It's over! So now I want to know how much!"

"Five hundred dollars!" he said.

"Five hundred!" she screamed. "Oh, my God, Salvador! That's more money than I ever heard of! What was this favor?" she asked, suddenly remembering the young man that she'd seen at Luisa's house with the gun sticking out of his back pocket. He'd reeked of violence, and yet he'd looked so at ease. "You weren't hired to . . . to kill someone"—she swallowed— "were you, Salvador?"

And here she held, heart in mouth, hoping to God that she hadn't married a murderer on top of all these rumors. Because she'd then have to leave this man immediately! No two ways about it. For she would not bring children into the world where the Devil was part of their lives.

Salvador took a deep breath and looked at this young, beautiful bride of his, and he saw her fear, her absolute terror, and yet she'd had the guts to ask this biggest of all questions. He breathed again. This was a woman who could stand up and speak her mind no matter what.

He'd won the prize when he'd married this young woman before him.

"No, *querida,*" he finally said calmly, "I didn't kill anyone. That wasn't my job. My job was to smuggle a Chinese doctor into the United States. It was an emergency, you see. This man's wife had died and his daughter is sick now, too. There's a sickness going on in Chinatown and they can't go to the authorities, because, well, the *gringos* are always just itching—I don't know why—for any excuse to come in burning and killing the Chinese like they've done in the past few years to almost every Chinatown all over the West."

"Then you were hired to smuggle in a doctor so he could help his people?"

"Yes, and in the past I've smuggled in many mothers and their daughters. I'm that smuggler that Archie spoke about at Long Beach when we were eating Chinese food. There's a big price on my head."

"I see," she said, and he could see the wheels turning inside of her head. Oh, she was tough, but also, she was really kind of hooked on the idea of the money he was bringing home. "And Archie doesn't know?"

"Not about my Chinese smuggling, but about my other kind of jobs, yes," said he.

She nodded. She was really trying to understand.

"Also," he added, reeling her in a little tighter, "I'd like you to know, *querida,* that I'd never take a job to kill anyone for any amount of money. Life is sacred, and so to take a life in cold blood is the greatest of all sins."

Hearing these words, tears came to Lupe's eyes, because she'd been raised the same way; to take a life *con sangre fria,* in cold blood, was the greatest of all sins. Only in hot blood, meaning self-defense or in the heat of battle, was taking a human life not the worst of sins.

"Then," said Lupe, "there is, also, no other woman?"

This last question, made Salvador's whole heart leap into his throat. "Oh, Lupe," he said, now understanding the entire situation, "of course not. There's only you! I've been driving all this time. I've been—oh, *querida,*" he said, taking her in his arms, "don't you know? You are my heart, my soul, my love! There's no one else! And this time, Lupe, when I got in trouble, oh, I could feel your love coming to me! You were right, it wasn't the *quesadillas* that gave you that stomach pain last time, it was your feelings for me—and this time I could feel your prayers coming to help me, and a great peace came to me from you!"

"I was praying so hard for you, Salvador, so hard!" she said, crying all the more. "It hurt me here inside so much again as I prayed, because I just knew you were in danger once again!"

"I know! I know!"

"You could've called, Salvador."

"Called?" he said. "But how?"

"On the phone."

"But Lupe," he said, "we don't have a telephone."

"No, we don't," she said. "But Eisner's little market down the street has a phone."

Salvador pulled his head away from Lupe and stared at her as if she'd just spoken the most fantastic thing that he'd ever heard. "Why, I guess you're right, Lupe, a person could do that," he said. "My God, I'd never thought of that. A telephone call. That's incredible. But hey, just wait, I don't know the market's number."

"You could've asked 'Information.' "

" 'Information,' what's that?"

"The operator, you know, when you call zero, she can give you the information of any number you want."

"Even in another town?"

"Yes, she connects you to the operator in that other town," said Lupe.

"Really? I didn't know that. I'll be!" said Salvador. "What will they think of next?!"

"Then you'll call me next time?" she asked.

"Yes, of course," he said. "I don't like you being worried, *querida.* You see, when I left that morning, I really thought that, well, I'd only be gone a few hours. I was just going over to Lake Elsinore to check on a job. Then Luisa's husband, Epitacio, told me that my mother had to see me, *pronto!* And when I drove over to Corona, she told me that this Chinese restaurant owner from Hanford had come by looking for me, saying it was urgent, and he'd be in San Bernardino's Chinatown waiting for me."

"Then your mother knew that you'd be gone for days?"

"No, I never went back to tell her, either. I had to immediately go down to Mexicali."

"Then your mother still doesn't know what happened, either?" said Lupe.

Salvador nodded.

"Well, don't you think she's killing herself with worry?"

Salvador burst out laughing. "My mother worry," he said. "Oh, no, the Stars in the Heavens will worry first! My mother never worries or panics over anything. God is her constant Companion! In fact, it's often God, Himself, who comes to her for advice—she tells us. But, of course, not directly. God, like all males, always likes to send His wife, the Virgin *Maria* in His behalf to speak to *nuestra madre* when He's uncomfortable."

"God can be uncomfortable?" asked Lupe.

"Well, yes, of course," he said. "Why do you think that Creation even exists. It's God, all God, a'growing as we grow, a'learning as we learn, that's why we have freewill. That's why we went out of the Garden, to help the Holy Creator."

"Salvador!" snapped Lupe, feeling that they were talking blasphemy. "We left the Garden of Eden to help God?"

"Sure," said Salvador, "this is why He created us in His image."

She swallowed. She held, breathing and swallowing. "Tell me," she said, "who told you all this? Certainly not a priest."

"No, of course not. My mother told me all this."

Lupe's heart went racing now. Not just pounding. This was so contradicting to everything she'd ever been taught. "And your mother, she also says that God . . . Himself, comes to her for advice?"

"But of course, Lupe. He's male, isn't He? Why do you think He got together with *Maria* to have Jesus? Certainly, He could've made Jesus out of nothing, if He'd so chose. No, God has been a male for some time now, and so that's why He comes to my mother for advice—and then ends up owing her a favor now and then."

"God owes your mother favors now and then," repeated Lupe, feeling so stunned that she could now feel herself going numb. She had to grip the table to steady herself. Her head just couldn't take anymore.

Salvador nodded. "Sure. How do you think we got across the Rio Grande at El Paso? God owes favors to every woman who's ever given birth and built a nest."

"You mean, that your mother parted the sea like Moses?" said Lupe.

"Oh, no," said Salvador laughing, "the Rio Grande is only knee deep in most places, so you can just walk across. What *mi mama* did was part all of the *gringos'* hearts—which is, of course, much harder to do than parting water. Every night, the *gringos* put huge alligators in the river to stop our *gente* from crossing, and that night they didn't."

He could see Lupe's eyes had glossed over, she was so lost.

"Look," he said, "you don't need to worry, Lupe, this male part of God is soon ending, and He then goes back to being a woman once again. Ask *mi mama,* she'll explain to you how it all works. God is hard like a man to leap us ahead, then soft like a woman to gift us wisdom. It works in cycles, see, like the day and the night, no big mystery."

"Your mother told you all this?" asked Lupe.

"Of course," said Salvador. "Ever since I can remember. And her father told her. You see, Creation works in fifty-two thousand year cycles. And thirteen is the sacred number, going into fifty-two four times, just like the four seasons of the year. And in order to keep balance, the Torch of Light has to go from male to female, then from female back to male within a *familia* just as it is with *Papito Dios,* Who's both sexes at the same time."

Lupe nodded, and she nodded again. Before, she would've thought that all this was blasphemy, or she would've laughed, thinking that Salvador was just being ridiculous.

But now that she'd met Salvador's *gran mama*—days before their wedding—and she'd heard that old Indian woman speak to her with a voice that seemed to come straight from the Heavens, Lupe truly did believe that this old lady and God had a very special relationship, indeed.

Why, my God, this old woman talked to Salvador as if she and God were best friends.

Lupe made the sign of the cross over herself just in case *Papito Dios* was listening. She didn't want to seem presumptuous, after all. Also, ever since she was a child, just making the crisscross motion of the Holy Cross across her body seemed to bring an immediate peace to her.

"As I've told you, Lupe," continued Salvador with the *gusto* he always had when he spoke of his *mama,* "I'm the nineteenth child of *mi familia.* I came to my mother at the age of fifty, and so she had more time to talk with me. And fourteen of us nineteen children grew to adulthood and my mother saw that my other brothers, who were raised by the males of *nuestra familia,* became hard, except for Jose, who'd been cast from our home at the age of twelve to be raised by the animals. So she took an oath before God to not make the same mistake with me and leave the raising of me to the men. In fact, she told me that when I was born she swore to raise me up like a woman so I'd have the ability to think, to talk, to keep an open heart and be as cunning as the She-Fox, and not just leap forward like the bull to settle matters with muscles and violence like most men do."

Lupe nodded. "Your mother, Salvador, is a very special woman."

"Oh, yes! She's my life!" he said with *gusto*.

Tears came to Lupe's eyes. "That's how I feel about *mi mama,* too. But she never told us children about any cycles of creation, Salvador."

Salvador took a big deep breath. "Lupe," he said, "my mother is no ordinary woman. She was educated in the Sacred Teaching of our people from Oaxaca." He breathed again. "Her role, like her father's, is to be the keeper of our language and history that Europeans tried to destroy. As a child I remember going with my mother to where the old ones would gather, hiding in the woods so they could talk in their native tongues without persecution."

"What would they talk about?"

He breathed deeply once again. "The Spirit World and that we humans aren't who we've been taught we are. We are much greater. We're Angels, Lupe. We're Walking Stars."

"Oh, this we were told, too!" she said excitedly. "Back home in our canyon our story tellers would point to the sky, telling us what stars we'd come walking from."

"Exactly," he said. "Then you'll understand why my mother always explained to us—that we don't have five senses as we were told by all that flat, world-thinking that came from Europe. The Mother Earth is Round, we were told, and the Universe is Alive and Whole and always Growing and Changing in Sacred Cycles. Men have six senses, and women have seven, and when a man and woman come together, they then have all Thirteen. This is what love is really all about, a man and a woman coming to their full senses when they Unite their Love with the Holy Creator."

"I'd never heard it quite said like that," said Lupe, smiling.

"In *nuestro amor,*" said Salvador, "is where we will learn of God's Power through the Thirteen Senses."

"I see," said Lupe. "Well, then, Salvador, tell me, what are the Thirteen Senses?"

"You should really ask *mi mama,*" he said. "She knows how to explain all this really good. But I can tell you, that the sixth sense, she has always told us, is the key to all of the other senses."

"So, then, what is the sixth?" asked Lupe.

"The sixth is balance," said Salvador.

"Balance? Plain old balance so you don't fall over?"

"Exactly. And can you believe that the Europeans left this one out?" said Salvador, laughing. "Incredible, eh? But they also thought that the earth was flat."

Lupe nodded.

"Balance is everything, Lupe," Salvador continued. "All living life has it equally. Trees, animals, water, and even rocks, everything must anchor itself to the Mother Earth and reach for the Father Sky. Look at a tree growing out of a cliff; out it goes, but then turns upward to find its own balance as it reaches skyward.

"Where balance was known, it was considered the key to all our other senses, my mother told us. In fact, it was used for measuring our intelligence. Thinking didn't measure a person's intelligence. Balance was the measure. Half the people I know who think they're so smart are always getting in hot water because they have no sense of balance."

Lupe nodded. "Yes, I can see that. So, then, what's the seventh sense?"

"Oh, the seventh is really good," said Salvador. "It's our intuition, which women automatically have more than men, and so this is why my mother tells me that women were always the leaders back when the world lived in harmony."

"When was that?" asked Lupe.

"In the Garden of Eden," said Salvador.

"But that was only near the Holy Land, wasn't it?"

"Lupe," he said, "every piece of Mother Earth is Holy in the Eyes of God. The Garden was everywhere and still is. Truly, talk with my mother, then you'll see. And you better do it soon, Lupe, because we're married and when a woman marries and starts making her nest and preparing for children," continued Salvador, "she gains her strongest sense of intuition, this little secret feeling, this little quiet voice from deep inside of her that tells a woman how to pick her mate, where to build her nest, and then gives her this feeling of knowing when all is safe in her home or not."

"Yes, this is exactly how I knew you were in danger, Salvador," said Lupe, excitedly. "I had this secret little feeling here in my heart, and it moved down to my stomach and exploded! Then I could hear a quiet voice inside of me telling me to start praying for your safety."

"Yes, to pray, my mother always says, is to join in with the Holy Force of Creation," said Salvador. "And once you have the sixth and seventh senses going, you can get into the eighth sense real easy. It's only with the ninth, tenth, eleventh, and twelfth that we need help, says my mother."

"What is the eighth, Salvador?"

"The eighth is simple," he said, smiling. "You take balance, the key to all the senses, and combine it with feeling, hearing, and intuition and you enter into the sense of harmony with all of Creation. And this eighth sense of harmony is where here, in your heart, you find the Music of God. Everything is music, see, everything is of the Holy Voice of the Heartbeat of Creation."

Tears came to Lupe's eyes. Ever since she was a child, she'd loved music and how it seemed to touch her very soul. "Then with the eighth sense we can actually hear God's Heartbeat?" she asked.

"Hear, feel, and even know. You see, Lupe, we learn to do this as infants inside of our mother's womb, hearing our mother's heart beat, beat, beating, giving us reassurance. It's the same thing out here after we're born, if we use all of our senses. God is real, Lupe, and with us with every breath we take, with every beat of our hearts. Talk to my mother, she'll explain all this to you. You see, when God created the Universe, He created One Song, Lupe. That's what the word 'universe' means. 'Uni' is 'one,' and 'verse' is 'song,' so everything is alive with God's Music," he said, smiling with *gusto*. "Which is, of course, the Universe's Heartbeat."

Lupe's eyes were bright with excitement. "Yes," she said, "this my mother taught us, too! That the plants, the trees, the stones, everything sings to us with the Love of God when we close our eyes and listen with Open Hearts!

"The other day I was drinking coffee on my parents' porch with the Sun just coming up—Salvador, I swear I could hear the plants whispering to me and giving me their love, just like back in Mexico when I was a child," she said, wiping her eyes—she was so happy.

Salvador took her hand in his. "Exactly," he said. "The whole world is beautiful when we can feel the Heartbeat of God singing to us here inside. The hills, the flowers, the birds, the trees, all become so beautiful. This is how our mothers—God bless them—were able to get us through all that starvation and killing of the Revolution, by keeping us strong in the Beauty of the Song of God."

They stopped their words. They just held, looking at each other in the eyes. Time stood still. All was Wonderful. All was Blessed.

"You know, Salvador," she finally said, "my mother told us all this too, but in her own way. I don't think that she ever made mention of us having so many senses, though."

"Well, maybe she'd also never been told that we only had five," he said.

"My mother told me that she never realized that all our senses were in question until they came to the capital, Mexico City, with Benito Juarez's people, and she was put in the academy of the arts, and they told her that we only had five."

"Oh, your mother went to that grand school?" said Lupe. The whole thing was finally beginning to make sense to her. She'd never realized that Salvador's *familia* had known Benito Juarez, the Greatest President of Mexico, or that they'd traveled with him to Mexico City.

"Then your mother's father, Don Pio, didn't just fight alongside Benito Juarez, but he knew him, too?"

"Yes, of course, they came from the same village, and were cousins, in fact."

"I see. But it wasn't until your mother was told that we have five senses—as they teach in school—that she realized that our thirteen were in question?" He nodded. "Well, then, tell me, what's the ninth," she asked, "and what does this sense do?"

"The ninth is really juicy," he said. "You take balance again, the key, and combine it with feeling and smell and seeing—but here you close your eyes so that your Heart-eye can open, and suddenly your seventh sense of intuition explodes into the psychic sense. This one you should really talk about with my mother, because with the ninth, then you're on your way to understanding everything, especially God," he said excitedly. "See, God is only a mystery and not understandable when you have five senses and see the world flat."

Salvador then asked Lupe if she ever had dreams of flying.

"Yes, of course," she said. "Especially when we lived in Mexico and the soldiers would strike our village, then at night I'd often dream of flying away like an eagle and being all safe and good, soaring above the treetops."

"Exactly," said Salvador smiling. "This is the tenth sense, having the ability to leave our earth-body and travel to the Heavens and gain rest in *Papito*'s arms. We all do this a little bit, but the ninth and tenth are really for healers, *curanderos*, my mother tells me, so they can travel in their dreams and help heal people and the world.

"You know, I should have asked the Chinese doctor I smuggled if he uses more than five senses," added Salvador. "I bet he does, because my mother has always explained to us that all healing ultimately comes from the Grace of God.

"Lupe, dozens of times I've seen *mi mama* put her hands on a sick person, close her eyes, then start feeling and smelling the person's body, and then boom—that person's body will start speaking to her, telling her where it's sick and what it needs in order to get well. Then she'll go outside, turn in each of the Four Sacred Directions, palms out, smell the air, and walk off into God's Garden and find the exact herbs and clay to heal the person. Talk to my mother, she'll tell you that there's *un arreglo,* a deal, between all living-life to help one another within the Sacred Circle of Life. It's only when we step out of the Sacred Circle that all of our *problemas* start," he added.

Hearing this, Lupe nodded. Yes, of course, this made sense. She'd heard so much of this from her own mother and that foul-mouth old mid-wife from their village back home. She rubbed her forehead. She felt a lit-tle bit overwhelmed.

Salvador soothed her hand with both of his. "It's okay if you don't understand all this," said Salvador, seeing her eyes go sleepy. "*Mi mama* always told us, 'Does the newly hatched chick need to know why she just starts scratching the ground and searching for seeds and bugs? Does the child need to understand why she immediately starts looking for a breast to suck on when she comes into the world?' No, the child and chicken don't need to know any more than a human needs to know—until that Holy Sacred Circle is broken and our natural powers are taken from us. Then yes, we immediately need to examine and understand so we can reclaim our full Human Being Powers. We are Angels, Lupe. We are all Walking Stars of pure magic."

She nodded.

He breathed deeply. "And this I truly needed to know, Lupe, because believe me, there wasn't a day that passed that my father—a big, handsome European—didn't hit me on the head, calling me a big-headed, stupid Indian without reason, yelling at me that my beloved mother wasn't noth-ing but an ignorant . . ." He stopped. His eyes were running with tears. ". . . and yet who had the power to go on when everything got destroyed!" he added. "It was *mi mama*! That short little Indian woman! KNOWL-EDGE is POWER, Lupe! And Knowledge with the VISION of our full Thirteen Senses is GOD! And God IS my Mother, because," he added, "with my own two eyes I saw her perform miracles day after day—*CON EL FAVOR DE DIOS!*"

Salvador stopped. He could say *nada, nada,* nothing more.

And Lupe, she just held, looking at Salvador, at his eyes, his face, his whole being. Yes, at first, it had truly frightened her when Salvador had said that his mother was God . . . but then, well, she remembered that the same thing had happened in her home.

Her father, mostly European, had also fallen apart, when everything had gotten destroyed, and it had been her mother, a Yaqui, who'd held their *familia* together. But she'd never realized it until now, that this extra strength of her mother's had come from her Indian heritage of knowing all of our Thirteen Senses.

Lupe breathed, and breathed again. Then it was true, she could now see so clearly, that all mothers who took up ground, putting their two hands on their hips, declaring the piece of Mother Earth on which they stood Sacred, did, indeed, become God—for they were then living in the Holy Grace of Creation, which was the exact meaning of the Mexican saying—*con el favor de Dios*!

Lupe made the sign of the cross over herself.

Oh, she loved this man, her husband, who was standing before her! They were BLESSED—*gracias a Dios*!

AND AT THIS VERY SAME INSTANT, Doña Margarita was going inside the stone church in Corona and making the sign of the cross over herself with holy water. She walked up the left aisle toward the front of the church. In the third pew from the front, Doña Margarita sat down by the statue of Mary.

"Good morning, my dear Lady," she said to the Blessed Virgin. "How have You and Your Family been? Good, I hope. Because I need Your help once more. You see, last night the Devil came to me in a dream, and in no uncertain terms he let me know that if he couldn't get one of my sons, he'd get the other. So here, in the safety of your church, where no evil can come to overhear what we are talking about, I'd like for you and me to work out a plan—woman-to-woman—so we can outmaneuver the Devil and send him back to Hell once and for all!

"Eh, what do you say, *Maria?*" said Doña Margarita, smiling to her good old friend who'd been guiding her all these years. "Are you ready for us to give the Devil a good *chingaso a las todas!*"

FIVE HUNDRED MILES to the north, Domingo, Salvador's great big, tall, handsome brother, could see that the six White prisoners were up to no good as they came walking across the yard. But Domingo didn't really give a good goddamn. All his life, trouble had come searching for him, and so if these six prisoners were looking for trouble, then they'd have no *problema* finding trouble with him!

It was midmorning, and Domingo was with his friend Herlindo, a handsome Black Latino from Veracruz, Mexico. They were with some of the other Mexican prisoners over on their side of the prison yard. They were laughing and telling jokes, smoking a little good *yerbita,* and really having themselves a very smooth-happy time.

Domingo hadn't smoked much *marijuana* before. Back home in Mexico, it had always been only for the old people with pains in their joints, or to help them with their appetite or bowel movements.

Laughing good-naturedly, the first big White came right up into Herlindo's face and asked him when he was going to get tired of hanging out with these doped-up half-wit "Mex-ee-can greasers" and go be with the other "niggers" where he belonged.

Then this same tough-looking Anglo turned to Domingo, who was big and blue-eyed and red-headed, just like his father, Don Juan. He asked Domingo when he was going to smarten up and come over to their side— the White side, the right side—and bring along a little of that special medicinal weed that he was having smuggled in through his Chinese connections.

Domingo's face almost dropped. How in the hell had these tricky bastard *gringos* already found out about his Chinese connection that Salvador had just gotten for him. Then it hit Domingo like a thunderbolt. They were the ones who'd knifed that Chinese guy the night before.

Seeing the surprised look on Domingo's face, the second White guy laughed, flashing a knife in the bright sunlight. If Herlindo hadn't leaped in front of Domingo just in time to divert the blade, it would've found its mark into Domingo's belly.

HAVING WORKED OUT A PLAN with her good friend the Virgin Mary, Doña Margarita went back home feeling pretty good. She always felt good after she'd talked to the Blessed Mother of Jesus. No *problema* was then too big. All then seemed possible and quite workable, when you had the backing of Heaven.

At home, Doña Margarita had a little breakfast, then she went next door and told her daughter Luisa and Luisa's children to not let anyone bother her because she was going to go back to bed and take a nap.

But Doña Margarita didn't go to her home to take a nap. No, she went home to set a trap for the Devil, who loved to come to people as they slept.

Doña Margarita hid her rosary under her pillow and lay down to sleep. But she wasn't sleeping; oh, no, she was ready. The Virgin Mary and she had worked out this plan. And then here it began again, just as it had been the night before; these two great big eyes were staring at her from the little fire in her wood-burning stove.

The old woman held, not moving. She knew that these two great big eyes belonged to her old friend the Devil. So Doña Margarita didn't panic. No, she simply went slip-shifting to that soft, easy, relaxed "place" halfway between being awake and being asleep, to that state of complete availability to God.

And so the Devil continued talking, thinking that he was getting past her conscious mind and into her soul-consciousness because she wasn't resisting.

Time passed, and more time passed, and she lay there on her little bed so still for so long that finally the Devil couldn't tell if she was asleep or if he'd convinced her of his wicked ways and she was now his.

Not moving a muscle, the crafty old She-Fox now watched with her Heart-Eye as these two great big eyes in her little wood-burning stove got larger and larger, braver and braver, as they continued dream-talking to her, telling her inside of her mind to relax and stop acting so surprised, because it was well-written in the stars long, long ago that evil would triumph over all the whole world in the end.

This was when she got the full smell of *el Diablo* as he came out of the fire of her little wood-burning stove, hoping to snatch her soul.

Then here he was, the Devil, himself, ready to possess her, when Doña Margarita suddenly leaped out of her bed with the agility of a young maiden, and grabbed hold of *el Diablo* by his long tail and swung him around and around and threw him out of her home with such power that old Devil flew past the clouds to the stars, SCREAMING as he went!

"Vieja condenada!" he shouted. "You tricked me again!"

"Vieja yourself! You will not have either one of my sons!" she screamed! "So help me God, you come sneaking on me while I sleep again, and it's not your tail I'll grab! I'll grab you by your *tanates* next time, and rip them out by their roots!"

"VIEJA PENDEJA!" screamed the Devil. "I thought you were too old to get hold of me anymore!"

"Old I am," she said, "but slow I will never be in dealing with you! And I still got one good tooth to tear your heart out, too!" she added.

"Damn the day you women were created. I swear, I left Our Lord God's side only because of you women!"

"Thank you for the compliment! *Gracias por la flor!* For I'm proud to know it was us, the women, who separated the likes of you from God!"

Hearing this, the Devil slapped his own mouth! "I didn't mean that as a compliment, *vieja cabrona*, you tricked me again!"

She laughed. "Of course, I tricked you again. Because come on, admit it, you love me, particularly when I trick you, my sweet!"

"*Mujer escandalosa,* don't call me 'sweet'! You must fear me!"

"That's for men who don't know the joys of birthing!" yelled Doña Margarita, blowing kisses to the Devil to finish driving him crazy.

Instantly, he took off in a mad fit of rage!

Doña Margarita awoke laughing! She just loved tormenting her old *amigo el Diablo.* But also, she well knew that she could never drop her guard when dealing with this Force of Evil.

The drums were beating!

The drums were beat, Beat, BEATING!

The One Collective HEART-*CORAZÓN* of HUMANITY was BEAT BEATING, POUNDING *CON AMOR!*

IN CARLSBAD, Salvador awoke with a start.

"What is it?" asked Lupe.

"Nothing," said Salvador, trying to catch his breath. "Just go back to sleep. It's early yet."

The drums were beat, BEAT, BEATING!

"Salvador," said Lupe, "tell me what it is? I can feel it, too. Something is wrong."

He sat up in bed, holding his forehead with both of his hands. "My mother," he said, finally, "I can hear her; no, I mean, I can feel her very clearly. It's a calling," he added.

"A calling?"

"Yes, you know, when you just know that a loved one is calling you."

Lupe breathed deeply, knowing exactly what Salvador meant. All her life, her own mother had also gotten callings, *llamadas.* For instance, when they'd gotten word that her older sister Sophia's ship had gone down in

the Sea of Cortez and she'd died along with all the hundreds of other people, their mother, Doña Guadalupe, had simply closed her eyes, placed
both of her hands on her belly, just below her heart, and breathed deeply
two or three times, then she'd opened her eyes and said, "No, Sophia
lives," just like that.

The months had passed and become years, and they'd come from
their box canyon in Mexico to work in the cotton fields of Arizona, but
never once had their beloved mother changed her mind. For the heart
spoke a language that the mind didn't know, and this language of the
heart-*corazón* knew no earth-distance or barriers, for it came straight
"through" God!

Lupe would never forget how everyone had given up on Sophia, feeling
that she was dead for sure, and they'd thought that their mother had just
gone crazy. But no, the old Yaqui Indian woman was not crazy. No, she'd
just hold herself here, in her center, close her eyes, breathe in of God, then
tell everyone—that no, one thousand times no, Sophia was alive and well.
She could feel her "calling" from here within her womb as sure as the day
she'd been born!

Their mother had been absolutely right. Three years later, when they'd
come to California following the crops, miracle of miracles, they'd found
Sophia and her new husband, Julian, in Santa Ana, California. Their
mother had finally planted her white lilies that she'd brought with them
from *la Lluvia de Oro*, giving thanks to God.

"So what will you do?" now asked Lupe.

"Well, I'll go," said Salvador.

"Right now?"

"Yes, immediately."

"Good. Then I'm going with you."

"But, Lupe, I don't know what this is all about. It could be, well—"

"Dangerous?" she asked.

He nodded.

"Salvador, is there something that you're hiding from me? Are you a
bootlegger?"

"My God!" he said. "Not now, Lupe."

"Well, just say yes or no."

"No," he said.

"Really?" she said.

He was up and getting his boots and clothes. "Yes, really, I'm not a
bootlegger."

"Well, if you aren't a bootlegger, then how did you end up with that pint bottle I found under the pillows?"

"Lupe," he said, trying to be as patient as he could, but he was in a hurry. "I have trucks, and well, now and then I haul things for some people. I do many things to make a living, Lupe. Find me something that needs getting done, and I'm right there to do it, especially for the right price."

Lupe was getting her own clothes. She'd heard the men talk like this before. After their mine had closed down back in their box canyon, men had begun doing many things just to make a living. Her own godfather, who'd married Sophia, had gone down the mountain through bandit-infested *barrancas* to get supplies for his little grocery store.

Quickly, Lupe dressed and was ready to go out the door with Salvador. She'd never been like Carlota and Maria, who took hours to make themselves ready to go out the door. All of her life, Lupe would be ready to go at just a moment's notice, like any man or her older sister Sophia. After all, she never wore any makeup. This was just her natural good looks, even her beautiful, reddish lips.

But then, going out the door, was when she saw it in Salvador's face.

"You don't want me to go with you, do you?" she said.

He breathed. "No, I don't," he said.

"But Salvador, you've been coming and going ever since we came down here to Carlsbad," she said, with tears coming to her eyes, "and I've just been here locked up inside of the house."

He nodded. "I know, I know, and under normal circumstances, I'd love for you to come, but like I said—"

"Then take me to my parents' house and drop me off," she said, "and afterward, you can get me when you're ready."

"But that's a couple of hours out of the way, Lupe."

She didn't say one single word. No, she just gave him such a look with her left eye, that he knew there was no more talking.

"I'll get the can of money," she said.

"Oh, good thinking," he said. My God, he hadn't thought of the money. "But hurry! I'm going to be driving fast!"

"In Kenny's truck?"

He smiled as he watched her go back inside to get their money. He hadn't thought of that either, that his Moon was still at Kenny's. My God, this bride of his was really a very fast learner.

"We'll stop by Kenny's," he said to her when she returned with the money. "Maybe the Moon is ready."

———

ALL HIS LIFE Domingo had heard the very Mexican saying, *"Que unos nacen con estrella y otros estrellados,"* that some are born with a star leading them through life while others are born crushed by a star from the start.

And now at this moment, Domingo felt the full impact of this very Mexican statement. For he knew damned well that he was the biggest and most capable fighter of all the Mexicans here in San Quentin, and so he wanted to be the one to take on the big, powerful *Animal Alemán*—as the *Mejicanos* had nicknamed this giant white guy, the German Animal. But the dark little twins from Guanajuato said no, taking Domingo aside so they could speak to him in private.

"Look, Domingo," said the first little twin, "as we've told you before, *hermanito,* we both know that you have heart and that you're with us, and we're family, but please, understand: this fight was coming between us and these *gringos* way before you got here to San Quentin, and it will be going on long after you are gone. My brother and I are in for life, not just five little years, and so we got to take care of it ourselves . . . not you. Do you understand?"

But Domingo didn't understand. Because this whole thing had gotten started because of him. Hell, one day, Domingo had refused to clean the toilets if the Whites didn't do it, too. But he'd just done it mostly for fun. He'd never expected it to blow up into a whole race riot thing.

And now because of that, it was these little twins who were planning to do battle with the monstrous White Enforcer. Why, Domingo, himself, was just about six feet tall, but this *Animal Alemán* towered over him and outweighed Domingo by at least sixty pounds, too.

And the man wasn't fat, either. He was a mountain of power! Only two nights before, he'd killed a "nigger" with his bare hands, just as he'd killed six other men since he'd been here in prison. In Domingo's opinion, one of these little twins had no more chance of beating this huge White in a fight than a flea had the chance of impregnating a mad dog!

But what could Domingo do? The Mexican council had voted, and these twins had been elected as their leaders, and so their word was final.

"Okay," said Domingo, "but I'll tell you the truth, I've fought many men in my life, but this one, my God, I think he's the first *cabrón hombre* that I fear! He's mad! Didn't you see his mouth foaming like he had a mouth full of *baboso*-snails when we refused to clean the toilet for him?"

Domingo was absolutely right. When *los Mejicanos* had gotten together and announced that they would no longer do any job in the prison that Whites did not also do, White prisoners had gone mad, completely raging insane with hate, killing three Mexicans and two Blacks in the first two days and trying to intimidate anyone else who wasn't all white and blue-eyed.

And it wasn't just the prisoners who'd done the beatings and killings. No, it was well known that the White guards had joined forces with the White prisoners to put all the non-Whites back in their place of doing the subservient jobs within the prison system.

And now, with a death total of over ten people in less than three days, a truce had been drawn between the opposing sides, and an agreement had been reached. *Los Mejicanos* would come forward with one champion to fight on their behalf, and the Whites would come forth with their own champion—who, of course, everyone knew would be Max, the mad-dog *Alemán,* who had never been beaten in a fight during his eight years in prison.

Why, the man was indestructible!

A God-given brute of pure muscle!

The guards, of course, were all behind Max. Because for years it was well known that Max was the warden's special man who did for the warden what he legally couldn't do for himself.

Regularly, the warden and the guards used Max to enforce their ways, and they gave him special treatment and special food—including beer—so that they could keep him strong.

Max, the enforcer, was a second-generation German from upstate New York. His father had had a dairy, and Max had milked fifty cows for the first sixteen years of his life until he'd killed his own father in a mad rage over his father's young, new wife. And Max's hands were so huge and thick and powerful—from milking cows morning and night—that it was said that he could break a man's neck with just one mighty snap alone!

The guards adored Max, and he and his group of White prisoners were the real authority of the prison. They ran the prison for the guards and the warden with absolute control.

It was the same with every prison throughout the country. The White prisoners ran the prisons, and this was the way it was supposed to be. And the wardens and guards didn't care if the Mexicans, Indians, and Black prisoners outnumbered the White prisoners in Texas, Arizona, and California by ten to one; the White prisoners were their people and they could trust their own and so, of course, it was out of the question for these slimy, little, tricky, bastard, greasy Mexicans to now say that they refused to do the dirty "nigger" work of the prison system unless the Whites did it, too.

"Look," said Domingo to the twins, "I'm not challenging the vote, but I warn you that you should think on it again. My God, if the one of you who fights him fails, then we'll all be worse off than before!"

The second little twin now spoke up.

Each twin was exactly five feet five and weighed about 135 pounds. And they were strong and fast and very capable, but they were certainly no match for Max, in Domingo's opinion.

"Whichever one of us goes," said this twin calmly, "we will not fail. I promise you, Domingo, we will not fail."

"God, I hope not," said Domingo, towering over the twins by half a foot and outweighing each by fifty pounds. "Look, I'm good, I tell you! I think I can maybe even take the *Animal Alemán!*"

The twins glanced at each other, realizing Domingo just didn't understand.

"Look, we know you're good, Domingo," now spoke the first twin again. "We've seen you fight. But understand, you're too White-looking and too big. So if you do win, then the *gringos* will just say that you won because you're really White and not *un Mejicano,* and they'll still have no respect for us as a people. That's why one of us—who's short and small and dark and *puro Indio*—must do it. So the *gringos* will have respect for all of our people, no matter how small or dark we are. Do you understand now?"

"Yes, I understand what you're saying, but good God, that *Alemán,* Jesus Christ, he's a MONSTER!"

And so, Domingo watched as the twins stripped to the waist and lit candles and burned *yerbitas* and prayed to *Papito Dios.* And he felt so helpless, because if they lost this fight, then they were all going to end up being slaves to these White guards and prisoners forever!

Estrellados! Crushed by a star!

AT KENNY'S, Salvador and Lupe found their Moon automobile ready. Kenny was very happy to see them. Lupe decided to walk down the street to the grocery store as Salvador gassed-up their car. Carlsbad was just a little town two blocks long back in these days. Everyone knew everyone. People didn't even take their keys out of their cars at night.

THIRTEEN SENSES [167

HAVING RUN THE DEVIL out of her home, Doña Margarita decided to go back to the Stone Church and thank the Virgin Mary.

"Thank you very much, my dear Lady," said Doña Margarita to the Mother of Jesus, "but I think the time has come for us to do something about the Devil on a more permanent basis. We can't just keep fighting tooth and nail every day. Look, ever since the arrival of these Europeans, You've been asking for us to rise up and show these lost strangers the way back to their hearts and souls, but we can't keep doing it alone, do You hear me, my Lady, we need help. And now!

"My son Jose rose up in Your Most Holy Name, only to be captured and tortured just like Prince Cuauhtemoc, himself. You know what I'm talking about, *Maria,* You lost Your Son to torture and crucifixion, but I have lost eleven. You hear me, ELEVEN! And yes, I know Your Son was Jesus Christ, Himself, but show me a mother who doesn't believe her own child to be a Holy Gift from the Almighty.

"There in the desert of Sonora with war and killing and death, and star-vation, You appeared to me one Holy Night after my children were all asleep. Do You remember, I was down, I was ready to give up and let my old bones die. But You came and said 'Margarita,' using my first name, 'the Father and I have spoken, and We're not ready for you to come home to Us yet. No, Margarita, We need for you to go north, to help build a great nation for all of the world to see what *la gente del pueblo* can do when they arise as one people from all over the world and open their hearts and souls to the Second Coming *del amor de Dios*!'

"And that Holy Night, there amid war and destruction, I said to You, 'But, *Maria,* I've already given eleven children in this struggle of trying to awaken the Soul of Humanity and I'm old and weak and tired, so I can't continue helping You and Your Husband alone. I need help, I told You, I can't continue alone!'

"Remember, eh, *Maria,* and I reminded You that to nineteen I gave birth, baptizing each in Your Most Holy Husband's Name, but these last three, I said to You," said the old, dried-up Indian woman with tears streaming down her face, "I would not allow You to take from me.

"Eh, do You remember, this was our agreement, *Maria,* woman-to-woman. And I didn't ask anything for myself, but for my children; that not another be taken. For since it appears that You have, indeed, chosen us to be like the Jews of old, leading humanity back around in the full circle to

Your love once more, then we must survive, too, just like the Jews, and so You agreed that my last three would not be taken—remember?

"Eh, DO YOU HEAR ME!" yelled Doña Margarita suddenly standing up in her pew there inside of the Stone Church and shouting! "And I don't care if one is on his voyage of milk and honey, and the other is in prison, it's all the same to me—prison or honeymoon—I will not allow You to break Your word and take one more of my children! DO YOU HEAR ME? Not one more, *Maria*! NOT ONE MORE!

"And yes, I fully realize that in old age, we mortals are supposed to become more and more patient, more and more tolerant, and leave matters to You and Your two Husbands, but to be perfectly frank, my Great Lady, the truth is that the closer I get to my proper age of passing over, I get MORE IMPATIENT!

"So please forgive my outburst, but, well, I am talking to YOU! We cannot continue this struggle alone! I need ten thousand Angels, and I need them NOW! Not tomorrow! Not next week! But right now! A full legion, DO YOU HEAR ME? No Burning Bush this time! No Parting the Sea! But ten thousand ANGELS! And now! PRONTO! For *el caldo esta muy calientito horita*—DO YOU UNDERSTAND?"

AND WHY, Domingo had no idea, but he, five hundred miles to the north, suddenly felt something like a great hand grip him and put him on his knees. Quickly, Domingo then made the sign of the cross over himself, and he began to pray. And he hadn't prayed in years!

Not since he'd left their beloved mountains of *los Altos de Jalisco* and he'd gone north in search of their father, hoping to surprise him, work with him, so that then they could both come home with money and be able to help the family.

But in Texas, those son-of-a-bitch, tricky *Rinche*-Ranger bastards had tricked him and sent him to Chicago with a boxcar full of other ignorant *Mejicanos* to be strike breakers in the steel mills—he now prayed!

He now prayed as he watched the little Indian twins prepare to do battle with the huge White Enforcer.

He now prayed as a handful of Black prisoners joined them, and then the two Chinese men joined them, too. But the White prisoners only laughed at them, calling them superstitious fools, as the other *Mejicanos* made the sign of the cross over themselves and joined Domingo, and now they all prayed together.

The first signs of daylight were now coming up over the mountains to the east of San Quentin, giving light to the great, flat sea waters of the Bay of San Francisco; glistening, smiling at the coming new, glorious day—another Holy Gift straight from God!

IN CORONA, CALIFORNIA, Doña Margarita was still praying.

In San Diego, Fred Noon was on the phone, calling here and calling there, but no one would tell him anything. Every contact that had always been open with him in the past—but off the record, of course—was now clammed shut.

Quickly, Noon decided to drive up and see Salvador. Something really big was going on in San Quentin, but he had no idea what.

At this very moment, Salvador was dropping Lupe off at her parents' home in Santa Ana, so he could then drive over to Corona to see his *mama*.

THE TWINS WERE FACING toward the east, giving thanks as they bathed themselves in the coming light of the new day, rubbing the salty ocean breeze into their bodies.

It was cold and they shivered, feeling alive! They chewed the cactus hearts that the *curandero* had given them to thicken their blood, and they drank the tea that one of the Chinese prisoners had brewed for them to numb them deep inside so when the deep cuts came, they could keep their strength.

One twin's name was Jesus-Maria, and the other twin's name was Maria de Jesus. They were both almost-pretty boys, they were so darkly handsome and delicately made. Their mother had had them at fifteen years of age and she'd never married, and so in time she'd come to believe that they were Holy Gifts from the Almighty!

Domingo watched their calmness, and he remembered how they'd told him that at the age of nine—when the Revolution came to their valley—they'd helped kill the son of the *hacendado* who'd sexually abused dozens of young, poor Indian girls, including their own mother.

Domingo watched them eat their cactus hearts and sip their tea. Finally, he couldn't stand it anymore! They were such small, delicately-made men.

"You can't fight that *MONSTRUO!*" he yelled. "Look at you two! You're nothing but little angels! You don't have a chance! I'll fight! I'm the only one who has a chance!"

The twins glanced at each other, and then Maria de Jesus took Domingo aside once again and spoke to him. Calming down, Domingo wiped the tears from his eyes and he embraced the little twin with all his heart, and then kissed him. They were *MEJICANOS*! They were *hombres* of the Mexican Revolution!

Then it was time, and the *curandero* led them in song, then they all made the sign of the cross over themselves. The rest of the prisoners were already in the central yard. Everyone knew that this was it, the showdown, the battle that was going to forecast the future of prisons across the entire nation.

Max and his group of white friends were over on the west side of the prison yard. They were talking and laughing, acting very confident, as if this was no big deal, as if this was just a normal day and it would all be over in a few minutes—done, finished—and then the business of American life could go on as it had always been going on for as long as they could remember.

The Mexicans, on the other hand, were gathered over on the east side of the yard, and were very quiet. For this was not a normal time for them. No, their entire existence depended on the results of what happened in the next few minutes.

In the middle of the people, the twins were stripped to the waist, and they were ready to draw straws. Everyone was anxious to see which Jesus would draw the shortest straw. The one with the shortest straw won and, therefore, would be the one who got to do the fight.

The twins loved each other more than life itself, and so each had prayed all night long that he would be the one to do battle so that his beloved brother could then live on for both of them and, maybe, someday could then get out of prison and marry and have children for both of them.

Opening their hands, Jesus-Maria drew the shortest straw.

"STRETCH US IF YOU MUST, dear LORD!" yelled Doña Margarita inside the little Stone Church with her eyes closed as she stood tall, here on the left-hand side, two pews back from the front row; palms up, arms spread out. "This I give You, I GIFT YOU, dear GOD, from my LOINS! STRETCH my blood, my flesh, my children . . . to do Your most Holy Work for You here on this *TIERR-RRRA FIRME*! But do not take Your living Holy Breath away from my sons even for one second! This, I will NOT PERMIT!

"STRETCH THEM! We are your instruments of LOVE! To help You with this ongoing Creation of Light into Darkness! Do you HEAR ME! I AM SPEAKING! We are Your INSTRUMENTS, and so use us! USE US, but do not take Your Blessed Breath from Us!"

PULLING INTO CORONA, Salvador didn't find his mother, so he quickly drove over to the church, and coming inside, here he saw his old, wrinkled-up Indian mother standing up at the front of the church, arms open, palms up, and shouting at God! Tears came to his eyes. Oh, his *mama*, his *mama* was just never going to stop helping God 'til her last breath!

AND IN CARLSBAD, Fred Noon was pulling into Kenny White's garage. Kenny immediately told Fred that Salvador had left, taking Lupe to Santa Ana, then to go over to Corona. "If you hurry," said Kenny to Fred, "you can probably get into Corona just about the time Salvador arrives."

Fred thanked Kenny and took off in his big Buick.

THEN HERE CAME the additional guards, boots pounding as they lined up on the tall walls. Seeing this, Max and his group of White prisoners now walked across the yard. Max and his group were laughing, joking, grinning.

And Max was loosening up his huge muscles and opening and closing his mammoth hands. Spotting Domingo, Max figured that Domingo was the man that he'd be doing battle with, and he began to laugh.

"Lookie here," said Max. "They got themselves a White man to do their fighting for them. Don't that beat all! Last year the niggers would have gotten a White guy, too, if they could've found one stupid enough!"

Max and his friends roared with laughter.

Then all of the White guards were set, and the officer in charge nodded to Max. Oh, the tension, the excitement was so great that there wasn't a bladder among all the men that didn't want to burst, feeling halfway between pissing and screwing.

The guards, the warden, they were all very proud of themselves that it had come to this instead of just more random killings. And now it would all be over in just a matter of seconds. This was the real thing! Not a phony fight with boxing gloves! There wasn't a swinging cock in all the yard that wasn't ready to climax—they were all so excited!

Max and his group walked toward the center of the yard, and they were ready. Max signaled for his friends to move away from him, and then there stood Max, all alone. Once he was alone, all the grinning and smiles left his face and suddenly, instantly, he was a raging bull, a mad-dog ready to fight, to kill, to devour his opponent! And his bright blue eyes turned white at the pupils, he was so crazed with rage!

Seeing Max's eyes, Domingo couldn't stand it. He knew damn well that these little twins meant well, but he also knew that they didn't have a chance in Hell! And so, not wanting to end up a slave to these abusive *gringos* for the rest of his life, Domingo now bellowed right back at the big German, screaming like a mad-dog, too, saying, "You're mine, you son-of-a-bitch! I got *TANATES*, TOO!"

And instantly Domingo started for the German, but he never got two steps, for three *Mejicanos* jumped him from behind, knocking him to the ground.

All the Whites started laughing. "Crazy, fucking Mexicans are now beating up on their own champion!"

Domingo kicked and screamed, trying to get loose. But one Mexican had a rope and they quickly hog-tied him and dragged him away. And once Domingo was dragged away, the *gringos* saw the strangest sight they'd ever seen. Why, there were two little Indians, stripped to the waist, looking like no more than kids, and they were hugging each other in the longest *abrazo* they'd ever seen and . . . with so much love.

Then one of them turned, coming toward Max. The big German couldn't figure out what was happening. This was crazy. What did the little dark Indian boy want? Certainly not to fight. But here he came, coming straight toward Max, who was easily three times bigger than him.

The White guards started laughing and so did most of the White prisoners, too. One even yelled, "Watch out, Max; he might try to kiss you to death!"

But Max wasn't laughing. He was confused. With the big one, Domingo, he had known how to fight, but what the hell was he supposed to do with a little Indian kid? Put one hand behind his back to make it fair? But then he bellowed, not giving a flying shit, and decided to just break this little Indian's neck with his bare hands and bring the whole thing to a quick end.

But just as he was about to charge, another strange thing happened. Someone tossed the little Indian a shirt and a little knife.

Seeing the knife, Max burst out laughing. Why, the blade was so small and insignificant, it looked more like a damned letter opener.

Someone rushed forward and handed Max a much bigger knife and a shirt, too. Max took the knife and shirt and watched the little *Indio* wrap the shirt very carefully around his left hand and forearm. Max laughed and threw his own shirt away, not bothering to wrap himself; then he raised up the big knife and came rushing toward Jesus-Maria, ready to cut him to pieces and finish the fight, showing these tricky little greasy bastards once and for all who were the rightfully superior people on the planet and get them back in their place!

But when he slashed at the little *Indio*, he wasn't there. And when he cut and stabbed and slashed and charged again, he was gone each time.

Domingo wasn't resisting anymore against the men who'd dragged him back. No, he was now staring at this battle of battles in absolute silence. Why, this Jesus-Maria was fighting like a priceless little fighting cock of the finest breeding.

And he was so fast, so agile, so smooth and easy, that the big German was missing time and again and getting angrier and angrier. And all the prisoners and guards were glued to the action with their eyes, their hearts, seeing what they'd only dreamed of seeing in their wildest of dreams: gladiators doing battle to the death with no holds barred.

This was every man's secret dream, secret love, secret desire, wondering how he, himself, would do under similar circumstances.

Max was out of breath. He'd had enough of this game of trying to catch the tricky little Mexican, and so he now took up ground in the center of the ring of men and shouted, "Come on, you tricky little bastard, stop and fight like a man! *Un hombre!* You greasy little chickenshit!"

Jesus-Maria stopped and smiled a big, beautiful, calm smile, like this was what he'd been hoping for all along. And at that moment, the Sun, himself, came over the tall eastern wall and bathed the whole courtyard in a pure Golden Light. And Jesus-Maria's sweaty, naked torso now glistened like an Angel, a Messenger sent by Almighty God.

"Okay," said Jesus-Maria, taking up ground, too. "But you come to me, *amigo!*" And he smiled. He didn't hate the German, he really didn't.

"All right, I'll come to you, but no more of this running, dodging shit!"

"No, no more running," said Jesus-Maria, and he stopped smiling. "We'll fight *mano-a-mano,* each one of us holding on to the end of this shirt."

"You got it!" yelled Max, quickly coming forward.

And so Jesus-Maria unwrapped the shirt from around his hand and forearm and, holding on to his end, he tossed out the other end of the long-sleeve shirt to Max.

With eyes full of lust and greed, Max grabbed up the other sleeve of the heavy cotton shirt, never taking his eyes off of Jesus-Maria. Then he suddenly jerked the smaller man toward himself and he slashed out with his large knife, drawing blood.

The crowd went WILD—screaming, yelling, LOVING IT!

This was more like it! This was the REAL THING! No more joking around! This was now the DANCE of DEATH!

Max was in ecstasy! And so with a grin, he rolled his powerful hand over and pulled in another good, big chunk of cloth so he could get himself in closer to Jesus-Maria. What a stupid fool this little Indian was to have tied up with him in hand-to-hand combat. He, Max, was bigger, stronger, had a larger knife, and so now everything was completely to his advantage.

So Max now jerked and pulled and slashed again, drawing blood once more, but the poor little Indian wouldn't let go and run. No, the brave little fool kept holding on, not realizing that he was too far away and his little knife was too small to ever do Max any harm.

Max now let out a screaming shout and came in for the kill. There was no more use in torturing the little fool, thought Max. He'd done the best he could. And he was a game little bastard, like so many Mexicans, but the truth was that no Mexican was ever really a match for a big, strong White man, and they never would be, so to give this little guy any false hopes was cruel.

Slashing and pulling, Max now wrapped the shirt around and around his hand as he pulled the little man in closer and closer, cutting him and cutting him as he brought him in for the kill. And Max was now going to go for the little fool's throat and finish him off, when suddenly the little Mexican did the stupidest thing. He ducked and rushed in on Max, impaling himself on Max's big knife, and then he bent down, locking Max's knife into himself with his own body as he now went to work, slashing at Max's lower body in a quick frenzy.

Max couldn't believe it; he couldn't understand what was happening until suddenly the little Mexican came up with Max's cock and balls and part of his lower stomach in hand, raising them up to the Heavens!

"You will call me MISTER!" screamed Jesus-Maria to all the White prisoners and guards. "You will call me MISTER JESUS-MARIA!" he shouted as he showed Max's balls and cock to all. "For we, too, are HUMAN BEINGS in the Eyes of GOD!"

And the Mexicans took up the chant, screaming, bellowing, "You will call us Mister! You will call us Mister! For we, too, are HUMAN BEINGS *en los Ojos de DIOS!*"

The whole White population then realized that it had been a setup from the start, and they bolted in absolute terror as the Mexicans came racing at them.

Max was still stumbling about, grabbing at the place where his balls and cock had been, not understanding what had happened, and then he fell. . . . Jesus-Maria now pulled Max's big knife out of his own side and drove it into Max's gut as he squirmed about on the ground, shrieking and wallowing in his own blood!

The screaming of the Mexicans grew and grew as they came rushing with knives in hand. Everywhere, Max's friends were running in horror, in absolute horror, and they were getting knocked down and castrated on the spot.

The screams, the screeches were so great, so unexpected, that even the White guards got caught up in the frenzy and were running away, too. Mexicans were everywhere—on the walls, up in the buildings—and they were stripping guards of their weapons and rounding them up.

The other twin, Maria de Jesus, now came up and lay his dying brother down on the ground so he could go gently into the Holy Night.

Then, with tears streaming down his face, he picked up Max's cock and balls in his right hand and, looking identical to his fallen brother, he took up *EL GRITO!*

When the guards and White prisoners saw him coming, they couldn't figure out what was what! Only moments ago, that same little Indian had been bleeding and losing the fight, so how could he now be sound and well, unless he'd risen from the ashes of the dead and he was Jesus Christ, HIMSELF, now coming to get their very Souls?

Domingo was knocking down guard after guard, disarming them! They weren't even fighting back.

They'd lost it; they'd just seen their greatest of all fighters go down like so much nothing!

And the screams of joy, the bellows of absolute *gusto* that came from the *Mejicanos* and Blacks and two Chinese men were deafening!

For their shouts came from the Heart, the Soul, their VERY GUTS, and they echoed across the yard with the POWER of HEAVEN'S THUNDER!

And that was when Domingo looked up and saw the legion of Ten Thousand ANGELS, Singing to them in Unison!

He dropped to his knees before the Hand of God even touched him, and he was Praying!

Yes, he was Praying—he'd seen *la LUZ!*

Part Five

LA VIDA LOCA

8

And so the Gates of Heaven opened wide and a flash flood de
AMOR *came pouring forth out over all the land —*
BURSTING *with* VITALITY!

Early that morning, Salvador and Fred Noon were at the gates of San Quentin, trying to gain entry, but the guards at the guardhouse were giving them a hard time. Finally, they were told to return the following day. Fred Noon and Salvador could feel the tension. Something really big must've happened, but no one was talking.

Early the next day, Salvador and Fred Noon returned. Fred Noon did all the talking and finally they got past the guardhouse and into the visiting room. They could still feel the tension. Everyone was being very careful and extremely courteous. And when Domingo came into the visitors' room, it was written all over his face. He looked like somebody had just given him a million dollars—he couldn't stop grinning.

"Salvador!" said Domingo, taking his younger, shorter brother in his arms, giving him a big, wonderful *abrazo* and kissing him. "So how is *mama* and Luisa? Good, I hope! And how did your honeymoon go, eh, *hermanito*?!" And Domingo hugged Salvador close again. "It's so good to see you!" he added radiantly.

Salvador looked at his brother suspiciously. Domingo never acted like this, unless he was drunk or—then it hit Salvador. His brother must be completely *loco*-happy and out of his mind on *marijuana*. "So our friends were able to get you the good little weed for your medicinal tea, eh?"

"Oh, yes, they were!" said Domingo, still grinning from ear to ear.

"And this is why you're so happy, eh?" continued Salvador, nodding at Domingo with a knowing little look.

"Oh, no!" said Domingo, seeing how his brother was regarding him.

"This isn't why I'm so happy! Haven't you heard?" he added. "Surely, you've read about it in all the newspapers!"

"Read what?"

"The *pinchi* news, *hermanito*!"

"What news?" said Salvador. "Fred Noon has been calling all week, but he can't get anyone to say nothing. So no, I don't know what the hell is going on, Domingo!?"

"Well, I'll be damned!" said Domingo, scratching his head as he swayed back and forth on his feet. "Then I bet that these tricky *gringos* didn't let the news get out. You really don't know, do you?"

Salvador shook his head. "No, damnit! I don't!"

"Why, we've taken over the prison," said Domingo, grinning with joy. "Us, *los Mejicanos*, have taken over the *pinchi* prison."

Salvador was taken aback. "You took over the prison? You, *los Mejicanos*, now run the place?"

"*Orale*! Now you got it! And we've come to terms with the guards and warden and we, too, now don't do no work that the *gringos* don't do!"

"What?" yelled Salvador, absolutely shocked by this last statement. "*Los Mejicanos* now don't do any work that the *gringos* don't do?"

"*Orale!*" said Domingo, full of *gusto*. Then he opened his mouth and shouted, mouth open wide, giving *un grito* here in the visitors' room. "We are ALL now EQUAL!"

Salvador's eyes went huge. He could hardly believe what he'd just heard. "My God!" said Salvador, now understanding the full impact of his brother's words. For he, Salvador, had been in jail enough times in this country to know how things were inside the prisons. Why, this was incredible! This was the most far-reaching news that Salvador had heard since he'd crossed the border coming into this country, more than thirteen years ago! The *gringos* had lost their all-abusive power!

"But Domingo," he said, "how did this miracle come to pass? My God, this is what our mother was praying for! A miracle with ten thousand Angels!"

"She was!" Domingo now yelled. "Well, I saw them! All ten thousand! Tell *mama* that her prayers came true! Oh, Salvador, I tell you," added Domingo with tears coming to his eyes, "it was a visit straight from Heaven! That's exactly what it was, a visit of TEN THOUSAND ANGELS straight from HEAVEN who came to save the day for all the world to SEE!

"You tell *mama* when you see her that I will never, never again doubt her powers as long as I live!" said Domingo. "And you tell her that I will never use the Lord God's name in vain again or tease her anymore when she says that she talks to God, for I saw the Angels that she sent here to us in this prison as well as I see you right now!

"I saw them come down from the Sky and one of them—brighter than the rest—entered into the body of the tiny, little dark *Indio* as he went to do battle with this giant Goliath, just like little King David! I swear it, God as my witness! I saw the Heavens open and smile down upon us, Salvador! God loves us! And He's *pinchi* real *a toda madre*!"

As Domingo spoke, Salvador watched his brother's eyes, and he could see that this brother of his had truly been touched by the Hand of God— just as their beloved *papagrande* Don Pio had been Touched by the Hand of God back in their mountains *de Jalisco*!

And so Salvador now listened to his brother, Domingo, tell this incredible story about these twins from the state of Guanajuato and how one brother gave his life—deliberately impaling himself—so that all of his brothers could live on with respect and equality!

"I saw his soul!" said Domingo. "His *pinchi* SOUL!" Tears were streaming down Domingo's face, but he didn't bother to wipe them. "And the White Enforcer, he saw none of this! He was just so full of hate and rage, like a sickness, that he couldn't see the miracle that was happening before him."

Domingo continued and the story brought tears to Salvador's eyes. Little by little, he was beginning to see why Domingo had used the words "we, *los Mejicanos*, have saved the whole world!"

Yes, indeed, something extraordinary had come to pass.

His hardheaded brother was a changed man! You could see it in his eyes. Domingo's eyes were now all alive with heart and love, compassion and wisdom, qualities he'd never had before.

And the tears that now ran down Domingo's face weren't tears of fear or anger or those of a doped-up *marijuana* user; no, these were the tears of joy, of *gusto*, of—why, they were the tears of *un hombre* who'd finally seen the Light of God! That Light, that Luz their mother had always told them about, that 'til you saw this Light, you weren't even ALIVE!

The tears continued streaming down Domingo's face, and Salvador took his older, bigger brother in his arms, and they held each other in a big *abrazo* for a long, long time.

"So, then, you're okay?" asked Salvador.

"I'm more than okay!" said Domingo with power! "They feed us good three times a day, 'cause we now got a head Mexican cook, and we got a good roof over our head that don't leak. I swear, for the first time in all my life I feel, like, well, I'm alive, Salvador! And the future is good!" he said, pounding his chest. "Here, inside my heart and soul! And you tell *mama* that when I get out, I'm going to find my children that I left scattered to the winds like a dog, and I'm going to make *mi casa*! For now I really do see *con todo mi corazón* that God loves me! He does, and I'm going to be *un hombre de los buenos* from now on! Hell, we're good people, Salvador," he added. "If we can turn a prison around like this, imagine what we could do for this whole *pinchi* country!"

Laughing, Salvador wiped his eyes. "I'll tell *mama*," he said. "And she's going to be so proud of you!"

"Good," said Domingo, "it's about time, damnit!"

And so they hugged again, *corazón-a-corazón,* feeling more love for each other than they'd ever felt before!

DRIVING BACK THAT AFTERNOON, Salvador tried to explain to Fred Noon all that Domingo had told him. But it was difficult, especially the part about the Angels and the Light of God.

Finally, Fred Noon just said, "Stop talking to me in English, Sal. Hell, there's no way a man can talk about *milagros* and angels in English without sounding silly."

"Hey, I think you're right," said Salvador, and so he switched over to Spanish and the whole story instantly became much easier to believe and understand.

Noon had been right, there was really no way a person could talk in English about miracles and angels without sounding, well, kind of phony, or holier-than-thou.

Hearing the whole thing in Spanish, Fred was stunned. "My God," he said, "no wonder they won't let out a peep. Do you realize what this means, Sal? If word ever gets out, there's going to be rioting in every prison across the entire country." He took a big breath. "Mark my words, Salvador, your brother is right, the truth cannot be kept secret for very long. Entire social upheaval is going to start happening everywhere. Like it or not, this country is going to be forced to start living up to its own ideals; of the people, for the people, the land of the free."

And so feeling ten feet tall, Fred Noon and Salvador drank coffee and whiskey the whole way back to Southern California, and they talked and laughed and became even better *amigos*. They, too, were now both rooted in the reality of the Light of God, a Doorway once opened, then All was Possible within the Miraculous Wonders of Creation!

LUPE WAS AT HER PARENTS' HOUSE in Santa Ana. Salvador had dropped her off a few days before, and ever since that time, Lupe had been talking non-stop with her mother, asking her mother all kinds of questions, like how had she, Lupe, been born, and how had her mother felt during the pregnancy.

"Well, tell me, *mama*," said Lupe, "how did you and *papa* get along when you first married?"

"*Mi hijita*," said Doña Guadalupe, "are you trying to tell me that you think you're pregnant already?"

Lupe's whole face flushed.

They were on the front porch, overlooking the street. It was midafternoon. Lupe's brother, Victoriano, and her sister Carlota still hadn't come in from working in the fields. Lupe's father, Don Victor, had gone for his afternoon walk around the neighborhood.

Lupe had been shocked to see how much her parents had aged when Salvador had first dropped her off. Why, her parents had really gotten old in the month and a half that she'd been away. She'd never noticed that her father stooped, looking almost hunchback, and that her mother had all this loose skin hanging below her chin on her neck.

Lupe had almost been embarrassed to look at them at first, for fear that they might read her thoughts.

Taking a deep breath, Lupe nodded. "Yes, *mama*," she said, "I think that I might be pregnant."

The old woman's eyes exploded with excitement, and she looked at her young daughter—this baby of the family—and she was overjoyed with *gusto*. "Oh, *mi hijita, mi hijita*," said the old Yaqui Indian lady, "but why didn't you just tell me when you first got here?"

"Because, well, I don't know . . . but I haven't told anyone yet, not even Salvador," said Lupe. "And why, I don't know, but it's almost like I don't want to share this feeling I have here inside of me with anyone. You're the first person I've told, *mama*," added Lupe.

Doña Guadalupe marveled at her daughter's words. "Oh, this is exactly how I felt with my first pregnancy, too, *mi hijita*."

"Really?" said Lupe.

"Yes, of course," said her mother. "Remember, *querida,* that for us, the women, so much of our life's work is done quietly, almost invisibly. We make love, and from the man's seed life is planted here, inside us, to grow a child like the land grows *maíz.* Truly, *un milagro de Dios*! This is our sacred destiny, *mi hijita,* the knowing how to grow a child here inside of us." Tears came to the old woman's eyes. "I'm so proud of you, *querida.* And when your time approaches, you won't know why, but suddenly you'll be so wise and strong and full of . . . well, you'll even be afraid of spiders and snakes, and you'll want to wash your hands constantly. It's nature telling you that it's time to clean your nest for your coming child.

"We've come full circle, *mi hijita,*" added the old woman, looking at her baby of the family with so much love. "You are now the parent and then—boom, the years will just fly by, and one day you'll awake and you'll be here like me, the grandmother."

Lupe nodded, and for the first time in her life, she truly understood that all Life, *la Vida,* was, indeed, Round and Circular and Complete! Why, only yesterday she'd been the child!

"Yes, *mama,*" she now said, "like you've always said, acorn, plant, growing up so fast, then harvest, and acorn again. Child, parent, grandmother, and child again. It's like, well, *mama,* finally . . . here in my *corazón* all these things that you've been telling me again and again all of my life are now beginning to make sense. Not just here in my mind, but here in my heart, too, and it's like, I suddenly see all these things that I'd never really seen before. And I have this hunger to learn everything I can so I'll be ready to teach my child like you taught me!" Tears came to Lupe's eyes. "Oh, *mama,* the whole entire world looks so different to me now. Teach me. Oh, please, tell me everything. How did you feel during pregnancy? How did *papa* and you build your nest? Was your honeymoon so, well, wonderful that sometimes you began to fear that you were losing your mind?"

Seeing her daughter's excitement, Doña Guadalupe looked at her with a new kind of love, respect, honor, and yes, adoration. Her baby was planting her feet into the rich soil of her female ancestry and starting to grow. And grow she would in the next nine months. "Your words are music to my heart, *mi hijita.* After so many years of struggle, it seems that God is finally taking us back into His arms once more. I loved my every pregnancy," she said, "and especially with you.

"I swear, only in pregnancy," continued the old lady, smoothing out the apron on her lap, "do we, women, know here inside of us that we are the soil to which the Seeds of Creation were entrusted. I remember the first time I got that little feeling that I had life here inside of my body. I swear, I could feel it within the hour. And so I, too, went to my mother, just as you've come to me, and I asked her to tell me everything, and I just couldn't stop talking, either.

"But I want you to know, *mi hijita,*" continued the old woman, "that you have nothing to worry about. You've seen much life, much joy, much heartache, and so in your heart and soul, you already know everything that you'll ever need to know. This is the miracle that was given to women by God as we went out of the Garden, that we, here, instinctively know how to love," she added, patting her chest. "And with love, we, humans, can then gain wisdom very quickly."

"I hope so, *mama,*" said Lupe. "But sometimes I just don't know what's going on inside of me. Like when I realized that something strange was happening to me, here inside, I didn't know what this little tickling was. But then, suddenly, I just knew. Just like that, I knew that—oh, my God, I was pregnant! And I wanted to tell Salvador, because he's been wonderful, *mama,* but I don't know why, I just couldn't bring myself to tell him. And I felt awful that I wasn't telling him, but, well," she said, laughing, "the truth is, that I wanted to come and tell you first, *mama.*"

Hearing this, the old woman took Lupe's hand, stroking it. "*Mi hijita,* I felt the very same way."

"You did?"

"Yes, of course. I didn't tell my husband for weeks. Lupe, the truth is that we, women, sometimes feel like that big black spider that kills her husband and feeds him to her young—that's how possessive we are about this feeling of life we carry here inside of our bodies. And men know this, *mi hijita.* They can feel it, that's why they're always so determined to come between us and our children.

"They become doctors, priests, whatever profession they can invent, but the one time that they can't come between us and our child is when we have our child here, in our womb," she said, smiling a glorious smile. "Oh, I tell you, when I was *embarazada,* I would have killed any man, if he had tried to come between me and this gift. So yes, of course, I went to see *mi mama* first. After all, that's where life had begun for me, too."

"Yes, that's it, *mama!*" shouted Lupe. "That's exactly how I feel! That's why I've come to see you—because my life began with you. And now I need for you to tell me everything, so I'll be able to protect this little soul that's deep inside of me. Because, well, I feel so, so un-unready and—" Tears came to Lupe's eyes. "What if I don't know what to do when my time comes, *mama*? And this pregnancy is so important, *mama*. It's like I'm, I'm—holding the greatest, most precious gift of all the universe and maybe I won't know how to—oh, I'm scared, *mama!*"

Taking a deep breath, the old woman kissed her daughter's hand. "Just close your eyes, *mi hijita*," she said, smiling, "and remember back to those days and nights in our beloved box canyon, and keep in mind how the Moon was full on the night that those twins were born."

Lupe closed her eyes, and her mother took her back in time and retold her the story of the Sun and the Moon and the stars and of . . . of that magic night when the meteorite came shooting across the Heavens and kissed the Mother Earth above their home in the box canyon, setting the white pine forest afire, and how she and Don Victor had made love that night, because they'd thought it was the end of the world.

"But then, to our surprise," said the old woman, "nine months later to the day, you, Lupe were born—just as the Mexican Revolution came into our mountains. And so you are *nuestro* child of the meteorite, the Gift from a Shooting Star.

"And so I don't want you thinking for a moment, *mi hijita*, that your father and I always knew what we were doing, either. No, many times we were as scared and frightened and confused as any young couple. But we had *nuestro amor*," she said. "And with love, *mi hijita*, then two people can always find a way to live. After all, we are children of the stars, planted here on *Tierra Madre* like *el maiz*, to grow and reach up for the Heavens from which we came!"

"Oh, *mama*," said Lupe, "that's so beautiful! But really you mean that you and *papa* were—"

"Yes, that's right," said the old lady, smiling. "Strange as it might seem to you, your father and I were once young and inexperienced, too!"

Lupe started laughing and laughing. Why, this was absolutely true. All of her life she'd never really, really realized—until now—that her parents had once been inexperienced and young, too.

She continued laughing uproariously. She was so glad that she hadn't shared with Salvador these secret feelings. Her mother was absolutely right, these feelings, this miracle of life that she felt down deep inside of her, could only be shared with one's own mother—the person with whom her own life had begun.

Poor men, no matter how much they loved their children or wished to share in a woman's pregnancy, they never really could. Not the way a woman did.

Lupe took a deep breath. She loved Salvador, she truly did, and she would've loved to have told him about their coming child, but no, she just knew that she'd done the right thing to have come to tell her mother first.

Lupe now took her mother in her arms, feeling so close to her. It was like her mother had suddenly become so much younger, and she, herself so much older, and they were now almost the same age—mothers, yes, mothers, both of them, *madres sagradas!*

EARLY THE NEXT AFTERNOON, Salvador was driving down the street lined with tall, green trees to pick up Lupe at her parents' house. Immediately, Lupe came rushing out of the house, telling Salvador that her father was in the hospital.

"What happened?" asked Salvador.

"We don't know," said Lupe, "but we think he maybe had a heart attack! When he went for his walk yesterday, he came back looking pale, then collapsed. Where have you been?" she added anxiously. "You've been gone three days, Salvador! And you said you were just going to see your mother in Corona!"

"You're right, Lupe," he said. "I'm sorry. But, well, I had to make a quick trip up to San Francisco with my attorney Fred Noon."

"To San Francisco?" said Lupe. "You mean way up north?" She was astonished.

He nodded. "Yes, but everything turned out fine. We'll talk later. Right now, just tell me, can we go and see your father?"

"Yes," said Lupe. "He's been asking for you. But first come inside and say hello to my mother, and then we'll drive over."

But even as Lupe spoke, trying to remain calm, her heart was pounding. Why in the world would a fertilizer mover drive all the way to San Francisco? And take an attorney?

Suddenly, Lupe felt like she was looking straight down a long, black gun barrel . . . at something that she'd never allowed herself to really see before. But she held, she swallowed, refusing to think about it anymore right now.

Right now she had to attend to her mother and father. Her *corazón* was going crazy! It felt as if the Devil, himself, had just entered her body. And good God, she was pregnant!

She swallowed again, determined to keep calm.

Going inside, Salvador could see that his mother-in-law was also upset, but she was very glad to see him. "Salvador," she said, "how things get twisted *en la vida.* Here, at last, I thought Don Victor and I were finally going to have a few days of rest and peace, then this happens."

"Yes, these are the twists of life, my mother always says, *señora,*" said Salvador to Doña Guadalupe.

"And how is your mother, good I hope."

"Yes, good," he said.

"As Lupe must've told you, we don't quite know what the situation is with my husband," she said. She was at the stove, cooking. "Are you hungry? I'm preparing a little meal for Carlota and her brother when they get in from work."

"No, thank you, I just ate," said Salvador.

"Good, sit down and have just one little bite, for no one passes through my kitchen without having at least one *bocadito.* Sit."

Salvador wasn't hungry, but he did as he was told, sitting down. And each time Lupe passed by him, he'd secretly try to catch her eye or stroke her leg. And of course, the old woman knew what was going on, so she diverted her eyes, pretending that she didn't notice.

Then, after eating two *tacos,* Salvador and Lupe were finally able to get out the door. At his car, Salvador put his hand to Lupe's butt, rubbing the fullness of her *nalguitas* as he helped her into the Moon automobile.

"Don't!" she snapped. "Please, not 'til we're out of sight! Besides, I'm pregnant," she added angrily.

"You're what?!" he said, completely taken back.

"Pregnant," she snapped again. She was pissed! First, this man had gotten her pregnant, then it seemed to her as if he'd deliberately brought *el Diablo* of doubt and fear home to her, too.

"You mean, you're going to have a—" He swallowed, not being able to say it. He jumped in the car and quickly drove around the block, then pulled over to the side of the road. "Lupe," he now said, "what are you talking about? That we, you and I, are really going to have a baby?!"

"Yes," said Lupe, "we are."

"My God!" he said full of excitement. "But how did it happen?"

"How?" she repeated. "Well, how do you think?"

"No, no, I don't mean how," he said, confused with happiness. "I mean when. When did it happen, or when did you find out?"

"Well, I had a feeling that maybe I was pregnant before you left, but I wasn't sure until my mother and I went to see my sister Sophia's doctor."

Lupe took a deep breath. "But now tell me, Salvador, why did you go all the way up to San Francisco . . . and you, you took an attorney? Why Salvador? I'm pregnant," she added, tears suddenly bursting to her eyes, "and I need to know what is going on!"

Salvador took a deep breath. It was he who now felt like he was looking down the long, black barrel of a gun. "I went to see my brother, Domingo," he said, simply.

Lupe had met Salvador's brother, Domingo, before their wedding at one of Archie's dances. But then, she'd never seen him again. Not even at their wedding. "And why did you take a lawyer?" she asked.

Her heart was pounding. She was sure she was now going to hear that which she'd never wanted to hear. She closed her eyes, instinctively asking *Papito Dios* for help.

"Because, well—" Salvador's heart was now pounding, too. He hated this damn lie that he was living! And now they were going to have a baby. A child. The Miracle of Life, *la Vida.* "Domingo is in prison," he said.

"In prison, your brother?!" said Lupe completely shocked. "But why?"

"Because of liquor."

"Liquor? Oh, then he's the one who's the bootlegger in your family," said Lupe, suddenly looking greatly relieved.

Seeing her reactions, Salvador nodded.

"Oh, then that's why you didn't want to speak about it," she continued. "You didn't want to speak badly about your own brother."

Liking this, Salvador nodded again, giving an open door to the Devil.

"Salvador, you should have trusted me," she said.

"Yes," he said, "I should have." He swallowed. Damnit, he'd really done it once again. He could feel *el Diablo* smiling. "And about the baby, then this is for sure?" he asked, wanting to get the feelings of the Devil away from himself.

"Yes, Salvador," said Lupe. "This is for sure. We are starting our very own *familia!* And you're not a bootlegger!" she added, eyes dancing with merriment.

"Lupe," he said, seeing her trust and love and happiness. "But, also, you should know—" He stopped. He held. He breathed. There was so much that he wanted to tell her, to stop all this damn lying, but he was afraid of losing her. "Lupe," he said again, "I want us to go to see *mi mama*. Come on, let's go. She's going to be so happy for us!"

And he turned and took hold of the steering wheel so they could go, because he damn well knew that his *mama* was the only living person in the whole world he could talk this whole thing over with and get some help before the Devil took over their lives.

"Salvador," said Lupe, smiling, "aren't you forgetting something?"

"What?"

"We were on our way to see my father in the hospital."

"Oh, that's right! I forgot. I'm sorry," he said.

Driving across town to the hospital, Salvador couldn't stop looking at Lupe. Why, she looked even more beautiful than ever before! But oh, deep inside, he felt like such a big damn liar. And of course, *el Diablo* loved it. One of the sons of the old She-Fox had managed to slip away, but this one the Devil had ahold of by his *tanates*!

Deep inside of himself, Salvador could now hear the Devil speaking to him as clearly as he'd heard the voice of *Papito Dios* so many times. And *el Diablo* was saying, "You've really screwed up, you no good, lousy, lying, backstabbing, *cabrón,* son-of-a-bitch, and you're going to ruin everything! And she's going to hate you! And you deserve it, *pendejo!*

"Unless, of course, you just keep on lying and hiding . . . then I'll make it easy for you, and you'll go far," the Devil added. "After all, look around and tell me who are the successful people of the world—certainly not the saints or any of the good-hearted people. No, the really successful people are the tough-hearted, the strong, the clever, all our kind of people, just like you and me, *amigo,* people who have the guts to face reality and do what it takes to get it done, now! *Pronto*! Hell, you and I both know that it took real guts for me to leave the side of the Almighty and go out on my own. I'm *un macho a lo cabrón!* And look, I'm doing GREAT! The future is OURS, I tell you!"

Salvador shook his head, taking a deep breath, he didn't want all this going on inside of his head. And he was just about to tell his mind to knock it off, to stop all this bullshit thinking, when the Devil SCREAMED out inside of his brain!

"GET SERIOUS, *amigo*! All nations are built on lying and greed, and manipulation! You're doing perfect! And I'm here with you to ensure your success! Hell, show me a man or nation that isn't founded on my princi-ples of success and I'll show a failed, hungry land!"

Hearing this, Salvador nodded, seeing that this was absolutely true.

The Devil leaped with joy, feeling so good to have at last gotten a good hold on Salvador.

"Good," said the Devil, "wonderful, just look up into the sky on any given night, *amigo*," continued the Devil, speaking so smoothly inside Salvador's mind that he couldn't help but listen, "and tell me what do you see—more stars or more darkness? Darkness, of course. For the powers of darkness are infinite! And every generation brings more and more people to our side. Lying is just a tool. There's nothing wrong with lying, Salvador, be a man! She's just a woman after all, an afterthought, a thing that had to be created so that man could reproduce. That's all. Nothing more. Remember Eve was Adam's downfall, *amigo*."

At the hospital, they had no record of Don Victor. But finally, after much insistence, they located Lupe's father in a small back room with five other men. All five men were bunched up together like fish in a can. And Don Victor was glad to see them, but he looked awful, with a yellowish tint to his face. They could hear screams coming from another room down the hall. The room smelled terrible. The window was closed, and there was no fresh air.

"I'm so glad that you two could come," said Don Victor, smiling the best he could to Salvador and Lupe.

"Of course, we could come," said Lupe, kissing her father. "How could we not? Are they treating you well, *papa?*"

"Well, what can you expect?" he said. "They got us all packed so close together that we smell each other's farts, and they don't speak Spanish and they don't have *frijoles* or *tortillas*, then they take all the salt away from my food, so how can I be? Weak, of course, and starving for real food instead of all this tasteless, awful mush that they serve us here."

The old man had told the truth, the whole room did, indeed, smell of stale farts and sick, decaying bodies. It was hard just to breathe. Salvador went to the window and tried to open it, but it was stuck.

The screams continued coming from down the hall.

"Salvador," said the old man, seeing his son-in-law's anxiousness, "remember this, as long as you live, never come to any damn hospital unless you're in perfect health! Because if you do, and you're just a little bit weak, they'll be sure to do you in!" And he laughed, trying to be brave, but he just wasn't able to bring it off. His hands were trembling.

Stepping out of the room to catch his breath, Salvador found a chair in the hallway and brought it inside for Lupe. It was a tight squeeze for Salvador to put the chair by Lupe's father's bedside. Sitting down, Lupe took her father's hands and began stroking them. The old man smiled and little by little, his hands finally stopped trembling. The simple act of being touched felt like Heaven to the old man.

The screams continued. Finally, two male nurses came rushing past their door.

"Well, Salvador," continued Don Victor, "I guess it looks like maybe you and I aren't going to go to get that gold up in *La Lluvia* after all. And oh, I tell you, I know exactly where those nuggets are. Damnit, I would have liked to be rich at least once in my life before I died. So rich that all the family would be proud of me!"

"But, *papa*, we're proud of you already," said Lupe, taking his hand to her lips and kissing his fingertips.

"See how she lies to me," said Don Victor, turning back to Salvador. "Proud of me, why? Because I left them. Because I refused to work below my station of a finish carpenter, and so their mother had to work day and night to keep *la familia* together."

"But I'm not lying," insisted Lupe. "We were always proud of you. Every day I went to school and sat in one of those chairs you made, I felt so proud of being your daughter. Every day I looked around at our little home, I'd feel so proud that you'd built it for us with your own two hands."

"But it was a shack of a house," said the old man, "and those little chairs at the school were so coarsely made."

"Yes, our home was made mostly of sticks and mud and our little school chairs were made of coarse wood, but, *papa*, you made all those things with your ax and saw and with your love, from here in your heart. Don't you see, *papa*, all of our life we've already been rich with love *de nuestra familia*."

Seeing his daughter's sincerity, tears burst forth from the old man's eyes. Reaching out, he now took Lupe's two hands with both of his two wrinkled, old, twisted, callous hands, and he now carefully brought her hands to his old, weathered, dark face, trembling as he hugged her two hands to his cheek.

And Salvador watched, and it was so beautiful. Daughter and father and such open real feelings *de amor*.

But *el Diablo* didn't like this one little bit! Because with Salvador seeing all this love and forgiveness crap, then he could start thinking that maybe Lupe could forgive him, too!

Women, and especially good-hearted women with their stupid, ignorant love, had been a thorn up the Devil's ass since the dawn of time!

What he, the Devil, liked was a woman with vanity and arrogance!

Women who were cunning, ambitious, and self-serving!

Women who could bring out the worst in men!

Women who were untrusting, especially of love, and were LUSTFUL!

These BEAUTIES were *el Diablo*'s POWER! Women, who'd bring him the head of a man on a silver platter! Oh, how he hated thoughtful, sincere women!

"You're right, *mi hijita*," Don Victor was saying. "You're absolutely right, but we men just keep forgetting this simple truth of life. Thank you, *mi hijita*, we were rich with love, weren't we?"

"Yes, *papa*, we were, and we still are," she added.

And she was crying and he was crying and together they took each other into their arms. Lupe now rocked her father just as Salvador had rocked his own mother on many nights. Holy. Complete. Full circle. The baby *de la familia* now babying her own parent *con amor*.

The other patients in the tiny back room didn't have any visitors, and they were being affected, too. Love was contagious.

So now it was *el Diablo* who was squirming and getting so upset that he could scream! The Devil rushed down the hall in a fit of anger, and suddenly, a ruckus was heard down the way, then a screaming, a horrible shrieking! But then it all stopped. Just like that. No more shrieking or screaming. All was silent.

Don Victor nodded. "That's the third time that I've heard that since I've been here," he said. "*Te juro,* what I've seen and heard here in this hospital in the last two days, I would have never believed if I hadn't seen it with my own two eyes. They neglect us 'til we start screaming, then . . . oh, oh." He licked his lips. "Money, only money is what gets you respect here in this country. A smile alone from a nurse, I think costs half a day's wages.

"Look, Salvador, you and Victoriano are going to have to make that trip without me. He knows where the gold nuggets are, too. Because I swear, life has so many twists and turns that I'm beginning to think that maybe we would've been better off to have remained in Mexico, instead of coming to this country." He glanced about at the other patients, then pulled himself close to Salvador, whispering, "*Te juro*, I swear to you, they look down their noses at us as if we're nothing but dogs. We need money, Salvador, we need gold! But also don't be stubborn like me, realize that these twists and turns of life don't all have to do with the curves and twists of Lady Luck as men like to think. I swear, if only I'd known then, what I know now, what a difference it could have made for me. My child loved those little chairs I made for the school. I didn't know. My pride made me blind. Truly, the heart is where we really live, Salvador."

Salvador nodded, thinking of how his own father had abandoned them, too. "Yes," he said, "I think you're right. The *corazón* really is where we live."

"Yes, exactly, but I couldn't see that when I was young, that even the twists and turns in life help *el corazón* to grow strong," said Don Victor. "I was so stubborn that, well, I actually thought that it was my duty to control life. What a fool I was! Thinking if only I just had enough money. I swear, the sad truth is that God saves wisdom for our old age, when it's too damn late!"

"That's what my mother always tells me," said Salvador. "God is afraid of us, so that's why He saves our wisest years for last."

The old man laughed. "Why, I'll be, I think your mother is maybe right," said Don Victor, his old eyes lighting up. "God fears us and the Devil tempts us, because with what I know now—I'd be a man of love and patience and not," he added, looking into his daughter's eyes, "a lost old fool."

"But you're not a lost old fool, *papa*," said Lupe, still holding her father's left hand and stroking it gently. "You're a rich man, surrounded with love!"

Hearing this, the Devil came crashing back into the room. If a person died at peace, then he lost them to Heaven. He needed for Don Victor to be full of self-righteous rage and blaming and hating—for these were the ingredients that kept the fires of Hell burning!

But Doña Margarita had also come into the room—having taken on the form of a flower among the flowers that had been delivered to one of the other patients—and she was now set, watching the Devil's every move. She wasn't about to let Lucifer get his way with her loved ones. Oh, she was crouched and ready as a tiger!

"Mi hijita," the old man was saying, "if only I'd known then what I know now, I wouldn't have gotten upset so easily when life tossed me a turn or twist. For instance, maybe I wouldn't have taken it so hard when they didn't have any more carpenter work for me at the mine. Maybe I wouldn't have left . . ." He bit his lower lip. "I would have swallowed my pride and stayed, because . . . oh, I missed you children so much, especially you, Lupe, whom I hardly got to know."

The tears were flowing from his old eyes. "Forgive me, *querida*," he said, taking her hand to his lips and kissing her fingertips once more. "Please, forgive me for abandoning you."

At this point, the Devil stepped forward to put the words of resentment into Lupe's mouth so she wouldn't give forgiveness to her father, but

Doña Margarita was a warrior of the highest order, and so when the Devil stepped forward, she leaped, shoving a long branch of rose thorns up his ass with such power that *el Diablo* jumped aside. Lupe was freed.

"But, *papa*, there's nothing to forgive," said Lupe, wiping the tears from her eyes. "Everything has worked out for the best. You're here with us now, and I love you very, very much."

"Really, *mi hijita*, you forgive me and . . . and you love me?"

"Of course," said Lupe, "with all of my *corazón* I love you and I forgive you and . . . and, well, we have a surprise for you," she added, turning and taking Salvador's right hand. "*Papa,* Salvador and I . . . are going to have a baby."

"A BABY!" shouted the old man with a flood of tears bursting forth from his old eyes! "A baby," he repeated with such joy. "A little baby from my baby! Oh, what a miracle life is! Good God, I'm so happy to have lived to see this Holy Day!"

And Don Victor strained to sit up in bed, so he could take Lupe into his arms. Quickly, Salvador moved forward, helping the old man to upright himself. He could feel that Don Victor's back had become nothing but bones.

"Oh, *mi hijita, mi hijita!*" said the old man, taking his daughter in his arms. And he held her, with his eyes closed for the longest time, breathing deeply, then he opened his redshot eyes—from crying so much—and he saw Salvador looking at them. "Oh, aren't women wonderful? Eh, Salvador, aren't they the true wonder of our lives?" The tears streamed down his face, but he didn't bother to wipe them away. "I love you so much, *mi hijitos*. Both of you so very much." He pulled Lupe in closer to himself as he stretched out an old, wrinkled-up hand to get hold of Salvador, too. "You girls and your mother are the absolute best thing that ever happened to me. Oh, my God, my God, I love you so, so much! And now here you are married and with child. These are the true riches of life, but I just couldn't see them until now that it's almost too late. God forgive me, God forgive every man who's ever abandoned his home!"

"Salvador," he now added, "you are now going to be a father, the one who protects and keeps your home alive and full of love against the ways of the Devil, who's so quick to deceive us men with dreams of glory and—"

But Don Victor wasn't even able to finish his words.

For hearing these jewels of wisdom coming from one who'd been on his way to Hell, the Devil became so enraged that he SCREAMED, kicking the window open and rushing out of the room!

A sweet, delicious breeze of fresh air came into the room, surprising everyone how the old window had just suddenly opened up by itself—a window that obviously hadn't been opened in years.

Salvador breathed in deeply, totally accepting Don Victor's words that yes, he, himself, was now the responsible father of his home.

And outside—much to the Devil's disbelief—here was Doña Margarita still after him. And she now grabbed hold of the Devil by the throat, with such force and conviction of Soul that she half choked him to death before he could escape, howling as he went—up, up, over rooftops and toward Heaven before he realized where he was going, and so he quickly shot back down into his own domain of Eternal Damnation!

Doña Margarita was flying through the clouds, laughing *con carcajadas*!

"Almost got you, eh, *Diablo*!?! I surprised you so much that you almost went to Heaven again, instead of Hell!"

"You son-of-a-bitch—no, DAUGHTER-OF-A-BITCH!" screamed the Devil back at Doña Margarita.

"Oh, come on, why curse me any longer," she calmly said to him. "Admit it, you're in love with me."

"IN LOVE WITH YOU!" screamed *el Diablo*, spitting in disgust at the leaping red-orange flames all about him. "I hate you! Look, what I've done to you and your children, you stupid, ignorant INDIAN WOMAN! I've raped and killed and starved and mutilated your children for hundreds of years! I DID IT! I found ways to get it DONE!"

"Yes, I know," said Doña Margarita with tears coming to her old, wrinkled-up eyes, "and I . . . I forgive you, Don Lucifer."

"But you can't forgive me, I'm the Devil! YOU MUST HATE ME!"

"Hate you?" said Doña Margarita oh, so softly. "But how can I hate you? For you, too, once came from God. Come, my poor, lost Child of Darkness and let me hold you, and hug you, and mother you with Love. You must be so tired and weary with all the bad, evil deeds you do. Come, let me mother you."

"NOOOOOOOOOOO! *VIEJA CONDENADA*!" screamed the Devil. "You will not trick me again! Oh, I pray to God for the day all you ignorant, backward *Indios sin razón* are finally killed off the face of the earth, so I can then be free at last to do as I damn well please in the name of progress and greed and—stop it! STOP BLOWING ME KISSES, you imbecile! Jesus, I hate you!"

The Devil stopped dead in his tracks. Suddenly, realizing that he'd just used the Sacred Name of "Jesus" and before that . . . he'd, well, actually prayed to God . . . and so *el Diablo* now slapped himself across the mouth, and took off for the depths of Hell, hoping to find some peace at last!

And Doña Margarita was left here with clouds all about her and tears running down her face. For truly, she could see that her Love was finally beginning to get to the Devil, himself.

She made the sign of the cross over herself, thanking *Papito*.

And God smiled.

LEAVING THE HOSPITAL, Salvador and Lupe drove back across town to get her things from her parents' house, so that they could then drive over to Corona to see Salvador's mother and tell her the news of their baby. Carlota and Victoriano, who'd just come in from working in the fields, were both eating at the kitchen table like young, starving wolves!

"Hello," said Salvador, smiling happily. "So how does it go?"

"Hot as always for those of us who work for a living!" said Carlota.

"Mi hijita!" said Doña Guadalupe.

"Oh, don't *'mi hijita'* me," snapped Carlota angrily. "Victoriano and I work hard while the princess, here, and her no-good, fish-poisoning husband do nothing all day long!"

"Fish poisoning?" said the old lady, surprised by this remark.

"Yes, I told you, *mama,* Salvador tried to poison me with a fish when we went to dinner to Long Beach and he talked Chinese, hiding the truth of his actions from us."

"Oh, Carlota," said Lupe. "But how can you talk like this? You ate no fish, and we who did, didn't get poisoned."

"See!" yelled Carlota. "That's how tricky the Chinese are! But I knew, I knew, that's why I was smart enough not to eat any fish!"

No one knew what to say. Carlota's logic was one of a kind.

"Excuse me," said Victoriano to Salvador, "but I need to know if you've seen *Señor* Whitehead lately?"

Mr. Whitehead was a local farmer for whom Victoriano had been working for several months now.

"No," said Salvador, "in fact, I haven't seen him for quite a while."

Originally, Salvador had introduced Victoriano to Mr. Whitehead, months before he and Lupe had gotten married. Whitehead was a drinking man that Salvador had met years ago through the Moreno brothers from Corona. For more than ten years, Whitehead had been one of the top foremen for old man Irvine, but then a few years back, he'd bought some property and started farming on his own. He'd planted an orchard of oranges and started growing tomatoes, cucumbers, string beans and other vegetables.

Whitehead was a good man. Anyone who'd ever worked for him had nothing but the highest respect for *el hombre.* Whitehead paid all of his workers on time, and he never tried to cheat them on their hours, as did so many of the other farmers in the area—including old man Irvine.

And Irvine was one of the largest and richest landholders in all the area. His place stretched from the sea of Newport to the mountains of the Trabuco Canyon on the back side of Orange County. Originally, Irvine's place had been a Spanish land grant, just as the O'Neil place and the huge Santa Margarita *Rancho* had also been Spanish land grants.

"Why do you ask?" asked Salvador.

"Because Whitehead is gone," said Victoriano. "No one has seen him in days. And his wife is worried, not knowing if he's . . . well, last year she said that he got himself a few bottles and tried drinking himself to death, when he lost that crop of oranges."

"Yes, I remember that," said Salvador, thinking back. "And there wasn't a freeze or anything to kill those orange blossoms. Strange. Very Strange."

"Exactly," said Victoriano, "and this afternoon his wife asked me to go and find him for her. Poor woman, she told me last time they found him in a hotel room out by Long Beach on 17th Street, and he was just about dead. Could you help me, Salvador? My little truck isn't running very well. I think I loaded my *troquecito* a little too much too many times."

"Of course, Whitehead is a good man," said Salvador, taking a deep breath. "But what happened? Did he lose another crop?"

"Yes, his string beans, and now . . . they're going to lose everything, his wife said."

"String beans!?!" said Salvador. "But tell me, how in the hell can a man lose string beans? *Ejotes* are tough, especially in our climate here, they always manage to live! Damn, what bad luck!"

Salvador kissed Lupe good-bye, and he then followed Victoriano out the door.

"Good riddance!" yelled Carlota as Salvador and Victoriano went out the door.

"Carlota!" said their mother in a stern voice. "You will do the dishes for being so disrespectful!"

"No, make her do them! She's not working! I'm too tired!"

"But not too tired to insult a guest under our roof!"

"But he's no guest anymore! The no-good is her husband now!"

"Start washing! Now!"

"Oh, I could kill with this frying pan!"

"Salvador," said Victoriano once they had gotten away from the house, "his wife also told me that he took his gun."

"His gun?" said Salvador, opening the door to his Moon. "But what would Whitehead do with a gun? He's one of the nicest, easiest-going *gringos* you'll ever meet."

"Yes," said Victoriano, "but the rumors in the *barrio* are . . . that, well, old man Irvine poisoned his crops."

"No!" yelled Salvador. He also knew old man Irvine very well. And Irvine could be tough, but this was beyond words!

"Yes, they say that old man Irvine's still so mad that one of his best foremen quit working for him and went out on his own, that he actually got the county sprayers to poison Whitehead's crops when they did their seasonal spraying for insects."

"I'll be damn," said Salvador. "But how did you find out?"

"Because, Salvador," said Victoriano, "one of the men who actually did the spraying is *Mejicano,* and he talked, saying that he had no idea what they were doing at the time."

"Then you think Whitehead took the gun to kill Irvine?"

"No, Salvador, *Señor* Whitehead is one of these good guy *gringos de todo corazón* who doesn't believe that the Devil lives inside people's souls, even if he saw him eye to eye, staring him in the face."

Salvador nodded, and they got into the Moon and took off. Salvador knew exactly what his brother-in-law was talking about. It just seemed like some *gringos* were so good-hearted that they couldn't believe the simple fact that the Devil lived Here on Earth as sure as the Sun came up and the Sun went down.

"Well, then tell me," said Salvador, "why would Whitehead take a gun with him if he isn't going to kill Irvine?"

"To kill himself," said Victoriano.

"WHAT!" screamed Salvador, almost driving off the side of the road, this surprised him so much! "But no man ever thinks of killing himself!"

"Among the *gringos* they do," said Victoriano, making the sign of the cross over himself. "His wife is going crazy. They've lost everything."

"So what! Most of us live our whole life with having nothing!"

Victoriano laughed. "Yes, us, the Mexicans. But among the *gringos*, Salvador, most of their lives they've always had something, so nothing is something that they know nothing about."

"Well, okay, but to kill yourself over nothing, it just makes no sense."

Victoriano nodded. "I agree."

"My God, my God," said Salvador. "Then you mean, that this poor crazy fool is really suffering over maybe ending up with nothing?"

Victoriano nodded again. "Exactly."

"But still," said Salvador, "how can he think that killing himself is the answer? Shit!" yelled Salvador, hitting the steering wheel and the muscles of his neck coming up like thick cords. "Hell, I'd kill Irvine in a second, then burn his house down, and drag his body through the streets behind my car for all to see, having *gusto a lo macho cabrón*, before it would ever even enter my mind to kill myself!"

"But of course," said Victoriano, laughing, "you're un *Indio sin razón*, not a good-hearted *gringo!*"

Hearing this, Salvador burst out laughing! Oh, life, *la vida*, really was so full of wild contradictions. Hell, he'd actually started thinking that only *los Mejicanos* had any *problemas!* Why, the poor *gringos* were all caught up in the struggles of living, too!

Nearing Long Beach, Victoriano spotted Whitehead's truck parked in front of a little hotel.

Salvador and Victoriano came bursting in on Whitehead, just as the tall, handsome man in his early forties, was putting the long, black barrel of the .38 Special to his mouth.

Victoriano screamed, and the .38 Special EXPLODED!

Hundreds of birds took flight from the inlet of water behind the little hotel that came in with the tide from the beautiful green sea!

9

---

*The Devil was tired, really exhausted, but still he was a long
way from giving up. One way or another, he was determined
to slip past that old She-Fox . . . but then he heard the
Singing of the Stones!*

I T   W A S   D A R K by the time Salvador and Lupe got to Corona, but Salvador's mother wasn't at her house, so they could tell her about the baby. Luisa told them that she was probably still at church, but when Salvador and Lupe drove over to the church, made of river rocks, they found the place already closed up. Then they spotted one of Doña Margarita's old church friends and the old woman told them that she'd gone off with the young priest a few hours ago.

"Do you know where they went?" asked Salvador.

"No," said the old lady, "but I did hear that your mother found a purse full of money inside the church."

"Really," said Salvador.

"Yes, a lot of money!" said the old woman.

Salvador thanked the old lady and he and Lupe drove back to Luisa's house. Inside, Luisa was feeding her boys.

"Weren't you able to find her?" asked Luisa.

"No," said Salvador. "They told us that she drove off with a young priest hours ago. That she found a purse with lots of money inside the church."

Salvador was all upset. He really wanted to tell his *mama* about the baby, before Lupe and he had to go back to Carlsbad.

"But why in God's name are you worried, Salvador," said Luisa to her brother in her loud, happy, vociferous way, "our mother is too old to get pregnant, so what harm can it be that she's out late with a priest, having fun with all that money she found."

Saying this, Luisa burst out laughing and laughing, truly enjoying herself. But Lupe wasn't laughing, she was shocked for a woman to talk like this, and especially in front of her own children.

Seeing Lupe's shocked look, Salvador yelled at his sister. "Luisa, damnit, do you always have to talk so wild?"

"Wild, how? That I'm realistic enough to admit that priests are human and have fun, or that our mother is capable of—"

"Luisa, shut up!"

"No! Not in my house! Now, sit down and eat and have a drink so you'll calm down! Our mother is fine. She'll be back in no time."

"Luisa!" said Salvador, turning his eyes at Lupe.

"Ah, bullshit!" said Luisa. "Stop hiding from Lupe. She's no fool! She knows that—well, you and I have a drink now and then. Don't you, Lupe?"

"Yes," said Lupe. "Especially since I found that bottle, Salvador," she added.

"See!" said Luisa. "I told you so!"

And so Luisa poured herself and Salvador a drink from a bottle that she kept under the sink and she offered Lupe a drink, too. Lupe declined, saying no, thank you, and she watched Salvador and his sister have their drink. Also, Lupe was beginning to notice that every few minutes a different man would come by with an empty jar and Luisa would take the jar to the back of the house, then meet the man outside. Lupe wondered if maybe Salvador's sister Luisa, like Domingo, was in the bootlegging business, too, and she was selling jars of whiskey out of her home.

But no, Lupe didn't dare ask this question. Besides, it was no business of hers what people did in the privacy of their own home.

It was nearly midnight when the young priest drove up with Doña Margarita in a Model T. Lupe had long ago gone to bed in the living room where Salvador's two older nephews, Jose and Pedro, normally slept. Benjamin, the baby, slept in Luisa's bed.

Ever since Lupe had lain down, Luisa and Salvador had begun drinking and talking wild. And now it was Luisa who was worried about their mother's whereabouts and Salvador was the one trying to calm her down. All her life Lupe had seen how alcohol changed people so much. She prayed to God that this type of behavior wasn't Salvador's normal way of life. Luisa was acting like a crazy woman.

"*Mama*," yelled Luisa, running to the front door when the priest drove away, "where have you been? It's almost MIDNIGHT!"

"*Calmate, mi hijita,*" said the old Indian woman coming into the house, "I've been out doing God's work. And look what I brought you. The rich don't live like you and me. No, they have the softest, smoothest, best-feeling ass-wiping paper I have ever felt! And their toilets are so comfortable that any king would feel honored to make his daily calling!"

"You and that priest bought toilet paper with all that money you found in church?" asked Luisa, looking at her mother suspiciously. "Oh, my God, I'm scared to even ask what you and the young priest were doing all this time."

"Then don't ask," said Doña Margarita, laughing happily.

"But *mama*," said Salvador, "where have you been? Lupe and I have been waiting for you so we can—"

"Are you HUNGRY, *mama?*" yelled Luisa, cutting in. "I saved you some dinner!"

"Of course, I'm hungry! Doing God's work while He sits on His behind up in Heaven, relaxing like the lazy male He is, is tough some days! You know," continued Doña Margarita, sitting down to eat, "after wiping myself with this fine paper, I got to thinking why so many of us *Mejicanos* don't know how to read so well. Hell, we've been putting the printed word to the wrong end of our body for so long, that the words now all look backward to us when we put them to our eyes to read!"

Saying this, the old lady burst out laughing with such *gusto* that Lupe—in the next room, lying down—now knew where this whole family got their loud voices and blasphemous attitude. Why, if Lupe didn't know better, she'd think that Salvador's mother was a wild Indian. How could any sane person accuse God of sitting on His lazy—oh, she couldn't even have the thought inside of her head, it was so awful!

Now they were all talking at the same time, Salvador, Luisa, and Doña Margarita—when Salvador finally yelled the loudest of all! "WE'RE GOING TO HAVE A BABY!"

The whole room suddenly went silent. Not another sound. Then Doña Margarita was the first to speak.

"A baby?" she asked, oh, so softly.

"Yes, a baby," said Salvador full of excitement.

"A baby from my baby," said the old woman. "Oh, Lord God, thank You! *Gracias!* My prayers have been answered! And where is Lupe? Where is this wonderful woman full of the Holy Grace of God!"

"In the next room sleeping," said Luisa.

"Let's go and peek in on her. Sssssssh!" added Doña Margarita.

Lupe could now hear them sneaking into the room, trying to be quiet. But Salvador and Luisa were drunk and bumping into things, snapping at each other, and making so much noise that Lupe was having a hard time not laughing.

She closed her eyes, pretending to be asleep. They came into the room smelling of whiskey—just as her father had smelled when he'd come home drunk.

"Just look at her, Salvador," said his mother in a soft voice, "she's an angel! My God, no prettier woman has ever lived!"

"Well, yeah, sure," said Luisa, "and we, too, would all be better looking if it wasn't for you, *mama*."

"Well, I did the best I could," said their mother. "I married a very handsome man."

"Sssssh," said Salvador. "You two will wake her!"

"Wake her, HELL!" said Luisa. "She's out like a fart amid the sounds of thunder!"

"Sssssh! Both of you shut up! *Callense!*" said Doña Margarita.

They were now all tiptoeing back out of the room, bumping into things. Salvador hit the wall, face first, almost fell, and his sister, Luisa, had to help him out.

With one eye open, Lupe watched and Doña Margarita stopped at the door before closing it, and she watched the old lady make the sign of the cross over herself. "Dear Lord God," Lupe heard her mother-in-love say softly, "Holy Be Your Name, please give this young mother peace of mind so her heart can then keep calm, feeding this child in her Sacred Womb the Holy Rhythms of Your Eternal Love!"

Lupe now watched the old woman make the sign of the cross once again, touching the center of her forehead this time, then kiss her fingertips and blow Lupe a kiss. "From our family to Your Most Holy *Familia*," she said, "as it is in Heaven, it is Here on Earth, too.

"And don't worry, *Papito*, I might be getting a little deaf and illmannered in my old age, but *mi familia* and I are still strong, and so You and Your Loved Ones can continue depending on Us to Do Your Earthly Work.

"And about Your lazy behind, God, well, I was just a little tired and hungry, so don't You get too upset. We're doing Good, You and I, God, We're doing Good. So Good Night, *Maria, Papito, y Todos los Santos!* And help Lupe sleep the sleep of an angel so that then her milk will be as sweet as honey!"

And saying this, the old woman made the sign of the cross over herself even once again, then closed the door softly.

And Lupe watched.

Lupe watched, and she could now see that this old woman truly spoke to God as if they were best friends.

Lupe wiped the tears from her eyes. This, too, she wanted for herself—God as her best friend, especially now with a child growing inside her womb. Suddenly she felt like she could feel a little movement inside of herself. But it was so faint that she thought that maybe she was just imagining it. Or maybe not. A miracle was growing inside her.

EARLIER THAT AFTERNOON, Doña Margarita had been praying at the little stone church when two well-dressed Anglo women walked in. But Doña Margarita had given them no importance for she well knew that her struggles with *el Diablo* were a long ways from over and so she continued to pray aloud with all her heart and soul.

". . . yes, *Maria,*" she was saying, "I fully realize Your Most Holy Husband God came through for me with Ten Thousand Angels to save the immortal soul of my son Domingo who's in prison, and You, Yourself, assisted me so I could be at the hospital to get hold of *el Diablo* by his long weasel tail, but You and I both know that *nuestra* struggle is far from over here upon this *Tierra Madre.* For now my son Salvador—even while he's on his journey of milk and honey—is still being pursued by *el Diablo.*

"And this, I will not tolerate! Do you hear me, *Maria!*" she said, standing up. "Because You and I both know that marriage is difficult enough without the Devil coming to us on our honeymoon when our hearts are open and we are most vulnerable. So You and I, woman-to-woman, have to come up with an even greater plan than last time and turn this whole situation around!"

Then Doña Margarita stopped her praying, figuring that she was maybe getting a little too heavy-handed with Heaven, especially since They kept coming through for her, and so she decided to ease off and tell Our Great Lady, *Madre de Jesus,* a joke, because she well knew how *Maria* always liked getting the latest jokes to take up to Heaven to share with Her Two Husbands, Saint Joseph and God.

"And this one, My Dear Lady," began Doña Margarita, speaking a little more calmly, "is about Don Cacahuate, Mr. Peanuts, and how he came home after being gone for a year. And upon entering his house, he threw down a *peso* on the table."

"One *peso*?!?" yelled his wife, Doña Cacahuate. "After being gone for a year?!?"

"And if I'd been gone a million years," shouted Don Cacahuate, standing up as tall as the little man could, "it would be a million *pesos!*"

Saying this, Doña Margarita burst out laughing and laughing. That's when she noticed that the two Anglo women, who were across the aisle from her on the right side of the church—the side the Anglos used—gave her a dirty look and got up, going out the side door.

Doña Margarita shrugged and just kept talking to the Virgin Mary.

"Don't You get it, my Lady," asked Doña Margarita to the statue of the Mother of God who wasn't laughing, "we, *los Mejicanos* have so much faith in the eternal goodness of life, that we now all think that we're on our way to being millionaires; see, it's only a matter of time!"

"Oh," said *Maria*, and now She was laughing, too.

"I tell You, my Lady, every day we, *Mejicanos,* awake and we're breathing, we think we're in the great danger of getting rich because—down deep inside, we are either crazy-*locos*, or You and Your two Husbands have, indeed, Blessed us with an indestructible faith!

"And now that we're talking about faith," continued Doña Margarita, truly enjoying how she'd brought the whole conversation back around to where she'd really been wanting to go all along, "I want to talk to you a little bit, about revisiting the deal that us mortals have with You up in Heaven. Because you see, the way I've been thinking lately, faith, *la fe*, goes two ways. And so it's not enough for us here on Earth to have faith in You up in Heaven, but the time has come for You People up Here, to also have faith in us. Not just us to You, eh?'"

Hearing this, the stone statue of the Virgin Mary burst out laughing with such force that the rocks of the stone walls that surrounded the sacred statue now began vibrating with the laughter of Holy Mother, too. Stone to Stone! Making Holy Music.

This was when two well-dressed Anglo ladies came in with Father Ryan in tow. Father Ryan had been eating and he was still chewing his food and wiping his mouth with his napkin.

Seeing that it was Doña Margarita at her regular pew up near the front on the left-hand side of the church, he almost laughed, but didn't. After all, he and Doña Margarita were very good friends. It was she who'd gotten her son to deliver whiskey to him and other priests. Also, he'd been the one who'd married Salvador and Lupe. Father Ryan now coughed his best priestly cough, straightened up, and signaled for the two women to stay behind while he handled this situation.

"*Buena tardes*," said Father Ryan in Spanish, coming up to Doña Margarita. She was still laughing.

"You should have been here a few minutes ago," said the old, wrinkled-up woman to the tall, well-dressed man. "Earlier today the Devil and I had one of our best! But in the end I grabbed him with such force, that in his confusion, he almost went back up to Heaven, he was taken by such surprise! Then I came to church to visit with the Blessed Mother and I told her a joke that got her laughing so hard you could feel the walls of the church singing with joy!"

Father Ryan laughed. "So you're still busy doing the work of the Lord, are you?" he said in perfect Spanish.

"Of course," said Doña Margarita. "Is there any other work worth doing?"

"*Señora*," Father Ryan now said, "I need to speak with you."

"Good," said Doña Margarita in a very pensive voice, "because I need to speak to you, too. You see, Father, lately, I've found the Devil to be very weary, so I've begun to send him my love."

"You've been sending the Devil your love?" asked the priest, taken aback.

"Of course, Father, after all, he was God's Greatest Angel at one time."

"Yes, *señora*, but to love the Devil—"

"Oh, no, I never said that I love the Devil, Father. I said that I send him love, and of course, I send him this love through Our Savior Jesus Christ. You see, it's time for God and the Devil to make up. I mean, how does God expect us to get along with one another here on Earth, if He's still angry with the Devil."

The priest nodded. In the last few years, he and Doña Margarita had spoken in depth about many religious issues. He found it so refreshing how her mind worked.

"You see, Father, lately I've been telling *Maria* that it's not enough for us to have faith in Heaven anymore. That the time has come for Heaven to start having faith in us, too!"

"And what has *Maria* said about this?"

"Well, at first She just laughed, humoring me, but then as I continued and She got the full impact of what I was saying, that a day doesn't pass by that Lucifer doesn't find himself feeling lonely and lost since he was driven out of Heaven, She has started to agree with me."

"Very interesting," said Father Ryan, "but I hope you realize that it wasn't God who drove Lucifer from Heaven. It was the Devil's own doings."

Doña Margarita laughed. "Yes, but who condemned him to Hell for all eternity? God is pretty famous for His wrath, you know."

"Well, yes, but—oh, I—"

The priest would've continued talking, he was so interested in this conversation, but then he suddenly remembered the two women who were still waiting for him to get rid of this old lady. He glanced in their direction again. They were looking quite antsy.

"Look at it this way," said Doña Margarita, "today when I was praying with the Virgin Mary, I closed my eyes and placed my two hands here on my Heart and I prayed for the salvation of *el Diablo* through the power of Jesus, and I could just feel it here, deep within myself, that the Devil's separation from *Dios* is only temporary. For a great sense of peace and love swelled up within me. God is Love, Father. His wrath is only our own childish misunderstanding of the past," she added with her eyes closed in concentration.

"Then you really do think that the time has come for the Devil to return home to God?" asked Father Ryan.

"Absolutely, Father!" she said, opening her eyes. "When I close my eyes, I then see with my Heart-Eye and I just know that all Life is Round and Whole and Circular; Sacred, in fact, and so the further and further we think that Lucifer is traveling away from God, the closer and closer is he, in Truth, coming around back to *Papito Dios* once again! Earth was never flat, Father."

"Is this, then, the Second Coming that you are talking about, *señora?*"

She smiled a great big smile. "Father, that's for you and the Pope to say. Not me. I'm just a mother and a grandmother who has a lot at stake here on Earth. Don't you just feel it Here, Father, inside of your bones, that the Love of God is forever Circling about all of us in sheer abundance! Eh, haven't you ever broken a bone and felt every little change in weather? Bones are instruments of feeling, especially broken bones. It was no accident that they drove those nails in Our Lord God Savior's wrists. Broken wrists are one of our highest levels of feeling."

"But how do you know this," asked the priest, "that the nails were driven through Jesus's wrists and not his hands?"

Doña Margarita looked at the priest as if something was wrong with him. "His mother told me," she said.

"His mother, Mary, told you?"

"Yes, of course, Father."

The priest was staring at Doña Margarita as if he'd never really seen her before. "And all this happened today when you were speaking to the Virgin Mary?" asked the priest, glancing once more in the direction of the two women who were still waiting for him to remove the old Indian woman.

Doña Margarita turned and saw the women, too. "Look," she said, "I've been talking with Our Sacred Lady *Maria* for years. She's very well-connected up in Heaven, you know, and so it's easy for Her to find out anything I want to know. Are you all right, Father," she added, leaning in a little closer to him.

He glanced in the direction of the two women once again. He could see that they were upset. "Excuse me," he said to Doña Margarita, "but well, how would you like to do me the honor of joining me for a drink at the back of the church, so we can get deeper into this matter. This is very interesting!"

"Of course," said Doña Margarita, licking her lips. "But only a short drink. I don't like walking home drunk with that new little dog down the street. That *cabrón*," she added laughing, "bit me last time I went home after drinking a few with you."

"I'll have our young priest drive you home today," he said.

"Then let's drink!" she said. "And I'll lay out the whole *enchilada* for you! Besides, I've always found that one or two good belts after tangling with *el Diablo*, feels pretty damn good!"

With his best priestly smile, Father Ryan nodded to the two well-dressed women as he escorted Doña Margarita down the aisle and into the rectory.

FATHER RYAN AND DOÑA MARGARITA had had quite a few drinks when they first heard the knocking on the door. The young priest was shocked to find Father Ryan laughing uproariously and hugging the old Indian lady.

"I've come to drive you home," he said.

Before leaving, Doña Margarita asked the young priest to help her put Father Ryan to bed. The young priest was outraged that Father Ryan was so drunk, but Doña Margarita just ignored his outrage, and helped the older priest lay down in his bed. Then she slipped off his shoes, massaging the soles of his feet, making sure that the deep crevices of his male mind were opened up to his own female powers. For only in opening up to our own opposite sexual being could single people balance themselves and begin to make use of their full Thirteen Senses.

Vigorously, Doña Margarita massaged the inner part of Father Ryan's big left toe. Soon she could see that he was moaning, letting go, then traveling through the Tenth Sense back to Heaven as he Dreamed. Visiting Heaven as she slept was what had saved Doña Margarita from losing her mind during those awful days of the Revolution. To sleep with an open mind was to bring the Powers of the Almighty into one's Heart and Soul.

Going down the front steps of the church, was when Doña Margarita saw the billfold bulging full of money on the bottom step. Picking it up, she turned, and the look that she saw on the young priest's face shocked her. Why, he was looking at her as if he thought she was going to steal the billfold.

She forgave him, then she remembered the two well-dressed women that Father Ryan had been concerned about in the church.

"Come!" she said, taking charge. "For this is a sign straight from God, giving us the opportunity to do greatness!"

The home—that the young priest drove Doña Margarita to—was all the way over in Santa Ana. It was a huge, imposing farmhouse with a row of towering eucalyptus trees leading up the driveway. The woman who answered the door was the younger of the two women whom Doña Margarita had seen at the church.

"Yes," said the woman. She was a slender, pretty Anglo in her late twenties. She was shocked to see the little Indian woman at her door. "Can I help you?"

"No," said Doña Margarita, "you cannot help me. How can you? I come with God so I need no mortal's help! Here is your billfold that you dropped in church. And yes, all the money is here, but since I can see that you are looking upon me with great distrust, then by all means count the money. For all Doubting Thomases have a difficult road to maneuver inside the dark crevices of their small, frightened minds."

"Who is it?" yelled an older woman's voice from inside.

"Doña Margarita *a su ordenes!*" shouted the short, dark, skinny, little, half-drunk Indian woman. "At your service with daily miracles! Who's sick and dying! I can smell their stink from here!" she added, sniffing.

Understanding Spanish, the young woman was outraged to hear Doña Margarita speak like this of her uncle, and then she was even more shocked to now have the little Indian woman walk right past her into their home, smelling the air like a bloodhound.

And here was old man Irvine, himself, the most powerful landowner in all California, propped up with a dozen pillows in a bed in the middle of the living room. This was his sister and his niece who'd come by to see him. For weeks he'd been sick, but the doctors couldn't find anything wrong with him.

Doña Margarita walked right up to him and said, "You stink of death! You need to be bathed in herbs and put on a specific diet. I don't know what you did, but you have poisoned yourself severely."

"Who are you?" asked the old man.

"She's the one who was laughing and shouting in church," said his niece.

"Yes, even God gets bored and needs a little entertaining now and then," said Doña Margarita, laughing and doing a quick little shuffle.

Just then, Irvine's sister walked in and when she saw Doña Margarita dancing and laughing as she'd been doing in church, her whole face exploded with rage! But before she could calm down enough to speak, the young priest walked through the door.

Catching herself, Irvine's sister said, "What is going on? Who brought this woman here?"

"She returned your billfold, mother," said the daughter.

"Yes," said the young priest. "I brought her. Doña Margarita is, well, a personal friend of Father Ryan's and—" He stopped his words. He was totally embarrassed.

The older woman looked like she was going to shit—she was so upset! But old man Irvine was smiling, enjoying the whole mess. Chaos was his forte.

"Are you *una doctora*?" he asked in Spanish. "*Una curandera?*"

All the Irvines spoke quite a lot of Spanish.

"Yes," said Doña Margarita, "I am."

"Do you think you can help me?" asked the old man.

"Really?" said his sister. "You aren't seriously going to pay attention to this . . . this dirty, little Indian, are you?"

Refusing to take insult, Doña Margarita simply said, "Dirty I may be, but little with the Spirit of God, I am not! Do you have some whiskey?" she added.

"How dare you! Liquor is illegal!" said Irvine's sister.

"Oh, pipe down," said the old man, "and get me my bottle."

"It's for your feet and back," said Doña Margarita, smelling of him, "to rub on you. All this *caca*-shit is stuck inside of you and poisoning you. I can smell it. You stink very bad," she added, laughing. "No decent, or even indecent woman would want to sleep with you."

Irvine started laughing, too.

When the bottle came, Doña Margarita took it, shot down a good-size swig, said it was very good, then she began to massage his feet with the whiskey, working vigorously between the toes and the ball of each foot.

At first it hurt old man Irvine, and he asked her to please stop, but she just squeezed the inside part of his big toe all the more, sending a lightning bolt through his whole body. "Quiet!" she said. "And take it like a woman!"

Little by little the release points below all five toes began to hurt less and less, then soon he began purring like a kitten—it felt so good!

"Oh, now this is wonderful!" he said.

"Yes, because, you see, the five toes are the entrance into our Holy Being. Our five toes, five fingers, five limbs—the head, two legs, two arms—is Our Sacred Human Key of five for getting us into Harmony of the rhythm of this *planeta*."

"I have absolutely no idea what you are talking about," he said.

"Of course you don't. You're an ignorant, old man who's just used to giving orders. Power doesn't equal knowledge, any more than muscle equals strength. Balance is key to the real power of body, mind and soul. And mind, you have, but very little soul, so you've ruined your balance of body like a fool. But you're beginning to feel pretty good now that I've worked on you, eh?" she said, taking another swig of whiskey.

"Can I have a swig, too?" he asked Doña Margarita, not really understanding much of what she'd said.

"Sure," she said in English.

"But the doctors have all told you not to—"

"Ah, pipe down!" he told his sister. "They haven't done beans for me!"

"Beans?" said Doña Margarita. "Oh, yes, *frijoles de la olla* with a little clay added will be *muy* good! You're weak! You need to have—"

"A young woman!" he said.

"No, a goat," she said.

"A goat?" said he.

"Yes, goat's milk," said she.

"Oh, okay," said he, "goat's milk and whiskey sounds pretty damn good after all the expensive crap that these damn doctors have been giving me."

"And a hot bath to make you sweet," she said.

"Sweet!" he said. "Like candy, make me sweet?"

"No, sweet," said Doña Margarita.

"Oh, sweat! *Sudar!* Oh, yeah, to get my stink out!"

"Yes," said she, "get your stinking *caca*-shit out!"

By the time Doña Margarita got to his back, old man Irvine was feeling no pain. And she wasn't either, taking a swig now and then as she worked his body, massaging him with her hands, her elbows, her fists, her feet, like a strong, little, wiry monkey, crawling all over a hard rock.

She had the young priest and Irvine's niece get eucalyptus leaves from trees in the driveway and boil them with salt and tomatoes and clay from the creek. Then she put the whole mess into the tub for old man Irvine to soak.

Then when they were alone, Doña Margarita explained to Irvine, in no uncertain terms, that the reason that the doctors hadn't found anything wrong with him was because nothing was physically wrong with him. And American doctors, she explained, only knew how to heal the body like a mechanic fixing a car, and so they knew nothing of how to get into the heart and soul.

"And you, you stinking old man, are sick in your heart and soul," she said to him, "because you did something very bad, and now it's coming back to get you. You see, the Devil is tired, so he doesn't wait for us to die anymore to get us down into Hell for our misdeeds. No, he now lets us have our own personal Hell here while we're still on this *Tierra Madre*. And you, you're so rich and stubborn and used to having your own way, that now you have the Devil's horn up your ass, eh?" She laughed. "You're *muy burro*—stubborn, so your head doesn't let your *corazón* know you are sick in your soul. This is why you feel that you're choking."

"It's true," he said. "I have been feeling a choking pain in my chest."

"Of course, smart people who only listen to their head are the biggest *pendejos* of all, and you know what I'm talking about, because you are very *pendejo-estupido* when it comes to the matters of the heart, eh, *cabrón*!"

"I'll be damned," said old man Irvine, smiling, "I haven't had someone insult me so much in years. And you do it with such *gusto*!"

"*Gusto* your ass!" said Doña Margarita, laughing. "Don't you start getting all excited on me, *viejo condenado!* You listen to me, you did something very bad, eh, so terrible that you are poisoning yourself. The Devil is just waiting to take you to eternal damnation if you don't wake up. So

don't be getting excited on me just because I've given your feet a little pleasure!"

And saying this, Doña Margarita stopped laughing and looked straight
into his eyes, and when he started to look away, she grabbed him by the
face and held him eye to eye.

Looking at her, eye to eye, he finally breathed, then he breathed again.
Then he reached up and gently took both of her hands in his. "You're
right," he said, becoming serious for the first time, "you're absolutely
right. I did something that even surprised me. But it's done," he said, "it's
done. So I can't do anything about it now."

Soothing his hands like a mother does with a child, Doña Margarita
said, "I see, I see, you can't do anything, because it's done. But I ask you,
does the Spring say to the Summer, 'Look, I did it, it's done, so I can't do
anything now.' Does the Summer say to the Fall, 'Look, I did it, it's done,
so I can't do anything about it now! Does the Fall say to the Winter, 'Look,
I did it, it's done, so I can't do anything about it.'

"No, the Spring, the Summer, the Fall, the Winter, all know that Life, *la
Vida,* is Circular, Sacred and Never Ending, and so what goes around comes
back around, so when you poison your neighbor, you poison yourself."

Suddenly, old man Irvine went pale. "But how did you know!?!"

"What? That the seasons of the year go around and around, working
together like the five fingers of the hand?"

"No, about the poisoning—you know, of my neighbor?"

"Oh, that? Everyone knows that."

"They do?"

"Sure, we can smell it. You stink of poison. And people don't normally
poison themselves."

"I see," he said. "I see. Then it's that easy for you Mexican people to see
these kinds of things?"

"Sure, back home in the mountains, we didn't have telephones, but still
we knew how to call long distance. We'd put our two hands over our heart
and send our feelings to the person that we wished to talk to. The heart
knows no distance when we go through God. How could there be? God is
everywhere, and so are we when we're God-Connected. And now you're
old and dying, no doubt about it. You stink of death."

"My God!" he said. "Do you call these your bedside manners?"

"God, yes," she said, "manners no. Because unless you're willing to
open up and talk to *Dios,* you're one dead, smelly, old duck!" she added,
laughing with *gusto.* "And you know it!"

He started laughing, too.

"Good, laughter is the first step toward getting sickness unstuck from a closed-up body like yours. Then the next step is that you face up to what you did, admit it, then ask for God to please forgive you. This is what freewill is all about, us choosing to be in good Graces with the Almighty. Sickness is no accident ever since we left the Garden, *viejo.* And sickness never starts as an ailment of the physical. No, sickness starts as a disharmony of the Soul that then goes on for so long that finally even the body succumbs to it."

His eyes went large and he held, looking off into the distance, to a "place" where he rarely went, then he nodded and nodded again, and his eyes began to water as he lay in the tub full of hot water, boiled eucalyptus leaves, tomatoes, salt, and clay.

"You're not a bad man," she continued in a soft, soothing voice. "No one is born bad. It just happens that we pick up a lot of fears in passing through this rugged, hard terrain of this Life as we journey back Home to *Dios.* You are a good *hombre*, a very good old man, you just need to rest a little, trust a little, or all these riches and power you have will come to *nada, nada,* nothing. Now rest, and close your eyes, and know that *Papito* loves you very much."

"Really, even after all that I've done?" he said.

"Yes, even after all that you've done."

"I've done terrible things to your people, too," he said.

"Yes, I know," she said. "Many of their Souls are Here in this room right now. In fact, the elders of the tribe that you ran off their Sacred Lands are here, in full dress, visiting from the Other Side."

"You can see souls?" he asked.

"Of course, and speak with them, too."

"How is that possible?"

"Can you hear the radio, and doesn't the radio come from a great distance? It's the same thing. Back at one time, we were all like cats and dogs who can hear and smell what humans can't hear and smell. We could see and hear the Spirit World. All of our senses were intact."

"These souls, they've come to see me suffer and die, haven't they?" he said.

"No, they've come to pray that you might finally see the Light," she said.

"Really?" he said.

"Yes, really," she answered him. "There's no greed or revengeful feelings on the Other Side, unless those are the seeds you planted here. You see, Here IS Everywhere once you give up the Ghost. The Devil and God aren't far away, living in Hell and Heaven. Both live Here, within us, that's why it's our daily task to meet *el Diablo* head on, face to face and do battle with him—not with fear or hate—but with the *gusto* of Living! Life, oh, what a Joy!

"You are not a bad man, only a man who's resisting the Light. You see, Here could be no Light without Darkness, Sound without Silence, Life without Death, God without Devil—for All is Round, Complete, and Whole." She kissed him on the forehead. "You are a good man, a very good man, and now the time has come for you to Balance yourself in Love."

He was crying like a baby. He, this man, who was so used to being all hard and mean and completely in charge.

"It's okay," she said, holding his head and massaging his back. "It's okay. Show me a rich man, and every time I'll show you a man whose fear is that of never having enough tit. Show me a powerful man, and I'll show you a boy frightened to death of his *tanates* being too small. Show me—eh, this bottle has only a little left, so let's drink it, okay?"

"Help yourself."

"Oh, yes, that I always do!"

And so she stopped massaging him with the whiskey and finished off the bottle, giving a loud burp.

"How much do I owe you?" he asked.

"How can you pay me," she said back to him. "Money and I have no interest in each other, and money is all you have and drove you to your present sickness."

He nodded, and she could see that she'd hurt his feelings. "Look, you want to pay me," she said, "then pay me by giving me some of your toilet paper that you have here. This is the softest, best-feeling ass-wiper I've ever felt, and I'll think of you every time I—"

The laughter that burst forth from the old man was so huge, so full of *gusto,* that everyone came running to see what was the commotion!

The young priest had to almost carry Doña Margarita to the car, she was so tipsy and tired, and yet happy. Big Happy!

THE STARS WERE OUT by the million in Corona. It was way past midnight. Lying down in the front room, Lupe could hear Salvador and

Luisa visiting with their mother. They were such a different family from hers. It shocked her how they treated each other, yelling so much.

"But *mama,* Luisa has a point," Salvador was saying with *gusto,* "if you're so close to God, then why is it that you're so ugly?"

"UGLY, ME?" yelled the old woman, laughing so loud that it even startled Lupe in the next room. "Why, *mi hijito,* don't you know?" she shouted. "I am the STANDARD from which all beauty is measured! If it wasn't for me, there'd be no beautiful people! Why, coming down the street what do people say—and sometimes even aloud—'look at that dirty, ugly, little, old woman.' But in truth, they are saying, 'hey, I look pretty good and young compared to her.' I make their day! I put a smile on their face! Why, the rich, arrogant, beautiful people of this world would all be lost without me! I am the BASIS of all BEAUTY!"

Salvador and Luisa were laughing *con carcajadas.* Their old mother could just never get rattled. In her world, she was as Complete and Round and Whole as Creation.

Doña Margarita finished eating. Luisa's boys were asleep with blankets on the floor. "Okay, I'm tired," said the old woman. Walk me home, Salvador, I need to go to sleep. I had a long day doing God's Work today."

"Yes, *mama,*" said Salvador.

"Good night, Luisa," said the old woman, "and may you all sleep with the angels. Ah, just look at your boys, Luisa, they are such good, handsome boys. God bless them."

Luisa and her mother hugged and kissed, then Salvador walked their mother out the back door and to the outhouse, where he relieved himself under the avocado tree while his old *mama* went inside the little outbuilding.

The air was crisp and cool and the Stars were blinking close and bright; smiling.

Finishing, Salvador buttoned up his pants and went inside of his mother's little shack, lit the kerosene lantern, and started up the little, wood-burning stove to get the chill out of the air.

"You must be so happy," said Doña Margarita, walking inside of the little shack.

"I am," said Salvador. "I love Lupe so much and now we're with child. Would you like a cup of *yerba buena* to warm you, *mama?*" She nodded, going to her bed. It was really cold. "*Mama,*" continued Salvador, "I'm in trouble."

"How is that?"

"Well, I'm still lying to Lupe about what it is that I do for a living."

"I see," said the old woman, getting under the covers to get warm. "And this worries you, eh?"

"Well, yes, of course, *mama*."

"Why," she said chuckling, "aren't you man enough to be a good liar?"

"Well, yes, I guess so, but *mama,* I don't want to just keep lying to Lupe forever."

"Why not?"

"Well, because—oh, *mama,* we're married now and I'd like to be truthful. Besides, sooner or later she's bound to find out the truth."

The old woman burst out laughing. "Isn't this the truth! Lying doesn't really bother most people, it's the fear of being found out that really troubles most souls!"

He turned all red. "*Mama,*" he said, "but must you always be so blunt?"

"And why not," she said. "I don't fear life or death, God or Devil, and I'm too old to start pretending now! Hell, at this age even my own *pedo*-farts sometimes slip out without me being conscious of them. So no, I will not worry about what comes out of my mouth!

"So you've been lying to Lupe, eh, lying about everything you do, and now it's not your conscience, but your fear of being exposed that is putting all these well-placed lies—that you built your marriage on—in jeopardy? Oh, I tell you, I feel sorry for the poor Devil with so many people starting to out-devil the Devil!"

"But what in God's name are you saying, *mama,* it was you who suggested for me to lie to Lupe about my liquor making in the first place!"

"And did I put a gun to your head, eh, forcing you to follow my suggestion? Oh, no, you did as I suggested because it fit into your way of thinking. Don't try out-deviling me with the Devil, for I know *el Diablo*'s evil ways as well as I know the ways of God!

"But I do have compassion for you, *mi hijito,*" she added, "just as I am now beginning to feel compassion for the Devil, too."

"Compassion for the Devil, *mama,* even after all the killing and evil that was done to our *familia?*"

"*Mi hijito,*" said the old woman, "you should have been with me at this poor, rich man's home."

"What house?"

"Where I took the wallet full of money to a grand looking house just south of Santa Ana with a long lane of eucalyptus trees."

"That's the Irvine place," said Salvador.

"Errr-eevin who?" said Doña Margarita. "I don't know. I never asked the old man his name, but he was all poisoned inside."

"Deserves him damn right!" snapped Salvador, leaping to his feet. "He poisoned the crops of Whitehead, a fine man who's worked for him for years!"

"*Mi hijito,*" said the older woman, making the sign of the cross over herself, "I've told you a thousand times that it is not for us to judge or to blame. Each person is his own world, and each world must find their own light, like any other Star in the Heavens."

"But Whitehead tried to shoot himself with a gun because of what Irvine did to him, *mama!*"

"And this Errr-eevin tried to kill himself with poison," she said. "Be compassionate, *mi hijito,* these poor lost *gringos* are a very self-hating people. I tell you, this Errr-eevin smelled worse than a week-old, dead skunk when I arrived. But then I massaged his feet and bathed him in herbs, giving him a little pleasure, and the old goat got all excited on me!"

"Excited on you, *mama!*"

Doña Margarita laughed *con carcajadas*! "Are you saying this, *mi hijito,* because you are morally outraged for me, or do you say this because you find it impossible for a man to get aroused for me?"

Salvador didn't know what to say.

Doña Margarita continued laughing. "Oh, what little you have seen. You still see me with eyes of child. Your old *mama* is a very sexy old woman! Why, today alone, Father Ryan himself was hugging and kissing me all he could until I had to stop him!"

"*Mama!*" said Salvador.

"Oh, stop it, and grow up! How do you think I got your father to marry me? How do you think I was able to wrestle him away from all the other girls of my village who were all crazy-*locas* about this tall, handsome, red-headed stranger! Why, I moved my eyes like this, walked with perfect posture, so that my cute little behind would then sway back and forth with such—"

"*Mama,* please!" yelled Salvador.

"—advertising that here moved the hottest little *nalgas de salsa* in the world!" She laughed. "Your father's tongue was hanging out three feet by the time we got married, and did we get to work making love! Oh, it was beautiful for the first fifteen years of our marriage, two, three, four, five, six times a day! But then, came that bad, awful winter and all the highlands turned white with snow and wolves came down in packs—you know the rest of the story well. He lost faith in God and life, and then even in *nuestro . . . amor.*"

She wiped the tears from her eyes. "I loved your father so much. So very much," she said. "But don't worry, this old Eeeervin and I did nothing yet. I just showed him a little love and understanding and the old fool's tool got aroused. Why, it even surprised him," she said, laughing. "I don't think he'd experienced a good big, hard one in years," she added. "These *gringos,* they seem to know so much about money and power, but then they are so lost when it comes to finding peace here in the heart." She breathed. "I could see it in his eyes; why, he'd done something that even the Devil, himself, hadn't thought of doing."

She made the sign of the cross over herself. "Forgive Eeeervin, dear Father, for he doesn't know what he does. And forgive the Devil, too, he's feeling lonely and wants to return Home to You, *Papito.*"

"*Mama*, you are really confusing me!" shouted Salvador. "You mean that the Devil now wants to return to Heaven and be with God?"

"And why not? Don't we all, including this old Eeeervin?"

"Well, yes, I guess so, *mama*," said Salvador.

"*Mi hijito,* now that you and Lupe are about to have a baby, you must understand that you can no longer live separated from God. You must give your lives over completely to the Holy Spirit of Creation or you will always be suffering Here, in your Hearts and Souls."

"And how do we do this, *mama?*"

"You do it with every Holy Breath you and Lupe now breathe in and you breathe out," she said, making the sign of the cross over herself and kissing her fingertips. "God is the Light, you are the Message. God is the Sea, you are the Wave. God is the Thought, you are the Doing. God is the very Atmosphere you breathe in and out."

Salvador said *nada, nada,* nothing. He just sat looking at his mother.

"And don't worry, *mi hijito,*" added the old woman, "you don't need to understand what I've just said. You are right on schedule, especially with you not wanting to lie to Lupe anymore. Because, listen closely, lies and love don't make good companions for very long. By the way, I told this old Eeee-rrrvin that I'd be sending you over with a few goats."

"Goats?" said Salvador.

"Yes, milk goats, *mi hijito.* And you can get these milk goats from the Morenos over in Moreno Valley, but now no more of this, I need to get some sleep. Oh, I tell you, doing God's Work can get very tiring, especially when He sits up Here in Heaven on—"

"—on His lazy Ass?"

In a flash, the old woman was out of bed and in her son's face. "You will never speak of *Papito Dios* like that again!" she said angrily. "I, who have been in His service for seventy-six years now, having completed thousands of Miracles, only said this about *Nuestro Señor* in jest 'cause We're old *Amigos,* He and I! But you, who still has so much to learn, will speak of Our Heavenly Father only in deepest respect, or I swear, your children will pay for your actions for thirteen generations!

"Do you understand me, the Forces of Creation are to be respected and honored, and this includes the Devil, too, who of his own freewill volunteered to come into this *Tierra Firme* to give us choice between Light and Darkness!"

"Okay, *mama,* okay, I didn't mean to—"

Just then, the front door burst open and the smell of fresh flowers filled the room. Going to the door, Salvador found a bunch of freshly cut red roses tied with a red bow, but glancing about, he saw no one. He picked up the flowers and brought them inside.

"I found these roses, *mama,*" said Salvador, coming back to her. "But no one was there."

"Just put them in some water," said Doña Margarita, getting back in bed under the covers and pulling them up over herself. "I'll see you in the morning. Good night, *mi hijito.*"

"But who would bring you roses, *mama,* this late at night?"

"An old admirer," said the old woman. "Don't worry about it. We'll talk *mañana.* Besides, I'm too old to get pregnant," she added, with a little, happy giggle.

Salvador did as he was told. And the roses were, indeed, the most beautiful he'd ever seen, and so aromatic!

DOWN THE CANYON from Corona some twenty miles away at Lake Elsinore, Epitacio, Luisa's husband, who took care of Salvador's distillery for him, awoke with a start. He'd heard something right outside the window. And it was probably just a cat once again, but oh, all these months of working the distillery had finally gotten to his nerves.

He was sweating.

Rubbing his hand across his forehead, Epitacio felt the sweat pouring down his face.

The fire of the stove, on which they did the distilling process, gave an eerie glow to the room where Epitacio slept on a mattress on the floor, watching the stove day and night.

He got up to go to the bathroom. That's when he saw all these huge eyes staring at him!

He screamed, and he continued screaming! Ever since Domingo had gotten arrested up in Watts and he'd been sent to the penitentiary, Epitacio kept having this recurring dream of the sheriff's department suddenly rushing in with axes in hand and breaking everything . . . huge uniformed giants with yellow eyes, looking more like a pack of wolves than humans, ripping him to pieces with their teeth!

Epitacio ran out of the house still screaming, leaving the front door wide open! *Coyotes* howled in the distance. Epitacio kept running. Overhead, the Father Sky was full of stars. It was a glorious, wondrous night!

"CAN'T YOU SLEEP, *mi hijito,*" said Doña Margarita, waking up and seeing her son Salvador sipping a cup of coffee there alongside the little wood-burning stove.

"No, I can't," said Salvador, shaking his head. He looked very pensive.

"You love her very much, eh?"

"Yes," he said, nodding. "Very much. And I've been thinking about what you said."

"About what?"

"Well, about your new compassion for the Devil. My God, *mama,* we starved coming north through the Revolution. I saw my brothers and sisters—" Tears came to his eyes. "How can you find compassion for all evil that we've been through, *mama*?"

The old woman breathed deeply. "Listen closely, *mi hijito,* if we don't find compassion and love with the twists and turns of life, then we only end up poisoning ourselves with hate and bitterness. What did our Lord Savior do on the cross, He forgave even his tormentors."

"But *mama,* you can't compare us to Christ!"

"And why not? Shouldn't we strive for the finest that Our Lord God has sent to us here on Earth to witness? Look, you love Lupe very much, right?"

"Yes," said Salvador.

"And it's been good between you two, eh?"

"It's been Heaven, *mama.*"

"Good. Good. And now you're afraid to tell her the truth about your business dealings, because you fear it will ruin the love that you and she now have?"

He nodded again. "Yes."

The old woman breathed. "*Mi hijito,*" she said, sitting up, "there are lies and there are lies, and the truth is that all people lie—especially the people who protest so loudly to never lie. And so lies are not what destroy a home. It is the lie about love that embitters a woman's heart. And about your love for Lupe you have never lied, *mi hijito.*"

"Oh, no, *mama*, about my love I've been completely truthful," said Salvador. "That's why I don't feel good about lying to her anymore."

The old She-Fox reached out for her son's hand. "Good, *mi hijito,*" she said, "this makes perfect sense. For you and Lupe have now passed through the needle's eye of truelove and have entered into the Light of God." She breathed. "You have planted your first Sacred Seed of the Thirteen Senses, *mi hijito,*" she added with *gusto*. "You are now on your way to giving root to all our God-Gifted Senses and learning how to make your own Miracles Here on Earth."

"I hope so," he said.

"Trust me, you are," she said, smiling. "And this Love you now have is so intoxicating, that you and Lupe are now slipping, sliding into that Sacred Place of God's Song, the Heartbeat of the Universe, from where all young couples find the wisdom to build their own World."

She stopped. She breathed. She could see it in her son's eyes that he was now finally beginning to comprehend what *Amor* was truly all about—a Human becoming a Spiritual Being.

"Look," she added, "who do you think was with you running at your side the day you ran after the train back in Mexico? You were only ten years old, and yet you ran without water or food, barefooted through the desert heat further than any grown man could ever hope to run."

Tears came to Salvador's eyes. "I was so scared that I'd lost you, *mama*, and I'd never see you again, so I chased the train."

"Yes, exactly, fear pushed you from behind, *mi hijito;* but also, see," she said, closing her eyes in concentration, "love was pulling you, too. These are our Two Great Forces on this *Tierra Firme*: Love and Fear."

His eyes lit up. "Yes, I can see that now. I was so scared of losing you, *mama*! And . . . and you are my Love, my Everything! I didn't want to lose you! So I ran! And ran!"

"Further than any human being can run, you ran! Further than any man on horseback can run, you ran! Further than the Sun held in the sky, you ran! Non-stop, well over a hundred and fifty kilometers, you ran! And you were prepared to keep running forever, for you had Fear and you had Love—in Balance—and when we have Fear and Love in Balance, then we are of the Complete Power of God!"

Salvador's eyes shot so huge—he didn't know what to think, then Here he held, not making another sound.

"And what do you have pushing you and pulling you once again?" she asked.

"Oh, *mama, mama, mama,*" were the sounds to finally come from his mouth, "I have Fear pushing me once more, and Love pulling me. Oh, my God! MY GOD! I hadn't seen it before, *mama.*"

"But now you do," she said.

"Yes, now I do. Both are needed, *mama*! This is our Power, when both Love and Fear are in Balance within us! Oh, *mama,* all of Life makes so much more sense for the first time!"

"Exactly, for you can now see that Here, there can be no Light without Darkness, no Sound without Silence, no Good without Evil, and no God without Devil. English is a very interesting languaging that shows us this more readily than any other languaging I know. Tell me, what is 'live' spelled backward in English? Yes, that's right, e-v-i-l, and what's 'lived' spelled backward; that's right, d-e-v-i-l."

"Then the Devil is just God going backwards?" asked Salvador.

She nodded. "Yes, Here, there are no accidents, *mi hijito,*" she said. "But drop 'the' before Devil. We don't use 'the' before God, do we? 'The' is a treacherous word. None of our Native languaging has it that I know of. In fact, I'm beginning to find out that only European-based linguistics use this 'the' form. The rest of the whole world is free from this illusion, see?"

But she could see that he didn't see. "It's okay that you don't under-stand at this time, *mi hijito.* The only thing you need to comprehend is this, can you now see why it was so foolish for your father, poor man," she added, making the sign of the cross over herself, "to ever think that God had abandoned us when we'd lost everything back in Mexico during the Revolution?"

"Well, yes, because if we understand Balance," he said, "then we see that bad times are needed for good times just like darkness is necessary for having light, so then God can never abandon us. The Devil, I mean 'Devil' is just a part of God."

"Exactly!" she said with *gusto.* "And how does it feel to know this, eh?"

"Wonderful!" he said. "I feel free!"

"Yes, exactly! And look at this word 'wonderful' that you just used. It originally meant being full-of-wonder, and being full-of-wonder IS this Sacred Place of Freedom from where we ARE all Miracle Makers. You see, *mi hijito,* it's only been six to seven thousand years, that as a whole, we humans languaged ourselves out of being Daily Miracle Makers with *Papito.*"

"And that's when the Bible says we ate of the Forbidden Fruit?"

"Exactly," she said. "Before that God was no mystery, but instead our Best *Amigo.* It's no accident, *mi hijito,* that we lost our Full Senses and were reduced to five. As it is, the Sense of Feeling has been under attack for nearly four thousand years. If humans could ever be reduced to just sight, smell, taste, and hearing, then we'd be perfectly obedient machines to do whatever the state wished us to do, including the killing of women and babies—for we'd have no feelings. And without feelings, we'd then have no compassion."

She closed her eyes in concentration. "It's no accident, *mi hijito,* that the Sense of Balance wasn't recorded in Europe and the Sense of Intuition was taken away from women."

"Oh, *mama,* I see it all so clearly now! Only with five senses do we then live in fear of Devil!"

She smiled. "You got it. In fact, Father Ryan told me that it wasn't until the Thirteen Hundreds with the Black Plague in Europe that 'hell' was made into the concept that it is today and *'el'* Devil became so terrifying. Before that, 'hell' and 'devil' weren't all horrible and mean, but more like pranksters.

"Imagine whole towns were put to fire with human bodies piled ten high. The Thirteen Hundreds were a Living Hell on Earth. And the Jews, because of their clean, kosher cooking, didn't get the plague, so they were hated more than ever. Understand, the unknown puts terror into the hearts of people who aren't using all of their senses. And how can it not, it takes all of our God-Given Senses to face the 'unknown' with the Vision *de Papito.*"

"But *mama,* why didn't you tell me all this before?"

"Were you ready to listen?"

Salvador took a deep breath, then shrugged.

"Let's not play the constipated fool. *Mi hijito,* you are very headstrong! Wasn't it me, eh, who first saw Lupe, but you didn't want to hear anything about it, so you had to go and meet her somewhere else? And you had no idea that she was the one that God and I had already picked out for you?

"Here are no accidents in Life, *la Vida, mi hijito,* but the constipated *pendejadas* that we refuse to learn in any other way!"

"Oh, *mama,* you are tough!"

"Thank you," she said with a little bow. "And now that you and Lupe have passed through that first needle's eye and reached this Sacred Place where all couples Dance the Wild Steps of Heaven, you have no more *problemas, mi hijito.* Now all you have to do is open your eyes and 'see' with Eyes of Creation, and understand then all *problemas* are already solved." She breathed. "And why is this true, because, simply, All of Life is already Perfect, *mi hijito.* Tell me, who does Lupe trust and pray to, eh?"

"Well, God, of course."

"And through which organization does she do this?"

"Well, through the Catholic Church."

"And on Whom is the Catholic Church founded?"

"On Christ, the Son of God."

"And what was Jesus Christ's first miracle?"

Salvador shrugged.

"Come on, it was His Mother who asked Him to do it."

"Oh," said Salvador, his eyes suddenly opening wide. "He turned water into wine, *mama.*"

"Yes, exactly. Jesus Christ, the Son of God, turned water into wine, and not just ordinary wine, but the best of wines!"

"Yes, *mama,* the best," said Salvador.

"Yes, *mi hijito,* and who do you know that's a member of the Catholic Church, who says that your whiskey is the best?"

"Why, Father Ryan, of course, *mama,*" said Salvador, suddenly so full of *gusto* that he leaped up! "He thinks my whiskey is the best he's had since he left Ireland! Oh, *mama,* I see it now! I see it! I'll just take Lupe to see Father Ryan, and have him explain everything to her, because with him, she will have trust!"

"Exactly!" said the old woman. "For what is happening Here, at this Holy Moment, isn't that you are lying to Lupe; no, you are educating her. You are exposing her to the world you know, and little by little with patience—take that damn grin off your face immediately!

"Don't you dare think that I am saying that it is for a man to teach his wife! For believe-you-me, *mi hijito,* the lessons you are going to learn from Lupe, will, in the end, make pale what you have taught her! Thirteen Sacred Seeds you two will plant in the first three years of your marriage—whether you like it or not—and the ones she will put down deep into the soil of your marriage will dwarf yours! For remember men come into a marriage with only six senses, and women come with seven! And the Seventh of Intuition is from which Balance grows WINGS, leaping us into the Arms of Creation, gifting us the Eighth, Ninth, Tenth—all Thirteen! Do you understand?" she added.

"Yes, *mama*, I understand, you've told me this a thousand times, the Female is the basis of all Life, but why—why do you get so angry?"

"Because, *mi hijito,*" she said with tears suddenly bursting from her old, wrinkled-up, lizard-looking eyes, "this is good-bye. This is good-bye for us. The life that you and I have known together . . . is done, gone, completed, and now it is for you and your young wife to leave our Garden of Eden, eat from your own Tree of Knowledge, and go out into your own World. The story of Creation never finished with the Jews of old, but is ongoing, right now, Here, forever. Adam and Eve ARE YOU!"

Tears were streaming down her face. "*Te amo con todo mi corazón, mi hijito.* You are a good son, a fine man. You are everything I ever hoped for you to be when I took my oath to raise you up like a woman. In you is the future of *nuestra gente.* For you are the sculpture, the painting, the symphony that I worked so hard to Create, *con el FAVOR de DIOS!* And you are Perfect, my Love. Perfect with all your faults and contradictions. In fact, these I love best, your imperfections.

"You lied to Lupe," she said, suddenly laughing, "just like a typical man, and now you're worried! Oh, I can hardly wait to see how you two will work this out!

"I love you, *mi hijito,* and I will always be with you, Here, inside," she said, tapping his chest, "in your Heart, beating like a great drum just like when you were within my womb and you could hear my Heart beat, beat, beating, pounding *con amor*—you, my Love, will hear me—ALWAYS!"

She started laughing once again.

"But what's so funny, *mama*?"

"That luckily the whole world is still all a big beautiful mess and it's your beautiful mess to deal with, and not mine!"

"You find this funny!"

"Oh, this!" she said. "Hilarious, in fact!"

And she was laughing *con carcajadas*. "But!" she said. "DON'T you EVER blame Lupe when *Papito Dios* comes asking you why you ate of the Forbidden Fruit! For you are *un Mejicano* who was raised by *UNA INDIA DE LAS BUENAS!* And *Mejicanos,* God forgive them, have many faults, but believe me, stool-pigeons THEY ARE NOT!

"And so when the time comes that you meet God, face to face, you will say, with your *tanates* in hand, 'I DID IT, GOD! I take FULL RESPON-SIBILITY!' And you will not blame the woman you love! Or it will not be Devil or God who comes looking for you, IT WILL BE ME! Your MOTHER, the *GARRRR-AAA-PATA* up your SPIRITUAL ASSHOLE for all ETERNITY!"

Salvador was laughing and crying, both at the same time!

"I promise you, *mama,* I promise you, I will not blame Lupe when *Papito Dios* comes asking."

"Good! Because—oh, that story alone shows me, that not only was the Bible—as we know it—written by men, but by weak, scared men, too! For no man with *tanates* blames his Love like Adam did to poor *Eva*!"

Crying and laughing, Salvador took his old mother into his arms. "Oh, I love you, *mama*! I love you so, so, so much!" he said.

"Of course, I was the first pair of tits you sucked!"

"Oh, you are awful, *mama*!" he said, laughing.

The Stars were Dancing!

The Stars above were Singing, Dancing, Rejoicing—GOD'S SMILE!

IT WAS DAYBREAK when Epitacio came running to the house in Corona. He was dropping dead on his feet. He'd run the whole way from Lake Elsinore. And he wasn't a young man anymore. He was a fat, middle-aged man who'd just run the run of his life!

"I CAN'T DO IT ANYMORE!" he was screaming to Luisa. "Salvador will have to do it himself!"

"Epitacio!" Luisa was trying to tell him, "Lupe is here! Lupe is here!"

But the frightened little man just couldn't shut up. This was when Salvador came rushing in, gun in hand.

"What the hell's the commotion?" he yelled.

"I can't do it anymore!" screamed Epitacio. "They killed my two older brothers right in front of me!"

"Who killed them!"

"*Los rurales!* The soldiers! Hanging them, and cutting their guts out!"

"You mean back in Mexico?"

"Yes, in the Revolution! I'm tired of running, Salvador! I'm tired of being afraid of every sound! I don't want to go to prison like Domingo. I'm not brave! Ask anybody. They'll tell you! I've never been brave!"

"Okay," said Salvador, seeing Lupe staring at the pistol in his hand. "It's okay. Calm down, and come outside with me so we can talk." He put the .38 snubnose Special in his back pocket.

"No, the *coyotes* are outside! I want to go to bed. Luisa is fat and round and all warm and I want her to hold me! I'm not brave! I'm not brave! Ask anyone!"

Salvador took a deep breath and looked at his sister Luisa, who was now ready to take the frightened little man into her arms and give him love. And he turned and looked at Lupe, his young bride, lying in bed and looking at him, not knowing what to think, but having so much love and compassion for this scared little man, too.

And so Salvador knew that this was a time for him to back off, a time for him to be soft and understanding, especially here in front of these two women, but he couldn't! For he, too, had been a child of war—years younger than Epitacio—when he'd, also, seen his brothers and sisters raped and killed before his eyes, by the soldiers in the name of justice! But, still, he hadn't run out on his responsibilities!

No, he'd stood up at the age of ten, becoming the head of his *familia*!

And so he, Salvador, now leaped forward, grabbed Epitacio by the throat and swung him about, and shoved him out the back door, over Luisa's screams of protest! And past Lupe's startled eyes!

"Get in the car!" bellowed Salvador, dragging Epitacio to the Moon. "We have business to do! And I don't care if you're brave or not brave! You will finish what we started, and do it now, you son-of-a-bitch! Does a woman have choice when she's birthing! Does the deer have choice when the lion has him by the neck! Business is business, and we will finish our DAMN BUSINESS!"

Luisa was bellowing like a cow who'd lost her young. Then she picked up a rock, trying to hit Salvador on the head with the rock as he shoved Epitacio inside of the car!

"Stop it, Luisa!" yelled Salvador, ducking the rock and shoving his sister so hard she fell on her ass. "Stop acting like a cow losing her calf! I'm not going to kill the *cabrón*! I'm just teaching him BUSINESS responsibility!"

Leaping to her feet, Luisa grabbed up another rock, a huge one, and she threw it with all her might, shattering the rear window of the Moon as Salvador sped away in the Moon with Epitacio.

Lupe stood by the back door, watching the whole thing. She just didn't know what to think or do.

In heart-crushed agony, Luisa turned, still crying, and when she saw Lupe looking at her, she bellowed even louder than before! "What the HELL are you LOOKING AT! Nobody asked you to be watching!"

She charged Lupe like an enraged cow, shoving her off the steps of the door as she ran back into her home, slamming the door closed, and bolting it.

But Lupe was quick, so she was able to leap out of the way before Luisa could put a good shove on her.

Behind the closed door, Luisa continued crying in heartfelt agony!

Lupe stood all alone in the early morning light, still not knowing what all this was about, rubbing her arms to keep warm. This was when Lupe heard a voice singing quietly over by the avocado tree. It was a beautiful voice and sounded so happy and at peace.

Walking over, Lupe discovered that the singing was coming from the outhouse. Then she saw this little movement underneath the partial door, and she realized that she was seeing the bottom of Salvador's mother's skirt, rocking back and forth as she sat in the one-seater.

"Is that you, Lupe?" asked the old woman.

"Yes, Doña Margarita," said Lupe.

"Well, I'd invite you to come in to join me, *mi hijita,*" said the old woman, "but this is only a one-seater."

Saying this, the old lady opened the door and she was sitting with a shawl wrapped about her, her Bible and rosary in hand, a homemade *cigarrito* hanging from her mouth, a cup of coffee in her other hand, and she looked so happy. A lit candle was at her side with a picture of Jesus and the statue of the Virgin Mary.

Lupe almost laughed. Without any hint of embarrassment, Doña Margarita was doing her daily calling.

"Isn't it a beautiful new day," said the old lady. "Look at that soft, early morning light coming down through those large, beautiful branches of the avocado tree. You know, this big, wonderful tree and I have been helping each other every day for years now. I shit in this outhouse a good, nice *caca* everyday, feeding her roots, and she in turn gives me the biggest, tastiest, juiciest avocados in all the area. Aaah, we're so happy together, this tree and I," she said, smoking her homemade *cigarrito* and looking so much at peace as the outhouse filled with little white clouds of smoke. "And God works with us both each day, blessing this tree and I with light and warmth—all day long. Aren't we just lucky. Then I make myself a fresh *tortilla de maiz* for breakfast, cut a few slices of avocado, add a little salt and salsa, and oh, it's Heaven Here on Earth, I tell you! Mmm mmm! So tell me, how did you sleep last night, *mi hijita,* good, I hope?"

"Well, yes, I did, but excuse me, didn't you hear the commotion, *señora?*"

"Oh, that? Well, yes, of course, I heard it. But haven't we all heard these commotions before?" She yawned, stretching and giving a happy little laugh. "*Mi hijita,* when it's all said and done, these disturbances are no more than a *pedo*-fart in the wind. You are with child. Don't let any of these ups and downs of life, *la vida,* disturb you from your task at hand. What you are doing—what is happening to you inside of your body—is a Sacred Miracle, is a Blessing straight from *Papito Dios,* and not to be disturbed."

"Then you aren't worried by this fight that just happened and how Salvador grabbed that poor man so violently?"

"Worried, me? Oh, no, the Stars in the Heavens will worry first! My only worry I now have—or concern to be more exact—is this big, nice, long, juicy *caca* that I can now finally feel come-come-coming—oh, feeling so good! Aaaaa! Ooooh, yes! Yes! Aaaah, yes! I tell you, *mi hijita,* at my age, a good bowel movement can bring the pleasure to a body that sex once brought when we were young.

"Look at these ants," continued Doña Margarita as she put her cup of coffee down on a shelf next to the lit candle by the statue of *Maria.*

"The ant season is over, but still they work on so industriously. You know," she said as she now took the candle to relight her homemade *cigarrito* with big, air-sucking sounds, "the queen ant, she runs the whole show. And all the males are so well behaved. I just love watching them, and learning from them. We talk together, you know, the ants and I, just like this tree and I talk together, too. And last year, we came to an agreement, the ants and I, and now, well, I've started feeding them outside during the summer months when they're so active, and that way they don't come into my house. Except, of course, during the time of those wood-eating termites, then nothing can keep the ants out. Oh, they really clean the wood-eating termites out of my house for me. Isn't it wonderful," she said, smiling, "how everything in all the world works so wonderfully together in the Sacred Circle of Living if we just relax, and watch, and learn, and keep out of the way, realizing that everything is perfect already, and has been perfect for millions and millions of years, and will continue to be perfect . . . forever!

"And us, and our short little stay, is less than a *pedo*-fart with all of our accumulated knowledge. Why, this tree is smarter than we will ever be. And these ants are smarter than us, too."

She laughed, picking up her cup of coffee and saluted to the statue of *Maria* and the picture of Jesus, but then—when she went to sip—she found the cup empty. "Ah, *Maria,* You-Trickster-You, You drank my coffee again when I wasn't watching, eh? You saw that, eh, Lupe?"

"No," said Lupe, shocked, "I didn't see the Blessed Mother drink your coffee."

Doña Margarita laughed. "No, I mean, you saw that my cup still had coffee in it when I set it down, didn't you?"

"Well, yes, I thought so," said Lupe.

"You did. Don't ever doubt your own senses. *Maria,* here, she has developed quite a few bad habits staying around with me. Would you like some coffee yourself, Lupe?" asked the old lady.

"Well, yes, I would," said Lupe.

"Good, would you then go inside of my home and get yourself a cup, and get *Maria* and I a refill with plenty of sugar—what, *Maria*? Oh, no, not now, *Maria,* later. It's too early to be drinking. Yes, that's right. Okay, okay. You see, *Maria* likes a little whiskey in our coffee, but I told her no."

"I see," said Lupe. "The Virgin Mary drinks whiskey?"

"Wine mostly, you know that, but I don't want any *whiskito* right now. Hurry, Lupe, and oh, yes, *Maria* also says to please come out and join us, Lupe, in our discussion if you'd like.

"After all, you are now a married woman with child, *Maria* says, and so it is time for you to know the secrets of our—our trade," said the old lady, laughing with *gusto* as she handed Lupe her cup. "Oh, now *Maria* is calling what we women know 'our trade'! Oh, *Maria* is so funny! Every day *Maria* and I trade *cuentitos*. So go on, *Maria,* as You were saying."

Taking Doña Margarita's cup, Lupe turned and headed for the little shack in back. In many ways Salvador's mother reminded Lupe of the Tarahumara Indian woman who'd been the midwife of their village. She'd been the outrage of their settlement—old and foul-mouthed and married to a man half her age.

Opening the door to the little shack, Lupe was instantly taken back with the fantastic smell of roses. The fragrance was pure Heaven. Then she saw them, the most gorgeous bunch of roses she'd ever seen!

"THAT DAMN SISTER OF MINE!" screamed Salvador as he and Epitacio sped out of the *barrio.* They took the road around town and down into the canyon that traveled from Corona to Lake Elsinore. "I'll kill her when I get back! And you, how could you just leave our distillery like that, Epitacio? You did at least lock up the place, right?"

Epitacio didn't answer. No, he just sat looking petrified.

"Oh, my God," said Salvador, glancing at him, "you didn't lock it up, did you? You son-of-a-bitch! You just ran out the door because you heard something!"

"And saw something, too, Salvador!"

"What?"

"Eyes!"

"Eyes?"

"Yes, and they were big, Salvador! *Grandisimos!* And they were everywhere! Two eyes here, two eyes there! Two eyes all over the place!"

"You were drunk!"

"I don't drink, Salvador. You know that."

"Two eyes, my ass!" said Salvador. But still, hearing this story, he reached under his seat, getting hold of his .45 automatic.

It was a narrow, twisting dirt road all the way down the canyon from Corona to Lake Elsinore. There was a little stream, oak trees, and an occasional grouping of sycamores.

Calmly, Salvador lit up a cigar. "All right, now tell me everything, Epitacio, and especially anything unusual in the last few days. I don't want us getting caught with our pants down. A man with his pants down is in a very dangerous position."

Epitacio's whole face turned red. "Well, once, when I went out for groceries, they, well—ah," but the frightened man didn't finish his words.

"EPITACIO!" screamed Salvador, grabbing him by the throat. "TALK! DON'T FUCK WITH ME! Our life is on the line!"

"They gave me a ride home," he added quickly, "because I'd bought so much."

"And why did you buy so much!?!"

"Because, well, I—"

"Did you invite them inside!?!"

Epitacio was swallowing. He just couldn't stop swallowing.

"You did, didn't you!?!"

"No! No! No! Salvador! They never came inside."

"But they saw where you live, Epitacio," said Salvador. "In a good house on the *gringo* side of town. That looks suspicious! Damnit, damnit,

damnit," added Salvador, but he wasn't yelling anymore. "You're out, Epitacio," he said calmly. "You're out. You were right. I can't have you working for me anymore. You're looking to get us caught.

"You've reached that place in the poker game of life where a man no longer cares about winning or losing. All he wants is out, one way or another. I've seen it a thousand times. There are no accidents. Domingo was asking to be caught. He'd lost his nerve, and that's why he fought and acted so brave against the cops once they had us. Cowards, not brave men, are the ones who always go looking for wars."

And saying this, Salvador breathed deeply again and again. "And who were they, these people who brought you home?"

"The people of the grocery store."

"Man, woman? Come on, talk! Explain! DAMNIT!"

"A brother and a sister."

"Okay, but they never came inside, right?"

Epitacio nodded.

"Good," said Salvador, "but you're out, you were right, you're not brave."

"Never have been," said Epitacio.

"Okay, I understand, but now, I still need for you to help me. We'll ride by the place, look around, then go over to that grocery store and see how they treat you. I'll read their eyes, especially their left eye, and then we'll decide what to do."

Epitacio nodded. "Then I can go back to Luisa?"

"Yes, then you can go back to Luisa."

"Oh, good!" he said full of warmth and *gusto*!

Salvador almost laughed. Hell, it was he, who was on his honeymoon, not this middle-aged, fat, old man.

Driving by the house, Salvador saw that the front door was wide open. His eyes shot huge! He glanced at Epitacio.

Epitacio was swallowing so fast, he could hardly speak. "I think I, well, might have left it open when I ran out," he said.

"My God," said Salvador. "My God!" And he was now swallowing, too. But not out of fear, but with rage! He felt like killing this idiot who was sitting here beside him! "Now, where is this grocery store?" he asked as calmly as he could.

Epitacio told him and they drove over and went inside. Salvador had his .45 under his shirt and his .38 in his back pocket. Who knew, maybe these people had set up Epitacio, stolen all the barrels of whiskey, and were now selling it out of their store. But he had to keep calm, calm as a reptile in the desert, eyes half closed and hardly breathing, so he could study these people in a calm manner.

Watching carefully, Salvador saw that the store people really liked Epitacio, especially the woman. And they weren't nervous at all. They seemed very relaxed and straightforward. Epitacio and Salvador bought a few things and went back out to the Moon. Seeing the car's shattered window, Salvador remembered his sister Luisa and took a big breath.

"You've been playing *el coo coo cooooo* with that woman in there, haven't you?" said Salvador to Epitacio. "That's why you bought so many groceries, to impress her, eh?"

Epitacio said nothing. He just turned all red once again.

Salvador shook his head in disgust.

"You're not going to tell Luisa, are you?" asked Epitacio as they got back in the Moon.

"I'm not thinking about that right now," said Salvador. "Now, we got business to do."

They drove back by the house, then parked in a large, open field way behind the house. They watched the place as they ate some of their groceries. They never saw any movement. Finally, this was it. Here was no more waiting or watching or hoping. Salvador opened the door of his Moon and got out, brushing the crumbs off his pants and shirt.

"You know, Epitacio, I don't even know how a man like you thinks inside of his head. And I'm not saying this with anger or malice, I'm just saying that I can't understand how you, or my brother Domingo, really think. My God, Epitacio, we had a good thing going, a little gold mine, so how could you be so stupid and careless?"

Epitacio sat in the Moon just nodding and listening. "Maybe, Salvador," he finally said quietly, "Domingo and I don't think. Maybe that's the whole thing."

Salvador's left eyebrow went up. "I'll be damn," he said. "Very good. Maybe you're right. Hell, my father didn't know how to think, either."

"Most people don't, Salvador. Not all people had a mother like yours."

Salvador's eyebrow arched up once again. "I'll be damn," he said. "Maybe you're right. But no more talking, this is it, Epitacio. You get in the driver's seat of the car and drive around to the front of the house, park, get out, and go to the front door. If everything is okay, you'll see me inside of the house, already."

"But how will you know to go inside or not?" asked Epitacio.

"Why, I'll do what my sister did," said Salvador, smiling. "I'll throw a big rock in the window, and if there's no shooting, we're home free! Damn, I owe Luisa one for teaching me this."

"That's it!" yelled Epitacio, excitedly. "That's it, Salvador!"

"That's it, what?" asked Salvador.

"That you think!"

"That I think?"

"Yes," he said excitedly. "Don't you see it? Luisa threw a rock at your car and broke your window and even from this you think about it, and learn! And most people wouldn't. No, they'd still just be so mad at their sister for ruining their car, that they couldn't think about it any other way. See, you and Luisa have learned how to do this from your mother, how to see things so differently than other people see."

"I'll be damn," said Salvador. "I think you're right. I think, you're really right."

"And this, you and Luisa learned to do since kids, to think, to see all of life so clearly from so many different angles. And most people don't know how to do this, especially not big, strong men who always try to get their way by force."

"I'll be damn," said Salvador again. "I think you maybe really got something. Because my mother always said to us that the great cunning of the She-Fox came to her—not because she was so smart—but because she was so small. That the *coyote* was so big and strong that he never had to learn how to be cunning. Oh, you are one smart *cabrón,* Epitacio!"

The short little man got all embarrassed. "I was never brave, Salvador, and so I've had to figure out other ways to live, too."

"I see, and you really love Luisa, don't you?"

He turned red faced again, and nodded.

"Fat and round and warm, eh?"

"And smart, too," added Epitacio. "She knows my weaknesses, but she doesn't hate me for them. She forgives me my other women."

"Then, about this other woman," said Salvador. "Luisa knows?"

Epitacio breathed. "Luisa knows everything! She's a *bruja,* a witch, you know, just like your mother. And believe me, I don't mean this in an offensive way, but well, this is what we men call women who are so capable."

Salvador nodded. "I guess you're right. Okay, no more of this. Let's get back to business, and do it, *a lo chingon*!"

And so Salvador checked both of his weapons, put them under his belt, then calmly lit another cigar.

Epitacio got in on the driver's side, started the motor and drove the Moon around the field to the front.

Smoking with his cigar in mouth, Salvador now began walking directly up to the house in a steady, well-measured stride, watching for movement at the windows very carefully.

Once he was close, he quickly tossed his cigar, picked up a rock, and threw it through the closest window as he rushed up on the side of the house, getting in so close that now no one from inside could open fire on him.

Heart pounding, he held. He breathed. He could hear no shots or cops inside, so he then nodded to Epitacio, who was out in front. Salvador went crashing in the back door as Epitacio came in the front door. To their shock, there was a family of raccoons scrambling out a hole in the cupboards of the kitchen.

Salvador burst out laughing and laughing. "These raccoons, they were the eyes that you saw staring at you!"

"Oh, no, Salvador, they were great, big, huge eyes!"

"Sure, great big, *grandisimos*! Come on, let's load everything up and get the hell out of here! I'm married, I'm not taking any more chances!"

It was almost midnight by the time they got back to Corona. It had taken five trips in the Moon to get everything out of the house and into the hills. And not one barrel of whiskey had been stolen. Everything was there, except for all the groceries that Epitacio had bought, which the raccoons had, of course, devoured.

Getting to Corona, Salvador stopped by the stone church before going home.

"Oh, you're going to give thanks to Our Lady," said Epitacio.

"No, not exactly," said Salvador. "I'm going to give a case of this whiskey to the priest, and ask him for a little favor."

10

LOVE was in the Air! Amor was Everywhere! The Wilds of Life, la Vida, were now leaping with the FIRES of HELL and HEAVEN Here upon MOTHER EARTH!

Then you lied to me, Salvador!" shouted Lupe. "Oh, my God! And I asked you if you were a bootlegger, I asked you, Salvador! And you lied to me! YOU LIED!"

"Yes, I did," said Salvador quietly, "you're right, I lied."

"Oh, Salvador, I feel like you drove a sword into my heart, I feel so much pain inside of me!" she said, with tears streaming down her face.

They were parked in a grove of oak trees just south of Temecula, about halfway between Corona and Carlsbad.

"Everyone knew, Salvador," continued Lupe, "but I refused to believe them, because I trusted in you. Tell me, how can I ever trust you again? Oh, if I wasn't pregnant, I'd leave you!"

And saying this, she stared at him eye to eye. "And, also, how dare you compare what you do to my mother having a drink now and then. What you do is dirty! All of my life my mother explained to us girls that liquor and cards ruined more homes than even war! I'd thought we were special, Salvador. I'd thought that people could look up to us in the *barrio* and we could—oh, I feel so dirty, so, so—my God! My God! Tell me, Salvador, at least you're not a gambler, right?"

Salvador breathed and he breathed again. He could hear a little creek running down through the rocks beyond the oak trees. These were huge oaks with big, thick roots going down to underground waters of the streambed. These trees had seen a lot of life; a lot of floods and a lot of droughts. Their roots were exposed where the soil had eroded.

"Lupe," said Salvador, "gambling is my main profession."

Her eyes went huge! She tried to speak, but nothing would come out of her mouth. No, all she could now do was just sit in the Moon, staring at this man, this person whom she'd married, but didn't know!

Suddenly, she couldn't stand the feeling that he'd ever put his hands on her, or that she'd ever allowed his "thing" to come into her body.

She began to hiccup, and when he reached out to help her, she lunged at his hand, biting him with such power that she thought she'd torn off his fingers. Then she was out of the car, and running as he screamed in pain!

The whole world was whirling, turning, tossing!

The oak trees were swaying, dancing as she made her way through them, trying to run, but unable to get her legs under herself.

Oh, how she hated that she was pregnant!

She should have married Mark! Her sister Carlota had been right! Salvador was a no-good liar!

She could feel herself going crazy-*loca* as she continued running further and further into the oak and brush. Then the underbrush got so thick, that she had to get down on her hands and knees to crawl.

She stopped. She was pouring with sweat, and she couldn't breathe. She felt like she'd been stabbed in her chest. She began gasping for air. She felt she was dying.

Then she thought she heard something. She held her breath so she could hear better, and yes, she could hear a waterfall. It sounded like the wonderful waterfalls they'd had back home in their box canyon of *la Lluvia de Oro*. This was when she also heard the rustling of leaves and she turned and saw that it was Salvador coming after her through the brush, bent over like a bear as he dodged in and out of the thickets.

"No!" she screamed!

She got up off her hands and knees and took off as fast as she could, running through the brush crouched over, then leaping out and running in the open places just as she'd done back home when she'd been a girl and she'd gone racing up and down *las barrancas* with her pet deer.

And she was fast! And it felt so good to be free again, running in the wild!

Why, only the Tarahumara Indians back home, the greatest runners in all the world, had been faster and more capable than her! Salvador could never catch her! No man would ever catch her again! She was her mother's daughter, after all, a long-legged Yaqui and she hated Salvador!

She hated that she'd ever loved him!

Salvador was leaping through the brush, trying to head her off. But he wasn't watching where he was going and he went running off the embankment of the oaks and brush. The *loco* fool hadn't stopped to listen for the waterfall. Out, out, out off the cliff-like *arroyo* with the stream way down below, he went screaming, "LOOOOOO-PEEE!"

Lupe ran out of the trees and brush to a large clearing at the edge of the steep, narrow wash and there was Salvador, still rolling and falling, and the little waterfall was about a hundred feet beyond him. "Looooo-Pee!" he still screamed!

She could see that he was going to end up rolling into some cactus plants. She began to laugh, loving it as he hit the cactus, SCREECHING in bloody murder!

"Serves you right," she said. "Maybe you'll kill yourself! Good riddance!" But then she remembered Salvador's mother and how much she liked her and she didn't want him to die. What would she tell his mother? Tears came to her eyes.

"Lupe! Lupe! Please, help me! I've got cactus thorns all over me!" Salvador yelled.

"Good!" she yelled back down to him. "I hope they hurt!"

And saying this, she looked beyond Salvador, down into the wide, deep wash, and she could see the little stream and the small waterfall. She realized that never before in all of her life had she ever thought of killing herself. Never in all of their suffering back in the Revolution had anyone in her family ever thought of giving up on life, because, well, simply, they'd always had so much love and trust between them.

Trust, she could now see was, indeed, a very big word. Maybe even larger than Love.

Her eyes filled with tears and she thought of their wedding vows and of the words that they had used. They'd said that they'd promise to be True to each other in good times and in bad, in sickness and in health, to Love and Honor all the days of their Lives. And then they'd also said, to have and to hold for better, for worse, for richer, for poorer, in sickness and in health, until death did they part. But never had the word "trust" been used. And yet she could now "see" so clearly that the whole wedding ceremony had been based on Trust. Trust was, indeed, a very important word, and she no longer had this with Salvador.

Tears continued coming to her eyes and she breathed and held, here on the edge of the *arroyo*, ignoring Salvador's shouts for help, and she looked at the waterfall. It wasn't a very large waterfall; no, it was just a little, tiny fall compared to the great falls of their box canyon, but oh—it would, indeed, be so peaceful for her to now just jump off and go slipping, sliding with the water over the fall and have no more worries, no more *problemas* with these two . . . so very important words, Trust and Love.

And she'd had both of these fine words with Salvador! Both of these heartfelt words. Completely! With all her Heart and Soul!

Her eyes continued crying, but no, she wasn't crazy-*loca* anymore.

After all, her mother had told her time and again, that a Woman of Substance never puts all her Love in the man, but in her nest, in her family. For men were of the wind, the rock, the fire, and so they had no real understanding of the woman who came from the water, the tree, and the very *Tierra Madre* of the Earth, herself!

Then wiping her eyes, Lupe suddenly remembered the little song that she and the girls of her village had sung when they'd played jump rope.

"Who moves who?" the song had said. "Does the rock move the tree, or does the tree move the rock? Why, of course, the tree moves the rock, as little by little her roots reach for water and soil!

"Who moves who?" the song had continued. "Does the fire move the water, or does the water consume the flame? Who moves who? Does the male wind move the trees, the water, the sand, or is it the female trees and water and sands who heat up with the rays of the sunlight and leap up, gifting dance and meaning to the wind?"

"Who moves who?" Lupe now found herself saying as she stood on the edge of the deep *arroyo*. "Does the Mother Earth with her rich soil and great waters move the Father Sky, or does the Father Sky with his great clouds and storms move the Mother Earth? Why, it is God Who moves All! It is *Papito Dios* Who came down Here to this *Tierra Madre* through the Miracle of the Virgin Mary and moved the Hearts of all Humankind!"

Having said this, Lupe took a breath and felt so much better. Everything made so much more sense now. Everything felt so much more understandable.

Ever since she could remember, she and all the girls of her village had sung these songs that told them how strong and special were the Female Forces of the World.

Lupe could now see that Salvador had finally gotten himself free of the cactus, but he was still yelping in agony like a hurt *coyote* pup.

She paid him no attention, and sat down to take a little rest. She was tired. And she was with child, and so she was going to do as her mother-in-law had told her to do and not let these little ups and downs of life, *la vida,* disturb her.

Sitting in the shade of an oak tree, Lupe pulled up a blade of grass and began to chew on it. Yes, men were Fire and women were Water. Men were Wind and women were Soil. Men were Rock and women were Tree.

Breathing, chewing, humming, Lupe looked about herself seeing the great Mother Earth all around her and the huge Father Sky above her. And she saw the boulders in the creek below her moving the current this way and that way, and she saw the soil of the embankments holding the water and boulders in place.

Tears came to her eyes, but she was no longer upset. No, she was calm. A breeze came up and began singing in the tree branches above her. Lupe looked up and saw the great tree's limbs dancing against the startling blue sky. She saw the leaves, the dark bark looking so beautiful against the infinite vastness of the Father Sky, and suddenly, Here in her Heart, she knew again why her mother had always explained to her—back in *la Lluvia de Oro*—that every woman needed her own Crying Tree in order to endure the hardships of life and marriage.

A great peace swelled up inside Lupe's Heart-*Corazón*. And she could now "see" so clearly that water, boulders, roots, everything was all-intermingled together just like the hate and love, hopes and expectations that she had for this man Salvador whom she'd married for better or for worse . . . for rich or for poor, in sickness and in health until death did they part.

Tears of pure joy came to her eyes. Wiping the tears from her eyes she breathed and placed her right hand over her Center, holding herself, and she now too began to sing, just like the breeze in the trees. And her sweet, young voice carried out over the *arroyo* and up the steep mountainside above the rocky *barranca*, just south of Temecula.

Instantly, in her mind's eye Lupe could now see that she and all her girl-friends from back in *La Lluvia* were no longer little girls playing jump rope, but grown women living life. And all over the Mother Earth—no matter where they were now located or what they were doing—Here in their Hearts, these women, her Sacred Sisters, were also singing these songs of their youth.

Songs that gave them Hope!

Songs that gave them Power!

Songs that kept them anchored on the Eternal Goodness of Life, *la Vida*, no matter how many stones the men of their lives put before them!

Songs that taught them how to move with ease and dexterity just like this little stream down below her.

Salvador and Lupe Villaseñor at their fiftieth wedding anniversary, 1979

Villaseñor familia at Rancho Villaseñor, 1979

CARLSBAD, CALIF.

Downtown Carlsbad, California, 1930

Catholic Rock Church in Corona, California, 1920

Salvador and Lupe, 1930

Salvador, 1931

Carlota and Archie, Mexico City, 1932

Lupe with Hortensia, 1930

And streamwaters could put out fire so easily, and so yes, Women of Substance had to be very, very careful of their Special Powers and not kill off the men in their lives, but work them, help them, nurture them, round them out like the river waters did to the stones, making them Smooth and Whole and yes, finally Complete.

This is what her mother had done with her father. This was why her father still adored her mother; she'd worked him, she'd forgiven him, and she'd never stopped loving him—even when he'd abandoned them.

This was a woman's calling.

This was a woman's treasure, the knowing of her own incredible strength!

Who moved who? Oh, what an innocent little song that had been that they'd sung back home while playing jump rope.

And so Lupe could now so very clearly see what it was that their mothers had done back home in their box canyon.

They'd stepped forward as Women of Substance in the middle of those terrible days of rape and plunder—called a Revolution by the men—and they'd come forth with the Power of Water crashing over a great fall, spreading Hope and Love, Wisdom and Warmth to All!

Tears poured down Lupe's face, but no, she was no longer sad. She was happy! She was joyful! She was full of *gusto*! She now well-knew, deep inside of herself, that she wasn't the first—or the last—woman to come to this painful "place" of deceit, where she felt like her truelove had lied to her about everything!

No, she wasn't alone.

Why, right now, at this very moment, she could actually feel the Mother Earth, herself, breathing under her, as she sat on the ground underneath this Great, Old Tree!

She could feel the Mother Earth breathing and she could see the Father Sky smiling and she could hear the She-Tree singing in the soft, gentle breeze.

No, she would never panic again.

After all, she was her mother's daughter, and she was pregnant, and so she had to keep in mind, like her mother had always told her, that men came and went just like the Wind and Fire, and so it was up to a woman—whom God had entrusted with the carrying of the child—to keep the Holy Waters of Creation going.

Lupe breathed again, and she felt full.

God was with her.

God was Here, right now, as surely as He'd been with the Virgin Mary, Mother of Jesus, when She'd been pregnant with Sacred Life, too!

Lupe began to Pray.

She'd found her Crying Tree.

She'd found her Crying Tree, Here in this strange land, and so she was good now as her mother and her grandmothers had also been good before her—*con Papito Dios*!

THAT NIGHT back in their home in Carlsbad, Lupe helped Salvador get the cactus thorns out of his legs and hands and backside. But the little, tiny, fine thorns that were between his fingers they couldn't pull out and so these, they rubbed with a mixture of lemon, garlic, and *masa de maiz*. But still, the itching of these tiny thorns between Salvador's fingers kept him awake most of the night, giving him terrible nightmares.

In the morning, Salvador immediately suggested to Lupe that they go and see the priest who had married them. "And whatever he says, I'll do it, Lupe," said Salvador, "because all I want is for us to be happy. I don't want another night of bad dreams. We've been so happy, Lupe, and that's what I want for us: happiness."

"Oh, this is wonderful," said Lupe. "And this way we can give all the money to the Church and cleanse our souls!"

"What!" yelled Salvador. "Just wait! Hold on! I never said anything about giving all our money to the Church!"

"But it's dirty money, Salvador," said Lupe. "So it needs to be blessed and made pure. Come on, let's go, so we can be clean once again, here inside."

"You mean right now?" he said.

"Yes," said she. "I mean, go give all of our money right now!"

Now it was Salvador who wasn't so sure he wanted to go to see the priest.

"Look, Lupe," he said, swallowing, "maybe we should just work things out for ourselves."

"But Salvador," said Lupe, "you're the one who said we should go see the priest, and that you'd do whatever he said because you want us to be happy."

"Yes, I did say that," said Salvador, scratching the left side of his head as he tried to think. And he'd set up everything with Father Ryan on how to handle this situation of his liquor making with Lupe, but my God, this young bride of his had put a wrench into the whole thing with her idea of giving their money to the Church.

"Well, then I agree with you," she said. "That's a very good idea, so let's go, and while we're there, we'll talk to the priest about your gambling, too. Oh, this is wonderful! I'm so happy for us, Salvador, we are going to be people *de honor* once again!"

Now, it was Salvador who wasn't quite sure who was moving who. It took three more days of Lupe talking to Salvador before he finally agreed to go and see the priest who'd married them.

Salvador was sweating nails as they drove from Oceanside to the little stone church in Corona. Lupe, she was so excited, she couldn't stop smiling.

Getting to the Church later that morning, Salvador started to feel a little more confident that maybe, just maybe, things would work out in his favor. Because when he'd stopped by late that night a few days before, he'd given this man of the cloth a case of his finest bottles of twelve-year-old whiskey, telling him that he wouldn't be able to bring him any more whiskey, because Lupe thought that alcohol was the tool of the Devil and she didn't want him making any more.

"I see," had said the tall, dignified man of God. "Well, this being the case, why don't you bring Lupe by to see me, before you do anything rash."

"Well, if you insist," had said Salvador, acting very innocent.

And so now, here they were, he and Lupe, parking their car in front of the church, and he felt pretty sure that maybe everything was still going to go his way, since he'd stacked the deck in his favor.

On the other hand, Lupe had really nailed him to the wall with her wanting to give all their money away.

Inside, the old priest was waiting for them, and with a big, generous smile, he greeted them and ushered them down the aisle and past the altar to his private quarters. Lupe had never been inside this part of a Church before. She could hear their footsteps echoing on the shiny hardwood floor. She walked on her tiptoes, not wanting to offend God.

At the end of the long hallway, they came to a large, heavy door. Inside was the priest's study, next door to where he and Doña Margarita had done their drinking. He closed the huge door behind them with a heavy thud. He saw how Lupe immediately started looking at the walls lined with his books. He also noticed how she watched him go behind this desk, sit down and put his hands together like a tent on top of his desk.

"Please, be seated," he said.

Lupe and Salvador did as they were told. The man of God took a big breath.

"Do you like books, Lupe?" asked the man of God, seeing how Lupe was now reading the different titles of his books.

"Oh, yes!" she said with excitement, feeling so good to be near so many legendary titles!

"I'm glad to hear that," he said, taking several deep breaths. "I'm a great lover of books, too, especially the classics. You see, I never had the good fortune to travel much but I can't tell you all the places that I've been because of books. Books were my first love as a youngster. I do believe that they are what kept me out of trouble and eventually took me into my studies for the priesthood."

Lupe had never heard a priest talk about his personal life before. Suddenly, she felt very much at ease. "That's what my best friend and I used to do up in our box canyon in Mexico, too," said Lupe. "Every chance Manuelita and I had, we would read, especially books of geography and we'd travel all around the world! I used to love my reading and learning about how other people live in faraway places!"

"But I hope you haven't stopped reading, have you, my dear?" asked the priest.

"Well, yes," said Lupe, becoming embarrassed. "Books are, well, you know, expensive, and my family and I were always moving from place to place, following the crops."

"But you're not moving anymore," he said. "Salvador has told me that you have a fine home in Carlsbad now."

She nodded. "Yes, that's true," she said, feeling very proud. But, then, she remembered why they'd come to see the priest. "But you see, Father—" She didn't know what to say. She felt all nervous inside. "—I haven't been feeling very well," she added.

"Oh, and this is why you haven't been going to the library to get books to read, my child?" he asked.

Lupe turned to Salvador. "I've been too upset," she said. "Tell him why, Salvador."

"Well," said Salvador, sitting forward in his chair, "you see, Father, Lupe and I have come to you today because, well, we took our vows of marriage very seriously, but, you see—" He stopped and glanced at Lupe. "Lupe, you're the one who's upset. I think you should tell him."

She shook her head. She felt so ashamed she could die. Here, they were, inside the Holy House of God, and Salvador was proposing that she talk of things of the Devil. "No," she said, "you do it."

"Well, okay," said Salvador, a little taken aback. "You see, Father, I make liquor for a living."

"You do?" said Father Ryan, licking his lips.

"Yes, and Lupe, here, she wants me to stop making it."

"I see," said the priest, nodding several times, as if he were digesting all this information for the very first time. "And this, my dear," he said, turning to Lupe, "is what is troubling you?"

"Well, of course," she said, completely surprised by the priest's question.

"And why does it bother you?" asked the priest.

"Why?!?" said Lupe, much louder than she'd expected.

Salvador squirmed in his chair. This man of God was really good and smart, and sneaky! Hell, he could be a Cardinal!

"Yes," continued Father Ryan. "Why does this bother you, my dear?"

"Well, because, Father, liquor is the substance of the Devil!" she said quickly, then she continued speaking in a fast, frightened voice. "And when you married us, Father, you said we're responsible for each other, so that when we die, our love will continue even up in Heaven. But this liquor, Father," she added, tears coming to her eyes, "is going to get Salvador sent to Hell for all eternity, so he's not going to be able to be with me up in Heaven!" And saying this, she burst into tears.

Salvador stared at Lupe. He'd never realized that all this was going on inside of her mind. Why, the poor girl had been suffering all this time beyond his wildest dreams. He took her hand, soothing it. He, too, wanted to go to Heaven and be with Lupe after he died.

"Well, my dear," said the priest, "then, if I understand correctly, you believe that alcohol is a great evil in itself. Am I right?"

"Well, yes, of course!" said Lupe, full of self-righteousness. "My mother always told us that liquor and cards ruined more marriages than even war!" she added louder than she'd intended. She was so scared, talking about these horrible things inside the House of God!

"And your mother was very wise in telling you this," said the man of the cloth. "For, all through the ages, the abuse of liquor and cards has been one of our biggest problems."

Lupe turned and looked at Salvador, as if saying, "See!" Oh, she was truly enjoying this priest now.

"But, also, my child," continued the priest, hands sweeping smoothly across his clean, wide desktop, "we must consider the fact that God, in His infinite wisdom, gave each of us freewill, so we could choose between good and evil and, therefore, make our own way—I repeat, our own way—as responsible individuals through life on earth and into His kingdom of Heaven." He stopped, replacing his hands on his desk like a tent once more. "Do you understand, my child?"

Lupe shook her head. "No," she said, "I don't."

"Well, child, simply, if there was no evil or temptation in this world, then what grace would there be in choosing the good?" he said.

"Then, you are saying that liquor is good, because it's bad, so then we can choose?"

Hearing this, he considered her words carefully, then he nodded. "Yes, I am," he said. "Or, now, look at it this way, I'm also saying that each one of us, in the act of choosing, becomes the person that we are. Take, for instance, this: what was the very first miracle that Our Lord Jesus Christ performed on earth?"

He stopped, licking his lips once more, but never once took his eyes off Lupe. "That's right," he said, "you remember; I can see it in your eyes. It was at the wedding feast. Yes, go on, say it. Their hosts had run out of wine and so, not to cause them any further embarrassment, Our Beloved Lady asked her Most Holy Son to please change—"

"Water into wine?" said Lupe.

"Exactly. And did Our Lord Savior refuse?" asked the priest. "No, he certainly did not. He chose to grant his mother her wish, and He didn't make just ordinary wine. Oh, no; He changed that water into the finest of all wines—just as your husband, here, does with his fine whiskey—or so, I've been told," he added quickly, coughing a few times.

Lupe felt her mind reeling. Why, all her life she'd absolutely known, without a doubt, that liquor was bad, was an evil tool of the Devil's; and now this man of God was reminding her that Christ, Himself, had made alcohol, too.

"So, as I was saying," continued the man of the cloth, "I do believe that God, in His infinite Wisdom, knew what He was doing when He gave your husband his special powers for making liquor, and even I might add, gave him the namesake of Salvador, meaning Savior, in honor of His only begotten Son, Our Lord Christ, the Savior!"

Lupe just didn't know what to say or think anymore. She felt like she was losing her mind. "Well, then, Father, do you mean," she said, "that my husband is like Jesus, doing God's work when he makes liquor?"

"Well," said the priest, rising up his left eyebrow. He hadn't expected to hit a home run. "I wouldn't quite go that far. But, I will say that what Salvador does isn't against the laws of God."

"But it is against the law in this country," said Lupe. "And I don't want him getting caught and going to jail. We're going to have a child and—oh, my God!" she said. "I'm so, so, so confused!"

"Then let us pray," said the priest calmly, "that your husband never goes to jail and that you come to understand that alcohol isn't evil in itself. Also, keep in mind many of our Church's finest people have been imprisoned over the centuries. Wasn't Christ Himself put in chains and forced to carry His own cross?

"What I think you should do, my dear, is pray every day for your husband's safety. After all, these are difficult times for all of us. Some people, as I'm sure you know, are even having trouble keeping food on their tables."

"Well, yes, I know that," said Lupe, "but, well, I just don't know . . . I'd thought that we were living in sin, Father," she added.

"And so you came to me and I think that's most commendable," he said. "So many young couples, after they are married, forget all about their spiritual needs. I congratulate you, Maria Guadalupe, on your thoughtfulness. But now, unless you have some other matter that you wish to discuss, I have other people waiting."

And saying this, the priest stood up. Long ago, the man of God had learned that it was best to cut things off quickly so people could go home and digest things by themselves.

"Well, thank you for your time," said Salvador, thinking it had gone well and now he and Lupe should quickly get the hell out before she remembered that she'd wished to give the Church all of their bootleg money.

But Lupe wasn't to be sidetracked. She remained seated and said, "Father, I almost forgot; we also came to give you the money from all the liquor that Salvador has sold."

"Oh," said the priest, turning to Salvador. "And how much might that be, my dear?" He could see that Salvador was now squirming in his chair, shitting square bricks.

"We want to give all of it to you," she said. "It's nearly three hundred dollars."

Salvador, who'd been rocking back and forth in his chair, now crashed backward to the floor, shattering the back of the chair.

"It's all right," said the man of God, getting to his feet, "it was an old chair. Are you okay?"

"Yes," said Salvador. He was all shook up.

"Look," said the priest, realizing that this was a fortune they were talking about, "that's very generous of you, my dear," he added, turning back to Lupe. "But, now that we've spoken together on this matter, I think that you and Salvador need to talk. But a small donation of, let's say, sixty dollars, which is twenty percent, is acceptable at this time."

"I thought the Church took ten percent!" said Salvador, getting to his feet and reaching into his pocket to bring out his money. Hell, he figured that he'd already given this damn priest well over his ten percent in liquor over the years, but what could he do? He couldn't very well tell Lupe that the man drank like a damn fish and was a costly expense every month as it was.

"Here's twenty dollars," said Salvador to the man of God. "I don't have any more money on me right now. All of our money is in the bank," he added, lying to the priest.

"As it should be," said the priest, taking the twenty and slipping it into his own pocket. "And this is more than enough," he added. "Forget the other forty." He didn't want to anger Salvador and have him cut off his whiskey supply. "Thank you very much. And remember, Lupe, yes, bootlegging is against the laws of this land, but not against the laws of God! Go in peace, my children!"

Walking out of the church, Lupe didn't know what to think. The whole world was going crazy all around her. This priest had said that liquor wasn't bad; that Jesus Christ, Himself, had made wine, and that God had, also, given people freewill so that they could choose between good and evil and make their way through life and into the Kingdom of God.

Oh, she felt like her head was bursting—she was so confused!

And Salvador, he was working hard not to grin. My God, it hadn't turned out as bad as he'd expected. And this freewill stuff, he really liked it. It was exactly what his mother had told him all his life, that even God needed help in making miracles here on Earth. And a miracle had, indeed, just come to pass—he was now a bootlegger with God's Blessing!

AFTER THEIR VISIT with the priest, life still remained strained between Salvador and Lupe. Salvador was running out of whiskey and so he had to set up his distillery again, but he didn't want to tell Lupe. He decided to go across town, over to the *barrio de Carlos Malo,* and talk to Archie. Lupe said that she'd come along and buy groceries at the little Mexican market across the street from the poolhall.

"So what are you asking me?" said Archie to Salvador. They were in the back room of Archie's poolhall. The poolhall—not the Church—was the real center of the *barrio*. It was the place where all the single men hung out and received their mail. Also, owning this place made it easier for Deputy Archie to keep watch over things and enforce the law. "Are you asking me for protection, or just advice?"

"I guess a little of both," said Salvador.

"Then it will cost you a barrel a week."

"Hey, Archie, I can't pay you that much!" yelled Salvador. "I don't have anyone who I can trust anymore to help me make the liquor! I'm small! I'll have to do it all alone, and also, remember, I'm married now!"

"Yeah, I saw Lupe going into the market across the street. So how is that cute little sister of hers? Man, she's a hot little *chile*!"

"The less I see of that woman, the happier I am," said Salvador.

"Does Lupe know your business yet?"

Taking a deep breath, Salvador nodded. "Yeah, I had to tell her, and *mano*, she hardly talks to me anymore."

Slapping his own leg, Archie burst out laughing! "So you're finally a real married couple!"

Salvador didn't think it was funny.

"Look, you can set up your distillery in Escondido," said Archie.

"And you'll talk to the sheriff over there?"

"No need to," said Archie. "That's so close to the border nobody bothers looking for bootleggers." In Mexico, liquor was still legal.

"And I'm going to pay you for this?"

"Yeah, you are. One barrel every . . . let's say, two weeks, or now that I know where you'll be, I'll haul you in myself!"

"That's blackmail, Archie!"

"Yeah, don't you just love it? Getting the horn from your wife one way, and from the law the other!" Archie's whole face filled with *gusto*, laughing and laughing, truly enjoying himself! "It's a screwed-up world, eh? Your best friend, sticking it to you, and your wife not giving you any!"

"How can you sleep at night, Archie?"

"Like a baby! I'm thinking of running for mayor. Or maybe governor and my slogan will be 'Dirty Archie—your straight-shooting, double-dealing, crooked politician!' Hell, I bet you I win by a landslide!"

"You're worse than any priest!"

"Thank you," said Archie. "Those con artists would've taken over ownership of all of California if they'd had their way."

Finishing up his business with the big lawman, Salvador was going out the front doors of the poolhall when he saw a big, tall Anglo walk up to their Moon automobile. Lupe was putting her groceries inside of their car, and the big, tall Anglo stooped over, putting his head inside the window of their Moon, smooth-talking to Lupe.

Salvador's heart EXPLODED! He went for his gun, but he didn't have it. It was under the seat of the Moon.

"Hey, *amigo*!" yelled Salvador, charging up.

The tall man turned around, smiling a big, lecherous grin full of huge white teeth and straightened up to his full height, towering over Salvador by a good foot. But Salvador wasn't to be intimidated, and he leaped up, hitting him under the chin with all the power of his short, thick, compact body.

The force was so great that the man's two feet came completely off the ground, and he went flying backward, hitting his head against the side of the Moon. Archie came rushing up.

"Get out of here, Sal!" said Archie. "This is an Anglo, you dumb son-of-a-bitch! A *gringo*! Good thing I saw how he attacked you first, so you had to hit him in self-defense!"

Salvador was shaking, he was so worked up. Oh, he'd gone crazy-*loco* when he'd seen that big man sticking his head inside of their Moon, flirting with Lupe. All those years of wanting to protect his mother and sisters came bursting up inside of him!

"Get the hell out of here!" said Archie again. "I think you really hurt him!"

"Come on, Salvador!" said Lupe.

Finally, Salvador got into the Moon and they were off.

"There was no need to hit that man, Salvador," said Lupe once they were out of the *barrio*. "He was just drunk. He didn't mean anything. Besides, it's probably your liquor that got him drunk."

"LUPE!" screamed Salvador. "Don't talk to me like this! Ever since we saw that priest, you've been mouthing off at me!"

"And why not? You lied to me, Salvador! You lied to me about every-thing!"

"Stop it, Lupe! Stop it! I warn you!" he added.

"You warn me?" she said. "You warn me that you'll do what! That you will hit me, too! That you will grab me by the neck like you grabbed Epita-cio that morning? Oh, no, Salvador, I'm your wife, and like it or not, I will speak!"

Screaming, Salvador slammed on the brakes and leaped out of the Moon! He didn't know what to do. He wanted to kill! He wanted to kill Lupe!

He continued screaming and bellowing like an enraged bull. Then suddenly he turned on the tree next to him—a great big, tall, beautiful eucalyptus—and he began kicking the tree as hard as he could, then pounding it with his thick, heavy, iron-driving fists.

"I saw my sisters raped and killed by soldiers in front of my eyes!" he bellowed. "And I was too little to do anything, Lupe! I was too little! And I was going to kill that son-of-a-bitch, if Archie hadn't pulled me off!

"He was a drunk Anglo, Lupe! A drunk Anglo! And what do you think drunk Anglos have been doing to our women for all these years! DON'T PLAY the FOOL WITH ME, LUPE! I LOVE YOU! You're *mi esposa*! And you will be respected, Lupe, do you hear me, I'll kill this ENTIRE NATION!"

He gouged at the tree with his nails, tearing off bark, biting at the bark, and kicking the tree again and again . . . until he finally hurt his right foot and could kick no more, and he started crying. He fell down, hugging the base of the Great Tree, weeping like a child.

The drums were beating!

The One Collective Heart-*Corazón* of Humanity was beat, Beat, BEATING!

"They raped my sisters," added Salvador quietly, "right in front of me and my mother, wanting to torture us, too, and I was too little to do anything. Too little, Lupe, too little." He swallowed. "My sister Emilia finally went blind with shame, Lupe. War is no good. No good, ever. The women and children always . . . lose, both sides."

The tears were running down Lupe's face as she sat in the Moon, watching Salvador hugging the base of the huge eucalyptus as he, too, cried in agony.

Lupe knew exactly what Salvador was talking about. It had been the same thing in her box canyon. It had never mattered who won, Villistas or Carrancistas, in the end they, *la gente,* always lost. War was, indeed, no good. Ever! Only men—far from their homes—could think war was great and adventurous!

A delicious, gentle breeze came up and Lupe glanced up and saw the leaves of the Great Tree Dancing in the sunlight, turning into a Sea of tiny Angels.

She breathed and breathed again, then opened her door and got out of the Moon to go to Salvador. The Angels were humming. Lupe could feel their humming in her Heart-*Corazón*!

"I'm sorry," she said, squatting down on the ground beside him. "I'm sorry, Salvador, I didn't understand."

She brushed the hair out of his eyes and they looked at each other in the sunlight coming down to them through the branches of the Great Tree, and they now saw each other all new and with so much . . . Love and Warmth, and Goodness.

Their Hearts were open.

The Garden of Eden was now, Here, within them, and all about them!

He breathed. "Lupe, what kind of men do this? Rape a daughter right in front of her mother's own eyes. They did this to my mother . . . again and again." His eyes flowed with tears. "Didn't they have mothers and sisters of their own?"

"They weren't men," said Lupe, "they were lost souls, Salvador."

He nodded. "Yes, you're right," he said, the tears still flowing from his eyes. "They weren't men. This is the same thing that my mother says, too, and then . . . she forgives them. Oh, Lupe, we must take good care of our love. You are my wife, Lupe, *mi esposa*!" he added.

"I am," said Lupe, "and you are *mi esposo*."

He breathed. "I love you, Lupe!"

"And I love you," she said back to him.

They took each other in their arms, and the breeze picked up and the huge branches of the Great Tree swayed, and Here was the face of Mary, the Mother of God, up in the tall limbs of the eucalyptus. And the leaves—which had taken on the form of Ten Thousand Angels for all the world to see who had the Heart to See, and all the world to Hear who had the Soul to Hear.

Once more a married couple, had stepped forward through the needle's eye, reclaiming Paradise at the base of the Holy Tree of Life, *la Vida*. And Lupe now got up and reached down, giving her husband a hand up, and they looked into each other's eyes, and they kissed softly, gently in a whole new way.

Going to their Moon automobile, Lupe had to help Salvador. He'd kicked so much that he'd hurt his right foot, the male side, and he was limping.

Driving home, they never said another word, and that night they made love like they'd never made love before. Slowly. Gently. Never tiring. Never doubting. Hour after hour. Eyes open, feeling only the most open, tender feelings of Heart and Soul.

NOW, IT FELT VERY DIFFERENT for Lupe when she saw Salvador to the door each day. She hugged him and she kissed him, but that fear and desperation weren't here. No, now it was all right with her that he was going off to do his work and she was going to be alone. In fact, she was happy to see him go, so she could get things done by herself.

And so this morning Salvador left and Lupe began cleaning house, singing to herself and feeling very good, when she came across the can full of money under the sink. And suddenly like a lightning bolt, instead of getting frightened or angry this time, she saw everything so clearly, so differently. Why, they could put this can of money in a bank. That's what rich people did with their money. She didn't need to be afraid of money! Money was just paper, as Salvador had so well told her.

Lupe became lightheaded with just the thought, because nobody in all her *familia* had ever gone inside of a bank, much less put money into one.

She felt so excited and clear-minded for the first time in weeks.

She couldn't wait for Salvador to get home, so she could tell him.

That evening after dinner, Lupe looked across the table at Salvador and said, "*Querido*, today when I was cleaning house, I came across your—I mean, our can of money and—no, no, don't get upset. This isn't bad. This is good," she said, smiling with *gusto*. "And I figured out what we can do with it, so I don't feel scared when you go out and I'm left alone."

"What?" he said, seeing her joy, but still feeling apprehensive.

"Salvador," she said excitedly, "we can put it in the bank."

"The bank?" he said.

"Yes," she said, "just like rich—I mean, people with money—do."

And she stopped, expecting Salvador to be thrilled with her idea, but instead he now leaped up from the table, pacing the floor and saying that no, no, no, he was totally against this bank idea!

But in the last few weeks Lupe had gotten pretty tough, so she didn't back off. No, she now closed her eyes, so she wouldn't have to see his raging face, and spoke calmly, explaining to him in a slow, steady, reasonable way that he was gone a lot of the time and so she didn't feel safe being alone with all this money in their home.

"Salvador," she said finally, "you've worked hard for this money and I don't want to see us losing it. Remember," she added, opening her eyes, "houses do get robbed. And banks are safe."

Hearing this last part, Salvador sat back down. "Okay, Lupe," he said very quietly, "you've convinced me, but now Lupe, I'm forced to tell you something that I'd hoped to not ever have to tell you in all my life."

Lupe closed her eyes again. "What is it?" she asked, wondering what could possibly be worse than his gambling and liquor making. Was he a murderer, too? Did he kill people for hire also?

"Lupe," he said, feeling so ashamed that he could hardly speak, "I don't know how to . . . to read. So I can't go to any bank," he continued, "because they, they have papers for you to . . . to read." He was crying, shaking, looking sick—he was so upset.

"And this is it, Salvador?" asked Lupe, looking at him with complete astonishment. "This is what you were hoping to never have to tell me in all your life?"

Salvador nodded. "Yes," he said, with tears streaming down his face. "Because you see, for you to be mad at me, or to hate me, well, that I can handle, but if you were ever—" He couldn't speak. He couldn't say it. And tears continued pouring down his face. "—ever to be ashamed of me, I couldn't live, Lupe."

Looking at him, seeing this powerful man sitting before her, being so scared and child-like and vulnerable, Lupe's whole heart went out to him. "How can I ever be ashamed of you, Salvador," she said. "You are a fine, hardworking, responsible man. Yes, I've been, well, mad at you, this is true, but not blind. You're a wonderful man, and a good husband, and I'm proud to be your wife, Salvador."

"Oh, Lupe! Lupe!" he said. "Truly, you mean what you say?"

"Yes, of course," she said.

"These words are MUSIC to my EARS!" he shouted to the Heavens.

She swallowed. She, too, was all choked up. "But tell me one thing," she said, "why didn't your mother teach you how to read? She's always reading the Bible."

Salvador took a big breath and dried his eyes. "She tried, Lupe," he said, sitting down next to her, "but, well, for some reason, I just couldn't learn how to do it. And she explained to me that many people—from the Indian side of our family—were never able to learn to read. And these weren't the dumbest people in our family, either. Many times our nonreaders could well, see, you know, like a blind person, with special eyes from the heart, seeing things that all others can never see. Like my brother Jose, the Great, couldn't read, but oh, he could fly down the mountainside with his eyes closed and he could talk to the Clouds, the Sky, the Trees, All of Creation! I'm sorry, Lupe, I never wanted to be an embarrassment to . . . to you," he added, and tears streamed down his face from his eyes once again.

"Salvador!" said Lupe, taking him in her arms. "You can never be an embarrassment to me. You are *mi esposo.* And last week, when you loaned all that money to my brother for his truck, I could see you are a good-hearted, generous man, Salvador."

"Oh, Lupe! Lupe! I always wanted to tell you before we married that I couldn't read and I was a bootlegger, but, I was afraid of losing you, and I love you SO MUCH! Ever since the first day I saw you, you Are my LIFE! The ANGEL of my DREAMS!"

They drew close and they were kissing, gently, softly, cautiously, then they were making love once again and it was . . . Holy, indeed, a married couple, visiting Heaven.

THE NEXT DAY they drove over to Corona to take a barrel to Luisa so she could keep selling whiskey by the pint, and then they went to the bank in the Anglo side of town and Lupe did the paperwork so they could deposit $540 in cash, all their money in the world!

The date was October 20, 1929, days before the Stock Market Crash of Wall Street.

But of course, they knew nothing of this, not even when the Crash happened and people jumped out of windows in New York City.

They didn't read the newspapers or listen to the news on the radio. They were *gente* from the *barrio.*

Salvador watched Lupe as she filled out the forms on the big, wide desk of the banker, and he felt so proud of her! She could read, and she could write! Both in English and in Spanish! He listened to her pen sing as it scratched over the papers, making such beautiful, intriguing designs! Oh, his wife, Lupe, wasn't just beautiful, but educated, too! She'd almost finished the sixth grade, she'd told him.

They walked out of the bank, feeling ten feet tall! They'd really done it. Together they'd gone to a place where Salvador would have never dreamed of going.

Returning to Luisa's house, Salvador made the mistake so many young couples make when they want to share their happiness with the rest of

their family. He couldn't stop bragging about Lupe, his beautiful, educated wife, so much so that Luisa finally felt violated.

For what Salvador was really saying, in Luisa's opinion, was that before
Lupe they'd been nothing but a bunch of uneducated Indians *sin razón*.

Then to make things even worse, Salvador left Lupe with Luisa, and he
took off with Epitacio. He and Epitacio were going to go into the hills and
dig up a couple of barrels that Salvador had buried in a dry riverbed and
deliver them to Riverside. And Riverside was only partially Salvador's territory, so he had to be very careful not to cross over the line and end up in
a gun battle. After all, that damn *Filipino* and *Italiano* were still giving him
trouble.

When Salvador and Epitacio got back, Lupe was sitting outside by the
outhouse all by herself and she wanted to go home to Carlsbad immediately. Salvador could feel that something was very wrong, but when he
tried to question Lupe, she just shook her head and would say nothing.

They were halfway to Lake Elsinore when finally Salvador couldn't
stand it anymore. "Lupe," he said, pulling into a grove of oaks, "what the
hell is going on! I know something happened. When I was delivering
those barrels I had this feeling, here deep inside of me that something was
going on with you. Talk to me, please!"

"All right," said Lupe, "I'll talk to you, Salvador, but only on the condition that you don't interfere. This is for me to work out. Not for you, do
you understand?"

"Okay, okay," said Salvador. "I understand. Now tell me, what happened?"

"Well, after you and Epitacio left, I was there in the kitchen with
Luisa—because your mother had come in from church, feeling very tired
and went to her home to take a nap—and this man came by to buy, I guess,
some whiskey. And Luisa saw him looking at me, and instead of informing
the man that I was married to you, her brother, she told me to serve him
his drink and sit down and join him."

"LUISA DID THAT!?!" screamed Salvador. "I'll kill her! I'll burn her
house down! And what did this son-of-a-bitch look like! I'll castrate him
and drag him through the streets behind my Moon!"

"Salvador!" shouted Lupe. "You will do none of those things!"

"But I have to! I'm your husband! Your protector!"

"Listen to me, Salvador! Listen to me! You will do nothing! I need to
take care of this myself. Or Luisa will never have respect for me, if you step
in and protect me. Don't you see, she was just trying to get at me, because

you got at her husband Epitacio. And then you added to the whole thing when you couldn't stop bragging about me and the bank."

"Oh, so now you're saying that this whole thing is my fault, eh?"

And Salvador licked his lips and Lupe could see that he was getting ready to go into another one of his rages. But she wasn't about to let him get away with this. After all, not only had she toughened up a lot in the last few weeks, but her love for him wasn't blind anymore. No, she was now a woman in love, but with—both eyes wide open!

"Salvador," she said, "how do you expect me to speak to you if you get angry every time I talk? I'm not blaming you. I'm simply telling you what I think is going on. I sat out there by that avocado tree by the outhouse for a long time waiting for you, so I had a long time to think. Why, right now, as we speak, I bet you, that Luisa is, well, as you'd say it—dirtying her dress, she's hoping so much that I don't tell you what she tried to do.

"Look, Salvador," she added, "I know how to defend myself. I didn't serve that man his drink. I simply said, 'I'm married, and I'm with child, and I don't feel well. And even if I did feel well, I serve no man, but my own husband, Luisa's brother Salvador.'

"Hearing your name, the man immediately took off his hat, apologizing, bought his pint and left, and I went out the back door and sat there waiting for you. Luisa came out three times, inviting me back inside and telling me that she'd only been joking, but I just ignored her. And I'm very good at ignoring, Salvador. I did it to you for almost one month."

Grinning, Salvador got out of the car and walked about, breathing deeply. And every time he'd glance at Lupe, he'd shake his head and grin again. Then he suddenly leaped into the air, giving *un grito de gusto,* and he started dancing around in a little circle, howling as he danced.

"Oh, oh, oh, you're tough, Lupe! You are tough! Poor Luisa is probably shitting in her dress right now! My God, my mother was right all along!" he added, hopping about like a rabbit on one foot and then the other. "And now here you give Luisa the horn!" he added. "Oh, this is wonderful! You really do know how to take care of yourself!"

And saying this, Salvador drew close to the car. "Lupe," he said, looking at her quietly, "I love you. You hear me, I love you, and I respect you, and I'm so proud to be . . . your *esposo.* Our children are safe, Lupe, for you are one hell of a tough, smart, cunning woman!"

Seeing his eyes looking at her with such open, honest, earned respect, Lupe's whole heart moved, and they were just going to kiss . . . when they both spotted a little fox looking at them from across the dry creek. And the little She-Fox had two young ones with her, and she was actually smiling at them.

"That's *mi mama!*" shouted Salvador, beaming with joy. "Look at her, my mother, the old She-Fox, and that's you and me, the two young ones that she's taking out into the world to teach!"

And Lupe knew Salvador had spoken the truth. For she, too, had gotten a glimpse of a little fox the day she'd been crawling through the brush, trying to get away from Salvador. And that little fox had smiled to her just as this She-Fox was now doing.

She breathed. That day of crawling through the brush and seeing Salvador roll into the cactus seemed like years ago—so much had happened since then.

Suddenly, Lupe remembered one of the many things that Doña Margarita had told her the day that she'd visited with her and the Blessed Mother at the outhouse.

"*Mi hijita,*" had said the old She-Fox, sitting in the outhouse with her Bible in hand and a *cigarrito* hanging from her mouth, "always remember that *el amor* isn't eternal like the poets like to say. No, love comes and goes, *mi hijita,* so here there needs to be trust and respect in between, or love will lessen every time 'til poof, we just don't know where it ever was.

"Respect, *mi hijita,* is the foundation of all love. For respect is the flame that rekindles love. Why do you think that rich, old fool in Tustin keeps sending his car to come and get me," she added, laughing. "It's not because of my great looks, I tell you. No, it's because it has been years since anyone spoke up to him. He respects me. And that respect has now lasted long enough to have grown into trust. And these, trust and respect, cannot be purchased. That's why he was so lonely, *mi hijita,* like only the rich and powerful can be lonely—having everything, and yet nothing at the same time. And here I came, not impressed with anything of his but his toilet paper, and the old fool got so excited, rekindling his love of life with such *gusto,* that he now thinks that he's in love with me.

"His household has moved out, saying that I'm a witch who's cast a spell on him, and I guess I am, because when I bathe him with herbs, massaging his feet, he gets so happy that he doesn't care what people think." She breathed. "Also, *mi hijita,* respect and trust—thank God—cannot be gained from here between the legs like our wet, hot, fires of passion, but must be earned in the depths of our Souls. Respect is the healing side of jealousy, and Trust is the healing side of fear, and together they are the sweetness that keeps a couple strong through their hard times of living Life, *la Vida.*"

And Respect and Trust was what Lupe now had for Salvador when he drew her close, and they kissed. Respect, the sweetest of all kisses, Trust the sweetest of all caresses, she was now beginning to see that she had for Salvador more and more each day as she grew to know him. And yes, she could also see that he was beginning to have more and more Respect and Trust for her, too.

So, yes, she now allowed him to draw her close, and they kissed, then kissed again.

The drums were beating.

The One Collective Heart-*Corazón* of Humanity was beat, Beat, BEATING!

And Here was the old She-Fox, herself, the *garrr-apata* up their spiritual ass for all eternity, watching over them from across the little dry riverbed.

A FEW DAYS LATER, Salvador was out making deliveries to his retailers, when he happened to drive through Oceanside and he saw Archie with a bunch of people at the front door of the bank. One old Indian woman was screaming hysterically, and the other people looked like they were ready to start screaming, too.

Having seen desperate people all of his life, Salvador parked his car across the street, making sure he could get away quickly if need be, then he got out of the Moon, glanced around, and went over to see what was going on. He was ready. For just like the rabbit or the deer, Salvador well knew that survival for a human depended on caution and speed afoot.

"That was all my money!" screamed the woman from the Pala Indian Reservation, grabbing Archie by the jacket and shaking him with all her might. "What will I do, Archie? What will I do? I lost everything!" And she hugged the big lawman close, crying all the more.

Another big, tall, huge Indian was kicking at the front doors of the bank, bellowing all he could. "You bastards! You lying, double-crossing rich sons-of-bitches! We want our money back!"

"What's going on?" asked Salvador, coming up to Archie.

"Don't you know?" said Archie, turning to see Salvador while holding the old lady close. "All across the country, banks are going belly-up! The whole nation is falling apart!"

"You mean somebody stole the money from all the banks?" asked Salvador. "But how can that be?" Salvador just couldn't conceive of such a far-reaching bank robbery. "Why, that would take a whole army of thieves, Archie!"

The big, huge Indian who was busy kicking the bank's doors, turned and screamed at Salvador! "It was an inside job, you dumb son-of-a-bitch! The bankers and their rich friends back in New York City stole our money, and ran out of the country!"

"Jesus!" said Salvador, suddenly feeling his face go pale. He'd told Lupe that he didn't trust banks! Oh, my God, my God, then they, too, had lost everything!

"Don't you read the papers?" said Archie angrily. "Don't you listen to the radio?"

"No," said Salvador. "I don't."

"Well, then, you must be the only son-of-a-bitch in the whole civilized nation who ain't going crazy!" yelled Archie.

The woman was now gagging and going into convulsions. Archie took off his jacket and put it on the sidewalk and helped the old Indian woman lie down on it.

"You got any liquor on you?" asked Archie of Salvador. "This is 'Aunt Gladys.' She's lost every penny she owned."

Salvador glanced around. He didn't want to be talking about his bootlegging business right here in front of everyone. "Archie," he said, "I don't know what you're talking about."

"Damnit!" bellowed Archie. "Don't give me any of your secret bootlegging shit! I need liquor, and right now! These people have lost everything they own—EVERYTHING!"

And he, Archie, this huge, powerful giant of a man, now began to cry, too. "Sal, I swear, this is just like they did to us when they took everything away from us years back and moved us from our springs on the back side of Palomar Mountain over to this side in Pala. They took our land, our homes, our—our Sacred Healing Springs! Bring me some whiskey, Sal! Dear Lord God, bring me some whiskey, right now, damnit!"

"You mean a quart?"

"No! I don't mean a bottle! I mean a whole damn barrel! Or I'll arrest your ass for not reading newspapers!"

"Okay, okay, I'll be right back," said Salvador, realizing that Archie wasn't joking. "I'll go get it." And he got into his Moon and drove over to the San Luis Rey riverbed about half a mile west of the Mission, where he'd just buried a couple of barrels. He glanced around to make sure that no one was looking, then he dug up one barrel and drove right back into Oceanside.

Now, there were well over a hundred people, and not just Indians, but Blacks, Whites, Mexicans, Filipinos and Japanese—and they were all behind the bank in the alley, crying and screaming, or just sitting on the ground and staring in utter shock.

When Archie saw Salvador drive up, he rushed over and with huge power, just yanked the barrel out of the trunk as if it weighed nothing, then he bellowed!

"Free whiskey for everybody! Come on, let's drink! Everybody's got to get drunk! I'm having a steer brought in, too, and we're going to have a *barbacoa* on the beach by the pier, and everybody has got to get shit-faced drunk! What's money, anyway? Just a bunch of worthless paper when you got friends! Come on, let's get drunk! And eat Archie's *barbacoa*! The best! Shit, life is just getting started! Who needs money when you got friends, and food, and plenty of free whiskey?"

"You bet!" yelled a man. "With free whiskey, we got everything!"

And the people came to Archie in a mad rush, and he poured the liquor into their hats, their hands, and down their throats. Soon people were laughing, and a couple of men started throwing rocks at the bank windows. And Archie, who was wearing his gun and badge, only laughed.

Coming over to Salvador, Archie put his huge arm around him. "Thanks, Sal," said Archie, glancing around at all the drinking, laughing people. "Poor bastards, they don't even know the half of it yet!" He took a big breath. "It's just beginning. They're gonna lose their homes and little ranches, too. Businesses are going to start folding right and left . . . and there ain't going to be no jobs, Sal, and then these fine people—my friends, my family—will start robbing and . . . and . . . I'm the law, Sal, and I'll have to come after 'em."

The tears ran down Archie's huge, long face, and he hugged Salvador in a big *abrazo*!

"But Archie," said Salvador, trying to understand what was being told to him, "how did this all happen? I don't see no change. I mean, I drive down the road and I see everything the same as yesterday, fat cattle, lots of oranges in the trees, big crops of avocados coming in, and acres and acres of tomatoes and lettuce, and people working and doing good. So what happened? Is there a revolution going on, or what?"

"Yeah, I guess you could call this a revolution," said Archie. "You see, from what I've been told, all of our main banks for our whole country are all located back in New York City and, as someone tried to explain to me yesterday, those banks loaned out too much money on too little collateral to their rich friends for stocks and bonds, and now these rich people are broke and can't pay back the banks."

"Now I get it," said Salvador. "That's the oldest trick in gambling! You put out a bunch of extra chips on credit, then when the time comes for the house to cover the chips, they don't have enough money, so they go broke."

"Exactly!" said Archie. "So now our local bankers are just as broke and all screwed up as those big banks back in New York City, Sal."

"I see, I see," said Salvador, scratching his head, "but how can a country be so stupid? It don't make sense. Somebody knew, Archie. And this somebody who knew made a lot of money on everybody else going broke."

"Yeah, that makes sense," said Archie, "some of those rich people in New York must've known, so they just stole all the chickens from all the chicken coops across the country before the crash!"

Salvador nodded. "I've seen many a'gambling house do this. They just let the house go broke, because the house people, they aren't held responsible. Hell, if the law was that we hang the ones who run the house, then this would never happen!"

"Jesus, you're right!" screamed Archie, and he now picked up a brick and threw it at the bank building himself. "You greedy, scheming bastards ought to be hung 'til dead!"

Seeing Archie, the law, do this, the people cheered, and Archie laughed, throwing another brick.

Quickly, quietly, Salvador slipped off, got in his Moon, and drove away. He hoped to God that he and Lupe could get to their bank in Corona before it closed its doors, too.

He never should have listened to Lupe and put their money in the bank. This was exactly what the entire Mexican Revolution had been all about, too. Don Porfirio, the big wolf, instead of guarding the chicken coop for the good of *la gente,* he'd given Mexico away to all his rich foreign friends, piece by piece, all in the name of progress.

Getting to their little rented house in the avocado orchard in Carlsbad, Salvador breathed deeply, trying to calm down. But his heart-*corazón* kept racing. A large part of him just felt like rushing in and telling Lupe that it was all her damn fault that they'd lost everything! That he'd never wanted to put their money in the bank in the first place!

But, also, Salvador realized that this wouldn't help. That what he really needed to do was take both of his *tanates* in hand, face the Devil of

Blaming, and get Lupe out of the house as quickly as possible and to Corona to their bank.

Breathing deep, Salvador got out of the Moon and went inside of their home. And there was *Chingon*, their little dog, in the house.

"Lupe," he said, coming up behind her, "we got to go to Corona," he added as calmly as he could.

"But I have lunch ready," she said.

"Lupe, this is an emergency," he said, still trying to keep tame his heart, which was beating wildly!

"Oh, your mother! Why didn't you say. I'll just get my purse, and coat!"

"Good!" he said, grabbing up the food that she'd been cooking in the frying pan with a couple of *tortillas*. "And bring our bankbook!" He ate the food as they went back out to the car. As they drove, he told Lupe what he'd seen in Oceanside and how Archie had ordered him to get him a barrel of whiskey.

"The people were going crazy," said Salvador. "And Archie explained to me that this is just the beginning, that now people are going to be losing their homes and little ranches, too. And then that he, Archie, the law, will have to start coming after them when they start robbing and stealing to feed their families."

Lupe was silent. She didn't say one single word. Tears were running down her face.

"You hate me, don't you, Salvador?" she finally asked.

He took a deep breath. "Lupe," he said, "we don't know if we've lost our money yet. Corona is little, not big like Oceanside. So, well, maybe people out there don't read the newspapers."

"Thank you, Salvador," said Lupe.

"For what?"

"For finding hope," she said. "For not yelling at me, for not throwing it in my face how I got you to put our money in the bank."

"Don't be thanking me yet," said Salvador, taking in a big breath. "Let's just keep hoping right now, that we draw some good cards in this game that we're now in."

Hearing this, Lupe asked, "Then to you, Salvador, everything is a gamble?"

"Exactly. All of life! Completely! To live is to gamble."

"I see," said Lupe.

And they didn't say another word. Each retreated to their own world, trying to make sense of what was happening to them in terms that they could understand. And their "terms" were very different. *Cada cabeza, un mundo,* every head a different world.

Then getting into Corona, Salvador immediately drove over to the Anglo part of town where they'd deposited their money in a bank. Parking, they both quickly got out of the Moon and approached the bank. There was no one around, like at the bank in Oceanside.

Salvador grinned, figuring that maybe everything was okay. But then, walking up to the front doors, they saw that the doors were all boarded up.

Salvador's whole heart went crashing down into his gut, then came leaping up into his throat! And he was gagging, choking, tasting this sour-metal green gunk that came to his mouth from out of his stomach!

Their bank had already gone broke and closed its doors! They, too, had lost all of their money in all the world. My God, why had he ever listened to Lupe. Men did get weak and stupid in the head once they married!

If it weren't for the fact Lupe was pregnant with their child, he'd send her packing home to her parents right now! He couldn't afford to have a weak, ignorant woman around him who had absolutely no idea what went on in the world, and yet kept acting so high-and-mighty, trying to tell him what to do!

To hell with his mother's advice, too, about men needing to listen to women. He'd just lost all of his money, because he'd listened to a woman's advice! And he'd worked so hard for this money, putting in days of sixteen and eighteen hours, and he'd just been getting ready to finish paying off his friend Kenny White!

And Salvador now found himself ready to start screaming just as those people had been doing in Oceanside! He was devastated. And Archie had said that this was just the beginning, that businesses were going to start closing down right and left.

Holding his stomach so he wouldn't throw up, Salvador was just turning around go back to their car, when he saw that Lupe was reading a small sign over at the side of the doors.

"Salvador," she was saying, "come and look, this sign says that the bank has moved around the corner to a new location."

"What?" said Salvador.

"This sign says that the bank has moved around the corner to a new location," she repeated.

"My God," said Salvador, coming over and looking at the sign that had an arrow pointing toward the right, "then maybe, Lupe, just maybe, this bank hasn't gone broke like the one in Oceanside, but has, well, maybe, just moved to a new location!"

"Yes," said Lupe, "I think that this might be the case."

Suddenly, Salvador's whole heart came back down into his chest and it was pounding something fierce! He turned, walking briskly up the street in the direction that the arrow pointed, then . . . he was running! And Lupe, she was right behind him, running, too!

Rounding the corner, still running, Salvador and Lupe saw a new building halfway down the block on the other side of the street. Salvador didn't even bother to look right and left as he raced across the street through the traffic, causing vehicles to slam on their brakes!

Getting to the other sidewalk, Salvador stopped to catch his breath, then he took Lupe's hand when she came up. She was holding up much better than he. Oh, my God, he felt lightheaded! He'd been holding his breath the whole time that he'd been running. He was pouring with sweat!

Blowing out, Salvador caught his breath, then he and Lupe walked up to the new building together. And yes, this new building was, indeed, the bank, and yes, this bank was open. They could see people inside doing business.

Salvador had to take several deep breaths, before he could open the door for Lupe. Following Lupe inside, the blood was finally beginning to come back into Salvador's face.

It smelled so good inside of the new building. The paint, the wood, the marble flooring. They both had to breathe deeply several times to tame their *corazones*. Then their eyes met and—oh, it was like magic between them, they were so happy!

Salvador squeezed Lupe's hand. And she squeezed his hand back. There were just a few people in the bank, so Salvador and Lupe quickly walked up to the first available cashier. Lupe opened her purse and brought out their bankbook, and asked for their money. The teller didn't even bat an eye.

"Certainly," he said, "do you want it in twenties or fifties?"

"I guess, a few of each," said Lupe. "But mostly twenties. Is that all right with you, Salvador?"

"Oh, yes, that's very all right with me!" said he.

"Good," said the teller.

"Yes, good," said Salvador. "Very good!"

And Salvador and Lupe would never forget the joy, the absolute *gusto*, that came to their hearts as they stood there watching the teller pull open his drawer and bring out a pile of crisp, new twenties and fifties, counting out their money for them with a quick little snapping sound.

It was money music to their ears!

No man and woman had ever walked taller out the doors of a bank than Salvador and Lupe when they came strolling out arm in arm, with a bulge of money so big and fat that it was pressing to break the seams of Lupe's purse!

"Salvador," said Lupe, once they were outside and walking up the street, "I'm going to need to get a bigger purse if we keep doing this."

"Okay, honey, *no problema*. We'll get you a bigger purse."

They strolled up that street, there in the Anglo part of Corona, looking like the most proud and happy couple ever seen on *toda la planeta de esta Tierra Madre*!

11

HEAVEN was laughing con carcajadas! Love, love, AMOR
was now Creating *a whole new* PARAISO *on* EARTH *as it
was in* HEAVEN!

THE DRUMS WERE BEATING!
The Drums were Beat, BEAT, BEATING, POUNDING in Unison with the Heartbeat of the Universe! GOD'S One Song!

Salvador and Lupe were now in Love in a whole new deeper and fuller way. Theirs was now a life of being out on their own!

But their challenges were not to cease. Lupe was now getting morning sickness and she felt terrible half of the time. And Salvador was gone so much, that it was causing her a new kind of fear. What if an emergency came up and she had to go to the doctor? Their doctor was way up in Santa Ana, more than an hour away and she had no means of getting there.

To make matters worse, this morning Salvador left before daybreak, saying that he'd be gone a couple of days, that he was going to stop by and pay Kenny White the rest of the money that he owed him, then he was maybe going to have to go north to see a Chinese man way up in Hanford near Fresno.

Lupe had said nothing, for she could see how hard Salvador was working, but when he didn't come home that night—she got scared. He was in danger once again. She could just feel it here inside of herself. By the next day she was sick and lying in bed feeling so weak and terrible that she could hardly move. This was when a knocking sounded on their front door. Lupe listened to the knocking, trying to figure out what was going on. For *Chingon*, their trusty little dog, hadn't barked any warning.

Cautiously, Lupe got out of bed, wondering who it could be and if this person was coming to tell her that Salvador had been killed or put in jail.

Lupe had to put her left hand to the small of her back. She felt so weak and now, for the last few days, her back was hurting, too. She'd never had any idea what a woman went through with a pregnancy.

"Coming!" shouted Lupe, going to the bathroom, sitting on the toilet, then brushing back her hair. The knocking continued. Walking across the living room to the front door, Lupe could hear that their dog, *Chingon*, was happy with whoever had come.

Lupe licked her lips and tried to straighten herself up as best she could. "Who is it?" she said through the closed door.

"Helen," said the German woman. Helen and Hans rented this house to Salvador and Lupe. "Salvador asked me to come by and have a little look in on you, honey!"

"Thank you, but I'm all right," said Lupe, not feeling well enough to see anyone.

"Lupe," said Helen, "open the door, honey, I brought you some bread fresh out of the oven I just made and—LUPE!" shouted Helen, seeing Lupe as she opened the door. "Child, you've lost weight! And your color is gone! Come, let's put you back in bed and I'll kill a chicken and make you some good soup and get Salvador to take you to the doctor first thing!" she added with authority.

"But I'm all right," said Lupe. "Really, I don't want to bother you. I'm not that sick."

"Honey, you don't want to wait 'til you get THAT sick! We got to take care of you now, before you get all run-down! Come," she said, stepping inside. "I'm putting you back in bed and Salvador is going to get an earful from me when I see him!"

Helen did exactly as she said she was going to do. She put Lupe to bed, tucking her in, gave her a slice of hot bread with freshly-made butter, then went across the orchard, killed one of their fattest chickens and came back to make Lupe a pot of soup.

Lying in bed and hearing Helen working in the kitchen, Lupe felt like she'd magically been transported back to their home in their beloved box canyon, and she could now hear the sounds of her *familia*—her sisters, her mother, and her brother. Victoriano chopping wood with that chop-chop-chopping sound. And Carlota, Maria, and Sophia helping their mother at the wood-burning stove, making *tortillas* with that slap, slap, pat, pat-patting sound, and the smell of *nopalitos*, cactus, and other wild plants and game.

She hadn't realized how much she'd missed these sounds, and smells.

Why, the smell of Helen's cooking was Heaven, itself, a gift straight from God. No house could be a home without the smell of food cooking.

Lupe ate with *gusto* for the first time in weeks.

She devoured the hot bread fresh out of the oven and she loved the way Helen held her head to spoon-feed her like a baby. Oh, how she missed her mother and her sisters. A man's love was wonderful, but it could never replace those tender feelings between sisters and mother.

IT WAS LATE that second day when Salvador came home dog tired.

In Hanford, he'd talked to his friend, the Chinese Godfather, and it had been exactly as he'd feared, a head-on confrontation with the *Italianos* had erupted. But it had been the Chinese who'd come to Salvador and not the *Italianos*, whom Salvador had been doing business with on a weekly basis ever since he'd served time with Al Cappola in Tulare. Both sides realized that Salvador was holding the wildcard, because *los Mejicanos* now ran the prisons in the Southwest, and so if any of their people went to prison, they were going to have to deal with the Mexicans, whether they liked it or not.

It had almost come to a gun battle, but—unarmed—Salvador had finally gotten both sides to put down their weapons and come to terms where they could all do business.

But seeing Salvador come in dog-tired, didn't stop Helen one little bit.

The German woman had been having it out with her husband, Hans, since they'd gotten together when she was a teenager. She was on Salvador like a hawk, telling him that Lupe had to be taken to the doctor first thing tomorrow morning, that she was run-down and had to be fed properly and given attention!

"She's with your child, Salvador!" yelled Helen. "And you will stay here with her and be responsible!"

Salvador was speechless.

Lupe tried to get up and come into the kitchen and explain to Helen that she didn't have to be so angry with Salvador. Mexican people didn't go to the doctor for any little thing, and Salvador was being as attentive as he could when he was home. But Lupe felt too weak to get up, so she just lay back down in bed and continued listening to Helen telling Salvador off.

Also, there was a part of Lupe that was really feeling pretty good at hearing this woman telling off her husband. For it was true, here she was pregnant with their child, and he, the man, was just free to run around doing whatever he wished while she was stuck at home.

"And if you can't be here with her," continued Helen as if reading Lupe's mind, "then you bring Lupe's sister to stay with her, and you pay her sister to help you! A pregnant girl needs her family with her, so that she's not home alone!"

"Her sister!" shouted Salvador, speaking back for the first time. "Oh, no! You don't understand, Helen!"

"Oh, yes, I do understand! It's you who don't understand! You're a man, Salvador, and you don't know what it is to be pregnant and feel all alone and helpless! You will bring her sister, and you will do it right now, for the good of your family! And I'm telling Hans! So he, too, will be speaking to you. We're your friends, Salvador. And friends talk bluntly!"

After Helen left, Salvador was in a daze. His confrontation with the two armed camps had been easy compared to this. Bringing Carlota into his home was a terrible thought.

Breathing, he went into the bedroom to see Lupe. *"Mi querida,"* he said, "I had no idea that you were so sick. But now I can see that Helen is right, you have lost your color." He sat down on the bed beside her. "First thing in the morning we're going to the doctor. But, about Carlota, well, I just don't know, Lupe."

"I'm okay," said Lupe. "Helen was just upset when she found me alone. We don't need to bring my sister."

"Well, yes, maybe we don't," said Salvador, taking her hand and stroking it, "but maybe we do." And saying this, he breathed and he breathed again. "I love you, Lupe," he said softly, "and we'll do whatever we need to do for you, and our child."

Tears came to Lupe's eyes. These were the sweetest words she'd ever heard, because she well knew how much Salvador didn't like Carlota. She lay quietly in bed, looking at Salvador's eyes as he continued stroking her hand. "Come here," she said, "I want to kiss you, Salvador."

And so they kissed, soft and gentle.

IT WAS NINE O'CLOCK in the morning when Salvador and Lupe got to the doctor's office in Santa Ana. They'd left Carlsbad at daybreak, stopped in San Clemente, gassed up and had a big, delicious breakfast roll. But Lupe was having a hard time keeping the roll down.

Taking one look at Lupe, the tall, handsome nurse immediately took her in to see the doctor. Salvador was left in the waiting room. There were two other women with children in the small waiting room. One of the women was Mexican. It looked like she was in her early twenties, but she already had five kids, and the smallest was nursing from her. Salvador began making faces at the oldest boy, trying to get him to laugh, but he was about ten years old and ignored Salvador, acting like he was too old to play such a silly game.

Laughing, Salvador began making faces at the little three-year-old girl. But she only smiled and quickly got behind her mother, poking out her cute little round brown face now and then to glance at this strange-acting man, Salvador, who was making funny faces at her.

The mother was too tired to enjoy Salvador's behavior, and so she just kept quiet as Salvador continued playing with her kids for nearly an hour. Salvador began to get anxious. He got up, and asked the nurse if everything was all right.

"The doctor will call you when he's ready," said the tall woman.

Salvador almost felt like reaching over the counter and grabbing the nurse by the throat. He didn't like her coldness. He began to pace. He prayed to God that Lupe was all right. He didn't want anything to happen to her. What a fool he'd been to keep bringing home all that money, forcing it upon her when he damn well knew how she felt about gambling and liquor. If anything happened to her, he was totally to blame, because he was sure that it was all this worry that had worn her down.

"All right, Mr. Villaseñor," said the nurse, coming up to him, "please, follow me. The doctor will see you now."

Salvador followed the tall, slender woman who was dressed all in white down the hallway. He hadn't noticed before, but this nurse was an attractive woman, just too skinny. Opening the door at the end of the hallway, she told Salvador to please go inside and be seated, and the doctor would be with him in a moment.

"But where is Lupe?" he asked. "Is she all right?"

"Yes, she's fine," said the nurse. "The doctor just likes to see the prospective father by himself on a couple's first visit."

"I see," said Salvador, going inside.

Glancing around, Salvador figured that this was the doctor's private office. It had a large, dark desk and a huge leather chair behind the desk and two walls of solid books and magazines. He decided to go behind the desk and sit in the big chair, to try it out, but then he heard voices outside in the hallway, so he quickly took one of the small upright chairs in front of the large desk. The door opened and in came the doctor. He was a tall, slender, nice-looking man in his midforties. Salvador stood up.

"No, please, keep your seat," said the doctor, going behind his huge desk. He looked like he was in a big hurry, until he got to the huge chair. Then he took hold of the wide arms of the chair and lowered his body into the wonderful-looking chair with an ease and care that showed his true appreciation of this fine piece of furniture. "It's been a busy morning," he said. "Twice I've already been to the hospital."

"Lupe?" said Salvador. "She had to go to the—"

"Oh, no," said the doctor, seeing the fear in Salvador's eyes, "Lupe is fine. She had nothing whatsoever to do with my trips to the hospital. Sorry, that I didn't make myself clear.

"Look," he said, rolling back into the deep, soft, comfort of the leather chair, "I asked you in because I like to have a little talk with the fathers about their wives and the future of their family."

Salvador swallowed. "Okay," he said. "But I thought that you said that Lupe is fine."

"She is," said the doctor, obviously loving the feel of the fine chair.

Salvador tried to relax, but he was feeling more and more uncomfortable by the moment. His mother had never been to a doctor in all her life, and she'd had nineteen kids. He just couldn't figure out what was going on.

"Would you like a drink?" asked the doctor, seeing how upset Salvador was.

"You mean medicine?"

"No, I mean a shot of schnapps. It's a German liquor."

"Oh, liquor! Sure!" said Salvador, immediately licking his lips and salivating.

The doctor opened a drawer and pulled a bottle and two small glasses out of his desk. He served them each a drink. "Here," he said, handing one to Salvador, "to your first child!"

"To my son!" said Salvador, and he shot the whole drink down in one gulp, but it was so sweet and thick that it tasted like hell. He started gagging.

"You sip schnapps," said the doctor. "Sloooowly."

"Oh," said Salvador, his eyes beginning to water. "Good stuff," he added, still gagging.

"Here, I'll give you a little more, but sip it this time," said the doctor, pouring Salvador very little this time.

"Okay, sure," said Salvador, pounding his chest to clear his throat. He tried to sit back like the doctor this time, but his chair wouldn't lean back.

Someday he would like to have a chair like the doctor's but at the dinner table, so he could lean back between bites to chew leisurely like a bull eating off the fat of the land.

"Salvador—is it all right if I call you Salvador?"

"Well, yes, of course," said Salvador, watching how the doctor was sipping his drink slowly and looking so grand in his big chair.

"Salvador, I've been a doctor for nearly twenty years," said the man dressed in white, "and over those years, I've learned that to be a good family doctor, it's important for me to know all about my patients, and their entire family.

"For instance, I've been attending to Sophia—Lupe's sister—and her family for nearly five years now, and sometimes I know when they're going to come in sick, days before they even come in. You see, a family is like a living organism, a cluster of cells, a group of individuals who are united, even though they also have separate lives. I've come to respect that woman Sophia and her family very much. You have married into a wonderful family, Salvador, and you and Lupe can have a wonderful, long life together with lots of happiness and success."

He stopped and sipped his schnapps again. And Salvador copied him, sipping a little bit, too, and it was a fine, smooth drink when you took it down in this way.

"Tell me, Salvador," continued the doctor, "how long have you and Lupe been married?"

"Well, let's see," said Salvador, feeling a lot better now that the liquor was taking hold and smoothing him out. "It's the first of November, right? So we've been married almost three months," said Salvador.

"Almost three months, and you're already expecting your first child?"

"Yes, of course," said Salvador, wondering what all this was about. Hell, it normally only took one mounting for a bull to get a cow pregnant.

"Well, Salvador," said the doctor, "I've been here in California for ten years, and in that amount of time, I've seen many beautiful, young Mexican couples come to me, like you and Lupe—and believe me, these young people have no trouble whatsoever getting pregnant—and they get pregnant year after year, every sixteen or eighteen months, like clockwork." He stopped and leaned in close to Salvador. "How many children are you and Lupe planning on having?"

"Planning on having?" said Salvador. He was astonished. Why, he'd never heard of such a ridiculous question. "Well, I don't know," he said. "I guess whatever God gives us."

"I see," said the doctor, sitting back. "And, if God gives you twenty, you'll have twenty?"

"I guess so. My mother had nineteen."

"Nineteen!" said the doctor.

"Well, yes, sure, but her sister who married my father's brother had twenty-two, and all twenty-two lived. You see, only fourteen of my mother's nineteen lived, so we were a small family."

"A small family at fourteen!" said the doctor. And he was the one who now seemed upset. He finished off his schnapps and served himself another drink. He didn't offer Salvador any this time, and he put the bottle away. "Look," he said, "strange as this might sound, Salvador, children just don't come from God. A couple, also, has the ability of choosing how large or small a family they want."

"They do?!?" said Salvador. He was flabbergasted!

"Well, yes, of course. Tell me, do you have any idea how much strain each pregnancy puts on the female body? Does your mother have any teeth left?"

"Teeth?" said Salvador, taken aback. "Well, no, she doesn't have many, but she still walks to church every day and is in good health."

"Well, I'm glad that she's in good health and walks to church every day," said the doctor. "You're a very lucky man. But, you see, Salvador, with each pregnancy, a mother gives nutrients to the child from her body—calcium from her teeth and bones. A woman needs years to replenish her body after each pregnancy. Did you notice my wife—the nurse who brought you into my office? How old do you suppose she is, Salvador?"

Salvador shrugged. "Maybe oh, thirty-five."

"Patricia will be fifty next month. You see, I love my wife very much, Salvador, and I want her to live a long, healthy life, and so that's why we decided long ago to have only three children. And we would've had only two, if we'd had a boy and girl to start."

Salvador didn't know what to say. My God, he'd never heard such wild talk in all of his life! Who did this doctor think he was, anyway? Children were a gift straight from God, everyone knew that! Why, if his mother had stopped having kids at two or three, he, himself, Salvador, would never have even been born! This was terrible! How could this doctor be saying these terrible things? Everyone knew that to be a real *hombre*, you had to have as many children as you possibly could. Twelve at least!

Then the truth of the matter hit Salvador. This doctor was just jealous that he and his skinny, bony wife had only been able to have three kids. What kind of family was that, anyway? Three kids was nothing! Absolutely *nada, nada*! Salvador almost laughed. No wonder his skinny wife had been so arrogant with him, she was all dried up and jealous that she couldn't have more kids. This was what was really going on here. Jealousy!

"Here," said the doctor, "I'll serve you a little bit more. I imagine that a lot of what I've said to you might, well, sound a little strange."

"Yes," said Salvador, "very strange."

"But if you'll listen to me, Salvador, I assure you, that not only is it possible to plan how many children you'll have, but it will also be very worthwhile. Don't you have some brothers and sisters who have done better than others?"

"Well, yes, of course," said Salvador.

"Well, by limiting the number of children that you and Lupe have, you'll be able to spend more time with each of them and educate them in a way that just isn't possible with a larger family. Education, this is the key for success in this country."

And here the doctor stopped and looked at Salvador. "And, please," the doctor now added, "don't be too quick to reject all that I've said to you, Salvador. For I know that you love Lupe very much. She's a beautiful young woman, and I saw how concerned you became for her when I made the mistake of mentioning the hospital earlier.

"But, I am saying that if you and Lupe just keep having children year after year, not only will she lose her teeth, but she won't have a very long life. On the other hand, if you and Lupe plan the number of children that you and she have, you can keep her beautiful and young with all of her teeth for many fine, wonderful years."

Salvador was speechless. He didn't know what to say or even think. Why, this whole conversation was an outrage!

"When I first arrived here in California," continued the doctor, "I used to have all these beautiful young Mexican couples come in to see me and have six or eight children before I dared to even speak to them. But now I've found that when I speak to couples right away, with their first child, it works out best. Please, Salvador, I'd like for you to talk this over with your wife and, if you're interested, my wife and I will be happy to discuss matters with each of you so that you two can continue enjoying yourselves as a man and a woman and still have a long, happy marriage, and an affordable number of children."

Salvador's whole face turned red. Why, this doctor was now talking about sex. And no one discussed sex openly like this outside of their immediate family.

Seeing Salvador's reaction, the doctor added, "I hope you listened, Salvador, and that you will think about all this. And if not, that's all right, too. I will not be bringing up this subject again. This is your decision. Thank you for listening."

"Well," said Salvador, scratching his head, "I'd thought that you'd brought me in here to talk about Lupe, and if she's all right or not. I never expected all of this," he added.

"Lupe is fine at this point," said the doctor. "She's young, and she might have a little difficulty in the mornings during this first pregnancy, but Mexicans are a very strong people, and every day I see them go through difficulties that would put most other people in the hospital. Yes, Salvador, Lupe is fine right now."

"Good," said Salvador. "Because you were scaring me with all your talk of planning babies."

"Well, I didn't mean to frighten you, Salvador. But Lupe also isn't one of these powerful women who can just keep having children year after year. You think about everything that I've said, Salvador, and as I said, you and Lupe can still enjoy yourselves as a man and woman all you want, but what I'm saying is that each time you do this, you don't have to end up with a child."

Hearing this, Salvador had to take a big breath. His whole head was spinning. "But the priests," said Salvador, "they're always telling us that to enjoy ourselves—you know, as a man and a woman, without making children is a great—how do you say it, *un pecado*!"

"A sin?" asked the doctor.

"Yes, that's it," said Salvador. "A sin! A very bad sin!"

"Look," said the doctor, seeing how upset Salvador had become, "I was raised Catholic, too, back in Germany. But long ago, quite frankly, I stopped paying attention to men who have no children or a wife when it comes to matters of love and family."

Salvador was shocked. He began to sweat. This was an outrage! Even when he'd been at his angriest with God, Salvador would never have said that he wouldn't listen to what a priest had to say.

"Tell me," continued the doctor, "would you take your car to get fixed by a man who's never driven or owned an automobile?"

"Well, no, of course not," said Salvador, pulling at his collar and wiping the sweat from his forehead.

"Then I suggest that you listen to the priests about those matters that have to do with God, but not about women and children. What can any priest possibly know? The poor men live a very limited life, at best, Salvador."

Salvador was speechless. Instinctively, Salvador now felt like making the sign of the cross over himself to protect himself from this man. He wondered what his mother would say about this doctor's ideas. He wondered what Lupe would say when he told her. My God, he needed a real drink of his own whiskey, and right now!

The drums were beating.

The Drums were beat, Beat, BEATING!

And he, Salvador, now wanted to ask this man if he was still a Catholic, and if he still believed in God, but he was afraid to ask.

DOÑA MARGARITA WAS INSIDE of the little stone church on the left-hand side, two pews back from the front, and she was on her feet, shouting at the statue of the Virgin Mary. "Give it to us, *Maria*! Give it to us, *Maria de Guadalupe!* Don't be afraid! *Los chingasos de la Vida* are not new to us, *los Mejicanos*! We will not fail You! We are STRONG with FAITH!"

In her mind's eye, Salvador's mother could still see the cannons of the Revolution flashing in the darkening day as the tens of thousands of unarmed people—mostly women and children—made their way along the railroad tracks with their newborns in their arms and their little ones at their sides as the soldiers loaded their horses into the boxcars!

Homeless people!

Starving people!

Frightened people!

And all around them machine guns sang! Cannons blasted!

Both Americans and Germans trying out their newest wares of war in Mexico in the first glimpses of the First World War.

"*Santa Maria, Madre de Dios! Santa Maria, Madre de Dios! Santa Maria, aaaaaaa-yuuuuuudaaa-NOS! Santa Maria, Madre de Dios!*"

Doña Margarita continued singing, praying these sacred words in church, and in her Heart-Eye she saw herself and all these mothers continuing here alongside the railroad tracks going north, hoping to get to the border of the United States; that land, that country, that promiseland where dreams came true!

Carranzas's troops were on one side with their German-made machine guns singing! And their German-made cannons blasting open the whole sky!

Villa's troops were on the other side with their heavy, American-made cannons and machine guns spitting flashes of fire, too!

The Father Sun was just going down and the day was beginning to cool. A group of fine carriages came up on the north banks of the Rio Grande, and well-dressed people got down from their carriages and their Black servants . . . set out chairs and tables for a grand picnic—future American Generals of World Wars I and II learning their trade of death and destruction here in Mexico as young lieutenants.

The western sky streaked in colors of red and orange, pink and lavender, and the fine, well-educated people laughed and sipped champagne as they looked across the river, watching the masses of escaping *gente*!

Brown people. Not their people. "Expendable" was their new key word because they had the whole world in their hands! And what the hell, war was natural.

Doña Margarita kept praying inside of the little stone church, and in her Heart-Eye she could still see herself and all these mothers as they now came pouring up over a group of little white sand hills, crying with *gusto* when they at last saw the Rio Grande right down below them!

Drinking from long-stem glasses, the people across the river watched as the mass of brown-skin people left the tracks and came rushing across the sand hills toward the river like people to the promiseland.

The fine, well-dressed people continued drinking champagne, eating finger-foods as they heard the children screech with delight, and start splashing about in the shallow brown waters!

On the north side of the river, just below the people in carriages, stood the United States Army. Young soldiers watching the masses of people pouring up over the white sand hills, crying with *gusto* as they came rushing down toward the cool, wet river waters.

Officers barked orders to hold the line!

Sergeants shouted to keep steady!

But the brown skins kept coming and coming by the thousands!

Finally a couple of confused, frightened, young soldiers opened fire on the unarmed women and children!

The Rio Grande ran red with blood.

And inside of the stone church, Doña Margarita continued praying, remembering how she'd been crying in agony, reaching for this little child's body, only to come up with the child's intestines in her hands, and she'd SCREAMED up to the HEAVENS, and this was when she'd seen those people with their fine carriages across the river up on the embankment, laughing and eating and drinking in the cool shade of their umbrellas, while the *gente* were cut down all about her and she held this lifeless child in her arms!

"SANTA MARIA, MADRE DE DIOS!" Doña Margarita now continued praying, chanting with tears streaming down her face as she stood here inside of the little stone church, arms out, palms up, Singing, Chanting, Praying! "Give it to us, my Lady! Give it to us! For we are strong with faith! We will not fail You! WE WILL NOT FAIL YOU! For *los chingasos* of Life are no more new to us, *los Mejicanos*, than the Jews of old! GIVE IT TO US! For the sins of the world must be made pure once and for all! Prison or marriage, I don't care! My children will grow! For *mata-los-demonios* is why we are all here on this *Tierra Firme*! And we are a strong *gente con mucha fe! Y MUY CHINGONES!"*

And saying this, Doña Margarita finally sat back down. She was spent. She was done. But, still, she could hear the cannons and the machine guns and the people screaming in terror and she could still feel that child's warm, slippery, bloody intestines as she wrung her hands, trying to cleanse them.

And this killing of women and children wasn't new. In their voyage northward, when the soldiers of Carranza and Villa couldn't kill each other, they'd both turn their fine weaponry at the unarmed mass of people, firing on them.

Doña Margarita now continued mumbling, *"Santa Maria, Madre de Dios! Santa Maria, Madre de Dios! Santa Maria, Madre de Dios!"* over and over again, as the tears streamed down her face.

So many people she'd seen shot all around her.

She must've fallen asleep, for the next thing she knew, she awoke with a start. "Oh, I'm sorry, my Lady," she said. The Sacred Virgin, Mother of God, had come out of her statue and was now here, standing before her. "I must've gone to sleep."

"That's quite all right," said the Mother of God. "Rest, all We mothers need our rest. I'll wait here, keeping you company."

"Thank you," said Doña Margarita, "I know I got a little insistent on calling You, but we do need to speak."

"Fine, now rest."

And so the Mother of God began to hum like a turtledove, giving such love and warmth, that little by little, Doña Margarita drifted back off to sleep.

For this was, indeed, her place, her "spot," her sacred "station," on the left-hand side of the stone church two pews from the front, from which she spoke to the Spirit World, and found her strength to go on. And every woman needed such a "place" from which to view Life, *la Vida,* or it could all suddenly get to be too overwhelming to handle.

The Mother of God continued Humming, Singing, and this time when Doña Margarita awoke, she felt much better.

"Oh, that was wonderful, my Lady," said the old She-Fox. She stretched and yawned, then smiled. "By the way, my Lady," she said, feeling refreshed and full of mischief, "have you heard the one about Don Cacahuate, Mr. Peanuts, going to church on Good Friday?"

"No, I haven't," said the Virgin *de Guadalupe.*

"Well, there was Don Cacahuate," said Doña Margarita, "with all the people following the priest through the Holy Stations of the Cross, picture by picture, as they all said the rosary. And at every station that they'd come to, the priest would describe the picture before they prayed. 'And here,' would say the priest, 'we have Our Lord Jesus being whipped as he carried the cross up the hill.'

" 'Ha,' would say Don Cacahuate under his breath, 'I'd like to see Him married to my wife, Josefina, for just two minutes!'

"Then they'd go to the next picture and the priest would say, 'And here we have Our Lord God Jesus falling to one knee and struggling to get up as the soldiers whip him.'

" 'Ha,' would say Don Cacahuate, 'I'd like to see Him married for just two minutes to my wife, Josefina!'

"And so they went through all Holy Stations of the Cross, My Lady," said Doña Margarita, "and finally getting to the last one, not only did Don Cacahuate say—but all the people now said along with him—'Ha! That's nothing! We'd like to see Him married for just two minutes to Josefina!'

"Just then, Don Cacahuate's wife, Josefina, entered the church and everyone scattered, even the priest, running the fastest of all!"

Saying this, Doña Margarita was laughing and laughing. "Don't that beat all, my Lady, even the tortures that Your Son, Lord Jesus, endured are nothing compared to the fears that some people have of being married!

"And how did this human phenomenon come about? Eh, You tell me? Because as I see it, my Lady, it should be the other way around, and people should be most happy to be paired off together so that they can work out their differences in the Loving Union of Marriage.

"But so many of us aren't. Why, right now, as we speak, even my last-born, who I raised up like a woman so he'd have respect for women, still has trouble dealing with the *problemas* that arise in life, without wanting to blame it all on his wife, Lupe."

Just then, as the Virgin Mary and Doña Margarita were speaking, Jesus Christ came walking up.

"Oh, no, not now," said Doña Margarita, seeing Jesus. "Your Mother and I are busy talking and—well, You know how You get once You start talking."

"Margarita!" said the Virgin Mary.

"Oh, no," said Doña Margarita, closing her eyes in concentration, "it's true and I will not be intimidated by You, my Lady, or Your Most Holy Son. This conversation is strictly between Us, Women of Substance, and so Your Son, Jesus, can wait His turn, my Lady!"

Jesus started laughing and laughing. "It's all right, Mother," He said to the Blessed Virgin. "I'll be happy to wait and listen, and . . . learn."

And so Jesus lay back in a pew, relaxing as His Mother and Doña Margarita continued their conversation. And Jesus looked so happy and all at peace . . . like in a sunny meadow with Trees and Birds all about Him as He leisurely chewed on a Blade of Grass—truly enjoying Himself!

LEAVING THE DOCTOR'S OFFICE, Salvador was very quiet as they drove over to Lupe's parents' home.

"Is something the matter?" asked Lupe, as they drove down the tree-lined street in front of her parents' home.

"No," he said, "everything is fine." He just had no idea how to put into words all the things he was feeling since that doctor had spoken to him.

"Well, all right," said Lupe, "but ever since we left the doctor's office, you've been very quiet."

"Yes, that's true," said Salvador, and he wanted to speak, to tell Lupe everything, but he just didn't know where to even begin. His mind was still spinning with all of the things the doctor had told him.

Going inside of Lupe's parents' house, there was Sophia and her bunch of kids and Salvador immediately almost asked Lupe's older sister if the doctor had spoken to her and her husband about family planning, too.

But Sophia looked so happy and full of life and mischief, that he didn't want to bring up this terrible subject. My God, children couldn't be planned! That would be like planning to buy a car? Like figuring out which groceries to get? Or like deciding which animals to breed on the *rancho*? Oh, how disgusting! He had to spit, the thought was so repulsive!

"I was just telling *mama*," said Sophia to Lupe and Salvador, "that *mi esposo* and Victoriano will be in late today. They're with *Señor* Whitehead, who once more is working with old man Irvine."

"But didn't he die?" asked Salvador.

"No," said Sophia, "you and Victoriano saved his life when you surprised him. The shot only grazed his head and the doctors were able to save him."

"Oh, I didn't know," said Salvador. "He's a good man. I'm glad he lived."

Sophia started laughing. "The talk is that now the old man is living with a bunch of goats inside of his house."

"Inside of the house, itself?" said Salvador.

"Yes, that's what I was told," said Sophia full of mischief. "And his family has gotten so upset with him that they've left to live in that cold, smelly swamp with the mosquitoes of *Puerto Nuevo*, Newport, I think, they call it, because old man Irvine will not hear of getting rid of his goats.

"And I guess the goats have done wonders for his disposition," she continued, "because everybody says that Irvine has had a complete change of heart and he now treats his workers and *Señor* Whitehead very well. I guess the goats' milk did it."

"Of course," said Don Victor, playing with one of his grandkids, "men who didn't get enough breast when babies never find peace until they're put on goats' milk. And the goat's tits are even better," added Don Victor. "I bet you that this is why he keeps the goats in the house, so he can suck the milk directly from the she-goats," and Don Victor was laughing.

"I took him the goats," said Salvador.

Everyone turned and stared at Salvador.

Salvador now told Lupe's family the story of his mother and the wallet full of money, and how the young priest had driven his mother to the Irvine place.

Laughter echoed out of the little house and all through the *barrio* when Salvador finished his story.

But Lupe's mother, Doña Guadalupe, didn't think the story was funny and she made the sign of the cross over herself and led them all in a prayer for the troubled soul of the Irvine *familia*, the richest family in all the area.

IT WAS GETTING LATE and Salvador and Lupe decided to have their talk with Carlota about her coming with them to stay in Carlsbad with Lupe to keep her company while she was pregnant and Salvador was gone.

"Ha!" said Carlota, becoming suspicious, "you just want a maid to clean the house for you, I'm not going to be fooled! Besides, I make a lot of money in the fields and I have the responsibility of helping *mama* and *papa*!"

Salvador was ready to throw in the towel. "Forget her," he said to Lupe. "We'll find someone from the *barrio* to come and stay with you."

"No," said Lupe. "I don't want someone from the *barrio*. I want my sister. She's *mi familia*, and I want her support."

"Well, what can we do, she doesn't want to come," said Salvador.

Suddenly Carlota got a twinkle in her left eye. "You remember that red dress we saw in that window at Long Beach, eh, Lupe," said Carlota, "when Salvador tried to poison me with the fish," she added.

"Yes," said Lupe, "I remember the dress. It was very beautiful."

"But I didn't try to poison her with any damn fish," said Salvador. My God, now no one even bothered to question her about that fish poisoning story anymore. It was just being accepted as truth.

"And remember the red shoes, Lupe?" continued Carlota.

"Yes," said Lupe.

"Well, if Salvador buys both of these for me, I'll forgive him and come and stay with you, Lupe, but I will not do all the housework!"

"And nobody is asking you to," said Lupe. "I just need somebody to be with me when Salvador is gone and—"

But Lupe was never able to finish her words. Carlota was now leaping and yelling about her new dress and red dancing shoes that Lupe and Salvador had promised to buy her!

THAT NIGHT, Salvador and Lupe drove home very quietly back to Carlsbad. In two days, they'd return to pick Carlota up. She'd have to give notice where she worked with Victoriano and Sophie's husband. Work, after all, was becoming harder to find. The farmers weren't shipping as much produce and fruit east anymore. Going down the long driveway to their little rented house in Carlsbad, Salvador and Lupe both knew that something very big had just happened to them in their married life together.

Immediately, going into the house, Salvador went to the back of their home and got the quart bottle of whiskey that he kept hidden underneath his work clothes and boots. And he was going to have a good belt there, in hiding, when Lupe came up.

"Is that a bottle of whiskey?" asked she.

"Yes," said Salvador. It had been a long day and ever since that visit with the doctor, Salvador had been feeling desperate. "I thought I'd have a drink," he said, feeling caught. "If you don't mind."

"Of course, I don't mind," said Lupe, looking at Salvador and his bottle. "This is your house, after all. And if you are going to be drinking, then I think it's better for you not to be hiding. My mother, she kept a bottle to have a drink now and then, too. In fact, the first time I saw her drink was on the night when the twins were born."

"Well, then, let's just consider this a drink to our first child," said Salvador, following Lupe into the kitchen and serving himself his first drink in his own home, here, in front of his very own wife, and he gulped it down hard.

"I'll go change," said Lupe, leaving the room. Something really strange had been going on with Salvador all afternoon. She could just feel it here inside of herself.

"I'll be right here," said Salvador, serving himself another shot.

In the bedroom, Lupe took off her coat and then walked into the bathroom, getting ready for bed. And she just knew that whatever was troubling Salvador had to do with their doctor's visit, but she wasn't going to pry.

Having gotten ready for bed, Lupe came back into the kitchen and found Salvador sitting at the kitchen table with the moonlight coming in the window behind him. The big whiskey bottle was half empty.

"Salvador!" yelled Lupe. "But what is going on? Why are you drinking like this? Is it because you're afraid of my sister coming to live with us?"

His eyes were bloodshot. He looked absolutely awful. "Well, no, I mean, yes, but it's not just her, Lupe," he said, slurring his words and his eyes rolling about with drunkenness. "I love you so much!" he said. "And we've been so happy, especially in bed, but now, well—damnit!" he yelled, "it's all got to stop, *querida!*"

"But what's got to stop?" she asked, coming closer and smelling him.

"Us! Me and you! Our love-making! Everything!" he yelled.

Lupe looked at him, sitting there surrounded by the moonlight coming in the window, and she had no understanding of what he was saying. "But Salvador, why are you saying that we need to stop our love-making?" She felt like a knife had just cut into her heart. "I don't understand, Salvador."

"Because, Lupe," he said, staring at her, "I don't want you losing your teeth!"

"My teeth?" she asked.

"Yes, the doctor, he told me that lots of children don't fill out a woman like I'd always been told. No, that lots of children kill her. And when I told him that my mother had had nineteen kids, he asked me if she has any teeth. And, well, what could I say? I'd always thought that kids were a blessing from God, and we could never have too many, because God loved us, and He knew what was best for us, but this doctor said no, no, no, if we want teeth and a long, happy life, like him and his dried-up skinny wife, then we can't have a home full of kids!"

Lupe almost felt like laughing. All this sounded so ridiculous, so crazy. "Salvador," she said, "are you telling me that the doctor told you that we shouldn't have any children or I'd lose my teeth?"

"Oh, no, we can have a few children," he quickly said, "but not every eighteen months, or I'll wear you out. That nurse, you remember, the one who took you in to see him, she's his wife and she's in her fifties! But, my God, I thought she was maybe only thirty-five!"

"Yes, she told me," said Lupe. "She was very nice to me."

"Also, he told me that beautiful, young Mexican couples come to him after only a few months of marriage, just like us, and they keep coming back like clockwork every sixteen or eighteen months, like that woman out in the waiting room with me, and she's only twenty-six. So, I don't want that to happen to you, *querida.* I love you, and I want you young and beautiful as long as possible! Just like his wife! And they only had three children, and so maybe we should just have three or four and not too close together so your body can, can, you know, replenish, get strong again between children," he said. "Lupe, I don't want you losing your teeth like my mother."

Lupe was stunned. She'd never seen Salvador like this before. And the doctor hadn't told her anything about this. He'd just checked her to see if she was pregnant, and that was all. "But, Salvador," she said, "isn't it up to God how many children we have?"

"Exactly! Me, too, that's what I always thought, but the doctor told me no, that it's also up to us, that we can plan on how many children we want."

Lupe was flabbergasted. "But he's not a priest," said Lupe. "So how can he speak like this?"

"That's what I thought," said Salvador. "And then he asked me if I'd take my car to be fixed by a man who didn't drive or own a car. And when I said no, of course not, he then asked me why would I then talk with a priest about marriage and children when they aren't married and they have no wife that they love or children to raise."

"He said all that?" said Lupe, making the sign of the cross over herself. She was astonished. She had to sit down. "But he's Catholic!" she said. "This is why Sophia went to him in the first place!"

"Yes, I know," said Salvador, "and that's when he brought out a bottle and gave me a drink. I guess, I was beginning to look sick."

"You mean that he gave you a drink of liquor in his office?" she asked, getting even more shocked.

"Yes, German schnapps, or something like that. It was awful, but, still, it did the job. I got to feeling better."

Lupe gripped her forehead. This was just awful. She'd never dreamed that their doctor was a drinking man.

"Salvador," said Lupe, "I just don't know what to do. Maybe we're not going to be able to go back to that doctor anymore. How could a doctor possibly tell someone to not listen to a man of God?" She took a deep breath. "Come, let's go to bed, *querido*. This whole thing has made me very tired."

"Me, too!" said Salvador, trying to get to his feet, but he was too wobbly and fell back in his chair. "But Lupe, you got to promise me that we don't . . . don't do it, or, oh, *querida*, I DON'T WANT YOU LOSING YOUR BEAUTIFUL TEETH!" he screamed to the high Heavens!

Lupe began to laugh. "But, Salvador," she said, taking his hands and pulling him up to herself, "it's too late. I'm already pregnant."

"Oh, that's right," he said. "Then it's okay, we can still do it tonight!"

"Yes," she said.

And so they hurried down the hallway together.

A SOFT, TIP-TAPPING SOUND awoke Salvador. It was raining. Lying in bed alongside Lupe, Salvador listened to the rain. The raindrops were gathering together on the large, dark, green avocado leaves in the tree outside of their bedroom window, bending the leaves with their weight and slip-sliding down the large smooth leaves with quick-moving little waterways of sounding drip-dropping water.

Lupe stirred, and Salvador drew her close, and the rain continued washing the dust off the avocado leaves, brownish trickles of water drip-dropping off the ends of the leaves, making a ping-ponging music when they hit the cold, smooth metal of their Moon automobile. The soft, gentle rain continued, and soon the entire dirt driveway in front of their little rented home was filling up with small water puddles.

The whole world was changing all around Salvador and Lupe. They were in love, they were at peace, and yet it felt like their heart-*corazones* had been ripped apart. All of their cultural beliefs felt like they'd just been shattered. Like the very ground on which they stood had been plowed under.

The raindrops continued gathering on the avocado leaves outside of their window, drip-dropping in long, steady streamlets. Here and there, high overhead the clouds would break up and startling patches of bright night sky would burst through.

Salvador thought about what the doctor had told him and he moved his hand over the curves of Lupe's wonderful body, gliding his fingertips oh, so softly, gently, back and forth over her valleys and hills. The feel of her was intoxicating. And the smell of her sent him flying to Heaven. But still he couldn't get the doctor's words out of his mind. Because . . . if people could really plan the size of their families, then they could also do other things that he'd always thought were of the domain of God alone.

The clouds broke up and the last of the droplets of water cascaded off the large leaves of the avocado trees. Lupe awoke, and she saw that Salvador, her truelove, was awake and looking down upon her with such tenderness as he sat here in bed at her side.

Smiling, she reached out and touched his left cheek with her right hand. And as she soothed his face, she continued feeling his fingertips gliding back and forth over her back so gently, so softly, so just right. Why, he just knew how to stroke her body so perfectly. His touch was magic!

She breathed and breathed again, then snuggling in closer to him, she put her head into the crook of his arm, and now she could feel his heart beating to her ear. And in the distance she could also hear the last of the raindrops falling off the avocado leaves and ping-ponging on their Moon automobile parked outside of their window. Now and then a small patch of bright moonlight would come in and dance on the far wall of their bed-room.

Lupe also couldn't get the doctor's words out of her mind.

It felt to her as if the very soil on which they'd been raised, had been ripped out from under them, putting them on very unstable land.

She closed her eyes, listening to Salvador's heartbeat. She felt very unsure of their future. But, also, down deep inside, she just knew that they'd do fine, because she felt so warm and safe in his arms up against his thick, full chest.

And so the Mother Earth continued to turn and the centuries came and went, but the matters of the Heart-*Corazón* held fast.

Part Six

HEAVENTALKING

12

And so Humanity was now being called upon to Sing and Dance and Praise the SECOND COMING *of the* LORD!

IN THE LATE MORNING, Salvador and Lupe decided to go out for breakfast to the Montana Café. It felt very strange for Lupe to go eat in a restaurant in the morning. The morning was when people did their best work out in the fields before the Father Sun became so hot that it drained them of their strength. Also, she and Salvador had now eaten out together more times than Lupe had ever done with her family in all of her life.

Walking into the café, directly across the street from the famous Twin Inns, Helen immediately came to Lupe, taking her in her arms. "Oh, you got a little color again!" she said. "I knew you just needed to eat good and go to the doctor! And you, Salvador, you needed that talking I gave you, so you'd get smart! No woman can just be locked up all day, especially when she's pregnant!" added Helen with conviction!

Lupe laughed. Here was this German woman, telling Salvador off once again. "Helen, we already talked it over with my sister Carlota," said Lupe, "and this morning we're going up to bring her back to stay with me."

"Good!" shouted Helen, "I'm glad to hear that! Women need company. Not just men. Come, sit down, and let me feed you. The beef stew is very good today, Lupe!"

"Oh, no, I don't think I could eat all that," said Lupe.

"Then how about just some mashed potatoes with a little gravy and some veggie-tables?"

"That sounds perfect," said Lupe.

"I'll take the beef stew," said Salvador, "and plenty of your homemade bread, too!"

"Of course," said Helen. "Fresh from the oven, just like our butter is fresh from the cow!"

Hans and Helen had five acres with avocados, lemons, oranges, livestock and chickens. Their dream was to get a big 40-acre place inland in Vista where they'd have a house on a hill with an ocean view, so even on hot summer nights they could enjoy the cool ocean breeze as they looked down on their domain.

Salvador went to the kitchen to say hello to Hans, as Helen and Lupe visited. Lupe and Helen truly seemed to enjoy each other's company, even though the German woman was about twenty years older than Lupe. Also, Salvador wanted to run past Hans what the doctor had told him. Hans was a smart man and over the last couple of years, Salvador had truly come to value Hans's opinion. He wondered what Hans would now say to him about this crazy idea that children didn't just come from God, but that people could actually plan the size of their *familia*.

After saying hello to Hans, Salvador straight-out told him what the doctor had said and that they'd had schnapps together.

"So the reason I bring this whole thing to you," added Salvador, "is because, well, Hans, I'd always understood that each child was a gift from God; a blessing is what my mother always told me."

"Your mother is right," said Hans, becoming very excited by the conversation. Hans had wanted to be a teacher in Germany, but hadn't had the finances to complete his studies. "Children are a gift from God, a true blessing, exactly. But," added Hans, taking Salvador aside so they wouldn't be overheard by the others, "so are the fields and the hills and the trees and the flowers and everything else, a true blessing from God. And yet, we don't just run wild through the hills and fields anymore. No, now we cultivate the fields. We prune the trees and flowers.

"Just look at these new avocado trees that George—you know George Thompson—is grafting here in Carlsbad. These new avocados are going to revolutionize the entire avocado industry," said Hans, glowing with excitement. "Because these avocados have a thicker skin and can be shipped all the way east, and big money is going to now be made with the avocados.

"I tell you, Sal, we live in a very exciting time in history! The whole world has changed faster in the last ten years than a thousand years before. So, of course, I agree with this doctor that you can plan your family, Salvador! And nowadays, every civilized man and woman should start doing it!"

"Really, Hans?" said Salvador.

"Yes," said Hans. "Absolutely! You see, here, in California, people are spoiled, thinking that they have land that goes on forever! But I tell you, there are people bunched together in Europe by the millions, and once they find out about this fine weather we got in California, there is going to be a gold-rush of people coming—not by the thousands, like for the California Gold Rush—but by millions for the California weather! Those days of the big families are gone forever, Salvador. Helen and I have one boy, and we'd like to have a girl, too, but no more after that, because we want our children educated and ready to handle this world of changing times."

"I'll be damn," said Salvador. "I never would have thought of it like this, Hans. And this doctor, he also said that I wouldn't take my car to a man who didn't drive or own a car, so why would I go to a priest about matters of marriage and wife and children."

"And this doctor is German? And he's Catholic? Well, Salvador, I'll tell you, he spoke to you man-to-man. You see, Sal, not too long ago," continued Hans, "the farmers in Europe always used to kill to eat their biggest and finest cattle and chickens and ducks, and then what happened?" He was on fire, he was so excited! "Well, the runts would breed each other and pretty soon all the livestock on the farms began getting smaller and sickly.

"But then, one day, a man down the valley from my grandfather's place figured it out that in nature, only the strongest and smartest lived long enough to breed, and that's why the wild animals were always so strong! This farmer, like I told you, just down the valley from my grandfather's place, began to eat his runts—which people thought was a disgusting thing to do—and only bred his biggest and finest animals, and within a few years, this man had the finest livestock in all of Germany! Imagine, Salvador, the finest in all of Germany! And Germany is a very civilized country!

"And so now I tell you that the same thing can be with children. We need to have just a few and raise them well. Big families only worked when people were wild, Salvador, and most of the young got killed by wild beasts or disease.

"Nowadays, we, ourselves, need to do our own pruning, just like any good farmer. And you and Lupe can prune your family to two or three children and raise them up with time and money, and they will be the new generation of Mexican people with lots of *corazón*, as you say—and German discipline and know-how! The sky is the limit, Sal! The sky is the limit here in this fine California, if a *hombre* be smart!"

Hearing this, Salvador was speechless. He'd never heard of such fantastic thinking.

"I'll be damn," said Salvador, shaking his head. "But still, Hans, you and Helen are Catholics, so what about this not paying attention to the priest?"

"Salvador, in the matters of religion, I do not enter, for religion is a matter of belief, and with beliefs, well," he said, shrugging his shoulders, "there is no talking."

"I see," said Salvador, realizing that Hans was always a very smart and tactful man. "I see, and so it doesn't bother you that the Church says one thing and the doctor another?"

"Sal, every profession has its limitations."

"Limitations?"

"Yes, a way of thinking. Tell me, does your mother always listen to the priest?"

"Well, no, not always," said Salvador. "In fact, she often stands right up to them, telling 'em that she has read the Bible for more years than they've lived, and that God also gave her a brain with which to think."

Hans was laughing. "I rest my case. Listen to your mother, Salvador. As you've told me a dozen times, she's a very wise woman just to have gotten you and your sisters here in one piece. I'd bet on your mother over any priest, when it comes to survival. And you also listen to this doctor. He's a very smart man, Salvador. And, since he drinks schnapps, he must be a good German," Hans added with pride.

"Maybe you're right," said Salvador. "Maybe you're right. Thank you very much, Hans. But I'd always thought that kids were a gift from God."

"And they are, Salvador, they are, but also we got to think, to plan, to figure. That's why you and me get along very well; I talk, you listen, and we always agree!" added Hans, laughing a big belly laugh.

"That's true," said Salvador. "We always agree when you do all the talking, Hans!"

"Yes, because then we're both very smart!" added Hans.

They embraced in a big *abrazo*. They were truly good friends. It never failed to amaze Salvador that Hans and Kenny White were both Anglos, but they were Salvador's best friends, next to Archie.

And about Hans being overbearing and opinionated, this didn't bother Salvador. Long ago, he'd learned that you never argued with a man like Hans. You listened, and you asked questions, and you worked him, learning all the knowledge that he had to give.

After all, as a professional gambler, you never counted your chips halfway through the game.

AFTER BREAKFAST, Salvador and Lupe were going to their Moon automobile when Salvador suddenly gripped his chest and his eyes rolled over backward, looking all white!

"Salvador!" yelled Lupe, grabbing hold of him. "What is it?" My God, her father had had a heart attack just a few weeks back, and now here was her husband grabbing at his chest, too! "Talk to me!"

"My mother," said Salvador, feeling a pain so terrible here in his chest that he had to get hold of the tree under which their car was parked, "she's leaving! I can feel it here inside of me, she's leaving! No, *mama*!" he yelled at her. "No, DON'T YOU DO IT, *MAMA*! You stay here 'til our child is born, you hear me! You stay, *mama*! Don't you dare die now!"

Lupe made the sign of the cross over herself, thanking God that it was a "calling" and not a heart attack. She helped Salvador into the Moon. He sat down in the car, breathing 'til he felt better.

"Do you want us to go by and see your mother before we pick up my sister?" asked Lupe.

"Yes," he said, "I'd like that, but wait." He put his two hands over his chest as he'd seen his mother, Doña Margarita, do all her life when she wanted to check on a calling. "No," he said, after breathing a couple of times, "we don't need to go to see her. She's okay now. She says that she's not leaving us. She just went for one of her visits to see *Papito*." He laughed. "She's telling me that God and she have some deal cooking, but we got no worries. *Mi mama* knows how to handle herself in Heaven or in Hell." Salvador felt better now. The pain was gone. "Nobody gets their way with *mi mama*!" he added. "Have I ever told you the story of how my mother went to Guadalajara in the middle of the Revolution to get my brother Jose released from prison?" Lupe shook her head. "Well, let me tell you as we drive up to Santa Ana. Oh, *mi mama* is the Power of the Universe! Here she was dressed in rags, barefoot, and she needed help, but she knew no one who could help her, except the enemy of our *familia*, a man who hated us so much that he wished us all dead." Salvador smiled. "But did this intimidate *mi mama*, oh, no, she doesn't even know the meaning of the word Fear! I love *mi mama* so much, Lupe. She was our everything. Without her we would have all died, again and again."

He made the sign of the cross over himself and Lupe did, too. They were both much better now. They got in their Moon automobile and headed north, and Doña Margarita's Spirit was with them.

DOÑA GUADALUPE AND DON VICTOR were once more playing cards on the front porch of their home when Salvador and Lupe drove up. They each had a pile of *pinto* beans in front of them, but different than last time, it looked like Don Victor was winning.

"Come here quick, Salvador!" shouted Don Victor, seeing Lupe and Salvador come up the walkway. "Look, how I got this old woman by the neck this time! I got good cards—take a look! What do you think?"

Salvador nodded hello to Doña Guadalupe, then glanced at Don Victor's cards. The white-haired old man still looked pretty weak. Ever since he'd gotten out of the hospital, he hadn't looked his old self. The old man had two kings and two tens.

Salvador had the strangest feeling like, well, they'd been here before until he glanced at Doña Guadalupe and she winked at him. Why, the old lady was deliberately letting her husband win. And the old fool was so excited with what he thought was a change in his luck, that he wasn't catching on.

"They look good," said Salvador. "Very good!"

"Yes, that's what I think! I love gambling when I'm winning! So I raise you twenty beans!" he said to his wife Doña Guadalupe, putting a bunch of *pinto* beans in the pot.

"All right," said Doña Guadalupe, "and I raise you back twenty more."

"Okay," yelled Don Victor. "You want to play tough, eh? Well, I match your twenty, and raise you twenty more!" he said, with a gleam of excitement in his old eyes!

"Two queens," said Doña Guadalupe, turning her cards.

"Two queens!" exploded the old man. "Then I win! Two pair! Kings and tens!" And he was so happy as he raked in all the beans.

Salvador took Lupe's hand, squeezing it as he watched her mother quickly put her cards in with the rest of the deck. She'd had three queens, just like last time, but . . . different than last time, she'd only chosen to show two.

Salvador breathed deeply, holding Lupe's hand close to his heart. Lupe's mother was truly a fine, wise old woman. The doctor had been right when he'd told Salvador that he'd married into a fine *familia*.

Salvador's whole heart was over-running with love, compassion, and understanding. And all this, he was able to convey to his truelove—not with words—but with just a simple squeeze of the hand.

They were on their way, a married couple who communicated—not just with speaking—but with a touch, a gesture, a look of the eyes.

They were all laughing, when Carlota came rushing out the door. She was all dressed up and without even saying hello, she said, "I've decided that I don't want to leave Santa Ana, Lupe. All my girlfriends live here and, besides, I'm sick and tired of always moving. That's why I've never married, because we're always on the road, following the crops, and I'm not like you. I'm responsible! I take care of *mama* and *papa* and so I don't want to go," she added with righteousness.

But Lupe didn't take the bait that her sister had tossed her. She moved her hips, taking up ground as married women have been doing since the dawn of time and squeezed Salvador's hand, reassuring him that she would handle this. "Carlota," said Lupe, with all the patience she could muster, "but you'd already agreed, and so we fixed up a room for you and drove all the way back to get you. And Salvador has a lot of work to do and took the day off. Please, reconsider. I'd really like you to come and be with us."

"Carlota," said Doña Guadalupe, also stepping in, "your father and I can take care of ourselves, and your friends can drive down to see you. This is your sister, your *familia*!"

"Oh, all right," said Carlota, feeling outmaneuvered by her mother and sister, "I'll go if that's what you want, *mama*, but they'll have to buy me that beautiful red dress and red shoes first!"

Hearing this, Salvador was backpedaling as fast as he could inside of himself. In his estimation, Lupe's sister Carlota had once more proven herself to be the stupidest, most selfish, woman he'd ever met! And my God, if she did come home with them to Carlsbad, he was sure that their marriage was sure to turn into pure *caca*.

Salvador's heart was pounding. He was ready to say, "Don't come," to Carlota, "we don't want you," when he felt Lupe's hip rubbing up against his side—telling him to calm down, to relax, that everything was okay. He breathed. Just the touch of her hips told him volumes!

Just then, Archie drove up in his big black Hudson. He was all dressed up, too. Salvador and Lupe glanced at each other. No wonder Carlota had changed her mind. Archie and she had had this date planned all along.

"Hello!" said Archie to everyone as he came up the stairs. "Beautiful day, isn't it?"

"Yes, it is," said Salvador.

"How are you?" said Doña Guadalupe. "How is the family?" added the crafty old woman, giving Archie the full understanding that yes, indeed, they all knew he was married and had a family.

"Fine, fine, thank you! The kids are with their mother. And, well, I thought that I'd pick up Charlotte, I mean Carlota, early so we could have a bite to eat before she helps me with the dance."

They all glanced at one another. No one had ever heard Carlota called Charlotte before.

"So you're putting on another dance?" said Don Victor.

"Yes, right downtown here in Santa Ana. I brought in a group of musicians from Los Angeles. Your daughter is a good businesswoman. She catches every Tom, Dick and Harry at the door and gets them to pay before she lets them in."

"Tom, Dick and who?" asked Don Victor, feeling outraged by so many male names being connected to his daughter.

"That's just an expression," said Archie. He was talking fast and acting nervous. "I don't really mean Tom or Dick or Harry. I just meant that, well, Charlotte's tough, and people don't pull the sheep—the wool—over her eyes."

"Sheep, over her what?"

"Ah, hell," said Archie, seeing that he was digging himself deeper. "That's just another expression. It really ain't got nothing to do with sheep or wool, or Tom, Dick and Harry or anyone else."

"I see," said Don Victor. "No sheep, then? And no *gringos*, either?"

"No, not a one," said Archie, tipping his hat. "Well, nice talking to you. I'll have her back early." Then he turned to Salvador and Lupe. "Would you like to go with us? We're just going over to the amusement park in Long Beach to have a bite before the dance."

Now suddenly, Salvador and Lupe both understood everything all at the same time. Why, Carlota had set up this whole thing so that they'd go out to Long Beach where she'd seen that beautiful red dress. They'd been had by a very deceitful hand.

Lupe gave Salvador a knowing little look, then took his hand, squeezing it again. "All right," she said, "we could do that, couldn't we, Salvador? But, then, you will be coming down with us to Carlsbad, correct, Carlota?"

"Yes," said Carlota, "with my new red dress and shoes!"

"What new red dress and shoes?" asked Archie.

"The ones that Salvador and Lupe are buying for me," said Carlota, and she was beside herself with joy!

"Great!" said Archie, looking relieved, no doubt having thought that he was going to have to buy her a dress. "Why don't we just leave your Moon by the dance hall downtown, Sal, and we'll go in my bigger car like last time, okay?"

"That's fine with us," said Salvador, massaging Lupe's hand. Oh, he felt so totally in love with this wife of his.

They quickly left.

Archie didn't want to hang around "Charlotte's" parents' house a minute longer and be drilled with any more questions about his family.

Hell, he and his wife had been broken up for years. And also, it wasn't like he and Charlotte were really dating, after all. And so he didn't know why he had to put up with all this south of the border kind of crap. This was the United States of America, and at eighteen a girl was free. And hell, Carlota was almost twenty-four years old!

GETTING TO LONG BEACH, Carlota was screeching with joy! She'd never had a brand new dress from a store in all of her life. And she'd had beautiful dresses before, but that wasn't the point. Their older sister Sophia—who hadn't attended Lupe and Salvador's wedding because she and her husband hadn't had the proper clothes—was an excellent seamstress, so she'd made all of Carlota's dresses for her over the years.

This would be her very first dress purchased right off the rack!

Walking down the boardwalk to the little shop where Carlota and Lupe had seen the red dress and red shoes, they found the place boarded up. And they also saw that the amusement park was empty. None of the rides were even working anymore.

"I told you," said Archie to Salvador, "places are going to start closing down right and left. I bet you the Chinese place ain't open either."

But getting there, the Chinese restaurant was, indeed, open. And when Carlota saw this, she went into a rage, cursing Salvador, and accusing him of getting that dress shop to close down so she couldn't have her dress, but having the Chinese restaurant stay open, so he could try to poison her with fish again!

"But there's no way you'll ever trick me into eating fish! I know fish! You can always smell it!"

And so that night Carlota ate lobster for the first time in her life, and she loved it! And when someone said that lobster was fish, Carlota screamed.

"Oh, no!" she yelled. "You can't trick me! Lobster can't come from that dirty, smelly sea! It's DELICIOUS!"

After the dance, in Santa Ana, Carlota drove home that night to Carlsbad with Salvador and Lupe. They were all very quiet. There was a half Moon, and she, the Mother Moon, followed them, giving them light as they went along the seashore by San Clemente. They were on their way, a married couple—homeward bound!

SALVADOR AWOKE WITH A START!

It was raining outside, and his mother's face was flashing to him inside his mind. He lay in bed trying to calm himself, but he couldn't. To his bones he just knew that something very big was going on with his mother.

But he had no means of contacting her unless they drove up to Corona to see her. They had no telephone, and Luisa and his mother didn't have one either. Telephones were instruments for stores, for doctors, for only the very rich, according to the people of the *barrio*.

Salvador lay in bed breathing deeply.

"What is it?" asked Lupe, waking up. "Is it your mother again?"

Salvador nodded.

"Then you better go up and see her," said Lupe. "I'll be all right. My sister is here. She'll help me if I need anything."

"Thank you," said Salvador, sitting up and holding his forehead in both of his hands. "But I can't go up to see her today. I promised Archie I'd help him."

Archie had been right; people were losing their jobs, their houses, and little *ranchitos*. The times were desperate. No one knew what was going on. And this morning, Salvador had promised the big lawman he'd get a case of whiskey down to the lagoon for him and his deputy *amigos* at daybreak.

Every week Archie and his sheriff buddies were going down to the lagoon between Carlsbad and Oceanside and shooting the hell out of hundreds of ducks. Then they'd get the prisoners out of the jail in Oceanside and have the prisoners swim out into the cold water to retrieve the ducks, then the prisoners could either pluck the ducks and help roast 'em down by the pier in Oceanside in exchange for whiskey, or they could go back to jail.

In the last few weeks good people were now actually breaking the law so they could get arrested and be in on one of Archie's illegal duck hunts. They, too, wanted to get chosen to retrieve the ducks, pluck them, roast 'em, so that then they could eat and drink free whiskey down by the pier.

Rubbing his forehead, Salvador got up, went to the bathroom, washed his face, then did something he hadn't done in a very long time. He went outside to welcome the coming Father Sun and ask *Papito Dios* to please help him understand what was going on with his *mama*. Because he could feel it here, inside of his chest area, that his mother was into something far beyond her normal everyday doings. He began to pray.

And it was true, at this very moment, Doña Margarita was at the little stone church in Corona talking directly to God, Himself. Not the Virgin Mary, not Jesus Christ, but with the Almighty, and she was speaking with such power and conviction that the river rocks of the church's walls were Singing, Vibrating, coming Alive with the Spirit of Holy Creation.

"All right, God," Doña Margarita was saying to the Almighty, "I asked *Maria* to set up this meeting between You and me, because, as I told Her a few weeks back, it's no longer enough for us mortals here on Earth to have faith in You up in Heaven. It's time for You to also start having Faith in us. You see *Papito,* we're not children anymore, but fully developed Human Beings, who've been doing Your Blessed Work for You down here on this *Tierra Madre* for hundreds of thousands of years, so the time has come for You—like any Good Father—to hear what Your children have to say.

"What? Oh, no, God, there's got to be some changes made around here! Listen closely to me, I've been reading Your Holy Bible every day for nearly sixty-three years—which, I might add, is a lot in human time—and discussing Your Most Holy Works with every priest I've met. And I'll tell You, we've come a long way since those days of needing an angry *Papito Dios* Who's full of Lightning and Wrath.

"I mean, look at my case alone, dear God, I married a man who followed Your every word and said prayers three times a day but he—like so many of his people who came from Europe—got stuck on just the message of Your wrath, thinking that they had to spread Your Holy Word to the whole world with sword in hand. And when we tried to tell them about our own understanding of You, Our Same *Señor* Creator, they just cast off our beliefs, calling them savage ignorance and superstition.

"Well, *Maria* and I have talked this matter over in great detail, and the other day Your Most Holy Son, Jesus, joined Us. He was patient and listened to me, too, 'cause You see, God, it's easy to call another's religious ideas superstition. That takes no guts, that takes no great intelligence. What takes guts and high intelligence is to open up one's Heart and Soul to the possibility that others' religious knowledge is also True, no matter how foreign-sounding at first glance. And this is where we now are Collectively—no, please don't interrupt, God! You listen, and listen Good! Oh, You weren't interrupting? You were agreeing with me? Oh, thank You. I appreciate that, because Your Most Holy Son, Jesus, also agreed with me, too, like His Mother, then They both suggested that I come directly to You and present my case. Or more precisely, Our Case, the case in which all of us humans now find ourselves. And this case is simply this—a very big mix-up got started long ago with the Jews, Your Chosen People, which then, I'm sure, led You to not have much faith in us here on Earth.

"Because You tell me, how in the name of Heaven did these Jews figure that there were originally Twelve Tribes and that all the other tribes got lost, except for them, the Chosen Tribe. Eh, that makes no sense. Because any goat or pig or horse or cow on *el rancho* is smart enough to figure out that, if they suddenly find themselves all alone, then they are the lost one, and not the herd!" she added loudly.

"Eh, You see what I'm driving at *Papito*? So of course, You lost faith in us then and had to send Your Only Begotten Son a few thousand years later to talk to these Jews and bring them back to the fold, because they were the ones who'd gotten lost, right? And not the rest of us, all around the rest of the Mother Earth.

"Then to make matters worse, these other people, who weren't Jews, now came in and took over in the name of Jesus, creating Christianity, and condemning anyone who wouldn't believe in their way.

"I mean, God, let us get serious here, I can see why You're having trouble. We've been following a lost people who adopted the ways of a lost tribe, and so—"

But Doña Margarita wasn't able to finish her thought, because God started laughing *con carcajadas*! And Jesus and *Maria* were laughing, too. The whole little stone church began to Vibrate with the Holy Laughter of the Heavens!

Doña Margarita got off her knees and stood up to her full height of four feet ten. "I'm not finished!" she yelled. "And I will not be silenced with laughter, nor approval!

"God, I AM TALKING to YOU!" she shouted. "And only You! So pay attention, because *Maria*, Your Wife, and I have worked all this out, so You better listen to me good while I'm still down here on Earth, or I swear that You will get an earful when I get up to Heaven! Remember, we humans were made in Your Own Image, so we're *muy chingones*, too!"

The laughter ceased.

"*Gracias!* Thank You, God," said Doña Margarita. "Now, as I was saying, simply, dear Lord, the time has come for You to make up with Your Most Glorious Angel, the Devil. What? Oh, no, You listen to me! Lucifer has never stopped Loving You, *Papito*, and You know this, since you are All-Knowing, remember, eh?

"And so what if he made a big unforgivable sin years back. Didn't Jesus, Your Son, forgive those who crucified Him, eh? Have I not forgiven my children their trespasses? And have I not forgiven the people who destroyed *mi familia* in those treacherous days of the Revolution?

"We have, dear God, Jesus and I, we have forgiven again and again with all our Hearts and Souls!" Tears burst from her eyes. "Understand, Lord, I haven't just been reading Your Most Holy Book, the Bible, but I have been Living it, too! And so if Jesus and I can do it, then You can do it, too, *Papito*! And RIGHT NOW! This very moment!"

And it was here, at this moment, that Salvador, who was outside of his home in Carlsbad praying, felt his mother needing all the help she could get.

Salvador looked up at the Father Sky and he, too shouted. "She's a good woman, *Papito*! So You listen good!" Salvador could see his mother in his Heart-Eye standing up and talking to God with all her might. To pray with all your Heart and Soul, his mother had always told them, was to Unite as One with *Papito Dios,* then, and only then, the worst could become the best for *las extremidades del humano son las oportunidades de Dios*!

"For the Bible was never meant to be treated as if written in stone and that's it for ETERNITY!" Doña Margarita was now saying. "The Bible was meant to be used as a Living, Breathing Testimony with each Holy Breath we take, bringing in each generation closer and closer to Your Most Holy Self, so that then we, together, Your Children are all Your Chosen People, equally, and can help You in the act of Creation Itself!

"So I, your daughter, now ask, beg, demand, dear God, that You step forward and make amends with Lucifer, Your Most Holy Messenger of Darkness, and Together as One Holy Family, You Two then lead us all forward *con Amor*, and no more of this Fear and Wrath!

"I did it! Jesus did it! And so You will now do it, too, My Lord God *Papito*! For I refuse to anymore have a stubborn, unwilling-to-change

Father who's revengeful and full of wrath! I LOVE YOU! Do You hear me! You are my Father, my Light, and so We will now go forward with Love, hand-in-hand in full Partnership, You and Us, here within Our Hearts and Souls.

"Because it was never us, the Other Eleven Tribes who got lost and scared! Okay, I'm done," she added. "I'm finished. I have nothing more to say, and so I'll see You here in, ah, okay, three days, and You'll have Your answer first thing in the morning. Thank You. *Gracias.* And hello *a todos los Santos y Angelitas. A Dios, Maria y Jesus.*

"Oh, and by the way, dear God, I almost forgot, I already talked this over in great detail with Lucifer, and he, too, anxiously awaits your answer. And he's picked some beautiful roses for You—and between You and me—I checked them out, and they smell beautiful, and also they have no thorns. He's really serious about wanting to make up with You, dear God. He never stopped Loving You. Remember, *Papito, no hay mal que por bien no venga.* Thank You, *gracias,* and I remain Your humble, but not too humble servant."

SALVADOR FELT BETTER NOW. His mother's "calling" was done. He could feel it here, inside of his chest. Over and over during the Revolution his old mother had brought God down Here to the Mother Earth to interact with their *familia* through Holy Prayer.

Walking back inside, Salvador told Lupe good-bye and took off for the day. He had to get that case of whiskey to Archie. The prisoners looked blue, they were shivering so much as they came out of the lagoon. Quickly, Archie gave them each a blanket and a bottle of Salvador's whiskey to pass around. Archie and his deputy buddies had shot well over a hundred ducks. They were going to have a feast!

"Salvador," said Archie, taking him aside, "thank you for getting down here in time, but now I'm gonna have to ask you for another favor. And I know that it ain't part of our original deal, but things have gotten worse in the last few weeks. So, well, I want you to get me a barrel of whiskey—as your donation to all the hungry people of the north county, okay?"

"Do I have any choice?" asked Salvador.

Archie just laughed.

Salvador nodded. "I thought not."

So Salvador went to get Archie his barrel of whiskey, and while Salvador was gone, Archie deputized some of his wild relatives from the Pala

Reservation and told them to cut the fence of the Santa Margarita *Rancho*—which would one day soon become Camp Pendleton Marine Base—and to confiscate the first couple of fat steers who wandered off the ranch and onto city property.

Then that same afternoon, Archie had his relatives from Pala kill the steers that they'd herded onto city property, butcher 'em, and barbecue 'em *a la* Archie Freeman to feed all the hungry, homeless people of the whole north county of San Diego. "Ranching Tax" was what Archie eventually called this line of work, when he got his ass arrested by the big boys from downtown San Diego for cattle rustling.

After delivering the barrel of whiskey to Archie and his sheriff buddies, Salvador told Archie that no, he wouldn't be able to stay for the barbecue, that he'd see him later, and he took off for Escondido. Salvador had to attend to his distillery and then to go on his deliveries. It was tough working alone, but also, he didn't know anyone that he could trust that wouldn't start stealing whiskey from him.

IT WAS LATE AFTERNOON the following day when Salvador finally got back to the Oceanside-Carlsbad area. He'd worked all day and night and was dead tired when he got home. Coming inside, he found Lupe washing a big stack of dishes. Carlota and two of her girlfriends were dancing and laughing in the front room. Salvador almost went through the ceiling. Carlota was here to help Lupe, not to be creating more work for her!

But then, when he took Lupe aside to talk to her about this, instead of her seeing that he was on her side and trying to help her, Lupe said, "Oh, Salvador, why do you always have to get your way? Don't you see that they're only having fun and enjoying themselves?"

Salvador was stunned. "But Lupe, I'm not trying to get my way! I'm thinking of you and that she came here to help you . . . not to be making more work for you. Look at all these dishes that you're washing for them!"

Lupe gripped the small of her back, cringing with pain. "Oh, please, Salvador!" Quickly, he quit his words and took her by the arm, helping her to the bedroom to lie down.

"Carlota!" he shouted into the next room. "Lupe isn't feeling well. Come in here and help!"

"Salvador," said Lupe, "please, calm down! I'm all right!"

Carlota and the two young women came into the room. Their faces were all flushed from dancing and their breasts were going up and down. They looked at Salvador and Lupe like they were people from another *planeta*—that place called married people.

"Carlota," said Salvador, "you were brought down here to help your sister, not to be dancing and piling up dishes for her to wash!"

"Salvador, please!" said Lupe.

"I'll go and get our mother," said one of the other girls, and the two girls took off.

"See what you did, you just chased away my girlfriends!" shouted Carlota. "I'm leaving, too!"

"Damnit, Carlota!" yelled Salvador. "Stop thinking of yourself for once in your life, and come and help your sister!"

"You don't want help!" said Carlota. "You just want to be yelling at me!"

And Carlota turned and ran out the door, too, and there was Salvador left alone with Lupe and he didn't know what to do.

"Should I go get Helen?" asked Salvador, feeling completely useless.

"No, you've done enough," said Lupe. "You've chased everyone away!"

"Oh, now you're blaming me, Lupe, for their behavior and I'm just trying to help! Good God, what's wrong here! It's like the Devil is here in this house with us, twisting our every word!"

"Please, Salvador, stop shouting. Just sit with me, and be quiet. I'm okay."

But she wasn't. And she was throwing up by the time Carlota's two friends came back with their mother. Their mother was a woman from the *barrio* in her forties and she immediately put the back of her hand to Lupe's forehead, then told one of her daughters to put the herbs that she'd brought to boil on the stove, then she told Lupe to not have anything to eat for a couple of days, except tea and soup—*menudo* would be best.

Salvador had fallen asleep, mouth open, on the floor alongside Lupe's bed. He'd been dead tired and barely able to keep his eyes open as he'd come up the long, driveway to their home in his truck.

After the woman left, Lupe struggled to get out of bed, and she put a pillow under Salvador's head, loosened his belt, and covered him with a blanket. Salvador slept for sixteen hours, and when he awoke, he couldn't remember where he was. Then, when he realized that he wasn't at his distillery in Escondido but here at home in Carlsbad with Lupe, he leaped up but tripped over his own clothing, falling back down to the floor.

"What is it?" asked Lupe.

"The time, the time?" yelled Salvador.

"It's about nine in the morning," said she.

"But how can it be morning? Didn't I come home in this afternoon?" he asked.

"Well, yes, but you fell asleep, so I covered you with a blanket and you slept the whole night through."

"Oh, my God!" he said. "I got to get to Escondido quick, Lupe! The stove could've blown up!"

"What stove?"

"In my distillery."

"You cook liquor?"

"Yes, that's how it's made," he said, putting on his clothes.

"I'm coming with you, Salvador," she said.

"No, you're sick! You need to stay home!"

"Salvador, I'm not sick, except for a little while each day, then I'm fine. And I'm your wife, and if this is what we do for a living, then I'm going to help you. I will not let you work yourself to death!" she added. "My God, I thought you'd died the way you passed out asleep!"

"Okay," he said, "but hurry! We got to go right now. And what about Carlota?"

"She can wait here for us."

"I can wait for who?" asked Carlota, walking in the front door.

"We're going to Escondido," said Lupe. "You can wait here for us until we come back."

"Will you be back tonight?"

"Maybe not," said Salvador. "It all depends on a few things."

"Then I'm going, too," said Carlota. "I'm not going to be left here all alone in this house in the middle of nowhere. We weren't brought up to be ranch people, you know."

Salvador cringed. He was sick and tired of this reference to "ranch people" that Carlota always seemed to make, but he said nothing. They got a few things together and were out the door in a matter of minutes.

Getting to *el Valle de Escondido*, meaning the Hidden Valley, a town just twenty-some miles inland from Oceanside, Salvador drove up to a large, two-story house on the south side of town.

"Who lives here?" asked Carlota.

"I do," said Salvador.

"Oh, so you have a whole other hidden family, eh?" she said, her eyes suddenly lighting up with joy.

Salvador didn't even bother answering her, and got out of the car and went into the house.

"Carlota," said Lupe, "when will you ever learn to hold your tongue and think before you speak?"

"Well, he's the one who said this was his house. I didn't."

"Yes, but he never said anything about another family."

"No, because he's hiding it," she said excitedly.

"Carlota, if he was hiding it, then why would he bring us here?"

"Because he's scared that we'd find out," she said. "I told you that he was a no-good, cheating coward ever since the beginning!"

"Carlota, please, just shut up!" said Lupe. She'd had enough. And she was just too tired to argue with her sister.

"There you go again, siding with him against your very own blood!" snapped Carlota.

Lupe didn't bother to answer her sister anymore.

Salvador came back, after going in to check the stove. "We're all right," he said. "By some miracle of God, the fire went out or—boom, the whole house would've gone!"

"What are you talking about?" asked Carlota.

"Just please keep quiet and watch," said Lupe. "And you can learn a great many things, Carlota, by just watching. Please, I'm tired, I don't want to hear you talking or asking any questions for a while."

Carlota made a face at Lupe, then pursed her lips together. She was sick and tired of her sister always acting so superior.

Going inside, Carlota and Lupe immediately saw that the house had no furniture. The whole place was completely empty. They also saw that there were a dozen big barrels in one room, but they were up against the walls; there were no barrels in the center of the room.

"It stinks in here worse than a pig pen!" snapped Carlota.

Lupe turned and gave her such an eye.

"I know! I know!" said Carlota. "I'm supposed to shut up! To think before I talk. But who needs to think when you can smell? It does stink. It stinks awful! Okay, I'll shut up. Not another word," she said, and put her hand over her mouth.

"Why are the barrels all against the wall?" asked Lupe.

"Good question," said Salvador. "You see, they're really heavy, so if I put all those barrels in the middle, the floor might give out."

"Has that ever happened?"

"Yes, once in an old house up in Watts; the floor caved in on me."

"I'll be," said Lupe. "And what is that smell?"

"That's the fermentation process. You see, those barrels are full of water and sugar and yeast, so the yeast—"

"Oh, like when yeast makes the bread rise and gets that little sour smell?"

"Yes, exactly."

They walked down the hallway to another room and, in this room there was a big tank on a stove in the middle of the room, and the tank had a pipe coming out of the top, spiraling in large curls to a small barrel.

"You see," said Salvador, "once the barrels have fermented in that other room, which takes about two or three weeks, then I pour that fermentation into this tank and bring it to a boil. And the steam that comes out through that coiled tube on top is straight alcohol; and as it cools off, it drips into that smaller barrel.

"Then, over in that other room, I have the finished alcohol which I then age with a big special needle that was made in France, and this way, I can have twelve-year-old whiskey in about, oh, I'd say six hours, and very smooth-tasting."

"I see," said Lupe. "Then it must take hours and hours to just make one barrel of whiskey?"

"Yes," said Salvador, loving how Lupe's mind worked. She was really quick and smart and knew how to get to the point.

"Whiskey?" said Carlota. "You mean you make whiskey here?" she yelled. "Oh, my God! Let me out of here before we all go to jail!" And saying this, she ran out of the room. "Why did you bring me? Why didn't you just leave me in Carlsbad?"

"We tried to leave you," said Lupe, going into the next room also, "but you insisted on coming."

"I wouldn't have if you'd told me that you were bootleggers!" said Carlota.

"And if we'd told you that, you would've told everyone in all the *barrio* by the time we got home," said Lupe.

"Oh, you're just DIRTY!" yelled Carlota. "Ever since you met Salvador, you've become dirty, Lupe! Why can't you be like other law-abiding, decent people, like Archie! No, you had to go and marry a bootlegger, when I told you he was no good from the start!

"Do you realize that, Lupe? Your husband is a—oh, my God!" She couldn't even talk anymore, she was so upset! Quickly, she now headed for the front door. "I'm getting out of here right now! I don't want to die and go to jail!"

Lupe almost laughed on hearing this, but she didn't. Salvador watched his young wife now cross the room in quick, well-measured steps and grab hold of Carlota before she got to the front door, saying, "The expression isn't 'to die and go to jail,' but 'to die and go to hell!' And you will not go out that door, screaming like a fool! Do you hear me, Carlota, you will stay put and get hold of yourself. You will not endanger us!"

"Yes, but Lupe—he's an outlaw," she whispered.

"Stop it, Carlota," said Lupe. "Salvador and I went to a priest, and the priest told us that liquor making is against the law of this country, but not against the law of God. That Jesus, Himself, turned water into wine. And who do you think sells most of his liquor, Carlota? It's Archie, that's who!"

"Archie?" said Carlota, her eyes getting huge.

"Yes, Archie, and let's not play the fool. You knew it. At every dance he puts on, there's always liquor being sold in the back."

"Well, then," said Carlota, eyes wide with disbelief, "Salvador tricked Archie, too?"

Hearing this, Salvador had had enough and so he stepped forward, blocking the front door with his body. "Do you still want that red dress?" he simply asked.

Suddenly, Carlota's eyes stopped jumping all about. "Well, yes, of course," she said.

"Well, then, you keep still like Lupe said, so I can finish my work here and then I can buy you that dress."

"And the shoes, too," said Carlota. "Remember, you promised me red shoes, too."

"Red shoes, too," said Salvador. "Now help me move a couple of barrels, Carlota, so I can get the stove going again, then we'll go out for dinner."

"To a restaurant?" said Carlota.

"Yes, to a restaurant," said Salvador.

"Oh, good. But no fish this time."

"But you loved that lobster," said Lupe.

"Well, yes, but lobster isn't fish," said Carlota.

"Well, maybe it isn't, but it does come from the sea."

"Don't talk to me like that, Lupe, you're just trying to trick me."

Lupe started laughing, there was just nothing else to do. Then Salvador started laughing, too.

"You two are crazy!" snapped Carlota. "Here we are, in hell itself, and you two think it's funny! Come, let's move these barrels, so we can get out of here!"

IT WAS MIDMORNING, and Lupe and Carlota were alone at the house in Escondido. Salvador was out on a delivery. The three of them had been working around the clock for weeks now. And this morning, Lupe was sweeping the kitchen floor and humming to herself. Carlota was doing the morning dishes and singing happily. They'd become like a little factory of dedicated, hard workers.

But then, Carlota suddenly looked up, and through the kitchen window, she saw that the sheriff's car had turned into their driveway. Her eyes exploded with terror! And she tried to talk, to warn Lupe, but she couldn't speak.

"L-L-Lupe!" she finally said, crouching down to hide in terrible fear. "It's *el shed-ififi!*" And saying this, her legs gave out from under her, and she fell to the floor like a wet rag.

Instantly, Lupe rushed across the room, glanced out, saw the sheriff's car, then ran to the front door to make sure that it was locked. She hurried back, just as Carlota was regaining consciousness.

"Lupe!" cried Carlota. "I don't want to die and go to jail!"

"They don't take dead people to jail," said Lupe, as she got hold of her sister, pulled her to her feet, and escorted her past the stove and counters to the back of the house. "And I've told you a dozen times already, Carlota, that Salvador and I talked to the priest who married us, and he told us that making liquor isn't a sin against God!"

"But it's not God that I'm WORRIED ABOUT!" screamed Carlota. "I don't want to go to jail and die a virgin!"

"But you're twenty-four, Carlota, and you and Archie sometimes stay out half the night," said Lupe.

"Yes, but I don't let him put it—you know, Lupe, in! Oh, if I die now, I'll never know *amor*!" And Carlota was crying and crying.

Lupe almost burst out laughing, but didn't. "Quiet!" she said. "I don't want you here when I open the door."

"Open the door!" screamed Carlota. "Don't do it, Lupe! Please, for the love of God, don't open the door!"

Just then, the lawman started knocking on the front door. Carlota went to scream again, but Lupe covered her mouth with her apron, muffling most of the sound.

"Carlota!" said Lupe, feeling her own heart starting to go wild! "You've got to get hold of yourself, or you'll get us caught for sure!"

"But it's not our liquor!" said Carlota, pulling the apron out of her mouth. "We'll just tell him that Salvador forced us to stay here. That he's the bootlegger! And the sheriff will only take him to jail, and let us go!"

"Carlota," said Lupe evenly, "Salvador is my husband! Now shut up!"

And with this, Lupe suddenly gripped her older, stronger sister with such power and determination that she was able to drag her down the long hallway and throw her into a closet.

"No, let me out!" yelled Carlota.

"For the love of God," said Lupe, "keep quiet! Or I swear, you won't have to worry about jail, because I'll strangle you to death myself!"

Carlota saw her sister's eyes, and she believed her, and bit her lip to keep still. She began to pray as she'd never prayed before, asking God to please make her invisible.

Lupe closed the closet door, straightened up, fixed her dress and hair as best she could, then made the sign of the cross over herself, and started back down the long hallway. She could hear her sister praying behind her in the closet and the sheriff knocking on the front door ahead of her.

Entering the kitchen, Lupe saw that the water faucet was still on and the sink had overflowed. Quickly, she crossed the room, turned off the faucet, and then continued to the front door. The knocking had become so loud that it reminded Lupe of the soldiers back in their village of *la Lluvia de Oro* on their days of rape and plunder.

"Yes!" she said, suddenly opening the door.

Taken by surprise, the lawman stepped back. "Oh, hello! I was beginning to think no one was home, but I thought I saw movement when I first drove up." He tried to glance behind her, but she closed the door halfway.

"That was my sister," said Lupe. "She went to get me. She's just visiting for a few days."

"Oh, I see," said the lawman. And he now took a closer look at Lupe and saw her incredible beauty and natural elegance. He immediately took off his hat, as so many men automatically did when they saw Lupe's extraordinary beauty. "Well, ma'am," he now said respectfully, "you see, I've come by to collect the rent."

"The rent?" said Lupe. "A sheriff collects the rent?" She was trying to sound calm, but inside her heart was pounding so hard that she was afraid she'd burst. Carlota's fear had truly taken the nerve out of her.

"Well," he said, straightening up, "you see, my wife and me, we own this house, so I happened to be in the neighborhood and I thought that I'd just stop by to collect our money."

Lupe almost fainted. She couldn't believe that all this just had to do with the rent. Suddenly, she wasn't frightened anymore; no, she was angry!

"Officer!" she said, straightening up, "my husband took our rent money to your home this morning, which, I might add, isn't due for three days!" And saying this, she almost slammed the door in his face but thought better of it and said, "Now excuse me, but I'm with child, as you can see, and I was lying down when you came. I'm not feeling well."

And she closed the door, locking it, then went to the kitchen and stood there for a full two minutes, leaning against the counter and shaking like a leaf.

"My God!" said Carlota, coming out of the closet after the sheriff was gone. "I heard the whole thing, Lupe, and I never could have done that! *Dios mio,*" she said in awe, "why, you behaved just like *mama* the day she saved our brother Victoriano from the hanging!"

But Lupe said nothing, then she suddenly rushed to the bathroom, where she began to puke. She'd been scared to death!

SALVADOR DIDN'T GET BACK to their house in Escondido until late that afternoon. He was very happy. He'd just sold five barrels and gotten cash up front on three. Everybody and his sister wanted whiskey. He was making so much money that he and Lupe were going to be able to go home soon.

Walking into the house, Carlota came screaming at him with such raging anger that he didn't know what was going on.

"You tricked us, you son-of-a-bitch!" she yelled, trying to scratch his face. "You knew the sheriff was coming, so you ran off like the coward I always knew you were and left Lupe and I to pay for your crimes!"

"What the hell are you talking about?!" shouted Salvador, shoving her away.

"You know damn well what I'm talking about!" yelled Carlota, picking up a pair of scissors. "The sheriff came to the house while you were off whoring around and now Lupe is so sick she's going to lose the baby, and it's all your fault!"

Hearing this, Salvador's whole heart was filled with fear and he almost slapped Carlota's across the face. But he didn't. No, he just shoved her away again, avoiding the scissors, and rushed down the hallway to the bedroom. He found Lupe trying to get out of the little secondhand immigrant cot that he'd brought in for her.

"What happened?" he asked.

"Nothing," she said, cringing with pain. "It was just a terrible mistake. The sheriff came by to collect his rent money."

"The sheriff?" said Salvador, still not understanding.

"Yes, he and his wife own this house," said Lupe.

"Oh, my God!" said Salvador, looking up to the ceiling. "What are you doing to us, *Dios mio*? Sending the Devil and all his evil forces to test us?

"Come on," he said to Lupe, helping her sit up in bed. "Let me get you and Carlota out of here. Right now!"

"But we haven't finished with the distilling yet," she said.

"Forget that!" he said. "Let's just get you out of here!"

"But I got to make up for that barrel that Carlota let burn." Her sister had ruined a barrel of whiskey the week before.

"No," he said, helping her sit up. "That's not important. I need to get you home. Good God, I rented this house from a realtor! How in the hell was I to know who owned it? Jesus!"

"But Salvador, you also loaned money to my brother," said Lupe, tears of frustration coming to her eyes. "Let me do my part and finish the distilling for you. Please, understand, the sheriff only wanted his rent; he won't be back, Salvador." Then she added, "You did pay the rent for this house this morning, didn't you?"

He looked into her eyes, and he could see that she was in terrible pain, but still she had the presence of mind to push all that aside and ask him about the rent money.

"Oh, Lupe, Lupe, Lupe," he said, taking her in his arms. "Here, you just went through Hell, itself, and you still remembered the rent. I love you, I adore you, I respect you! You are a woman among women! Jesus, I'm so proud to be your husband!" he added. "You are made of iron! The way you stood up to your sister the first day we came here, grabbing her and speaking to her with such common sense—oh, I love you more today than the first day I saw you—and then I thought that you were an Angel straight from Heaven! You are *una mujer de poder* who knows the Power of God!"

And he started to kiss her, but she held him away. And out in the hallway, Carlota was sneaking toward their room with that pair of scissors in hand, clenched in her fist like a knife.

"The rent," Lupe said again. "You did pay it, right?"

He laughed. "Of course. First thing this morning. That damn sheriff is just a greedy bastard, coming by so early. What is he going to want next? That people start paying their rent a whole month ahead of time?"

"Probably," said Lupe, and she now let him kiss her.

"We're going to go home," he said to Lupe between kisses and hugs. "You and your sister don't need to be here with me anymore. You've helped me enough to pay off Kenny the last of the money that he'd loaned me, and a few other debts that I had, too. Now, I can do it alone. Look, I even brought some money home. I sold five barrels today. Everybody wants whiskey. Ever since those bank problems started, people are drinking more."

Saying this, he took out a roll of money from his pocket, handing it to Lupe. She sat up on the little migrant worker's cot and began to count the money, putting the ones in one pile, the fives in another pile and the tens and twenties in their own piles, too.

"But I thought you got sixty to eighty dollars for each barrel," she said, after counting the money.

"I do," he said.

In the hallway, Carlota was holding her breath and hearing their every word as she held, back up against the wall.

"Well, there's only enough here for three barrels at sixty dollars each."

"Two I gave on credit. I get eighty dollars for those."

Hearing this, Lupe puckered her lips together, making a face of pure disappointment. Salvador burst out laughing.

"What's so funny?" she asked.

"Your face! You look so upset, because I didn't bring home all the money!"

"Well, I am," she said. "We worked so hard making those barrels. Don't laugh at me! It's not funny!"

"But it is," he said *con gusto*. "You, who hated my liquor money, are now fighting to get all the money!"

"Well, the priest said that even Christ made wine, and—well, what if they don't pay you for our two barrels, Salvador?"

"They will," he said. "And we make an extra twenty dollars with each barrel that we sell on credit."

"But what about that fool who hit you with a piece of wood 'cause he didn't want to pay you? Will that happen again?"

"Oh, no, that was my mistake. I'll never try to collect money from a man in bed with his woman ever again. He apologized afterward, Lupe. He's a good man."

"But he could've killed you! And then my child would have no father. You have to take better care of yourself, Salvador. Please, we both have to live, so we can build our home together and be *una familia de—*"

"Stop it!" screamed Carlota, leaping into the room with the scissors in hand! "I've been listening to you two, and you're sick! What do you think Salvador is, a saint? He's a no-good bootlegger! He's a liar! He's the Devil! He married you on falsehoods, Lupe!"

Lupe was staring at the pair of scissors in her sister's hand.

"Carlota," said Lupe very calmly, "but what are you doing with those scissors?"

"I'm going to kill him, Lupe. He hit me! And he had no right!"

"I didn't hit you. You were trying to scratch my eyes out and I pushed you away!" said Salvador. "You want to see a real hit? I'll show you! You big-mouth fool, calling me a coward and saying that I'm whoring around when I'm out working!"

"I saw you two counting all that money!" yelled Carlota. "Don't think I'm stupid! Lupe and I do all the work and you're out having a good time like all men do, and now you're rich and we're poor!"

"You're crazy-*loca*, Carlota! I'm not rich, you whoring little bitch, going out with Archie, who's a married man, and all those other men, too! This is just my working capital!"

"You lying bastard!" screamed Carlota. "You're just trying to get out of buying me my red dress and shoes!"

"Stop it! Stop it! Both of you!" shouted Lupe.

But they wouldn't stop. Carlota now stepped in slashing at Salvador with the scissors, and they continued yelling at each other like two enraged carnivores!

Lupe gripped her stomach and was going to faint. "Oh, my God, my God, please, stop it! With all your yelling, the sheriff will be sure to come back!"

Instantly, Carlota lowered her scissors and was by her sister's side. "Look what you did!" she yelled to Salvador.

"Me? It was you who came in with those scissors!" he yelled back at her.

"For the love of God, stop it! Both of you!" said Lupe. "Just stop it!"

"Me?" asked Carlota. "But what did I do?"

"Well, first of all, you went crazy when the sheriff came," said Lupe. "He wasn't my problem! It was you, Carlota!"

"Oh, my God," said Carlota, eyes going wide with disbelief. "Look, she's gone crazy, Salvador. She doesn't know what she says, and it's all your fault. I'll never forgive you for what you've done to my beloved sister." And Carlota dropped her scissors and began to cry. She cried the whole way back to Carlsbad.

Salvador took the back road through San Marcos in case the sheriff was out looking for them. He buried two barrels in the brush at the entrance of the Leo Carrillo *rancho*.

Getting to their house in Carlsbad, Lupe immediately went to bed. She was in great pain, and every few minutes she felt like she needed to throw up again, but nothing was coming up anymore.

"My poor child," said Lupe, body twisting with pain, "what's the poor thing feeling? This is just terrible! I so much wanted a quiet, loving home so that my child could—oh, my God!" she said, cringing once again.

"You see what you've done?" said Carlota to Salvador as she fixed the pillows behind her sister's head. "You've ruined my sister, and I'll never forgive you for this!"

Salvador turned and walked out of the room. He just didn't know what else to do. He wanted to kill this woman. Ever since Carlota had come to live with them, it seemed like the Devil had put a curse upon their home.

He went into the kitchen and got down the big quart bottle of whiskey, serving himself a full water glass. He could hear Carlota talking to Lupe in muffled tones.

"Lupe, you have to come home with me right now. He's no good—I told you that the first day I saw him."

"No," said Lupe. "Please, understand, he's the father of my child, and this is my home now."

"Oh, no, Lupe!" said Carlota. "You can't possibly mean that! He's no good! He lied to you! He's a monster! You should leave him right now and come home and have the baby with *mama,* who knows how to care for you. There is no other way. Believe me, he's evil!"

"Yes, there is," said Lupe to Carlota. "For you to leave, Carlota, and let me and Salvador work things out for ourselves."

Salvador couldn't believe these last words.

"But, Lupe, I'm your sister! We're of the same blood!"

"Carlota, you're going to need to go home," said Lupe, softly but firmly. "It was a mistake to have ever brought you, knowing how you've always felt about Salvador."

Carlota SCREAMED!

And hearing this scream was truly the most beautiful sound that Salvador had ever heard. He poured the glass of whiskey back into the bottle, tears coming to his eyes—he was so moved. His young bride was going to stick by him, after all. She really did consider this place the House of her Heart.

High above the Angels sang and the Heavens rejoiced; once more a married couple had planted their roots deep into the rich soil of Mother Earth's Soul!

ALL NIGHT Salvador drove back and forth from Escondido getting everything out of their rented house and hiding it at the entrance of the Leo Carrillo *rancho* and also over near the Kelly ranch. Then early the next day he drove Carlota back home to Santa Ana. The whole drive, Salvador couldn't stop whistling, he was so happy.

"I'll get you," said Carlota as they came into Santa Ana. "Don't think you can get away with this! You're no-good! You've just tricked my poor sister, but I'll get you! I'm going to tell my parents all about your bootlegging!"

"Sure, go ahead," said Salvador, "and I'll tell them about your whoring around with Archie and Juan and all those other guys."

"You *desgraciado*!" she screamed. "That's not true!"

"What's not true?" he said. "That you're too stupid to get paid for it, or that I didn't mention enough men?"

The shout, the bellowing scream that erupted from Carlota, was so loud that it even took Salvador by surprise, and he swerved, almost going off the road. If she'd had those scissors, he was sure that he'd be dead. "I'LL GET YOU IF IT'S THE LAST THING I EVER DO!" she bellowed, mouth open wide with such force that her neck muscles stood up like cords.

Coming into the *barrio* of Santa Ana, Salvador was feeling pretty bad. Even though he hated Carlota, he really shouldn't have said that last remark to her. After all, she and Lupe truly had been through a pretty big scare in Escondido and, also, it wasn't going to help his life with Lupe for him and her sister to be at each other's throat.

"Look, Carlota," he said, "I'm sorry about what I said, because, well, we're going to be together for a long time, and for Lupe's sake, I think that we should try—"

"You should be sorry, you lying coward!" she screamed into his face. "You made a damned fool of my entire family, lying to all of us! But oh, don't worry, you and Lupe won't be together for long, once I finish telling my mother and father the truth about you!"

"Carlota, please," said Salvador, taking her arm, "can't we just drop the insults and try to get along, you and me?"

"Oh, now you want me and you to get along, do you?" she yelled, jerking her arm away in pure repulsion. "Do you really think I'd have anything to do with you, you ugly fool? You're nothing, but a dirty-smelling old man!"

"Hey, just wait; now what are you saying?" asked Salvador. "Do you think for a minute that I'm trying to have something to do with you? Oh, my God, you are crazy!"

"Yes, so crazy that I knew from the beginning that you really wanted me, but I knew you were no good, and I was right, so you then went after Lupe! You are a bootlegger, you are a liar, and you are no good! But you couldn't trick me so you tricked my innocent sister like you tricked Archie!"

"Oh, sweet Lord Jesus," said Salvador, shaking his head. He dropped Carlota off at her parents' home and kept going. He didn't even go inside to see his in-laws. My God, he just couldn't figure out what was going on. Everything was becoming so crazy-*loco*.

He decided to immediately drive over to Corona to see his mother, the wisest, most practical person in the whole world.

13

The Devil himself had now come Full Circle and he, too, was anxiously awaiting with Flowers in Hand for the SECOND COMING of the LORD!

THE FIRST THING Lupe did when Salvador drove off with Carlota, taking her home to Santa Ana, was to go for a walk. Here, they only lived a couple of blocks from the ocean and yet she'd never taken a walk down to the sea. She had a lot to think about. My God, she'd sent her sister home. How could she have done this? No one in all of her family had ever ordered a relative to leave their home.

Walking down the long driveway between the avocado trees, Lupe turned left, and went half a block to the corner, then turned right. She went by the main part of downtown Carlsbad, crossed the railroad tracks, and continued up the small slope to the highway. There she watched the traffic for several minutes, wondering where all these people were going, then she walked by the big, beautiful Carlsbad Hotel, and down toward the beach.

Climbing down the steep bluff to the sand, Lupe saw some well-dressed people whom she assumed were guests of the grand hotel. They were sitting under large umbrellas. Looking more closely, Lupe could swear that she'd seen one of the young women in the movies.

Lupe tried hard not to stare at the woman's beautiful clothes and just keep walking, but it was difficult. She could feel the people were now looking at her, too. Lupe put her head down and kept walking, wondering why such fine, well-dressed people would bother to even look at her. She hoped that they weren't making fun of her. After all, she wasn't dressed up like they were. She was wearing a simple white dress that her sister Sophia had made for her. The dress had two red roses embroidered over her heart.

Before she realized it, Lupe had walked all the way north into Ocean-side. And she hadn't meant to go that far. But she'd enjoyed watching the waves and the little, quick-legged seabirds so much, that she hadn't been paying attention.

She sat down. She was tired and needed to decide what to do. After all, not only had she sent her sister home, but her sister was also so mad at Sal-vador that Lupe was sure that Carlota was probably right now, at this very moment, telling their parents about Salvador's illegal business. Lupe just didn't know how she'd ever be able to look at her parents in the eye again. All their lives her family had been such law-abiding people.

Feeling overwhelmed with anguish, tears welled up in Lupe's eyes and she looked out at the sea and she saw that the Oceanside pier wasn't very far away. She wondered if she had the strength to walk to it and then all the way back to Carlsbad, but then she realized that she was hungry and that she hadn't brought her purse or any money, either.

Lupe continued sitting on the sand by the edge of the concrete road that ran along the beach to the pier. She looked out at the waves, and the waves began talking to her, singing to her as they rolled in like tall, smooth, blue-green hills; slowly, gracefully, but then suddenly they'd speed up, and flip forward in a roar of thundering power, turning white and full of foam as they climbed up on the seashore. Lupe sat there on the sand and watched the waves as they came to the shore again and again.

Time passed and more time passed, and the sound of the waves mas-saged Lupe's mind. She yawned and lay down by the side of the cement road on the soft, warm sand. She began to relax and soon she was thinking *nada, nada,* nothing as the waves kept coming to the shore with sound and fury. A few yards behind Lupe, a car would pass, and people would look out of their car windows and see Lupe sleeping in the sunshine on the sand, looking so beautiful.

When Lupe awoke, she could hardly remember where she was. She sat up, glancing around. She felt so refreshed and wonderful, and yet, well, kind of confused, too. She truly felt as if she'd traveled out of herself and had gone back to her childhood.

Lupe sat for a full five minutes, breathing easy.

They'd always been so happy back in *la Lluvia de Oro*—no matter how poor they'd been—but here in a land of peace and abundance, the whole world had turned black and awful . . . she'd ordered her sister to go home.

She'd broken the Sacred Circle of *la familia.* But what else could she have done? She, too, had been terrified when the sheriff had knocked on their door, but she hadn't panicked. And later she'd also come to understand that it hadn't been Salvador's fault. How could he have known that the sheriff and his wife owned the house when he'd rented it from a real estate office?

A group of tiny birds came flying up in front of Lupe. Quickly, they landed on their fast-moving little legs and began looking through the sand as each wave receded, trying to find something to eat. No, there was just nothing else that she could've done. She was with child and this child's father was Salvador and so she had to make her home with him . . . for better or for worse, for rich or for poor to death did they part.

Watching the quick-footed little birds working so hard to make a living, tears flowed from Lupe's eyes and she thought of how her mother's family must've felt when her mother had followed her husband high into the mountains of *la Barranca del Cobre* to find work in a gold mine. That too had been a breaking of the Sacred Circle for her mother.

Lupe breathed, watching the sea and the little birds and how the tiny birds just seemed to barely get away with their lives every time a new wave came crashing into the shore. Little by little, Lupe began to see that if she just opened her eyes, then here, in the present, was also a very wonderful place. The soft, warm sand felt so good under her legs and her hips, and the ocean smelled so clean and glorious. And the waves were dancing, singing as they came to the shore, offering a feast to the little, quick birds.

Lupe sat, breathing easy, remembering how her mother-in-love had told her—the day of Salvador's fight with Epitacio—how she and the great avocado tree by her outhouse helped each other every morning; she by giving the tree substances when taking her daily calling and the tree by giving her the biggest, juiciest fruit in all the area.

Smiling, Lupe took off her shoes, wiggling her toes in the sand. The sand was so warm and itchy good feeling that little by little she began to feel all back together again. Then, feeling complete and whole, she got up, and began to hum to herself as she walked back south toward Carlsbad. And as she went, she felt like she was going in a soft glow, in a special place of warm dream-like knowingness. The smooth, wet sand under her feet and the breeze on her naked legs truly felt of Heaven, itself.

Listening to the waves as she went, Lupe also remembered what her mother-in-love had wisely said to her, that same day at the outhouse when she'd asked her if she hadn't heard the fight between Salvador and Luisa and Epitacio, "Of course, I heard it, but *mi hijita,* when it's all said and done, these disturbances are no more than a *pedo*-fart in the wind. You are with child, so don't let these ups and downs of life, *la vida,* disturb you from your task at hand. What you are doing here, inside of your body, is a blessing straight from *Papito Dios* and not to be disturbed."

And it was true, what Lupe was now feeling going on inside of her stomach, as she walked along the seashore, was every bit as huge and powerful as the Mother Sea, herself.

Lupe continued walking, watching the waves, the seabirds, and feeling the wet, glistening sand under her feet, and she just knew that somehow she would face her parents eye to eye and everything would be all right. After all, the world was huge and the world had many ways and she was a married woman with a husband and a child on the way and so she wasn't going to allow anyone, not even a member of her own *familia,* to cause her any unnecessary worry.

She was feeling stronger now, feeling a confidence that she'd never felt before in all of her life. It really was like her mother had told her, once a woman married and started her home, then every woman needed to find her own way so she could find her own special answers to the twists and turns of life. And Lupe could now see that this great body of water, the sea, had helped her find her way as her mother's Crying Tree had helped her mother find her way. After all, women came from Water, just as much as they came from Tree.

Suddenly, Lupe felt like shouting, like dancing—she felt so very good! She could now see clearly that she was glad that she'd sent her sister home, even if Carlota did tell their parents everything.

Lupe walked on, eating up the miles, and she was strong and good now. Up ahead in the distance, she saw the brightly-colored umbrellas of the people that she'd seen earlier from the Carlsbad Hotel. But they were so far away that they looked like bite-sized, individually wrapped chocolates, just like the ones her sister Sophia had gotten from her suitor back in *La Lluvia.*

Lupe laughed and kept walking, feeling stronger with each step. The brightly-colored umbrellas got closer and closer and, finally, she was close enough to see that the people under the umbrellas were sitting down and reading books.

Lupe's whole face lit up with joy. "Oh, what a splendid idea," she said to herself, seeing what these fantastic *gringos* were doing. "Why, I'd never thought of that! To come down to the seashore and read a book while you listened to the ocean!"

Lupe began to walk even faster. She would find the local library and she would start to read once again.

"Yes, I'll read to my child here inside of me!" she said excitedly. "Sure, books can become our best companions!"

Suddenly Lupe felt so happy, that she wanted to get home to their little house as quickly as she could. She was so glad that she'd come down to the seashore alone. Being alone was wonderful, especially when you could feel the Seed of Life, *la Vida,* inside of you.

As Lupe passed by the well-dressed people under the umbrellas, the beautiful young film star glanced up and saw her. And to Lupe's complete surprise, the young woman now gave her a beautiful smile and waved a big, "Hello, there! What a gorgeous sundress!"

Lupe turned a thousand shades of red, she was so embarrassed. Why, she was just dressed in the simplest of dresses, and she felt so plain and ordinary compared to these fine people. But still, she smiled back to the movie star and said, "Thank you!" Then she flew up the bluff from the beach in large, graceful bounds, as she'd always raced up the *barrancas* back home in *la Lluvia de Oro.* She hoped that she could get out of earshot before the people started laughing at her. What in God's name had ever possessed her to smile back at such a well-dressed famous woman.

Lupe hurried down the road, past the Carlsbad Hotel, and back down the short slope to the railroad tracks. She wanted to fix a special dinner for Salvador tonight. She and Salvador had been so happy when they'd been alone together.

She felt excited as she started up the driveway to their *casita.* She'd get her purse and she'd go to the *barrio* market and buy groceries just like a married woman. She was so happy that she began to sing. And at the market, Lupe couldn't believe it, there was a canary for sale, and so she bought the bird, too. Song was in the air—she could feel it in her HEART!

WHEN SALVADOR GOT to his mother's house, he found his sister, Luisa, screaming like a crazy woman. "Salvador," she yelled, "I've been praying that you come! Our *mama* has gone *loca* and endangered us all!"

"What are you talking about, Luisa?" said Salvador.

"Come over here by me, away from her, and I'll tell you," said his sister, making the sign of the cross over herself. Doña Margarita was sitting across the room from Luisa and her boys in the kitchen calmly drinking a cup of tea. Luisa made the sign of the cross over herself again, making sure to keep her distance from their mother as if she was expecting a bolt of lightning to come down from the Heavens at any moment.

"Go outside, boys," Luisa said to her children, "and don't come back 'til I call you!" After getting her boys safely out of the house, Luisa turned on her brother. "Our *mama*," she said to Salvador, "spoke to God, Him-self, demanding that He make up with the Devil! Can you believe that, Sal-vador? Our mother did this horrible thing, completely ignoring that we're supposed to be afraid of the Holy Wrath of God?"

"*Mi hijita,* calm down," said Doña Margarita.

"I will not calm down!" said Luisa with tears streaming down her face. "You tell Salvador what you told me, *mama*! And I'm sorry to say this, *mama,* but I have children to worry about, so unless you're willing to take back what you said to God, then I'm going to have to ask you to go to your own house and not come to my home again. My God, you're lucky *Dios* hasn't struck you DEAD with a bolt of LIGHTNING! How could you have done this, *mama,* endangering us all! Don't you remember that woman in the Bible—what's her name—who God turned to stone just because she turned to look back? I'm scared, *mama*!" added Luisa.

"Oh, *mi hijita,*" said Doña Margarita, "woman of such little faith, don't you see that—"

"Faith? Oh, I got faith, *mama,* lots of faith, that's why I don't put my nose in where it don't belong, because I have FAITH that it will GET CUT OFF!"

Hearing this, Doña Margarita started laughing. "*Mi hijita,* that's not faith, that's fear."

"Well, then I got FAITH in my FEAR, *mama*! Because just look at me, I'm a nervous wreck, shaking like a leaf ever since you told me what you did, and that you didn't ask—but demanded—that *Papito Dios* have an answer for you *mañana*. Yes, He'll have an answer for you—*UN RAYO DE LUMBRE* down our throat, *mama*!"

"Luisa, Luisa, *calmate,*" said the old lady, "or better still just come with me in the morning, and you'll see that God is—"

"Oh, no, *mama*!" yelled Luisa, cutting her off. "I followed you down the mountains into the battles of war! I followed you across the desert without water or food! But I will not go to church with you tomorrow to see what God has to say about *el Diablo*!"

"And why not, *mi hijita,*" said the old woman kindly. "God is already Here . . . all around us, showing us His Eternal Love. That's all God is, *querida, Amor* above all else. Who do you think was with us through all those difficult times of the Revolution, Luisa?"

"God, yes, I know that, *mama,* but He was, well, invisible . . . you know, what I'm saying. But this, well, this—oh, no, no, no! I'm not pure, *mama.* I can't go with you to see God face to face! I don't even own new UNDERWEAR!"

Hearing this, Salvador started laughing. "Look, Luisa," he said, "if that's what all this is really about, I'll buy you new underwear."

"Oh, yeah, sure, make fun of me!" said Luisa. "You haven't heard all the stories that are going on around the *barrio*! *Mama* has told God what to do, don't you see, and she's not the Pope! She's just a poor, ignorant woman!"

Hearing these words "just a poor, ignorant woman," Doña Margarita closed her eyes in concentration. "*Mi hijita,* after all these years of struggle, haven't you come to see that it is us, the poor, ignorant women of the world, who've been saving the day since the dawn of time?"

Breathing, Doña Margarita now opened up her eyes. "We are the Power, *mi hijita,*" she added. "We are the Sacred Power of all Creation. Tell me, where would the Almighty be without us? Didn't even God need *Maria* so He could give us Jesus, eh?"

"Oh, I just don't know," said Luisa, wringing her one hand with the other. "I hear you, *mama.* But tell me, what if God is in a bad mood? I mean, yeah, sure, I know He's All Love and All Good, but what if He just happens to have a bad night tonight, then what?

"Look, *mama,* I'll tell you what," added Luisa, looking so scared and nervous that she could pop. "I'll go for you and tell the priest to tell God that you were just joking, okay? That you didn't really mean to start up all this trouble."

"You'd do that for me, *mi hijita,*" said Doña Margarita. "You'd go to the church feeling the way you do?"

"Well, yes, of course, *mama,*" said Luisa, her eyes suddenly filling with tears. "Because—oh, *mama,* you are our sacred mother, and I love you with all of my heart!"

"Oh, Luisa, come here, and let me hold you, you are a fine, brave daughter."

"Well, no, not quite so brave, *mama,*" said Luisa, "because I won't go inside of the church. I'll go to the priest's door in the back, hoping God doesn't see me."

The burst of *carcajadas* that erupted from the old woman filled the house with the sound of laughter. "Come here," she said to her daughter. "Come here, and let me hug you and give you love!"

Quickly, Luisa went to her skinny, little, old mother and knelt down on the floor, putting her large, tear-wet face on her mother's tiny lap, crying and crying as her mother soothed her head with her old, wrinkled, dark hands. Salvador breathed easier. They looked so beautiful together. And he was thinking that they were both finally calming down, when Luisa suddenly jerked her face up from her mother's lap.

"*Mama*," she asked, "you didn't invite the Devil to come and see you tomorrow morning in church, too, did you?"

"Well, of course," said Doña Margarita, "the whole reason why I've set up this meeting is so that the two of—"

But Doña Margarita was never able to finish her words, because Luisa now let out a blood-curdling SCREECH of pure terror, then she was up and racing out the back door, scattering chickens, goats, and the mother pig and her little piglets!

Luisa continued screaming in wild hysterics 'til the neighbors came out of their homes to see what was the commotion. And when Luisa told them of her mother's predicament, that she'd set up a meeting between God and the Devil for tomorrow morning at their little stone church, many of *la gente* quickly made the sign of the cross over themselves and hurried back into their homes, closing their doors, thinking that this crazy old Indian woman had finally done it and she was now bringing about the end of the world for sure!

But a few didn't rush away in fear and some of these neighbors came to Doña Margarita, found her sipping her tea quietly in the kitchen, and they told her that it was about time that someone had spoken up to God, because it was true what she'd been saying all week long; how did the Holy Creator expect them to get along with one another Here on Earth if He couldn't make up with the Devil up in Heaven?

Salvador walked his mother to her own little shack behind Luisa's house. He built a little fire in the wood-burning stove and asked his mother if she was all right.

"I'm fine, *mi hijito*," she said. "You don't have to worry about me. Everything's going well, perfect in fact," she added, kissing the crucifix of her rosary.

"Then why is Luisa so upset?"

"Because, *mi hijito*, until a person has made peace with the Darkness we each carry inside of ourselves, then our Fear of the Devil is greater for us than our Love of God. Balance, remember, is the key to all of our senses."

"I see, it's as simple as that, eh, *mama?*"

"Of course. Show me a person who Fears the Devil and I'll show you a person who hasn't brought Peace and Harmony to their Soul."

He thought of Carlota and how she was so full of fear and that she thought he, Salvador, was the Devil. "So, then, how do you deal with a person who has so much fear, *mama?*"

"This is the very reason I have set up this meeting between God and the Devil, *mi hijito.* So once people see that God, Our Father, has made up with Lucifer, then Fear of Death and Fear of the Devil will be uplifted off the whole Mother Earth like a bad dream and we will then burst forth into a Sense of Harmony and Peace across the whole land for thousands of years!

"Tomorrow, *mi hijito,* is the day we've been waiting for a very long time. I thank the Blessed Mother and Jesus that they allowed me to join them in this great event," she added, making the sign of the cross over herself. She was glowing.

Salvador nodded. "You know, I came to see you, *mama,* because I was all mixed up," he said. "Lately so many things have been going wrong with Lupe and me that I didn't know what to think, but now I'm here with you just a little while and I swear, everything seems so easy and understandable. I can now even see why Lupe's sister Carlota always attacks our marriage every chance she gets. She's just jealous and full of fear, *mama.*"

Doña Margarita laughed. "Well, then by all means thank Carlota every night before you go to sleep. For in her doings she saves you and Lupe a lot of heartbreak."

"How is that?"

"Because," said the old woman, closing her eyes in concentration, "if it wasn't for Carlota, then you and Lupe would be fighting each other to learn the lessons that life destined for you. Carlota, *mi hijito,* is your Holy Cross, thank God," she added.

Salvador burst out laughing. "Never in a million years, *mama,* would I have ever dreamed that I'd be thanking God for my loud-mouth sister-in-law! You are the best! I adore you, *mama!*"

"Of course, I was the first pair of tits you sucked!" she said.

It was getting late when Salvador realized that he should start for home. Lupe was by herself and he didn't want her to be alone. But then he remembered that he'd promised Lupe to call her if he was ever going to be late, that he'd call Eisner's little market up the street from their house and have someone deliver the message.

"Mama," said Salvador, "I'm going to go into town so I can call Lupe. She hasn't been that well and I want her to know that I'll be late—or should I stay over, *mama,* and go with you to the church in the morning?"

"No, you go home to Lupe," said the old woman. "I don't need your help Here, *mi hijito.* Everything is already done. Do you really think that I could have talked to the Almighty the way I did, if He hadn't, in fact, already conceived that Thought inside of His Being? Remember, He is the Thought, we are the Doing. He is the Sea, we are the Wave. He is the Symphony, we are the Note. Everything is already Perfect Here, *mi hijito.* You go home and be with Lupe. Yours is the true test of my bringing the Devil and God Together, for you are in the midst of the storm of Living Life, *la Vida.* Go with my blessing, *hijo de mi corazón.* And when you get home, Lupe and you pray for me," she added, making the sign of the cross over herself.

"We will," said Salvador, hugging his mother, "we'll pray with all our heart and soul."

Then he was on his way and he was feeling ten feet tall! Oh, his old *mama* just knew how to bring Heaven down Here to Earth!

THAT EVENING when Salvador came into Carlsbad and turned in to the avocado orchard, he could feel a difference half an orchard away. The Father Sun was going down and the whole western sky was painted in beautiful colors of pink and gold. Lupe and their little dog, *Chingon,* came out to greet Salvador. It became a magic moment of hugs and kisses with the windows of their little *casita* all lit up behind them.

"Thank you for calling that you'd be late. That was wonderful, Salvador."

"You're welcome, *querida.* I didn't want to cause you any worry after all you went through with the sheriff. My God, Lupe, we were making whiskey in the sheriff's own house. Can you beat that?" Then it hit him like a *rayo*—a lighting bolt. "Lupe!" he yelled excitedly, "this is what my mother is talking about! You, Lupe, brought peace to your soul when you faced that sheriff. That's why you were able to think so clearly, see. The Devil didn't have a hold of you."

Lupe had no idea what Salvador was talking about. It was quickly getting cold. The last of the Sun was blinking in and out of the avocado leaves as it slipped down into the sea.

"Hurry," she said. "Come inside with me. I have a surprise to show you."

Walking in, Salvador could smell something very delicious cooking. And there was a bright yellow canary singing in a cage.

"I bought a canary," said Lupe, whistling to the bird. "Our mother always had one back home in her kitchen. And guess what, I'm cooking *chiles rellenos* again!"

"Oh, no," he said, laughing.

"Oh, yes!" she said with conviction. "And this time, I know how to do it. I asked the woman at the grocery store. And she told me that I'd had the pan too hot last time, and that's why they exploded.

"You know," she said, turning down the fire a little on their two-burner camp stove, "because I'd eaten so many of my mother's wonderful *chiles rellenos,* I thought that I knew how to cook them, but I didn't. Okay, get back!" she now said. "Here comes the first *chile*! A big, fat, long one and he better not jump!"

Saying this, she put the stuffed *chile* into the sizzling pork lard, and the big green *chile* danced about the frying pan, but didn't explode. No, it just settled in and began to cook in quick little jerks in the hot clean pork fat, singing a little hissing tune.

"I did it!" yelled Lupe excitedly.

"Yes, you did," said Salvador.

"This is wonderful," said Lupe. "But now, if only I can turn it over and cook it on the other side without it—oh, no, don't do that, you lousy fat *chile*! You stay over there on that side of the pan," ordered Lupe, "so that there's room for me to get your friend into the pan, too."

Salvador started laughing.

"What's so funny?"

"Well, we used to have a witch in our valley who everybody thought was crazy because she spoke to her fruit trees, and now here you are—"

"So you think I'm a crazy-witch because I'm talking to my big, fat—oh, no, don't you dare!" she said to the first *chile.* "You stay over there!"

"Here, let me help you," said Salvador. "I think that the stove isn't level and that's why it keeps sliding to that one side of the pan."

Salvador got a plate and turned it upside down and slipped it under the lower side of the stove. "There, is that better?"

"Yes," said Lupe. "Now get back! Here comes *chile* number two! And he better behave, too!"

And she put the next *chile* in the pan, and it didn't explode, either.

"I did it again!" yelled Lupe, feeling so proud of herself. "I really did!"

"Yes, you did," said Salvador. He was so happy to be home all alone with Lupe. It was a dream come true. This was all he'd ever wanted—a home with the woman he loved.

"Oh, Lupe," he said, coming up behind her and slipping his arms around her waist and kissing her neck, "I'm so happy that we're alone in our little *casita*."

"No, don't do that now!" she yelled, pushing him away. "I'm busy cooking! You go over there and sit down!"

He laughed and sat down at the table. This was truly wonderful. He could actually feel the walls of their whole little house singing with joy. Something had truly changed.

"Where'd you get the bird?" he asked.

"At the market," she said. "And I know I should've asked you first—because it cost a lot of money—but, well, he was singing so beautiful, that I just couldn't resist, Salvador."

"*Querida,* you don't have to be asking me if you can spend a little money here or there, you have your house money, remember."

"The bird cost three dollars," she said.

"Three dollars!" he said. "That's a fortune, Lupe! Most men are lucky if they make a dollar a day. But, but, well, I'm glad you did it," he added. "He does sing like an angel."

"Then you really aren't angry?"

"No, of course not, Lupe. This is your house, *mi amor,* our home, the nest that you are making for our *familia*."

"Oh, Salvador!" she said, hugging him.

"By the way, Lupe, I forgot," he said as they hugged and kissed, "I promised *mi mama* that we'd pray for her. You see, she's doing a great miracle tomorrow in church."

"In Corona?"

"Yes."

"Well, then we better pray for her right now, Salvador," said Lupe, putting down her big spoon and knife.

And so Salvador and Lupe prayed for Doña Margarita as the last of the Father Sun went blinking over the horizon and the whole western sky turned silky-soft with colors of pink and gold and silver. Hundreds of red-shouldered blackbirds came swooping overhead on their way to the lagoon just north of Carlsbad. Another glorious day had come to pass.

THAT HOLY NIGHT IN CORONA, meaning the crown, there was a wondrous display of shooting stars flying across the Heavens, then in the early morning—just before daybreak— came some great big, soft clouds with gentle rain, washing the Earth and Rocks and Trees, gifting New Life to all the Land.

Hearing the raindrops drip-dropping outside of her window, Doña Margarita stirred in her sleep, beginning to awake little by little. She stretched and yawned and listened to the soft, gentle rain washing the Earth. She'd had a wonderful night. She'd slept like an Angel.

Sitting up, Doña Margarita saw that the cat was curled up at the foot of her little bed. It was Luisa's cat, but of late the little female cat had been coming over more and more to bed-down with her. After all, pets instinctively knew when family members needed help in their spiritual quest.

"Okay, wake up, *gatita,*" she said to the cat. "We have work to do today, eh?"

At first the little calico cat didn't want to move, but finally she was up on all fours, stretching and yawning, too. Doña Margarita and the she-cat actually looked quite a bit alike. They were both old and mangy-looking, but still pretty quick once they got their old bones warmed up.

The soft, gentle rain continued making a quiet drip-dropping music outside Doña Margarita's window as she walked across her little shack in the dark and lit a candle with a big wooden match. It was cold, so she put some paper and kindling into the wood-burning stove, lit the paper with the candle, then got some water going for coffee.

She smiled. Today, after so many years, she was finally going to meet with *Dios,* Himself, in the little stone church, and the Almighty was going to have an answer for her concerning *el Diablo.* She laughed, shaking her head. Sometimes she really couldn't believe the situations into which she got herself. Luisa was right. She really wasn't anything but a crazy-*loca* old woman.

She laughed again and blew on the little flames that had taken hold. Little by little she got the fire in the stove going pretty good. She added some sticks, blew a couple more times, then got her shawl and put on her old *huaraches* so she could go out to the outhouse.

At the door, she picked up her rosary, her Bible, and took her candle and went out the door. Outside, Doña Margarita was taken by surprise. Standing in the rain were a half dozen *gente*—mostly women—with lit candles, too, waiting for her under the avocado tree.

"Eh," she said, with a little happy smile, "but what are you all doing, standing in the rain? Did you come to accompany me to the outhouse? Well, I'm sorry, but it's only a one-seater. So out of my way."

Laughing, the people parted like the Red Sea and the old Indian woman hurried past them into her outhouse. Closing the door, her sounds came instantly; big, full, strong *pedo*-farts and *caca* without any embarrassment.

One of her old lady friends had a cup of coffee waiting for Doña Margarita when she came out of the little outhouse. She accepted the cup and got underneath the big avocado tree with *la gente* and she sipped her coffee in big air-sucking sips as they all watched the birthing of the new day. There was thunder and flashes of lightning in the distance.

Little by little Doña Margarita got to feeling better once again. Last night, the Devil had gotten pretty unsure and he'd caused quite a stir. But Doña Margarita had held strong with her Faith in the Eternal Goodness of the Almighty, and she'd held the Devil's hand through his outbursts and gotten him to calm down.

"All right," she said, finishing her coffee, "I'll just wash my face, then we're on our way *con el favor de Dios*."

She put down her cup on the stack of firewood under the avocado tree, went inside, washed her face, then came back out. More people had gathered. They now walked briskly to church.

From inside of her home, Luisa watched her mother and her dozen old friends go up the dirt street and out of the *barrio*. Luisa wanted no part of them. In her opinion, they were just a bunch of old, toothless women and a few crippled, old men with a herd of grandchildren. Some of these women and men were even older than her mother—*gente de la Revolucion*—with missing legs and arms and scarred faces. Luisa just couldn't understand why they'd be starting up all this trouble with God, Himself. Hell, they were lucky just to be alive!

Luisa came out of her house and watched them continue up the street with their limps and crutches as lightning illuminated the whole Father Sky in the east. Part of her really wished that she had a little more faith so she could join them, but she didn't. She'd just seen too much terror to have much faith in the eternal goodness of life or God. Tears came to her eyes. She'd seen her brothers and sisters killed all around her, and her first husband Jose-Luis, the love of her life, shot at their dinner table by two little thieving soldiers trying to steal their food.

Then Luisa saw a huge terrible Bolt of Lightning EXPLODE with a THUNDEROUS ROAR just beyond her mother and her friends, and overhead patches of startling bright Father Sky burst through the clouds in glorious rain of gold! Quickly, Luisa made the sign of the cross over herself. Her heart was pounding wildly as the soft, gentle rain continued drip-dropping all about her.

Now Luisa couldn't tell where Earth ended and the Heavens began.

"*Mama,*" said Luisa, putting her hands together in prayer. "Oh, what have you gone and done?"

Doña Margarita was singing as she and her friends went out of the *barrio,* going into the well-paved streets of the Anglo part of Corona. *La gente* took up the Holy Song of Glory Be To God, and they continued across the Anglo part of town, raindrops coming down from Heaven, Blessing them.

Some Anglos—hearing the singing—came to their windows and they saw a sorry-looking lot of poor, old Mexicans singing in the rain and cupping their free hand over their candle so that the rain wouldn't put out their flame.

Seeing one old Anglo lady looking out her window at them, Doña Margarita gave her a glorious smile, feeling so happy that she gave a little dance, shuffling her old feet. The old Anglo woman laughed and ran across her house to get her coat. By the time they got to the steps of the little stone church half a dozen Anglos had joined them. They had no candles with them, but they did have umbrellas and raincoats.

Doña Margarita and all her people could feel the Singing of the Stones of the Church as they started up the stairs. This was when Luisa suddenly came rushing up, yelling, "*mama,* we're coming with you, too!"

"Oh, this is wonderful," said the old woman, seeing her daughter rushing up with her grandchildren. "You have finally seen the Light!"

"Light, hell!" said Luisa. "I just don't want to be left out!"

La gente burst out laughing, and Doña Margarita took her daughter in her arms. "You are a good daughter," she said. "A fine daughter, and I admire your honesty. Welcome, *mi hijita,* to this New Glorious Day that's long overdue!"

Then she turned to her three grandchildren. "Thank you for coming, too," she said.

"Is God really waiting for you inside of the church, *mamagrande*?" asked Luisa's middle son.

"Isn't He always waiting for us, *mi hijito*?" asked the old woman. "And today Our Holy Father, awaits especially happy . . . for He sees that we are finally stepping forth, beyond our childish self-imposed illusions of fear and separation and rejoining Him in His Full Glory—across the entire land! Come, give me your hand, and you'll see!"

Saying this, she turned with Luisa and grandchildren in hand, and they continued up the steps to the entrance of the church, and that was when the thick, heavy oak doors of the Stone Church suddenly opened wide all by themselves and they saw that the entire Holy Structure was jam-packed Full of Angels!

Angels were Everywhere, gliding this way and that way, over *la gente* as they all came pouring into the Church!

Then Doña Margarita saw that everyone, from all of her past, was Here, too!

Her father, Don Pio, who'd died more than a dozen years ago, was Here!

Her mother, Silveria, who'd passed over almost twenty years ago, was Here, too!

And Here were also all of her children whom she'd lost in that terrible Revolution!

Doña Margarita's old, wrinkled-up eyes overflowed with tears!

Why, Everyone was Here for those who had the Eyes to See!

And it was the same for all of *la gente* who'd had the Faith to come this morning—they, too, now had Here, before them—Everyone from out of their Earth-Past!

It was GLORIOUS!

WONDROUS! MIRACULOUS!

HEAVEN and EARTH were UNITED as ONE!

And then Father Ryan was ready to begin mass, and he looked so handsome.

Doña Margarita gave *un grito de gusto*—she just couldn't help herself! For Here was also her old *amiga,* who'd given her life for them back in their mountains *de Jalisco* when those soldiers had turned their dogs loose on them!

And Here were also the two giants—her nephews Basilio and Mateo—grinning ear to ear like the happy children that they'd always been!

EVERYONE was REALLY HERE!

And their torn bodies were intact!

Then Here was also that child—who's lifeless body she'd taken in her hands in the river the day the American soldiers had opened fire on them in El Paso and those well-dressed people had watched from the shade of their grand carriages—and she, this child, was now whole!

Doña Margarita and this Angel Child now hugged in a big *abrazo,* and this Child now stepped forward and began to Sing, leading all the Angels in chorus!

A million Light Years of Illumination was coming to Be!

And Doña Margarita now knew that she, and all the people who'd come with her, had just passed through the Gates of Heaven and they were now United as One in this Holy Place where Angels Sang the Song of God—Here on Earth as it is in Heaven.

But then she suddenly remembered the Devil. "Excuse me," she said, "I'll be right back." She hurried back out the front doors of the stone church. In her excitement, she'd forgotten all about Lucifer. She hoped to God that he was still waiting outside with his roses in hand.

Glancing around outside, Doña Margarita didn't see him at first, but then Here he was, standing under a tree with roses in hand in the soft, gentle rain drip-dropping all over him. She called to him. "Come on," she shouted, "everyone is waiting!"

But Lucifer didn't move. He just stood Here looking very unsure of himself.

Doña Margarita walked over to him. "Look," she said, "come on, we can't very well go on without you. Remember, as I told you, you are the whole reason we put this together. Come, give me your hand, and I'll walk inside with you."

But the Greatest Angel ever Created still wouldn't move. He was scared. For truly, he'd never stopped Loving the Almighty.

"Look, Lucifer," said Doña Margarita, "you and I have had a lot of run-ins over the years, but frightened or shy I've never found you to be, so come on."

But still he wouldn't move. No, he just stood, roses in hand, kicking the dirt like a nervous young boy.

"Lucifer," said Doña Margarita, finally growing impatient, "you take my hand and come inside right now! Let's face it, what other choice do you have, eh? Nobody is afraid of you anymore. Hell, little kids are now starting to out-devil the Devil, so basically, you did your work so well for so long that now you're out of a job unless you take my hand right now and we take Creation to a Whole New Level!"

Hearing this Lucifer smiled a big beautiful smile, looking at Doña Margarita with such Love and Respect, then he started laughing *con carcajadas!* No one, but no one, had ever spoken to him like this. "Okay," he said, taking her old, wrinkled-up hand, "lead the way. I'm all yours, Margarita!"

"You bet your sweet ass you're mine," she said, "because I'm a grandmother and I got children and grandchildren, and all this fear *caca* has got to stop! The world was never flat, and we're no longer going to pretend that it ever was!"

And so the Whole Stone Church was Rocking, Singing, Dancing *con gusto* when Doña Margarita came in the doors with Lucifer in hand.

And Here was Father Ryan and *Maria, la Virgen de Guadalupe*, the Mother of God—just as she and Doña Margarita and Father Ryan had planned it—and *Maria* now came forward, greeting Lucifer. And she, Doña Margarita, a Woman of Substance, handed over Lucifer to *Maria*, and together the priest and the Mother of Jesus led the Angel of Darkness down the aisle back to God.

You could smell the "fear" coming off Lucifer.

You could hear the Heart of the Universe Beat, Beat, Beating.

The One Collective HEART-*CORAZÓN* of All Living Life was Beat, BEAT, BEATING! POUNDING *con AMOR*!

And Lucifer, holding the Holy Mother's hand, looked as nervous and anxious as a young handsome groom going to his wedding, as the Blessed Virgin led him up the center aisle.

Father Ryan Prayed and Blessed them with his smoking ball of incense.

At the altar, *Maria* gave Lucifer a small kiss on the cheek, patted his hand in reassurance, and sent him up alone to the altar to re-meet with the Almighty and Our Lord Savior Jesus Christ.

Everyone inside the Church held their Breath.

The Whole Stone Church was now Vibrating with so much Love that the Mother Earth, Herself, began to purr!

The soft, gentle rain continued all over the land, and all living life rejoiced!

And Jesus, the Pure Note of Creation, now stepped forward to take both of Lucifer's hands in His.

But Lucifer was so frightened that he looked like he might bolt, until Jesus smiled. And His Holy Smile was so warm and Full of Compassion that Lucifer's Heart-*Corazón* melted and he was able to hold.

Jesus kissed Lucifer on the right cheek, then the left cheek, and said, "Welcome, Home, Our Greatest Angel! You've done your job, my Holy Brother, so the time has come for you to rejoin *Nuestra Familia*."

Tears BURST from Lucifer's eyes. "Thank You, my Lord God's Son!" he said.

And Jesus then turned, gift-giving Lucifer's right hand to the Lord Almighty, Who stood up to receive!

And when Their Holy Hands Touched, HEAVEN EXPLODED WIDE OPEN!

MOTHER EARTH WHIRLED, STARS BURST, and ALL of CRE-ATION joined in with One VERSE, One SONG, One SYMPHONY OF GODING GOOD GOD!

And over to one side the Blessed Mother took Doña Margarita's hand and said, "Thank you, *señora*!" For she could see how thrilled was Her Husband, GOD ALMIGHTY!

"Thank you!" said Doña Margarita to *Maria*. "We did it!"

"Yes, we did," said *Maria*.

"We kicked Heaven's Ass!"

Maria laughed. After all these years there was still just nothing she could do to get this earthly old woman from using such spicy language.

God drew Lucifer close, looking at him Eye to Eye, then gently drew him forward in an *abrazo de corazón*!

And thusly Father Ryan began High Mass.

Part Seven

EARTHTALKING

14

GOD was Happy! PAPITO was Smiling! Singing "through"
every Stone, Tree, Raindrop, Blade of Grass — HE was
SO MOVED!

SALVADOR AWOKE WITH A START. His heart was pounding, but he wasn't scared. He was happy. Wildly happy! But he didn't quite know why.

"What is it?" asked Lupe.

"Mi mama!" said Salvador, excitedly.

"What about her?"

"I think she did it. I think she really did it! She brought God and the Devil back together once again!"

"Salvador!" snapped Lupe.

He laughed. "Put your hand over your heart," he said, putting his right hand over his own *corazón*. "Don't you just feel it—like we've come full circle," he said. "Look, it's sprinkling outside, and yet there's bright sunlight coming through the clouds."

"So then there's bound to be a rainbow," said Lupe.

"Yes," he said, smiling with *gusto*. He felt of Heaven. "Come on, let's go see."

Slipping on clothes, they hurried outside and yes, there was a big, beautiful rainbow to the north of them. They hadn't even bothered to put on shoes—they'd gone out so quickly. Standing in his bare feet, Salvador itched his toes back and forth in the wet soil as he held Lupe in his arms. The whole land was alive with color and light. Birds were chirping in the trees above them. Then they heard a SCREECH and a huge Redtail Hawk came swooping down by them, giving sound to all the world. The Red Eagle landed in an avocado tree right in front of them.

"Lupe!" said Salvador with tears bursting from his eyes. "This is *mi mama* and she's telling us, that yes, we now have a whole New World!"

"I'm glad to hear this," said Lupe, "because yesterday, when you took Carlota home to my parents, I took a long walk on the beach by myself, Salvador, and I was able to think." She took a big breath. "Carlota is going to tell my parents, Salvador."

He nodded. "Yeah," he said, "she told me she was."

"Yes," said Lupe, "and I've been thinking of how *mis padres* are going to take it. We must prepare ourselves," she added.

Turning Lupe about so he could see her face, Salvador had a twinkle in his eyes. This young bride of his was just never going to stop surprising him. Here she was taking hold of the bull of life by the horns in the middle of a storm. She wasn't complaining or getting hysterical. No, she was thinking calmly with the same iron that she'd used when the sheriff had come knocking on their house in Escondido.

"Lupe," said Salvador, "*mi mama* told me yesterday to come home to be with you. That she didn't need me to go to the church with her this morning, even though Luisa was going crazy with fear, because *mi mama* said that the real proof of her bringing God and the Devil back together again wouldn't be inside that church, but here with us, me and you, two married people in the thick of living life, and you've just done it, *mi amor*. You are telling me of this situation that we now have with your parents with such fearlessness. You are the best, Lupe! You are the woman of my dreams! I adore you, *mi amor*! The Devil has no hold on you!"

He went to kiss her, but she held him away. "No," she said, "none of that right now. I need to talk to you. I did a lot of thinking yesterday on the beach."

He smiled. "Talk, Lupe. I'm listening."

"Good," she said.

And so they went back inside to talk and the Red Eagle watched over them, giving yet another cry.

AND YES, the night before Carlota had, indeed, told her father and mother about Salvador's being a bootlegger and how he was a coward who'd deliberately endangered Lupe and her. Doña Guadalupe and Don Victor listened very carefully and Carlota told them the story about Escondido and how they'd barely escaped with their lives.

"If it hadn't been for my bravery," Carlota told her parents with tears streaming down her face, "we would have all been caught and sent to prison!"

Hearing the whole story, Doña Guadalupe and Don Victor were very upset. But Don Victor said nothing and simply excused himself and went outside. He sat down in his rocking chair on the porch, and he tried to light a *cigarrito,* but couldn't. His hands were shaking too much. Ever since he'd come home from the hospital, his hands had been shaking.

Finally, after several attempts, Don Victor was able to light his smoke. Rocking and smoking, he began to calm down. Something just sounded a little fishy about this whole story. But, still, had he, Don Victor, ever asked his wife to climb down into the mine when he'd gone down into the depths of hell to do his carpenter work? Did a *ranchero* involve his wife when he was chasing wild cattle through the *chaparral*? There was no excuse for what Salvador had done! A man's work, was a man's work!

Don Victor was still rocking and smoking, when his son Victoriano drove up. For the last month Victoriano had been working with Mr. Whitehead once again. Don Victor looked at the truck that his son was driving. If Salvador hadn't loaned Victoriano those two hundred dollars, he wouldn't even be working right now. The times were hard and getting worse. The date was late January 1930, and the holidays had come and gone without anyone noticing. And yet, there was one thing that Don Victor couldn't get out of his mind; it just didn't sound like Salvador's style to get his two daughters involved in a man's business.

That night Don Victor and Doña Guadalupe had a big fight. Don Victor was determined to confront his son-in-law and tell him in no uncertain terms how dare he put their baby daughter, Lupe, in such a terrible situation. But Doña Guadalupe thought differently of the situation and she told her husband that he was going to have to hold his tongue.

"We can't interfere," she said, lips trembling, "we must not even say one single thing unless Lupe asks us. It will embarrass her and cause her great shame. We must act," continued the wise old woman, smoothing out the apron on her lap, "like we don't even know. Besides, remember, our daughter Carlota has always exaggerated, so who knows what the truth really is? We must keep calm, *mi esposo,* and be reassuring. After all, these are hard times and Salvador is bringing home the money."

Don Victor turned his eye on his wife. "Are you saying this because of my gambling?" he snapped. "At least I never endangered your life by having you go down into the mine with me! HE WAS IRRESPONSIBLE!"

yelled the old man, red-faced with rage. "Oh, I just don't know if I can hold my tongue—I'M SO MAD!"

"Me, too," said the old woman. "But, well, what can we do, she's with child and every young couple must find their own way. Let us pray," she added. "Come on, *viejo,* let us go and pray that *con el favor de Dios* this, too, will come to pass."

"I don't feel like praying!" shouted Don Victor. "You pray! I'm going for a walk!"

He went out the door in a huff. Dona Guadalupe remained inside. She lit a candle, put a shawl over her head, and began to pray for God's guidance. She well-knew that the world was often not what one thought, so only with God's help could we humans comprehend that good really did, in fact, come from evil if we just remained open of *corazón.*

AND SO THAT YEAR, the spring came in with a torrent of rain and thunder and lightning. Lupe was now in her seventh month, and she was still looking pretty skinny, but their doctor in Santa Ana said that she was in fine health. Doña Guadalupe, on the other hand, didn't like seeing her baby daughter that thin, so one day she shrewdly asked Salvador if Lupe could come and stay with them so she could attend to her personally for the next few months.

Salvador looked at Lupe. They'd just been to see the doctor, and he could see it in her eyes, she loved him, she was committed to him, but still she really wanted to be with her *mama*. And also, it was now time for him to start making liquor again, so he was going to be gone a lot of the time.

"Of course, Doña Guadalupe," said Salvador to his mother-in-love, "no daughter should be away from her *mama* when she's getting ready to give birth to her first child."

"Thank you," said the old woman, glancing at her husband.

"Thank you, huh!" said Don Victor, mumbling to himself as he went out of the room.

Watching the old man go out in a quick rush, Salvador damn well knew that Lupe's family knew all about his bootlegging. Carlota had definitely told them. But Lupe's parents hadn't brought up the subject, so he sure as hell wasn't going to bring it up, either.

Salvador and Lupe drove back down to Carlsbad that day, then Lupe packed up all her personal belongings, including the canary, and the following morning, Salvador took her back up to Santa Ana and dropped her off at her parents'.

"Salvador," said Lupe, "we don't have to do this. I'm your wife, remember."

"I know," he said, loving her for saying this, "but I really think this is for the best right now. I also have a lot of work to do and I don't want you alone in Carlsbad without your family. Helen is right, a woman with child needs her *familia.*"

"Okay, Salvador," said Lupe, "thank you."

"Thank you, Lupe," he said, taking a deep breath.

They kissed and the canary began to sing. After seeing Lupe inside, Salvador was immediately on his way over to Archie's. The big lawman had long ago separated from his family and was staying by himself in a house across town in Tustin. He and Carlota were now openly dating.

Getting there, Salvador found the front door wide open. He could hear Archie singing to himself somewhere in the back of the house.

"Archie!" shouted Salvador.

"Come right in!" yelled Archie. "I might be a *cabrón* son-of-a-bitch, but I live with my front door wide open!"

Salvador came in. "Open for who?" he asked.

"The whole damn world!" said Archie. "A lot of people think I'm a rotten son-of-a-bitch because I moved out of my home, but hell, I still pay the rent for my wife and kids, and see them all the time!

"Now, tell me," he said, "what can I do you out of this fine morning?" Archie was in a good mood. He was in the bathroom, looking at himself in the mirror as he lathered his face with a bar of shaving soap. He had his pistol and holster on the back of the toilet for easy reach and a half-empty bottle of whiskey, too.

"Well," said Salvador, "it's time for me to start up the distillery again, and so, well, I was wondering where the best place to set up would be."

"Well, Escondido sure as hell is out," said Archie, strapping the straight razor. "Man, you really screwed up, Sal." He began shaving. "I told you to be careful or that Sheriff Georgie-boy would get suspicious. Then he came back a few days later, found the place a mess, and he was pissed when he realized that he'd rented his house to a damn bootlegger and hadn't got his cut." Archie laughed, washing the shaving soap off the razor.

"Sal," he said, continuing his shave, "you're going to have to set up here in Tustin, where I can keep an eye on you. Things are getting pretty hot all over the country." He washed off the razor again, then strapped it a few more quickies before continuing. It was really very interesting for Salvador to watch a man shave himself with a straight razor. The hot water, the soap bar, the razor-sharp knife, the smell. It was the only good memory that Salvador had of his own father.

"Personally, I think that it's because of all these damn cheap gangster movies that don't know shit about real life, so they make it look like the bootleggers and the law gotta be shooting at each other like crazy fools, instead of getting along hand in hand and working things out together. You know what I mean," added Archie as he twisted his face this way and that way, shaving the last of the lather off of his face and continually rinsing off the razor, "it's that damn cowboys and Indians mentality all over again, that shoot 'em up, stupid ignorance of don't live and let live."

Salvador just nodded, not saying a word, and he watched Archie finish shaving, wash his face, look in the mirror, then grin this great big shit-eating grin.

"Man, Archie," Archie said to his reflection in the mirror, "why weren't you born rich, instead of so damn good looking!" And he threw himself a kiss with his big, loose-moving, puckered lips, making a low, rolling, gut-sound like a studhorse. "Aaaah, what a man!"

Salvador had to laugh. In his estimation, Archie had to be one of the homeliest-looking men he'd ever met, but this was what Archie said to himself in the mirror every morning.

Archie reached for the bottle of whiskey on the back of the toilet, took a good pull, then poured some in his left hand and slapped it on his face. "Best damn shaving lotion in town!" he said, still admiring himself in the mirror. "Ah, to feel as good as I look—damn, I'm lucky! So, do we got a deal, Salvador?"

Salvador nodded. "Yeah, I guess we do. But what's it going to cost me, Archie?"

Archie turned and looked at Salvador for the first time. "Not much, Sal," he said, grinning ear to ear, "just a leg and arm! And for chrissakes, make it a farmhouse this time," he added as he put on his shirt, lowered his trousers, tucked in the tail, hitched up his belt, and slipped into his shoulder holster. "And rent it from the farmer himself, too, damnit!" He put on his Stetson, took one last good look at himself in the mirror. "Man-o-man, and to realize that before the Sun sets today, some lucky woman gets to have this real stud of a man with gun and all!" He pointed his index finger at himself like it was a gun. "Pow! Pow! Pow! Man, I love me! Okay, now take me out for breakfast, Sal," he added. "Man, I'm hungry enough to eat a steer!"

It took Salvador a week to set up his new distillery in a good-sized farmhouse just a little southeast of downtown Tustin. And after setting up, he told Lupe where he was in case she ever needed him. But, of course, he and Lupe didn't tell her family where his new plant was located.

Salvador now went to work like a madman once again, working around the clock day and night. He, also, made a deal with Kenny White and had the old man make some of his deliveries for him. Kenny wasn't getting much work in his garage anymore, so he was happy to drive for Salvador. Everywhere, people were out of work. They didn't have the money to get their vehicles worked on, but they did have the money to drink whiskey.

LUPE WAS ONLY HOME with her parents for a few days, when she came to realize just how much the whole world was changing all around them. In Santa Ana, entire Mexican families were packing up their belongings and going back to Mexico. All the banks had closed down. There was no money anywhere. Now, hardly any ranchers had the means to pay people to do their picking and packing. Shipping from California back to the East Coast by rail had almost come to a standstill.

Wages dropped to nothing. People fought to get the few jobs that were left. Blacks and Whites now came in, competing for the jobs that the Mexican people had always done.

Fights broke out, and big, strong white men—called Okies—were brought in with clubs by the truckload, and they beat workers, so that they'd quit their jobs, and then their own people could get the work.

One day Sophia's husband, Julian, got so beat up that he was hardly able to walk home. He'd asked for his wages, and the farmer had him beaten up by two big men instead of paying him.

The next day Lupe and her family went to the surrounding hillsides to trap rabbits and look for wild cactus and other edible things. Julian tried to get out of bed to do his part, but he couldn't move—he'd been beaten so badly. Lupe's sister Sophia cried that day up in the hills as they searched for food as she hadn't cried since they'd left their ragged, war-destroyed homeland. How could God have allowed this to happen to her beloved

Julian, a good-hearted, little, tiny man who'd never lifted a finger to hurt anyone in all his life.

The following weekend when Salvador came to visit, Lupe asked him if he had any money so that they could go shopping for groceries for her family. All of her people were hungry. Victoriano had also been beaten. Salvador said, sure, he had money. Lupe thanked her lucky stars.

Then that Sunday, when Lupe went to church with Salvador and her *familia,* she was shocked to see that half of the Mexican families that they usually saw at church were gone. It felt like a death had happened inside of the very house of God.

Mexican communities all over the Southland were returning to Mexico. But back to what? Mexico was still a land of ragged misery, trying to heal from its terrible Revolution. The word *repatriando* now began to be used in almost every conversation—meaning that people were returning to their native land.

That week, the farmer who'd had Julian beaten came with his hat in hand bearing gifts and paid Julian the wages that he owed to him, and he apologized over and over again for the terrible misunderstanding, saying that this situation would never happen again, and that Julian had a job if he wanted it, and Victoriano, too, of course.

"It was like a miracle," said Lupe to Salvador, the following weekend when he came by to see her and take her shopping for groceries for her *familia.* "That farmer just couldn't stop apologizing. Isn't it wonderful, Salvador, how life can change so quickly and so much good can come from a bad situation?"

Salvador nodded. "Yes, I agree. Life is really full of surprises."

And he, the man who'd long ago befriended the Devil as well as God, said nothing more as he listened to his wife go on about this miracle that had come to pass. For he, too, believed in miracles here on Earth, but he also well-knew that now and then, they needed a little help. And that farmer, who'd come hat in hand, would never again ever even dream of having one of his workers beaten up. He was a changed man. He, too, had seen the Devil and the Devil's name was Juan Salvador Villaseñor.

This week, Salvador and Lupe found out that even having money wasn't much help. The grocery store that they normally went to hardly had any merchandise.

"Don't worry," said Salvador, "I know a big grocery store across town where the owner has lots of everything!"

But then, getting to the store in the Anglo part of town, they went inside and found that shelves were mostly empty. And there was a hollow-looking old *gringo* at the cash register.

"My God!" said Salvador.

"What is it?" asked Lupe.

"That man, he's the owner," whispered Salvador to Lupe. "He helped me once, years ago, when I was first getting into the liquor business and didn't know how to get the big quantities of sugar that I needed. Jesus, he used to be so full of life! This store was his pride and joy, and it was always so full of piles of food!"

Salvador almost felt like turning around and leaving, but he didn't. He took a big breath and walked up to the man. "Hello, my friend!" he said, with a big, happy grin, trying to uplift the man's spirit.

But the man didn't recognize Salvador and only responded with a weak "Hello."

"Don't you remember me?" asked Salvador. "You helped me!"

"Good, I'm glad I did, and now what can I do for you?"

"Food!" said Salvador. "My wife and I want lots of groceries!"

"Do you got any money?" asked the man cautiously. "I can't just keep helping people, you know."

"Sure, we got money!" said Salvador. "Cash! Lots of cash!"

"Really? Cash?" said the old worn-out-looking Anglo, who was probably only in his early forties. "Well, please, do come right in."

Salvador watched him try to gather his strength, and be the confident man that he'd once been, as he showed them what he had left, but he just couldn't bring it off.

Salvador bought boxes and boxes of groceries—things that they really didn't even need—and he told the man that he'd be back. "So order more merchandise, my friend, because I'll be coming in from now on, once a week!"

"Really?" said the man. "And you'll have cash?"

"I'll have cash for you every week, *amigo!*" said Salvador.

"Oh, good!" said the old man, and he thanked Salvador again and again for having come in. But the following week, when Salvador and Lupe came by, the store was all boarded up.

"Good God," said Salvador to Lupe.

"What is it?" asked Lupe.

"He killed himself," said Salvador, feeling a chill go up and down his spine.

"But how do you know?" asked Lupe.

"I can feel it here inside of me," he said, taking a deep breath and blowing out. "*Gringos*, they do this, you know. Your brother, Victoriano, explained it to me, Lupe; they're afraid of ending up with nothing."

"Oh, no," said Lupe, "it's not nothing that they're afraid of! It's that they love money more than they love their *familia*!" she added with anger.

"But why are you getting angry," said Salvador. "The poor man must've been suffering awful to kill himself."

"I don't care how much he was suffering!" snapped Lupe. "I'm with child and I'll do everything I can to keep alive so my child can be BORN! He had no right to be so selfish! May he BURN IN HELL, the coward!"

"Lupe, Lupe, please, calm down," said Salvador, laughing. He'd never heard her speak like this. "He was a good—"

"No, I WILL NOT CALM DOWN, Salvador!" she shouted. "I will live! And you will live, too! And that's that, do you hear me? THERE ARE NO EXCUSES!"

Seeing her anger and determination, Salvador tried to stop his laughter. Every day, this young wife-of-his was surprising him. "Okay, okay, I'll live," he said. "I promise you, I'll live."

Salvador could still see in his mind's eye how he'd gutted that screeching pig right there in bed with that farmer, then he'd put the flaming torch to the man's face, explaining what's what about life. He'd tossed the torch to the terrified man's bed and the horror-stricken man had had to fight to stop his house from going up in flames!

"Salvador," she said, taking his hand, "I may not know much about a lot of things, but I do know that life is sacred, and we have no right to take it, especially our own."

His whole chest came up. "Couldn't agree with you more," he said. "No one should ever take their life, especially when the other guy is still breathing."

Saying this, he looked into Lupe's eyes and he could see that she and he had truly come a long ways since they'd married. Why, she was becoming his hero like his very own mother.

"Lupe," he said, "the more I get to know you, the more I love you."

"You better," she said, "I'm with your child."

Her strength was truly becoming the Food of his Soul. "My God," he said, laughing again, "just look at you, Lupe, at how far we've come in the last few months. You're a woman of IRON!"

"Salvador, that store keeper didn't know how to be poor of purse, but rich of Heart," she said. "And that's what's happening to this whole country, too. These people just love money too much, and that's not right, I tell you. All families see hard times. That's just part of *la vida*."

Salvador nodded. "You're absolutely right, my *familia* and I sure have seen our share of hard times and yet, well, we always found a way."

"Of course, you found a way, Salvador, you found the way of God," said Lupe, making the sign of the cross over herself. "Look what happened to Sophia's husband; they beat him so they wouldn't have to pay him, and he was so hurt that he could hardly make it home, and still that day he found a dead rabbit on the road that had been hit by a car and a bunch of onions that had fallen off a truck. My sister cooked up a feast!" she said, with a smile full of pride. "Then a week later that same farmer came by and apologized. Life is full of miracles, Salvador. No one has the right to kill themselves!"

"I completely agree," said Salvador, flashing in his mind's eye on the fear of that man's face as he'd thrown the flaming torch at him and the screeching gutted pig beside him. "We *Mejicanos* are pretty damn good, tough people, eh?"

"*Con el favor de Dios,*" she said, bowing her head.

Yes, *con el favor de Dios,* Salvador thought to himself, but also with a little help from the good, old Devil, too.

"You're a good man, Salvador," she said, soothing his big, huge, thick hand in hers and looking at him in the eyes.

"Thank you, *querida,*" he said.

And he felt so happy, and all at peace, but God help him . . . oh, how he loved to see the terrible fear that he'd put in that farmer's eyes that night.

Heaven was theirs, but the Gates to Hell were wide open, too.

THEY FOUND another grocery store, bought a few things, then drove over to the farmhouse where Salvador had put up his distillery. Looking at the setup, Lupe realized that her husband was working day and night, around the clock. He had a mat and a couple of blankets on the floor right next to the stove.

"That's where you're sleeping?" she asked.

"Yes," he said. "That way I can keep watch on the stove night and day and make sure it doesn't blow up."

"But wouldn't you be safer in another room?"

"Not really," he said. "If she blows, Lupe, she blows as big as a bomb, taking the whole house."

"Good God," she said. "I never realized that. Then let's go outside," said Lupe.

"Okay," said Salvador.

And so they took the straw mat and blankets outside and put them under the pepper tree in front. It was a beautiful, warm spring day. They lay down and ate, truly enjoying themselves. Then Salvador noticed a large bush with huge purple-violet flowers across the yard over by the side of the toolshed.

"Do you know what those big flowers are called, *querida*?" he asked, pointing across the yard.

"Hortensias," said Lupe. "They're some of my mother's favorites."

"I'll be," he said. "Look, how they take in the sunlight. I've never seen a flower like this before. They're so big and beautiful. You know," he added, "if we have a girl, I'd like to maybe name her Hortensia, just like those flowers."

"Hortensia, why that's a beautiful name," said Lupe. "And you know, if you look at one of those flowers real closely, you'll see that they aren't just one flower, but hundreds of tiny flowers."

"No, really?" said Salvador and he got up, brushed off the seat of his pants, and walked over and picked one of the huge, round hortensias and brought it back across the yard. He was carrying his .38 in the front pocket of his loose-fitting pants. Their closest neighbors were two fields away. The farmer who had rented this place to Salvador had been overjoyed to get the cash. Salvador figured that he had nothing to worry about, but still a man in his business could never afford to be too relaxed.

"You're absolutely right, this flower is made up of hundreds of small, tiny flowers," said Salvador, lying down once again beside Lupe. The bright sunlight was surrounding them in delicious warmth. "You know," he said, "if we have a boy, I'd like to name him Jose, after my brother, *el gran Jose.*"

"But I like your name Salvador," said Lupe. "So why don't we call him Salvador or, well, Jose Salvador?"

"Yeah, I like that," he said. "Jose Salvador. I'll be damned, it's like a miracle, isn't it, how life just goes on and on, never ending, eh?"

"Yes," she said, smiling with *gusto,* "around and around, generation after generation, never ending, forever. And I was just thinking of this the other day, that I come from a long line of women who've been getting married and having kids since the dawn of time. We're not alone, Salvador, I can feel it, right here inside of me," she said, patting her little popped-out stomach. "All of our ancestry is guiding us."

"Yes, I feel that, too," he said. "But I don't really want to think about my own father." He took a deep breath. "I like to skip over him and think about my grandfather. Now, there was *un hombre*! Hey, if it's a boy, I think I'd like to call our baby Pio for my grandfather, instead of Salvador."

"No," said Lupe, "I want us to use your name, Salvador."

"Really, you want to use my name, Lupe?"

"Yes, yours and your brother Jose's. You are a good man, Salvador."

Hearing this for a second time, that he was a good man, Salvador breathed in so deeply that he had to look up at the Father Sky. This was all he'd ever wanted to hear, coming from the woman he loved. A car passed by.

"Okay," said Salvador, having seen the car before, "then if it's a boy, we'll name him Jose Salvador; but if it's a girl, we'll name her Lupe Hortensia, after you, *mi amor,* and this gorgeous flower, that's not just one flower, but a treasure of hundreds of tiny little flowers—just as our child is sure to be a treasure in a hundred little ways, too!"

Lupe drew close to Salvador, kissing him. A flock of crows came flying by overhead, coming off the produce fields. They landed on the top branches of the huge pepper tree, and instantly, they began making a racket of sound.

"Lupe," said Salvador, hearing the birds, "after so many years of suffering it looks like the world is finally beginning to be at peace for us, so let's have the biggest baptism celebration that this country has ever seen!" he added with his whole face lighting up with *gusto*. "Yes, let's do it, Lupe, like people did back in *los Altos de Jalisco* before the Revolution! I remember my grandfather Don Pio slaughtering a steer, killing a couple of pigs, and people would feast for days at a child's baptism!"

"Can we afford it?" asked Lupe.

"We can't afford NOT TO DO IT!" shouted Salvador, grinning ear to ear. "Even during the Revolution we still celebrated. I'll never forget, our village was burned to the ground, Lupe, women and children had been slaughtered like beasts, but, still, that night, after we buried our loved ones, we celebrated. And my parents even danced! We need to always dance, Lupe! We need to always celebrate! We need to always laugh and love and live no matter how twisted and awful things seem! So let's have a baptism for our first child, marking the beginning of the many celebrations for *nuestra gente* here in this new country of ours!"

Tears of joy were now also running down Lupe's face. "Let's do it!" she said.

Instantly the flock of crows in the tree turned into Angels for those who had the Eyes to See. God was Happy! His children were at long last beginning to Awaken.

The drums were beating!

The Drums were Beat, BEAT, BEATING! Singing *Papito*'s One Song *de AMOR*!

ARCHIE CAME ROARING up in his big, black Hudson to Salvador's distillery in Tustin—fifty-some miles west of Corona—honking to beat hell. "Come on," he yelled to Salvador, "the circus has come to town!"

No matter how broke people were, they always seemed to have money enough for the circus. But Salvador didn't want to go. He was dead tired. He'd been working around the clock for nearly two weeks now. He needed to go to sleep. Also, all day he'd been having strange feelings about his mother.

"No, Archie, I'm too tired," said Salvador.

"Bull! Get dressed! You look like hell! We'll pick up Lupe and Carlota and take them with us, and have a great time!"

"Oh, all right," said Salvador, "but I'll have to bathe and shave."

"I hope so," said Archie, "you stink like shit!"

Bathing, Salvador got to feeling a lot better. He hadn't been out of the house in thirteen days. He was almost done with his distillery job. Tomorrow he'd go over and see his mother. Ever since yesterday morning, he'd been having these quick-little flashes about his *mama,* and a huge roaring fire. Coming out of the house, Salvador found Archie loading a barrel of whiskey into his trunk.

"Were you going to tell me, Archie," said Salvador very carefully, "or was this just one more leg and arm that I've lost?"

"Of course, I was gonna tell you, Sal!" said Archie, closing his trunk lid. "What do you think your sheriff is, a damn crook! I'm the law, damnit! I'm as honest as the day is long, which I might add—" he said with a twinkle in his eyes—"gets a little too damn long for me in the summer months!"

Saying this, Archie burst out laughing to beat hell. He and the Devil were really very good friends.

Before getting in the big Hudson with Archie, Salvador went over to the bush of hortensias alongside the toolshed, and slipped his revolver behind the bush. He had this little feeling. Then he got in the vehicle with Archie and they drove over to pick up Lupe and Carlota. Sophia and her husband, Julian, and their kids were visiting, so Archie—always being the big-hearted man—said, "Come! Everyone's invited! Kids and all! Salvador is paying!"

Just then, Maria, Carlota and Lupe's other sister, arrived with her kids and Archie invited them, too. And how they did it, they'd never know, but that day twenty-some people got into Archie's Hudson and Victoriano's truck.

The circus was in the riverbed just outside of San Juan Capistrano. It was the tightest drive that Salvador and Lupe would ever have in all of their lives. But no one was complaining. Not even the kids who had to ride in the trunk of the Hudson—with the lid wide open.

At the circus, they all were truly enjoying themselves, hearing the music and seeing the lions and elephants and clowns, and smelling all the candy and food and strange animal odors.

The main attraction was announced by a huge, gigantic, fat man wearing the tallest black hat ever seen and sporting the longest, thickest mustache ever imagined. He had a bullhorn and he shouted that the main attraction only cost fifty cents extra per person, but was too frightening for shy-hearted women and children under eighteen.

"For the first time in modern history!" bellowed the huge man, "a wild man has been captured from the highest peaks in all the Sierra Madre mountains! A human beast so wild, so untamed and uncivilized that he refuses to wear clothes, and he spits and growls and puts terror into anyone who dares set eyes on him!

"And also, so that you men won't be shocked or put to shame, I'll tell you that some people might look at his feet and call him bigfoot, but if you look closer, it's not his feet you'll call big! This human beast puts most studhorses to shame!"

"Damnit!" said Archie, grinning. "This sounds like one of my relatives from Pala! Come on, baby!" he said to Carlota. "Let's go see!"

"I'm not going," said Carlota, "not on your life!"

"Why not," said Archie. "You ain't no shy-hearted woman!"

"Shut up, Archie!" said Carlota.

Archie only laughed. "Hell with it, let's go, Sal, and you, too!" he said, turning to Victoriano and Sophia's husband, Julian. "Let's the four of us go see how this beast stacks up to us *machos*!"

Victoriano declined. He didn't want to waste any more money. As it was he'd thought that they were fools to have come to the circus. Sure, the farmer had come and he'd apologized and given them back their jobs, but hell, now the farmer had nowhere to ship his produce. People just weren't buying. Whole fields of produce were being left to rot. Victoriano didn't even have the gas money to get home.

And so Archie paid the extra buck fifty for the three tickets, then they got in line with the couple of other men who were lined up to see this horror of horrors. And the kids wanted to go see, too. None of them had ever seen a wild man before who spat at you and growled—and who knew, said one small boy, the beast might even piss on you!

"I'll piss right back on him with my big thing if he does," said Archie, laughing. "I'll just jump right in the cage with him and see who's more wild!"

Archie and Salvador and Julian were laughing uproariously as they went into the tent. Then, they'd no more than disappeared into the tent, when Lupe and Carlota and Victoriano and Sophia heard Archie's huge, BELLOWING VOICE screaming something terrible!

A crowd gathered at the entrance of the tent. Now everyone was trying to pay their fifty cents as fast as they could to get inside. My God, if the wild man had put such terror into their local sheriff's heart, then he was truly worth seeing!

But what happened inside the tent, was that Archie took his pint bottle out of his coat pocket and took a drink, and was handing the bottle to Salvador when he turned and saw the wild man. And the wild man was none other than Archie's own nephew from the Pala Indian Reservation at the base of Palomar Mountain.

Immediately, Archie began to protest, to say that he'd been robbed and wanted his money back, but just at that moment, the wild man saw his uncle Archie, and so he picked up some shit that they'd put in his cage with him, to make him look authentic, and he threw it at Archie to shut him up.

Getting a chunk of shit in his face, Archie let out a ROAR that terrified everyone in the tent. Then Archie threw himself at the cage, trying to reach in to get hold of his naked relative by the throat and kill him. But his nephew just grabbed hold of Archie's hand and bit it, growling like a wild man.

Archie let out a bloodcurdling scream, trying to lift up the whole cage and tear "Aunt Gladys's" boy, limb by limb. It took the announcer and two other men to pull Archie off the cage.

The people were screaming, shouting, and the tent poles were getting knocked down with the pressure of the mob of people who were trying to get inside to see what was going on. Inside, Archie hit the gigantic announcer right in his big stomach with all his might. But the huge announcer just took the punch like nothing—in one show, they shot cannonballs into his stomach—and he asked Archie if he could do this every day and twice on weekends.

"He's my DAMN NEPHEW, you crook!" bellowed Archie.

"Even better!" said the announcer. "We could bill you both! The wild beast and his uncle, the lawman!"

Salvador was laughing hysterically.

By the time Archie and Salvador and Julian finally got out of the tent, people were lined up by the hundreds, fighting to get inside. Sophia's husband was saying that he hadn't laughed so hard in years. Archie didn't think it was funny one little bit. He was pissed and still wiping the shit off his face.

All the women and children wanted to know what had happened.

"What happened," said Julian, "is that I just found out that we, *los Indios,* will never starve! If we can't make money working, we can always get money by just acting wild!"

All the kids wanted to go in and see.

"Just look at Archie," said Salvador, falling off his feet with laughter, "and you'll see everything! It's his damn nephew!"

"Was his thing like a horse?" yelled one little kid.

"Ask Archie to show you!" roared Salvador with laughter. "It's his relative!"

Salvador continued laughing. Archie was the best damn show in town!

AFTER THE CIRCUS, Archie stopped by a friend's bright yellow house in downtown San Juan Capistrano right by the railroad tracks and bought a fine, strong, young billy goat and threw it in the trunk of his Hudson along with the kids.

Back in Santa Ana at Lupe's parents' home, Archie started a fire in the backyard and let the kids play with the goat for a while, so that the animal would calm down, then right there in front of everyone, Archie pet the goat gently and slit his throat, the whole while talking to him in a soothing voice as he bled him. Then one, two, three, Archie had the cute little animal skinned-out, gutted, and on the fire, smelling of Heaven.

Neighbors started coming because of the fine smell, and Archie showed the kids how to stretch the goat's skin and salt it down. Every kid in the neighborhood now wanted his own vest made from this goat's fine skin that they'd played with and had so much fun!

Archie set up the barrel of whiskey right in plain sight. This time no one would be hiding from Doña Guadalupe and Don Victor. Archie was sick and tired of hiding. He'd fallen in love with Carlota the first time he'd laid eyes on her back down there in Carlsbad over two years ago when he'd put on that dance across from his poolhall. Just the sight of her caused him to start snorting like a studhorse.

The Sun was going down. Salvador was looking off into the distance and being very quiet. He just knew that something very big was going on with his *mama* once again. He could feel it in his gut.

"You know, this is one hell of a country," said Archie, coming up to Salvador, as he sipped his whiskey. "That crazy nephew of mine is now making more money acting wild than he's ever made in all his life. He's a hell of a good boxer, too. In an exhibition bout a few years back down in San Diego, he knocked down Jack Dempsey himself."

"Dempsey?" said Salvador. He was still looking off into the distance.

"Jack Dempsey," said Archie. "You know, the champ! Hey, what's going on with you, Sal?"

"I just don't know," said Salvador. "But I got this crazy little feeling, Archie."

"Hell, you just need a drink," said Archie. "What's wrong with you? Has the wife told you to lay off? That's what my ex was always telling me. Man, that got old fast."

"No, this has nothing to do with Lupe," said Salvador. "It's *mi mama*, I keep—" But he stopped his words. Suddenly, he had a flash of a huge roaring fire and people were dancing around the fire.

"Salvador!" Archie was yelling at Salvador. "Come on, we need to talk! I finally got word to old man Palmer," said Archie, leaning in close to Salvador. Palmer was a big-shot Chief Deputy Sheriff down in San Diego. "And he said to tell you that yes, he'll sponsor Domingo so he can get early parole, but it will cost you."

"How much?" asked Salvador. For months now, he'd been working with Archie to get Domingo released early, but it was costing him more and more every time they spoke. He was beginning to get suspicious.

"Two hundred," said Archie.

"Two hundred!" screamed Salvador. "Archie, I'm doing good, but not that good!"

"Keep your voice down," said Archie. "Maybe I can talk Palmer down to one-fifty."

"Bullshit!" said Salvador. "I'm better off telling Domingo to stay another year in prison and I'll give him the one-fifty when he gets out!"

"Well, all right, if that's how you feel about it, Sal," said Archie. "But a year is a long time."

Just then, Victoriano drove up with a truckload of melons that a farmer had left to rot in his fields. The whole neighborhood had gathered. The free whiskey had brought all of *la gente* out of their homes.

Lupe and her three sisters came out of the house with freshly made *tortillas* and a huge pot of *frijoles*. The goat was ready, and everyone's mouth was watering. Archie's homemade barbecue sauce smelled of Heaven. Lupe and her *familia* weren't used to seeing a man cook. Archie Freeman was truly a very strange individual, in their estimation. But what could they say, he was a big, happy, good-hearted guy, and he and Carlota now really seemed to be becoming a couple.

A couple of men strolled up, playing their guitars.

Salvador said nothing more to Archie. Long ago he'd learned that this wasn't the end of the situation. It was just the beginning. He was finally understanding how to deal with a greedy man like Archie. You had to work him very slowly, and then he'd come around.

Hell, maybe this Palmer wasn't even asking for this much money. After all, Palmer was an educated man and educated men, Salvador was beginning to find out—as he did more and more business with them—were usually pretty straight-forward, honest people. Hell, nobody was more honest than his attorney, Fred Noon.

"All right, come and get it!" yelled Archie, turning to everyone. "The cute little maaaaaa-goat is ready!"

From everywhere, the people came. They were starving. Archie's whole face lit up with joy as he watched the people fill up their plates, licking their fingers. He'd seen a lot of hunger in his day, and it was truly a pleasure for him to see people with lots to eat.

The Sun was down, and Salvador kept seeing in his mind's eye a huge roaring fire. His mother's face flashed in the fire's flames. The flames were leaping twenty-thirty feet into the Father Sky and she was dancing about the fire with a group of people with painted faces. It gave him shivers, it all seemed so real. He took a deep breath and asked the Almighty to please look after his old *mama*.

15

LIGHTNING flashed across the land and THUNDER roared through the canyons with the HOLY VOICE of CREATION!

SALVADOR DIDN'T KNOW IT, but for three days and nights his mother hadn't been home. She'd disappeared late one afternoon with three young local Indian boys, saying that she'd be gone for just the afternoon. Driving over to Corona, Salvador could hear his sister Luisa's screams as soon as he got out of his car. Going inside, he found his mother once more sitting quietly at the kitchen table, sipping her *yerba buena* and humming to herself as Luisa continued screaming at her at the top of her lungs.

"You were gone nearly a week! No one knew where you were! I was going crazy, *mama*! I can't keep living this way! You don't seem to know or care what you put me through! I swear, I've aged TWENTY YEARS this last week!"

"Well, then, I guess that pretty soon we'll be the same age, *mi hijita*," said the old woman cheerfully.

"THIS ISN'T FUNNY!" screamed Luisa. "You were gone! I thought that they'd STONED YOU TO DEATH!"

This was when Luisa finally noticed that Salvador had come into the room. Luisa whirled on Salvador with vengence!

"And where have you been!" she bellowed! *"Mama*'s been lost! She just walked in! And you were lost, too! I'd thought that the Earth had opened up and swallowed you both!"

Luisa slapped Salvador across the face with all her might, then she was crying and hugging him so hard that it looked like she was going to break his back.

It was well over an hour before Luisa had finally calmed down enough to go to bed. Salvador now walked his old mother out the back door of Luisa's house and to her own little shack in back. The Mother Moon was out and she was beautiful!

"Oh, just look at Moon, *mi hijito,*" said Doña Margarita. "If Luisa would only have looked at Mother Moon with an Open Heart, she would have known that here inside there was no reason to worry about me.

"What do you think people did for all those thousands of years before the telephone? They'd just put their hands to their Heart and look at Moon and Mother Moon would tell them about their Love Ones. Always talk to Moon, Salvador, especially when difficulties come up between you and Lupe. Mother Moon is your guide in the matters of Heart and Soul. Moontalk is the languaging of *la familia,*" she added, making the sign of the cross over herself.

"I'm tired," said Doña Margarita, once they were inside of her shack. "Help get me into bed, *mi hijito.* We did so much Holy Work. Everyone was there. Everyone! And you know, *La Gloria,* herself, is blind."

"La Gloria?" asked Salvador.

"Oh, didn't I tell you, *mi hijito,* God sent down Three Holy Angels to take me up to Heaven to visit. It's just up the mountain behind San Bernardino at a beautiful lake surrounded by huge, old pines. That's where I met *La Gloria*—God's Own Self in the New Sun of Creation into which we are now entering."

"And She's blind?"

"Yes, totally," said his mother. "And so I asked Her how this happened, and She told me that She'd gone blind with rage. I asked how long had this rage lasted to make Her blind, and She grinned and said not too long, just a little over one hundred years. We both started laughing and laughing, *mi hijito,* this is how I will always remember this Great Woman of God, Her laughing eyes rolled over back, looking all white, and the whole land filling up with Her Great Laughter.

"You should have been with me, *mi hijito,* it was so beautiful up in that high country of Heaven. We could see forever and the waters of the Holy Lake were so crystal clear that you could see each little pebble down at the bottom, no matter how deep."

Salvador stopped listening as he tucked his mother in. She just seemed to have no idea how upsetting it was for everyone that she'd been gone for all these days and nights without a word. Why even he, who hadn't been here in Corona waiting for her, had still felt pains in his stomach.

"Why aren't you listening to me, *mi hijito*?" she stopped and asked.

"You want to know the truth?"

"Of course."

"Because sometimes I think you're just crazy, *mama,* the way you don't seem to realize how you upset people," he said.

"I upset people, eh?"

"Yes, you do. We love you, *mama,* and you just disappeared. This time I side with Luisa. She has every right to be angry with you."

"I see, it's not the people who upset themselves with their own fears and doubts?"

"*Mama,* don't twist my words. You know what I mean."

"Am I twisting your words to question what it is you say, *mi hijito*? Oh, no, you and your sister are the ones who upset yourselves, and you seem to think that because you love me, you have the right to say I upset you."

"But *mama,* you disappeared. What was Luisa to think?"

"So, then, stop thinking," she said. "Do you still not get it? Thinking, here in the head, is how we lost the Garden we had all over the Earth. It's only when we return to the Heart, Here in Our Center, that we can regain all of our lost senses and step through the illusion of separation and return to the Garden. *Mi hijito,* we've come Full Circle. What we did in the Church isn't some isolated reality. Our Sacred Unity of Light and Darkness is now Circling the whole Mother Earth with Sun and Moon, even as we speak."

Salvador said nothing. He just stood there looking at his old mother.

"Then, *mama,*" he said, "you're telling me that for all these days that you were gone, you were really up in Heaven visiting with *Papito*?"

"Aren't we all once we return to Grace?"

He nodded. "Yeah, I guess so," he said.

And so she now told Salvador how Beauty, Harmony, and Peace had come down from Heaven in the form of Three Handsome Young Indian boys to get her one morning. They went by truck to the foot of the Big Bear Mountain where their old truck broke down and they had to go up the mountain by foot.

"I flew up the mountainside, I was so full of power!" said Doña Margarita to her son Salvador. "And on top of the mountain, we came to a beautiful Holy Lake that the local *gente* call *Ojo-de-Dios,* Eye-of-God, because the waters are so clear that they reflect the Sky, putting Heaven Here on Earth.

"It was so cold, that we built a huge fire the first night," she added.

"I know," said Salvador. "I saw these people dancing around a huge fire with painted faces and stones in their hands."

"That was us!" said Doña Margarita. "That first night we heated up big stones, then we went into a cave-like structure half underground and put herbs and water on the hot stones. The whole cave heated up so hot with steam that it was like returning to the womb.

"The second night we built another huge fire, and I showed *la gente* how we dance on hot-burning coals back home. People came in from hundreds of miles all around. *La Gloria* used Her Spring Festival to Honor me for what I'd done down here in the lowlands with the Devil and *Papito Dios.*

"It was beautiful, *mi hijito,* they, too, knew that what I'd done was nothing new. Each of us, in fact, needs to bring Peace between God and Devil for us to Balance our Cycle of Harmony. Then *Diablo* can once more be viewed by us mortals as the happy-joking-prankster who volunteered to walk in Beauty into the Darkness of the Unknown.

"*La Gloria* led us in Holy Chant and the coyotes came to join us in Song, and Golden Eagles Screeched from the Heavens and the Great Old Trees around the lake stepped forward and joined with the Holy Singing of the Stones! Everything was in Symphony, Everything was Being Touched by the Blessed Breath of Creation!

"Oh, I could go on for days, telling you of the Sacred Places that we Voyaged Beyond as Guests of God, but I'm tired now, *mi hijito,* so we'll talk *mañana*. Good Night. I'm sorry I caused so much worry, but if only Luisa would've checked in with her Heart, instead of her head, she would've known that I was fine. By the way," she said to her son as he tucked her in under the covers, "She walks on water."

"Who?" said Salvador.

"La Gloria," said his old mother.

"You saw *La Gloria* walk on water?" asked Salvador.

"Yes, we all did. In the early morning as Mother Moon was going down and Father Sun was coming up, giving Light to all the land, we on the shore all watched Her walk out upon the lake with the dignity and stride of a woman in her prime of life and—my God, they say that She is close to two hundred years old!"

"Then is *La Gloria* a Spirit, *mama*?" Salvador asked.

The old woman laughed. "Aren't we all once we finally realize the Fullness of Being?"

"Well, yes, I guess so, but then—I mean, was She, also, of real flesh and blood, *mama*?"

"Of course, She is of real flesh and blood," said Doña Margarita, smiling as she closed her eyes to go off to sleep. "Wasn't Mary and Joseph and Jesus? *Mi hijito,* Our Holy Story of Creation never stopped. We are still all Walking Stars Living in the Sacred Breath of the Almighty." And she looked so very happy and all at Peace—Dreaming.

La Gloria was now walking . . . across the Holy Waters of Creation up above San Bernardino under a Star Filled Sky.

SHE, *La Gloria*!

SHE, *LA GLORIA*!

SHE, *LA GLOOOOOO-RRRRRR-EEE-AAAAAA!!!* Star Walking upon Water!

WHEN SALVADOR GOT BACK to his distillery in Tustin, he found Kenny White all upset. And Salvador well knew that Kenny White wasn't a man who panicked easy, so something very unusual must've happened.

"They were just kids, Salvador," said the old man. He was half drunk. "Little, blond, blue-eyed girls no more than twelve or thirteen, and they were selling themselves, Salvador, with their parents looking on, hoping to make enough money to eat.

"It made me sick," said the white-haired old man with tears running down his face. "What has this country come to? They were decent people, Sal! Good people, Christians, and yet here they were willing to sell their own flesh and blood for a dollar. So when I seen those two guys drive up in that beautiful new roadster, willing to pay for those little girls, I went crazy, Sal, and I know I shouldn't have done it—but, hell, those parents could be going in the hills like your people and trapping rabbits and quail and living off the land, instead of selling their—"

"What did you do, Kenny?" said Salvador, cutting him off. He, too, had seen this same kind of stuff going on for some time now, especially in those areas that had been the more affluent, and had the most to lose.

"I rammed their car with your truck and kept going 'til I'd pushed their new roadster off into the ocean below. Then I gave a barrel of whiskey to the parents of those little girls and told 'em that we'd set them up in the liquor business, but if we ever heard of 'em selling their kids again, you—the Al Capone of the Southland—would have them torched and buried alive!"

Salvador started laughing and laughing. It had been Kenny White whom he'd taken along with him the night that he'd taught that farmer what was what. He'd wanted a white man with him so that the farmer would see that it wasn't a racial issue. "Al Capone of the Southland, where the hell you get that, Kenny?"

Kenny shrugged. "I don't rightly know, Sal," he said. "It just came out. 'Capon,' don't that mean in Spanish 'he who castrates?' "

Salvador's left eyebrow went up. "I'll be," he said. "I'd never thought of that. You're right, 'capon' does mean in Spanish 'he who castrates'!"

"See," said Kenny with a big shit-eating grin, "nobody deserves that handle more than you. Hell, you probably deserve it more than Al Capone, himself! Besides," he added, "I wanted to put some real fear into those parents' hearts real quick and I couldn't come up with anything else." He breathed. "I think you'd better take a look at your truck, Sal. I really, well, put the gas to the metal when I hit their roadster."

"Don't worry about it, Kenny," said Salvador, still laughing. "Just get it fixed for me, or get us a new truck."

"A new one will probably be better. You should see it. I put it in reverse and I was flying when I hit those two guys. Then I was after 'em with the .45 you keep under your seat." He was laughing now, too. "They ran like hell! Man, it felt good! They'd seen the Devil!"

"Good for you, Kenny, showing the Devil to some people is the only language they understand. So what do you think, will they really sell that barrel for us?"

"Hell, Sal, they're gonna be your best retailers! They're working the main street right there in San Clemente!"

"Damn good location!" said Salvador.

DAIRYMEN WERE MILKING their cows and throwing the milk away. Farmers were plowing under their crops of string beans, squash, and melons. Victoriano was driving around as fast as he could collecting milk in buckets and vegetables in crates and taking everything to the *barrio* to distribute among the people, who now didn't even have the gas to drive their old vehicles around to get the free food.

On one trip, Victoriano came home with a truckload of beautiful, ripe watermelon—a new seedless variety that Whitehead had invented. But there was no market for anything, no matter how wonderful. Now all the ranchers were just letting their workers help themselves. Victoriano parked the truck full of the gorgeous melons in front of his parents' house and told everyone on the street to just take all they wanted. Quickly, it became a watermelon party. Adults and children, goats and chickens, everyone was eating to their heart's content.

Then, that same afternoon, just as the day was beginning to cool, Lupe—who was now staying inside most of the time—felt a little warm and decided to go outside and get some fresh air. Going out to the backyard, she saw that her brother was cutting another great big beautiful melon in half under their walnut tree. She walked over and sat down on the bench next to him. She was feeling a little strange.

"Can you stay here by the melon," said Victoriano to his sister. "I'll be right back. I'm going to go inside and let it cool for a few minutes. In warm weather like this, it usually only takes about ten minutes for a melon to get ice-cold."

"Okay," said Lupe, knowing full well how this evaporation process worked. "I'll stay here and keep the birds off of it."

"Thanks," said Victoriano, going back into the house.

Lupe sat there under the big tree alongside the watermelon. Glancing around, she remembered that this was the exact same spot where she'd been on the day that Salvador had come with the priest to ask for her hand.

Lupe put both of her hands to her stomach. Something was going on inside of her. Two days ago, she'd gone to see the doctor and he'd told her to start taking castor oil, and ever since then she'd been going to the bathroom constantly.

She breathed easy, trying to relax and enjoy the last of the going sunlight. Huge flocks of birds came by, swooping down and up in unison as they flew home. She could smell the orange trees behind her and hear the birds flying by overhead. Truly, Santa Ana had become a wonderful place for Lupe and her *familia*. The orange trees gave fragrance of Heaven, and the ocean, over there in the distance, gave a sweet coolness to the late afternoon.

Victoriano came back outside to check on the watermelon. "Oh, it's cold," he said, cutting himself a big, juicy slice. "Here," he said to Lupe, cutting her a slice, too. "Taste it! I swear, these are the sweetest melons I've ever tasted, and they're rotting by the thousands in the fields, yet people in town are starving."

"That's true," said Lupe, taking the slice and beginning to eat it. But then, she felt a little funny feeling on the left side of her face, and she stopped eating. Something very strange was happening to her. The watermelon had no taste for her, whatsoever.

"Poor *Señor* Whitehead," said Victoriano, shaking his head, "he's a good man, and this is the best crop he's ever had, but still he's going to go broke again. 'The finest watermelons I've ever raised,' he said to us, 'but I got no place to sell them, boys,' he said to all of us workers. 'So help yourselves!' And the poor man just drove off. I hope that he doesn't get drunk again. Poor *hombre*. But at least it wasn't old man Irvine that poisoned his crop this time."

Seeing their older sister, Victoriano yelled into the house. "Sophia, come on out with your kids! This melon is sweeter than honey! Come on!"

Lupe had to cover her ears. She just didn't know what was going on inside her. She felt like maybe she had to go to the bathroom again. But she couldn't move. The whole left side of her body was now going numb. So she just sat here, listening to Victoriano talk as he cut more watermelon slices for Sophia and her kids.

"I swear, Lupe," continued Victoriano, "this season alone I've already brought home truckloads of the finest avocados, the best tomatoes, cucumbers, string beans, melons and oranges. Hell, all we need is a little salt and a few *tortillas* and we got everything here in the *barrio* for free!" He turned to the house again. "Hurry up, everybody!" he yelled.

Sophia was laughing and playing with her kids as she came across the yard. Getting under the huge tree where Victoriano was slicing the watermelon, she took just one look at Lupe, and exploded! "Oh, my God, Lupe, you're having your baby!"

"I'm what?" said Lupe.

"You're having your baby," repeated Sophia. "Come, quick, let's get you inside before the Devil does any more mischief. Victoriano, help me! And you!" she said to her boys, "run to the corner store and have them call the doctor immediately!"

The two boys took off, eating their watermelon as they ran.

"I want Salvador," said Lupe, as Sophia led her into the house.

"Don't worry, he'll be here," said Sophia.

"No, I want him right now!" said Lupe, realizing that these were contractions that she'd been feeling for some time. "My God, Sophia, please get me *mi esposo*!"

"Hurry, Victoriano," said Sophia, "help me get her inside, then you go find her *esposo* immediately!"

"Sure," said Victoriano. "I'll get him, Lupe."

By the time the doctor arrived, thirty minutes later, Doña Guadalupe and Sophia had everything well in hand. But Lupe, on the other hand, didn't know what was going on. It was all happening so quickly, and Salvador wasn't at her side. "Salvador!" she called. "Salvador!" Then she began to mumble something about a watermelon.

"Oh, please, dear God," Lupe kept saying between contractions, "let it be a small watermelon. Please, dear God, a very small melon!"

"But what are you talking about?" asked Lupe's mother.

"Oh, don't you remember?" said Sophia, laughing. "She's just saying what that old midwife always used to tell us all back home in *La Lluvia*, that having a baby is like making love to a watermelon."

"That foul-mouthed old woman, I never liked her!" snapped Doña Guadalupe. "Now don't worry, *mi hijita*, everything is all right. Just relax and don't fight the pain."

But the contractions were coming closer together and Lupe could swear that she could actually feel her bones beginning to move. She began to sweat. Her sisters Maria and Sophia were talking to her and massaging her legs, her hips, and telling her to keep calm, to relax, and let the pain go.

Her mother was with her, too, and Lupe was sweating more and more. Sophia began to wipe the sweat off Lupe's face with a cool cloth that felt so good to Lupe, but for some reason, Lupe could only feel the cloth on the right side of her face. It was like she didn't have any feeling whatsoever on her left side, the same side that had felt a little funny when she'd tried to eat that watermelon outside in the backyard a little while ago.

VICTORIANO DROVE OVER to try to find Salvador. He'd heard that he had a house somewhere just south of Tustin where he made his liquor, but he'd never been there. Finally, a few miles southeast of town, just this side of the big old Irvine house, he spotted Archie's big black Hudson parked in front of a farmhouse and figured that Archie was maybe visiting Salvador.

Driving up, Victoriano could now see Archie and Salvador under a big pepper tree to the side of the farmhouse. They were talking and seemed very upset about something. Parking and running toward them, Victoriano heard Domingo's name mentioned. And rumor had it that Salvador's brother was in prison at San Quentin.

"Salvador," said Victoriano, "Lupe is having the baby!"

"She's what?!" said Salvador.

"She's having your baby!"

"Oh, my God! Is she all right?" asked Salvador, feeling his heart beginning to pound. He fully realized that this had been a difficult pregnancy for his young wife.

"Yes, she's fine," said Victoriano, lying. He didn't want to be the one to tell Salvador that Lupe had completely lost the feeling of the left side of her face and they were worried that it was now traveling down that whole side of her body and could affect the birthing. "But she's been asking for you!"

"Okay, Archie," said Salvador. "I just won't tell him a damned thing! Not where I'm located, or nothing! Believe me, I don't want Domingo in my business again when he gets out, either!"

"Good," said Archie, "because we can't afford another screw-up! Now, get the hell out of here, and go see Lupe!"

"Yeah, but you go first!" said Salvador. "I don't want you staying behind and just helping yourself to my barrels."

Archie only laughed. "Damnit, Sal! Where's your trust? When are you going to trust your fellow human being?"

"Never! You're the law, and since the beginning of time, lawmen have been the worst thieves! Too damned lazy to do their own robbing, so they shave the good, honest robbers like sheep, hiding behind their badge!"

"Sounds pretty good to me," said Archie, grinning.

"You bastard!" said Salvador, getting in his Moon and taking off behind Victoriano.

"Yeah, but MY DOORS are always WIDE OPEN!" yelled Archie back after Salvador. "Front and REAR!"

THE BABY WAS BORN before Salvador and Victoriano got to the house. She was a big, healthy girl, and Lupe would never forget how the doctor cut the cord and handed the baby not to her, but to her mother. Lupe wondered if this was how she, herself, had looked in her mother's arms when she'd been born. The baby looked like a skinned-out rabbit.

Then the baby was crying, and so Doña Guadalupe wrapped her in a little blanket and handed her back to Lupe. Lupe immediately put her to her breast, and the infant began to search around with her little hands and tiny mouth, and then she was nursing, just like that—so naturally, like she'd been doing this all her life.

Salvador and Victoriano came rushing in. Salvador saw Lupe with the baby on her breast, and his whole face filled with pride.

"Is it a boy or a girl?" he asked.

"A girl," said Sophia.

"A girl! Oh, how wonderful!" he said. "And she looks just like my mother. All wrinkled up!"

"She was just born, Salvador," said Sophia, laughing. "She'll fatten up and in a few days all those wrinkles will smooth out. Come and hold her."

Sophia took the baby from Lupe, handing her to Salvador, but at first he didn't know how to take the tiny infant in his arms. Then, once he was holding his baby, he noticed that Lupe's mouth was cocked at an odd angle to the left, and it looked like she was trying to talk to him, but she couldn't form her words.

Salvador didn't know what to do. He handed the child back to Sophia and came close and kissed Lupe on the forehead and stroked her hair. The doctor walked in and told Lupe to just rest and that everything was all right. Then he took Salvador to the kitchen.

"Look, I don't want to alarm you," he said to Salvador, "but you're going to have to keep Lupe here at her mother's house for at least a week so I can check on her every day."

"Yes, but what's wrong with her face?" asked Salvador.

"It's not that unusual," said the doctor. "But if it doesn't clear up by itself in a few days, I'll start giving her shots. Don't worry, everything is all right. This happens quite often," he said, lying. "And Lupe and the baby are both very healthy. Congratulations, Salvador," he added. "You have a fine little family started. Now let's see if we can't keep it small?"

Salvador nodded and walked the doctor to his car and gave him a quart of his finest whiskey.

"Oh, thank you!" said the doctor. "That's very kind of you."

"And this one you don't sip," said Salvador, grinning. "You drink it down in big, quick shots!"

The doctor laughed, remembering how he'd told Salvador to sip his schnapps. "Okay. Maybe I'll be willing to try that. And like I said, don't worry, everything is fine. Lupe is young and she'll be back to normal very quickly."

Salvador nodded, then he went back inside. Lupe's whole left side looked cock-eyed. It was difficult for him to look at her without showing how worried he was. He silently prayed for her. Oh, how he wished that they'd used his mother for this pregnancy instead of a male *doctor Americano*.

THE NEXT DAY, Lupe had no feeling whatsoever on her whole left side. They called the doctor, and he came and gave her a shot. Now Doña

Guadalupe was worried, too, and wanted to know what was going on, but the doctor, once again, just said not to worry and that everything was all right.

For two more days this continued, and neither Salvador nor Doña Guadalupe could find out what was going on from the doctor. Then Salvador had to leave to go on a whiskey run. While he was gone, Maria, Lupe's other older sister, came by with her husband, Andres, in a big rush and told everyone that she'd had this terrible dream that night and so Lupe's baby had to be baptized immediately!

"But what was your dream?" asked Doña Guadalupe.

"I can't tell you!" said Maria. She was upset and kept making the sign of the cross over herself. "All I know is that we have to baptize the baby RIGHT NOW! IMMEDIATELY!" she shouted.

"But just wait," said Carlota. "I might not like Salvador, but you can't just do this without him."

"I agree with Carlota," said Sophia. "Dream or no dream, I will have no part of this, Maria."

"Okay," said Maria, "think as you like, but the baby's immortal soul is in danger, and with Lupe in her condition, she can't think straight, and so I'm not going to let my little sister's child's Soul go to Purgatory for All Eternity!"

And saying this, Maria—a powerful bull of a woman just like Salvador's own sister, Luisa—pushed past everyone and took the baby from Lupe, who was sound asleep, and said, "Come on, *mama,* quickly, you go with us, and be the *madrina,* and you be the *padrino,* Andres!"

No one knew what to say. It was all happening so quickly. And to baptize a child was a big event. What Maria was doing was completely against all customs. The parents were the ones who were supposed to choose who the godparents would be—not an aunt. An aunt didn't just come in and kidnap the child like this. But here was Maria, going out the front door and up the street to the church where Salvador and Lupe had been married, before anyone could figure out how to stop her.

And at the church, when the priest asked for the child's parents, Maria simply said, "Lupe, my sister, the baby's mother, is sick, and the father is gone! So they couldn't come, and we need to do this right now. Immediately!"

Seeing how anxious they all were, the priest took them to the small, dark room where they performed baptisms in the front part of the church. And when the man of God asked for the child's name, Maria didn't know what to say, but luckily Doña Guadalupe was here and so she stepped forward.

"I overheard Salvador and Lupe saying something about hortensia, the flower."

"Oh, that's beautiful," said the priest. "Hortensia. So, then, we'll baptize this child Maria Hortensia for the Blessed Mother."

And so this was how Lupe and Salvador's first child was named and baptized—without either one of them being present or even knowing anything about the event.

WHEN SALVADOR CAME in the following day and was told what had happened, he went into a screaming rage. "But how in the name of God could you have done such a thing?" he asked his mother-in-law, who'd met him at the front door and told him the news.

"I don't know, Salvador," said Doña Guadalupe, feeling full of guilt and grief. "But it happened so quickly. Maria just came in, saying that she'd had this terrible dream and—oh, I'm so sorry, Salvador! I'm terribly sorry!"

"And that's how my daughter got the name Maria? Because of Lupe's sister Maria and her dream? Good God!" he screamed. He wanted to kill, to strangle Lupe's sister Maria, but he was able to control himself. He turned and got back in his car.

"But don't you want to see Lupe or the baby?" yelled his mother-in-law after him.

"NO!" he screamed, and he sped away in his grand automobile.

When Lupe awoke and heard that Salvador had come and found out about the baptism and that he'd left in a rage, she had them call the doctor.

"Doctor," said Lupe, as soon as he arrived, "you must make me well today. I cannot stay here another day. I need to go to my own home and be with my husband."

The doctor began to argue, but then seeing her determined look, he simply nodded. "All right," he said, "but I don't like this." And he increased her dosage.

WHEN VICTORIANO DROVE Lupe and Maria Hortensia back to their home in Carlsbad the following day, they found the kitchen table broken into pieces but Salvador wasn't home.

Victoriano wanted to go to the poolhall in the *barrio* to ask if anyone had seen Salvador, but Lupe said no and asked her brother to please just stay in their little house and wait with her. She wasn't feeling well. But then, as the day began to darken, Victoriano became nervous.

"Look," he said, "you stay here. I'm going to go and have a look around for him. Please, I know what I'm doing, Lupe."

"Okay," said Lupe. "But please don't be gone too long." She was still having problems with the left side of her face. The shots that the doctor had given her had taken away the pain, but had not helped the situation.

"I won't," he said, and drove off. He was afraid that maybe Salvador was out on a *parranda* and might come in all drunk with another woman. Salvador had been fit to be tied, when he'd left the day before. But asking around the *barrio*, Victoriano found out that no one had seen Salvador for several days.

SALVADOR HAD BEEN KILLING mad the day he'd left Lupe's parents' home. He'd been helping Lupe's *familia* for months, and then they'd done this to him. He felt like everyone was taking advantage of him right and left. He'd had such big plans for his first child's baptism. My God, how could Lupe and her family dare do this to him! Then it hit him like a thunderbolt! Carlota must've been behind the whole thing. "Yeah, sure," he said to himself. "That's what happened! That damn woman hates me and wants to ruin our marriage!"

Getting to Carlsbad, Salvador kicked the kitchen table again and again, then drank down a whole pint bottle of whiskey, grabbed an ax, broke up the table, then went out the door and chopped a fruit tree down, raging and screaming! All his life this had been his dream, to have a huge baptism celebration for his first born! He drank down another bottle, then got in his car and drove up the hill directly over to Palmer's ranch. He was going to talk to old man Palmer about Domingo's parole, face-to-face, without having Archie as his damn go-between.

"PALMER!" yelled Salvador, pounding on his back door with his fist. "Open up! I want to talk to you, MAN-to-MAN!"

Salvador's heart was pounding a million miles an hour. He knew damn well that if he wasn't drunk and so mad at Lupe's family, he would never have gotten up the nerve to do this.

All his life, Salvador had known how to handle men with guns and knives, but to speak to authority, especially to educated Anglo authority, was still a thing so far beyond Salvador, that he was almost pissing in his pants as he pounded on this man's back door! And he and Chief-Deputy Palmer had drunk whiskey together and they knew each other, and yet Salvador was still frightened down deep inside. After all, this was a *gringo*!

"Yes!" said Palmer, coming to his back door with huge, pounding steps. He was the only man in all of Carlsbad who was even bigger than Archie. "What the hell do you want?!" he yelled, opening the door. "Oh, it's you, Sal!"

"Yes, it's me!" shouted Salvador right into his face, not backing up an inch. "I want to know why you're charging me two hundred dollars to help me parole my brother out of prison!"

"Two hundred dollars!" shouted Chief-Deputy Palmer, rubbing his eyes. It looked like he'd been asleep. "What the hell are you talking about?! I told Archie two cases of whiskey and that I had to speak to you, because, well," he said, yawning and rubbing his eyes again, "I talked to my cousin Jeffrey up in San Quentin, and the only way we can parole your brother early is for me to say he's an agriculture specialist—you know, one of these modern damn avocado doctors—and say that we need him down here for the avocado industry right now. I never said anything about two hundred dollars, Sal."

"I'll be damned," said Salvador, "my brother an avocado doctor!" He almost laughed, but his mind was still reeling in a liquor-kind-of-swirl.

Then instantly, he saw Archie in a whole new light. Why, that son-of-a-bitch half-breed had been hustling him, trying to do him out of two hundred dollars to put in his own pocket. And Archie was his friend, damnit, his best friend, and was always so ready to help his fellow *Mejicanos* and *Indios*. The dirty, double-dealing bastard was really a thief with a badge, just like Salvador had jokingly told him the other day.

"So what is it?!" said Palmer. "Did Archie tell you that I'd asked for two hundred dollars?"

It took all of Salvador's power to stop his thinking and look at old man Palmer in the eye. And, in this next millionth of a second, Salvador made a very important, far-reaching decision; a decision that would eventually help him become one of the most powerful businessmen in the whole area. "No," he lied. "I guess, well, I just got it all mixed up."

"Are you sure?" asked Palmer. The big man was really concerned.

Salvador took a deep breath, looked at Palmer right in the eye again, and he lied again, "Yeah, I'm sure, Palmer, it was my mistake."

And why Salvador said this wasn't because he was a good guy and wanted to protect Archie; no, it was because he'd seen it in this big law-man's eyes—that even though he truly wanted to get down to the bottom of this situation—there was also fear in his eyes of finding out the truth.

And truth, his old mother had told him time and again, scared most good people even more than death.

"Okay, good," now said Palmer, exhaling deeply and rubbing his eyes once more, "then Archie didn't ask you for two hundred dollars?"

"No, he didn't," lied Salvador for the third time. "You see," Salvador added, "my wife, Lupe, and I just had our first baby, and, well, the doctor says that she's having a little trouble, and so I'm just upset."

"Oh, I see," said the huge chief-deputy, looking even more relieved. After all, Archie was one of his main deputies and so he didn't want to think that he had a double-dealing deputy under his command. "Sorry to hear about Lupe," he added, looking all relaxed now. "Come on in, Sal," he said, opening the door wide open. "My wife, Mildred, is gone up to see her family in San Francisco, so the house is a mess, but if you don't mind that, then come on in and we'll have a drink to your baby. Is it a boy or a girl?"

"A beautiful little girl!" said Salvador proudly. "Looks all nice and wrin-kled, just like my mother!"

"Girls are great," said Palmer. "They hug and kiss you much more than boys. I got one of each. I'm sorry that Lupe is having trouble. I hope it's nothing serious."

"Oh, no, the doctor said she'll be fine."

"Good," said Palmer.

They went into the kitchen. It was a big, expansive kitchen with a beau-tiful view all the way past downtown Carlsbad to the ocean. Salvador had never been inside a rich Anglo's home before. He now knew that he'd done the right thing to give old man Palmer what it was that he'd wanted to hear, and that was that Archie was okay.

Mi hijito," Salvador's mother had told him more than a thousand times, "ever since the loss of the Garden people all over the Earth need to believe in something. Politicians in politics. Lawmen in law. Doctors in medicine. Soldiers in war. Businessmen in business. Men of the church in a church. And rich people in money. No one, and especially men, can stand naked without some belief that they are willing to even die for. So always give to *Cesar* that which is of *Cesar*'s and here, from this Sacred Place of Giving, is where we, the people, can then perform miracles as well as Jesus Christ, Our Savior.

"This is the place where I was when I went to get your brother Jose released from prison in the middle of the Revolution. I had nothing but rags on these old bones, but to each—even our enemy—I gave them what they wanted, and they then opened their hearts wide for me, maneuvering doors open that otherwise would have been closed to a poor old Indian woman."

Salvador could now see that this was exactly what he'd just done. He'd had the cunning to give this rich powerful Anglo what it was that he'd wanted, and it had then turned out just as his mother had said. Here he was now inside of a powerful *gringo*'s home and this big lawman was washing his face with cold water at the kitchen sink as if they were best old friends.

Salvador couldn't stop smiling. Every day he lived, he came to realize how smart his old She-Fox *mama* really was. He'd come over here to this man's house in a wild drunken stupor, not giving a good shit about *nada*, and he'd ended up performing his first "official miracle" as a married man!

Having washed his face with cold water from the sink, Palmer took a hand towel and dried off. He looked much better. Salvador now very clearly understood what it was that rich, powerful people wanted above all else: peace and quiet. Palmer really hadn't wanted to hear that there were any *problemas* going on between him and Archie.

The big lawman now brought out a half-empty quart bottle of whiskey and served them each a good-sized shot. It was Salvador's product. For years, Palmer had been one of Salvador's steadfast customers.

"Here's to you and your wife and baby," said Palmer.

"Thank you," said Salvador.

They finished off the quart, and Salvador went out to his Moon and brought in a fresh quart, and they drank long into the night. Palmer told Salvador he and his wife were originally from San Francisco, that his wife's family had money and were highly educated. His wife didn't like it down in Southern California, saying it was a cultural desert and that San Francisco was the only really civilized city in all the western hemisphere except, of course, for Mexico City, where they'd gone to visit college friends on their honeymoon.

Palmer spoke Spanish fluently and he asked Salvador if he'd ever been to Mexico City.

"No," said Salvador, "I was born in a little village in the mountains of Jalisco not too far out of Guadalajara. Then came the war, and we migrated to the United States along with lots of other poor people. My mother and father knew Mexico City and Guadalajara, but not us kids."

"So then you only know Mexico through war?" asked Palmer.

Salvador nodded. He'd never thought of it like this. "Yeah," he said, "my wife and I, that's almost all we've ever seen."

"Well, that's too bad," said Palmer, "you should visit Mexico someday as a tourist. It's a beautiful country, Sal!"

Palmer then began telling Salvador about Guadalajara and Mexico City, comparing both of these fine cities to San Francisco. He explained to Salvador how his wife had gone to a private school in San Francisco with the daughters of some of the finest families from all over Mexico. Salvador had never heard such talk and was very fascinated. He absolutely knew nothing of how the wealthy of Mexico lived.

"You know," said Palmer, "we, *gringos,* did a very stupid thing in this country when we put up the border between Mexico and the United States. These two countries belong together more than the eastern and western U.S. Hell, I get along better with the Mexican people than I do with all those damned easterners, who think everything west of the Mississippi is still a wilderness."

They talked until the early hours of the morning, and Salvador didn't go home that night. He just rolled up with a blanket that Palmer gave him on the couch in the living room and went to sleep. And down deep inside, Salvador well knew that if he'd told Palmer the truth, that Archie had lied and tried to trick him, Palmer would never have invited him into his home and gotten so friendly. Salvador's instincts for survival had been correct, when he'd told this big lawman what it was that he'd wanted to hear.

Sleeping that night on the couch, Salvador knew he'd passed through a very important needle's eye. He was sleeping in the home of his enemy, a *gringo*—and a lawman to boot—and he was an outlaw who'd come knocking with rage and vengeance on the back door.

Salvador started laughing with *carcajadas* because he could now see so clearly that if Maria hadn't taken their newborn to be baptized, then he, Salvador, would have never gotten so raging angry that he'd come home, broken the table, downed two pints, chopped down a tree, and had the nerve to come knocking on Palmer's back door!

SALVADOR AWOKE WITH A START.

He glanced around, at first not remembering where he was. Then remembering, that he was at old man Palmer's house, he gripped his forehead. What had ever possessed him to think that he could just come knocking on a rich *gringo*'s door? He hoped to God, Palmer wouldn't have him arrested. He sat up, holding his head. *Mano,* did he have a hangover!

"Bathroom's down the hallway," said Palmer, coming into the room. He looked washed and shaven and ready to go. "I'll make us breakfast, *compadre!*"

Hearing this word *"compadre,"* Salvador felt a rush of feelings go shooting up and down his spine! My God, Palmer was calling him family, like last night they'd really celebrated his child's baptism, and so now he, Palmer, was Hortensia's Godfather.

Salvador got up and went to the bathroom. Palmer was in the kitchen, cooking bacon and eggs. It smelled wonderful! The bathroom was the biggest bathroom Salvador had ever seen. It, too, had a beautiful view all the way down the hill to the sea. Never had he ever thought of a kitchen or a bathroom being built to have a view. This was a new world for Salvador. Maybe he and Lupe could also someday build a house on a hill with a view from every room.

He washed his face with cold water, used the smallest towel he could find, then he took a long, loud piss. He was glad that the big chief-deputy was whistling as he cooked. All this felt so strange to Salvador. Never in his wildest dreams would he have ever dreamed that someday a *gringo* would call him "godfather," and then he'd be cooking breakfast for him, too!

"Come and get it!" yelled Palmer.

"You bet!" said Salvador, yelling back.

"Sit your ass right down, *compadre!*" said Palmer with *gusto*!

"You got it, *amigo,*" said Salvador. He was all excited, but still felt a little too self-conscious to use the word *"compadre"* himself.

And so they had a fine breakfast together with plenty of eggs and thick cuts of freshly cured bacon and plenty of hot, black coffee. Then Palmer took Salvador outside to his avocado orchard to show him how to "doctor" the trees. As the huge old man spoke to him, Salvador truly felt as if they'd entered into paradise.

Hell, his own father had never treated him this well!

Salvador no longer saw Palmer as a *gringo,* or even a lawman. No, he now simply saw the huge man as a fellow human being! For the first time Salvador very clearly saw that this country of the United States could now also be his home as much as *los Altos de Jalisco,* or anywhere else.

"You see, Sal," Palmer was saying, "you're going to have to explain all this grafting business to your brother, Domingo, that I'm showing you, so if anyone asks him anything, he won't look completely ignorant."

"Okay," said Salvador, trying to concentrate.

"To begin with," said Palmer, "we graft these trees because the original avocado trees produce a fruit with too big of a seed inside and also the skin isn't thick enough so we can ship east. But when we cut these old trees back to a stump, then graft on this other variety of avocado, we get a lot more meat on the fruit and the type of tough, thick skin that we need for shipping."

"Oh, I see," said Salvador. "Very good!"

Old man Palmer and Salvador worked side by side in the hot Sun, and as they worked, the lawman-farmer kept talking, and Salvador found out a lot more about his family and that his children didn't come by to see him very often, or at least not as often as he would like.

Around noontime, Hans, who also owned avocado trees, came by with a basket full of food and some of his homemade beer—which was terrible but cold—and they ate and drank together in the shade of a big eucalyptus tree.

Salvador couldn't remember having had such a wonderful time in all his life—not since he and his *familia* had had to flee from their beloved homeland *de Jalisco*.

LATE THAT SAME AFTERNOON, Salvador went to his car and got a bottle of his best whiskey, and he and Hans and Fred Palmer shot down a couple of good-sized drinks, and kept right on working. And work they did, fast and hard, learning this new trade of "avocado doctors"—and not as hired hands—but as *amigos, compadres,* FREE MEN!

Oh, Salvador had never had such an experience in all of his life! Why, work could be fun! Sweating could feel good! This was Paradise when you were a free human being working on your friend's place with your own two GOD-GIVEN HANDS!

"You know," said Hans, when they finally went in for the day, "a lot of my friends and relatives back in New Jersey still aren't liking these avocados that I ship to them."

"Hell, that's just because they don't know how to eat them," said Palmer. "Avocados are delicious! George Thompson's dad was a damn genius to have brought in these babies from Mexico! In not too long, avocados are going to be the number-one crop in this whole area!"

"Yaaa, I'm sure that may be true," said Hans with his heavy German accent. "But we got to first figure out an angle on how to sell 'em, or we're just going to lose our pants and shoes like those men did with all those eucalyptus trees east of town. Tell me," he said, turning to Salvador, "how do you people eat these avocados back in Mexico?"

"Well," said Salvador, feeling good to be included in this conversation with two such educated men, "we put them in our *tortillas*. But also we mash them up and mix 'em with *salsa,* and they're *muy* tasty!"

"How? Show us," said Hans. "I'm a cook. I love learning new recipes."

"You got any tomatoes and *chile*?" asked Salvador.

"Is the Pope Catholic?" said Palmer. "Hell, I grow my own *chiles* and tomatoes just for this very reason. I love *salsa!*"

So Salvador cut open three big avocados and mashed them up in a big bowl, then added lots of freshly-chopped tomatoes, onions, and *chile,* then salt and pepper and squeezed in one big juicy lemon. Hans's and Palmer's mouths were watering when they finally tasted it.

"Hey, this is delicious!" said Hans. "What's it called?"

"*Guacamole,*" said Salvador, "but we need a little *cilantro.*"

"Guac-a-what?" said Hans.

"*Guacamole,*" repeated Salvador.

"Gua-qua-hell!" said Hans.

"Here, take a few more shots of whiskey," said Palmer, laughing. "You have to loosen your lips to get hold of Spanish. That's why the Mexican *señoritas* always make the best damn kissers in all the world. They got loose, fast-moving lips and tongues. My wife learned that from her Mexican girlfriends. They'd practice kissing in the mirror for hours!"

The Father Sun was going down into the sea and Hans kept drinking more and more whiskey, trying to loosen his German tongue so he could say *guacamole,* but he could just never get hold of the word.

Salvador and Palmer laughed and laughed, matching him drink for drink. Then Salvador suggested that they go to the *barrio* and get a couple kilos of corn *tortillas, carne asada,* then they could really see what *guacamole* was all about!

Coming back, they almost ran head-on into old man Kenny White and the truck he'd found for Salvador. Kenny could see that they were half drunk and up to no good. He loved it and followed them in Salvador's new truck back to Palmer's place.

Walking into Palmer's house, Kenny put his arm around Salvador and whispered to him that his brother-in-law was looking for him. Salvador nodded, but said nothing. He was still pissed. Then Kenny told Salvador to be careful because every time Palmer's family left town, Fred Palmer got Mexican Wild.

"Mexican Wild?" said Salvador. "What's that?"

"You just watch and you'll find out," said Kenny, "a few more shots and he'll start barking and howling to the Moon! Hell, he's the best coyote-howler in the region! Even the chickens run from him once he gets going. You see, originally, Palmer's people came from Tucson, Arizona. They were in the mining business on both sides of the border and made tons of money. All his people speak Spanish like natives. But his wife, hell, she's even richer than him, but she don't think her shit stinks."

"I'll be damn," said Salvador, laughing, "then this is what you call Mexican Wild, eh? A man howling and being happy?" And he thought of all the money that Archie's nephew was making, acting wild. Also, he wondered what it could mean that Victoriano was looking for him. He hoped to God that Lupe and the baby were okay.

In Palmer's huge kitchen, Kenny and Salvador put the *carne asada* in a pan, then they cut up a dozen big, juicy avocados and made a huge bowl of *guacamole*. Kenny and Salvador had become even better friends since the old man had started driving liquor-runs for him. Salvador just couldn't believe it—here he was with three Anglos—educated men, men who could read and write—and he was having one of the best times of his whole life!

Then Kenny and Salvador heated up the corn *tortillas,* and the four of them now pigged out with *tacos de carne asada* and the whole bowl of *guacamole*. Hans and Palmer were sure that they'd come upon the best damn appetizer that any drinking man would ever want!

"We've struck gold!" said Palmer, giving a coyote howl!

"I agree, this *guaca*-hell and *tortillas* is the best!" said Hans, kissing his fingertips, then giving a howl, too. "But you know, I'm still gonna have trouble selling it to my relatives in New Jersey. Because, well, fruit just don't sound like it'd go well with drinking whiskey or beer, eh?"

"Well, then, hell," said Kenny, laughing, "just call these avocados a damn vegetable! What the hell would they know back in New Jersey?! Hell, myself, I'd call it the Mexican vegetable especially grown for the drinking man so he don't get a hangover! A cure, I'd call it, *una cura para tu cruda,* as they say in Mexican. Eh, Sal?"

"That's right," said Salvador. *"Una cura para la cruda!"*

"Yaaa, that I can sell if we just say it in good English like I speak," said Hans, butchering each word as he spoke. "We really could call it a vegie-table! You know, like the potato that you can eat baked or mashed and goes so well with beer, wine, or whiskey."

"So that's it," said Palmer, "from now on the avocado will be known as a vegetable, as the miracle vegetable from old Mexico that helps with bowel movements, arthritis, hangovers, and everything else," added Palmer, howling to the Heavens again. He was getting more Mexican Wild by the moment. "And its natural oiliness gives longevity, too!"

"Yaaa, that's it!" said Hans, taking Palmer's suggestion seriously. "But Sal, do you really know any people in Mexico who drink whiskey, and eat avocados and have lived a long time?"

"Well, yeah, sure," said Salvador. "My mother, she eats lots of avocados, because, well, they're soft and easy on her gums and stomach."

"Then old people do eat them for their health," said Hans. "By God, we're all going to become millionaires!"

"Sounds good to me," said Kenny. "And I'll fix your trucks and farm machinery and get rich, too!"

"And I'll sell lots of whiskey!" said Salvador.

And so the four of them got shit-face drunk, drinking to the avocado, the new miracle vegetable from Mexico that gave people a long, healthy life.

Soon they were all HOWLING to the Mother Moon, while all around them, the whole country was going to pieces. Nobody had money. Entire communities were going under.

PARKING, Salvador could see Lupe through the kitchen window with her brother. His whole heart came leaping up into his throat! His truelove was home, and their child was in her arms. He breathed and breathed again, sitting in his car, just looking in the window. Then he got out of his Moon, thanked the stars above, and approached the front door.

He was trembling, he was so happy. Lupe and Hortensia looked so beautiful, inside their well-lit kitchen, visiting with Victoriano

"Lupe!" he called, coming inside. "When did you get home?"

"This afternoon," she said. Her face was still having trouble when she spoke, but at least she could form her words pretty well now. "Where have you been? My brother searched for you everywhere!"

"Up at Palmer's ranch on the hill," he said. "Hi, Victoriano. I grafted avocado trees with Hans and old man Palmer all day long. I'm becoming an 'avocado doctor,' " he added.

"A doctor?" said Lupe.

"Yes, that's what they call the men who know how to graft avocado trees," said Salvador. "You know, someday I want us, Lupe, to buy a ranch and raise avocados. They're the future, Victoriano. They're going to be the number-one crop in all the area." He glanced at their child. "How's Hortensia?" he asked.

"I'm glad you finally remembered to ask," said Lupe.

"Lupe," he said, "don't do that. I'm not the one who forgot. It was you. Eh, how could you have done the baptism without me, *querida*? Our first child, and you did it without me?"

"But I didn't do it," said Lupe. Suddenly, she was having a lot of trouble speaking once again. "I was sound asleep when Maria came and took our baby."

Salvador could hardly understand her now. She had to say the whole thing over again and much slower.

"Oh, then you didn't know, either?"

"No, how could I, Salvador? I was sick and half out of my head. I would never have permitted them to do what they did if I'd been well," she added, having difficulty with each word.

Victoriano, who'd been sitting down watching this whole exchange, now got to his feet. "Well, I'll be going now," he said. "I can see you two are now acting like a real married couple and have a lot to talk about. And the doctor said not to worry about her, Salvador; within a few days she'll be fine."

"Why don't you stay the night," said Salvador, really wanting him to go. "It's late."

"No, I need to get back. Whitehead and I are meeting with old man Irvine tomorrow morning. The old goat-man has an idea."

"Well, then, I'll see you out," said Salvador, walking his brother-in-law outside to his truck. He was really glad that Victoriano was going. He wanted to be alone with Lupe and their baby. "Here," he said, slipping Victoriano a five-dollar bill. "For your gas. Thank you for bringing Lupe home."

"You don't need to pay me, Salvador. She's my sister. I did it for her."

"I know. I know. But here, gas is expensive. We can't get gas free from the farmers."

"By the way, talking about farmers," said Victoriano, smiling, "was it you, Salvador, who got that farmer to come apologizing to our house?"

"Me? Oh, no," said Salvador. "God just works in mysterious ways."

"I see. I see. But you didn't give God a little help, did you?"

"Well, maybe my prayers did reach the man."

"Your prayers, eh?" said Victoriano, laughing. "Yeah, I think I've heard about your prayers. They can be very convincing."

Salvador nodded. "Yes, I agree, I do pray a very convincing prayer sometimes, Victoriano."

They said nothing more. They both just stood looking at each other with a twinkle in their eyes. They, too, had come a long ways in their relationship as brothers-in-love.

"Take good care of her, Salvador," Victoriano finally said. "The doctor, he told Lupe that she was still too weak to come down today, but she insisted once she heard how you'd come and left so angry. She loves you very much, Salvador."

"I know, and I love her very much, too. Here, take the five. I know that you're using your gas to bring food to the *barrio.*"

"No, Salvador," said Victoriano. "I don't want to be one of these people who always keeps taking from you. You helped me to buy my truck, that was more than enough. I'm just glad that I was able to pay you back a little."

"All right," said Salvador, putting his money back in his pocket. "See you, *compadre. Buenas noches.* You're a good man, Victoriano, a very good man."

"You, too," said Victoriano, "and I'll tell my family that you send them your best."

Salvador breathed. "Yeah, sure, please do say that."

Victoriano drove off. Salvador took another deep breath, glanced up at the Heavens, and then went back inside their *casita.* Lupe was in the kitchen. Their baby was nowhere in sight. Lupe had put their child down for the night.

"Your brother is a good man," said Salvador.

"What did he tell you?" asked Lupe. "That I'm still sick? That the doctor told me not to come? Well, I'm not sick, Salvador. I can, well, almost talk straight again." She took a big breath. "I just don't know what got into everyone. I guess they were afraid because of my condition, so they didn't know what to do when Maria came in saying that our baby had to be baptized immediately."

"Oh, so then it really was Maria who did it? I had guessed it was Carlota."

"Well, you guessed wrong. Carlota defended you, Salvador. Both she and Sophia told Maria that you should be there and they'd have no part of it."

"I'll be damn," said Salvador. "Carlota defended me. That's incredible. Then who exactly was at our child's baptism?"

Lupe hated to tell him, but she came forward. "My mother and Maria and Andres. Maria made my mother and Andres our child's godparents."

"I see," said Salvador, trying to not get upset again. "And so this is why they named our daughter Maria Hortensia, instead of Lupe Hortensia, for your sister Maria."

"No, the priest, I was told, added the name Maria to Hortensia, for Our Holy Lady."

"Oh, I see," said Salvador, pacing around the room. "My God, our first child, and we didn't even get to name her! The Devil sure is playing some wild games with us!"

Tears came to Lupe's eyes. "I'm sorry, Salvador. I'm really sorry, but it's hard arguing with people's dreams. No one knew what to say to Maria."

"But why not? Is your family superstitious? Don't they know there is no evil on the other side, except that which we carry in our own hearts? My God, *mi mama* would've stopped Maria in a second!"

"Salvador," said Lupe, "I'm every bit as upset as you, but there's no need to insult my family."

"I'm not insulting them," he said. "I'm just saying that when it comes to matters of the spirit or confrontation, your family runs or doesn't want to discuss matters. Look how your father treats me ever since Carlota told them of our situation in Escondido with the sheriff."

"Salvador, I didn't come home to fight with you," said Lupe, starting to have trouble speaking again. It seemed that every time she became upset she began having trouble forming her words. "Look, when I found out what had happened and that you'd come and left in a hurry, I had the doctor come and give me a—a—a shot to make me—" She had to stop speaking and take several deep breaths before she could go on. "Salvador," she said with tears of frustration, "I wanted to come and be . . . be with you. I'm your wife, Salvador, and you're my husband, and I . . . I . . . I swear to you, no matter how sick I am next time, this . . . this will never happen again," she added with tears streaming down her face. "I'm sorry. I was sick and out of my mind. I didn't know, Salvador, I just didn't know!"

Salvador's whole heart came up to his throat. He came close, taking Lupe in his arms. "I'm sorry, too, *querida*. I did wrong to drive off. I was just, well, so disappointed. I wanted to be there. I'd missed the birthing, too, and so I was planning a big celebration for Hortensia's baptism."

"Me, too," said Lupe. "Me, too. Now hold me, please. I've missed you so much!"

"You have? Really?"

"Of course," she said, "you are my husband 'til death do we part," she added, taking a big breath.

"Yes," he said, taking a big breath also, " 'til death do we part. Oh, I Love you so much, Lupe. You are my life, my love, my wife!"

They now kissed and kissed again, holding each other in a big *abrazo de corazón*!

And in the next room was their child, and even though Hortensia was sound asleep, in her heart, she, too, could feel the Love of the Home she'd picked to be hers when she'd been up in *Papito*'s arms, looking down from Heaven.

16

The DEVIL was Whirling, Swirling, Dancing — he was so
HAPPY! He was still working the Earth, giving choice
between Good and Evil, but Now each Night he, too, went to
be with PAPITO DIOS!

IT WAS EARLY Sunday morning when Archie came wheeling down the long gunbarrel driveway between the avocado trees to Lupe and Salvador's little rented house in Carlsbad. Salvador was in the back, but he was ready. He'd been expecting Archie ever since he'd gone over to old man Palmer's home and confronted him about those two hundred dollars.

"Hello, Lupe," said Archie, sweet as honey when she opened the front door for him. "How are you and the little one?"

"Much better, thank you," said Lupe. Her speech was almost back to normal again. Taking herbs and feeling so good to be alone with Salvador and Hortensia in their own home had helped Lupe heal immensely.

"That's wonderful," he said. "Is Salvador home?"

"Yes," said Lupe, "he's in the back. We're just getting ready to go out the door."

"I see," said Archie.

"I'm over here," said Salvador, coming in the front door.

"Hi, friend," said Archie, with that same wonderful smile that he'd used on Lupe. "I drove down 'cause I need to talk to you, Sal," he added, still smiling.

"Sure," said Salvador, almost laughing. He'd been in enough poker games to know what was really going on. Archie was mad as hell because he'd gone to see Palmer without him and now he was trying to set him up by acting friendly. "I'll be right back, Lupe," Salvador said to Lupe. "You go ahead and get things ready. I'll only be gone a couple of minutes."

Now that Lupe was feeling better, Salvador wanted them to drive over to Corona to show off Hortensia to his mother and sister, Luisa, and her boys.

"It might be more than a few minutes," said Archie.

"I don't think so," said Salvador, putting the spurs to Archie's ribs.

Then Salvador led Archie out of the house and around to the back.

Suddenly, when they'd no more than turned the corner and were out of sight, Archie grabbed hold of Salvador by the shoulder and whirled him about, screaming into his face like a mad bull. But being ready, Salvador kept as calm as a reptile in the noonday Sun, refusing to be provoked.

"What the hell do you think you're doing, going over to see Palmer behind my back, you son-of-a-bitch?! You think you're the only deal I got cooking with him?! I do business with him all the time! And I'm not going to let you screw that up for just a few lousy dollars, damnit!"

"Two hundred is just a few lousy dollars?" said Salvador, smiling.

"Two hundred isn't that much!" screamed Archie. "People are dying! People are killing themselves! The whole country is going to hell and I've been protecting your ass, and I don't get paid shit for being a deputy! I do all my work just to help our people. I got no money coming in like you, Sal! Hell, you're doing better than anyone I know!"

Salvador said nothing. He just looked up at the big lawman as he raged on and on. He now knew that he was, in fact, holding all the aces, or Archie wouldn't be this mad. He let the lawman scream on and on. After all, he could now afford to be calm. There was nothing that Archie could ever do to him again. Because he, Salvador, now not only had the money, but he also had the contacts.

Archie had cooked his own goose.

"I've known Palmer since high school!" continued yelling Archie. "Do you really think he would have ever even talked to you, if I hadn't introduced you?! Hell, no! His family comes from San Francisco!"

"I thought they came from Tucson, Arizona," said Salvador, rubbing in a little salt.

"What? Tucson? Oh, yeah, that was before San Francisco, when they was into mining. They're one of the oldest, most influential families in the whole West! You had no right going to him behind my back, you bastard! I ought to pound you into the ground right now!" screamed Archie, raising up his huge arms as he continued cussing out Salvador and threatening him with bodily harm.

Finally, Salvador had heard enough and put down his first ace. "You just got a little too greedy, Archie," he said calmly.

"What did you say?!" yelled Archie, not quite having heard him because of his own screaming.

"Too greedy," repeated Salvador. "Your game is a good one, and it could've gone on forever, Archie, if . . . you just hadn't gotten so greedy."

Archie stopped his rage and took a deep breath, pulling up his gunbelt and taking a good, long look at Salvador. "Too greedy, eh?"

"Yeah," said Salvador, putting down his next ace, "if you had asked for fifty, I would've never gone asking questions, Archie."

"Fifty, eh?"

"Yeah, or maybe even a hundred, and I would've just paid it, because you're right, Palmer never would have spoken to me if you hadn't introduced us, and so you did have money coming, but not two hundred."

"Okay," said Archie, easing off and gripping his long nose with his huge hand and pulling on it. "So maybe I did lean on you a little too much. But what do I got coming now, eh? Seventy-five?"

"No, nothing," said Salvador, putting down his third ace.

"Nothing?!" yelled Archie. "Why, you son-of-a-bitch!"

"NO, YOU'RE THE SON-OF-A-BITCH!" Salvador now bellowed! He'd had enough and he was going to now show Archie the full power of not just three aces, but all four! "You go around acting like you're our people's hero, always doing this and that, giving food and drink and everything, but all the time you're lining your own pockets with our money! You lie to us, Archie, telling us that we can't go to the *gringo* and talk to him ourselves, but have to go through you! You act like only you know how to do this great *gringo*-magic, and it's no magic at all! Palmer's just a regular, good guy! Why didn't you just have the guts to deal me an honest hand, Archie, and tell me that you wanted some money for yourself for setting up the deal?!"

"Because, well, I . . . ah," faltered Archie, not knowing what to say.

"Because the truth is, Archie, that you like to keep us—your own people—weak and scared so you can then look big and smart and strong.

"You're like the Catholic Church at its worst! Like one of those angry, bad priests back home who always preached of hell and damnation, telling us all about the Devil and the end of the world, so he could keep us all in slavery with TERROR!

"I owe you NOTHING, Archie! *Nada, nada*, NOTHING! You hear me, not one damn little dollar! In fact, it's you who now owes me!" added

Salvador, putting down his final ace with all the power of a man who long ago had befriended the Devil as well as God, and so Here 'there' was no way anyone could scare him with either.

"I owe you?!" said Archie, still not understanding. "And how in the hell do you figure that, Mr. Smart-Ass?!"

"Because I did you a favor," said Salvador. "The biggest damn favor any man can do for another human being in this country."

"And what might that be?" asked Archie. "You told Palmer that I'm a crook and tried to shake you down?"

Salvador only smiled. He loved it. He'd won. He'd saved himself two hundred dollars and Archie was going to go along with it. "No, Archie," he said calmly. "I did the opposite; I told him nothing. That's what I did for you, I told him nothing."

"Nothing?" said Archie. He was completely baffled now.

"Yes, *nada, nada,* nothing."

"You mean you didn't tell him anything about the two hundred that I was charging you?" he asked.

"Exactly, I didn't tell him nothing," said Salvador.

Archie still didn't quite get it. "Why not?" he asked suspiciously.

"Because," said Salvador, "Palmer likes you, Archie, and he respects you. And so I didn't want him knowing about our own *problemas.*"

"I'll be damned," said Archie, now catching on to what Salvador was telling him.

"I didn't want him thinking badly of you or of me," continued Salvador. "No, I want this rich, educated, powerfully-connected man thinking only the best of us, that we're both honest, hard-working, good people, Archie, so he can then feel good and safe about working with us and our people now and in the future."

Hearing this, Archie grinned. "Why, you slick son-of-a-bitch!" he said, laughing. "You know," he added in all sincerity, "sometimes I think I got you all figured out, Sal, but then you throw me a fast one like this and I see that I don't know you at all. My God, you're one hell of a smart *hombre*! And you're right, I do agree I owe you one! I really do, you bastard!"

"Yes, and this is a big one that you owe me," added Salvador with a little-happy grin.

"Hey, slow down 'em horses," said Archie. "You better not be getting any wild, greedy ideas on me, you son-of-a-bitch!"

Salvador only smiled. "I won't," he said. "I'm a professional, Archie, and a professional card player never rides too much on one hand. No, a pro likes to ride home on many hands so no one feels the burn."

Archie roared with *carcajadas.* "Well, whatever that means, all I know is that you cut one hell of a mean deck, Sal! Yeah, I have to admit that you got me this time!" he said.

"No, Archie, understand, you got yourself."

"I got myself?"

"Yes."

"Look," said Archie, "I ain't no professional gambler or nothing, so all I know is that I'm out two hundred and in debt to you, you son-of-a-bitch! But I'll get you next time!"

And Archie laughed and laughed, and Salvador could now see that this man had missed the whole point. There would never be a "next time." That game was over. Archie truly had cooked his own goose. He'd just lost all of his power over Salvador for a cheap, little, greedy two hundred dollars.

Greed had no respect or understanding of Power.

For long ago, Salvador had learned that Greed was based on Fear and Fear, of course, had no lasting power.

Salvador glanced up at the Heavens and thanked the Stars above that he'd had the good fortune to have been raised by a woman who'd taught him that the Real Power of Life, *la Vida,* wasn't measured in muscle, or weapons, or from one's feet to our head, but from our head TO THE SKY for we were GIANTS who knew how to "live" without Fear of Life or Death, Devil or GOD!

"LUPE!" SAID SALVADOR, coming back into the house after seeing Archie off, "let's get all dressed up in our best clothes! I want to celebrate! I just saved us a big chunk of money, and put the law in my pocket!"

Salvador and Lupe got dressed in their finest clothes, the clothes that had been tailor-made for them by that exclusive little dress shop owned by Harry in downtown Santa Ana. He put on his beautiful navy blue pinstripe double-breasted suit and his fine white panama hat with the wide black band and the tiny red feather that he'd gotten off a red-shouldered blackbird. She wore her beautiful royal blue suit and her coat with the soft, dark fur around the collar.

"As soon as we get a little ahead," said Salvador, as they went out the door with their daughter and got in their grand Moon automobile, "I want to go back up to Harry's shop and get us some more new clothes, *querida*! That Jewish man, Harry, was always good to me. He's the first man to ever give me credit. Credit, Harry explained to me, is the future!"

"But my clothes are just fine," said Lupe.

"Yes, but I want for us to spend some money just for the hell of it!" said Salvador. "Besides, Harry and his wife, Bernice, probably need the business. Everyone is hurting real bad, Lupe!" It was midmorning by the time Lupe and Salvador left Carlsbad, going over to Corona to see Salvador's *familia*. Then just this side of Lake Elsinore, Lupe asked Salvador to please pull over, so she could change Hortensia.

"I want to put on her pretty little dress that Sophia made for her," said Lupe, "so she'll look her best for your mother, Salvador."

Salvador pulled over, under a group of large California sycamores. Hortensia was almost a month old now, and she was filling out, just like Sophia had said that she would. She was a beautiful baby. She had her mother's wonderful, good looks and her father's dark eyes and long, thick eyelashes.

Salvador got out of the car to stretch his legs and relieve himself. Just looking at Lupe and his daughter, he felt overwhelmed. He took several deep breaths and watched Lupe baby-talk with their daughter as she changed her, and he just had this sudden urge to hug them, squeeze them, to eat them all up and take them into his body.

There was so much that he wanted to tell his wife and child, so much that he just wanted to take out of his brain and heart and soul and hand over to them, so they could then understand once and for all how much he truly loved them!

He watched Lupe finish changing their little daughter, and he saw Hortensia's tiny feet and tiny hands and those tiny, little, cute nails on each toe and finger . . . tears of joy came to Salvador's eyes. This was, indeed, a Blessed Holy Moment.

He wiped his eyes and hoped to God he could live long enough to see his child grow. He prayed he could maybe even get to the age of forty without getting killed or ending up in prison. No male in his *familia* had ever gotten past the age of thirty, who hadn't ended up behind bars.

Salvador breathed and watched Lupe finish putting knitted shoes on their daughter that Sophia had also made, and he was so grateful to be alive after all these years of running and hiding and dodging bullets.

Tears of joy continued streaming from Salvador's eyes.

DRIVING INTO THE *BARRIO*, a young black billy goat ran across the road. Salvador had to swerve not to hit it. The owner of the goat came running out of his house, yelling. It was the old schoolteacher from Monterey, Mexico, Rodolfo Rochin, who'd been having trouble with his eyesight the last couple of years.

"Watch where you're going! Or you'll be paying for a goat!" yelled Rochin.

"Okay!" said Salvador. "I'll pay for the goat right now!"

"Oh, it's you, *mi general!*" said Rochin. He'd been calling Salvador "his general" ever since they'd tried to put on that strike at the rock quarry outside of Corona years back. "How have you been?"

"Pretty good," said Salvador. "Lupe and I have just had our first child. So why don't I buy that goat from you, and then you bring him over to the house and we'll barbecue him. Eh, come and bring your whole family, and we'll have a *fiesta!*"

"The honor will be mine," said the elegant old man. "Good to see you, *señora,*" he added, addressing Lupe with a tip of his hat.

Lupe nodded to him. He'd been at their wedding. "Good to see you again," she said.

Rodolfo bowed respectfully to her. "And the goat," he said, "will be a present from me to your first child, Salvador."

"That's very generous of you," said Salvador. "But these are hard times, Rodolfo. Let me pay you for the goat."

"Well, all right, if you insist," said the schoolteacher.

"How much?"

"Oh, let's say fifty cents," said Rodolfo.

"How about fifty cents and a pint bottle," said Salvador, fully knowing that the man liked to drink. "And then you help me with the killing and the barbecue?"

"That would be my honor," said Rodolfo, and he tipped his hat again to Lupe.

Lupe nodded to him once again, too, then she and Salvador drove on to his mother's house, just up the block.

Parking their Moon automobile, Salvador's whole *familia* immediately came rushing out to see them—Luisa, Epitacio, Jose, Pedro and little Benjamin. Then came the grand old lady herself, Doña Margarita. She had a white bandage wrapped about her head.

"Oh, she's so beautiful!" everyone was saying about Hortensia.

"Here, let me hold her!" said Doña Margarita, reaching for the baby.

"No, *mama*," said Luisa, cutting in. "You better sit down first. You know how you've been lately."

"What happened to her head?" asked Salvador of Luisa.

"Oh, at the church, you know, one of her old lady friends stoned her just as I knew they would."

"Sssssh!" said Doña Margarita. "She only stoned me because you half choked her to death and put that idea in her head."

"Now you're blaming me, *mama*! Me, who saved your life!"

"But what are you two talking about?" asked Salvador. "What woman stoned you, and why?"

"Does it ever really matter why," said his mother. "The important thing is that it's over. Now let me hold your baby. Oh, she's so beautiful! Just look at her eyes!"

Salvador turned to Luisa.

"Don't look at me," said his sister, "it was our mother who was holding court with Moses and brought this whole catastrophe upon herself!"

"You were talking to Moses, *mama*?" said Salvador. "The Moses of the Bible?"

"Yes, why not," snapped the old woman. "But enough of that. I want my granddaughter," she added, pushing Luisa aside and reaching for Hortensia once again.

But as she took the infant from Lupe, she lost her balance and almost fell. Jose caught his *abuelita* in his arms and helped her to sit down on the running board of the old, abandoned truck in their yard. The old woman never let go of the child, holding her to her heart.

"What are you going to name her?" asked Doña Margarita. "Have you decided yet?"

Salvador glanced at Lupe, then back at his mother. "We, ah, already named her. Her name is Maria Hortensia. But, well, it wasn't really us who named her, *mama*."

Everyone went silent. They were all staring at Salvador, trying to understand.

"It was Lupe's sister Maria," continued Salvador, "who took the baby from Lupe while she was sleeping and baptized her Maria Hortensia without our knowledge." He swallowed. He felt so ashamed. He could see his whole family was shocked. "You see," he added, "Lupe's sister had a terrible dream, and I guess the dream scared her so much that she—"

"All right, no more!" said Doña Margarita, seeing how uncomfortable the whole story was making Salvador and Lupe. "The important thing is that she was baptized, and with such a beautiful name! Why, she has the name of the Mother of God and then she was blessed with the name of a big, beautiful flower! How perfect for such a gorgeous child! Now get away, all of you! I need to speak to my newest granddaughter alone!"

"But, *mama*," said Luisa, "you really shouldn't—"

"GET!" snapped the old woman. "Get away all of you! Or I'll take a stick to you right now! And don't think I can't! I'm still very quick!"

And she laughed, truly enjoying herself, and began to sing to Maria Hortensia. Lupe didn't know what to do. She didn't want to just leave her little daughter with this old woman, whose head was all bandaged up.

"Come on," said Salvador to Lupe. "She's raised dozens of children. She knows what she's doing."

Reluctantly, Lupe began to go with Salvador and the others, but she didn't like it. Then Doña Margarita, who was rocking Hortensia in her arms as she sat on the running board of the old rusty-red truck, saw Lupe leaving with the others, and said, "No, not you, Lupe! You stay with me!"

"Oh, okay," said Lupe, quickly coming back to the old woman and her child.

"You see, Lupe," said the old woman, pulling Lupe in close on the running board, "we—the mothers—need to welcome this little woman-child into the world!"

Hearing this, Maria Hortensia screeched with joy, kicking her feet.

"See, she understood me," said the old woman, kissing the child again and again. "Please understand, Lupe, that children—no matter how young—truly comprehend what people say. In fact, I'll tell you, many a child's life has been ruined by parents not realizing this and saying hateful things in front of them. I swear, Lupe, children actually understand more of what we are really saying than we, ourselves, understand. Just like dogs and cats understand what is going on within a *familia*—even before the family knows itself—so do children. For they are our latest messengers straight from God.

"Eh, isn't that right, *mi hijita*?" said the old woman, turning to Maria Hortensia, "you already know everything there is to know, don't you? For you are an Angel, our latest little *Rayo*, Lightning Rod, from the Heavens." Maria Hortensia looked straight up at the old woman and started kicking wildly once again. "See, Lupe, she knows, she Knows!"

Lupe was astonished. "I've never seen her kick like this before," she said.

"Watch this," said Doña Margarita. "Hortensia, do you remember flying about in Heaven with *Papito Dios* and the Angels?"

Hearing this, Hortensia's eyes lit up with joy and she began waving her arms like they were wings, screeching to the Heavens!

"Listen closely, Lupe," said Doña Margarita, closing her eyes in concentration, "the more and more we move through the Sixth Sun to the Seventh, our children will be born with fuller remembrances. The Holy Day is not too far away when the bulk of Humanity will be Awakening. This, even the Incas and the Mayans still did know. Isn't this right, Maria Hortensia," added Doña Margarita, turning back to the child, "it is now safe for you, *querida,* to be here on this *Tierra Madre* with your *familia* and keep your memories of Heaven, for you are surrounded *con Amor*! Tell her, Lupe, she needs to hear this from you, her mother."

"Why, yes, of course," said Lupe, "but she already knows that she's loved, *señora.*"

"Yes, but you must also tell her in words, Lupe," said Doña Margarita. "Words, you see, Lupe, were originally sounds, chants, Vibrations that fed Love from one Heart to another Heart, so these Sound-Vibrations must be fed to a child several times a day from the one who nurses her and gives her warmth, in order for the child to feel anchored.

"There's so much I need to tell you, Lupe. I should've started telling you months ago, as all wise midwives have been doing since the dawn of time with every young mother. Men, you see, they just don't understand this Voyage that Hortensia just completed of coming Here to the Earth from the Stars.

"Each Child, *mi hijita,* is a Sacred Blessing, having traveled here on the Breath of God. Each is the Reflection from that Star from which they traveled. This *planeta* is a school, if you will, for the unveiling of the Understanding of Creation, God and Ourselves. And so, Lupe," she added, "when you lay down to rest always put Hortensia on your chest so she can feel your Heart, beat, Beat, Beating, then she'll grow up Knowing the Heartbeat of Creation wherever she goes.

"Isn't that right, *mi hijita,*" said the old woman, turning to the infant once again. "Your mother's Heartbeat was your First Song of the Universe, beat, Beat, Beating to you while you were inside of her womb. It would Sing, Sing, Sing to you Night and Day, sending you Love and Good Tidings, teaching you to Relax and Trust the Universe as you slept. Well, *mi hijita,* I want you to know that out here in this world the same is true and here is also a heartbeat and this is the Heartbeat of the Holy Creator, that will also continue teaching you of the Universe every time you sleep and your Guardian Angel takes you up to visit *con Papito Dios.* Eh, you remember, don't you. You Know what your grandmother is talking about?"

Suddenly, the child was screeching once again as if she'd truly understood every Holy Word.

Lupe had never seen an adult, much less a young child, behave like this before. Tears came to Lupe's eyes. She felt so Blessed to have a mother-in-love such as Doña Margarita.

"Always remember, *mi hijita,* you are God's One Singular Note in His Great Symphony!" continued the old Indian woman. "You are Special, you are Unique, no one, but no one like You was ever Created before in all the Universe! And each night when you go to sleep, always Know that your Guardian Angel will come and take you hand-in-hand back up to Heaven, so that you can sleep with *Papito Dios.* And then when you Awake in the morning, you'll feel good and wonderful! Welcome to our *familia,* little woman! Welcome to your short stay here on *planeta* Earth!"

Maria Hortensia screeched again, kicking and kicking.

She'd been ANCHORED!

Her Soul had been REAFFIRMED!

Lupe was beside herself with joy. She had all but forgotten that her own mother, a Yaqui, had done almost this exact same thing with her when she'd been born.

Each and Every child needed to be presented to the Stars and the Mother Earth to have their Soul Reaffirmed, or they'd be lost and floundering about all of their Life!

Tears were streaming down Lupe's face.

"What is it, *querida?*" asked the old woman.

Lupe shrugged. "Oh, I don't know. It's just that every time we get together, *señora,* I just feel so good! I'm so sorry that Maria took Hortensia and baptized her without you being present, but—well, she'd had this terrible dream, and—oh, I just don't know!" Lupe added with frustration.

"Lupe, what's done is done," said the old woman, "and who knows, dreams can foretell the future, so maybe your sister did the right thing. There are no accidents. Now, give me your hand and place it gently here on Hortensia's stomach.

"Now," added the old woman, "feel the child's breathing? Breathing is the single most important thing we can teach any child. To breathe slowly, slowly, calmly, especially when things aren't going well; this is the True Baptism a mother gives her child. These priests and their fine robes know nothing of baptizing children. That's all just show. But we, women, must forgive them, Lupe. They're just men, they never had the miracle of Life, *la Vida*, pulsating here inside of them like you did for those nine months. Oh, Lupe, you are now the Miracle Maker *de tu Casa*!

"So forgive your sister Maria," continued Doña Margarita. "I, too, was young once and had many powerful dreams and didn't know what to do. In fact, this is why Moses and I have been spending so much time together."

"Then you really did see Moses?"

"Well, yes, of course," said the old woman, laughing. "I just don't understand why this surprises people. Talking with the Virgin and Jesus is accepted quite easily in *nuestra cultura,* but then people are so shocked when anyone says they've had a conversation with Moses."

Seeing Lupe's reaction, the old woman laughed again. *"Mi hijita,* it's okay. I'm really no more crazy-*loca* today than I was day before yesterday. You see, Moses and I are re-doing the Ten Commandments."

"You and Moses are re-doing the Ten Commandments?!?" said Lupe in astonishment.

"Of course. What do you think, that they were written in stone?" added Doña Margarita, laughing *con carcajadas.*

But she could see that her daughter-in-love wasn't laughing. Lupe truly looked very frightened.

"But why are you frightened, *mi hijita?*" asked the old woman.

"Well, because," said Lupe, finding it hard to believe that her mother-in-love wasn't shaking with fear, "the Ten Commandments are the LAWS of GOD, *señora!*"

Doña Margarita burst out laughing again. "And so is Breathing. And so is Birthing. And so is Loving. And so is—I could go on for hours, for days, *mi hijita.* All Living are the Commandments of God. These Ten," she added, "just got more attention. And they aren't even the main ten."

Lupe nodded and nodded again. "And Moses, he went along with you on this?"

"How could he not, I had him by his *tanates.*"

It was very hard for Lupe to hear anything after this. Just the image of her mother-in-love to have hold of the Great Man of the Bible by his private parts was too fantastic for her to—but then Lupe remembered what she'd learned about men since she'd married, and she couldn't believe what came out of her mouth.

"Did he enjoy it?" she asked.

"Did who enjoy what?" asked Doña Margarita.

Lupe turned a dozen shades of pink, she became so embarrassed.

"Oh, Moses?" said Doña Margarita. "When I had him by the balls? Oh, yes, he loved it! Nobody had fondled him in years!"

And now they were both laughing *con carcajadas.* Salvador and Luisa were watching them through the kitchen window. The two women looked so beautiful, laughing together on the running board of the old abandoned Model T with the missing doors and motor. This was an old wrecked truck that the people of the *barrio* had been cannibalizing for parts for years.

"How did you get stoned, *señora?*" Lupe asked, wiping her eyes.

Doña Margarita ran her hand over her bandaged head, taking in a deep breath. *"Mi hijita,"* she said gently, reaching out to caress Lupe's hand, "I wasn't alone when I spoke to Moses. Many of my church friends wanted to talk to Moses, too, so I invited them to join me. And well, birthing has frightened women since the dawn of time. And you see, to meet with someone like Moses, from the Other Side, is to Birth One's Self out of the flat and narrow five sensory world and back into the Whole, Complete, Wide Universe of our Full Thirteen Senses."

Hearing this, Lupe said nothing. She just looked at her mother-in-love, not really knowing what to think or even feel—anymore.

"So, then, who stoned you, *señora,* these other women?"

"No, it was my old friend Dolores who felt left out when she wasn't able to make the Voyage with the rest of us, God Bless her troubled Soul."

The old woman stopped her words and made the sign of the cross over herself. Lupe sat still. A breeze picked up, sweeping across the yard with a beautiful little swirl of leaves.

"Señora," said Lupe, "I can understand some of what you've just said, because back home in Mexico my own mother also told us about Creation while we were growing up. But still, a very large part of me can understand your friend Dolores' fear because at first, when you mentioned what you did with Moses, my whole stomach felt like it had been—"

Lupe stopped her words. She just didn't know how to say what she wanted to say without sounding awful.

"You felt like a sharp knife had been stuck into your stomach, and a part of you then also felt like doing me harm."

Lupe turned red with embarrassment.

"It's okay, *mi hijita,*" said Doña Margarita. "Why do you think Our Lord God Jesus was crucified? People attack that which they don't understand."

"It hurt so much here inside of me when you said that Moses and you re-did the Ten Commandments, that I didn't know what to think or do. All my life we were taught that these laws came straight from God and that they are the whole basis of civilization and beyond reproach!"

"Then comes along this old, toothless, crazy woman undoing everything!" said Doña Margarita, laughing.

Lupe nodded.

"Well, *mi hijita*," added the old woman, "I can fully understand your feelings. Emotion is what this *planeta* is all about. This is why we have so many wars. And what does the word 'emotion' mean, simply 'feelings-in-motion, feelings-in-change.' And men fear to change their feelings even more than women. This is why even Moses himself, the Great Man, had difficulty with me at first, too." She closed her eyes in concentration. "Truly, all people Fear the Pains of Change, and Change is nothing but the Birthing of New Life. And Life is Birthing. And All this Birthing is what we call Creation, and Creation is . . . the Almighty. Remember, *mi hijita, la extremidad del humano es la oportunidad de Dios.*"

The old woman opened her eyes. "Poor Dolores couldn't have behaved any differently with her name being Dolores, meaning 'Pain.' She had to fulfill that which she was named.

"Do you see what I am saying, *mi hijita,* Words are Holy. They make us Who We Are. Give us ten commandments full of 'don't' do this and 'don't' do that, then these 'don'ts' are exactly what we become. Give us a god full of wrath and vengeance and this is how we are destined to treat each other no matter how much we are preached at to not do that. Does this make sense, *mi hijita?*"

Lupe took in a big breath, then she shrugged. "Yes, I guess it does, but I don't know, *señora.*"

"Perfect. Because when the day comes that you do know all this, to the depths of your Soul, you, *mi mujer,* will never be intimidated by men and all their doings again," said Doña Margarita. Then she once more closed her eyes in concentration. "Feeling left out is why men created the story that god is only a male. Feeling left out is why men had to invent that women came from adam's rib, instead of directly from god. Feeling left out is the very reason why wars and empires and power are the most loved children of every male. And I'm sorry to say, this also includes my own son Salvador," said the grand old woman, opening her eyes, "whom I Love with all my Heart!"

Smiling, she reached out and took Lupe's hand. "To you, *mi hijita,* I now entrust Our Future." She Breathed in of God. "And not because I don't love and respect my fine son, but, simply, because—just see how your daughter looks at you, Lupe. Already she knows your smell, your voice, above all others. You are her Everything! And no man can ever experience this miracle, Lupe.

"This is why, Lupe, in the end, it was finally Jesus Christ, Himself, Who came forward and told Moses, in terms that he could understand, that the time has come for us to move the Commandments out of stone and into Flesh and Blood," said the old woman. "This is what the Crucifixion was all about, God sending His Only Begotten Son down here to us to put the Flesh and Blood of Forgiveness, Compassion, and Understanding on the Commandments.

"This is what each generation needs to do with their Own Flesh and Blood in order for us to continue adding to Our Understanding of the Almighty," she added, pointing into the air with her index finger with each word she spoke. "Moses, the poor man, really could do *nada, nada,* nothing but agree with us. He really had no idea that Creation is ongoing. He was truly trapped—no matter how much God spoke to him—in the flat and narrow world of the Egyptians' way of thinking. It was absolutely beyond his comprehension that one day soon the Holy Creator would need to send His Own Flesh and Blood to Save the World of Humankind from yet another kind of slavery. Understand, Creation continues even as we speak and we, humans, aren't the end of Creation. Hell, the Ants know more than us."

"Señora," said Lupe, "how come you know so much?"

"Oh, no, *mi hijita,"* said the little old lady, laughing, "long ago I gave up knowing and simply gave my Life over to Spirit."

Saying this, she kissed the Crucifix of her rosary, then touched the Holy Cross to her daughter-in-love's forehead, Blessing her. A pool of Golden Light came all around the Three Generations of women. "Isn't this right, *mi hijita,"* she turned and said to Hortensia, "you Know what your *mamagrande* is talking about, eh? We know *nada, nada,* nothing, except that which comes to us Here, within ourselves, directly from God!"

She kissed the Crucifix again, touching Hortensia lightly on the chest this time, then mumbled a little Prayer. The child kicked her feet and waved her little arms. She'd understood perfectly.

Lupe took in a deep Breath. "So, then, tell me, *señora,* what are these new—" She stopped. She still couldn't quite bring herself to say the word. "—that you and your friends came up with," she added.

"You mean the Commandments?" said Doña Margarita.

"Yes," said Lupe, still feeling a little nervous.

"Mi hijita," said the old woman, "we didn't come up with any—what

you'd call—new commandments. That would have been no improvement. To command, rule, or control these are *hombre*-ideas, created out of fear. You tell me, what did we come up with, Lupe?"

"I don't know, *señora,*" said Lupe, surprised that her mother-in-love would even ask her.

"Oh, yes, you do," said the old woman, closing her eyes as she continued speaking with a cadence of calm, deliberate concentration. "You are married, you have given Birth, so now all you have to do is . . . Breathe in of God, and All the Knowledge of the Ages will come Birthing into you!"

Saying this, Doña Margarita herself Breathed in deeply of *Papito,* too. "Now, tell me, *querida,* what did we come up with? Go on, speak. You Know."

Tears came to Lupe's eyes. "You came up with Love, *señora,* that we must Love each other with all of our Hearts and Souls as One *Familia*! That no one is better than anyone else! That we are all the children of God. And God Loves Us All Equally—no matter what!" she added, almost yelling.

"Perfect," said Doña Margarita, making the sign of the cross over her daughter-in-love. "This is, in fact, the First Understanding that we also came up with to Moses. Now go on, what was our Second Understanding?"

Lupe shook her head. "No more, please, *señora.*"

"Come on, *mi hijita,* they all come out so easy once we get past our personal fear of this *Tierra Firme.*"

Lupe still didn't want to go on.

"Come on, *mi hijita,*" she said, smiling, "dig into yourself. You know. You Know! Every woman does, particularly once she marries, and Births."

Lupe just shook her head. "You ask too much of me, *señora.* I have no idea. There are so many *problemas* in the world of hunger and war and hate, so where do I begin?"

"Okay, and while you're at it, then add in prejudice and racism—like my poor husband had for *nuestra familia.* And greed and abuse of women, and the rape of the Mother Earth, and of course, the worship of power and money above all else. Where did all this great big mess come from? Many of us like to think that it started when the Europeans came to our shores.

"But no, *mi hijita,*" she said, laughing, "we had many of these *problemas* already here. Lots of our people were already going in the direction of conquering, enslaving, and wanting to build empires, and why . . . because, simply—come on, say it, they'd lost their Trust in God.

"Close your eyes, *mi hijita,*" Doña Margarita added. "It's no accident that Our Lord Jesus, Himself, chose to go blind for thirteen years so He could open His Heart Eye to See Here in this *Tierra Firme*. The two eyes of our head are so dominant that they become our distraction. Now, Breathe in of *Papito Dios*. Go on Breathe, Breathe, and close your eyes, and open wide with Vision from Here, within your Heart."

Lupe did as she was told. She closed her eyes and Breathed in of the Almighty, and suddenly, in a flash, she was BURSTING! "*Señora,* all those *problemas* simply began when people stopped Breathing in of God with every Holy Breath they took!"

The old woman smiled.

"I see it so clearly now that I have my eyes closed," continued Lupe. "Then losing God, man became frightened, then to hide this fear he began thinking that he was better than the rest of Creation. Why, he actually began to think that he alone was made in god's image."

"You got it. Go on, *mi hijita!*"

"That was our Fall from Grace, *señora,* and after that man—in his false arrogance—began to think he was better than . . . than his own sister, too."

"Exactly! This is where separation began! Greed isn't part of human nature. Fear of heights and death isn't part of human nature, either. All this came after Separation. Before Separation all of Creation was Together, part of God, and hence able to communicate with one another. The Trees, the Rocks, the Birds, the Animals, the Sea Creatures and the Humans All had a Common Languaging. All was in Balance, in Harmony, in Peace within the Sacred Circle of Our Holy Thirteen Senses. Here, at this place—now known as the Garden—there were no mysteries. All was understandable. To rule, to control, to command weren't concepts even comprehended. So then what happened, *mi hijita,* go on, tell me, you Know Everything!"

"Well, after the Separation," said Lupe, closing her eyes once again, "I see, well, a darkness." She began to tremble. "A huge, awful Black Darkness," she added, "here deep inside each of us—I can feel it inside of me so clearly—oh, my God, the DEVIL! He's SMILING!" she said, gasping!

"Yes," said Doña Margarita. "Go on. The Devil came to Be. You got it. Beautiful!"

"Oh, *señora,*" said Lupe, opening up her eyes. "I saw it all so clearly, but then I lost it." She was crying. The sight of the Devil's smile had truly frightened her.

"No, you didn't lose it, *mi hijita,*" said the old woman, closing her own eyes. "We never lose anything. It's just that we sometimes reach places inside of us, where we don't want to see . . . what it is that we saw and this place—since our Separation—we call evil.

"And Lupe, believe me, I'm not blaming you or criticizing you. We all do this. I've done it. Your mother has done it. It's all just part of gaining confidence, then passing on through that needle's eye of Darkness. Now just relax and Breathe in of *Papito, mi hijita,*" said the old woman, "and you'll be able to go on and see again. Lucifer, remember," she added, "was also originally just another part of God, and so we had no fear of him, either. In fact, Lucifer, the Light, awaits to show you safe passage through this Darkness back to the Almighty."

"No," said Lupe, shaking her head. "This is too confusing for me! Lucifer is bad! Why would he take me to God? I don't want to do this anymore, *señora.*"

"All right," said Doña Margarita, "I can understand, fear is frightening. But—and this is the biggest 'but' of your whole life, *mi hijita*—deal with this Fear you will. And if not now, here with guidance, then later. For this is where God," she said, closing her eyes in concentration once again, "came asking Adam about the forbidden fruit and Adam couldn't handle it, so he blamed *Eva,* his Love. Why? Because Lupe, he, too, had come eye to eye with this Smile of the Devil and it terrified him.

"He didn't realize that it's from Here, *mi hijita,* from the Fear of this Smile inside of our own Darkness, that comes all of our Powers. I lost sixteen children, Lupe," she added with tears bursting from her eyes. "How do you think I was able to not go crazy? Because I faced that Smile eye to eye Here in the Darkness of my own Heart with the Complete Trust that the Soul is Eternal and God is Good. That's when I was able to understand that each of my children had done their Sacred Work no matter how short was their stay Here on this *Tierra Madre.* The Devil could not trick me. I had indestructible Faith in the Eternal Goodness of the Universe, understanding that Darkness is just that part of Heaven that hasn't been Illuminated yet."

She breathed. "You see, *mi hijita,* the Bible is a much, much Greater Book than even the Pope, himself understands. The Bible isn't the story of a people who lived a long time ago. No, the Bible is the Key for the Comprehension of the Ongoing Story of All of Humanity, including Our Cousins on Our Other Six *Planetas.* Noah didn't load up a little boat on this *planeta* with all the animals of the world, but on Our Twin Sister *Planeta* on a Great Sky Sailing Mother Ship of well over sixty kilometers around. And you know this, Lupe, Here inside of yourself, we all do, once we accept who We really Are—Walking Stars of Illumination!

"So, no, you don't need to go on right now, Lupe, but do understand this, *mi hijita,* when Adam comes blaming you like he blamed *Eva,* you stand up in your marriage and face that Fear of the Unknown, putting both of your feet deep into the Mother Earth, and speak up for yourself, because if you don't, believe me, no one will, and that's a Woman's Truth straight from the Bible that you can depend on!

"Your mother, she told me how she had to stand up and take hold of the reins of your *familia* when your father left you in search of work. And I, then, told her how I had to stand up and take up the reins of our *familia* when my husband returned from having left us in search of work, and he disowned us because he thought all his blue-eyed sons were gone and all that was left of our *familia* were females and one Indian-looking son."

Tears burst from Doña Margarita's eyes. Lupe began to cry, too.

"Are you saying, *señora,* that I, too, will one day have to take up the reins of my family because Salvador is going to—" Lupe couldn't finish her words, the thought was so scary for her.

"No, I'm not saying this," said the old woman, "because I raised my son to respect women and his family above all else with all his heart and soul, so he will never abandon you, but—*desgraciadamente,* he is a man and so he will drift away from you with dreams of power and riches and maybe other—"

"Don't say it, *señora*! Please, don't say it!"

"Why? To not say it, do you think will cause it to not come true?"

Lupe shrugged, then nodded vigorously.

The old woman laughed. "Oh, no, *mi hijita,* men have been men for millions of years! What they are, they are already! So we, women, must face this and—"

"But not now! We're so happy right now, *señora.*" Tears streamed down Lupe's face.

"Exactly," said the tough old She-Fox. "You are happy right now, so this is exactly why you can now see what you must see, without Fear or Bitterness. A Woman of Substance does not put all of her Love in the man, *mi hijita.* A Woman of Substance understands how the Universe works and puts her Love in God first, then in her child, then in her nest, so then when that day comes—which it will—that she finds him with another woman— no, don't pull away! Listen!—whether this woman be Power, Riches, or a young coquettish girl, she doesn't panic and run, saying 'Oh, he has betrayed me!' For no man has ever betrayed any Woman of Substance! A Woman of Substance is a Prepared Woman who realizes that the man has simply done what is in his nature here between his legs.

"So what does a Woman of Substance then do, *mi hijita,* when her husband has drifted off? She digs deep inside of herself, drawing up her most primitive of Wild Powers and she leaps forward and grabs hold of him by his *TANATES* and she says, 'These are MINE! And I LOVE YOU and I'm your WIFE and we have CHILDREN, and I'll walk through fire and Hell for you, but you bring home to us WHAT IS OURS! Your BALLS!' This is a language that all *hombres* understand, especially when you got a good hold on their *tanates*!

"So Believe me, Moses is re-working the commandments even as we speak because of the grip we women got on him between his legs. Open your eyes, Lupe, now while you're happy, and realize that love is no little, cute, romantic game. To Love is to leap with both feet into the middle of the Storm of Creation, in this already emotional *planeta,* and come up laughing *con gusto* and hot juices running down between our legs! You are the VOLCANO! You are the HURRICANE!

"Never beg a man! DEMAND! And YOU WILL BE RESPECTED! Particularly when you take him back to bed without blaming or being a crybaby! I did it! Time and again! Your mother, what did she do after all those years of abandonment? She wrote your father a letter and then got all dressed up and received him in her bed when he returned."

Lupe wasn't crying anymore. No, she was now wiping the tears from her eyes and remembering that it was true, it was all true, what her mother-in-love was telling her. Lupe took in a long, deep breath and looked at this old woman sitting beside her on the running board of this old abandoned truck.

"Thank you, *señora*," she said, "with all my Heart and Soul, *gracias*!"

"The thanks are mine," said Doña Margarita. "You are Our Future, *mi hijita, con el favor de Dios,*" she added, bowing her head.

ACROSS THE YARD, a huge fire was roaring, leaping, snapping. Salvador had changed clothes and he and the men were teaching the boys how to kill the goat.

"Now, no one make any sudden movements," said Salvador, "and keep your voices down. Ssssh, we want the animal relaxed and breathing easy, so his meat will taste sweet."

Salvador had a .22 rifle ready and was now looking for a clear shot as the young pretty goat ate the corn they'd put on the ground for him to nibble. Rodolfo had the knife ready to cut the throat and do the bleeding. The boys were nervous, especially the ones who'd never been in on a killing before. One boy made the bad mistake of giggling nervously and two others joined him. Salvador whirled on them.

"Grab ahold of your *tanates*!" he said under his breath, putting his face into the young men's faces. "I said, GRAB THEM! That's right, and now squeeze! Hurts, eh? Will you keep this in mind when you give death or make Love. Life is tender just like your *tanates,* so don't be getting too cocky, because right here, below your cock, are your balls! And it was no accident that men were made in this way! Do you understand?"

The three boys nodded and one made the sign of the cross.

"Good, now you can let go of your balls. We respect life, and above all else, we never kill an animal in view of the other animals, especially his own kind. You boys watch and you'll see, that in families where they don't know how to kill with respect and honor, they also don't know how to live with respect and honor!"

Turning back to the little goat, Salvador now pet him gently. The goat looked up at Salvador. The little animal had big, dark, beautiful eyes. Salvador spoke calmly, quieting the animal right down again. Then he carefully took aim, and shot the cute little goat between the eyes, at such an angle that the bullet went into the brain—and not downward into the mouth and nose area.

The billy went down in a heap, not knowing what had happened.

Instantly, Rodolfo cut his throat under the chin and put a pan to gather the blood, petting the animal as his blood came out in spurts with his still pumping heart.

"There," said Salvador, smiling, "another job well done. And next time, you boys do it, then you'll know here in your balls respect of death and life. Now, let's have our first drink," he said, turning to Rodolfo.

"Orale, mi general!" said the schoolteacher from Monterey, Mexico. "The honor is mine!"

And so all the grown men now had a drink to Salvador's firstborn child, and then some of the older boys were included in their first drink among men, too.

Back in those days, there was no such thing as a teenager. A boy was a boy until the age of twelve, then on his thirteenth birthday, he was a man with pubic hair, capable of impregnating a girl, and so he was expected to be responsible, go to work, and know how to behave!

The same thing with girls. No exception. Then two years later, at fifteen— on her *quinceañera*—a girl was given a coming-out-party and made available to the world as a woman, with a woman's respectability and responsibilities!

After passing the bottle around, Salvador took his nephew Jose aside, spoke to him, then gave him the keys to his Moon automobile. The young man quickly went to his uncle's grand car and took off.

"Now it's time to check the fire while the goat's blood cools down and he quits kicking. Two of you stay here with sticks and make sure that the dogs don't help themselves to the goat. And be stern. Don't let the dogs even start sniffing, or they could become livestock killers. Dogs, cats, they're just like people; only one day away from being loving angels or wild killers. This is why our eyes are up front and not to the side like pastoral animals—the cows, the goats, the sheep, the deer, the rabbits. Eyes to the side, watchful grass eaters. Eyes up front, focused killers. There are no mistakes. Creation is Perfect. When people say that they're making improvements on nature, that's bullshit!"

And so the men now went over to check the fire, to move the burning wood about, and put the stones—which they'd dug out of the hole—back into the hole so that the stones would now heat up and distribute the heat evenly once they began cooking.

Having fixed the fire, the men and young boys all went back to the goat. Now it was time to skin-out the little animal, gut him, quarter him, cover each piece of meat in salt, pepper, and *salsa,* then wrap each piece in clean cloth, then wrap these pieces into a wet burlap sack.

Then, when the wood had all become burning coals and the rocks were breaking from so much heat, the bulks of wrapped meat were lowered with shovels very carefully down into the three-foot deep hole. New green poles were put diagonally across the hole, palm branches were placed over the poles, then wet burlap or old cloths over the palm leaves, and now the whole thing was covered over with about three inches of dirt, until not one little puff of smoke was escaping.

They were done!

The Mother Earth would now cook this goat into a mouthwatering feast within a few hours.

This was the way humans had been cooking all kinds of large mammals for thousands of years all over the globe.

And as the men did this work, the women—inside their homes—cooked up huge pots of *frijoles* and rice, and made up big platters of cut fruit and vegetables.

And most important of all, a flat piece of metal was put over a little fire and here stood three women making *tortillas* by hand and cooking them over the little open fire.

And the women didn't drink their *tequila* straight. No, they squeezed sweet limes, added a little honey or sugar, then spiked this with their alcohol. A mixture of this tasty lemonade was taken out to Doña Margarita and Lupe.

All the people were working together. It took a whole *barrio* to put on a *pachanga*!

Two men came up with guitars and they began to play *rancheritas*. Another man joined them with a heavy wooden crate for the citrus and he began to beat the crate like a huge drum! Automatically, the people began to clap their hands and move their bodies to the beat as they continued preparing the feast.

The Father Sun was just starting to go down when Lupe saw Salvador's nephew Jose drive up in their Moon automobile with her parents and Sophia and her kids. And her brother, Victoriano, had Maria and Carlota and a whole truck full of nephews and nieces.

Lupe had thought that Salvador had sent Jose to get some groceries in town, not all the way to Santa Ana to get her *familia*. Oh, what a surprise!

Lupe leaped up screeching with joy to see her mother, Doña Guadalupe, getting down from their car.

"*Mama! Papa!*" yelled Lupe, feeling a sudden hot rush go all through her. "Carlota! Maria! Victoriano!" Then she started giggling. "What a wonderful surprise!"

"*Mi hijita,*" said her mother, hugging her, "have you been drinking?"

"Of course not!" said Lupe. "Just lemonade! I don't drink, you know that, *mama*!"

"Just lemonade," said her father, licking his lips. "I'd like to have some of this 'just' lemonade, too!"

"We call them *Margaritas* because of our mother," said Luisa, coming out of the house with a big jar of this special drink designed for hot weather. "My mother swears that *Margaritas* bring you close to God!"

"I love being close to God!" said the old man, taking a cup.

The Father Sun was just beginning to touch the far horizon when they uncovered the hole. Instantly, the whole neighborhood smelled of the underground feast! Huge pots of beans and rice were brought out of the different homes! The homemade *tortillas* were already piled high!

"Salvador," said Lupe, taking him aside. She was tipsy. "I want to thank you sooo much for sending Jose to get *mi familia*." She laughed. "I love you."

"Thank you, *te amo también*, Lupe."

Others had joined with their homemade instruments to the drum Beat, BEAT, BEATING of the wooden crate!

The Heavens Opened and ten thousand Angels began to Sing!

GOD was HAPPY!

The whole HOLY FAMILY was SMILING!

Another *familia* had put the Flesh and Blood of Compassion, Forgiveness, and Understanding on their Personal Crucifixion!

Father Ryan showed up and gave his Blessing. By now, everyone's mouth was watering. Even the dogs were licking their chops and just waiting to be thrown bones.

The Father Sun winked his last as he now disappeared into the West. Another Glorious Day was coming to close Here on *PAPITO DIOS'S PARAISO*.

Then the Stars were out by the thousands and Doña Margarita—having drunk many *Margaritas*—stepped forward and began to sing.

"PARTERAS!" she shouted.

"Hay parteras,
   Parteras que parten sus niños!
"Hay parteras,
   Parteras que parten sus sueños!
"Hay parteras,
   Parteras que parten el mundo que conocemos!
"Hay parteras,
   Que parten sus niños, sus sueños, el mundo que conocemos, y las
   Estrellas
   Que nos dan Luz en el Oscurecer del Universo—EL SUEÑO DE DIOS!
"Y estas parteras somos nosotras,
   Las mujeres con ojos, carne, sangre, y amor!
"Por eso levantense todas mis amigas, parteras!
   Este baile es para nosotras,
   Hemos partido sangre, niños, sueños, Estrellas—El SUEÑO DE DIOS,
   "SOMOS PARTERAS!"

The HOLY FAMILY was down from Heaven, Dancing, Singing—*EL SUEÑO!*

Everyone was Now Here! EVERYONE! God and the Blessed Virgin, Jesus and Lucifer, All the Saints, and Angels by the Tens of Thousands!

You couldn't tell where the Earth ended and the Heavens began!

Part Eight

ILLUMINATION

17

GOD was Whirling, Swirling, Dancing! His Children were
finally Awaking to the Light and Loving each other as much
as they LOVED HIM!

NEXT WEEK Domingo would be getting out of prison. Hortensia was nearly a year old. Salvador and Lupe were in the back room of their little rented house in Carlsbad. It was Sunday morning and Lupe was getting Hortensia dressed so they could go to church.

Salvador had just put a chair sideways across the door on the floor between the kitchen and the living room. The week before, *Chingon* had been killed by a car when he'd dragged Hortensia out of the vehicle's path. They'd quickly found a little black and white puppy for Hortensia so that she'd continue to have someone to take care of her. She'd loved *Chingon*. He'd been her best friend. And now they were training the puppy to stay in the porch and kitchen area when they were gone. Putting a chair sideways on the floor did the trick.

Suddenly, they heard a banging at the front. Salvador and Lupe were in the tiny bathroom. They could hardly move—they were so crowded together.

"Did the puppy knock something over?" asked Salvador.

"I don't know," said Lupe. "But you finish getting dressed, Salvador. I'll go check."

Lupe couldn't believe it. All her life, she'd always heard that it took women forever to get dressed, but ever since they'd been married, she'd noticed that it took Salvador about twice as long to get dressed as it did her. And now with the baby, she could still dress herself and the baby before Salvador was ready.

"Please hurry and finish getting dressed, Salvador," said Lupe as she went to the front of the house. "I don't want us to be late for church again!" She stepped over the chair that was blocking the doorway of the kitchen, and she was going past the stove and sink toward the back door of the porch, when suddenly she stopped dead in her tracks.

Through the glass of their back door, Lupe could see the form of a big man with a rifle in hand. He was screaming like a wild man! At first Lupe thought that it was their good friend, Kenny White, but then she didn't think so. He was waving the rifle wildly and hollering like a madman and Kenny was always so soft-spoken.

Lupe froze. Instantly she was back home in their beloved box canyon in Mexico, and armed men were breaking into their home to rape and plunder. She began screaming as loudly as she could!

"Salvador!" yelled Lupe at the top of her lungs as she went running back through the kitchen and leaped over the chair on the floor. "There's someone with a gun!"

"No, Lupe!" the man outside the back door was screaming. "It's me, Kenny, for CHRISSAKES!"

And saying this, Kenny White busted the glass out of the door with his rifle's butt, reaching inside to unlock the door.

Salvador had been looking at himself in the mirror and whistling happily, tying his tie, when he heard Lupe's shouts. Then he heard the glass being broken out of their back door and Lupe's racing footsteps. He ran for his gun.

Opening the top drawer of their dresser, he took out his .38 snubnose Smith & Wesson, and raced down the hallway, pistol in hand. Lupe shot past him, picking up Hortensia in her arms. The little puppy was in fast pursuit, barking happily, thinking that they were playing. In the kitchen, Salvador came standing face to face with Kenny White. The old man's 30/30 rifle was pointing straight at Salvador's stomach. Salvador didn't know what to do.

"Jesus Christ!" said Kenny, seeing Salvador's .38 in hand, "put that gun away! I'm your friend, Sal! I just killed Eisner, and I don't want to DIE SOBER!"

And yelling this, the white-haired old man slapped down ten dollars on the kitchen table. "Give me a bottle of your best!"

Salvador couldn't figure out what the hell was going on. Eisner was the *gringo* who'd come into town about two years back and he'd opened up a little grocery store. But Salvador sure as hell wasn't going to argue with a man with a rifle. Kenny looked completely *loco*!

Quickly, Salvador got Kenny a quart bottle of whiskey from under the sink. Hungrily, the old man opened it, putting it to his lips, and he drank down six long gulps, each gulp shooting past his reddish-brown Adam's apple like a quick-moving steel ball.

"Damn, that's good!" he said, blowing out with power. "You've always made the best damn whiskey, Sal! You've never cheated no man with your liquor! You're a good *hombre*!"

Just then, Hortensia came crawling back into the room, trying to catch the little puppy that had gotten through the chair's legs.

"Oh, isn't she cute, all dressed up in her Sunday best," said Kenny, smiling happily. "And look at that puppy; he's a good one, too! Just like *Chingon*!" He bent over, putting his 30/30 in the crook of his left arm as he made baby talk with Hortensia and the little dog.

Lupe was at the doorway. She and Salvador glanced at each other, not knowing what to do. Salvador thought of maybe trying to wrestle the rifle away from the old man, but then thought better of it. Somebody could get shot.

"Well, I best be going," said Kenny, straightening up. "The cops will be here any minute, and I don't want you folks getting in any danger because of me.

"But I'm glad I killed that son-of-a-bitch!" added Kenny, bringing up his lever-action 30/30 Winchester. "I loaned him five hundred dollars when he first came to town, just like I loaned you, Sal, man-to-man, on a handshake. But you know what that son-of-a-bitch told me today when I went to his grocery store to get my money? He said to me, 'What money?' So I said to him, 'Hey, don't joke me, Eisner! I need that money, or I'm gonna lose my garage!'

"Hell, it's bad, Sal, you know that! Nobody's got money to pay me their bills, except you and maybe a couple of other guys in town.

"But you know what the snake then told me? He said, 'You got any witnesses that you loaned me that money? You got any written note?' I said, 'Eisner, you know I don't. We shook hands on it, man-to-man. Don't bull me like this!' Well, God as my witness, he just looked at me straight in the eye, Sal—I couldn't believe it, right in the eye—and said, 'Get out of my store! I owe you nothing!' Just like that. The store I helped him get started. So I said, 'All right, I'm going, but I'm coming back with my 30/30, and I'm going to kill you, you son-of-a-bitch!'

"So I went home and got my rifle and went back to his store and shot that snake five times—the dirty, lying, double-crossing son-of-a-bitch! And

I'm sorry that his wife and kid saw me do it—I really am—but, my God, I love my little garage, Sal! I didn't want to lose it!"

And Kenny lifted up the bottle and drank again, then levered a round into the chamber of the Model 94 Winchester and said, "Thank you, folks; you've been like family to me! God be with you. *Adios, amigos mios!*"

"Lupe," said Salvador, "take Hortensia and the dog into the next room."
Lupe quickly did.

"Wait, Kenny!" said Salvador, catching the old man at the back door. "Did anyone see you come here?"

"Hell, no, when the shooting started, people scattered!" he said, laughing.

"Then there's still time, Kenny," said Salvador. "Give me that rifle and I'll get rid of it for you, and I'll be your witness. I'll say I was with you all morning and you never shot the bastard!"

"You'd do that for me?" said Kenny, his blue eyes sparkling with *gusto*.

"You damn right!" said Salvador. "We're amigos! You saved my life before I got married! We're *compadres!*"

"Damnit, Sal," said Kenny, tears bursting from his eyes, "you're a real man! And I love you dearly for it, Sal, but like I said, there were witnesses; it won't work! His wife and kid saw me do it and, good God, I wish they hadn't, but what could I do?!"

"Look, I'll get fifty people from the *barrio*!" said Salvador. "We'll all say that you were drinking all night with us and never left us! Hell, *la gente* love you! You're a *macho de los buenos,* Kenny!"

Putting the bottle in his coat pocket, Kenny reached out with his 30/30 in one hand and took Salvador in both of his arms. "Give me one of 'em *abrazos,* you son-of-a-bitch!" he said with joy. "I love you with all *MI CORAZÓN, AMIGO!*" And he hugged Salvador with power. "Hug me! Yeah! Harder! HARDER, JESUS!" The tears streamed down from Kenny's eyes. "My old man, we never done this! And, my God, I loved him! But we just didn't know how to touch, or hug, or—shit, life is so much easier with *abrazos,* ain't it?"

"Yeah," said Salvador, hugging Kenny with all his strength. They held each other for a long, long time.

"Well," said Kenny, letting go of Salvador and wiping his eyes, "it was a good life; good friends, good whiskey, a little good loving now and then, and now a good rifle to end it all!"

"But, Kenny," said Salvador, "it will be Archie and our friends who'll have to come after you!"

"Don't worry, Sal," he said, pulling out the bottle of whiskey again. "I'd never shoot to kill a friend!" And he drank, nearly emptying the whole bottle. "See you in Hell, Sal!" he said. "Hell of a life! Damned shame it's got to end like this, though! Damnit, I was working on two cars! People from Oklahoma and they need their cars fixed *pronto*, and I needed the money to get the parts. Damn snake ruined a lot of lives!"

And saying this, he turned and quickly went out the back door, 30/30 in hand. "See you, *amigos! Vayan con Dios!*"

And just then, as Kenny went out the door, Salvador saw that Archie's big black Hudson was parked at the end of the driveway in the avocado trees. Instantly, Salvador ran back into the front room, yelling, "Get down! Get down!" But Lupe was already down. Ever since she could remember, she and her *familia* had been dodging bullets. "Archie and some deputies are in the orchard and—"

The huge explosion of Kenny's big 30/30 stopped Salvador's words.

"Archie, damnit," bellowed Kenny. "Don't come any closer! I don't want to kill a friend! But I ain't going to jail for killing a snake!"

"Kenny!" yelled Archie with his huge, booming voice, "you didn't kill him! Give yourself up!"

"Don't lie to me, Archie!" said Kenny. "Goddamnit, I shot the son-of-a-bitch five times!"

"That's true, you shot him, but he's alive!" yelled Chief-Deputy Palmer. Palmer and George Thompson were in the orchard, too.

"Damnit, Fred," Kenny said to his good drinking friend Palmer, "you and Archie are my friends! Don't try and trick me!"

"We ain't. Honest. Eisner's alive!" yelled Archie.

"Bullshit!" said Kenny, and he raised up his 30/30, firing two more quick shots into the eucalyptus tree beyond the orchard way above Fred Palmer's and Archie's heads. "I'm drinking this bottle down! Then I'm going to my garage, getting in my car, and driving off to Mexico and find myself a couple of *señoritas*! So nobody try to stop me, for chrissakes! I don't want to kill no friends!"

"Kenny, put that rifle down so we can talk!" yelled Fred. "We can't let you go, you know that! We're the law!"

"And you really didn't kill him!" yelled Archie. "The bastard is still breathing!"

"Bullshit! I killed him, sure as Hell! In old Mexico, I'd get a medal!" shouted Kenny. "Shit, a song, a *corrido,* would be sung about me, because there ain't no loss of honor in shooting a rattlesnake!"

"That's true!" bellowed Archie. "And I'd sing it, true as Hell, because, personally, I'm glad you shot the son-of-a-bitch, the way he treats folks! But he's still alive, so you got to give yourself up, Kenny, so you can shoot him again next year, and finish the job!"

On this one, Kenny BURST OUT LAUGHING. "Archie, you slick-talking Pala Indian son-of-a-bitch, I just don't know how the white men ever out-tricked you-breeds out of nothing! But, goddamn, I know I killed that son-of-a-bitch Eisner, and so I'm not going to jail for killing a rattlesnake!" He fired two more quick shots.

At that moment, a car came screeching up behind Archie and Fred Palmer. Two young cops from Oceanside leaped out of the car, opening fire. Kenny never moved. No, he just stood out there in the middle of the driveway, firing over their heads, as the two young cops—one named Davis—continued shooting at him.

A couple of the rounds came flying past Kenny and hit the windows where Salvador had been watching. Salvador dove for the floor again.

Lupe SCREAMED!

Salvador turned and saw a mass of blood covering his daughter's face and her little, white church-going dress. Crawling over to her, he saw that Hortensia was holding the puppy in her arms. Its head was missing.

The shooting continued, and more bullets came flying just barely over their heads. Salvador tore the bloody puppy from his daughter's grasp, throwing it as far as he could.

Then the shooting stopped as quickly as it had started. And now you could hear Archie's huge, bellowing voice, "You stupid son-of-a-bitches! He wasn't shooting to kill nobody! You had no reason to open fire on him, you stupid, ignorant, trigger-happy young BASTARDS!"

Then Archie rushed over to Lupe and Salvador's front door. "They killed him," he said, "Jesus Christ, those stupid, young Oceanside trigger-happy bastards killed him! Those stupid son-of-a-bitches! I kept yelling for them not to shoot!" Then seeing the blood, he finally asked, "Hey, is everyone okay here?"

But no one answered Archie.

No, Salvador was sitting on the floor, holding his wife and daughter in his arms. And they looked absolutely petrified.

"Jesus H. Christ," said Archie, seeing Hortensia all covered with blood. And across the room lay the splattered, bloody remains of the little black and white female puppy. And on the lime-colored wall, about three feet above the puppy's body, was a big, bloody mess where the puppy's body had hit the wall when Salvador had thrown it with all of his might.

The drums were beating!

The Drums were Beat, BEAT, BEATING! POUNDING! SINGING with the FORCES of CREATION!

SALVADOR WAS WAITING for his brother, Domingo, at the Carlsbad train station when the train came down the tracks from Los Angeles. Salvador had just driven down from Tustin where he and Lupe were now living in the ranch house where he made his liquor. He had a lot of things to explain to Domingo.

The whole country was going to Hell!

Everywhere businesses were closing their doors. Kenny White wasn't the only good, decent man who was taking the law into his own hands to settle money matters.

Watching the people get off the train, Salvador was excited with the prospect of seeing his brother. He wanted to tell his brother how hard he'd worked to get him out of prison a year and a half early, and that Chief-Deputy Palmer had explained to him that Domingo would have to be very careful, or this whole early parole business could backfire on them.

But, then, Salvador no more than saw Domingo get down from the train and he knew that he was in for big *problemas*. His brother looked wild. He didn't have any of that calm healthy look that Salvador had seen when he'd visited him in prison.

"Salvador!" yelled Domingo, rushing up to him with a big, rawboned grin. "Damn, it's good to see you, *mano*!"

They hugged in a big *abrazo*, chest-to-chest, then, they'd no more than stepped back from each other to get a better look, when Domingo said, "You got a drink?! I need one quick! All the way down on the train I was wondering what I'd want first—a woman or a drink! But then I got to thinking that a woman takes at least an hour, so I figure that I'd have a few drinks first! Eh, so you got some whiskey with you, *mano*?"

"Keep your voice down," said Salvador as he glanced around. There were people all around them. "Remember," he added, "it's Prohibition."

"Prohibition?" shouted Domingo, laughing to beat Hell. "Who the hell gives a shit about Prohibition! I wanna drink!"

Salvador rolled his eyes to the Heavens.

"Where's your car?" continued Domingo, licking his lips like a starving wolf. "You always got a pint under the seat!"

"Look, don't you have a bag or something?" asked Salvador.

"Hell, no!" said Domingo. "I threw everything away! And as soon as I can, I want to throw away these clothes that I'm wearing, too!" He put an arm around Salvador, turning him about. "Come on," he said, "I need for you to get me all new clothes, and a car, and a roll of money, and—"

Salvador stopped listening. My God, this man was crazy-*loco*. Nothing had changed. This was exactly how Domingo had been behaving just before they'd been caught and he'd gone to prison. What in the world had happened to all that peace of mind that Domingo had found in prison when he'd seen those ten thousand angels?

"All right," said Salvador. "Let's go."

"*Orale!*" said Domingo, grinning ear-to-ear.

Getting to the Moon, Salvador decided not to take Domingo to Palmer's place, where he'd be working. The man was just too dangerous. He'd first take him out of town, around the lagoon between Carlsbad and Oceanside and try and talk some sense to him in that eucalyptus forest east of town.

At the back side of the lagoon, Salvador parked the Moon and led Domingo up a trail and across a little swampy area on a couple of logs. They could hear the frogs in the water behind them.

"You got some barrels buried out here?" asked Domingo, licking his lips as they continued up a small embankment.

"Yeah," said Salvador. "A couple."

"Oh, good!" said Domingo. "That's a start! Let's drink a whole damn barrel, then go chase us some women with nice, big, *nalguitas*!"

"Okay," said Salvador, uncovering the first barrel. He had no intent of going anywhere with Domingo. He had a plan. He was going to let Domingo get stinking drunk, then he was going to call in Archie to come and run a bluff on Domingo, telling him in no uncertain terms that he had to watch his step or his parole officer—old man Palmer—was going to put him right back into prison. He couldn't afford to have his brother out here in the world without reins. Why, the wild fool could destroy everything that he and Lupe were working so hard to put together.

But it didn't work out as Salvador planned.

After a few drinks, Domingo didn't want to hear anything. He wanted to fight!

"Whadda the hell you mean, I got to go to work for Palmer and you got no money for me?!" bellowed Domingo. "I've been locked up, you hear me?! Locked up *como un perro*! I don't wanna work! I want to live!"

"Domingo, we got you out of prison early on the condition that you'd be an avocado doctor, don't you see?"

"No, I don't see shit! I only know that I've been locked up and you've been free all this time! You owe me!"

"I owe you?" yelled Salvador. "Hey, you just hold on to your horses, Domingo! I don't owe you NOTHING! It was your own doings that got you caught in the first place!"

"Bullshit! If that was true, then why have you worked so hard to get me out!"

"Jesus Christ!" said Salvador, shaking his head in disbelief. "I try to help you and now I owe you once again."

"Help me!?!" yelled Domingo. "Hell, it was me who helped you get your liquor making operation going! I, Domingo, who learned all about *la bootlegada* in Cheee-cago!"

Salvador rolled his eyes to the Heavens again. There was just no talking to his brother. Domingo hadn't taught him anything about liquor making. He'd learned how to make liquor from Al, the *Italiano.* His brother had snake eyes, meaning eyes that saw everything in reverse, so he could then blame everyone for everything.

"Look, Domingo, you better understand this right now," said Salvador. "You've cost me a fortune. First to pay my attorney to defend you when you got us caught, then I paid more to get you out early, not to say anything of the money and liquor I lost because you got us caught when you took that damn agent over to our distillery for a drink."

Salvador stopped. His brother was staring at him with this strange, far-away look, like he was maybe really seeing things for the first time from another human being's point of view.

"Well, if this is all true," said Domingo, "then why'd you wanna get me out early if I'm such a terrible expense to you every time you turn around? Eh, you tell me?"

Salvador bit his lower lip and tears suddenly came to his eyes. He shrugged. "I don't know," he said, "I guess, it's because, well, we're brothers, Domingo."

Seeing his brother's tears, Domingo burst out laughing. "Well, then, you fool, you should've left me in prison, *pendejo,* if you really got no money for me!" yelled his brother. "I had everything I wanted there in San Quentin! Food, bed, *amigos,* the best *amigos* I've ever had, and respect!

Real respect! And plenty of *mota a lo cabrón*!" His face was all red and his eyes were bloodshot. He licked his lips.

"Oh, no," he added, not laughing anymore, "you got me out of jail, *hermanito,* and now you got to come through for me. You're not going to cheat me, you cheap son-of-a-bitch, and just leave me hanging as you did our father!"

And shouting this, Domingo leaped forward like a wild-looking wolf, trying to grab Salvador by the throat and choke him to death, but he was too drunk and Salvador was able to shove him away. Domingo went falling backward over a log into the grass and mud.

"Don't start all this," said Salvador. "I've told you a dozen times, we didn't leave our father, Domingo. He left us!"

"Bullshit! How can a man leave his *familia,* eh, you tell me that?"

"How could you leave children all the way from Texas to Chicago?"

Hearing this, Domingo eyed his brother with his red, bloodshot eyes. His eyes truly did look like a snake's eyes. "Oh, you're really looking for a beating, aren't you," said Domingo, putting his left hand on the log and pushing himself up to his feet—never once taking his eyes off his brother.

And here they stood face to face, two brothers ready to grab hold of each other and go down fighting.

AND IN CORONA, California, some sixty miles to the northeast, Doña Margarita was just lying down to take a little rest when in her Heart, she felt a pain, but she didn't quite know what it was at first. She Breathed in of God, then she Knew. The story of Cain and Abel was at work once again.

SUDDENLY, with this wild-eyed scream, Domingo lunged at Salvador again, ripping his left sleeve halfway off his coat as he tried to wrestle him to the ground. But the mud and grass were slick and mushy, so Salvador was able to break loose from his brother's grip and shove him away once again.

"You owe me!" yelled Domingo, grabbing a tree limb so he wouldn't fall this time. He looked desperate. "You hear me, I want half of everything that you and Lupe made while I was locked up! That's only fair, you son-of-a-bitch!"

He shook his head in grief. "Back home in Mexico we had everything when I left to go find our father. Everything! Cattle, horses, a home, and when I got back—after being trapped in Cheee-acago like a slave—everything was gone. There was nothing left, but burned out ruins!"

"Domingo, Domingo," said Salvador, "we've been over this a hundred times. It was wartime. Everything got destroyed. We thought you were dead. You just disappeared one day without saying anything."

"I wanted to surprise our father who'd gone to work, you know, on that highway from San Diego to Del Mar, California, but those tricky son-of-a-bitch Texas Rangers arrested me at the border for nothing, and sent me to Chicago to work off a crime I never committed in the steel mills. I was fourteen years old! I KNEW NOTHING!"

"Look, Domingo, we can't just keep going over this or we'll go crazy," said Salvador. "We got to stop this and figure out what to do here, today, right now. What happened to that peace you had when I saw you in prison? You were making so much sense then, Domingo."

"Well, yeah, sure," said Domingo in a drunken slur. He was still holding on to the thin tree branch for support. "Everyone finds peace and makes sense when they're locked up, Salvador. But turn that dog or horse loose, and he goes crazy again, wanting everything! It's only natural. That's what's wrong with the *pinchee* world! We're all starving with greed!

"Oh, I tell you, God as my witness, I'm going to get rich, *hermanito*!" he said, slipping and sliding in the grass and mud as he held on to the thin branch. "I can feel it here in my bones! I'm going to find that gold mine—the one I told you about before I went to prison—and I'm going to get so damn rich, that I'm going to be able to re-buy all the lands that our grandfather Don Pio settled, and I'm going to rebuild our village and be 'mister' out here in the world, just as I was in prison!"

And he smiled this wild, drunken smile. "Mister *Señor* Domingo Villaseñor, they'll call me. And . . . and then I'm going to find all my children from Texas to Chicago and . . . and . . . what's wrong with you, Salvador," he said, seeing his brother shaking his head. "Why, I swear you're looking at me like some pussy-whipped *hombre* that has forgotten the realities of life?! Men want everything! And you know that, *cabrón*! It's our *pinchee* nature, so don't play the fool with me! I want it all, Salvador! *Todo! TODO! TODO!* Now empty your pockets," he said, "and give me half of your money, and then let's go find some women with plenty juicy, hot *nalgas*! Oh, I love a woman *con carne* on her ass, so I can grip her close with two hands full!"

Salvador could see there was just no speaking with his brother. He reluctantly brought out his roll of money, and he was just beginning to count it out, when Domingo leaped forward, grabbing it.

"Good," said Domingo, his eyes wild with greed. "I knew you were just holding out on me! I'll take it all! And after I spend this, I'll want half of what you and Lupe have hidden at your house, too!"

Salvador swallowed. This was all the money he and Lupe had in all the world, but his brother would never believe him. No, he was now caressing the money as if it was the most beautiful woman he'd ever seen.

Suddenly, Salvador realized why a good man like Kenny White had taken the law in his own hands and shot old man Eisner with his 30/30. There was no doubt about it, he, Salvador, was going to have to kill his brother. There was just no way around it. Domingo was right, he should have left him in prison.

Salvador pretended to walk off to a private distance to take a leak, but instead he opened up his coat—which was ripped and muddy—and brought out his pistol. It was getting late. The last of the big mallards were coming into the lagoon. The frogs and crickets were getting louder and louder. The Sun had just gone down and the Sky was full of spectacular colors of blue and pink and orange with streaks of gold.

Domingo sat down on the fallen log behind Salvador and began to sing an old *ranchera* from their beloved mountains of *Jalisco,* clutching the money close to his heart. Salvador took a deep breath. This was it. His brother was crazy and dangerous, so there was no other way. He turned, pistol in hand, coming up behind Domingo.

"NO!" SCREAMED DOÑA MARGARITA, sitting up in her bed in her little shack behind Luisa's house. The Father Sun had just gone down and she'd lain down to take a nap. "You will not! Do you hear me, Salvador! YOU WILL NOT!"

And in her mind's eye, the old woman saw Salvador holding his pistol to the back of his brother's neck ready to fire. Quickly, Doña Margarita stopped her yelling and began to pray. For only in Prayer did One then Unite with the Almighty, and hence were able to bring the Heavens down Here to the Earth.

THREE GREAT WHITE BIRDS came out of the evening Sky in Carlsbad, California, circling above the rosy-colored waters of the lagoon.

Pistol in hand, Salvador looked up and saw the magnificent birds. He lowered his pistol. He couldn't do it. The three great white Snow Geese came
in with a flare of flapping wings and lit upon the water. Salvador took a
deep breath, feeling overwhelmed with the Beauty of the closing Day and
coming Night. He slipped the pistol back into his pants and sat down on
the fallen log beside his brother.

Still singing, "*Jalisco no te rajes,*" Domingo turned with a drunken
smile and put his arm about his brother's shoulders. Watching the ducks
and geese out on the water, Salvador opened his mouth wide and began to
sing, too, joining his brother.

LATER THAT WEEK, Lupe was in the front bedroom sleeping with
Hortensia. Salvador was down the hallway in the back bedroom sleeping
on the floor on a mat. For three days and nights Salvador had been working around the clock at the distillery process. He'd lost a lot of time helping his brother Domingo to settle in and get to work as an avocado doctor.

It was just past midnight and the flames of the fire underneath the cop-
per kettle were singing, burning blue-hot when the kettle suddenly
EXPLODED like a BOMB!

Salvador's body was thrown across the entire room against the wall,
knocking him unconscious.

Lupe, in the next room, was knocked out of her bed. Hortensia was
SCREAMING! The whole room of the distillery had erupted into flame!
Lupe was on her feet and rushing down the hallway to see what happened,
but she couldn't get the door open to their back bedroom no matter how
hard she pushed. Salvador's body was blocking the door. But Lupe didn't
know that. All she knew was that her daughter was screaming in terror and
the whole place was becoming a burning *infierno*!

Lupe finally turned and rushed back down the hallway, picked up Hortensia, wrapped her in a blanket, then she saw Salvador's gun and why,
she'd never know, but she picked it up. Then she remembered their can of
money and she rushed out of the bedroom, down the hall, into the kitchen,
got their money and was out the front door with money, gun, and daughter.

Lupe raced across the yard, put Hortensia in their car and closed the
door. Then for some reason, she put the gun and money up in a fork of the
tree under which their car was parked. She turned, and saw that their
whole house was now engulfed in huge flames, shooting twenty, thirty feet
up into the night sky.

Lupe made the sign of the cross over herself, and never hesitated once as she ran back across the yard and into the burning *infierno*. She rushed back down the hallway and put her shoulder to that door again and again with all her God-given power, shoving and pushing. Finally it opened up just enough for her to see that something on the floor was blocking the door. And when she got down low, under all the smoke and flames to see what it was, her whole heart leaped up into her mouth. It was Salvador's leg.

"Salvador!" she yelled. "SALVADOR!"

But he didn't answer her. She reached in through the crack, grabbing hold of his leg and shook it. There was no response, so she figured he was already dead until she heard his voice.

"Lupe," he said, ever so softly, "Looo-pe."

Hearing him call her name, filled Lupe with a power that she'd never known before. She was now her mother who'd gone down to the plaza in their village back in Mexico to save her brother, Victoriano, from being hung by renegade soldiers. She was now her Yaqui Indian grandmother who'd also been touched by the hand of the Almighty when she'd had the faith to send her youngest child out of their burning hut to find a man whose eyes were filled with the Holy Light of the Creator.

Lupe stood up and put her shoulder to the door again, and with the power of all her ancestry, she gave a SCREAMING shove, and the door opened enough for her to get down low and crawl into the room as the flames shot over her head.

She got hold of her husband's foot and dragged him away from the door so she could open it all the way, then—gagging and coughing—she dragged his body out of the burning Hell and down the hallway. This was when the first barrel of whiskey exploded, shattering walls and windows like toys!

The siren was coming!

Lupe could now hear the siren screaming closer and closer as she dragged Salvador's body off the porch and across the yard to their car. He was still unconscious and truly heavy. Lupe opened the driver's door and tried to get Salvador up into the Moon so he could drive them off before the firemen and the law arrived. But he wouldn't come-to and he was all loose, like a bag of water.

Finally realizing the hopelessness of the situation, Lupe dragged Salvador around the car to the passenger side. And how she did this she'd never know, but she just suddenly grabbed Salvador up in her arms and threw him into the Moon, closing the door. Then she ran around and got into the driver's seat. She tried to remember how she'd watched Salvador start the car a hundred times. But every time she'd press down on the starter, the Moon would just leap forward and die. Finally, pushing the clutch all the way down to the floor, she got the car started and was backing up so she could take off when she remembered the gun and the money.

She braked, trying to figure out what to do, but the fire truck was almost at their driveway, and Hortensia was crying once again. She couldn't get the gun and money right now. She tucked her daughter in with her blanket, soothed her face with a loving touch, got hold of the steering wheel again, and drove off just as the siren came screeching into their driveway. She almost hit the fire truck head-on, but didn't, and she sped off—eyes closed, praying as she went.

Half a mile down the road, Salvador began to regain consciousness.

"You almost got yourself killed!" Lupe yelled at him. "You almost got us all killed, Salvador! Oh, I'm so mad at you that I could kill you!"

She pulled off to the side of the road. They could see the leaping flames of the fire even from this distance, and every time another barrel of whiskey exploded, the whole *infierno* would leap hundreds of feet into the night sky!

"What happened?" asked Salvador. He still didn't quite understand what had happened. "Did the stove blow up?"

"Can you drive, Salvador?" asked Lupe.

Two sheriff's cars were coming toward them, their sirens screaming in the night.

"I don't think so," said Salvador.

"Oh, my God," said Lupe, tucking in her daughter once again, then she took hold of the steering wheel and got their Moon automobile back on the road. She didn't know how to drive, but she had no choice. Once more Salvador was unconscious.

Lupe continued down the road, driving toward the oncoming sheriff's cars; eyes focused, face determined. After all, she was a mother now, so come Hell or high water, miracles had to be of her makings, just as they'd been for her mother, and her mother's mother.

Lupe drove on, passing right alongside the two screaming sheriff's cars.

DOÑA MARGARITA had both of her hands over her eyes. She was exhausted. She didn't want to keep seeing what it was that her Heart

Vision saw. But oh, she was so proud of Lupe. Her daughter-in-love was truly on her way to becoming *el eje,* the hub of her *familia.*

"Thank You, Lord God," she said once again. "Thank You with all my Heart and Soul. Your Will is being done!"

"Thank you," she heard the voice of the Almighty Creator say right back at her.

Tears of joy came to the old woman's eyes. "We're doing pretty good, You and I, eh, *Papito*? We're doing very good."

"Yes, We Are."

LUPE DROVE UP to her sister Maria's house, which was just a few miles up the road. Even though Salvador hadn't spoken to Maria since she'd kidnapped their daughter, Hortensia, and taken her to be baptized, Lupe wasn't going to let herself be concerned with this.

Maria and her short little husband, Andres, were standing in their front yard when Lupe drove up. The two of them had woken up when the sirens screeched past their home. And even from this distance, they could see and hear the explosions of the whiskey barrels.

"Oh, my God," said Maria, rushing up to her sister as Lupe came wheeling into their driveway and crashed into their front porch. "What happened? Is that your house that's on fire?"

"Yes," said Lupe, "and Salvador is half dead and they'll be looking for us. But I can't drive."

"You're telling me!" said Andres, looking at the damage that she'd done to their porch.

"I almost ran into the fire truck, too, and then the two sheriff's cars!" added Lupe. She was beside herself.

"Andres can drive you," said Maria. "He can take you where you want, but where will you go, Lupe? This fancy car will be recognized anywhere you go."

"I don't know," said Lupe. "If only we could just get to Corona and maybe hide before they start looking for us."

"No, Lupe," said Maria, getting her sister out of the car, "you're not going anywhere. Just look at you, *mi hijita.* You're all burned, Lupe. This is exactly what my dream was all about when I came and took Hortensia to be baptized. You and Salvador and your child were burned to death in your home! I've been praying for you every night since. Ask Andres, he'll tell you! For weeks I've been telling him that you and Salvador need to get out of your *bootlegada* business," she said, making the sign of the cross over herself. "Come, we got to get you and Salvador into the house and get some pig fat on these burns."

"But what will we do with the car?" asked Lupe. "They'll see it here."

"Andres," said Maria, "you get in the car and drive it off right now!"

"But to where?" asked Andres.

"You figure that out! Now go! Go! And far, too. And leave it. Just leave it!"

"All right, all right, I'm going," said the small-boned man. He was really scared, but he knew better than to argue with his wife, who was a bull of a woman, just like Salvador's sister, Luisa.

Andres got in the Moon and drove off as Maria helped her sister and Salvador and their child into her house. Andres was so scared that he wasn't driving any better than Lupe, swerving from side to side. Another fire truck was speeding down the gravel road with a sheriff's car in fast pursuit. Andres almost hit the fire truck, and went off into a ditch as the two screaming vehicles shot past him.

By the time Andres got to the highway, he was sweating nails, but he now did a brilliant move. And not because he'd figured it out, but because, simply, luck would have it that he saw no traffic toward the south, and so he turned left, going toward San Juan Capistrano.

INSIDE, UNDER THE LIGHTS, Maria saw the immensity of Lupe's and Salvador's burns. Only their child, Hortensia, wasn't burned like Maria had seen in her dream.

Salvador was finally becoming conscious and the first thing out of his mouth—once he realized that Lupe and Hortensia were alive—was "Lupe, did you get my gun and our money?"

Lupe nodded. "Yes, Salvador, I got them both," she said.

"Good," he said, "good, then we'll be okay."

And saying this, he dropped back off into unconsciousness.

"Men," said Maria, putting an herbal pack on Lupe's face, "they're such fools! Who thinks of guns and money at a time like this? He's lucky to be alive!"

"I do," said Lupe.

"You do what?" said Maria.

"After wrapping up Hortensia in a blanket," said Lupe, "I don't know why, but I thought of Salvador's gun and our money even before—God help me—I thought of my husband."

Maria laughed. "Really, but that's awful, Lupe! Whatever possessed you to think of a gun and money at a time like that?"

Lupe shrugged. "I don't know."

"You did good," whispered Salvador.

Both women turned to see Salvador. His face was all swollen and blistered with burns and his eyes were closed and covered with soot. He looked awful.

"You did good," he repeated, "you did very good. Promise me, *mi amor,* that you'll always think first of our child and your survival before you think . . . of me."

"Oh, Salvador," said Lupe, getting up and coming to his arms, "I didn't want you to hear that. I feel so terrible that I first went after—"

"Sssssh," said Salvador, reaching for Lupe with his eyes all swollen and closed, "you did good, *querida;* in this world of men, a woman needs a gun, and money. My sisters, my mother, I couldn't help them. I was only ten years old."

"This, I can understand," said Maria. "Only women like me, who are stronger than any two men, got a chance without a gun. You're right, Salvador, but I'm surprised that you know this." Maria made the sign of the cross over herself. Her terrible nightmare had, indeed, been turned around by Lupe and Salvador's Love for each other. In her dream she'd seen her baby sister and her *familia* burned to death.

ANDRES DROVE THE MOON to the train station of San Juan Capistrano, parked, glanced around, then got out of the vehicle and ran for the train that was headed south. He pretended to get on the train, but he slid between the cars and disappeared into the little Mexican *barrio* of San Juan on the other side of the tracks. Then he headed north on foot.

It was daybreak by the time Andres came walking into his yard. Victoriano's truck was parked in front. Every day Victoriano came by to pick up Andres so they could go to work together. This day Victoriano and Andres decided to not go to work and stay home and fix the porch that Lupe had run into and keep working around outside in case the authorities came by asking any questions.

Twice that day the sheriff's cars came shooting by and once it looked like they were going to stop, but they didn't. It was evening before Salvador was clear-headed enough to ask Victoriano to contact Archie.

The next morning when Victoriano came by at daybreak, to pick up Andres so they could go to work, Lupe took her brother aside and asked him to please drop her off at her house on their way to work.

Victoriano glanced at Salvador. He was sound asleep on a mattress on the floor in the front room. "Have you talked this over with your husband?" asked Victoriano. Lupe shook her head. "Well, then, no," said Victoriano, "I can't take you back there without his agreement. My God, Lupe, you two are lucky to have gotten away!"

"All right," said Lupe, refusing to discuss the matter, "then I'll walk. It's not too far."

Victoriano looked at this baby sister of his. Ever since she'd been a child she'd been hardheaded, especially once she'd made up her mind. "All right," he said, "we'll drive by and if it looks safe, I'll drop you off. But why in God's name do you want to go back?"

Lupe didn't know how to explain it to him. But the night before the explosion, she'd taken off her wedding ring—either while she'd been doing the dishes or washing up to go to bed—and she wanted to go back and find it. Also, she'd left her Colonel's card. The card that her first love had given her when she'd been seven years old . . . back home in their box canyon in Mexico. All these years she'd kept her Colonel's card along with her rosary and the rolling pin for making *tortillas* that her mother had given her when she'd also turned seven years old. And of course, she wanted to get Salvador's gun and their money from the tree fork. Oh, how she hoped to God that the authorities hadn't found them.

She got in the truck with her brother and Andres and they drove down the road to where Salvador and Lupe had set up their distillery. It was the longest couple of miles Lupe had ever traveled in her life. Each tree, each clump of brush stood out, looking at her as if they were alive. She remembered back to their box canyon, to the day when she'd hid in the thick foliage down by the creek as the shooting and killing and raping had gone on all above her in their village. She'd hid there for so long praying for God to please help make her invisible that she'd finally seen the foliage all about her breathing in and breathing out.

Three times Lupe and her brother and Andres drove by the old burned-down ranch house before they pulled into the driveway. Up close, Lupe could see that all that was left of their house was the rock chimney of the fireplace and the iron stove in the kitchen. The rest of the place had burned to the ground. It looked like the fire had also almost gotten to the barn, which was across the yard. The ground itself in front of the house was covered with ashes. Pieces of the distillery were all over the place. The initial explosion had been devastating!

"Are you sure you want to do this?" asked Victoriano.

Lupe nodded, saying, "Yes."

Andres got out of the passenger's side and helped Lupe out. As soon as they'd left, Lupe walked over to the pepper tree under which the Moon had been parked. She could see the dark handle of the gun and the top of the can with their money. But she didn't go near them. She breathed. Something had happened to her deep inside when she'd gone rushing down the hallway in that burning *infierno* to get her daughter. It was like she'd opened up inside herself and she now had this extra sense about knowing what to do and what not to do.

She just didn't know how to explain it. But after she'd made the decision to go down that hallway to get her daughter, the whole world had slowed down, and she'd then seen everything with such utter clarity. She wasn't alone anymore. It was as if she now had a holy self friend, hovering above her about twelve or fifteen feet in the air, and this Holy Self Friend had a Vision and a Voice of her own, telling Lupe and showing Lupe what to do so clearly.

Like right now, at this moment, Lupe could hear a car coming, and this Voice from deep within her was telling her that it was the law and so she should hide immediately.

Without question, Lupe did what this Voice told her, slipping into the barn.

Looking through the cracks of the barn door, Lupe saw that it was Archie and another car with a couple of officers whom she'd never seen before. She thanked her Holy Self Friend and watched these officers get out of their vehicles along with Archie—who towered over them—and go over to the house and kick around in the ashes. Twice Archie looked over toward the barn. Each time Lupe cringed, closing her eyes in concentration, and prayed with all her might that they didn't come over to the barn and find her.

Then the lawmen were gone, just like that, and Archie, too. That's when Lupe knew that someone was, indeed, watching her from above. She turned and saw that behind her was a big-eyed owl in the rafters of the old barn watching her.

Lupe began to hiccup. The owl, *el tecolote,* was a very powerful omen among her mother's people, the Yaqui. Quickly, she made the sign of the cross over herself.

All morning Lupe looked through the ashes of the burned down ranch house for her wedding ring and her Colonel's card, but she couldn't find either one. Everything was gone. They had *nada, nada,* nothing left. No clothes, no shoes, no furniture, not even their cooking utensils. Everything had been burned or blown to pieces. Tears came to Lupe's eyes. She felt like once more her whole world had been destroyed. But she didn't lose hope. The Voice within her kept her calm. Without knowing it, Lupe was now instinctively learning to work her Ninth, Tenth, and Eleventh Senses.

In the early afternoon, Lupe walked across the yard and got Salvador's gun from the tree fork along with the money, and started for her sister's house. She walked across the fields and through the orchards, keeping away from the roads.

The moment Lupe walked in through the front door, Salvador went into a rage. Seeing how upset her husband was, Lupe started laughing.

"This isn't funny!" yelled Salvador.

"Oh, yes, it is," said Lupe. "How many times were you gone for days without a word, Salvador, and I was supposed to just stay home and keep my faith in God and not get upset?"

"That was different!" yelled Salvador.

"Why, because you're a man?"

"Yes! I mean, no, but because, well, I was out working, bringing home the money!"

"So what I do isn't important, then?"

"Well, no, I'm not saying that, it's that, well, Lupe—damnit, I don't want you going back there again, and that's that!"

"Salvador, I'm going back tomorrow," she said, calmly fixing her hair with her fingertip as she'd seen her mother do when dealing with difficult situations with her father.

"But why in God's name would you do that!" he yelled. "You already brought back our money and my gun!"

"Because," she said, "I didn't find what I was looking for."

Salvador stared at her. "And what is this that you're looking for?" he asked.

"Salvador," she said, "I lost my wedding ring in that fire and . . . and I'm going back to find it."

He took a big breath. He'd worked so hard to get her that ring. It was a real diamond. Harry, his Jewish friend from Santa Ana who'd made their wedding clothes for them, had helped him get it. This diamond was the first in their families' history. "But Lupe, I'm afraid for you," he said quietly. "I'll buy you another one someday."

"No, Salvador," she said, "that would not be the same."

The tears were flowing from her eyes. He didn't know what to say.

"I'll go with you, Lupe," said Maria.

"Oh, no!" said Salvador. "Don't say that, Maria! Talk some sense into her! Diamond or not, a ring is just a ring! Didn't you do enough when you took our daughter to have her baptized without us!"

Maria walked right up, getting into Salvador's face. "You will not intimidate me with guilt or reason, Salvador! Do you hear me, my baby sister dragged you out of burning fire, turning disaster into a miracle just like our mother, against all reason! My baby sister *es una mujer de poder*! I will go with her tomorrow if she goes, and THAT'S THAT," added Maria.

There was nothing more Salvador could say. He could barely move without screaming in pain. And Maria was every bit as powerful and stubborn as his sister, Luisa. These were women that would've been better off being men. They had *tanates* so huge that they dragged on the ground!

For three days Lupe and Maria went every afternoon with Hortensia to the burned-out house up the road and searched among the foot-deep ashes. On the third day, Lupe not only found her wedding ring, but miracle of miracles, she also found the rolling pin that her grandfather had made for her mother. And she found her rosary, too.

Suddenly, Lupe remembered that she'd taken off her wedding ring and placed it and her rosary alongside of the rolling pin on the windowsill of the kitchen above the sink as she'd begun to do the dishes after dinner.

And she'd found the three of them together, ring, rosary, and rolling pin! This was, indeed, a sign straight from the Holy Creator!

Lupe gave a *grito* of *gusto* to the sky, then made the sign of the cross over herself with the crucifix of her rosary, giving thanks to the Mother of God to whom she'd been praying every night since the fire.

Maria also made the sign of the cross over herself. There were no accidents.

The old Mexican saying was really true, *las extremidades del humano son las oportunidades de Dios!*

18

*And so Adam and Eva stepped forward, not blaming each
other but united in Love, Respect, and a Natural Awe for
One another — REFLECTIONS of the CREATOR.*

SALVADOR WOULD NEVER SEE Lupe the same ever again. She
just wasn't the same young, innocent girl that he married. Coming in
that afternoon with their wedding ring all intact, she walked up to him
with her eyes glowing with a power he'd never seen before. Her whole
body moved differently.

"Look, Salvador," she said, with tears of joy running down her face, "I
found our ring."

"My God!" he said.

"And she found the rolling pin that our mother gave her, and they were
both with her rosary."

"It's a miracle," whispered Salvador.

"Of course," said Maria, making the sign of the cross over herself. "I
told you so. There is no other way for us women to survive, but in the
making of miracles."

Lupe now moved with the grace of an inspired woman, *el eje,* of her
familia.

Salvador watched Lupe scrub the ring with such care and love and
devotion, that it brought tears to his eyes. He was truly in awe of Lupe.
From her would come all of his children. From her would come their
whole future. His mother had been absolutely right. The lessons that
Lupe would teach him about Life, *la Vida,* would dwarf his in the end.

He felt so proud to be married to this creature that just the curve of her
hips, her breasts, the tilt of her neck sent chills of fire to his groin.

Once the ring was scrubbed and clean, Lupe brought it over to Salvador—

who was still lying down on the mattress on the floor—and he took it, admired it, kissed it, and put it back on her finger, then kissed her fingertips, his eyes glowing.

THAT SAME NIGHT Archie came by and asked which one of them had been over at the house a few days back and had been hiding in the barn.

"And I can see that it wasn't you," he said to Salvador, "because you're still pretty well fuc—I mean, screwed up, but one of you was in there."

"How do you know that someone was in the barn?" asked Lupe.

Archie looked at Lupe and licked his big, loose lips. "An owl told me," he said.

Lupe turned all red.

"Look," he said, "you can't take any more chances like that, Lupe. It's a good thing the two guys I was with don't talk owl. You see, Domingo has disappeared on old man Palmer, revoking his parole, and so maybe I can turn this whole thing around and pin it on him—the damn fool—since he's going back to prison anyway. But you two are going to have to get the Hell out of the whole area so I can pull this off. You see, the sheriff's department of Orange County has decided to make an example out of you, Sal, and is combing the whole area. Can you travel, *amigo*?" added Archie.

"Do I have a choice?" said Salvador.

Archie only laughed.

"No problema," said Doña Margarita, who'd come in a few hours earlier and she was attending to Salvador's and Lupe's burns with chicken fat and herbs and having them drink gallons and gallons of her special tea. "They won't have to travel very far to disappear."

"Whadda you gonna do," asked Archie, laughing, "kill 'em with your medicine weeds or use your witchcraft like Salvador told me you did to make those barrels of whiskey disappear?"

Refusing to be insulted, Doña Margarita looked straight up at the huge, towering lawman and said, "No, Archie, when you need miracles, you go to God, but when you need protection from the law, you go to the man who owns the law."

"And who might that be?" asked Archie, still laughing. "The governor up in Sacramento?"

"No, that's too far for me to travel," she said, "so I won't go to him, but that doesn't mean I wouldn't go to the governor to get my way." And saying this, she turned and asked Epitacio to get their truck and drive her.

"We'll be back within the hour," she added, going out the door, "and the Will of God will be done!"

"Hey, did I upset her?" asked Archie. "I didn't mean anything. I was just having fun."

Salvador shook his head. "You're not big enough to upset her, Archie. You just showed her how small of faith you are. She'll move mountains, you'll see. And within the hour, as she said."

Archie blew out, tipping back his Stetson. "Yeah, I believe it. My grandmother, she was the story-keeper of our people back in Texas. The keeper of our language and—oh, her chants could move mountains, too! I just don't see how we lost to the White Man with all the powers of our old people."

"My mother says we didn't," said Salvador. "It's just taking us a little time to gather ourselves up again."

Hearing this, Archie laughed so hard he almost choked.

ONCE THEY WERE OUTSIDE and on the road, Doña Margarita told Epitacio to take her to see her old *amigo* Irvine. "He owes me one," she said, "just as God, Himself, has owed me many in the past. And it's late and so he'll be home with his goats at this hour. I don't care what people say, Eee-rvine is a very good *hombre* in his *corazón*."

And so Doña Margarita was back within the hour and Salvador and Lupe disappeared from the face of the Earth, hiding out on the back side of Irvine's huge ranch in the Trabuco Canyon while the law hunted for them everywhere.

All over the Southland, the Mexican people were being rounded up by the thousands like cattle and being shipped back to Mexico. Many of these people had been born here in the United States and had never even set foot across the border, but the authorities didn't care. The whole country was falling apart, so someone had to be blamed and there just weren't enough Jews in the area to take it out on.

Everywhere *familias* were being broken up.

Among all this, Salvador and Lupe's Moon automobile was stolen from the parking lot in front of the railroad station at San Juan Capistrano. And when Salvador was told, he started screaming like a madman with vengeance. He'd loved his Moon! He wanted to kill, to put a curse on that damn car thief!

But his wise old mother, Doña Margarita, only said, "Be happy, *mi hijito,* that you had such a fine car to get stolen. Most people will never have such a fine, beautiful car even for one minute in all their lives."

"But *mama,*" screamed Salvador, "how can you say this! My coat was in that car! Cash was in the glove compartment! Lupe's coat with the fur collar was in the back!"

"All the better," said his mother, refusing to be turned. "Look what a great find these people will get to enjoy who stole your car. Maybe they were hungry. Maybe they have a bunch of children. Maybe they have never had such good fortune in all their lives. No, *mi hijito,* let that car go. It's gone, and so now just enjoy, here inside you, the good memories you had *con tu carro.*"

"But *mama,* how can you talk like this?" he yelled.

"But how can I not talk like this," said the old Indian woman calmly. "This is exactly what I had to do with each and every child I lost . . . in the Revolution."

Her eyes filled with tears. They were under a grove of oak trees, camping on the little creek that ran through the Trabuco Canyon. Salvador and Lupe were now living like wild Indians, hiding from the law. Epitacio and Doña Margarita had just driven out with some groceries for them and gave them the news of their Moon automobile.

"I loved each child so much," she continued. "Alejo, tall and strong and brave and blue-eyed like your father; Teorodo, looking so much like Alejo but a poet here inside of his heart; Emilia, as beautiful and delicate as an angel; Jose, small and dark with his whole soul here in his liquid-black eyes; Lucha, always laughing and dancing ever since a child; Jesus, Maria, Lupe—sixteen children in all I lost, each one a passing here between my legs with sacred blood, each one a joy of hope and dreams—*esperanzas*! And then, just like that, they were brutally taken away from me by that Revolution. So, of course, I hold, here in my heart, only the joy I had with them, *mi hijito,* or I would've gone crazy-*loca* with grief long ago."

She Breathed in of *Papito.* "Let these next people enjoy your *carrito, mi hijito.* Wish them well, in fact, for only then will you be free and fate can then stay open to you, giving you no end of surprises. Do you see, *mi hijito,* to close in with hate and anger is to kill yourself. I know, I tried that, too, and it doesn't work. We must keep open, in order to Breathe of *Papito* with each Holy Breath we take."

She smiled, making the sign of the cross over herself. And Salvador—didn't want to—but he started smiling, too. He just couldn't help it. His old mother was truly the wizard of the whole UNIVERSE!

"All right, *mama*," he said. "I'll do it! May those no good dirty son-of-a-bitches who stole my car have a great time! May they find that money in the glove compartment and have a feast with their kids!"

"There, that's it, *mi hijito!*" said the old lady with *gusto*.

Just then, as if on cue, old man Irvine himself drove up in his truck and he had a side of beef with him, a sack of flour and vegetables, and also his last jug of Salvador's whiskey.

Laughing and drinking, they gathered up fallen oak wood, swept clean an area with brush so that they wouldn't start a range fire, and got a barbecue going.

Old man Irvine just couldn't stop laughing when he visited with Doña Margarita.

And it was said that he was a man who never laughed. But around Doña Margarita, the rich, powerful old man laughed and laughed *con carcajadas,* finding *gusto* in all of life's awful twists. Also, he'd brought Doña Margarita a case of toilet paper—which was hard to find these days. And why this was so funny, nobody could figure out.

Then as if this wasn't a big enough turn of events, the next day, Archie drove up. Salvador was making jerky with the rest of the beef. Archie took Salvador aside and told him that he had a deal for him. But no, it had nothing to do with Domingo or the law. In fact, this deal had everything to do with a situation outside of the law. It had to do with Salvador's reputation of having castrated those two little pigs in Carlsbad to teach Tomas a lesson and then cutting that hog open in bed with the farmer in Santa Ana to teach him a lesson, too.

"But this job is a little more delicate," said Archie, pulling at his big nose. "This involves a rich, powerful man who has a horse ranch just north of Los Angeles. It seems that this rich man was originally from back east and he needs to be reminded that money alone don't buy you security out here in the wild west with us Indians still running loose."

"And how much is this job worth?" asked Salvador.

"It's worth, well, I won't lie, I'll be truthful with you, Salvador, five hundred big ones, with two hundred up front in cash."

Salvador's heart leaped. This was very serious money. Hell, in the can that Lupe had saved from the fire they'd only had sixty dollars, which was a fortune compared to what most people had nowadays. But still Salvador now just looked at Archie in the eyes, not saying a word, because if Archie said that he wasn't lying and was being truthful, then this meant that he was really lying, and big time. And if he said that this was a delicate job and was worth $500, then this meant that the job was probably almost impossible and going for at least a thousand dollars and that Archie was pocketing $500 right off the top.

Also, Salvador figured if these people, who wanted this job done, had gone to all the trouble of finding out who it was who'd done those pigs' balls in Carlsbad and then had put the pig in bed with that farmer, then these were very powerful, intelligent, well-organized people.

"But I'm not supposed to kill anyone, right?"

"Yeah, no killing. Just put the fear of the Devil into this man."

"Okay, Archie, but for a job like this, I'll need to hire a couple of good men to go with me," said Salvador. "Men who really know horses, so we'll be able to get some jobs on the ranch, learn the ropes, and pull off the job with no *problemas*. So I'll need a couple more hundred, because, after the job is done, we'll all need to disappear for a while."

And saying this, Salvador never took his eyes off of Archie's eyes, looking to see if this lawman's eyes would go to the left to prepare another lie, or if they'd go to the right to really think the matter over carefully.

But Archie's eyes held, not moving either way, meaning he was an experienced liar. Then they quickly went to the left, and then to the right, so this meant he was considering the matter, but also preparing another lie.

"Okay, I'm sure I can get this for you once I explain the situation to these two men," said Archie. He pulled up his gunbelt and reached into his pocket, handing Salvador the two hundred dollars in cash.

Salvador felt the blood come back to his face. He and Lupe had already spent all their money and they'd been getting desperate. Salvador now began caressing this money like a beautiful woman, just as he'd seen his brother, Domingo, do that day by the lagoon. Money really was like water; when you had none, that was all you could think of, but once you had some, then just like water, it wasn't that important anymore.

That same night, Salvador took Lupe and their baby over to her family in Santa Ana and dropped them off, not really telling her what was going on. He then took off with Epitacio and his mother over to Corona to drop them off, too, and he went to go see the Moreno brothers. He made a deal with the two Moreno brothers—the same two level-headed horsemen he'd used in Carlsbad—and they headed north to this big exclusive horse ranch on the other side of Los Angeles.

Salvador and the two Morenos had no trouble getting jobs grooming horses and cleaning out stalls. Within a week, they knew the whole layout of the place, and so the night of the Full Moon with the *coyotes* howling, they beheaded a big, beautiful, newly imported stallion, cut off his balls and cock, and served them up at the breakfast table for the owner of the ranch.

At daybreak, the screams of the rich man were heard all through the house. Their job was done. Salvador and the Morenos took off immediately. The story of the horse amputation exploded all over the Southland, adding to Salvador's reputation that the Devil lived and he walked on two upright legs and his name was Juan Salvador Villaseñor!

Buying some clothes and a new, used truck, Salvador came by later that week to pick up Lupe. They were going to have to get out of the country and return to Mexico. And there was a good chance that they'd never be able to return. Salvador and Lupe were now wanted people.

Lupe's sister Sophia, who was normally so sweet and cheerful, went into a rage, cursing Salvador for being such an awful beast that he was taking Lupe, their baby, away from her *familia*! And Carlota, who'd never liked Salvador at all, surprised everyone by now standing up and defending Salvador and assuring her sister Sophia and their parents that everything would turn out for the best, because Archie, her fiancé, would be helping them.

Salvador brought out a hundred dollars in crisp, new twenty-dollar bills and tried to hand them to Don Victor. But the old man was so vivid with rage that he just shoved the money away.

"You can't buy our daughter!" he said.

"I'm not buying her," said Salvador. "Please, be reasonable. Times are hard. I'm doing the best I can. Here, take it."

But Don Victor didn't take the money and he watched his youngest child and his granddaughter go to the truck to go off with this beast whom now everyone knew was the real *el capón,* the castrator of the Southland!

Doña Guadalupe was crying with tears running down her face, but she kept her opinions to herself. "Go with God," she said, giving her daughter a final *abrazo de amor,* "go with God here in your *corazón, mi hijita,* and everything will always turn out for the best. Did not my mother with her last dying breath, tell me to run into the arms of our enemy who were shooting at us, and I'd be safe when I saw the Light of God in one man's eyes? Miracles do happen, remember this above all else, my angel, *milagros* are a woman's sustenance."

"I know, *mama,*" said Lupe, pressing the money into her mother's hand that Salvador had handed her. Her mother received it. "Not only did I find my wedding ring, but I found my rosary that you gave me and the rolling pin that *papagrande* made for you out of that rosewood."

Hearing this talk about the rolling pin that his father-in-love—also a finish carpenter—had made for his daughter with his own two hands, Don Victor hugged Lupe, too, kissing her again and again with trembling hands. Then he stepped back, dried his eyes, and took his wife's arm.

Doña Guadalupe and Don Victor continued crying as they watched their youngest drive off with her husband and child. It was starting to rain.

"Vayan con Dios!" yelled the old Yaqui Indian lady.

"Yes, *con el favor de Dios*!" yelled back Lupe, waving out the window to her father and mother and sisters.

Salvador and Lupe drove in silence. There was nothing either one of them could say.

19

*Of their own Freewill Adam and Eva now chose to go out of
the Garden, away from their familias, and into the Wilds of
the World — for they had absolute Faith in GOD and
in their AMOR!*

L UPE WOULD NEVER FORGET as long she lived the night they
drove out of Santa Ana. It was storming. Lightning was striking all
about them as they started to climb over the mountains to the east. It
seemed even worse to Lupe than when she'd been a child and she and her
family left their box canyon back in Mexico and she'd thought it was the
end of the world. At least, then, she'd been going with her *papa* and
mama, her sisters and brother. She'd never, never been away from her
familia before.

The wind was sweeping across the road in freezing cold gushes at the
top of the mountains. It felt like their little truck was going to be blown off
the road and down a cliff. Coming around a sharp curve, they almost
crashed into a fallen tree that had been split in half by lightning and lay
across the road. Lightning flashed all about them. Twice a landslide of
rock and mud almost devoured them. The narrow, little, two-lane road
just didn't give a driver much room to move from one side to the other.

Lupe held Hortensia close and prayed with all of her Heart.

Then suddenly, it looked like they'd come to the end of the world, and
they were driving straight down into Hell, as they descended from the
steep mountains, toward the desert way down below. Suddenly they were
hot. Lupe couldn't believe it—just like that—they'd gone from freezing
cold to muggy hot, and yet it wasn't raining anymore.

The storm was behind them and out before them like a dark roof, and
underneath the roof, was the coming of a whole new day in bright colors
of yellow and glorious blue sky.

They smiled, looking at each other, feeling blessed that they'd gotten safely through the terrible storm. But then, before they had time to really enjoy this marvelous feeling, they lost their brakes and now . . . they were SCREAMING down the last part of the curvy mountain road at a reckless speed!

Salvador was all eyes as he tried to brake and steer the runaway truck with a bottomless cliff on one side and a rock wall on the other. Lupe held Hortensia in her arms, wondering if she wasn't better off to open her door and jump, maybe just breaking her arms and legs instead of plunging over one of the thousand-foot canyons to sure death!

Wrapping Hortensia in her blanket, Lupe got hold of her door handle.

"NOOOO!" screamed Salvador. "DON'T JUMP! We'll get out! Believe me, this road straightens up in just few more turns—I think!"

Taking in a deep Breath of *Papito,* Lupe decided to trust her husband's judgment. She let go of the door handle and they continued speeding down the road and around the hairpin turns. Lupe was getting sick, but trying hard not to vomit. Then it looked like they were coming out to the bottom of the grade when they were suddenly hit from behind.

A huge old truck was right behind them. He'd obviously lost his brakes, too, and was up against their bumper, ramming them off the road toward the boulders and cactus.

Seeing themselves being pushed off the road to certain death, Salvador threw a kiss to Lupe, and gave their pickup all the gas, going even faster so he could get away from the runaway truck. Lupe was holding Hortensia to her chest, trying not to scream so she wouldn't terrify their little child anymore. Oh, their poor baby, she'd been through so much Hell in Life already and she couldn't even talk yet!

Then, Lupe couldn't believe it, here among all this endless terror, what did her husband now do, he suddenly gave a *grito de gusto,* "AAAAA-YYYAAAYAAAIIII!" with such joy, that Lupe found herself laughing as they continued barreling around the last couple of curves and then hit the straightaway of the desert.

Lupe was peeing in her dress, she was laughing so hard! But they'd made it! They'd done it! They hadn't been killed!

"*AAYIII QUE VIDA LOCA,* eh?" yelled Salvador.

"Yes," said Lupe, "*LOQUISIMA!*"

But the truck behind them didn't make it and went flying off the road into the deep canyons of boulders and gray-green cactus, crashing, rolling, and EXPLODING into FIRE!

Salvador used the handbrake, trying to stop so he could go back and maybe help the truck driver, but it felt like he had no handbrakes left, either. They continued going down the steep straightaway. It took all of Salvador maneuvering with what was left of the handbrake to finally get the truck going slow enough so he could pull into the little gas station about three miles further down the road at the foot of the mountain.

Salvador told the gas attendant about the truck. The man told Salvador that this was the third truck that had gone off the road this month, and he immediately sent his assistant with their tow truck to go and see what he could do.

It took several hours for the gas station owner to fix their brakes with some used truck parts and a length of barbwire that was lying around. He was an old Anglo, a good guy a lot like Kenny. He suggested for Salvador and Lupe to hold up under the trees by his gas station and wait out the heat of the day before they continued east across the desert.

Underneath the trees was an Anglo family sitting around their old truck looking pretty beat down.

"They're Okies," said the gas station owner, "can't get rid of them. They broke down, got no money, and nowhere to go. But they wouldn't bother you. They're good people, too."

"What are Okies?" asked Salvador.

"People from out of Oklahoma, a state east of here out towards Texas. Thousands of them lost their ranches 'cause of a drought, then an endless dust storm. They're coming out in droves to California, hoping to find work. Damn poor sight, but the transmission they need for their truck, I'd have to buy, and so I can't help 'em."

Salvador could see that these "Okies" had three little blond kids with them and an old woman who reminded Salvador a lot of his own mother.

"How much would that transmission cost?" asked Salvador.

"Even used they're expensive," said the station owner. "About six dollars, my price, then another two or three dollars to put it in."

Salvador thanked the gas station owner for his offer that he and his family could stay underneath the grove of trees, but he told him that they had to go on. What Salvador didn't tell the man, was that he was afraid that any minute the law was going to show up and question them because they'd been the ones who'd seen that truck go off the road.

"All right," said the old desert rat, "but then you'd better take along a couple of extra water bags."

"We got water for the baby," said Salvador, not wanting to spend any money that he didn't have to. Between buying this truck and giving money to his mother and Lupe's mother, he didn't have much left out of the $500 he'd been paid.

And they'd need money to set themselves up in Mexico. After all, his bootlegging trade would be worthless across the border. Mexico wasn't a dry land. Liquor was legal down there.

"No, this isn't for you or your child. This is for your truck in case it overheats. You're going to have to be careful," added the man, spitting a stream of chewing tobacco juice on the ground. "Very, very careful, *amigo*, especially in those damn sand hills. People die out there."

Salvador paid the man for his work on the truck and the two canvas water bags. The bill came to $2 and the man had worked on their truck for well over an hour. This gas station owner had charged Salvador 20 cents an hour for his labor. Just like Kenny, this Anglo was a good, honest man.

"And here," said Salvador, "six more dollars for that transmission for those people and two dollars for you to put it in."

The gas station owner was stunned.

"You've saved that family's life, *amigo*!"

"We all need a little saving now and then," said Salvador.

And Salvador got in his truck and he and Lupe were gone.

Part Nine

REBIRTHING

20

In the Wilds beyond the Garden, Adam and Eva now found themselves bringing the Light of God to friend and foe alike—Lucifer and Papito were Working as One once again!

I T W A S H I G H N O O N when Salvador and Lupe came out of the rocky, granite desert and hit the sand hills of California. Here, nothing grew, and there were no rocks whatsoever, either. These were the famous floating "death" hills of pure yellow and white sand just west of the Colorado River, which divided California from Arizona.

Salvador and Lupe hadn't seen one single vehicle for well over an hour. Several times they'd stopped to add water to their truck's radiator. The first time it had cost them a lot of valuable water. Because Salvador made the big mistake of turning off the motor so the radiator would cool off, but instead of cooling off, the damn radiator had gotten hotter, erupting with boiling water when Salvador had taken off the radiator cap.

Salvador could now see why that old desert rat who owned the gas station had told him that no one, but no one, moved during the heat of the day; not even the rattlesnakes or scorpions. But also Salvador figured that maybe he could be able to turn this whole situation around in their favor, if he just kept level-headed. Maybe this would then be the perfect time for Lupe and him to get across the border into Arizona without any questions being asked.

But, then, they'd no more than come off the two-lane, solid gravel road of the rocky desert and hit the first stretch of the wooden-plank road of the sand hills and Salvador realized that he'd been very naïve. He'd really miscalculated the whole thing.

These yellowish-white hills of smooth, soft sand stretched in all

directions for miles and miles without one single blade of grass or a clump
of brush or cactus. Here, there was nothing but sand as far as the eye could
see. And this tiny, toylike, single-lane road—made of wooden-planks, like
the planks of the railroad laid down one next to the other—looked like a
joke, like a little worm inching its way through this infinity of gullies and
sand hills. The whole place had an eerie feeling of another world.

It was said that so far, no engineers had been able to figure out how to
build a permanent road across these sand hills, because the sand was so
fine that it never stayed long enough in one place for a road to be completed.

Every time the wind came down from the great mountains in the west
or up from the gulf of the Sea of Cortez to the south, the sand would be
blown from one place to another, moving an entire sand hill to another
location in a matter of hours. The roads that they'd tried to build in the
past had sometimes disappeared before they'd even completed them.
Years ago, a dozen people and their cars had been found dead underneath
tons of sand after one of these terrible sandstorms. The wooden-plank
road was the best thing that the engineers had come up with so far. But the
wooden-plank road definitely had problems. For one, the road was so narrow that oncoming vehicles couldn't pass one another, so one car would
have to back up to the nearest little turnout to let the other car by before it
could proceed on its way.

It was high noon when Salvador and Lupe came off the good, solid,
two-lane gravel road of the rocky, cactus desert and started across the
single-lane, wooden-plank road. Salvador didn't tell Lupe, but oh, how he
truly wished that he had his Moon. Now that fine automobile had never
once overheated on him, no matter how fast or hot he'd run it.

It was a scary feeling getting on the planks with the truck's tires going
boom, boom, boom, making noise like driving on the railroad tracks,
except these planks of wood were constructed closer together and so the
boom, boom, boom sounded much faster. It was said that the reason the
engineers had finally decided to use wooden ties for this road was because
they'd figured that the sand could blow through the wooden ties, and
hence, the road wouldn't get lost every few months, as had happened to
those old gravel roads that they'd tried to lay down.

The Sun was blazing bright white hot. Lupe had her straw hat over
Hortensia, protecting her little daughter from the Sun's rays. The breeze
coming in their window felt like an oven. Glancing at his wife and child,
Salvador saw that they were holding up pretty well and so he figured that

if they could just get past these sand hills and across the river to Arizona, they'd be all right. Once they were on the Arizona side, they could hole up for a few days and get some rest. It seemed to him like they'd been on the run ever since Kenny had been shot in front of their house in Carlsbad.

Then Salvador saw something coming toward them in the distance, but he couldn't figure out what it was because of how it kept jumping about in the dancing heat waves. It looked to Salvador like it was a brightly colored carnival.

He rubbed his eyes. He thought that he was seeing things. But then as this mirage got closer and closer, he saw that this wasn't a circus or a carnival of bright waving flags. No, through the sea of dancing heat waves came a long line of brand-new automobiles with colorful flags, loud whistles, and people acting like they were in a parade.

Lupe and Salvador glanced at each other, and started laughing. There were two people in each vehicle and some of the cars were convertibles. Seeing Salvador and Lupe out here in the middle of nowhere, a few of the people stood up in their bright, new convertibles with colorful Sun umbrellas in hand and waved their flags at them.

It was crazy! Completely crazy-*loco*!

Salvador braked, put his truck in reverse and backed up so he could get off the road on one of the little turnouts and let the long line of cars and trucks pass. This had to be one of the funniest sights Salvador and Lupe had ever seen in all their lives.

The second vehicle, a bright red convertible, stopped next to Salvador and Lupe's car, and a well-dressed, midget-size man stood up on the seat of the grand car and told them in a large, booming voice that the train had broken down back in the desert in Arizona, but that he had to get these new model cars and trucks to an auto show in Los Angeles, California, by tomorrow.

The short, little man then tipped his hat. "Sorry, for the inconvenience," he added, "but we'd been told that we wouldn't meet any traffic at midday. Onward," he added with flair, and he sat back down in his shiny new convertible and his beautiful woman driver drove on.

Thirty-some vehicles passed by before Salvador and Lupe stopped counting. It wasn't amusing anymore. Salvador had had to turn off his motor. The truck had overheated. They were hot and thirsty and felt miserable sitting on the little outlet of the wooden-plank road. Their daughter, Hortensia, was having a hard time of it. The midday Sun was blasting them with terrible heat.

Finally, the last new vehicle passed by and Salvador tried to start his truck, but the truck wouldn't start. He took a deep breath, refusing to lose his temper. He checked their water situation, figuring if they each took a little swallow, he'd still have enough to put some in the radiator. Hopefully, the truck would then cool down enough so it would start up.

"Take a drink," he said to Lupe. "Then give some to Hortensia." Their daughter was being a brave, good little girl as long as her mother held her close, but, also, it was just too hot for two bodies to be touching.

"No," said Lupe, "I'm fine, Salvador. You take a drink and I'll just give a little to Hortensia and wet a cloth so I can keep her head cool. A child's brain can boil if it gets too hot, you know."

"No, I didn't know," said Salvador. "I'd never heard that one."

"Well, we learned that one in Arizona when we were working in the cotton fields at Scottsdale. Two children's brains were cooked to death as their mothers worked picking cotton. You drink, Salvador, you're driving. I can just nap and keep cool," she said, smiling.

Salvador took a deep breath. He could well see that Lupe was having trouble hanging on, too. She'd never been one to do very well in hot weather, because she had a hard time sweating, and sweat was what cooled off a body and was therefore essential for survival in hot weather. Himself, Salvador was pouring with sweat. His whole shirt was all soaked through. Never in his life had he had any difficulty sweating.

"All right," said Salvador, lying. "I'll drink." But he had no intention of drinking any water. He was a man, after all, and so as the *hombre* of his *familia,* he could take it—for this was his job, to take it *como un macho de los buenos* for the survival of his *familia.*

He watched Lupe give water to their child; then he watched her wet a piece of cloth and moisten their baby's lovely little face and neck, cooling her off. Salvador's whole heart-*corazón* was filled with love. This was the child of their love, the flesh of their flesh.

Glancing up at the boiling hot Father Sun, Salvador stepped out of their truck to pour the remaining water into the truck's radiator. But first he needed to take a leak. He unbuttoned his pants and wondered if maybe he shouldn't save his piss, too, and put it in the radiator. Peeing, Salvador decided that his pee was probably too warm to cool off anything. And, also, it wasn't very much pee. He hadn't drunk any water since they'd left that gas station early this morning, and all this time he'd been sweating like a racehorse.

Rebuttoning his pants, he saw that his hands were shaking. He put his left hand to his forehead and took a deep breath. He was cold as ice and he felt lightheaded.

He took in several deep breaths, steadied himself, then poured all their cool, clear water into the truck's radiator. This was it now. There was no turning back. If the truck didn't start up and they didn't get out of here *pronto,* they were going to be dead ducks for the buzzards, or a good find—his mother would say—for people to steal everything from their dead bodies tonight when the road would be full of people crossing the desert.

Getting back in the cab, Salvador smiled to Lupe, not wanting her to know all the things that were going on inside of his head. "Okay," he said, "here goes!"

And saying this, he pushed down on the starter and wonder of wonders, the truck just started right up! Just like that! No *problema* whatsoever!

But then, as luck would have it, when he went to put the truck into first gear, his hands were shaking so much that he put the truck in reverse by mistake and off the wooden planks they went—backward!

Salvador leaped out of the truck and ran around to the back, and he saw that his right rear tire was buried in the sand. They were stuck! He put his right hand over his mouth, so he wouldn't scream in fear. He didn't want to frighten Lupe and Hortensia any more than they already were!

Suddenly, Salvador just knew deep inside of his being that they were going to die if they didn't get help. He turned to see if any of that long line of new vehicles were still in sight. The last vehicle had been a water truck with a dozen barrels. And there it was, the last vehicle, disappearing into the dancing heat waves to the west.

Salvador ran up the plank road, yelling, whistling, but they were too far gone. Glancing around, he truly realized for the very first time how all alone in the whole world were he and his little *familia.* There was *nada, nada,* nothing in all directions as far as the eye could see, but glistening bright white sand, and overhead, the huge, burning orange-red Father Sun!

Taking a deep breath, Salvador pulled his shirt out of his pants. He took several more breaths, trying to gather his strength. What could he do now? How could he get that tire back on the wooden road? If only there was a way for him to lift the truck high enough so that they could get something underneath the tire, then maybe, they could drive the vehicle back on the road. But he had nothing to put under the tire except their clothes, and the tire would just spin their clothes down into the sand. Salvador decided to check and see if they had a jack.

"What are you doing?" asked Lupe. "Is everything okay?"

"Everything is fine," he lied. "I'll have us out of here in a minute. I just got to see if we have a jack," he added as he went through their things in the back of the truck. But then he stopped. Who was he kidding, they had no jack. And even if they did have one, how would that help them? The fine, loose sand would just swallow up the jack.

Salvador closed his eyes in concentration as he'd seen his mother do a thousand times when they'd come up face to face with an impossible situation, and little by little, as he breathed in and he breathed out, a power began to fill up his chest and stomach. Then it was traveling out to his arms and legs. His mind suddenly felt strong. All that Doubting Thomas crap stopped, and this crystal clear clarity of thought began filling up his Mind, his Heart and Soul. Now he could Visualize everything here, in the present, of what was going to happen before it happened. He was *aprevenido*.

His hands stopped shaking. He was good now. Instinctively, he'd just used his Ninth, Tenth, and Eleventh Senses. The Force of Creation was with him.

"Lupe," he said, feeling confident once again, "we're going to be fine. All I need is for you to get in the driver's seat and start the motor, then when I lift up the rear end of the truck, getting that tire back on the planks, I'll need for you to drive forward, but only about two feet, so you don't drive off the front end of this little damn turnout." He laughed. He was loose enough to find humor. "Why they made these turnouts so short is beyond me. It's dangerous every time you get off on one of these little damn things to let that other car pass by you. I guess that this is why people are told to never travel these sand hills alone."

"All right, Salvador," said Lupe, her own heart beating a million miles a minute. "I think that can do that. I give it the gas to go forward, but then I'll brake and stop immediately, right?"

"Exactly," he said. "You got it, *querida*."

Lupe closed her eyes, saying a quick little prayer, then got behind the steering wheel. Hortensia was asleep, thank God. Lupe pushed down on the clutch all the way as she'd learned to do with their Moon—feeling good that she'd remembered to do this—then she tried the starter and the truck quickly started up. She smiled, feeling very proud of herself.

"Okay," she said, "I'm ready, Salvador."

"Good," said he, and he rolled up his sleeves and took in several more deep breaths, remembering back to the days when he'd worked as a dynamite man in the rock quarries and he'd been one of the strongest men in all of the quarries.

He flexed his arms and his hands, then rolled back and forth his thick shoulders several times. Then this was it! He got hold of the rear bumper, got his legs under himself, set his feet in the sand, and began to use all of his power!

And yes, the one side of the truck came up, and he then tried to inch forward with it so he could get it back on the wooden planks, but he just didn't have it in him, and so when Lupe went to give the vehicle the gas, the tire that was up in the air spun rapidly, but the tire on the solid wood didn't move one inch to help him forward. Suddenly, Salvador remembered that this was the way trucks were built, one tire could be spinning in the mud and the other would just keep dead still. He lowered his side of the rear end of the truck back down into the sand.

"Okay, Lupe," he said, catching his breath, yet still feeling confident, "I'm going to have to get in the middle and lift up the whole rear end of the truck, and then shove it forward at the same time."

"Can you do that, Salvador? I don't want you hurting yourself."

"I got to," said Salvador, glancing up at the huge boiling red-orange Sun. "We have no other choice, Lupe."

Sweat was pouring down his face. His whole shirt was soaked through and dripping. That was why he'd taken the shirt out of his pants, so the sweat could drip off onto the ground and not run down the inside of his pants. This was a trick that he'd also learned while working on the railroad up in Montana.

But when Salvador got hold of the truck in the middle, wanting to lift up both tires at the same time, he just didn't have enough power to do it. He was too tired, and his feet were also sinking deeper into the sand.

Still, Salvador gave it a try again and again until he finally just fell down into the hot sand in exhaustion, coughing and gagging, trying to catch his breath.

Lupe turned off the motor. She hadn't really realized how hot it truly was out in the direct sunlight until she'd stepped out of the cab.

"My God!" she said. "It's boiling out here, Salvador! You can't be doing this, you'll kill yourself, *mi esposo*!"

"Lupe," said Salvador, between gasps for air. "What choice do we have? I got to, or we're going to die," he added, not knowing how to put it any other way.

"Oh, no, we're not!" said Lupe, now realizing the gravity of the situation as she glanced up at the huge red-orange Father Sun. "We are not going to die! Do you hear me, Salvador, we are going to get through this alive and well, and that's that!"

"Not for long without water," he said.

"Well, then we'll find water," said Lupe, looking around at the infinity of sand, but she didn't panic. No, once more she had this feeling, this knowingness coming to her from this Holy Other Self—which just kept hovering above her like a Guardian Angel directly from God. And then she saw it, and she saw it so clearly. "But Salvador, we do have water," she said, "we have lots of water right here in the radiator!"

Salvador's eyes opened wide. "You're right," he said, smiling. "I never thought of that." And he looked at his wife, Lupe, with more love and respect than he'd ever dreamed of having for another human being besides his own mother.

"Come," she said, "let's get you out of the Sun, *mi esposo,* and I'll make a shade for us with a blanket on the other side of the truck. Then after you rest a little, you can then show me how to steal a little water from the truck and we'll drink just enough to keep us alive until some help comes by or the day cools off, so we can then go on. Either way, we are not going to die, Salvador! You hear me, we are going to live, and that's that!"

Tears would've come to Salvador's eyes if he wasn't so dehydrated—he was so much in love with this young woman before him. But he didn't cry and he could hardly move. Lupe had to help him up and get him to the north side of their truck where there was a little pinch of shade.

Salvador couldn't stop grinning. He'd married a good one! There was just no way that Lupe was ever going to let them die. His mother's evaluation of Lupe—that day when she and her *familia* had stopped by to milk Luisa's mean old she-goat—had been, indeed, correct. A mother truly could help a son in picking out the best wife.

Lying down on the wooden ties and leaning back on the driver's side of their truck, Salvador watched Lupe rip one of her dresses into ties so she could put up a blanket for shade. Salvador figured that they'd have to wait about an hour for the truck to cool down enough so they could get a little water out of the radiator without a lot of water boiling out.

When Lupe finished making the shade, she then got under it along with Salvador, holding their child on her lap. She looked so happy and proud of herself and full of confidence.

Salvador closed his eyes so he could rest. Time passed and more time passed and the silence of the land was so complete it was eerie. Nothing moved or made a sound. Then Lupe began to baby-talk with their daughter, sounding like a happy bird in the deadly silence.

Finally, Salvador figured that they could now draw out a little water from the radiator. When they did it, the water tasted hot and awful, but Lupe then ingeniously drained it with some cloth, and they were able to finally sip enough to keep their mouths from turning into cotton and their tongues from swelling up in pain.

No vehicles came. The Father Sun seemed to get hotter and hotter, instead of cooler. Dozing off, Salvador thought of his mother and wondered what she would do.

Then he suddenly realized that she was here, she was always here, and she was calling to him. He awoke with a start. *Dios mio,* Lupe had passed out. She was lying half out in the Sun with her mouth wide-open and her tongue hanging out. She looked dead.

Instantly, Salvador was on his feet, hearing his mother's voice inside his head. "Quickly, *mi hijito,*" she was saying to him. "Lupe is dying! Get that cloth she used for Hortensia and rewet it and get her to suck some water down her throat before she swallows her tongue!"

And as he got up to do what his mother's voice told him to do, he flashed back in his mind to those terrible days of the Revolution when his mother had saved his sisters and him from the jaws of death again and again!

Cannons had been exploding all about them, but his old mother had never panicked. No, she'd kept calm, clearheaded, and gotten him and his sisters out of the way of the stampeding hooves of the soldiers' horses and into the brush, then she'd given them little, round, smooth stones to suck on so that they wouldn't swallow their tongues from lack of water.

Salvador wet the cloth and put it to Lupe's mouth to suck on and he said to her—as his mother had said to him—"Lupe, wake up and suck on this cloth. Our daughter, Hortensia, needs you. We are going to get out of this hell *con el favor de Dios.* You are our *eje de nuestra familia,* Lupe. So suck on this cloth! Suck," he pleaded.

Coming around, Lupe began to suck on the cloth just like a newborn instinctively going to her mother's breast. And it was beautiful; Lupe had been dying, but then she'd heard her husband's voice calling her and she'd pushed herself beyond the dark shadow of death!

And she had no Fear. Above Salvador—a few feet in the air—Lupe could see Doña Margarita and the Virgin Mary and a whole legion of Angels and one Angel was far brighter than all the rest. And this brightest

Angel of all, Lupe knew, was Lucifer, himself, and once more he was at the Almighty's side. All Fear was gone! Our Holy *Familia* was Together again!

Seeing Lupe coming around, Salvador was overjoyed. "You've come back to life, *mi amor,*" he said, kissing her again and again—he was so happy!

Quickly, he got Lupe and Hortensia into the cab, threw the blanket into the back and got into the driver's seat, released the handbrake and put the truck in neutral.

This was it! His *familia* was dying! And he was rested, and he was *un Mejicano! Un macho de los buenos! Un Tapatio de los Altos de Jalisco!* And so he would now lift the entire rear end of the truck up into the air and give it one mighty shove, get them back on the road, then they'd drive off and get to the Colorado River.

He turned to the Father Sun. "Please, Lord God, help me! Give me the POWER of *MI PAPA!*"

Saying this, Salvador was shocked that he'd asked for strength of his father. But, then, he suddenly realized that this was, indeed, the type of strength that he needed right now; that brute power of his father that had enabled his *papa* to do so many great feats, like rope and drag the gigantic serpent that had held their village hostage with fear!

Salvador suddenly realized for the very first time in his life that he really did love his father, after all. That he did have good feelings for that tall, red-headed, blue-eyed Spaniard who'd always hit him on the head, calling him names because he, Salvador, was dark and short, and Indian-looking like his mother, and not tall and blue-eyed.

And instantly, with this feeling of Love for a man that Salvador had always assumed that he hated, he, Juan Salvador Villaseñor, now went to the back of the truck and grabbed hold of the rear bumper once again. He wiggled his feet solidly into the soft sand, then with a mighty SCREAM he yanked up the whole rear end of the truck, as he knew that his mighty father could have done! But still—oh, he just didn't quite have the strength to move the vehicle forward onto the planks, and he fell down! And now both rear tires were in the sand!

Salvador exploded, screaming to the HEAVENS! Bellowing with ALL HIS MIGHT! "Don't tease me like this, God! I saw it all so clearly for a moment! I had *amor* even for *mi papa,* damnit!"

He lay down in the hot, burning sand, panting like a dog. "God," he said between gasps for air, "I need help, don't You see? Right now! Not tomorrow! I was only inches away from getting the two tires up on the planks! But I'm not quitting, God, no matter how much You put me through! You hear me," he yelled to the Heavens. "I'm not quitting! I'm *mi mama*'s son, too, and she never quit on *nada,* not once, even when we were dying in the desert!"

Then he saw it so clearly: he was both Indian and European! Both bloods ran within his veins. He was *un mezclado, un mestizo,* a United Force from two different WORLDS!

Seeing this so clearly, Salvador leaped to his feet. He grabbed hold of the rear bumper with the power of both of his ancestries, and he tried again, and again and each time he almost did it, but he just didn't quite have that last little bit of power to put both of the rear tires up on the wooden ties.

Finally he fell down to his knees, crying and sobbing. He'd failed his *familia.* He was now ready to give up the ghost and start cursing God for having forsaken them just as he'd seen his father do when he'd returned home to their village and thought all his blue-eyed sons dead and everything in ruins. But no, Salvador did not do this!

Instead, he closed his eyes in concentration as he'd seen his mother do thousands of times when it looked like it was the end for them, and he said in a calm, even voice, "God, look at me, just take a good long look at me. Don't You see, I'm Here," he said, with tears flowing down his face. "I'm Here and I'm Your son, too, my mother told me, just as much as Jesus Christ. For my mother Loves You and Lives for You with her every Breath, just like her Best Friend, the Virgin Mary. Don't You see, God, We're All One *Familia*!"

He knelt in the sand. "And yeah, I know that I screw up a lot, God, but I do keep giving it my best. So come on, God, We're *Familia,* You and I, so give me a little help right now, *Papito*!"

Once more, Salvador got back up and set his feet and got hold of the rear bumper, because he hadn't lost Faith. He still fully Trusted that his Heavenly Father would come through for him and make a Miracle Here on this *Tierra Firme* just as God had for his mother time and again. But then—when he set his feet and got ready to give it his all once again—he heard a voice behind him say, "May I help you?"

Salvador turned, half expecting to see God, Himself, but it wasn't. It was Kenny White.

Salvador held, not quite knowing what to think. Kenny White was now a young man and he had long, dark hair like those pictures of Jesus. Salvador smiled.

"Yeah, sure, Kenny," he said. "I could sure use your help."

Grinning ear to ear with that grand smile of his, Kenny White handed Salvador a water bag full of dripping cool water, and said, "Move aside, *amigo*, you look a little tired." And Kenny then just got hold of the bumper and lifted up the entire rear end of the pickup as if it were a toy, and put the vehicle back on the wooden road.

Then he turned, still smiling that beautiful smile of his, and said nothing more as he walked off into the desert of sand hills, leaving footprints as he went. He disappeared as quickly as he'd appeared.

Salvador stood still for a full minute, thinking no thoughts, feeling no feelings.

Then with huge eyes, he uncorked the canvas water bag, took a sip, and it was the sweetest, coolest water he ever tasted. He drank down two good mouthfuls, but no more. Then he got in the driver's seat, wet a piece of cloth and reached across the seat, moistening Lupe's forehead. Little by little, his truelove came back around again.

"Here, Lupe," he now said to her, "drink. We have water, but no, no, not so fast. I don't want you getting sick."

Lupe drank and drank, catching her breath between swallows, then Salvador gave some water to Hortensia. She wasn't as bad off as her mother. Lupe had actually looked like she'd been dying.

"What happened?" asked Lupe after she'd gotten some color back to her face. "The last thing I remember—I'd thought we died, Salvador. Where did you get the water? It's so cool and delicious."

"Kenny," said Salvador. "Kenny came walking out of the desert from that direction over there, Lupe, and he gave me this bag of water, then he lifted up the whole truck and put it back on the road for us."

"Kenny!?!" said Lupe. "Our Kenny White from Carlsbad who got killed?"

"Yes, our Kenny White from Carlsbad," said Salvador. "But he's not old anymore, Lupe. He's young and he has long, dark hair, you know, like those pictures of Jesus."

"Oh, my God," said Lupe, making the sign of the cross over herself, "Maria told me that in her dream, Jesus came to save us, and that He was also the One who helped me push that door open and drag you out of that burning Hell!"

"Well, then, Jesus has saved us twice in the last few weeks," said Salvador. "And this time, He did it through Kenny, instead of through you." He drank some more water. "Isn't this the sweetest water you've ever tasted?"

"Yes," said Lupe, "just like our water back home that rained down the cliff of gold. Oh, Salvador, we are Blessed, aren't we?" Her eyes filled with tears of joy.

He nodded. "I think we've died, Lupe, and gone to Heaven."

Hearing this, Lupe felt a cold chill going up and down her spine.

"What is it?" asked Salvador. "Do you feel sick?"

She shook her head. "No," she said, "I have this feeling that maybe we really have died, Salvador, and now all of this is just a dream."

He swallowed. "This is what my mother says that people actually do when they let go of all their Fears and start Living in the Grace of God—they Die and are forever then in Heaven."

If anyone else had said this, Lupe would have dismissed it as wild talk. But feeling what she was feeling deep inside of herself, and hearing this had come from her mother-in-love, Lupe could see this had, indeed, been Salvador's mother's Power. The old woman had died and been reborn long ago, just as Jesus had done, only to ascend into Heaven three days later.

"*Mi hijita,*" she'd told Lupe once, "Jesus isn't some faraway unreachable Holy Being, but the Living Example of what We can all Be."

Taking in a deep breath, Salvador started the motor, drove out of the little turnout, and got them back on the wooden-plank road. They were moving along at a good ten to fifteen miles an hour again. At this speed, they'd get out of these sand hills in no time and then they'd be at the Colorado River by sundown. They were good now, they were very good, they were a married couple who Knew of Miracles as well as they knew of *tortillas y frijoles*.

Salvador looked at the sand hills all about him as he drove. They looked beautiful. They no longer looked threatening. They were now actually Singing, Dancing, Sending their *Amor*.

Suddenly, Salvador knew how his mother had made the barrels of whiskey disappear. Truly, once a person gave up the ghost, then all of life was a dream and in dreams a human being could make of life whatever they desired—*con el favor de Dios!*

*They'd met Death and they'd found Death to simply be
another Holy Opening to the Creator's Corazón — Beat,
BEAT, BEATING throughout the UNIVERSE!*

THEY DROVE ACROSS THE RIVER. There was no one at the border to stop and question them. They'd gone from one state to another with such ease.

They drove into the tiny town of Yuma. They bought groceries and went down to the river to spend the night on the Arizona side of the border. They found a whole encampment of Mexicans and local Indians by the river's edge. Most of the Mexicans were headed back to Mexico, but others were simply playing it day by day and working in the fields outside of Yuma, trying to figure out what to do next.

When the Sun went down, the mosquitoes got so bad everyone went crazy. Salvador drove back into town and bought half a dozen big cigars and had the men light them up and blow smoke on themselves and on their families. The mosquitoes never came near them again that whole night.

Salvador said that he'd learned this trick up in Montana from the only other Mexican up there, who'd been from Veracruz, and he'd told Salvador that in the jungles, the lead man always puffed on a big cigar so that the smoke would trail back over the others and keep all the bugs away, not just the mosquitoes.

For two days and nights, Salvador and Lupe mostly slept, getting over the terrible ordeal that they'd had in the desert. When they shared their story with the *gente,* many of them came forward with similar stories. It seemed that every family—who'd crossed the river—had at one time or another been helped out by a dead friend or relative coming to them in their hour of need.

One local Indian woman told Salvador that he'd come face to face with the Spirit of the Sacred Sand Hills when he'd seen Kenny White. And that this powerful Spirit they, the locals, considered much like the Christians considered Jesus.

Hearing this, Lupe made the sign of the cross over herself. It was all becoming more and more clear to her every day. Her mother's last words to her had been so wise. "And always remember above all else, *mi hijita,* miracles do happen. They are a mother's sustenance."

Tears came to Lupe's eyes. Oh, how she missed her *familia*!

RESTING UNDER THE TREES alongside the Colorado River, Salvador and Lupe truly thought that they'd died and gone to Heaven the way they were being treated by the Mexicans and Indians alike. One person brought them some freshly made *tamales*. Another shared some of their beans and rice with them. An old, heavy-set Indian woman with large bare feet gave them a plate of wild quail baked in cactus fruit that had to be one of the most mouth watering dishes that they'd ever tasted!

Salvador and Lupe truly missed their *familias,* but they could now also see that they were, indeed, starting a whole new life of their own. Here, Hortensia had little kids her own age to play with and she was very happy. That terrible night of their distillery exploding like a bomb seemed so far away. And that night of the lightning and thunder and then losing their brakes as they'd come down the mountain almost seemed like it had all just been a bad dream.

On the third day, Salvador felt strong enough to go to work in the fields along with the other men. Here, not too many of the women worked. It was well over 110 degrees in the shade, but they weren't working in the shade. No, they were out in the direct sunlight—where thermometers couldn't even measure the heat without breaking.

Being a good sweater, Salvador was able to adjust to the heat and work very well in the hot fields. But by the end of the day, his feet were swollen and burning.

That night, Lupe took her husband's shoes off, and she massaged the soles of his feet with water and river clay, and Salvador was sure that he was in Heaven. Little by little, all those terrible days of their past disappeared and they became a happy little family living here in the trees and brush alongside the Colorado River.

That Friday night, a man got hold of some *tequila* from Mexico and they started up a poker game and invited Salvador to join them. Salvador said no, saying that he really wasn't into gambling, but after they kept insisting, he joined them. Quickly, Salvador realized that these men really weren't into the gambling, either. No, they were just drinking and relaxing. The art of playing cards wasn't a thing that they even knew existed. And so without really meaning to, Salvador began to win pot after pot until he had almost all of their money.

Then he caught himself. And they thought he was just being lucky. They really had no idea that he was a professional. Quickly, Salvador did something that he'd never done before in all of his life. He deliberately began to lose back all the money that he'd won, doing all he could to make sure that each man won at least one good pot.

He wasn't going to be a wolf, shearing the sheep this time. He wanted to give thanks to the Almighty for having gifted him His Son Jesus through the form of Kenny White in the desert.

That night Salvador and Lupe made love under the Mother Moon and Stars at the edge of the Colorado River. Salvador and Lupe hadn't known such peace and happiness since they'd married. Their *amor* was now anchored . . . deep with roots.

LUPE AWOKE WITH A START. It was half past midnight and her mind was running wild. "Salvador," she said, "quick, we got to get out of here! The police are coming!"

Seeing her eyes, Salvador believed her. They had no more than gotten in their truck when a horde of men with clubs descended on them, beating everyone in sight. People were screaming and running every-which-way, trying to escape. Women and children were being beaten, too. In their headlights, Salvador and Lupe saw one woman's head explode into pieces like a watermelon as she ran with her child in hand. And a big young man kept hitting her again and again with his club!

With pistol in hand, Salvador stopped to shoot the man, but then here came six others with clubs in hand, also swinging at anyone they came across. Salvador lowered his .38 snubnose and they drove on, and surprisingly, because they were in a vehicle, no one seemed to notice them. It was like, well, these people own a car and so they must be okay.

Up ahead, Salvador and Lupe gave witness to two grown White men knock down the old Indian woman—who'd given them that dish of cactus fruit and quail—and beat her as she tried protecting her grandchild!

Salvador slammed on his brakes and leaped out of his truck. His .38 snubnose BURST the night open with GUNFIRE! Then his .45 automatic sounded like a machine gun! The men with clubs were suddenly on the run, screaming in pain—as Salvador shot their legs out from under them!

Twenty-six years later, one of these same Okies would come to Salvador and Lupe in Oceanside, California, asking for a job at one of their retail stores. "We knew nothing," the man would tell Salvador and Lupe a couple of years later, after they'd become good friends. "I was nothing but a big, strong, fifteen-year-old kid off a farm in Oklahoma and the cops told us that we could get jobs once we run off those lazy, no-good Mexican-Indians who lived by the river. We was desperate, so that night we lit into you people there by the river under those trees, breaking heads, not caring if it was women or children—just being told they weren't White and really human like us who needed the jobs!

"But when that gunfire broke open, it was like we all of the sudden sobered up and realized that these were real people, too. I just don't rightly know quite how to explain it—I'm ashamed to say—but until some of us was screaming that we ourselves was in pain, it was like we hadn't had a clue that we'd been doing something wrong. That night still haunts me. One woman's head I felt shatter under the swing of my club. And the cops, they kept egging us on, and we were just so stupid and desperate that we thought nothing of it at the time."

This man's name was Thompson, he was an ex-Marine, and he worked for Salvador and Lupe, in Oceanside for fifteen years and every time he'd have a few too many drinks, he'd come back up with this story, feeling worse about this than any of the things he'd done in the service overseas.

But Salvador never told Thompson that it had been he, Juan Salvador Villaseñor, the Devil, himself, who'd taken aim on those running men with clubs in their hands that night and shot their butts, crippling them on the spot!

The next day Salvador and Lupe fled in the truck. Over twenty people had been killed with clubs—eleven of them women and children—and another dozen had been left with broken arms and cracked ribs. But of this, the authorities didn't care.

No, they were looking for the man who'd used a gun and shot the legs out from under half a dozen White people! The official story was that once more a bunch of drunk Mexican-Indians had started *problemas*. Hundreds of good citizens were deputized and brought in to round up all the trouble-starting half-breeds and put them on the train so they could be shipped back to Mexico where they belonged.

And half of these people weren't even Mexican. They were full-blooded Yuma Indians who'd never been south of the border before. This had been their home, here along the Colorado River for hundreds of years.

ABOUT 150 MILES EAST of Yuma in the little nothing place of Chuichu, right outside of Casa Grande, Arizona, a wind came up so strong that Salvador and Lupe had to pull off the road and take shelter by an abandoned barn. Things went flying out of their truck. Lupe's purse with all their money in the world was ripped off of her hand and went flying through the air along with anything else that wasn't nailed down.

Lupe screamed, "Our money, Salvador!" And Salvador—who'd been tying things down—went running after the purse, which was quickly disappearing into the dust storm.

Lupe was left alone with their daughter alongside a barn that was now being pulled apart, too, by the terrible winds of the dust storm. Lupe was sure that she'd sent her husband to his death. She began to pray, asking God to please not let Salvador get killed or lost in the storm.

He was gone for what seemed like hours. Lupe was just about to give up all hope, when here came Salvador struggling back against the wind, grabbing hold of fence posts to support himself.

Getting back inside of the truck with her, Salvador told Lupe that he hadn't been able to catch her purse, no matter how many times he'd seen it just ahead of him in the wind and he'd leaped, trying to grab hold of it. He'd failed once again. Now, they had no money, no gas, no food, no anything. What was going on? Why was God testing them again and again without mercy!

But then miracle of miracles, the next day when the storm died down and Lupe was out trying to trap quail, something in the distance on a little knoll, caught her eye. She called to Salvador, and together with Hortensia in hand, they walked out to the little knoll, and there caught on a lone piece of barbwire fence was her purse and their money was all intact.

Tears of joy came to Lupe's eyes. God loved them and was looking after them!

That night, under the Stars Salvador and Lupe built a fire, marinated the quail, that Lupe had caught, in the cactus-fruit-sauce like the big, bare-foot Indian grandmother had taught them, and they roasted the little bird. It was a delicious feast. Heaven smiling down upon them.

THE NEXT DAY, Salvador and Lupe had the confidence to make one of the most terrifying and important decisions of all of their lives. They decided to drive—not south as they'd been doing—but up north to the big town of Phoenix, so they could wire a message to Archie.

This was scary. They'd be wiring to the sheriff's office itself, exposing their whereabouts. My God, Salvador and Lupe were now wanted not just for bootlegging but maybe even for murder—if any of those men he'd shot in Yuma had died.

On the other hand, the whole country was going to pieces and so maybe Salvador and Lupe wouldn't even be noticed, especially since they no longer had a grand automobile and fine clothes and looked just like all the other poor Mexican workers.

On a blanket, Salvador counted out the bullets that he had left for his .38 Special and his .45 automatic. On the same blanket, Lupe counted out their money, including all of their change. Salvador had twenty-three .38s left, but he only had seven .45s. He'd need a couple of boxes of each, he figured, before they crossed over into Mexico, because once in Mexico, it would almost be impossible to get any ammunition unless, of course, you were in the military or a policeman.

Lupe counted their money and they had less than twelve dollars left. Where all their money had gone, she didn't know. Sometimes she just couldn't understand her husband, like when he'd given those six dollars to that gas station owner for those people's transmission.

My God, those were the same Okies who'd beat Sophia's husband in Santa Ana and had come in with clubs, trying to kill them by the river in Yuma!

"Lupe, Lupe, calm down," said Salvador. "We're going to be all right. There's nothing wrong in helping people here and there as we go."

"I know, I know," she said. "It's just that, well, I guess that I just miss my *familia* so much, Salvador! And now it looks like we're never going to be able to come back, because of that shooting you did!"

"But they were going to kill that old lady, even as she screamed, trying to protect her grandchild," he said. "It was my mother and sisters all over again, Lupe! They're lucky I didn't shoot them in their *tanates*!"

"Yes, I know!" said Lupe in frustration. "You did good, I see that, but only—I just don't know, Salvador. Where is all this going to end?"

"I don't know," he said.

"And," said Lupe, tears coming to her eyes, "I'm pregnant again, Salvador, and I don't want to be carrying all this fear around inside of me along with my new baby. I'd thought we'd left the Revolution behind us when we'd left Mexico."

Salvador smiled. "Don't worry, we'll find peace someday, Lupe, I swear it, we'll find peace, and make a home for our daughter and this new child."

"God, I hope so," said Lupe, making the sign of the cross over herself, then kissing the back of her thumb which was folded over her index finger.

DRIVING IN TO PHOENIX, they saw more Indians than they'd ever seen before, and these Indians were as poor and desperate as beggars. Going to the Western Union office, they wired Archie. It cost them a fortune, sixty cents for the telegram and then one dollar to have it hand delivered to Archie at the sheriff's office in Santa Ana.

They waited and waited, but they got no answer. They decided to risk everything and wire the same message to Oceanside to be delivered directly to the police station there.

They fully knew that they were playing with fire, trying to contact Archie at the sheriff's office and the police department, but they hadn't been able to come up with any other way of doing it.

Every few minutes, Salvador would walk out of the Western Union office to make sure that their truck was still free at the end of the street, so they could just jump in and take off if they needed. He had both weapons under his shirt in his pants. God, he didn't want to shoot at anyone anymore. Only little, scared cowards resorted to settling matters with guns. A strong man, who was *aprevenido,* could always find another way.

Inside the office, Lupe was holding calmly.

Seeing two cars full of men park across the street, Salvador quickly walked up to Lupe, took her by the arm, and he told the Western Union man that they'd be back in a little while for their answers.

Leaving the office, Salvador was surprised to see that these two cars full of men did not come after them as he'd expected, but, instead, they went into the bank across the street.

"My God," said Salvador, "it's going to be a bank robbery. Let's get the hell out of here!"

And they'd no more than gotten into their truck and were taking off, when the shooting started. They didn't go back that day to the Western Union office, and they didn't go back the following day, either.

When they did return on the third day, figuring that things had finally cooled off and maybe there'd even be a different man in the Western Union office, who did they run into, Domingo, Salvador's brother—and he was all dressed up and had his arm around an older, rich-looking woman with tons of makeup and lots of jewelry.

"Where the hell have you been?" asked Domingo. "We got here yesterday. Here, I want you to meet Socorro. We would've taken off and left if you hadn't come by today!"

Salvador was overjoyed to see his brother. He looked sober and happy and well.

"And here," said Domingo, taking his brother aside, "is the hundred dollars that you wired Archie for."

Salvador hadn't wired Archie for one hundred dollars. No, he'd wired Archie for all the monies that were still owed to him for the barrels of whiskey that he'd given to people on credit. If Archie had at all done his job, he should have wired Salvador close to three hundred dollars, after pocketing a hundred for himself.

"Are you sure that this is all the money that Archie sent me?" asked Salvador.

Suddenly, just like that, Domingo was red-faced, and raging mad like a bull! "Are you trying to say that I stole some!" bellowed Domingo, with his neck muscles coming up like thick ropes!

"No, I'm not saying that," said Salvador. "I'm glad to see you and that you brought me this money, but you see, Domingo, Archie owes me close to three hundred."

"Oh," said Domingo, calming back down as quickly as he'd gone up. "I now remember, he said something like that. Something about not having collected it all yet, and so for you to wire him again in about a week."

With that settled, Domingo was all happy again and so they went up the street to get something to eat, passing a whole bunch of Indian women who were squatted down on the boardwalk with a colorful blanket in front of them, showing off their wares of handmade turquoise jewelry.

Socorro's whole face lit up like a happy little girl's and she wanted to buy some of the beautiful silver jewelry. But Domingo was starving and so he just laughed and hugged her close.

"Look, you fool," he said, "you already look Indian enough. What you want is some *gringo* jewelry, not this Indian stuff!"

"But it's so beautiful!" insisted Socorro.

"Oh, all right, but after we eat," he said, pulling her in close and kissing her.

"Besides, it's my money," she said.

"Oh, no, don't start that," he said, suddenly getting angry at her. "You agreed to call it 'our' money, if I allowed you to come in with me to open up my gold mine in Mexico!"

"All right," she said, "but, then, if I'm willing to call it 'our' money, then why do you always call it 'my' mine, instead of ours?"

"Because, as I've told you why a thousand times," said Domingo, grinning a handsome smile, "a gold mine is worth much more than this little bit of money that you've brought into this deal of ours, see?"

And saying this, Domingo winked at Salvador as they went into the restaurant at the end of the street. He was happy showing off to his brother how he'd just handled this situation with his woman so cleverly.

After eating, Socorro did, in fact, buy several pieces of jewelry for herself, then one very plain piece for Lupe, which Lupe had been eyeing. Lupe told her no, that this wasn't necessary, that she'd just been looking, but Socorro insisted. She was a very child-like, generous person who just wanted to make everyone happy. God, for her, was a Gift Giver.

Lupe put the plain silver bracelet on her left wrist and it looked so elegant on her. Socorro, on the other hand, adorned herself with the biggest, most elaborate bracelets and earrings they had!

They drove out of Phoenix and headed south back down to Mesa Grande where Salvador and Lupe were staying a little ways out of town.

Domingo and Socorro were driving a big beautiful Packard, one of the finest automobiles of the day. Salvador and Lupe could hardly keep up with them in their little truck. At Mesa Grande, Domingo treated Salvador and Lupe to a room in a hotel with him and Socorro. Lupe took a long, hot bath, and it was Heaven! She and Salvador had been living in the brush ever since they'd left Santa Ana.

Once the two women were settled in, Domingo took Salvador outside to talk with him. Domingo was in great spirits. He now had money, money, money, not just to open up that gold mine in Navojoa, Sonora, but to live! To breathe! To feel FREE once again!

"Come on in with me, Salvador," he said, "and I'm willing to let bygones be bygones and for you to come in with me as a full partner—just because you're my brother!"

"But you have a partner already," said Salvador.

"Who, Socorro? Hell, don't worry about her. I only keep her around, because—oh, I'll tell you, she was old and worn-out looking when I found her. Her husband—who'd treated her badly for years—had just died and left her some money and her kids, the worthless *cabrones,* were killing her with their greed and fighting. But I could smell, like a good horseman can smell a fine horse, that there was a fire burning underneath the worn-out, old woman.

"And so I took her in with smiles as if she looked like an angel to me, and I worked her long in the nights with soft, gentle hands and whispers. I swear to you, Salvador, that within a week she was fifteen years younger and became the hottest woman I've ever had in my whole *PINCHE* life! I tell you, her powerful legs and those volcanic eruptions that she has—fill me with a love I've never felt before! And so now I do love her! But she's just a woman, Salvador," he added, laughing, "so don't confuse things. She'll get her money out of my share."

Hearing all this, Salvador nodded, wondering what this whole thing really meant. Their mother had always told them that to plant the seeds of love in a woman's heart but not take the woman seriously was a very dangerous game. Their mother had also said that this behavior told more about what was going on inside the man's heart than he'd ever know.

"So what do you say, eh, *hermanito*?" asked Domingo. "You wanna get rich?!? Hell, within a year, we'll be able to buy back all of our lands in *los Altos de Jalisco*. Our father—God rest his soul—will be able to look down upon us from Heaven and see how well we're doing!" Tears came to Domingo's eyes. "I love you, *hermano*! We're *familia,* you and I!"

Underneath the Stars of Mesa Grande, Arizona, Domingo hugged his brother, Salvador, in a big *abrazo,* and it was wonderful!

That night, Salvador told Lupe in the privacy of their hotel room about Domingo's offer, but he didn't add what Domingo said about Socorro. Lupe and Salvador could hear Domingo and his rich lady friend making love in the next room. They were so loud and wild, that the headboard of their bed was banging against the wall like a great drum! Lupe and Salvador were sure everyone could hear Domingo and Socorro's lovemaking throughout the hotel.

Then Domingo was howling, and Socorro was screeching, SCREAM-ING, again and again! Domingo and Socorro kept at it for nearly half the night before they finally went off to sleep.

Lupe thought this was scandalous! The woman was a grandmother in her forties, and Domingo was just being a show off, wanting the whole world to know how great he was because he could drive a woman crazy.

"This isn't love," said Lupe, "this is two poor, desperate people closing their eyes to what they are really feeling for each other inside!"

"Oh, Lupe," said Salvador, laughing, "don't be so hard. He was locked up for years and she was trapped in an abusive marriage, let them have their fun."

"I'm not stopping them," said Lupe, "but that doesn't mean that I have to like or trust the whole thing!"

Salvador took a big breath. He didn't want to admit it, but he also had this same little feeling of "mistrust" here inside of himself.

The more and more that Lupe heard about Domingo's proposal—as they made their way from Mesa Grande to the border town of Nogales, just south of Tucson, Arizona—the more Lupe thought that there was just something very wrong about the whole situation.

Each day there was less and less talk between her and Salvador.

Ever since Domingo had come into the picture, it was like Salvador and she, Lupe, weren't very close anymore. The feeling of those intimate conversations they had on the river's edge under the Stars in Yuma was all gone.

And they'd been so happy, she and Salvador, when they'd had *nada, nada,* nothing living under the trees and brush and Stars. Something had happened. It was like the arrival of his brother—with all this money and big dreams—was a tonic that was bringing out a side of Salvador that Lupe had never seen before.

She was frightened.

22

*Adam and Eva now both Knew that it wasn't the Devil
who'd ever tempted them — it was their own Mirror that
Reflected their Doubts and Fears.*

THEY HAD NO TROUBLE getting into Mexico. In Nogales, Sonora, right across the border, Lupe and Salvador went to the bank to wire Archie for the rest of their money. They couldn't just keep depending on Domingo's generosity for everything, especially since it wasn't really Domingo's money, but Socorro's with which he was being so generous.

Across the border liquor was legal, and so Salvador and Domingo began drinking beer like water and shooting down *tequila* with chasers of *sangre*, meaning "blood," and all they could now do was talk about how wonderful their childhood had been and that they were going to return to that wonderful place of their childhood when they got their gold from that mine in Navajoa.

Domingo purchased dozens of shovels and picks and iron bars for working the mine, then he got a case of dynamite smuggled in for him from the U.S. side of Nogales. It was decided that Salvador and Lupe would take all these things in their truck and all of their clothing and personal belongings would be put in the trunk and backseat of the big Packard.

The two Villaseñor brothers who'd survived the Revolution, would now be returning home to *los Altos de Jalisco* in style, driving side by side in their fine automobiles with their women at their sides and with enough gold to buy back all the lands of their once *rancho grande*. They weren't being deported back to Mexico like cattle as was happening to thousands of their *gente;* no, they were returning to their homeland of their own freewill like *hombres de estaca* with guns at the waist and money in their pockets.

Every day, Salvador and his brother continued drinking, singing, and celebrating, and each night Domingo and his lady friend could be heard screaming to the Heavens.

Then each morning, Salvador and Lupe would go down to the bank to see if their money from Archie had arrived or not. But by the end of the week, Salvador was no longer going to the bank in the mornings with Lupe anymore. Lupe was going by herself. Salvador was too hung-over from drinking so much.

One morning, Lupe went to the bank wearing a new dress and shoes—not expensive, but decent looking—that Socorro had bought for her. Socorro, Lupe was finding out, was one of these Mexican-Indian women who were all Heart-*Corazón,* thinking that "gift" giving was the ultimate human virtue, a reflection of the Almighty!

This day when Lupe went into the bank and asked the bank manager if their money had come in, he said, "Yes, it has," but then he added, "but not here, nor in the great empire of China will money be put into the hands of a woman. You'll need to bring in your husband," he added with arrogance.

Lupe was shocked, and a few months before she would have felt crushed and had no idea what to say or do. But she'd come a long ways in these last few days.

"Señor," said Lupe, feeling her heart-*corazón* beginning to pound like a great drum, "for nearly a week you have been seeing me come in to this bank with my husband every morning and you have been nothing but courteous to my husband and me, until now that our money has arrived. What do you mean by speaking to me in this manner? Do I look like an irresponsible person? And even if I did, that is not your business. That money is ours, and I want to have it right now!"

The well-dressed man was surprised, but not without words, either. *"Señora,"* he said in an arrogant, condescending tone of voice, "you have forgotten your place, my dear. You have been too long over there in that frivolous country of the United States. Here in Mexico, we know how to treat women, so I will not release this money or any other to you without your husband's presence!"

Maria Guadalupe Gomez *de* Villaseñor held, looking straight into the eyes of the man standing before her. He was a tall, slender man in his thirties, an educated man, a good-looking man, a man who thought he knew the ways of the world, and how things should be done. But she was also her mother's daughter and her grandmother's granddaughter, and so here in her veins ran the blood of women who'd been taking up ground and being accounted for since the dawn of time! Why, she'd seen her mother hold their *familia* together—after their father abandoned them—with nothing but her wits! She'd seen her mother fight tooth and nail to keep food on the table for them, so Lupe wasn't going to be intimidated, either.

"*Señor,*" she said, "then do I understand you correctly that you are refusing to give me our money? Money that belongs to my husband and me?"

"Yes," he said, "your ears are not dirty, you understand me."

And he now actually laughed at her, playing with his mustache as if he were flirting with her. A few of the other people in the bank laughed, too. Lupe glanced around. They were all men. There was not one single woman working in the whole bank.

And why Lupe took this vow, at the moment as she faced this bank manager all alone, she'd never quite know, but that Other Holy Self of herself now spoke up inside of her mind and said, "This isn't right. Women can count money and put it away as good as any man or faster. I've seen women do this with fast, agile hands every day in the packinghouses with the peaches, lemons, tomatoes all over the Southland. And we, women, have our dreams, too, just like Salvador and Domingo have their dreams, and so I now take an oath before God that I will one day be rich and I will help see to it that women get the chance to work in banks just like men, for my mother—God Bless her Soul—knew how to handle money for the benefit of our whole *familia* much better than my father, and so did Salvador's mother, too. We, women, need to have a say about money matters for the world to progress, and that's that! It will be done, so help me God!"

And hearing this Voice speak inside her, Lupe felt this great peace come over her and she now said to this man standing before her, "All right, I will return with my husband, but—you understand this right now—you and your other male friends are coming to an end."

"Is this a threat?" said the man, grinning with amusement as he turned smiling to his fellow male coworkers.

"No," said Lupe, "this is a promise from me, a woman."

Saying this, Lupe turned and started out the bank, and by the time she got to the front door to go out, she was shaking like a leaf—she was so enraged! She could hear the banker and his friends behind her laughing, no doubt congratulating each other on how they'd just put another woman in her place.

Suddenly, in a flash, *un RAYO del CIELO,* she knew that these men

were cowards! If she and Salvador had been driving up all week in their
fine Moon automobile and they'd entered the bank all dressed up in fine
clothes, none of this would have happened to her.

And in this same flash of insight, Lupe now also realized why she'd
married Salvador above all others. He, Salvador, was, indeed, his mother's
child, *un hombre* who truly respected women, and especially strong
women who spoke up for themselves!

Tears of joy came to Lupe's eyes. This was what made Salvador different from his brother, Domingo, and almost all other men. His mother had
raised him to be a woman-man, as her mother-in-love had so well
explained to her. Salvador's mother had showed him that a woman's
power, here inside of a male, didn't weaken that man, but instead strength-
ened him to be the strongest of all *hombres*!

Lupe was exhausted by the time she got back to the little hotel where
they were staying. That man at the bank had truly turned her stomach
with his arrogant, male airs. And how those other men at the bank had
enjoyed it. Not one of them had tried to intervene or lessen her embarrassment.

She was glad that Salvador and Domingo and Socorro were out.

She wanted to lie down and gather her thoughts. This was no longer
just about the money that they'd finally gotten wired to them at the bank.
No, this was now about a whole way of life, about her whole way of thinking ever since she'd grown up in *la Barranca del Cobre* and she'd given
witness to her mother getting up before daybreak day after day, performing miracle after miracle just to keep them alive during that AWFUL REV-
OLUTION of men's abuses!

LUPE MUST HAVE FALLEN ASLEEP, for the next thing she
knew she was waking up with such a clarity of thought that she Knew
Everything!

No, she and Salvador were not going to go back to Mexico. Both of
their *familias* were now in the United States, and so this was where they
were going to make their home and raise their children with cousins and
aunts and uncles.

But how would she be able to say this to Salvador with his big plans of
establishing a gold mine along with his brother, and getting so rich that
they would be able to buy back their lands in *Los Altos*?

Lupe took a deep breath, fully realizing that this was the turning point of her life. She was taking up ground! This was it! But she was going to have to be very careful in presenting herself to her *esposo,* especially with all of their *gente* being run out of the United States.

Lupe put both of her hands over her heart area, Breathing in and Breathing out of *Papito Dios.* She almost went to sleep, but not quite. She was in that place halfway between sleep and waking where she could feel the Power starting to come into her—as she lay in bed with her eyes closed. It was extraordinary, all fear and confusion quickly evaporated from her.

And she now knew that this was exactly what her own mother had done just before she'd gone down to the *plaza* with a gun underneath her dress and saved her brother, Victoriano, from that hanging by those no-good renegade soldiers. Her mother had gone to this Sacred Place, here inside of a woman, where God impregnated a Female with the Holy Force of Creation.

Tears of ecstasy came to Lupe's eyes as she kept Breathing in and out of *Papito.*

Her mother, Doña Guadalupe, and her mother-in-love, Doña Margarita, were now here with her, too, guiding her, helping her, and so was the Blessed Mother of Jesus.

THAT AFTERNOON SALVADOR CAME IN all drunk and happy, along with Domingo and Socorro. Immediately Socorro and Domingo went to their room next door and their headboard began to sound as it banged against the wall once more.

Coming into their room, Salvador saw Lupe sitting quietly at the end of their bed with the sunlight coming down all about her in a golden glow. "What is it?" he asked.

Hortensia was down the way, playing with the two little girls of another family who were also staying at the hotel.

"Nothing," said Lupe. "It can wait."

She didn't want to speak to Salvador about all this that she was feeling inside while he was drinking. But on the other hand, he now seemed to always be drinking. Tears came to her eyes. They'd been so close there on the banks of the Colorado River in Yuma.

"Lupe," said Salvador with a twisted, happy-liquor grin, "I could feel it all the way outside—even before I opened the door. Something very big is going on with you. Remember, we've been through a lot and so we're very close together, here inside, *querida,*" he added, tapping his chest area. "Talk to me."

The tears now flowed freely from Lupe's eyes. There was just nothing any finer that Salvador could have said, because it was true, they had been through so much together and they were, indeed, very close.

"Salvador," she said, "the money has arrived."

"Well, that's wonderful! So then why are you crying? Isn't it the full two hundred?"

"I don't know how much it is," said Lupe. "The banker wouldn't give it to me."

"That's okay," said Salvador, "we'll just go and get it together right now, before the bank closes."

"Salvador, the money isn't why I'm crying," said Lupe. "It's how the bank manager treated me that has upset me, because, well . . . now I understand why it is that I don't want us to return to Mexico."

"You what?" said Salvador, squinting his eyes, trying to understand what it was that Lupe had just said. "You don't want us going back to Mexico?" he asked.

"No, I don't," said Lupe, "I want us to use this money to go back to California so we can be with our *familias.*"

Lupe said no more. Salvador was staring at her as if she was crazy. He was swaying back and forth on his feet with a drunken, confused look until the whole idea finally seemed to come through to him. Then he EXPLODED!

"But what are you saying, *mujer*!?!" he shouted. "Have you gone completely crazy-*loca,* eh? We got a gold mine waiting for us just outside of Navojoa! We'll be rich within a year, and then we can do whatever we damn well please! That's what rich people get to do, whatever they damn well please, here or across the border!"

"No, Salvador," said Lupe, as calmly as she could. Her heart was pounding. She'd never spoken up like this in all her life. A real lady didn't behave like this. No, a real lady was cute and coy and indirect, or elegant and beautiful and knew her place. Those were a woman's two choices. Not this, that she was now Birthing here inside of herself!

"No?" said Salvador to her. "Is this what I just heard you say to me, Lupe, 'No, Salvador?' "

She swallowed. She could see that he'd been drinking far more than she'd realized and she knew he had a temper every bit as bad as his brother's, so she'd have to be careful in what she said. But this was her life, too, and so she wasn't going to be silenced.

"Yes, Salvador, I said no to you."

"You said no to me? Your husband? *El hombre de la casa?*"

"Of course, I said no to you, Salvador, you're *mi esposo,* the man I married," she said, getting louder than she'd expected. "I'm your wife, Salvador, the woman who loves you and is carrying your next child here inside as we speak. The woman who got down on her hands and knees, crawling into the fires of Hell to rescue you when I don't think any other rational human being would have. So yes, I said no, and I'll say NO AGAIN IN THE FUTURE, TOO!" She hadn't meant to shout, but she had.

Salvador held, just staring at her, then he started laughing. "Okay, okay, so you said no. You don't have to bite my head off," he added. "I just wanted to make sure that I'd heard you correctly."

"You heard me correctly, Salvador," she said, her heart pounding so hard that she felt the top of her head might come off. "We've been married for nearly three years, and I've followed you through Hell and fire and supported you with all my heart and soul without question, but I will follow you no more without speaking up. What happened to me at that bank is no small matter. And what is happening to you with all your drinking and celebrating with your brother is no small matter, either."

"All right," he said, feeling his mouth going dry with all the beer and *tequila* he'd drunk, "this has gone far enough! I don't want to hear any more! I, too, have put my life on the line TIME and AGAIN, LUPE!" he yelled. "So don't think you've been doing things alone!"

"Yes, I agree," she yelled right back at him, refusing to be silenced, "you have risked your life, too! But in the past, we always did things only your way, and we are not going to be doing it only your way in the future anymore! Do you hear me, Salvador?

"We were so happy on the riverbank of Yuma with me massaging your feet after work and . . . and the two of us talking about our dreams. Those were our dreams, Salvador, yours and mine, and yes, small, I agree, not big and grand like the ones you and Domingo now talk about every day, but they were ours. Do you understand? I'm in this marriage, too."

The tears were flowing down from her eyes and Salvador felt such heartfelt power for her as he looked into her eyes. Lupe was speaking right up to him in his face with all the passion of her *corazón.* He was touched to the core.

"Yes, Lupe," he said, taking in a deep breath, "we were happy, weren't we, *querida,* there by the river's edge."

"Yes, Salvador," said Lupe, her eyes looking like great, shiny, dark ponds as the tears continued streaming down her face, "you and I were together, here inside of our hearts, and every night when we'd make love, we'd speak about our dreams of making a home, of building a place big enough so we could take care of our mothers and my father in their old age. We were wonderful together, Salvador, there underneath the Stars along the river skin to skin, feeling so warm and good."

"Yes, I remember well," said Salvador, his whole chest swelling up. "My feet were swollen and burning after working in those hot fields and you massaged my feet with that cool, wet clay from the river and it felt like Heaven here on Earth!"

"Exactly, Salvador. We had nothing but our happiness, and our happiness was our EVERYTHING!"

Salvador's eyes were now crying, too. "Yes, I agree completely, but still, what is this all about? Are you afraid if we get the gold, then we can't be happy?"

She shook her head. "No, not at all, Salvador. I think people can have something and still be happy, it's just, that, well—" She didn't quite know how to put it in words, but she'd been raised in a gold mining town so she'd seen what gold did to people's minds. It was already happening to Domingo and Salvador. They could talk of nothing else. They were possessed by *el Diablo* of gold.

He could see that she was having difficulty. "Lupe," Salvador now said, "why don't you just tell me what happened to you at the bank. I just don't understand what is going on."

Lupe told Salvador the story of how the bank manager had treated her. At first Salvador just laughed, telling Lupe that she was being too sensitive and spoiled, because of how women were treated in the United States.

But, then, when Lupe reminded Salvador of how difficult it had been for his own mother in Mexico and how he, himself, had explained to her that his family would never have come to ruin if his mother, Doña Margarita, had handled their finances, Salvador remembered their days of starvation and he EXPLODED!

"You're right!" he yelled at Lupe. "A thousand times, you're right! We could have maybe even survived the Revolution if my mother had handled our money!"

"And also, Salvador," Lupe now said, "realize that this banker would have never treated me like this, if you and I had driven up all week in our Moon automobile and we'd been dressed in fine clothes. The way in which he talked to me made me almost ill, Salvador," she said with tears coming to her eyes again. "This is how women are always treated, especially poor women. Then you should have seen how all the other men in the bank also snickered at me. They were all just a bunch of cowards, but what could I do? The whole Mexican system supports them."

By now, Salvador could hear no more. He was ten feet up in the air, fighting demons, seeing his beloved mother in rags, looking all Indian!

He jammed his fist into his mouth to stop himself from screaming out in anguish! He'd been nothing but a child of ten years old when the Revolution had come raping and killing into their mountains. But he was a child no more! He was now a fully-grown man with his *tanates* hanging loose and his heart-*corazón* beat, Beat, BEATING like the mighty DRUM of the UNIVERSE!

"Come on!" he yelled to Lupe. "Let's go down there to that bank right now and get our money, and you'll get your RESPECT!"

"But no, Salvador," she said, "this isn't the point of what I've been talking about. This banker's behavior is in all of Mexico, don't you see?"

"Then all of Mexico is about to change right now!" bellowed Salvador as he kicked the door open, and Lupe was right behind him, yelling, but he wasn't listening to her anymore! He was *un hombre, un macho,* a man possessed!

Hearing the commotion, Domingo came running out of his room, pulling up his pants. "What is it?" he asked.

"Our money has arrived!" shouted Salvador. "But that stupid banker wouldn't release it to Lupe!"

"Do you need my help?" said Domingo, liking the sound of the action. "We'll hang the son-of-a-bitch by his tongue *a lo chingon*!"

"No, it's only one bank," said Salvador, getting in his truck. "I'll be right back!"

But Lupe wasn't going to be left behind and she got into the truck with her husband. "Look," she said, "you missed the whole point of what it is that I'm trying to say. This isn't about going after this banker, Salvador. This is about understanding how our life would be if we returned to Mexico."

"Exactly," said Salvador, "and you're my wife and so our life in Mexico or anywhere else on this whole damn *planeta* will be good, because every inch of the way we will have respect! You hear me, RESPECT, Lupe!"

"But we can't fight everyone, Salvador."

"No, just every son-of-a-bitch *pinchi cabrón* who doesn't show us respect!"

Lupe didn't know what more to say. Salvador just wasn't really hearing her anymore. No, he was drunk and wild with rage!

Getting to the bank, Salvador burst through the doors, rushing straight up to the manager who was sitting at his desk, talking to a customer.

"What do you mean, you won't give my wife our money!?!" he bellowed at the bank manager.

"Of course, I'll give you your money, *señor,*" said the manager. "I guess there's just been a misunderstanding. It's simply not our bank's policy to give money to women." He laughed, feeling a little bit nervous. "Where would our country be if we gave money to every wife who came in here?" he added.

But he'd added this last statement to the wrong man. Salvador's mother had begged his father not to sell their goats or they'd starve. His father, the arrogant fool, had sold the herd of fine milk goats anyway, because he, a man, couldn't go back on his word to another man, even if the man was a tricky businessman.

"I'll tell you where we'd be!" yelled Salvador, leaning over the desk right into the manager's face with the cords of his nineteen-inch neck coming up like a bull's! "We'd be a SMARTER, BETTER OFF COUNTRY! Now, give us our money, right now!"

"Of course, by all means," said the man, still refusing to be intimidated.

"And," added Salvador, "I want you to apologize to my wife!"

Now, this stopped the bank manager dead in his tracks. He'd had enough. He wasn't going to take any more abuse from these two poor, uncivilized, ignorant ranch people. Not taking his eyes off of Salvador for a second, he now pushed back in his chair, standing up to his full height, towering over Salvador and Lupe. He straightened his coat, buttoning it.

"Apologize?!?" he said. "I apologize to your wife!?! Why, it is your wife—just because she's pretty—who thinks that she can come in here and get her way! Oh, no, she owes me an apology! But I'm a gentleman and a professional, and so I'll let that go and I will be glad to give you two your money, but you two will burn in Hell before you ever get an apology from any member of this banking institution!"

Grinning, smiling that little tight grin of his, Salvador now said, "I see, I see," and he said this so softly, so calmly, that if the bank manager hadn't been so full of himself he would have understood that something very dangerous was up, but he didn't. "And we're just poor, simple people, right? We aren't rich, so we're really of no consequence to you or your bank, correct?"

And saying this, Salvador calmly turned around, grinning that little tight smile of his, and he took note of where all the other employees and customers were situated in the bank, because he certainly didn't want to do something that he couldn't handle.

Then, feeling satisfied that he now knew the lay of the place well, Salvador suddenly, without any warning, lunged across the huge desk, grabbed hold of the man by the throat and jerked him halfway over the desk. "I'm from *Jalisco,* you stupid son-of-a-bitch! A *TAPATIO!* A WILD MAN! And we INVENTED HELL for the likes of YOU!"

Saying this, Salvador drew his .45 automatic and rammed the barrel of the gun into the man's face. "You don't insult a man's wife—no matter how poor—and think that you and your friends can laugh and snicker without getting the bull's horn up your ass!

"And don't one of you son-of-a-bitches, who's behind me, even think of moving! I checked each one of you and know right where you're standing! MOVE, and I'll shoot your ass dead!

"And now you," he said, turning his attention back to the manager, "are you ready to start apologizing, or do you really want to start bleeding slowly on your WAY to HELL! For I will not kill you quickly, but shoot you in one foot, then the other, then shoot you in the *tanates,* so you'll feel the pains of giving birth before YOU DIE! Didn't you have a mother? Weren't you taught respect. Now, start talking!"

No one moved. Everyone was transfixed. And the banker didn't know whether to shit or scream! His eyes were all jumpy. He'd never expected this. He'd truly miscalculated who these people were. And he now knew that he was dealing with a totally wild man, a people who six years after the Mexican Revolution ended, were still fighting—not because of poverty—but because of personal pride and religious fanaticism. These people of Jalisco were crazy-*loco* Christians, willing to die on a moment's notice for their impossible beliefs of God, the Devil, and Eternal Salvation!

"Please, understand," the banker was now saying, "this had absolutely nothing to do with your fine wife, *señor.* I'm sure that your *señora* is a fine, intelligent woman," he added.

"Does this sound like an apology to you?" said Salvador, turning to Lupe. "Or does this just sound like more *caca del toro*!"

And why Lupe said what she said next, she'd always wonder about, because she'd never thought of herself as being one of those types of women who enjoyed egging her husband on to see him fight in her behalf. Those type of women, her mother had always told Lupe and her sisters, were low class women who were not thinking of the benefit for the whole *familia* and were just having a little personal fun in a stupid and very dangerous way.

But Lupe now found herself saying with *gusto,* "No, Salvador, that almost sounds like an apology, but not quite."

And with this word "almost," Lupe gave Salvador all the reins he needed to jerk the man completely across the desk and slam him down on the floor to his knees, bellowing at him like a WILD BULL!

"ALMOST isn't good enough!" screamed Salvador, cramming the barrel of the gun into the man's mouth. "Was your mother ALMOST pregnant when she gave you birth! Are you ALMOST full of shit when you pull down your pants to crap! No, your mother was fully pregnant when she gave you birth, and you're completely full of shit RIGHT NOW! Why, I can smell you shitting!"

"I apologize!" said the banker, tears coming to his eyes. He was terror-stricken! He, too, had now seen the Devil and the Devil stood here before him upright on two legs and his name was Juan Salvador Villaseñor, who'd seen his beloved sisters raped and killed before his eyes and he was the Avenging Angel of God, who of his own freewill had volunteered to take the Light to Darkness! And he was insane with hate because of all the Love that he carried inside of his Soul! "May I burn in Hell for all eternity if I don't take back my behavior! Please, accept my apology, *señora,* I didn't mean anything! Oh, my God! Please! Please!"

"Is this now an apology?" said Salvador, turning to Lupe. "Or do you want more!"

"This is a real apology," she said. "It's enough."

"Good," said Salvador, "and in the future you will treat every woman who comes in here with respect!"

"I will! I WILL!" yelled the banker. "I swear it on my mother's grave!"

"Excellent," said Salvador, throwing the man back across his desk. "Now, *señor,* please, give us our money. And understand that the only reason I'm being so kind to you today is . . . because you caught me in a good mood, you lucky *cabrón* son-of-a-bitch!"

Salvador and Lupe got their money, and were quickly out the door. No one followed them. They were all still too stunned.

23

*GOD and Lucifer were Dancing and Mary and Jesus were
Clapping — all the Forces of the Heavens were at last
working Together once more.*

Driving back to their hotel, Salvador figured that
everything was settled and they'd be able to continue on their way to
the gold mine in Navojoa, Sonora, until Lupe spoke.

"No, Salvador," she said again. "I still don't want us returning to Mexico."

"But I stood up for you," said Salvador.

"Yes, you did, and I love you for that, *querido,* but I still don't want to
go back to a country that treats women like this. My mother and sisters
worked too hard for too long for me to go backward, Salvador."

Domingo was grinning ear to ear when they pulled up to the hotel.
"Did you get your money, or should I go back down to the bank with you
and teach them how us *hombres de Los Altos* handle matters?"

"We got the money," said Salvador, looking beaten down.

"Then why the long face?" asked Domingo.

The door was open to Domingo's room and Salvador and Lupe could
see that Socorro was still in bed.

"Lupe still doesn't want us going back to Mexico," said Salvador.

"She what?!?" said Domingo, suddenly getting red-faced as a tomato
with rage. "Well, then, just slap her, Salvador!" he yelled. "Don't be letting
a woman tell you what to do! You got to be strong to be *el hombre de tu
casa*! You're not some little *puto cabrón* crybaby!"

"That's not it," said Salvador. "She's right, our *familias* are back in California, and it's also true what she says, we've been drinking so much and
dreaming so high, Domingo, that I'm afraid that it could all just—"

"OUR FATHER is DEAD!" roared Domingo. "We got no family until we've rebuilt our *rancho* with cattle as far as the eye can see! SLAP HER! Teach her her PLACE! Here, if you don't have the *tanates* to do it, I'll do it for you!"

And Domingo lunged at Lupe, to hit her, but Salvador stepped in, grabbing his brother in a bear hug. "DON'T, Domingo! Lupe's my wife! Not yours!"

"Then treat her like a wife, you fool! Or she'll ruin everything that's between us! Here, I'll show you," he yelled, breaking loose from his brother's grip, "I'm not afraid to show you my love, brother to brother!"

And saying this, Domingo rushed into his room like a madman, and yanked Socorro out of their bed. She screamed and tried to hide her nakedness with a blanket as he dragged her out of their room. Outside, he began to slap her across the face in an insane rage, trying to show his brother how much he loved him, and that no woman would stand in the way of their love.

The poor terrified woman screamed and SCREAMED. People came out of their rooms.

Salvador had to hit his brother across the back of the skull with his gun to stop him from killing the woman. But this didn't silence Domingo, he continued screaming!

Lupe took Socorro back inside, bolted the door and began to attend to her. Lupe just couldn't believe all this. In the last few weeks all Hell had broken loose!

"We got gold, *hermano*!" bellowed Domingo. "Don't you see, we got GOLD, the KING of the EARTH! We're going to be RICH! Don't throw it all away for a woman!"

Domingo's eyes had looked completely crazy-*loco* with hate when he'd lunged to strike Lupe. Obviously, hitting women was something he'd done many times before. Of course, Lupe fully realized that striking women went on in many Mexican households, but for all of her father's faults of drinking and gambling, he'd never once struck their mother.

Lupe now soaked a towel in cold water and put it to Socorro's face and the back of her head where Domingo had kept hitting her, even after she was down. My God, he might have killed her if Salvador hadn't knocked him down with his gun. Lupe just couldn't believe all that was happening to them ever since Kenny had been shot in front of their home. Where was all this going to end?

Socorro couldn't stop shaking.

"Lupe," she said, shaking like she was freezing to death, "my husband used to beat me, too, but at least I knew why. Domingo just attacked me like a wild dog! Oh, my God, my God! What did I ever do to deserve such abuse! All I've done is give him love and money!"

"You did nothing to deserve this beating," said Lupe. "My mother always told us girls there's absolutely no reason for a man to ever beat his wife. Do not twist things around and blame yourself. You are a fine, generous human being, Socorro, and I recommend that you get away from Domingo right now, while you still have some money left.

"Look, I was born in a gold mining town," continued Lupe, "so I know how men's minds get wild and twisted with the thoughts of getting so rich that now they are above all the realities of life. You need to get away from Domingo immediately, before it's too late!"

"Then you don't think there's really a gold mine?"

Lupe could see that this woman just didn't understand what she was saying. "Socorro, it doesn't matter if there is a gold mine or not. Men go crazy when they get to thinking of gold."

"Then I should leave him now?" asked Socorro.

"Yes," said Lupe. "And I'm going to get Salvador to take us back to the United States and I'm—I'm—I'm going to tell him that he can no longer do any more bootlegging, either. That I've followed him long enough, and now it's time for him to follow me, and I say that we are going to be law-abiding people and have a normal life, so help me God, or I will leave him and take my daughter and this child I carry here inside of me, and return on my own to my family, and that's that!"

Socorro was no longer shaking or crying or even seemed concerned with her bruises and pains. She was just staring at Lupe in utter shock. "You'd do this," she said, "you'd really face your husband and tell him everything to his face that—that you've just told me?"

Lupe nodded. "Of course, why not?"

"Oh, Lupe!" said Socorro, and both women now took each other in their arms, holding Heart to Heart.

Outside, Domingo was down on his knees, hugging his brother and crying with all of his might! "We had EVERYTHING, *hermanito*! Don't you see, we had EVERYTHING when our beloved father was alive! So how could you and *mama* have left him!"

"Domingo, I've told you a thousand times, we didn't leave our father," said Salvador.

"Of course, you did!" said Domingo. "Don't you see, or we'd still have everything, if you hadn't left him."

And in that moment, Salvador finally saw in a flash what it was that his brother was really saying. Domingo was confusing God with their own father. He had the story of Adam and Eve being put out of the Garden all mixed up with his own story of coming back to *Los Altos* and finding everything gone.

"Yes," said Salvador to his brother, "I can now see that we did have everything when our father lived and you're right, we did leave our father. We went down the mountain to find food and he chose to stay up on our *rancho* drinking and racing off on his horse to the distant mountaintops, screaming that God had abandoned him and all of his sons were dead!"

"See!" yelled Domingo. "You could have helped him if you hadn't abandoned him!"

"Domingo, I don't have blue eyes like you. He never acknowledged me as a son. It was you he wanted, it was you that he screamed for on every mountaintop!"

"Then I did it?" asked Domingo, his snake eyes suddenly being able to see in a whole new way. "Then I'm the one who abandoned our *papa*!" said Domingo, "and all I'd been trying to do was good!" he yelled. "To surprise him where he was working with a team of horses on that new highway that they were building from San Diego to Del Mar, but those *rinchi* bastard Texans beat me, arrested me for a crime they knew that I'd never done, and shipped me to Chicago to work in the steel mills! I LOVED OUR FATHER, Salvador! I never meant to abandon him!"

"SOCORRO!" he then screamed. "SOCORRO! I didn't mean to hit you! I'm sorry! I only meant GOOD! My mother didn't abandon my father! She, too, only meant GOOD!"

And Salvador could now see so clearly that at this moment, Domingo was forgiving—not just his own mother—but all women, including *Eva*, our original mother, for having lost the Garden of Eden for all Mankind!

Inside the hotel, Lupe couldn't believe it, hearing Domingo's shouts of agony, Socorro forced herself up from the bed. And against all the pain she felt from the beating, she began to grip the walls as she made her way out of the room and to the door so she could go and be with Domingo.

And when Socorro opened the door, there was Domingo kneeling on the ground by his brother with his arms open to her, shouting to her with all his heart. "Socorro! SOCORRO! Forgive me! Forgive me! I DIDN'T KNOW!"

"Domingo!" she yelled, staggering with pain as she went to him.

And they were then hugging and crying and kissing.

Domingo was begging for forgiveness, and she was saying yes, yes, yes, she'd forgive him, and he was saying that he loved her.

Lupe was enraged!

Salvador had tears running down his face.

And above both couples, hovering in the Sky, were Jesus and the Virgin Mary and Doña Margarita along with Moses and Lucifer. The Mother Moon was coming and the Father Sun was going. Another Day had come to pass Here on this *planeta,* passionately situated between Hell and Heaven!

24

The SIXTH SUN *was now arising fast for an* All New Day.
People would no longer be able to tell where the Heavens
ended and the Earth *began.*

L UPE DIDN'T WAIT. That very night she kept her word that
she'd given to Soccoro and she told Salvador, "No, not only don't I
want us going any further into Mexico, but when we return to the United
States, I also want you, Salvador, to not do any more of your bootlegging,
or any other illegal activities!"

Salvador was stunned!

"What in God's name has gotten into your mind, Lupe? Have you gone
completely crazy-*loca*? How in the world do you expect us to return to the
United States and make a living without my bootlegging? Everything in
the U.S. is stacked against us, *los Mejicanos,* from the word go. And Father
Ryan told you that—"

"I DON'T CARE about ANY of THAT!" shouted Lupe. "This is our
life! Not his!"

Salvador couldn't believe what he was hearing. She was flying beyond
reason.

"Look, Salvador," she now continued more calmly, "I want us to be
legal and have a home where we are no longer running from the law. I will
not bring another child into this world of violence like we did with poor
little Hortensia! She has nightmares, Salvador!"

"Lupe, you were born in the middle of the Revolution. You saw much
more than our daughter has seen, and you're fine."

"And because I had to witness our village being burned to the ground
time and again, we need to do this to our daughter, too?!? Oh, no, Salvador, WE WILL NOT!" shouted Lupe. "Because before we married,

Salvador, I asked you if you were a bootlegger, and you told me that you were not a bootlegger, and I took you at your word with ALL MY HEART and SOUL, and so now you will make that word of yours COME TRUE, and that's that, do you hear me!" she yelled. "I have spoken!"

Salvador looked at Lupe, not knowing what to think or do. It was true, she had, indeed, spoken. He could well see that she wasn't a woman who would be moved anymore. No, she was now a woman who'd taken up ground like he'd seen his own mother do so many times, declaring that this piece of Mother Earth where she stood was Holy and she, the Tree of Life, would move Earth and Rock with her roots and do whatever it took to Live.

But, also, he truly wondered if Lupe had any idea with whom she was dealing. He was also a man who wouldn't be moved! Did she really think for a minute that she could tell him how to run his life? If they were giving up a gold mine and returned to the United States, then bootlegging was his only possible livelihood. It was what got him—not just money—but RESPECT in a country that looked down its nose at his people.

"All right," he now said, "I quit my bootlegging like you say, Lupe, then how in the name of Hell do you propose that we make our living in the United States, eh?"

"Well, we can work in the fields like everyone else, Salvador."

He took a big breath, and blew out. "Lupe, a depression is going on. Our people are being run out of the country. Your own family would be starving if I hadn't given money to your brother to buy that truck. And that truck, remember, I bought with my BOOTLEGGING MONEY!" he shouted into her face!

"Salvador," she said, closing her eyes so she could avoid his wild intimidating look, "we will find a way. God will provide."

"Sure," he said, "but also God needs a little help in life, damnit!"

And saying this, he stopped talking, stepped back, and just stood, looking at this young wife of his. Long ago he'd learned that all demands in life, *la vida,* had a price, and most people weren't willing to pay that price. It took real *tanates* to put your life on the line day in and day out.

He now wondered if Lupe—for all her talk—was really willing to pay the price if she didn't get her demands. For to make any demand, without being willing to pay that price tag, then that demand was just a hollow and empty voice of a chickenshit, all-talk *pendejo*!

"All right, Lupe," he now said in a calm voice, "if I don't agree to your demands, then what?" He was feeling so damned tired of this whole conversation that he wasn't going to take Lupe seriously anymore unless she was really willing to pay the full price of being taken seriously. And to be taken seriously carried a formidable price tag, and this price tag had to be paid in full just as Jesus Christ, Himself, had paid it in full on the cross so that every mortal since then could feel it down here in his guts that Jesus was, indeed, real and not just talk.

This, one's wedding vows never addressed.

This had nothing to do with whether two people loved each other or not.

No, this, of being the lead horse of *la familia*, was not just an automatic part of the honeymoon package.

He took a deep breath. "So come on, Lupe," he repeated himself as he saw the tears streaming down her face, "speak up, what will you do if I don't agree to your demands?"

It was stuck in her throat. She didn't really want to say it, but here it came at last.

"Salvador, I will leave you," she said, finally stepping forward into the darkness of the unknown and becoming her own self lead horse and now each shadow, each fallen branch, every puddle along the trail was looking dangerous, but she still wasn't going to be stopped.

"I will take Hortensia," she continued, "and this child I carry here within me, and I will survive without you, somehow, so help me God!"

Seeing her face and knowing how she'd risked her life by going back into the burning *infierno* to save him, Salvador now knew that this woman, this girl, standing before him had truly come into her own. For she was now, indeed, willing to pay the price for the Song she wanted to Dance to in Her Life.

He blew out. And she wasn't just wild in her assessment of herself. No, instinctively she'd taken his gun and their money out of that burning Hell and had the presence of mind to put them up in a fork of a tree, so if they'd gotten caught driving off, their money and gun would still be safe. She was brilliant! A genius! And tough! She didn't panic when the chips were down! Rich or poor, in sickness or in health, this woman could be the best lead horse around!

"Okay," said Salvador, "so then what you are saying, Lupe, is either we now do things your way, or that's it. You will leave me and go home to your parents."

She nodded, and nodded again. "Yes, Salvador, that's it. I've made up my mind," she added calmly.

Salvador took in a big breath. He really couldn't believe all this that was happening to him and Lupe. They'd been to Hell and back, and yet the power, the strength, the conviction that was now radiating from this young woman before him was so great that most men would feel the need to slap her face and bring an end to this Formidable Force that Lupe now Possessed!

And a man could do this, a man had the brute strength within him to put the fires out of almost any woman, but then what would this man have—a shell. A frightened gun-shy horse.

And so no, he, Salvador, wasn't about to slap Lupe. For to do this, he fully realized that he, Juan Salvador Villaseñor *de* Castro, would be slapping his very own mother. And his mother had warned him that this day—where he now stood—would come to be. And his mother's voice now RANG OUT IN HIS HEAD like a great DRUM, saying:

"And when God comes asking who ate of that forbidden fruit of the Tree of Knowledge, you will not blame Lupe as Adam blamed *Eva*! Do you hear me, you will take it like a man, *un Mejicano de los buenos,* and with your *tanates* in hand you will say, 'God, I did it! I did it!' And you will take full responsibility, for believe me, this young bride of yours will then rise up with the Love of the Night Star and make all the lessons that you've taught her seem small by comparison to the great lesson that she will then teach you in ONE GREAT STROKE!

"And this will happen to you when you least expect it, and it will drive you to the wall! And all this I know, for when your father and I reached this point in our marriage—as all couples do—my poor lost husband, didn't hit me as so many men do, but he lost his love for me, and started blaming me for all of his *problemas,* saying that all these misfortunes had come down upon him because he'd married beneath himself.

"I was *Eva* being blamed all over again! But you will not do this, *mi hijito,* do you hear me, you will understand that at this moment—with your *tanates* in hand—you can now step forward and ARISE *CON AMOR*! Do you hear me, no slapping, no blaming!"

Salvador burst out laughing!

What else could he do? Here was his mother inside of his head, having brainwashed him, on what to do and what not to do ever since he'd been a child, and here was his wife, standing before him, and giving it to him right in the face with both barrels. He was trapped between two women. He was engulfed by WOMEN-LEAD-HORSES!

He laughed until his belly ached!

He laughed until he had tears rolling down his face!

He laughed until he was hopping about from one foot to the other, doing a little crazy-*loco* dance!

And he Knew to the bottom of his Soul that this was the exact Power that he'd been looking for in a Woman all of his Life! And that this was the Power that every healthy *macho-cabrón* searched for, too, whether he knew it or not.

"Anything else, Lupe?" he asked.

"No," said Lupe, "that's all I can think of right now."

Hearing this, he started laughing all over again, and this time she was laughing with him, too.

"Okay, Lupe," he said, "I don't know how, but we'll do it your way! Hell, my way hasn't turned out so good lately anyway."

The joy, the *gusto,* that erupted from Lupe's Heart-*Corazón* as she heard her husband's response was so great, so wonderful, that she didn't really know what she, Lupe, was doing until she realized that it wasn't Domingo and Socorro's headboard that was pounding against the wall!

It was theirs, Salvador and hers!

Why, she'd thrown him across the bed, and she was now on top of him, skin to skin and trying to get all of him up inside of her as deeply as she could!

She was a Wild Woman in HEAT!

She was a Wild Woman who'd come into her Own!

And she was starving, wanting to DEVOUR the WORLD!

Salvador's eyes opened wide and he now knew where the old Mexican saying came from that said, "Men do it until they can't do it anymore, but a Woman does it until she DIES!"

For the screams that Lupe now heard weren't Socorro's, either. Oh, no, Lupe was now screaming WILDLY with LOVE, and it was her husband, her *esposo,* for whom she was WILD *con AMOR*!

The headboard was Beat, BEAT, BEATING! POUNDING!

The One Collective Heart-*Corazón* of all Humanity was Beat, BEAT, BEATING—POUNDING!

25

*All was back in Balance, All was back in Harmony and at
Peace, generating Wisdom through our Thirteen Senses from
HEAVEN to EARTH — ALL ONE SONG!*

THE NEXT DAY each couple was ready to go their own way. Domingo had ripped the trunk lid off their beautiful new Packard and piled up everything in the trunk like it was a pickup bed.

"If you two change your mind, you know where to find us," said Domingo. "Just outside of Navojoa."

"Thank you," said Salvador, "but I think this is best for Lupe and me."

"You're giving up millions in gold!" said Domingo.

"Yes, we know," said Salvador. "But, well, we're already rich with something no money or gold can ever buy."

"Damnit!" said Domingo. "But what the Hell! *Cada cabeza es un mundo!*"

Salvador smiled. This was a saying that their grandfather Don Pio, on their mother's side, always used to say, each head was a different world.

They parted with a big *abrazo,* hearts pounding with love between brothers. Then Domingo and Socorro, who was wearing so much makeup that you couldn't see her black and blue bruises, headed south, and Salvador and Lupe headed north.

Getting to the border, there were a few cars in line ahead of Salvador and Lupe. The United States authorities weren't allowing anyone to cross anymore who wasn't an American citizen or couldn't show a means of support. Lupe could see that Salvador was getting very uneasy. She took his hand.

"Lupe, do you really realize what you're asking of me? To give up a gold mine, to return where they don't want us, and then to give up the one trade that I know can make us a living."

Lupe took in a large Breath of *Papito*. "No, Salvador," she said, beginning to feel much more comfortable with this word no. "I'm not asking any of that. What I'm asking is for us, simply, to have more Faith that everything is going to turn out well for us, because we have health and we have love and we have one beautiful child here and another on the way. We're a *familia*, Salvador. And *familias* have somehow been making a living since the dawn of time!"

Salvador had to smile. His mother couldn't have maneuvered him about anymore tactfully. "I hope you're right," he said.

"You know I am," she added.

He laughed. Then it was their turn to be asked questions by the border patrolman. The man looked tired and sweaty and in an awful mood.

Quickly, instinctively, Salvador prepared himself for battle.

But what did Lupe do, why, she just leaned across in front of Salvador, taking the lead, and said in a happy, bird-like, cheerful voice, "Officer, you must be burning up in this hot weather! Be sure to have your wife make you a big, tall glass of lemonade when you get home tonight!"

"Thank you," he said. "Pass right on through. Good to have you back!"

And that was that. The patrolman hadn't even noticed that they were Mexicans or that they were driving a beat-up, old truck. He'd just seen them as good people, and that was all there was to it, and they were back in the United States.

"Lemonade?" said Salvador.

"Yes," said Lupe, "I saw it in a movie, lemonade is very American, that and apple pie."

Salvador couldn't stop laughing, every time he'd glance at Lupe. She'd been so quick and ready!

"Do you know what day this is?" asked Lupe when they came into the outskirts of Tucson, Arizona.

"No," said Salvador, "I don't."

"It's my birthday," said Lupe. "It's May 30, 1932, and I'm twenty-one years old today!"

"Really, it's your birthday?"

"Yes, and I want us to go to the movies tonight, then afterward sleep underneath the Stars."

"Anything else? God, you're getting wild again, Lupe!"

"Yes, I'd like warm apple pie for dinner with vanilla ice cream and nothing else."

"All right, you got it!"

And so that Holy Night they had hot apple pie with vanilla ice cream and they went to the movies in Tucson, Arizona, and it was a wonderful, talking movie with music and dancing.

Then they slept under a million Stars, and when they made Love, Lupe and Salvador just Knew they were in Heaven Here on Earth—the happiest, richest couple in the Universe, GOD'S ONE SONG, ONE SYMPHONY!—OUR DREAM!

Afterword

YES, DOMINGO DID FIND the gold mine just outside of Navojoa, Sonora, Mexico, and he became very rich for about fifteen years. Then he sold the mine for a lot of money and started drinking himself to death, leaving women and children all over the place.

I remember meeting my uncle once when I was about eleven years old in Nogales, Mexico. He was a big, rawbone-looking man with a gorgeous smile. He reminded me a lot of the famous actor of the day, Burt Lancaster. My father and mother loaned him some money so he could go to the doctor, but instead he used the money to drink some more and he died a few months later. My father cried when he got word of his brother's death.

"*Mi hijito,*" he said, taking me aside, "if it wasn't for your mother's guts, I, too, would most likely be dead, just like my brother. We got wild with all of our ideas of the gold mine. But your mother forced me to give up the mine, quit my bootlegging and become law-abiding. A woman, I tell you, is hard to listen to at times, but she can be a man's salvation."

My mother told me that the day after they left Tucson, Arizona, they immediately began to have problems with their little truck, but they didn't panic. They just knew that everything would somehow work out for the best, if they just kept faith and kept going.

When they got to Santa Ana, my mother told me, that they found out that her father had died. He'd died of pneumonia in the hospital three weeks before, when he'd dirtied himself in bed because he was too weak to get himself to the bathroom. The head nurse had gotten so angry that she'd put him in a cold concrete room where he'd quickly developed pneumonia and died.

My mother told me that she felt absolutely terrible that she hadn't been home for her father.

My father told me that he and my mother went through some very hard times for about a year and a half when they returned to California, but then he told me that Franklin Delano Roosevelt—who everyone in the *barrio* thought was half Mexican because of his middle name—changed the whole country overnight. He closed the banks, then ninety-nine days later reopened them with good money, ended Prohibition, and suddenly everyone had jobs. There was nothing to fear but fear itself, my father told me were the words that President Roosevelt made famous—words that his own mother, Doña Margarita, had lived by all of her life.

Archie sold my father and mother the poolhall he'd built in the *barrio* of Carlsbad on credit and my parents became legitimate businesspeople. But my father knew nothing about bookkeeping and so it was my mother who took over the handling of the monies and going to the bank. The whole country began to prosper and my parents were on their way, too.

But, coming back to our original question:

Was it love?

Had it ever really been love between my parents, or had it just been two people surviving through the good times and hard times of life, *la vida*?

My father always told us children that it was love, no doubt about it, just as he'd stated on their fiftieth anniversary. But *mi mama*, I'm sorry to say, could never quite say this, for she always seemed to keep some resentments toward our father deep inside of herself.

In fact, it wasn't until 1990—a couple of years after *mi papa* had passed over to the Other Side and I found my mother crying by the huge, old pepper tree in our front yard—that this matter finally started to be addressed.

"What is it, *mama*," I asked my mother. "Why are you crying?"

"I miss your father so much," she said to me, gripping her chest.

"I do, too," I said.

"Yes," she said, "but I'm the one who could never bring myself to tell him that I loved him." She was in agony.

"You mean that you never once told *papa* that you loved him, *mama*?"

"When we first married I did, of course, but then as the years passed"— she shrugged her shoulders—"I never did anymore, because, well, of all the things I'd grown to not like about him. And now . . . it's those very same things he used to do that annoyed me so much, that I miss the most," she added.

"Oh, *mama*," I said, "I'm so sorry. I didn't know. This is terrible."

"*Desgraciadamente*, this is the tragedy of life that so many of us do with our loved ones, *mi hijito*." She gasped, taking in a big breath. "We let life's ups and downs separate us from our love. I loved your father very much," she added with tears running down her face, "but only now that he's dead and gone can I say this without resentments."

"Oh, *mama*," I said, "you must feel awful."

"I do," she said, "but what can I say, this is what women have been trained to do," she added, "to be afraid of giving all of our love completely, because once we marry, we think that everything is now suddenly supposed to be perfect, and so we then refuse to accept each other's imperfections. Oh, dear God," she added, "please *jurame, mi hijito,* promise me that you will never let a day pass by that you don't let your children and wife know how much you love them."

"I promise, *mama*," I said to her.

"Good, because I really did love him, *mi hijito*. I can now see this so clearly without any doubt, that I loved your father with all my heart and soul, but I just wouldn't let myself know this until he was gone—God forgive me."

I took my mother in my arms and she cried, sobbing like a child. Truly, this, I could now see, had been haunting her for years. "Please, *mama*, don't be too hard on yourself," I said, tears streaming down my own face. "*Papa* knew you loved him."

"Did he?"

"Yes, *mama*, he always told us you did, but you just didn't know how to say it in words."

"*Gracias, mi hijito,*" she said to me. "Your father was a good man, a very good man, and I now see that this is our worst sin of all, *mi hijito,* withholding our *amor* that we feel here, inside our *corazones* until it's too late."

I didn't know what else to say. My mother's truthfulness was causing me to take a deeper look at my own situation with my wife and kids. But, then, in the spring of the year 2000, my mother, God Bless her Soul, took me into an even deeper level of understanding Love. It was midmorning and she was on the back patio whistling to her canaries. It had been a long time since I'd seen her enjoying her canaries with such happiness.

"How are you, *mama*?" I said. "You look so happy."

"I am," she said, singing to her birds.

"Why? What happened?"

"I've finally forgiven myself, *mi hijito*."

"You've forgiven yourself of what, *mama*?"

"Oh, EVERYTHING!" she said with *gusto*. "Of your brother Joseph's death"—(I'd had an older brother who'd died of an internal injury because of football at the age of sixteen)—"of my not being there when my own father passed over, and, well, especially of not telling your father that I loved him."

"And this feels good, eh?" I said, smiling.

"Forgiving feels WONDERFUL!" she shouted with joy. "Especially when you finally even forgive yourself!"

I laughed. It felt so good to see *mi mama* being so happy after so many years mourning. I invited her to breakfast and she accepted and we ate together—*huevos rancheros,* her favorite. "I tell you, *mi hijito,*" she said to me as we ate, "I'm finally beginning to understand that it really does take a lot of living—as your father's mother always used to say—before we humans finally open up our eyes and begin to see. Why, only now that I approach ninety, do I see that so many of the things that I detested about your father—or I thought that they were of the Devil—were actually Blessings in disguise straight from God!"

Her eyes filled with tears again. But no, these were not tears of sorrow. These were tears of wisdom and joy—of insight. "For instance, all these years I've thought how disgusting it was for that woman Socorro—there at the border when we'd been returning to Mexico—to go to Domingo's arms all full of love after he'd beaten her and accept his apology. But now I can see that she did right. We all need to forgive each other our trespasses and quickly, too, or else our hearts harden and we lose our ability to love.

"Oh, if only I'd known how to forgive your father for all the things he did while he was alive, what a different life we could've had. I was stingy with my love, *mi hijito.* But don't think that I've suddenly come to all this, *mi hijito,* because I'm some saintly woman," she said, laughing. "No, I'm just a very practical woman who doesn't want to go to Hell. And I can now see so clearly that if I don't find it in my heart to forgive everyone, including your father, then how can I expect God to forgive me?"

She smiled. "Do you understand, *mi hijito,* it's as simple as that and it's all in Our Lord's Prayer: 'forgive us our trespasses as we forgive those who've trespassed against us.' But it's taken me all these years for me to finally drop my pride and open my eyes to see that it had always been me, myself, who saw all these things as wrongs in life. Your father and I had a wonderful life, but I just couldn't see it because I was so full of ideas of how a man should really be." She breathed. "I loved your father so much. Now, I can hardly wait to die, *mi hijito,* so I can meet him up in Heaven and tell him so. 'I love you, Salvador,' I will tell your father, 'I love you with all my Heart and Soul for All Eternity, *mi esposo de mi corazón!*"

I was now crying, too.

It was love!

It had always been love!

And that was all there really was, *nada, nada,* nothing but *AMOR* Here on Earth as it is in Heaven once people finally opened their Eyes to See with Clarity *del Corazón!*

I hugged *mi mama* close and we cried together. And she, *nuestra madre,* died three weeks later, June 2, 2000, and she was . . . smiling. She'd done it! She'd found Peace and Love and Harmony with God before passing over!

Victor E. Villaseñor
Rancho Villaseñor
Oceanside, California
Spring 2001

P.S.:

Now about our Thirteen Senses, yes, I deliberately didn't list them anywhere in the text, because if I had, then people wouldn't have experienced the book. Instead, they would have been checking to see if here, at this point, the Tenth was being used or the Eleventh or whatever.

You see, it was no accident that we were reduced to five senses during the last three or four thousand years. The five senses are the perfect "trap" to keep us going around in circles inside of our brain computer. It's only when we get out of our head and go into our heart and soul computers that we find freedom and begin to glimpse the wonderful world of abundance and infinite possibilities that we have all around us.

And to activate the Heart Computer, the Sixth and Seventh Senses need to be acknowledged, and these two are, of course, Balance and Intuition. Then to activate the Soul Computer we need to go into the Eighth and Ninth Senses, which are Music (being in Harmony, being Interconnected with all existence, which is then Alive and Breathing and Vibrating) and Psychic (being able to See the Future with utter Clarity). Then once these are activated, Balance, Intuition, Music, and Psychic, we burst into Tenth, Eleventh, Twelfth, and Thirteenth, which are Flying (space swimming/sailing), Form Shifting (all indigenous languaging that I know of have this one), Hall of Records (collective memory or consciousness—Carl Jung was barking up the right tree) and Being. The first six, of course, all men still automatically do. The first seven all women still automatically do. And the last one, Being, we all do every day of our lives or we'd go crazy.

You see, the question was never to be or not to be. To Be or not to Be is the Answer. For when we just relax after a hard day and breathe in easy, having no thoughts or ideas, we are utilizing the Thirteenth, of simply Being.

God, remember, originally was never called God in the Bible. He was called the Supreme Being, and we are human beings, and so when we utilize the Thirteenth, we are then of God with our every Breath.

There are no accidents in languaging. Language is the growing, changing, evolving process of our conscious development in the art-form of verbal communications. And who taught me this? It was my father and mother, and especially *mi mama* once my father had passed over and she was forced to come out of her head and into her Heart and Soul.

Now here you have all of the Thirteen and you can look back in the book and see where they were all used again and again—effortlessly. Why, because all Thirteen were a natural part of our daily living for hundreds of thousands of years, a time when the Garden of Eden was understood not to be "a" location, but our Breathing, Living, Relationship with the Holy Creator. Thank you, and please don't tell anyone what the Thirteen Senses are. Let each person experience the book first. *Gracias,* from *mi familia* to your *familia.*

Remember, we are all WONDERFUL, meaning Beings who are Full-of-Wonder. Life on this planet is just Awakening. And we are so incredibly Good and full of Love, Heart, and Soul—Reflections of GOD in CO-CREATION are WE!

Acknowledgments

First, I'd like to thank my agent, Margret McBride, who read this work in so many different forms for the last six years. Poor Margret, I almost drove you crazy when *Thirteen Senses* was entitled *Father Sun, Mother Moon and To The Sky*. Thank you, Margret, for not losing your enthusiasm. I'd like to also thank Margret's staff, who have been real troopers—Kris, Sangeeta, Donna, and Jessica.

Next, I'd like to thank my friend Bill Cartwright, whom I met in the early '60s and we were both going to be writers. Thank you, Bill, for hiking into *la Lluvia de Oro* with me when I had a broken arm and I was writing *Rain of Gold*. Thank you and Dennis Avery when we traveled to *los Altos de Jalisco* for researching *Wild Steps of Heaven*. And biggest thanks of all, Bill, for reading *Thirteen Senses* in its many forms and drafts over the last six years. You and Helen and Rob and Barbara were such big help during that mentally explosive time.

Thanks to Jackie, who runs my office and knows more about me than anyone will ever know, thank you, Jackie, thank you, Jackie, thank you, Jackie and I also thank your wonderful husband, Roland, that great attorney that you found in the yellow pages, brought him into our office, then married him to make sure that he stayed with us. Thanks, Roland, too.

Hal, my running partner with the sore neck, thank you for sticking with me on an almost daily basis, not only reading the different drafts again and again but also listening to me when I was jumping up and down, screaming, "Hal, I now see the Sixth! Hal, I now understand the Seventh! Hal, last night *papa* came to me with his *mama* and a dozen angels and now I finally see the Ninth, the Tenth and the Eleventh." Hal, thank you for not forsaking me. It was a long, marvelous experiencing of Good-Goding-God.

Thank you, David, my son, for being the wise solid rock that you are and keeping the *rancho* together even in the midst of great financial worry and mind-expanding times. You always manage to say the most reassuring words. And congratulations on your acceptance to med school.

Thank you, my son Joseph, and for being the bearer of light. You caused your mother, Barbara, and me to travel to India on a moment's notice and we got to participate in your Siddhartha experience of illumination—which no doubt one day you will put to pen or simply teach. No greater sons could parents ever hope to have than you, Joe, and your brother, David.

Thank you, Barbara, mother of our children, for your support and love that continues even now that we are no longer husband and wife but good friends and . . . family forever.

And I'd like to thank my sister Linda, whom I grew up with and have not had a close relationship with for almost twenty-five years but now, since *mama* passed away on June 2, 2000, we have been closer together than ever. For the last six months you, Linda, are the one that saved this book by typing with me, working with me, literally from six in the morning to late at night as I reworked the book over and over, sometimes one page, one paragraph for a week—stretching not just our minds but our languaging from the five senses into the Thirteen.

Now, I'd like to give thanks to René Alegria, my editor, who had the guts to buy *Thirteen.* This genius of an editor of HarperCollins (who'd been raised by his grandparents in Tucson, Arizona, and is of my own culture) had the *tanates* to drink red wine and work with me through five months of editing. Thank you, René, you are a great editor. *Gracias!*

And I'd like to thank Juanita Kramer-Hermoza for coming into my life with such flair and dance, teaching me the word *delicioso* in an all-new way, saying, "Isn't this just a delicious day!" and then smile with such *gusto* at the end of a long, hard day of teaching third grade and still want to go dancing that night. Thank you, Juanita, *mi esposa,* for all your love and support.

Also, thank you very much, my baby sister, Teresita, for supporting me with love and wedding rings and information about our life with *mama* and *papa.* Thank you, Tencha, my older sister with the wealth of information and photos that you have so generously given to me to help capture the mood of this book. And thank you, Gorjenna, for being the wild person you are, and your husband, Big Gary. Thank you, RoseAna, for being the loving person you are, and your husband, Jay. Thank you, Joe Colombo. Thank you, Teri, Joseph and Lyn, John, Kimberly, Skeeter and Alicia, Bryon, Billy and Stacy, Jason and Kady, Little Gary, Bill and Charlene, Erik, Lorraine and Greg. Thank you, Andres and Shannon, Jacinto, Diego, Melissa, Jessica, Callie, Adam Ray, Nicholas, Sara, Miguel, Madeline, Carlitos, Nina, Pablito, MacKenzie, Tyler, Trent, and all you others of *nuestra familia* that I might have missed at this moment, but will remember within the hour.

We are all *familia,* we are all God's children—Together Forever!

And of course, thanks to all of *Tia Maria*'s children and grandchildren and great-grandchildren. And thanks to Luisa's and Sophia's and Victoriano's and Domingo's, who are spread all over Arizona and Texas on both sides of the border and we really don't know who you are—like Dale, who just showed up at the *rancho* with his wife and kids last month and is a great-grandson of Sophia, who'd been adopted and found us after reading *Rain of Gold. Gracias!* There's no way that this book could've been realized without All of You!

And last but not least, I'd like to give a very special thanks to Gary Cosay and Chuck Scott, who've been with me more than twenty years, as my agent and lawyer. Thanks for the faith and perseverance. We've done it and are still doing it—*adelante!*